SOCIAL PROCESSES IN INTERNATIONAL RELATIONS

Advisory Editorial Panel

SOCIAL PROCESSES IN INTERNATIONAL RELATIONS

A Reader

Edited with Introductory Notes by
LOUIS KRIESBERG

JOHN WILEY & SONS, INC.

NEW YORK · LONDON · SYDNEY · TORONTO

Library of Congress Catalog Card Number: 68-30914
SBN 417 50795 4
Printed in the United States of America

Preface

The primary purpose of this book of readings is to provide material for courses in international relations that have a sociological or general social-science orientation. The availability of such courses reflects new developments in the study of international relations, as discussed in the introduction to this book. I also hope that the opportunities and advantages of an interdisciplinary approach to the study of international relations are sufficiently documented in this book to encourage and facilitate further efforts in this direction.

The criteria used for selecting papers, the organization of the selections, and the editorial introductions to the papers are all intended to meet these objectives. The major emphasis has been on empirical studies. I wished to present a wide variety of data and of methods of analysis. The presentation of data permits the reader to consider alternative explanations. The variety of methods used should provoke reflection about how we know what we think we know and how we may become more certain in our knowledge. This emphasis means that general reviews of the state of knowledge in a particular area are not included. Such reviews should be used in conjunction with the careful consideration of individual studies on which they are based. "Facts" as well as values can be contested.

The substantive topic covered was the other major criterion used in choosing the papers. The selections deal explicitly with some aspect of international relations or foreign policy and were chosen to represent a wide range of topics. The book is organized according to a comprehensive scheme for understanding international relations, and papers were selected to illustrate various aspects of that scheme. Some aspects are being more intensively studied than are others and the present organization should reveal which areas are relatively neglected and deserve more attention

The organization of the book reflects one theoretical approach to the study of international relations; the approach is developed in the introductory notes. Consequently, the editorial introductions place the selections within a meaningful context. In discussing the particular selections, furthermore, some implications of the findings are suggested and related issues for further inquiry sometimes are indicated. All this should increase the usefulness of each selection and also make the book sufficiently integrated so that it could be used in courses without an accompanying textbook.

The selections vary in difficulty. Some presume familiarity with complex modes of statistical analysis. Some presume information about events pertaining to particular places and times. Others presume familiarity with some general sociological ideas. Other papers do not presume special knowledge in any of these areas. In all cases, the major points in each paper are comprehensible to the general student, though additional knowledge will enhance understanding.

In using the set of readings for courses, the selections may be read in different order than that presented here. Indeed, several selections can be used in more than one context, as will be noted in the introductory notes. As it stands, this organization and set of selections represents a uniquely focused book, presenting a general social-science approach to the study of international relations and emphasizing empirical analysis. I have not included those kinds of material which are well represented in other books of readings. Thus proposals for solutions to problems in international relations are not included.[1] Papers emphasizing a psychological or social psychological approach are not heavily represented.[2] Selections presenting general social science findings relevant to but not dealing directly with international affairs are excluded.[3] Finally, expositions of different theoretical perspectives and orientations and overviews of particular areas of investigation have not been included.[4]

Syracuse University
August 1968   Louis Kriesberg

[1] Roger Fisher (ed.), *International Conflict and Behavioral Science*, (New York: Basic Books, 1964); and Quincy Wright, William M. Evan, and Morton Deutsch (eds.), *Preventing World War III: Some Proposals*, (New York: Simon and Schuster, 1962).

[2] Herbert C. Kelman (ed.), *International Behavior: A Social Psychological Approach* (New York: Holt, Rinehart and Winston, 1965).

[3] See J. David Singer (ed.), *Human Behavior and International Politics* (Chicago: Rand McNally, 1965).

[4] A large number of books of readings present more broadly ranging or more narrowly focused sets of papers. See, for example Leon Bramson and George W. Goethals, *War: Studies from Psychology, Sociology, Anthropology* (New York: Basic Books, 1964); Elton B. McNeil, *The Nature of Human Conflict* (Englewood Cliffs, N.J.: Prentice-Hall, 1965); Harry Eckstein (ed.), *Internal War, Problems and Approaches* (New York: The Free Press of Glencoe, 1964); James N. Rosenau (ed.), *International Politics and Foreign Policy*, (New York: The Free Press of Glencoe, 1961); and Richard A. Falk and Saul H. Mendlovitz (eds.), *The Strategy of World Order* (New York: Wintry Press, 1966).

Acknowledgements

The Committee on International Order of the American Sociological Association, under the chairmanship of Morris Janowitz, encouraged and aided the preparation of this book. Several members of the Committee served as an editorial advisory panel for the book; they are Morris Janowitz, Lewis Coser, Amitai Etzioni, William Gamson, Allen D. Grimshaw, Jerome Laulicht, Mayer Zald, Roger Little, David Riesman, and Louis Schneider. I am indebted to all of them.

Discussions with colleagues at Syracuse University and elsewhere, over many years, have contributed to the ideas expressed in the introductory notes and to the selection of articles. I wish to acknowledge especially the contributions made most recently by colleagues and students of Syracuse University: Manfred Stanley, Robert Gregg, Michael O'Leary, Michael Barkun, Alphonse J. Sallett, Jr., David Rosen, and Charles Shull. Mr. Shull ably assisted in many of the special tasks in preparing the book. Many of the papers included in this reader were used in my course in international relations. The students' comments and responses helped in making the final selections and preparing the editorial introductions. Susan Drucker, Audrey Lekutis, and Ruth Davis typed much of the editorial material and correspondence related to the reader.

The contributions of my wife, Lois Ablin, are too manifold to enumerate. My brother Irving made helpful suggestions.

My primary debt, of course, is to the authors and publishers who made their work available for publication in this reader. The acknowledgement is made in each case at the beginning of the selection.

Despite the advice and comments of so many persons, the responsibility for the selections and the introductory notes must remain with me.

L. K.

Contents

SOCIAL PROCESSES IN INTERNATIONAL RELATIONS

Introduction

Although the study of international relations has traditionally been within the jurisdiction of political science, the enterprise is becoming increasingly interdisciplinary. Many political scientists use the concepts and methods of other social scientists and urge their colleagues to do so. Economists, psychologists, and sociologists increasingly study topics that pertain to international relations. On the basis of the work done, even the disciplinary identities of some social scientists are difficult to assess. Books, journals, and research centers pertaining to international affairs are often interdisciplinary.

These developments are the result of changes in political science, in the other social sciences, and indeed, in the reality itself being studied. Among the changes in that reality, I shall discuss only a few. First, in a fundamental sense, the countries of the world are becoming democratized: popular support for government policies is important and vulnerable now in a way it could not be before mass education, mass communications, and mass armies had come into existence. Second, many nations are newly independent and are new participants in the international system. Most nations of the world are engaged in efforts directed at economic and social development. Partly as a result of these changes, technical assistance, cultural exchange, and international propaganda — both governmental and nongovernmental — have been added to traditional diplomacy as significant types of international relations. Finally, the advent of nuclear weapons creates a drastically new condition which requires new ways of thinking about international relations; past experience is a less useful guide than it had been. Economists, sociologists, anthropologists, and psychologists clearly can make contributions to these newly significant aspects of international relations.

Political scientists studying international relations have incorporated these changes in the object of their studies; this makes the work of other social scientists newly pertinent. The substance and orientation of other social scientists have been incorporated, in varying degrees, by political scientists. This has occurred also because many political scientists have moved away from a policy orientation toward a more value-free, scientific model for their discipline. Concomitantly, they wish to increase the precision and validity of their findings and interpretations. The work of economists, psychologists, and sociologists seems to have moved further along this path. Consequently, the methods of data collection, theory construction, and testing of hypotheses used in these social sciences are attractive. Along with the theoretical and methodological techniques developed in these social sciences, many of their concepts, hypotheses, and topics of inquiry have been taken into the realm of international relations as studied by political scientists.

Movement has also come from the other direction. Social scientists in other disciplines have become increasingly engaged in the study of international relations. This has occurred in part out of moral concern, in part because traditional discipline interests, under the changed circumstances, included international relations, and in part out of simple intellectual curiosity. The social sciences have varied greatly in this movement. After all, the interests, techniques, and professional concerns of historians, economists, geographers, psychologists, anthropologists, and sociologists are quite different. Some of these disciplines have had a long and intimate relationship with the study of international relations and have been closely allied with political science. Others have had a more peripheral relationship and are now having a major impact; this is notably so for psychology and sociology.

The study of international law has another tradition, long distinct from the social sciences. Norms regarding international conduct are crucial; yet, as long as they are studied only as rules without reference to sources of development, support, and deviance, their study will not have the necessary import. Some students of international law have drawn upon the social science orientation to enrich their work, and some social scientists have begun to study, or at least speculate about, the international normative system to the benefit of the general understanding of international relations.

At present, the study of international relations reveals a wide variety of directions and emphases. Eventually a new synthesis may emerge. It is also possible that the differences in emphasis will persist and there will be greater differentiation in the field. One way to keep options open and to build upon the efforts already made is to continually examine the work of people with different orientations. This is the crucial dialogue. This book represents an effort to facilitate that dialogue. A sufficiently wide variety of topics has been included so that the book constitutes a survey of the field of international relations from at least one general perspective. The work has been done by social scientists from a variety of disciplines, but studies by sociologists predominate.

SOCIOLOGISTS AND THE STUDY OF INTERNATIONAL RELATIONS

The attention of sociologists to the study of international relations has varied from little to hardly any and back again.[1] The reasons for the relative neglect of the issues related to international affairs and for the newly emerging interest deserve some comment.[2] They reveal important characteristics of the profession and of the subject of international relations.

The number of sociologists and the scope of their research efforts have increased greatly, particularly in recent years. Yet, along with this expansion, certain developments have seemed to inhibit the investigation of international affairs. The major development has been the increasing emphasis on sociology as a science. Sociologists have sought to collect data which could be measured and statistically manipulated. In order to use such techniques, many cases are needed. Such research also requires large-scale financial support. On all these grounds, the study of international relations has appeared to be an unlikely subject of investigation. Quantitative data relevant to international affairs seemed to be relatively inaccessible; access to pertinent sources is limited. Furthermore, the issues seemed complex and unique. In addition, financial support was plentiful in many subject areas, but not in the sociological analysis of international relations.

Related to the scientific emphasis, sociologists have striven to be value-free. That is, in doing research and in the construction of theory, they strive to eliminate personal biases and values. This does not necessarily mean that values and moral concerns should not enter into the selection of topics for exploration, but they should not distort the collection of data and the interpretation of the findings. Yet the desire to demonstrate the independence of one's research from such values and moral concerns deters some sociologists from inquiring into social problems. The study of international relations seems problem oriented, since the interest in such studies is usually related to a concern with international tensions, conflict, and war.

Until recently, particular features of sociological development have also inhibited sociological exploration in this area. The vast expansion of sociology has been particularly marked in the United States, and the concerns and style of sociological work here has become dominant. Aside from the concern with

---

[1] Robert C. Angell, "The Sociology of International Relations: Empirical and Experimental Studies," *Transactions of the Sixth World Congress of Sociology*, Vol. 1 (Geneva: International Sociological Association, 1966), pp. 67-97; and Amitai Etzioni, "Sociological Contributions to Disarmament and Arms Control in the United States," in P. F. Lazarsfeld, W. Sewell, and H. Wilensky, *Uses of Sociology* (New York: Basic Books, 1967).

[2] Kathleen Archibald, "Social Science Approaches to Peace: Problems and Issues," *Social Problems*, 11 (Summer, 1963), pp. 91-116.

empirical research, the choice of topics has been largely focused upon intrasocietal phenomena. International relations has had less visibility than in smaller nations and in nations with powerful neighbors.

Developments in theoretical orientations within the discipline of sociology have also directed attention away from a sociological concern with international relations. On the one hand, the general broad theoretical orientations have been concerned with consensus, functional interdependence, and equilibrium, and these would seem to make concern with conflict and its regulation peripheral to the major thrust of sociological theory. On the other hand, theories about particular sets of phenomena, such as industrial relations, reference groups, and leadership, must be based upon empirical generalizations from a number of studies. Yet a corpus of such studies in the area of international relations has not yet come into existence.

Sociological neglect of the study of international relations is not due to moral indifference on the part of sociologists. But moral concern is not enough. As members of a discipline, the techniques, interests, and theoretical orientations of the discipline channel the work. Otherwise there can be no cumulative effort. Only as the aspects of the study of international relations become relevant to the development of the discipline will a significant movement into the area occur. This is now happening, and this book bears witness to the emerging work in the sociology of international relations. A few comments are in order to account for this.

Quantitative research methods, as they have been assimilated into sociological work, have lost some of their novelty, but they have not displaced older methods of research. Meanwhile, advances in quantitative methods and computer technology have been so great that even international-relations topics have become more amenable to quantitative analysis. With the aid of the computer, vast amounts of data can be processed and analyzed with greater efficiency than before. In recent years, too, there has been a renaissance in the study of social problems by sociologists. In large part this is due to the significant theoretical contributions made in the study of deviance and social control. The intellectual contribution of these efforts has placed the study of such problems into the mainstream of sociology. At the same time, the successful establishment of sociology in the academic and political worlds as a respectable discipline has freed sociologists to devote their full concerns to substantive issues. More sources of funds have also increased independence.

Related to this development has been a resurgence of interest in the sociology of coercion and conflict. Efforts to integrate these interests with consensus and normative emphases have broadened both. The utilization of functional analyses in the study of international systems has demonstrated that this approach can be applied to a variety of international topics.

Furthermore, the provincialism of American sociologists has been breaking down. Funds for research abroad have become more readily available; sociologists in other nations have increased in number and have undertaken research comparable to the work done in the United States. The traditional sociological concern with comparative research can now begin to be fulfilled in consonance with the new levels of methodological and theoretical sophistication.

Finally, the moral concern of many sociologists with the paramount issue of war in a nuclear age cannot be overlooked. Convinced that sociological analysis can contribute to the study of war and peace, sociologists have undertaken a variety of research projects. As noted earlier, political scientists have seized upon many of the methods, concepts, and hypotheses of sociology and applied them to the empirical study of international relations. Psychologists have used the methods and approach of their discipline in the study of international relations and have demonstrated the relevance of their work both to psychology and to the study of international relations. As noted too, areas of traditional sociological concern, under contemporary international conditions, have become particularly relevant to the study of international relations. Consequently, an impressive and growing body of empirical studies and theoretical discussions are now available which utilize the sociological orientation or social science orientation in general in studying international relations. These developments are revealed by the inclusion of international relations in contemporary textbooks and special sessions of the annual meetings of professional sociological associations.[3]

One further observation should be made. There will always be a gap between scientific theories and practical applications. In applying knowledge in international relations, one is usually concerned about a single case. This requires a clinical approach and detailed information about the particular conditions that are pertinent. Theoretical knowledge about international relations, however, can help tell us what conditions are pertinent and what outcomes are more or less likely under specified conditions.

OVERVIEW OF THE BOOK

The previous remarks have suggested some of the ways in which sociology and the other social sciences can contribute to the understanding of international

[3]Howard S. Becker (ed.), *Social Problems: A Modern Approach,* (New York: John Wiley and Sons, 1966); Richard L. Simpson and Ida Harper Simpson (eds.), *Social Organization and Behavior: A Reader in General Sociology,* (New York: John Wiley and Sons, 1964); Alex Inkeles (ed), *Readings on Modern Sociology* (Englewood Cliffs, N.J.: Prentice-Hall, 1966); Irving Louis Horowitz (ed.), *The New Sociology* (New York: Oxford University Press, 1964); and Robert A. Dentler, *Major American Social Problems* (Chicago: Rand McNally and Co., 1967).

affairs. The selections that follow illustrate the range of contributions. In briefly reviewing the selections and their order of presentation, some of the major contributions can be indicated. The Introductory Notes develop a more detailed perspective within which the selections may be viewed and indicate their relationship to some of the basic issues in understanding international relations.

In Part I of the book, some basic processes and conditions of international relations are considered. Perhaps one of the most important aspects of the sociological orientation is the attention to general social processes which, presumably, underlie political institutions and actions. It is within the full context of social relationships — not only conflicting ones — that an understanding of the occurrence and termination of war is to be understood.

Part II is focused upon the society as a unit and the internal processes that affect its external relations. One matter of social science inquiry is the way in which attitudes about international affairs among various population segments are shaped. Another concern is the way in which various population segments influence each other in shaping a collective position in international relations. Although the society is the primary unit, the relations among groups in different societies are also studied.

In the remainder of the book, the selections relate more directly to interactions across political boundaries, to international relations rather than foreign policy. The selections are divided into two categories: relatively noninstitutionalized and relatively institutionalized international relations. In the first category (Part III) are processes and patterns of interaction that are relatively ungoverned by shared norms and enforcing sanctions. Following the social science orientation, attention is given to nongovernmental as well as governmental interactions and to efforts of governments to influence the people of other countries. Currently war is a relatively noninstitutional way in which governments deal with their conflicts with other governments. In this part of the book, then, the analyses pertain to the use of this mode of handling conflict and to the conditions and processes affecting its utilization.

In Part IV of the book, the focus of the selections is upon patterns of interaction which are relatively, though not absolutely, institutionalized. The selections, more specifically, deal with international organizations: their establishment, structure, and consequences. Informal processes of development as well as formal structure, nongovernmental as well as governmental organizations, and indirect as well as direct consequences are studied. The underlying interest is with institutionalized regulation of conflict.

The selections sample the major social science contributions in methodology, substantive research, and theory. In terms of methods, a wide variety of sources of data is utilized: public opinion surveys, informal interviews, biographies, documents, and simulations. The studies vary in the form of statistical and nonstatistical analysis. Substantively, the selections examine subgovernmental as well as governmental patterns; cooperative and complementary, as well as conflicting relations; and informal, evolving patterns, as well as formally enacted structures. Such topics indicate the general theoretical perspective of sociology and other social sciences. In addition, the selections utilize and sometimes test a variety of hypotheses related to concepts such as stratification, differentiation and integration, power and authority, cross-cutting ties, and consensus.

Part I
PROCESSES AND CONDITIONS

The primary concern in the study of international relations is conflict, and, more particularly, war. Conflict is not the same as war—war is a mode of expressing conflict. Since conflict is inevitable, however, the thrust of much thinking is to discover ways in which conflict may be expressed and contained without recourse to governmentally organized violence.

It is useful to consider international conflicts as part of a general process of international collective decision making.[1] In considering how regimes interact to determine the allocation of scarce resources among themselves, not only conflicting, but also common and complementary relationships and processes are pertinent. In this context, furthermore, war is only another way to arrive at a collective decision. There are inherent difficulties in forming collective decisions and these problems are compounded when independent, territorially based political units are involved. The basic difficulty is that any two parties attempting to reach a collective decision cannot measure what they both want on the same scale. It is even difficult for one person to assess the relative priority of what he wants; to objectively rank the goals of two persons seems impossible. Even assuming a shared desire to reach a collective decision maximizing the attainment of both parties' ends, no externally valid solution is attainable. Agreements can only emerge from interaction, from mutual testing and bargaining. In collective decision making among independent political units, those processes are complicated by the low level of mutually agreed upon rules for such interaction, the variety of objectives within each unit, the power differences among them, and, ultimately, the ability of each to use force.

Not all collective decision making is of equal interest in this book. We are most interested here in decisions about issues which entail a preponderance of conflicting relationships. Conflict is a fundamental social process and relationship; it exists in every sphere of social life; consequently, it has been subjected to

[1]See James S. Coleman, "Foundations for a Theory of Collective Decisions," *The American Journal of Sociology*, LXXI (May, 1966), pp. 615-627.

sociological inquiry in various settings.[2] Much of the sociological approach to international conflict reflects the insights acquired in studying conflicts between units other than the nation-state.

Definitions of conflict vary, but some elements are common to nearly all definitions and discussion.[3] Conflict entails at least two parties who want to occupy positions that are incompatible and who are aware of the incompatibilities. This view of conflict defines it as a relationship or condition among two or more parties. Conflict may also be viewed as a process, in which case the sequence of interaction between the parties is emphasized. Because of this distinction, it seems advisable to consider feelings of hostility and intent to punish, harm, or eliminate the other party as possible stages in the process of conflict development rather than as a necessary part of the condition of conflict.

Given this conception of conflict, many implications follow about the variety of conflicts and their bases. It is clear that having like objectives does not prevent conflict – if the parties did not both want the same resources, leadership positions, or other objectives, then there would be no conflict. The incompatibility of such objectives depends upon scarcity and limitations in the sought-after objectives. In that case, what one party gains, the other loses. This is what is meant by a zero-sum game—a game in which the total outcome remains unchanged, but the division may vary. Some conflicts would seem to be based upon dissimilarities. But even differences in ideologies, styles of life, or values would not be the basis for conflict unless at least one party had as its objective that the other party embrace similar ideologies, style of life, or values. If the parties were indifferent to each other, such differences would not be the basis of conflict.

---

[2] For example, see Ralf Dahrendorf, *Class and Class Conflict in Industrial Society* (Stanford, California: Stanford University Press, 1959); James S. Coleman, *Community Conflict,* (Glencoe, Ill.: The Free Press, 1957); Arthur Kornhauser, Robert Dubin, and Arthur Ross (Eds.), *Industrial Conflict* (New York: McGraw-Hill Book Co., 1954); and Raymond W. Mack and Richard C. Snyder, "The Analysis of Social Conflict – Toward an Overview and Synthesis," *Journal of Conflict Resolution,* 1 (June, 1957), pp. 212-248.

[3] Robert E. Park and Ernest W. Burgess, *Introduction to the Science of Sociology* (Chicago: University of Chicago Press, 1921); Vilhelm Aubert, "Competition and Dissensus: Two Types of Conflict and Conflict Resolution," *Journal of Conflict Resolution,* VII (March, 1963), pp. 26-42; Jessie Bernard, "Some Current Conceptualizations in the Field of Conflict." *The American Journal of Sociology,* LXX (January, 1965), pp. 442-454; Jessie Bernard, "Parties and Issues in Conflict," *Journal of Conflict Resolution,* 1 (June, 1957), pp. 111-121; Raymond Aron, *Peace and War: A Theory of International Relations* (Garden City, N.Y.: Doubleday and Co., 1966); Jessie Bernard, T. H. Pear, Raymond Aron, and Robert S. Angell, *The Nature of Conflict: Studies in the Sociological Aspects of International Tension* (Paris: UNESCO, 1951); Anatol Rapoport, *Strategy and Conscience* (New York: Harper and Row, 1964); Feliks Gross, *World Politics and Tension Areas* (New York: New York University Press, 1966); and Kenneth E. Boulding, *Conflict and Defense* (New York: Harper and Row, 1962).

All this sounds and is very static. When we view conflict as a process, we recognize that even the objectives sought by each party must in part depend upon what the other party wants. The relative priority each assigns to its objectives and the amount of resources each is able to utilize for his attainment determine whether or not each party will actively "want" a given objective. Since conflict includes recognition that the other party wants what is incompatible with one's own objectives, the price the other side might exact for trying to attain one's own objective may lower its priority to such a point that conflict can no longer be said to exist. Furthermore, whether or not particular like objectives or interests place parties in a conflict relationship depends on the context of their relationship. Consider students in a course all of whom wish to get good grades in the course — they have like interests. If they are graded on a curve so that only a few will get "A" and some will get "D," they may well consider that their competitive situation is also conflicting. If, however, they were graded as a collectivity or on some absolute standard, then their like interests would be the bases not for conflicting relations but for common or complementary efforts.

Although it is useful to consider the nature of conflict as a general process or condition, we are primarily concerned in this book with international conflict. As Holsti states in Selection 29, "Incompatible objectives and policy actions between interacting states form the basis of most international conflicts." States or governments, then, are the critical units, and they have special features. States have control over considerable means of violence. Domestically, their means are predominant; internationally, the relative amount is not so great, but in absolute terms they are awesome enough. This is why conflict between states is so ominous. Military force, even if not used to conquer or physically coerce the other state, may lurk as a threat or deterrence so that a particular conflict does not emerge into focus or if the conflict does, it is resolved by the withdrawal of one side. The possibility of force also affects the way in which various other modes of settlement may occur: bilateral or multilateral negotiations and bargaining, mediation, judicial awards, or actions by international organizations. The relative frequency of such modes of conflict resolution are provided by Holsti in Selection 29.

Although states are the interacting units, questions still arise about who speaks for the states and for whom within the society does the state speak. The bases, development, and resolution of particular conflicts, as already suggested, depend upon a variety of conditions and processes pertaining to (1) each party involved, (2) the relations between the parties, including nonconflicting relations, and (3) the entire system of nations, rules, and organizations within which the involved parties are interacting. Although each selection bears on some aspect of these conditions and processes, a few will be discussed now, in relationship to the selections in the introductory chapter.

The states of the world share the same world. None can act solely in terms of its internal characteristics. They are parts of a world system made up of other states, of international governmental and nongovernmental organizations, of flows of transactions such as migration, visits, and trade, and of identifications by people according to religion, ethnicity, and culture. From this welter of reality, we may abstract certain dimensions to characterize the system within which the states are interacting. Consider even the various ways of abstracting the system of states. We might view the international system as a bipolar one: divided into two blocks, the Socialist camp versus the Free World. But the world of states is not comprehended well by such an abstraction. Even taking into account the existence of other groupings and viewing the world as made up of three worlds or of several blocs is not sufficient.[4] States differ according to many dimensions: the societies of which they are a part differ, for example, in economic development.[5] Consequently, on one issue, some states may be aligned differently than on other issues. Some issues pertain clearly to the conflict between the East and the West. But other issues, pertaining to economic assistance, for example, may divide nations in terms of their economic development; such a division is sometimes called the North-South division of the world. (See, e.g., Alker in Selection 28). Presumably, if nations are divided differently on many different issues, no one issue is likely to be fought about as intensely; the adversary on one issue is likely to be an ally on some other issue. If conflicts and alliances cross-cut every bloc, the possibility of finding bases for bargaining and compromises is enhanced.

Moreover, states are not unitary wholes interacting like a bunch of billiard balls. Ties among the peoples of the various societies may cross-cut national and bloc boundaries. Again, such cross-cutting ties may limit the intensity of conflict. A state whose people have many bonds with people of an adversary state would suffer losses to its own people in inflicting harm on the adversary society.

Finally, emerging from the interaction between states and people in various societies are the mutual expectations and understandings that influence the conduct of the states. As Coser (Selection 3) points out, even the duration of a war depends in part upon some *mutual* understandings; the termination of most

---

[4]Morton Kaplan, *System and Process in International Relations* (New York: John Wiley and Sons, 1957); Wolfram F. Hanrieder, "The International System: Bipolar or Multibloc," *Journal of Conflict Resolution*, IX (September, 1965), pp. 299-308; and Irving Louis Horowitz, *Three World of Development* (New York: Oxford University Press, 1956).

[5]Gustavo Lagos, *International Stratification and Underdeveloped Countries* (Chapel Hill: The University of North Carolina Press, 1963); and Michiya Shimbori, Hidea Ikeda, Tsuyoshi Ishida, and Moto Kondo, "Measuring a Nation's Prestige," *The American Journal of Sociology*, LXIX (July, 1963), pp. 63-68.

conflict is a reciprocal activity. How is defeat to be recognized and acknowledged? It must be socially defined by both parties; it rarely results from unilateral imposition.[6]

Wirth (Selection 1) indicates the complexity of some of these phenomena and some of the processes by which interactions based upon ecological relationships provide the basis for the formation of a society. Presumably, upon stable patterns of interactions mutual expectations develop which in turn may become the bases for a normative order. Hodgson (Selection 2) offers a broad historical view which should be a corrective for the American (and "Western") provincial view of the world. He shows how societies have historically helped mold each other and form a complex, interrelated movement of peoples and civilizations.

The emergence and regulation of conflict, then, depend upon general social conditions and processes. In this introductory chapter, a few major ideas are outlined. Later chapters examine these and related ideas in more detail.

[6]Talcott Parsons discusses the possibility of an emerging world consensus and a two-party world system in "Order and Community in the International Social System," in James N. Rosenau (ed.), *International Politics and Foreign Policy* (New York: The Free Press of Glencoe, 1961), pp. 120-129 and in "Polarization of the World and International Order," in Quincy Wright, William M. Evan, and Morton Deutsch (eds.), *Preventing World War III* (New York: Simon and Schuster, 1962), pp. 310-331.

CHAPTER ONE

Some Perspectives

1. WORLD COMMUNITY, WORLD SOCIETY, AND WORLD GOVERNMENT: AN ATTEMPT AT A CLARIFICATION OF TERMS

Louis Wirth

I

The quest for a free, peaceful, and just world in which all men can develop their capacities to the fullest and enjoy the blessings of an advancing civilization is the professed aim of more than a few Americans and other members of the human race. This goal has been variously formulated, sometimes as the building of a world community or world society, and sometimes as the construction of a world government or world state.

These terms, while designed to aid us in defining the objective toward which we are to move, themselves introduce an element of confusion into programs of

SOURCE. Louis Wirth, "World Community, World Society, and World Government: An Attempt at a Clarification of Terms," in Quincy Wright, ed., *World Community,* Chicago, Ill.: University of Chicago Press, 1948, pp. 9-20. Reprinted by permission of The University of Chicago Press. Copyright 1948 by the University of Chicago. All rights reserved.

action and thus become obstacles to the realization of the ends which they symbolize. There are those, for instance, who believe that we already have a *world community* and that what is necessary is to develop a corresponding *world society*. There are others who take the existence of a world society—or at least an embryonic world society—for granted and regard the creation of a world government or world state as the urgent need of the present. And since a regime of law and order is the characteristic mark of government and is indicative of the existence of a state, they would proceed to formulate such a body of basic law or a constitution for the governance of the world and thus bring a world state into being.

Clearly, if a world community already exists, it is superfluous to spend effort to bring it into existence. If a world society is already at hand, it is obviously stupid to be waiting for it to emerge. This, of course, still leaves open the question of whether a world community or society is a necessary prerequisite for the effective operation of world government and the effective functioning of a world state. It also leaves open the question of whether the framing of a world constitution is a necessary or desirable step in the building of a world community. Furthermore, it leaves unanswered the question as to whether a world community can be deliberately built, or whether it is the unwitting product of growth and unintended activity. It also leaves open the issue as to whether, if a world community or society were in existence, a world government or state would be necessary at all for the attainment of a free, peaceful, just, and prosperous humanity.

Disagreements as to the ends to be striven for as well as to the most appropriate means to be employed in the pursuit of the ends will persist as long as this confusion continues to plague us. The confusion, however, by which mankind and the intellectual leaders of mankind are beset in the attempt to work out the problems of the contemporary world are of two kinds: (1) the ambiguity of the terms of discourse and (2) the differences in judgments concerning the facts and the relations between the facts. It is the purpose of this paper to deal only with the former, although it will be difficult to avoid at least some reference to the latter, especially since it is impossible to discuss terms and the relations between terms without alluding to the objects or phenomena which they designate and the relations that are supposed to exist between these objects or phenomena.

Agreements regarding objectives and programs of action will obviously be impeded as long as the parties to the debate talk *past* one another instead of *to* one another. There may still be disagreement as to the values to be achieved and the procedures to be employed to achieve them even after the terms used in discourse have been clarified, because there may still be errors of fact, of logic, and of theory. But the least we can do to facilitate the realization of such hopes as we share is to provide ourselves with fairly precise categories of thought and of communication in terms of which we understand ourselves and our fellows.

II

The controversy that exists concerning whether a world community must precede a world state, whether the two develop simultaneously, or whether the world community may be expected to arise out of a world government rests to a large extent upon the meaning ascribed to the term "world community." Though the terms "state" and "government" are by no means unambiguous, there is on the whole less confusion incident to their use than there is in the case of the term "community." The confusion in all these instances is, of course, largely due to the circumstance that these and most other words we use in social-science discourse are also terms current in common speech and often reflect the universe of "common sense."

But even the common-sense meaning of the terms "state" and "government" carry the connotation of more or less formal organization, whereas the term "community" connotes, if it does not actually denote, the absence of formal association and organization and of legally sanctioned or regulated living-together of men. Indeed, we even speak of plant and animal communities, where formal, deliberately contrived, and legally sanctioned organization is precluded.

When the plant and animal ecologist talks about a community, he is referring to the aggregation of living forms knitted together by symbiotic ties into a web of life. Through their involvement in the struggle for existence in a given habitat, the various individual members and species of organisms acquire a spatial position and a place in the division of labor which gives to each its peculiar character and function and to the total community the semblance of an equilibrium.

The sustenance and reproductive relationships which the individual organisms and types of living things develop with one another and with the habitat as a whole give the plant and animal community an internal interdependence and a distinctiveness from other communities which leave the external observer with the impression of the separate identity of each community. The bonds that bind the individual organisms and varieties of plant and animal organisms together are the functional interrelationships which are essentially competitive. When we talk about the "law of the jungle," we mean the war of each against all. This state of existence, if it can at all be called social, rests on what Kant has called man's "unsocial sociability," that is to say, upon a set of conditions under which each organism strives to achieve its own ends and only inadvertently confers some benefit upon other organisms, but through this inadvertent by-product of its own selfish striving creates ties of mutual interdependence with others. Such a condition of interdependence does not call for either awareness, communication, or the existence of or agreement on norms.

The symbiotic relationships which underlie every plant and animal community are either those of (1) *mutualism,* where the functions of one organism or variety of organisms are beneficial to others and vice versa; (2) *commensalism,* where the benefits derived by one are a matter of indifference to the other; or (3) *parasitism,* where the benefits derived by one imply harm to the other. Classical examples of each type of symbiotic relationship are readily available from plant and animal ecology.

A special case of an animal community often cited as a model for mankind is the peculiar symbiotic relationship obtaining among the members of colonies of social insects. Even there, however, the order and cohesion that prevail are based not upon communication, mutual awareness, and the acceptance of social norms but rather upon the morphology and elementary reflexes or instincts which are built into the organisms and which operate automatically.

III

The human community, too, rests upon a similar ecological base, but it should be noted that human communities are never merely ecological units. Upon the ecological base there are always superimposed economic, cultural, political, and moral or ethical levels of interdependence. The human economy is never without some rules of the game. There is always present some degree of awareness of the other. There is always some measure of conscious control. There is language, symbolic communication, and some approximation to mutual understanding. There are rights and duties, claims and expectations. There are not merely tropisms and reflexes but also habits and sentiments, customs, institutions, shared norms, and values. In short, there is not merely symbiosis but also some degree of consensus.

One of the persistent interests, however, among students of man is the attempt to differentiate between a community and a society. In a sense these two terms have become polar concepts in the efforts to understand human social life. When we use the term "community," we seek to isolate and to emphasize the physical, spatial, and symbiotic aspects of human group life, whereas by the term "society" we wish to bring into focus and to stress the psychic, deliberative, rational, normative, and consensual phases of group existence. When we are dealing with human beings as aggregates of population distributed in space and in relationship to resources, it is useful to employ the concept "community." When, on the other hand, human groups are thought of as held together by communication, by the bonds of interest, and when they move toward common collective goals for which they require a common understanding of symbols and a sharing of common norms, we are dealing with a society.

It should be noted, however, that every human community is always something of a society. It is difficult to conceive of human beings living together in close physical contact with one another without engaging in communication, especially if the physical contact persists over a considerable time. And, as Dewey has pointed out, there is "more than a verbal tie between the words *common, community,* and *communication.* Men live in a community in virtue of the things which they have in common; and communication is the *way in which they come to possess things in common.* "[1]

We do occasionally find instances of two or more groups of people living next to one another but having little if any direct physical contact. The etiquette of the classical caste system was a case in point, as was the "silent trade" in the course of which adjoining communities exchanged goods without communication or direct physical contact. The diffusion of modern technology through the more or less impersonal market on a world scale is another approximation to such a case. Although the market mechanism does involve communication of some sort among the participants in commerce, the physical and social distance between producers and ultimate consumers is immensely greater in the modern world market in capitalistic civilization than it was in earlier times. This is not to say that there are not some survivals of the intimate, personal market to be found today; but it certainly is not representative of typical economic relations in the modern world.

While every community tends to generate some element of society, the reverse is not so obvious. The people scattered over the face of the earth who share, let us say, a common interest in some esoteric belief or body of knowledge but who may never have met can perhaps be said to live in a simulated community, but the ties of such a community will at best be tenuous. In such instances where the bond of cohesion among individuals rests upon shared beliefs based upon communication, it is proper to put the accent upon the polar concept of society. Conversely, where the bonds linking individuals rest upon spatial contiguity, upon a division of labor, and upon competition in the market, it is preferable to put the stress upon community. What makes every community at least an embryonic society, however, is the fact that any involvement in reciprocal relations among human beings calls for some kind of communication and generates some degree of consensus.

IV

In a sense, the concept "world community" is a contradiction in terms, for the community is most frequently conceived as a territorially limited *local* unit. We do not ordinarily speak of an individual as belonging "to more than one community, except in so far as a smaller community of which he is a member is included in a larger of which he is also a member."[2] More particularly, it has been

[1] John Dewey, *Democracy and Education* (New York, 1915), p. 5.

[2] Robert E. Park and Ernest W. Burgess, *Introduction to the Science of Sociology* (Chicago: University of Chicago Press, 1921), p. 163.

taken as the mark of a community that "one's life may be lived wholly within it, that all one's social relationships may be found within it."[3] In that sense a community is an inclusive, relatively integrated territorial group as distinguished from the segmental and widely ranging ties and identification of society.

It appears, therefore, that in the traditional conception of community there are implicit the notions of territorial compactness and closeness, intimacy of contact, and relative self-sufficiency. These criteria apply readily enough to most human settlements in an earlier stage of civilization; but it is difficult to find modern communities which in their economic, social, and political life can be sharply delineated by narrow local bounds. Modern technology, economy, political organization, and even culture tend to encompass the earth. We can see this more clearly if we recognize and attempt to trace the intricate and far-flung networks of interrelations which are associated with such a relatively compact unit as a metropolitan region. The limits of such a region must be more or less arbitrarily defined in terms of retail and wholesale trade area, commutation area, newspaper-circulation area, and service area of the central city. To delineate the "communal" boundaries of an entity as large as a national state would obviously lead to even greater complications.

Barriers to the universal spread of technology, science, and culture are, of course, still formidable. Tribal, racial, national, linguistic, religious, economic, political, and other differences do still divide the world into separate regions. But, on the other hand, there remain few self-sufficient, internally homogeneous islands some inhabitants of which, at least, have not been drawn into the universal currents of modern life; and these few remaining islands are being rapidly submerged.

The overwhelming trend is from *Gemeinschaft* to *Gesellschaft;*[4] from social groupings based upon "status" to those based on "contractual"[5] relations; from homogeneous aggregates held together by "mechanical solidarity" to heterogeneous aggregates based upon "organic solidarity" and a division of labor;[6] from "primary groups"[7] to secondary groups; and from the "folk cultures"[8] to urban industrial civilization.

The bonds of the market certainly are not so personal and intimate as are those of *kinship* and close local association, but they do organize life over ever wider

---

[3]Robert M. MacIver, *Society: Its Structure and Changes* (New York, 1931), p. 9,

[4]See Ferdinand Tönnies, *Gemeinschaft und Gesellschaft* (5th ed.; Berlin, 1922).

[5]See Sir Henry S. Maine, *Ancient Law* (London, 1861) and *Village Communities in the East and in the West* (New York, 1889).

[6]See Émile Durkheim, *The Division of Labor in Society* (New York, 1933) and *Elementary Forms of Religious Life* (New York, 1915).

[7]See Charles H. Cooley, *Social Organization* (New York, 1909).

[8]See Robert Redfield, *The Folk Culture of Yucatan* (Chicago: University of Chicago Press, 1941).

areas approaching the limits of the universe. There are still local dialects, but there are also world languages. There still is rumor and gossip, but there also is ever greater reliance on news. There still are local cultures, but there is also an approximation to world civilization. There still are local, county, state, and national governments, but there are also emerging world political institutions, however, feeble. We even find more or less successful appeals made by statesmen to the court of "world opinion," to the "conscience of mankind," and to the loyalties and duties of "world citizenship." These phrases may as yet be merely figures of speech, but in critical situations in the recent past they have demonstrated their power to move men's thoughts and actions.

V

The central issue which makes the concept "community" relevant to the problem of peace, world order, and progress is the indispensability of a basis for effective co-operation and collective action among the nations and peoples of the world. In this connection it might be pointed out that the cohesiveness of a group derives, or is widely believed to be derived, in part from its antagonism to other groups. This function of external conflict as a factor making for internal integration has been dramatized by William Graham Sumner, and others before him, notably Gumplowicz, as the in-group versus out-group relationship. It has been suggested that if the whole world were to become a single community, the organizing and beneficent effect of conflict would be lost and, hence, that such a world could not long remain an integrated unity unless it picked upon some extra-mundane body for its opposition.

Here it may be in point to emphasize that such local community cohesion as we now have is sustained only in negligible degree by conflict with other communities. There is no evidence available to me on the basis of which students of local communities could arrive at the conclusion that intracommunity solidarity is significantly furthered by intercommunity conflict. It is highly questionable whether external conflict is an essential ingredient of internal community cohesion, and it is at least plausible that adequate equivalents for external conflict can be found in what Simmel calls the war against "inner enemies." And if we do not actually have ready-made "inner enemies" at hand, we can always invent them. We have, of course, a considerable literature tending to support the proposition that nation-states are never so strong as when they are threatened by external enemies. Whatever the facts may be on a national and international level, there is nothing to support the assumption that local communities gain an appreciable *measure of their internal integrity through external conflict.*

VI

If we are to apply the lessons we have learned from the structure of community life on a local scale to the problem of organizing the world, it will be helpful, then, to think of the community in terms of a series of processes and levels of interaction.

In its most elementary sense the community is a habitat which sustains a population. The symbiotic relationships or the competitive co-operation which the occupancy of a common habitat demands creates a common ecological base upon which social relationships may develop.

Upon this ecological base human beings tend to build a technological order, a division of labor, and an economy. Such an order inevitably calls forth a set of norms and institutions which control the participants. These controls are initially for the most part unconscious. Later they tend to become conscious and formal. When such an order becomes crystallized, it takes on political forms, of which the law, the state, and the police are symbolic. Throughout this process communication goes on, and a set of common understandings, values, and ideals and a body of loyalties develop, based upon participation in common experiences and the generation and dissemination of common symbols. From this foundation there emerges the beginning of a moral order in which individual and group conduct is controlled not so much by external coercion as by uncoerced consensus.

Thus we pass along the continuum from community to society, from a form of living together in which the members of the aggregate have not merely conflicting and parallel interests but also common or shared interests. A community thus might be regarded as a state of existence, whereas a society is a state of mind.

VII

A serious misunderstanding often stands in the way of rational discourse about the world community. It is naïvely assumed that likeness of characteristics makes for integration, whereas heterogeneity impedes integration. The fact is that similarity of traits may also be the occasion for more intense antagonism, whereas differentiation of traits may be the basis for a mutually beneficial division of labor. We see this situation in the plant and animal world, where we have what is known as "like commensals" and "unlike commensals." The hardest wars are often fought between "like commensals." If the trait of belligerency were universal among men, it surely would not make the creation of a peaceful world easier. All depends, therefore, upon what traits are similar and what traits are different.

Similarly, it is often naively assumed that the more contacts we have with one another and the more intimate these contacts, the less occasion there will be for conflict. It should be noted, however, that frequency and intimacy of contacts can become the basis of conflict as well as of harmony. To know one another better is often to hate one another more violently. To be sure, a common language and a common culture facilitates mutually intelligible communication, but it also makes possible conflict in areas of life in respect to which we were formerly indifferent. The more we know one another and the more frequent and intimate our relations with one another are, the more opportunity there also exists for disagreement, for irritation, and for overt conflict.

VIII

In building a world community or world society, we encounter the problem of "community organization." From what has been said before, community organization is in part an unconscious development in interaction on a symbiotic basis of competitive co-operation, but it is in part also a product of deliberate construction, of education, of facilitation, of communication, of the building of institutions and other formal controls, and of participation in organized life. Attention might be directed at this point to the history of the community organization movement. In the United States this movement is about two generations old. It began with the surveys and studies of actual communities as they existed in England and America, such as Charles Booth's survey of London. In the course of these studies it was found that communities had organization or structure quite apart from any deliberate and concerted effort to create such structure. The actual problems of social life of these communities were discovered, and organized efforts were undertaken to remedy some of these undesirable conditions of life by bringing incongruities into mutual accord and by building new programs of action and initiating new control devices. It was the deliberate effort to create and manipulate the institutions and services of communities in the interests of more wholesome life that became known as the community organization movement.

This takes us back to an interesting discussion which went on during the eighteenth century among the Scottish moralists concerning the relations between the "natural order" and the "civil order." They raised the question as to the extent to which a community was an organism or a natural entity, as over against the extent to which a community was an artifact, that is, a contrived entity. While a full discussion of this problem would take us too far afield, it is an issue of significance in the light of present-day discussion concerning the need for building a world society. It has been argued, for instance, that it is useless to attempt to build a world society, for, if one is to exist, it will come into being as the unintended end product of the participation of people in some common enterprises on a world scale. I am skeptical of this argument because we have learned from local experience that, whereas sometimes a formal organization may impede a natural development, it is also true that formal organization may facilitate and guide such natural processes.

In struggling for the emergence of a world community and a world government, therefore, it is well to keep in mind that we already have much to build upon. In many respects the world is already drifting toward a community. In other respects it can be helped to so do or can be impeded in this process.

There is, for instance, a reciprocal relationship between world trade and world political organization. The more trade we have, the more rules and regulations we will need and develop for carrying it on; and, in turn, the more we subject ourselves to commonly accepted rules and regulations, the more easily world trade can be carried on. I do not mean to suggest, of course, that these rules and regulations are always beneficent; they may be stupid and lead to the emergence of trade barriers. Similarly, the more of a common culture we have, the less we need formal law and the easier it is to enforce such law as there is. On the other hand, the attempt to create a common rule of law in areas where no such law existed before itself enlarges and deepens the sphere of a common culture. The formulation and adoption of the Constitution of the United States has probably been an important factor in the emergence of a "national community."

Even in highly integrated local communities we find some deviations from the accepted norms in the form of crime and other forms of social disorganization. The very issues, however, for public discussion and public action which such deviations pose furnish occasions for increasing community solidarity. Indeed, it has been pointed out by Durkheim that it is precisely in the attempt by communities to prevent and punish infractions of social rules that these communities reaffirm and strengthen their solidarity. We should not expect, therefore, on a world scale any more than on a local scale, to find complete and unvarying adherence to existing social norms. Rather, we should be prepared to use these occasions as opportunities for creating a world opinion, a world conscience, world-wide concerted and collective action, and a sense of belonging to a world entity.

In building the world of tomorrow, therefore, we must start with what we have. We must take the world as it is. We cannot expect to start with a clean slate. If we see the ingredients of a world community in a series of forms of interaction on a universal scale—actions which formerly for the most part were carried out on a local, regional, or national scale—we can measure the progress in world solidarity and integration as we go along. The world community upon which a world society will ultimately have to rest will not automatically come into existence by making a world constitution or even by having such a constitution formally accepted; but, on the other hand, neither need we wait until the world is ready for a universal regime of law before making progress toward peace and order. Between the inevitable and the impossible there lies a realm of the feasible. On this we must keep our eye, for it is this area that provides the opportunity for deliberate intervention and sets the limits for such intervention.

We have already a number of embryonic world institutions. They are indicative of the degree to which we have achieved a world community. For the time being they are still feeble; but they represent a great advance over what we have had before. We shall probably not achieve in our lifetime anything even approximating the ecological, the economic, the cultural, the political, and the moral integration which we have achieved in communities on a local scale. But even some progress in that direction on a world scale is better than war or the permanent division of the world into two potentially warring camps.

2. THE INTERRELATIONS OF SOCIETIES IN HISTORY

Marshall G. S. Hodgson

It has been long pointed out that the destinies of the various sections of mankind began to be interrelated long before the twentieth century, with its global wars and cold wars; or even the nineteenth century, the century of European world hegemony. Here we will study certain of the historical ways in which these destinies were intertwined; in this way we may distinguish more valid modes of tracing large-scale history and of comparing the societies involved in it, from a number of popular but unsound modes of trying to do so. I shall speak mostly of the ages before modern times. . . .

THE GEOGRAPHICAL WORLD-IMAGE OF THE WEST

It would be a significant story in itself to trace how modern Westeners have managed to preserve some of the most characteristic features of their ethnocentric medieval image of the world. Recast in modern scientific and scholarly language, the image is still with us; indeed, all sorts of scholarly arguments are used to bolster it against occasional doubts. The point of any ethnocentric world image is to divide the world into moieties, ourselves and the others, ourselves forming the

SOURCE. Marshall G. S. Hodgson, "The Interrelations of Societies in History," in *Comparative Studies in Society and History,* 5 (January, 1963), pp. 227-239 (slightly abridged). Reprinted by permission of the author and The Society for the Comparative Study of Society and History. Copyright 1963 by the Society for the Comparative Study of Society and History.

*This paper was delivered originally as a lecture at the downtown College of the University of Chicago in a series on "The Idea of Mankind," sponsored by the Committee for the Study of Mankind. It contains a sketch of ideas which the writer hopes to substantiate more fully; meanwhile, it constitutes an advance over the writer's "Hemispheric Interregional History as an Approach to World History" in *Cahiers d'histoire mondiale,* Vol. I (1954), pp. 715-723.

more important of the two. To be fully satisfying, such an image of the world must be at once historical and geographical. As in the Chinese image of the "Middle Kingdom" and the Islamic image of the central climes, so also in the Western image, most of this sleight-of-hand is performed through appropriate historical manoeuvers. Western Europe may be admitted to be small geographically, but all history is made to focus there.

But we must begin with the map. A concern with maps may seem trivial; but it offers a paradigm of more fundamental cases. For even in maps we have found ways of expressing our feelings. We divide the world into what we call "continents." In the eastern hemisphere, where more than four-fifths of mankind still live, these are still the same divisions as were used by Medieval Westerners—Europe, Asia, and Africa. As we know, Europe west of the Russias has about the same population as historical India, now India and Pakistan; about the same geographical, linguistic, and cultural diversity; and about the same area. Why is Europe one of the continents but not India? Not because of any geographical features, nor even because of any marked cultural breach at the limits we have chosen. The two sides of the Aegean Sea have almost always had practically the same culture, and usually the same language or languages and even the same government. Much the same is true of the Black Sea and of the Ural Mountains.

Europe is still ranked as one of the "continents" because our cultural ancestors lived there. By making it a "continent," we give it a rank disproportionate to its natural size, as a subordinate part of no larger unit, but in itself one of the major component parts of the world. Incidentally, we thus also justify outselves in evaluating it on a far more detailed scale than other areas. I believe it was the *New Yorker* magazine that published the *"New Yorker's* map of the United States," in which New York City, New England, Florida, and the West appeared as roughly comparable subdivisions. With our division of the world by continents, we allow ourselves a similar projection of our own interests. Italy is a country in the south of the "continent" Europe; India is a country (naturally "vast" and "mysterious") in the south of the "continent" Asia.

The *New Yorker* map of the United States went on to reflect the *New Yorker's* notions in the very sizes the several areas appeared to have on the map. Our Mercator world maps have done much the same thing for our Western world image. Some say the Mercator world map is so popular because it shows the correct *angles* essential for navigation (even though its *shapes* are almost as badly distorted as its areas). But if you use a map not for navigating but for placing and comparing at a glance different parts of the world, shapes and areas are more important than angles. Moreover, areas are more important than shapes, because they have cultural implications. What is objectionable about the Mercator world map in fact is not that it distorts the shape of North America, nor even that it shows Greenland so large—our conception of Greenland makes little difference.

Rather, it is that it shows India so small, and Indonesia, and all Africa. (I call such a world map the "Jim-Crow projection" because it shows Europe as larger than Africa.)

The point is not, of course, simply that we make Europe big or put it in the upper center. Such matters in themselves might be as irrelevant as the fact that we put the prime meridian at Greenwich. What matters is the peculiar way our perceptions get distorted by the map projection (as they are by no prime meridian). The fortieth parallel north has a curious significance for our world image. Historically, almost all the great centers of civilization have lain south of the fortieth parallel: all, that is, save Europe. Most of Europe lies north of that parallel. But it is precisely at about the fortieth parallel that the Mercator projection begins to exaggerate areas unconscionably. In consequence, that projection and others like it show Europe on a far larger scale than the Middle East, or India, or China. India does appear to the eye, on that projection, as a "country in Asia" on the order of, say Sweden in Europe. And it is possible to show on such a world map numerous details in Europe, towns and rivers that are famous among us, while India or Indonesia, say, are quickly filled up with only the most essential features—which, indeed, are all we have usually heard of.

No wonder, then, that despite all our awareness that Mercator distorts, and that many better projections are available, Mercator remains the most common form of world map outside geographers' classrooms. It confirms our predispositions. It flatters our egos. If we decide we must abandon Mercator because of its notoriety, we adopt a projection which may reduce the size of Greenland, but leaves India as diminutive as ever, compared to Europe; for instance, Van der Grinten, used by the National Geographic Society. Yet, what we really want is to face the world as it actually is, not as our Western self-esteem would like to picture it. We may study our own Europe in more detail than other areas—on appropriate separate pages of the atlas. But when we look at the world as a whole—when we look at mankind as a whole—we want our own parts of it to fall into place so that we can see ourselves in true proportion. We need an equal-area world map for any purposes for which we need a world map at all.

THE HISTORICAL WORLD-IMAGE OF THE WEST

So much for our geographical paradigm. An idea of world history is much less tangible than a map of the world. But much the same points can be made about the Western image of world history. Here too the very terms we allow ourselves to use foster distortion. We aim to overcome any parochial outlook, but so long as we do not radically overhaul our historical categories and our notions of the structure of the historical world, we find ourselves dragged back by older preconceptions the moment the center of our attention shifts to other concerns.

We know how the traditional story runs: history began in the "East"—in Mesopotamia and Egypt (but not in Paradise, still further east, as the medieval Westerners had said); the torch was then passed successively to Greece and Rome and finally to the Christians of northwestern Europe, where medieval and modern life developed. During the Middle Ages, Islam temporarily was permitted to hold the torch of science, which properly belonged to the West, until the West was ready to take it over and carry it forward. India, China, and Japan also had ancient civilizations but were isolated from the mainstream of history and "contributed" still less to it (that is, to Western Europe). In modern times Western Europe expanded over the rest of the world, so that Islam and India and China have ceased to be isolated, and have entered the orbit of the ongoing Western Civilization, now becoming a world civilization.

In this story, there are two key notions. There is a "mainstream" of history, which consists of our own direct antecedents. This includes all West-European history since it became civilized, of course; and before that time, selected periods from areas to the southeast: Greek history till the time of the Roman empire (but not since—the Byzantines do not count as mainstream); and the Near East till the rise of the Greeks, but not since. Note that this conception of "mainstream" is not identifiable with the history of lands of cultural creativity, or times of intensity of historical change. The "mainstream" of history, in the traditional image, runs through northwestern Europe in the Dark Ages of the Merovingians—although everyone knows that the Byzantines and the Muslims (and the Indians and the Chinese) were far more civilized then. The "mainstream" of history is simply our own closest historical antecedents.

In fact, all the lands of the "mainstream" are sometimes identified with the "West." Classical Greece is called "Western," though Byzantine Greece is often included in the "East." This brings us to the second key notion which allows us to construct a world history in which our own cultural ancestors hold most of the attention. All the other civilizations of the Eastern Hemisphere are lumped together under the heading "East," "Orient." This concept in history is the equivalent of the concept "Asia" in geography. It enables us to set up our West as conceptually equivalent to all the other civilized regions taken together—the "East"; just as the European peninsula is detached from the Eurasian landmass and made equivalent to all the rest of that landmass taken together—"Asia." Apart from Eurasia and the northern part of Africa (the latter is, of course, included in the "East," though Morocco is west of Spain), the more distant parts of the world were relatively sparsely inhabited and for the most part not highly civilized; their history does not force itself on our attention. Hence such a conception of Eurasia allows us to erect a classic ethnocentric dichotomy in the main part of the world—ourselves and the others, Jews and Gentiles, Greeks and Barbarians, "West" and "East." Since by definition the "mainstream" of history runs through the "West," by the same definition the "East" is isolated and static:

hence the West, already appearing as one half of mankind, is made the more important half also.

One of the most curious features of this modern Western ethnocentrism has been its superimposition on all the other ethnocentrisms of the world, generally compounding the confusion. Muslims or Hindus have tended to accept modern Western conceptions as indiscriminately scientific; they have commonly accepted their geographical and historical terms from the West, and the implications that follow from them. Sometimes the Western conceptions prove convenient, as when an Egyptian, identifying himself as "oriental," claims spiritual superiority to the West on the ground that Jesus, Buddha, and Confucius were all also "Orientals"; or, accepting the Western conception of "Africa" as a continent, finds an excellent excuse, as an "African," to meddle in Sub-Saharan politics without looking imperialistic. Sometimes the Western conceptions prove less convenient. I found displayed on the wall of an ardent Muslim in a government office in Cairo a map of the Muslim world, showing how widespread is Islam. But the map was a French one, drawn on the Mercator projection, and consequently drastically minimized the area of Islam as compared with Europe. The official was so used to the Mercator projection that he had not noticed this case of what might be called official imperialism.

Now just as the Mercator projection has been criticized so much that everyone is aware that it distorts, so the Western historical world image has been criticized; most of us are uneasily aware that "the East" is more important than we had thought. But just as most people think of Greenland as the best example of Mercator's distortion, failing to see just where the distortion is most misleading, and why certain related projections are just as bad, so it is rare for one to see the full implications of the distortions in the Western picture of world history, and to judge soundly of the various attempts to improve on them. Jim-Crow world maps continue to be the usual maps in newspapers, magazines, and general books; and few protest. Similarly, one or another modification of the Western world-historical image still underlies most discussions of mankind. This is true, unfortunately, even on the scholarly level, for some of the presentations of world history that try hardest to escape the traditional pattern still show its distortive influence.

THE CONTINUITY AMONG THE REGIONS OF THE EURASIAN HISTORICAL COMPLEX IN PRE-MODERN TIMES

I must limit myself here to discussing the major civilized regions of the Eastern Hemisphere. The overwhelming majority of mankind—until the last two centuries—lived within the region I am including. It was a zone of Afro-Eurasian lands extending from Atlantic to Pacific, but chiefly north of the equator, that most of those societies were to be found, before modern times, which had the developed agricultural and urban life which carried with them density of population. It is becoming conventional to articulate this Afro-Eurasian zone of civilization into four main nuclear regions, which we may call Europe, the Middle East, India, and the Far East of China and Japan. Such a division makes a good deal of sense from about 1000 B.C. on, at least, down to about 1800 of our era. Each of these regions presents a considerable continuity over some three thousand years of cultural development. More precisely, in each of these regions there was a core-area with reasonably persistent traditions, from which cultural influences have radiated more or less continuously into a wide surrounding region.

We must place these areas with greater precision, as we will have much to say of them. The core-area of what may be called Europe was the northern shores of the Mediterranean, from Anatolia to Italy especially. It had a Greek (and, later, Greco-Latin) culture which pervaded increasingly the lands to the north; but the Mediterranean lands remained economically and culturally dominant over the more northern ones, on the whole, from the time of the Minoans to the end of the Middle Ages. The core of the Middle East was the Fertile Crescent and the Iranian Plateau, to which lands north and south from Central Eurasia to Yemen and East Africa looked for cultural leadership, as did increasingly even Egypt, despite its distinct roots in its own past, and North Africa, and eventually all the Sudan. The great cultural languages of the Middle East were of the Semitic and Iranian families; though the particular Semitic and Iranian languages changed, much cultural lore was carried over from one period to the next. In the vast domain of Indic tradition east and south from the Hindu-Kush range, the Indus and Ganges valleys formed a somewhat similar core; there the Sanskrit and Pali languages developed, which became classical as far away as Cambodia and Java. Finally, the Hoang-Ho and Yangtze valleys in China formed a fourth creative core-area, from which cultural influences spread to an ever-increasing distance in all directions, within a constantly expanding China and beyond it to such lands as Japan and Vietnam.

Western scholars, at least since the nineteenth century, have tried to find ways of seeing this Afro-Eurasian zone of civilization as composed of distinct historical worlds, which can be fully understood in themselves, apart from all others. Their motives for this have been complex, but one convenient result of such a division would be to leave Europe, or even Western Europe, an independent division of the whole world, with a history that need not be integrated with that of the rest of mankind save on the terms posed by European history itself. But such attempts, if pressed consistently, leave us with a false notion of both world history and even European history. For even among the four great nuclear regions, the cleavages were not decisive enough to sustain such an interpretation. A brief survey of some of the more obvious cleavages will enable us to assess their significance.

If one tried to group these great cultural regions so as to divide the whole of the Afro-Eurasian historical complex into two portions (which is not often seriously attempted), the least useful division would be one in which Europe formed one portion, the "West," and the other three formed a second portion, the "East"; for the cleavage between Europe and its nearest neighbors was unusually slight. The lands north of the Mediterranean were always very closely linked with those of the Fertile Crescent and Iran. I have listed the Anatolian peninsula (the western half of the present Turkish Republic) as part of Europe, since it was one of the chief formative centers of Greek culture, and has always shared the fortunes of the Balkan peninsula; but it is commonly listed as part of the Middle East, and not entirely without reason. The Mediterranean Basin formed a historical whole not only under the Roman Empire but before and since; even at the height of the Middle Ages a land like Sicily brought together creatively Greek, Arab, and Latin. Greek thought became an integral element in the Middle Eastern tradition, while Middle Eastern religion had a central place in European life.

A somewhat sharper division existed between Europe and the Middle East on the one hand and the Indic lands on the other. Greeks and Arabs, Latins and Persians, have had much the same reaction to India, in medieval times, finding it alien to a degree they have not found each other alien. The Hindu-kush and the Baluchistan desert formed a more serious barrier than the Taurus. Yet even so the constant thriving trade between the Middle East and India was reflected in important cultural exchanges, which reinforced the fact of a partly common background. For, long before the coming of the Indo-Europeans assured a common origin to the languages and myths of India, Iran, and Greece, the Indus Valley civilization had been closely linked with that of Mesopotamia.

The greatest breach in continuity was between China on the one hand and the Indian, Middle Eastern, and Mediterranean lands on the other. The Himalayas were more effective even than the Hindu-kush. Until modern times, direct contact was usually limited to mercantile expeditions. Alexander invaded both Greece and the Punjab; the Turk, Timur, campaigned in Russia and on the Gangetic plain; but though Timur dreamed of China, he could scarcely have reached it. Yet the Mongol armies at one point mastered much of China and at the same time won victories in Germany, in Iran, and on the Indus. As we know, Buddhism, originating in India, colored deeply the life of China and Japan; while numerous important inventions, among them gunpowder, the compass, paper, and printing, apparently came at various times from China to the Middle East and so to India and Europe.

As Eurasian history is studied, it becomes clear that these interrelations were not purely external, accidental cultural borrowings and influences among independent societies. They reflect sequences of events and cultural patterns shading into each other on all cultural levels. The four nuclear regions are imperfect

historical abstractions. All regions formed together a single great historical complex of cultural developments.

Till modern times, the four core-areas were the most creative centers; but
there were always lesser creative centers beyond them, such as Tibet; and the
core-areas themselves cannot always be taken as units. Very early the cultural
traditions of the western and eastern Mediterranean regions began to be distinguished, till finally Greek and Latin, Orthodox and Catholic, developed relatively
independently of each other. Iran and Central Eurasia often seem to have had
their own history apart from the Fertile Crescent and Egypt. Northern and
southern India presented a major contrast to each other. Finally, there is no
point where the sort of differences that existed between the great regions could
be decisively distinguished from the sort of differences that existed between particular nations. Yet all our modern serious attempts at understanding world
history are based on the assumption of a series of distinct societies, distinct culture worlds, each with its own inner unity and with only external relations to the
others. Universalizing efforts, such as that of Ranke, are only seeming exceptions,
based on optical illusions which made Europe seem the world, and all other regions isolated and parochial.

As we consider the origins of the great civilizations, it will become evident both
why it is impossible to draw any sharp lines within the Afro-Eurasian historical
complex, and why none the less historians constantly try to draw such sharp
lines. As we know, literate culture arose very nearly at the same time, but in different (though usually urban) forms, in the Indus, the Tigris-Euphrates, and the
Nile valleys and probably somewhat later in the Hoang-ho and other less independent places as Crete. This process seems to have had a common, interdependent development at least from the Indus to the Aegean; that is, in the areas
which became the subsequent cores of the Indian, Middle Eastern, and European
traditions. Some sort of Neolithic life had been widespread for some time; when
once it crystallized into urban, literate forms in one place, it did so in many; and
then rapidly spread over wide regions. It was only when developing civilization
had come to a certain point—at about the same time in the main centers of the
Afro-Eurasian zone—that the great regional traditions can come to be distinguished.
They grew out of a relative breakdown of the local cultural traditions in a more
cosmopolitan setting, into which many local strains had intermingled, from the
Aegean to the Indus valley. The distinction among the different great regions was
secondary, and based largely on accidents not only of geography but of history,
even from the start.

This point is supported by the fact that in the marginal areas, such as Central
Eurasia, where influences from the several core-areas overlapped, the culture cannot be reduced to a mixture of those of the main cultural regions. Commonly,
all areas had their own traditions reaching back into Neolithic times, and forming
directly an integral part of the broader Eurasian cultural whole. The French have

emphasized this in the case of ancient Gaul; it is equally true of Malaysia or of Central Eurasia. In the Oxus-Jaxartes valleys, no doubt Semitic-Iranian influences had the greatest sway of any from outside; the writing systems came from the Fertile Crescent, for instance. For long periods, again, the Oxus-Jaxartes region was linked with northern India both politically and to a large degree in religion, literature, and the arts. Buddhism flourished there (it was from there that it came most readily to China). Chinese influence was strong recurrently, not only when the area was under Chinese political domination. Even Hellenism flourished there for a period. Yet the history of the Oxus-Jaxartes basin possesses its own continuity over time; it cannot be read simply as a function of the history of the several great cultural regions. Moreover, the historical context in which its history makes sense can be nothing less than the whole Eurasian civilized zone.

THE PLACE OF SUPRA-NATIONAL SOCIETIES IN THE AFRO-EURASIAN COMPLEX

Hence the more sophisticated have tried to make not permanent regions as such, but supra-national societies, defined purely historically and so limited in time as well as space, the desired independent historical worlds. It is in this sense that the phrase, "the Western world," has meaning, if it has any serious meaning at all. This attempt has its own limitations. Such societies are conceived as held together by some element of conscious solidarity, perhaps through spiritual pre-suppositions or through creative style. They are distinct "worlds" in the sense of realms of communication on the highest cultural level. Spengler's is the most famous of the many attempts at distinguishing such societies. Toynbee made a rather half-hearted attempt to do the same, with his doctrine of separate "intel-ligible fields"; but the weight of his material forced him to go beyond the usual limits, and in effect he abandons the attempt. If we examine Toynbee's work more closely we find that his alleged "intelligible fields" are not really independ-ent intelligible fields, nor even the most important intelligible fields of his own historical study. In the end what is most important in this system comes to be the development of the religions, and he shows the religions developing right across the lines of his nineteen civilizations, which he began by supposing to be independently intelligible fields. In the end most of his work makes no sense ex-cept in terms of one large intelligible field—the whole Afro-Eurasian historical complex, in which the several generations of his "societies" are variously related to each other.

This is necessarily so; for important as the various supra-national societies were as frameworks of historical life, they overlapped each other, and even so they did not exhaust the field among them. They were superimposed on a con-tinuum of historical life which recognized no insuperable geographical boundary anywhere between the two oceans. Commercial life, the patterns of urban and rural relations, and the spread of technology, particularly military technology, commonly evolved in relative disregard of the boundaries of religious or literary traditions; such matters were often determined more by local conditions on the one hand and by the general cultural level of the civilized zone on the other.

When historians speak of civilizations or societies, in such connections, they are usually referring primarily to certain limited, if very important, aspects of civilized life. Normally, before modern times, a given area was indeed associated, at any given time, much more closely with some neighboring areas than with others. These associations have been of three main types, political, literary, and religious. The political associations have usually been relatively transient, and only rarely come into consideration here except as reinforced by literary and religious associations.

In the early days of civilization, each language area seems to have developed with relative autonomy from every other; but fairly early certain languages came to be recognized as unusually rich in cultural values, and were cultivated as cultural languages even by peoples which did not use them as the vernacular. Thus Sumerian and Babylonian came to be classical languages for the Fertile Crescent and to some degree for Iran; all the peoples whose literate elite paid some degree of deference to that classical tradition formed in some sense a single civilization. They possessed common terms of reference and common standards, and sometimes the recognition of a classical literary tradition carried with it varying degrees of common legal forms, common political ideals, common artistic patterns. This became especially true by the end of the first millennium B.C., when local cultural traditions within the main geographical regions had been largely submerged.

But by the Middle Ages, the rise of the religions of salvation had established bonds which were as strong as, or even stronger than, those of literary tradition; such bonds sometimes cut right across the lines of literary association. In the regions from Europe to India, religious affiliation became more important than literary, and peoples came to be linked together as Christian or Zoroastrian or Buddhist, rather than as using Greek or Cuneiform or Sanskrit. In China and the Far East, religious affiliation was eventually outbalanced by literary affiliation, and Chinese society was ruled in the end in the name of the Confucian classics rather than of Buddhist or Taoist faith. In any case, on the "high cultural" level most educated men found themselves associated with a given lettered tradition, "literary" or religious, normally to the exclusion of any others.

The importance of such groupings for the development of human life can hardly be overestimated, particularly for that of the ideal and the imaginative life, religion, art, belles-lettres, and even law and political and social institutions. To some degree even the life of the peasant was molded by the ideals set forth in the lettered tradition cultivated by the educated élite of his area. But it is not because of any implications for peasant life, but because of literary and philological implications, that historians have concentrated attention on them. They are indeed the central concern of a humanistic historian. But in the course of giving them almost exclusive attention, many historians have misinterpreted them; they have absolutized these lettered traditions into "historical worlds" to an illegitimate degree.

Such societies were never closed wholes; there were always fields of activity, even important fields, that were but superficially molded by the central tradition in question. As in the case of the geographical regions on which they were often based, there were always territories where two or more traditions competed, and actual life, even on the high cultural level, was a synthesis of diverse elements. These were not anomalies, as our theorists have tended to count them. Indeed, different sorts of lettered tradition mingled in different degrees in given societies. Thus it is possible to regard Byzantine life on the one hand as a continuation of the ancient Greek culture and on the other hand as part of a Christian complex, wider in area, but more restricted in time. Revealingly, there existed lesser lettered traditions of the same basic sort, which had less extensive effects, but cut across other lines. Thus the society formed by the Platonic-Aristotelian philosophers, clinging to a particular strand of the Greek literary tradition, cut across the lines formed by Christianity, Islâm and Judaism; these philosophers lived lives largely molded by their common philosophical heritage, and often had more in common with each other than with any of their respective religious groups. More tenuous, but perhaps even more important, was the interregional tradition of natural science, originating in Babylonian and Greek writing, taken up in Sanskrit and later in Arabic, and transmitted still later to Chinese and Latin—a vigorous tradition of wide implications, which cut across all the main cultural lines of the Afro-Eurasian zone.

Islâm was the community which succeeded perhaps most strongly in building for itself a total society, demarcated sharply from all culture before and beyond its limits. Though it appeared relatively late in Eurasian history, as the religions go, it developed its own system of comprehensive law—where the Christian communities took over pagan Roman law. It created its own classical literatures, with only a limited reminiscence of earlier Middle Eastern traditions. Social organization, economic patterns, the arts, all carried an unmistakable Islâmic coloring. Moreover, though the Islâmic society was far the most widespread among its contemporary medieval societies, yet an unusually strong social solidarity prevailed among Muslims, from Morocco to Java and from Kazan to Zanzibar.

Yet even so, on investigation, it is clear that Islâm as a lettered tradition cannot be treated as a distinct historical world, an exclusive intelligible field. The Middle-Eastern origins of the Islâmic society are relatively obscure; we know too little about life in the Fertile Crescent and Iran in the immediately preceding centuries. But it seems likely that one central phenomenon of early Islâm had gotten well under way in the last generations of Sāsānī rule: the centering of power in urban mercantile communities, under the lead of an absolute monarch who could override and break down the locally rooted power of the landed nobility and gentry. The rise of the late Sāsānī sects and that of the classical Muslim sects both seem to be closely related to this situation. We are learning that we cannot really make out what was going on in early Islâmic political and religious life without a much fuller understanding of the Sāsānī life which preceded it. Moreover, the orthodox faith of Islâm itself, as it was created in the course of the first two or three Muslim centuries, cannot be understood simply as a fulfilment of the vision of Muhammad; that vision could have been fulfilled in innumerable other ways, or indeed (as might have seemed most likely) reduced to a merely political ideology, to wither away as the Arab ruling class became assimilated. The being of Islâm must be explained in terms of the aspirations of Syrian Christian monks and Mesopotamian Jewish zealots—aspirations which gave to early Muslim converts their very notion of what a religion ought to be, and which they fulfilled in an unprecedented way.

When later the Islâmic society expanded over half the Afro-Eurasian civilized zone, the persisting regional configuration of that zone reasserted itself despite all Muslim solidarity. By the sixteenth century, at the latest, Islâm in eastern Europe, Islâm in the Middle East proper, and Islâm in India were clearly pursuing their separate paths. Already when Bābur, founder of the Mogul empire, entered India, he seems to have found the local Muslims as alien to him as their Hindu friends; and despite the continued reliance of his descendants on Middle Eastern and Central Eurasian personnel, and despite a strong puritanical force within Indian Islâm which rejected its Indian-ness and eventually won over the Mogul emperor himself, Islâmic society in India under the Moguls increasingly developed its own Indian institutional framework and cultural patterns, and formed a relatively independent society. East-European Islâm, under the Ottoman empire in Anatolia and the Balkans, evolved in a like direction. The Ottoman empire, like the Mogul, reversed in its own area the long-standing trend of Islâm toward decentralization and toward reduction of the social role of political authority; it built up enduring central institutions, religious, legal, and political, though quite different ones from those of the Moguls. But the heart of Ottoman life remained its European center—the formerly Greek lands of Anatolia and the Balkans. The Arab areas south of the Taurus remained only half-subdued dominions, sharing relatively little in the creative sides of Ottoman life; Irâq, at least, tied its sympathies to the third great Muslim empire of the time, the Safavī empire of Iran.

Indeed, not only in these three empires, expressing the traditions of the three core-areas of previous millenniums, but throughout the Afro-Eurasian zone, Islâm was a microcosm of interregional civilization, containing within its society all the types of relationships which had formerly been carried on as between the several regions into which it had spread. In Malaysia, Islâm had powerful effects;

it overlay the earlier Indic traditions with the hemisphere-wide Muslim allegiance, and replaced the earlier Indic-type literary inspiration with a new inspiration expressed in a new alphabet, if not a new tongue. Yet even in their new faith, the Malaysians were inspired largely by *Indian* Islâm as they had been by Indian Hinduism; and their new literary traditions, so far as these did break with the old (which was not entirely), derived also from the mixture of Persian and Arabic heritage which prevailed in southern India. More important, Islâm in Malaysia (sometimes a bit to the scandal of orthodox Muslims there and elsewhere), rarely took on, before quite modern times, the rigorous severity which from time to time purged Islamic life in its more central regions; Islâm for Malaysia was a new and more universal mysticism, and was taught as such by the heirs of the Indic *gurus*. In fact, Islâm for Malaysia was the natural consequence of its position in the Afro-Eurasian zone as a whole. Malaysia lay at the crossroads of the Southern Seas. Its higher cultural life, from the time when civilization first came there, was ultimately adopted from the life of its ports. Yet these on the one hand remained somewhat apart from the life of the interior—never deeply rooted in local traditions, and on the other hand naturally remained open to the broad currents of culture from throughout the Southern Seas. When the dominant culture of merchants in those waters was Hindu or Buddhist, the port cities became Hindu and Buddhist, and eventually the hinterland followed them. As interregional trade gradually increased in volume and range, the Middle Eastern ports came to have a more pivotal role in the trade of all the Southern Seas; it was then the Middle Eastern culture which increasingly prevailed in the ports of those seas—especially in Malaysia. By the later Middle Ages this meant Islâm. But the fundamental pattern of Malaysian life persisted; and it can be understood only in the context of the Afro-Eurasian civilized zone as a whole.

It has become clear that historical life, from early times at least till two or three centuries ago, was continuous across the Afro-Eurasian zone of civilization; that zone was ultimately indivisible. The various regions had their own traditions; important social bodies arose, sometimes within a regional framework, sometimes cutting across regional life, which molded much of the cultural life of their constituents. But all these lesser historical wholes were imperfect wholes. They were secondary groupings. Local civilized life could go on without full participation in any of them; some of the most creative of historical activities, such as that of natural science, cut right across their boundaries. The whole of the Afro-Eurasian zone is the only context large enough to provide a framework for answering the more general and more basic historical questions that can arise. . . .

3. THE TERMINATION OF CONFLICT

*Lewis A. Coser**

Certain social processes are finite, i.e., they are defined by their transitory character and the manner of their termination is institutionally prescribed. Courtship ends when union with the beloved has been attained in marriage; formal education ends when the educational goal has been reached and examinations or commencement exercises mark completion of the process. Other social processes, however, such as friendship or love, have no precise termination point. They follow a law of social inertia insofar as they continue to operate if no explicit provision for stopping their course is made by the participants. Social conflict is such a process. While in a game, for example, the rules for the process include rules for its ending, in social conflict explicit provisions for its termination must be made by the contenders. If no mutual agreements are made at some time during the struggle, it "ceaseth only in death" or in total destruction of at least one of the antagonists. The termination of conflict hence presents problems that do not arise in finite processes.

Various types of conflicts can be classified according to the degree of their normative regulation. Fully institutionalized conflicts, such as duels, may be said to constitute one extreme of a continuum while absolute conflicts, in which the goal is the total destruction of the enemy rather than a mutually agreed-upon settlement fall at the other extreme. In the second type, agreement is reduced to a minimum; the struggle ceases only upon the extermination of one or both of the contenders. As Hans Speier has said, "peace terminating an absolute war is established *without* the enemy" (9, p. 223).

It stands to reason that conflicts of this kind—at least between contenders with a rough equality of strength—are exceedingly costly and exhausting. If the contenders wish to prevent their struggle from becoming a zero sum game in which the outcome can only be total defeat or total victory, they have a common

SOURCE. Lewis A. Coser, "The Termination of Conflict," in *The Journal of Conflict Resolution,* 5 (December, 1961), pp. 347-353. Reprinted by permission of the author and the Center for Research on Conflict Resolution. Copyright 1961 by the University of Michigan.

[1]This paper was written while the author was carrying out research at the Institute for Social Research, Oslo, Norway, under a Fulbright grant.

interest in establishing mechanisms which can lead to an agreed-upon termination of the struggle. The fact is that most conflicts do indeed end long before the defeated has been totally crushed. "Resistance to the last man" is almost always a phrase. As long as one belligerent survives in one's camp further resistance is always possible; yet combat usually ceases long before this point is reached. This is so because both parties agree upon norms for the termination of the conflict.

While absolute conflicts allow practically no agreements as to their termination, certain types of highly institutionalized conflicts have built-in termination points. Trials by ordeal, duels and other agonistic struggles are centered upon symbolic endings which give them game-like features and determine the outcome automatically. A score is kept, a goal line established, maximum injury is conventionally fixed. When the score adds up to a certain number, when a certain type of injury has been established, or the goal line has been crossed, the conflict is over and the loser as well as the winner can easily perceive the outcome of the contention.

In conflicts not fully institutionalized, assessment of relative strength is not an easy matter so that the loser may not in fact concede that he has lost, nor may he even be aware of it. Therefore, it is to the interest of both contenders that the point at which victory is attained or the point beyond which no more gains can be anticipated, be marked as clearly as possible so as to avoid unnecessary exertions on both sides. Termination of conflict becomes a problem to be solved by both parties.

The termination of conflict is a social process dependent upon, but not directly deducible from its pursuits. It is, as Georg Simmel has noted, "a specific enterprise. It belongs neither to war nor to peace, just as a bridge is different from either bank it connects" (8, p. 110). To be sure, the outcome of a conflict is related to the goals of the antagonists and to the means by which it is fought; its duration and intensity will depend on objectives and available resources plus the time and effort required to achieve a decision. But the termination of the conflict, that is, agreement as to what constitutes a true decision, highlights some factors which are not deducible from its pursuit and must hence be studied separately.

For all except absolute conflict, termination involves a reciprocal activity and cannot be understood simply as an unilateral imposition of the will of the stronger on the weaker. Therefore, contrary to what common sense might suggest, not only the potential victor but also the potential vanquished makes crucial contributions to the termination. As a military commentator has pointed out, "war is pressed by the victor, but peace is made by the vanquished. Therefore, to determine the causes of peace, it is always necessary to take the vanquished's point of view. Until the vanquished quits, the war goes on" (1, p. 18). Victory, in other words, involves the yielding of the vanquished. By the very act of declaring himself beaten, he achieves a last assertion of power. With this act, as Georg Simmel has said, "he actually makes a gift to the victor" (8, p. 114). The capacity of making gifts is a measure of autonomy.

If both victor and vanquished are to make a contribution to the termination of their conflict they must arrive at some agreement. Thomas Schelling has recently argued persuasively that "limited war requires limits . . . but limits require agreement or at least some kind of mutual recognition and acquiescence" (7, p. 53). This applies not only to the conduct but also to the termination of conflicts. In order to end a conflict the parties must agree upon rules and norms allowing them to assess their respective power position in the struggle. Their common interest leads them to accept rules which enhance their mutual dependence in the very pursuit of their antagonistic goals. Such agreements make their conflict, so to speak, self-liquidating. To the degree that such rules are provided, the conflict is partly institutionalized and acquires some of the features of the agonistic struggle alluded to earlier.

Agreements as to goals and determination of outcome shorten the conflict. Once a goal has been reached by one of the parties and this accepted as a clue to the acceptance of defeat by the other, the conflict is ended. The more restricted the object of contention and the more visible for both parties the clues to victory, the higher the chances that the conflict be limited in time and extension. Emile Durkheim's dictum concerning human needs, "The more one has, the more one wants, since satisfaction received only stimulates instead of filling needs" is applicable in this connection. Agreed-upon limits upon the "appetities" of the contenders place normative restrictions upon a process which does not inherently contain self-limiting properties. The history of trade unionism provides interesting examples.

Struggles engaged in by business unionism, given its limited goals, provide for the contending parties an opportunity for settlement and furnishes them at the same time with recognizable signals as to the opportune moment for ending a conflict. Revolutionary syndicalism, on the other hand, has always been plagued by the problem of ending strike action. Since its goal is the overthrow of the capitalist order rather than improvements within it, it cannot accept as the end of the conflict outcomes which would constitute victories from the point of view of business unionism. Revolutionary syndicalism is faced with the dilemma that no outcome of a strike, short of the overthrow of capitalism, can be considered an acceptable form of conflict resolution so that its strategy is foredoomed to failure. Not sensitized to clues which would allow them to conclude that a victory has been reached, unable to recognize peace overtures or concessions from the adversary, revolutionary syndicalists are not in a position to take advantage of partial gains. Paradoxically, in this case, those who are under ordinary conditions the *weaker* party demand "unconditional surrender" of the stronger so that they make it inevitable that the struggle can cease only upon total exhaustion.

The above examples illustrate how closely specific outcomes are related to the aims of the contenders. The smaller the sacrifice a party demands from the opponent, the more limited the aims, the higher the chances that the potential loser will be ready to give up battle. The loser must be led to decide that peace is more attractive than the continuation of the conflict; such a decision will be powerfully enhanced if the demands made upon him are not exorbitant (1, p. 253 *et passim*). When the war aims of the winning side are limited as, say, in the Spanish-American war or the Russo-Japanese conflict of 1905, the making of peace is relatively easy. Once the Japanese war aims—the stopping of Russian penetration into the Far East—had been reached, Japan could afford to make the first move for peace by appealing to Theodore Roosevelt to act as a mediator. Once Cuba was liberated and the Spanish fleet defeated, American war aims were attained and the United States had no interest in continuing the war through an attack upon the Spanish mainland.

It remains, however, that no matter how the activities of the potential winner have facilitated an early termination of the conflict, the final decision to end the war remains with the potential loser. How, then, is the loser moved to decide that he has, in fact, lost? Not only the objective situation but the perception of the situation is crucially important since only the latter will bring forth the requisite admission of defeat. "If an opponent," writes Clausewitz, "is to be made to comply with our will, we must place him in a situation which is more oppressive to him than the sacrifice we demand" (2, vol. 1, p. 5). This elegantly phrased dictum is, however, meaningless unless the criteria be specified that determine how the antagonist will in fact assess the situation. Different contenders might arrive at variant estimates as to the degree of oppressiveness of a situation and of the value of the sacrifice demanded. Since such assessments are difficult to make and do not depend on rational calculations alone, they are greatly facilitated by the availability of symbolic signposts.

Whenever wars have been strictly limited, as in eighteenth-century warfare, some visible event, such as the taking of a particular fortress, the reaching of some natural barrier and the like, symbolized to both parties that the desired objective has been reached by one of them and that the conflict could now be considered solved through the subsequent acquiescence of the loser. When such mutually acceptable symbolic clues are not available, the resolution of the conflict will be more difficult.

The nature of such symbolic clues may vary considerably[2] and it is hence important that the potential winner ascertain which clues will be accepted by the potential loser as symbols of defeat. If in the common consciousness of the

---

[2]One must further distinguish between purely symbolic events, such as the capture of a flag, and events which, as in the examples that follow, have realistic as well as symbolic significance.

citizens, the capital symbolizes the very existence of the nation, then its fall will
be perceived as defeat and will lead to the acceptance of the terms of the victor.
The Fall of Paris in 1871 and 1940 symbolized to the bulk of Frenchmen the
end of the war despite the fact that Gambetta had rallied significant numbers of
undefeated troops in the provinces, and that de Gaulle appealed for the continuation of the war from London. Only a relatively small number of Frenchmen refused to accept the Fall of Paris as a symbol of defeat. In less centralized nations,
however, where the capital has no such symbolic significance, its fall is not perceived as a decisive event. Pretoria and Bloemfontein fell to the British in 1900,
yet Boer resistance, rather to the surprise of the British, continued for two more
years. The British failed to understand that, to the rural Boers, the vast countryside rather than the cities symbolized the nation; to them the war ended only
when want of forage, capture, and overwork decimated the Boer horses. In a
country in which men were bred in the saddle, the decimation of horses symbolized defeat (1, p. 114). Similarly, the sacking of Washington in 1812 did not
signal defeat to Americans for whom the open spaces of the country rather than
the federal capital symbolized national independence. In other situations the
capture of charistmatic war lords rather than any taking of a locality will symbolize defeat.

The structure of the opposing camp furnishes clues as to meaningful symbols
of defeat and victory. It is hence of the utmost importance for both sides to have
as much knowledge as possible about the characteristic features of their respective
structure and symbols. When ignorant armies clash at night, their pluralistic
ignorance militates against their ability to come to terms short of mutual exhaustion.

The contenders' ability to make use of one another's symbols of defeat and
victory does not only depend on their awareness of the structure of the opposing
camp, but also on the dynamics within each camp. Internal struggles may be
waged over what set of events may be considered a decisive symbol of defeat. A
minority may consider that resistance can be continued even though the majority has accepted defeat. Subgroups may consider that the decision-makers have
betrayed the cause by agreeing to end the conflict. Peace terms provide ample
material for internal conflict within each of the contending camps. These terms
are, moreover, likely to be defined and redefined in the course of the conflict in
tune with the fortunes of battle. Different parties may disagree violently on
whether a given event is to be considered decisive or of only incidental significance. Such contentions are likely to be the more deepgoing the less integrated
the social structure. In integrated structures internal contentions may vitalize
and strengthen the groups' energies, but if divergencies as to appropriate action
affect the basic layers of common belief, symbolizations of victory and defeat
are also likely to be basically divergent (3, pp. 72-80). In highly polarized social
systems where a number of internal conflicts of different sorts are superimposed

upon one another, there exists hardly any common definition of the situation binding all members of the society to commonly held perceptions (3, p. 76 ff., 4, pp. 213 ff.). To the extent that a society or group is rent into rival camps so that there is no community of ends between the parties, if one party is not willing to accept the definition of the situation which the other propounds, the making of peace becomes an almost impossible enterprise. In such situations a prior settlement of scores within, an unambiguous definition or redefinition of the balance of power between contending groups, may be the precondition for concluding peace without. The Russian provisional government after the March 1917 revolution being continuously goaded and challenged by the growing Bolshevik Party, was unable either to wage war effectively or to conclude peace; once the Bolsheviks had seized power their definition of the situation prevailed and peace could be concluded at Brest Litowsk.

Even when such deepgoing fissures are not present in a social structure, the ever-present divergencies between the perspectives of the leaders and the led, between those in authority and those submitted to it (4, ch. 5), require considerable effort on the part of the leaders to make the led accept their definition of the situation. Just as at the beginning of the struggle the leaders must convince the led that the sacrifice demanded of them will redound to their benefit and that the conflict concerns wide interests of all rather than the narrow interests of the top stratum, so the leaders must also be able to convince the led that the acceptance of defeat is warranted and even desirable from the point of view of the total system rather than in terms of special leadership interests. To make defeat palatable may require as much effort as to make war desirable.

Leaders will typically differ from the led not only in terms of social perspectives but also in regard to their cognitive horizon so that leaders may be able to assess consequences and relative advantages more rationally than the led. A leader foreseeing a defeat which is not as yet visible to his followers must adjust his strategy to the need of convincing the followers. In such an effort it might be advantageous to him to construe partial defeat in such a way as to make it appear as at least a partial victory. Often the led, like the mark in a con game, might have to be cooled out by being told that what they experience as a loss is "really" a partial victory (5).

Contentions within enemy camps as to the proper definition of the situation once again highlight the importance of symbolizations. The leader will have to rely on his ability to manipulate the symbolic system by which the led define the situations if he is to soften the blow that defeat implies. In labor-management conflicts, for example, events which may appear to an outsider as having only peripheral importance may in fact have highly charged emotional significance to the participants. The return to work of a few strikers or, alternatively, the success of a demonstration or the support of public officials or the reactions of an organ of public opinion, may be invested by the rank and file with high symbolic significance and trigger off a return to work or a revival of the will to victory. This is why it is important for the leaders to manage the symbols that structure the perception of the led. The strike leader must know how to end a strike at the opportune moment, but his knowledge would serve him but little if he did not also have the ability to communicate his knowledge to the led. This may often involve the highlighting for the rank and file of a partially attained victory in order to divert attention from a partially suffered defeat.

This is the stuff of which compromises are made. Often seen by the rank and file as a "betrayal" by the leaders, they actually derive from the structural circumstance that the leaders' position allows them a view of the total situation which is denied to the led. Moreover, leadership roles require to so manage intragroup tensions as to keep the group united in adversity even though this might entail certain sacrifices insofar as the attainment of the group's goals are concerned. "System maintenance," to use Parsons' terminology, may sometimes require lowered task performance.

Indeed, most conflicts end in compromises in which it is often quite hard to specify which side has gained relative advantage. Hence, one must distinguish between the will to make peace and the will to accept defeat. Quite often the former may be present although the latter is not. The parties to the conflict may be willing to cease the battle when they recognize that their aims cannot be attained or that they can be attained only at a price which they are not willing to pay, or, more generally, when they conclude that continuation of the conflict is less attractive than the making of peace. In neither of these cases would they be willing to accept defeat although they are willing to stop short of victory. In such situations they may be impelled to explore the chances for a compromise. The willingness to negotiate a compromise, that is, to stop chasing the mirage of victory, will, of course, depend on correct assessment of the situation and such assessment, just as in the cases discussed earlier, will be facilitated by the availability of indices of relative standing in the battle. It is one of the key functions of the mediator to make such indices readily available to both parties. To the extent that the contenders share a common system of symbols allowing them to arrive at a common assessment, to that extent they will be able to negotiate. Symbols of defeat and victory thus turn out to be of relevance in order to stop short of either.

Relative appraisal of power is difficult before the contenders have measured their respective strength in conflict. But accommodation may be reached once such an assessment has been achieved. Such redefinitions in the course of a struggle often bring to the fore elements which remained hidden during its onset. Accommodation is facilitated if criteria are available which allow the contenders to gauge the situation. The chance of attaining peace without victory depends on the possibility of achieving consensus as to relative strength and on the ability to make this new definition "stick" within each camp. When the United States chose the neck of Korea as their symbolic standing place in the Korean war, they succeeded in conveying to the other side as well as to the American people their determination to hold it. When enough blood had been let and it became clear to both sides that the other could be beaten only at a cost that neither was willing to incur, negotiations got down to a compromise that took into account the real balance of political and military power and proved acceptable at home. "Peace through stalemate," writes B. H. Liddell-Hart, "based on a coincident recognition by each side of the opponent's strength, is at least preferable to peace through common exhaustion" (6, p. 370).

Although it is true that in many cases an assessment of the relative strength of the opponents is possible only in conflict, it is also true that their travail may be shortened if clear symbolizations of outcome and relative strength are readily available. When recourse to such measures of success or failure has been highly institutionalized, the duration of the conflict can be shortened and its intensity limited. In this sense, research directed toward an understanding of those symbols which move men to accept compromise or even defeat might be as valuable as research to uncover symbols which incite to war.

REFERENCES

1. Calahan, H. A. *What Makes a War End*. New York: Vanguard Press, 1944.
2. Clausewitz, Karl von. *On War*. London: Routledge and Kegan Paul, 1956.
3. Coser, Lewis A. *The Functions of Social Conflict*. Glencoe, Ill.: Free Press, 1956.
4. Dahrendorf, Ralf. *Class and Class Conflict in Industrial Society*. Stanford, Calif.: Stanford University Press, 1959.
5. Goffman, Erving. "On Cooling the Mark Out," *Psychiatry,* **15** (November, 1952), 451-63.
6. Liddell-Hart, B. H. *Strategy, the Indirect Approach*. London: Faber and Faber, 1955.
7. Schelling, Thomas C. *The Strategy of Conflict*. Cambridge, Mass.: Harvard University Press, 1960.
8. Simmel, Georg. *Conflict*. Trans. Kurt H. Wolff. Glencoe, Ill.: Free Press, 1955.
9. Speier, Hans. *Social Order and the Risks of War*. New York: George W. Stewart, 1952.

Part II

SOCIETIES AND INTERNATIONAL RELATIONS

In Part II the focus is on the society and its components as the units of analysis. Although the action of a state is not solely determined by internal characteristics of the state and its society, an understanding of international relations requires studying how members of a society individually and collectively develop foreign policy views and act upon them. Of particular interest are those characteristics of societies or states that affect the way in which collective decisions with other states are reached and, more particularly, the use of war as a means of reaching a decision.

Views of foreign policy among the population at large may affect the priority given to different modes of handling conflict in general or with particular other states. It is also necessary to understand how views of foreign policy are formed and to what extent they may be modified by the very processes of collective decision making utilized and by other international transactions. In Part III of the book we shall look at some of the variations in international transactions and the factors affecting them.

Much of the research relevant to international relations which has been done by sociologists and other behavioral scientists has concentrated upon foreign policy views of the population at large, of elite groups, or of other selected segments of the society.[1]

[1]In addition to the studies cited later in these introductory notes, see, for example, Gabriel A. Almond, *The American People and Foreign Policy* (New York: Harcourt, Brace and Co., 1950); Peter M. Blau, "Orientation of College Students Toward International Relations," *American Journal of Sociology*, LIX (November, 1953), pp. 205-214; Vilhelm Aubert, Burton Fisher, and Stein Rokkan, "A Comparative Study of Teachers' Attitudes to International Problems and Policies," *The Journal of Social Issues*, X:4 (1954), pp. 25-39; Kenneth P. Adler and Davis Borrow, "Interest and Influence in Foreign Affairs," *Public Opinion Quarterly*, 20 (Spring, 1956), pp. 89-101; Lloyd A. Free, *Six Allies and a Neutral* (Glencoe, Ill.: The Free Press, 1959); Johan Galtung, "Foreign Policy Opinion as a Function of Social Position," *Journal of Peace Research*, Nos. 3-4 (1964), pp. 206-231; Jerome Laulicht, "Public Opinion and Foreign Policy Decisions," *Journal of Peace Research*, No. 2 (1965), pp. 147-160; and Daniel Lerner, "French Business Leaders Look at EDC: A Preliminary Report," *Public Opinion Quarterly*, 20 (Spring, 1956), pp. 212-221.

There is abundant evidence that how individuals perceive and evaluate nations, agencies, and policies relevant to international relations depends upon experience which they deem relevant, as shaped and filtered by friends, leaders, mass media, and their general orientations, as well as by the raw reality encountered. The selections in Chapter Two illustrate and document some of these factors and processes.

Gamson and Modigliani (Selection 4) propose some alternative models for explaining foreign policy opinions and present evidence regarding them. Clearly, people are influenced by others in forming opinions about foreign policy; they are likely to accept the interpretations of authoritative leaders. But what happens when leaders disagree? At such times, popular sentiments tend to diverge as people adhering to each political party tend to be influenced by their respective leaders.[2] Party adherence apparently is usually based upon factors other than the party's stand on foreign policy issues.

The Gamson and Modigliani paper also points out the importance of considering variations among people in understanding how they will react to their experiences and to the views of others. They use level of knowledge of foreign affairs as an indicator of attachment to the mainstream in one model and as an indicator of conceptual sophistication in another model. They also more directly examine general beliefs about the Cold War and the U.S.S.R. Such social positions and belief systems play a role in interaction with other factors in molding opinions. Many other studies have been done which investigate personality factors related to general orientations and particular opinions about international affairs.[3]

Reigrotski and Anderson (Selection 5) investigate the effects upon national stereotypes of exposure to people of other nations. Despite differences in the consequences which undoubtedly arise from variations among the people involved in such international transactions and the settings in which they occur, their findings reveal some typical consequences.

As background, it should be noted that national stereotypes are learned through early socialization, experience with people in other nations (and what

---

[2]See, for example, Bernard R. Berelson, Paul F. Lazarsfeld, and William N. McPhee, *Voting: A Study of Opinion Formation in a Presidential Campaign* (Chicago, Ill.: University of Chicago Press, 1954), pp. 182-214; Louis Kriesberg, "Die Europaische Gemeinschaft fur Kohle and Stahl im Urteil der Deutschen, 1950-1956," *Kolner Zeitschrift,* 11:3 (1959), pp. 486-515; and Eugene J. Rosi, "Mass and Attentive Opinion on Nuclear Weapons Tests and Fallout, 1954-1963," *Public Opinion Quarterly,* 29 (Summer, 1965), pp. 280-297.

[3]See, for example, M. B. Smith, J. S. Bruner, and R. White, *Opinions and Personality* (New York: John Wiley and Sons, 1956); Daniel J. Levinson, "Authoritarian Personality and Foreign Policy," *Journal of Conflict Resolution,* I (March, 1957), pp. 37-47; and William A. Scott, "Psychological and Social Correlates of International Images," in Herbert C. Kelman (ed.), *International Behavior* (New York: Holt, Rinehart and Winston, 1965), pp. 71-103. 103.

they say about themselves), and from the media.[4] The stability of national stereotypes cannot be presumed nor can their independence of governmental relations. For example, in 1942 and then in 1948 a cross section of the United States population was asked to select those adjectives that best described the Russians.[5] In 1942 25 adjectives were presented, and in 1948 12 adjectives were presented; 7 adjectives were common to both lists. The percentage of the population selecting each of the 7 adjectives in 1942 and 1948 is as presented below:

	1942	1948
Hardworking	61%	49%
Intelligent	16	12
Practical	18	13
Conceited	3	28
Cruel	9	50
Brave	48	28
Progressive	24	15

Such rapid and profound changes in images of the Russians among Americans should caution one in attempting to account for national policy in terms of popular stereotypes of other peoples. The stereotypes reflect political relations between governments as well as more direct experience with the people concerned. Perhaps, if interaction between Americans and Russians was much more widespread than it was and is, and if governmental relations were more stable and the learning of stereotypes more widespread and constant, the stereotypes would have more resistance to modification by shifts in governmental relations. We do not know.

Russett (Selection 6) reports on a study of members of the United States Senate and the British House of Commons. He reveals how, people of nonelite status, transnational experiences and social relations with others—constituent and party ties—affect foreign policy views. Moreover, the study reveals how these factors differ in significance in different circumstances.

[4]See, for example, Jean Piaget and Anne-Marie Weil, "The Development in Children of the Idea of the Homeland and of Relations with Other Countries," *International Social Science Bulletin*, III (Autumn, 1951), pp. 561-578 and the other papers in the issue devoted to national stereotypes and international understanding. Also see Otto Klineberg, *The Human Dimension in International Relations* (New York: Holt, Rinehart and Winston, 1965).

For analyses of media coverage of other nations and their policies, see, for example, Martin Kriesberg, "Soviet News in *The New York Times*," *Public Opinion Quarterly*, 10 (Winter, 1946), pp. 552-557; Daniel Lerner, "Franco-German Relations: Politics, Public and the Press," *Journal of International Affairs*, 10:2 (1956), pp. 138-152.

[5]The 1942 survey was conducted by the Office of Public Opinion Research and the 1948 survey by Benson and Benson, Inc. The 1948 survey was part of a nine-nation survey sponsored by UNESCO. The findings from the nine-nation, 1948 study may be found in William Buchanan and Hadley Cantril, *How Nations See Each Other* (Urbana, Ill.: University of Illinois Press, 1953); the findings presented here are from p. 55.

Other selections in this book also indicate how different elite groups develop particular foreign policy views, given their special orientations and given their experiences with colleagues, adversaries, rivals, and followers within their own society and in other countries (see Selections 7, 11, and 27). The processes illustrated here also underlie the programs of governments in trying to influence the peoples of other nations (see Selections 17, 18, and 19). Hall and Whyte (Selection 15) emphasize additional processes.

Elite groups are of special interest in the study of foreign policy because they play an important role in forming and implementing policy. It actually is not so clear how many elites, which elites, or how limited a category within each elite play crucial roles in forming and determining foreign policies. Some writers argue that in the United States a military-industrial elite is decisive, whereas others argue that a much broader range of elites is involved in the formation of policy, but they have the power to veto each other more than to coerce or lead others.[6] Undoubtedly, valid descriptions will differ depending upon the society being examined, the historical circumstances of the society, and the specificity of the foreign policy issue under consideration. For issues, however momentous, which require a quick response to the actions of another government, a small group of persons—usually those officially responsible for decision making and their advisors—can be said to "decide" about the national policy. For example, in the Cuban missile crisis of 1962 (see Selection 19), nongovernmental elites played neither a determining nor a veto role. But, in a larger perspective, the opinions of political party leaders, business leaders, intellectuals, and the general public in this country and elsewhere limited the range of alternatives considered; the perceptions of their views by government leaders affected the weights given to the alternatives considered.[7]

In accounting for the foreign policy orientation of a country over a number of years, the role of more segments of the population becomes pertinent. For example, the state of public opinion supported and mobilized by Senator Joseph McCarthy affected the formation and implementation of foreign policy in the United States in the early 1950s. That state of opinion depended, in part,

---

[6]C. Wright Mills, *The Power Elite* (New York: Oxford University Press, 1956); David Riesman with Nathan Glazer and Ruel Denney, *The Lonely Crowd* (New Haven, Conn.: Yale University Press, 1950); William Kornhauser, "'Power Elite' or 'Veto Groups'?" in Reinhard Bendix and Seymour Martin Lipset (eds.), *Class, Status, and Power*, Second edition (New York: The Free Press, 1966), pp. 210-218; Marc Pilisuk and Thomas Hayden, "Is There a Military Industrial Complex Which Prevents Peace?" *Journal of Social Issues*, 21 (July, 1965), pp. 61-117; Arnold Rose, *The Power Structure* (New York: Oxford University Press, 1967), esp. pp. 89-98.

Also see Eugene Staley, *War and the Private Investor: A Study in the Relations of International Politics and International Private Investment* (Garden City, N.Y.: Doubleday, Doran and Co., 1935).

[7]Richard C. Snyder, H. W. Bruck, and Burton Sapin (eds.), *Foreign Policy Decision Making: An Approach to the Study of International Politics* (New York: The Free Press, 1962).

upon a wide variety of societal conditions as well as the changing role of the United States in the international scene.[8] If one tries to explain national policy about one issue rather than another, different elites become significant. Thus with the development of atomic weapons, physicists and other natural scientists became an influential elite on issues related to such weapons.

Even when particular elites or subelites are not participants in decision making, they can affect it by the information they provide and the alternatives they present. If objectives and their pursuit are in part dependent upon other parties' responses, accurate intelligence may lessen the likelihood of the emergence of a conflict formulated and pursued in a manner that makes war likely. In deciding how to pursue a particular objective, choices must be made among the alternatives which appear to be available. Within any political unit, some alternatives are planned in more detail than others, as contingencies. The failure of one effort requires falling back upon some alternative, and a planned one has increased chances of adoption. Often the planning entails commitments of various people to the contingency, which gives the plan additional weight. In many societies the military agencies are particularly likely to be charged with the task of making contingency plans, and they have the resources to make those plans in great detail and with the commitment of significant resources. In this case violent modes of pursuing a policy objective are more likely to be implemented than if contingency plans had also been developed by subunits committed to other modes of collective decision making.

The papers in Chapter Three deal with several aspects of these considerations. Janowitz (Selection 7), in his analysis of the military elite, shows how personal ties among the military elite and between military and nonmilitary leaders affect general policy orientations.[9] Keller (Selection 8) reports on some of the characteristics of United States and British ambassadors, observing that such characteristics may affect their views and how they interact with representatives of other countries. Dexter (Selection 9) assesses some of the limits, and reasons for the limits, in the pressure a nongovernmental elite may exercise in attempting to influence even an aspect of foreign policy which is directly pertinent to it. The Moores (Selection 10) directly confront the idea that major foreign policy decisions are made by a small group of the power elite. They argue that in the case of the decision of the United States to use the atomic bomb, physicists played a major role in all steps in the decision. On the other hand, one might argue that

[8]See, for example, papers by David Riesman and Nathan Glazer, Daniel Bell, Talcott Parsons, and others in Daniel Bell (ed.), *The Radical Right* (Garden City, N.Y.: Doubleday and Co., 1964); Edward Shils, *The Torment of Secrecy* (Glencoe, Ill.: Free Press, 1956).

[9]For other analyses of the military elite in other societies see: Morris Janowitz, "Military Elites and the Study of War," *Journal of Conflict Resolution*, I (March, 1957), pp. 9-18; Morris Janowitz, *The Military in the Political Development of New Nations* (Chicago, Ill.: The University of Chicago Press, 1964).

this is done within the constraints imposed by the power elite. Or it may be argued that once other major decisions have been made, even as critical a one as using atomic weapons might seem unproblematical.[10]

Chapter Four focuses on general societal characteristics. As noted earlier, societies differ in the relative importance different segments of the population play in forming national policy. The forces affecting the views have varying significance in different societies. Shils (Selection 11) analyzes the new nations and the role of intellectuals in them, discussing some of the important experiences of the intellectuals which shape their views.

Other writers, particularly during and shortly after World War II, have studied characteristics of society members resulting from certain child-rearing experiences and major patterns of institutional life.[11] Such studies of national character have sought to examine common cultural themes which are deeply internalized and widely shared by members of a given society.

Interest in discovering which characteristics of societies are related to involvement in war has resulted in studies examining societies varying in economic structure, demography, technology, and political organization, as well as culture.[12] Although not systematically studied, one other societal condition should be important in helping to account for the resort to war in reaching a collective decision. A high rate of growth in the relative power of one regime makes possible demands upon other regimes previously suppressed or not even acknowledged. Consequently, the rudimentary institutionalized patterns of collective decision making are not likely to be adequate for such rapidly changed circumstances.

Tanter (Selection 12), in examining the relationship between domestic and foreign conflict, tests several ideas about the relationship between war and in-group

[10]This is implied by considering the use of the atomic bomb as merely a means of ending the war quickly and saving American lives–it was only another weapon. Others may speculate that the bomb was directed in part against the U.S.S.R.–to end the war before the Soviet Union could enter and claim part of the victor's spoils or as a means of intimidating a potential adversary. Such interpretations of the meaning or intentions in using the atomic bomb are likely to be coupled with other views of which elites played a crucial role in the decision to drop the bomb.

[11]Arvid Brodersen, "National Character: An Old Problem Re-examined," *Diogenes,* No. 20 (Winter, 1957), pp. 468-486; Alex Inkeles and Daniel J. Levinson, "National Character: The Study of Modal Personality and Sociocultural Systems," in Gardner Lindzey, ed., *Handbook of Social Psychology* (Cambridge, Mass.: Addison-Wesley Publishing Co., 1954), pp. 977-1020; and Robert A. LeVine, "Socialization, Social Structure, and Intersocietal Images," in Herbert C. Kelman (ed.), *International Behavior* (New York: Holt, Rinehart and Winston, 1965), pp. 45-69.

[12]Tom Broch and Johan Galtung, "Belligerence Among the Primitives," *Journal of Peace Research,* No. 1 (1966), pp. 33-45; Quincy Wright, *A Study of War* (Chicago, Ill.: University of Chicago Press, 1942); Lewis F. Richardson, *The Statistics of Deadly Quarrels* (Pittsburgh, Pa.: The Boxwood Press, and Chicago, Ill.: Quadrangle Books, 1960); and Raymond Aron, *Peace and War* (Garden City, N. Y.: Doubleday and Co., (1966), pp. 210-242.

solidarity. The paper reveals that several dimensions of foreign and domestic conflict are distinguishable. This was revealed by factor analysis—which shows what items tend to go together with each other and not with other items. The analysis of the relationship between various dimensions of domestic and foreign conflict also reveals that the relationships vary in strength and direction. This was revealed by use of multiple regression analysis, in which various dimensions of domestic conflict in 1955-1957 were related to dimensions of foreign conflict in 1958-1960; also, foreign conflict in 1955-1957 was related to domestic conflict in 1958-1960. Some moderate positive relationships were found in both cases. Thus three domestic conflict variables of societies in 1955-1957 (antigovernment demonstrations, revolutions, and guerrilla warfare) together had a correlation of .12 with war in 1958-1960 and .40 with severance of diplomatic relations in 1958-1960. When such multiple correlations are squared, they indicate the amount of variation in the dependent variable which is "explained." The paper reports and describes a variety of ways in which domestic and foreign conflict tend to be related.

In the remainder of the book the emphasis is on international relations rather than the formation of foreign policy. We shall see, however, that just as a regime's policy does not merely express domestic considerations, neither is it explicable merely as a response to external circumstances.

CHAPTER TWO

Influence Upon International Views

4. KNOWLEDGE AND FOREIGN POLICY OPINIONS: SOME MODELS FOR CONSIDERATION

William A. Gamson and Andre Modigliani

There is a seldom cited but widely shared and appealing law of public opinion, which can be stated very simply: The more knowledgeable people are, the more likely they are to agree with me. This law would appear to be particularly applicable when one is concerned with public opinion on foreign policy, since these matters of state are far from most people's daily lives and highly complex. Unenlightened thinking will surely be more prevalent among those who have little information and understanding; those who are sophisticated and aware will tend to share the opinions of the prototype of these characteristics, oneself.

SOURCE. William A. Gamson and Andre Modigliani, "Knowledge and Foreign Policy Opinions: Some Models for Consideration," in *Public Opinion Quarterly*, XXX (Summer, 1966), pp. 187-199. Reprinted by permission of the authors and Princeton University Press. Copyright 1966 by Princeton University Press.

*An earlier version of this paper was presented at the Montreal meetings of the American Sociological Association, September 1964, under the title, "Competing Images of Soviet Behavior."

THE ENLIGHTENMENT MODEL

Many social scientists are strongly convinced of the inadequacy of military force or the threat of force as a means of influence in international relations. For such people, this "enlightenment" model leads to the expectation that, with increasing knowledge and sophistication, people are more likely to reject belligerent policies. An examination of public opinion data does not immediately disabuse one of this view. In one study, for example, the better-informed people were, the less likely they were to support the statement, "We should never compromise with Russia but just continue to demand what we think is right."[1] In a 1953 poll, 70 per cent of the college-educated favored United Nations atomic energy control, while 61 per cent of the high school-educated and only 52 per cent of the grade school-educated favored such an alternative.[2] Or, in a 1954 poll, only 9 per cent of the college-educated, against 16 per cent of the grade school-educated, felt we should give up trying to reach agreements with Russia on outlawing atomic weapons.[3]

On the other hand, certain results which show that more knowledgeable people are more likely to support a militaristic policy tend to come as a surprise to those who believe in the enlightenment model. Back and Gergen report some examples of such greater willingness to engage in war on the part of the more knowledgeable.[4] Of those who had opinions, 29 per cent who scored low on a measure of political knowledge, and only 9 per cent who scored high, favored decreasing the war effort in Korea. In a 1958 poll, 42 per cent of those who were poorly informed and only 18 per cent of those who were highly informed felt Berlin was not worth fighting over.[5]

THE MAINSTREAM MODEL

Such results give rise to a second explanation, more defensible than the enlightenment model. In this second explanation, education brings with it, not so much better understanding of the world as greater participation in it and attachment to the mainstream. The politically educated are not better analysts of

---

[1] Previously unreported data from Andre Modigliani, "The Public and the Cold War," Cambridge, Harvard University, 1962, unpublished undergraduate honors thesis.

[2] AIPO, May 24, 1953, reported in *Public Opinion Quarterly,* Vol. 27, 1963, p. 167.

[3] AIPO, Apr. 28, 1954, reported in *ibid.,* p. 168.

[4] Kurt W. Back and Kenneth Gergen, "Public Opinion and International Relations," *Social Problems,* Vol II, Summer 1963, pp. 77-87, report on Gallup Survey 474, April 1951.

[5] Previously unreported data from Modigliani, *op. cit.* The exact wording of the Berlin item was; "We should try talking to Russia (about Berlin) but avoid fighting no matter what since it's not worth it to get into a war over Berlin."

complex situations but are simply more aware of what official U. S. policy is. Being more integrated into their society, and more susceptible to the influence of its institutions, their opinions are more likely to fall within the narrow boundaries of open official discussion. This occurs at the expense of either more conservative *or* more liberal alternatives that are not legitimized by the support of major political officials. The two models are summarized in Chart 1.

CHART 1

Summary of Enlightenment and Mainstream Models

Enlightenment Model

Independent variable: The degree of enlightened understanding of the true and complex nature of foreign affairs. Such enlightenment tends to be a product of education and is reflected in sophisticated knowledge of foreign affairs.
Dependent variable: Willingness to use military force to influence international affairs.
Central hypothesis: The greater the understanding and knowledge of foreign affairs, the less belligerence in one's foreign policy opinions.

Mainstream Model

Independent variable: The boundaries and clarity of official government foreign policy.
Intervening variable: One's attachment to the mainstream and the resultant exposure to influences such as the mass media. Such attachment and exposure are highly related to education and are reflected in factual information about foreign affairs and knowledge of the nature of, and rationale for, official policies.
Dependent variable: The degree of conformity of one's foreign policy opinions to official government policy.
Central hypothesis: The greater the attachment to the mainstream, the greater the degree of conformity of one's foreign policy opinions to official policy.

Note that both of the above explanations of the effect of knowledge are *consensus* theories, i.e., they predict that increasing knowledge will move all groups toward the same point. Either because they gain better understanding (the enlightenment model) or because they are more subject to social influence (the mainstream model), people are similarly affected by increased knowledge. In these theories, there is a single pole toward which knowledge impels people regardless of their starting point.

The above issue is vital, because we intend to present some data that appear to support the mainstream argument. However, on closer analysis they reveal a contradictory result—a polarization of opinion with increased knowledge. The data are drawn from a probability sample of 558 residents of the Detroit Metropolitan Area and are part of the Detroit Area Study data for 1963-64.[6] The questionnaire included a sixteen-item measure of knowledge of foreign relations. The questions

[6]We are indebted to John C. Scott, Director of the Detroit Area Study, and Robert Hefner and Sheldon Levy, principal investigators for the 1963-1964 study, for allowing us to include several of our items in the questionnaire and making the data freely available to us.

were straightforward and factual but required considerable knowledge. Respondents were asked to state which among the following countries are located in Africa: Ecuador, Ghana, Afghanistan, Mongolia, and Morocco; which among West Germany, Algeria, France, Japan, England, and Russia have developed and tested their own atomic weapons; and which among Egypt, Poland, Spain, Mainland China, and India have Communist governments. They were scored for number right minus number wrong on the sixteen items and are here divided into high, medium, and low knowledge groups.

Respondents were also asked a number of items on particular policies toward the United Nations, trade with Communist countries, disarmament, and so forth. We have singled out for consideration here those with particular relevance for the mainstream theory. They are items in which respondents are asked to choose one among three alternative policies, one of which had official government sanction at the time the survey was conducted.

According to the mainstream argument, we should expect that, with increasing knowledge, individuals will tend to reject both of the alternatives that are not officially endorsed and accept the one that is. With this in mind, we can examine the data in Table 1. On all three policy items, there is a pronounced increase in the percentage picking the official "mainstream," or middle, alternative as knowledge increases. This is at the expense of *both* more liberal and more conservative alternatives on China and on trade. However, on the question of military strength there seems to be some shift from right to left, as one might expect from the enlightenment theory.

The most striking feature of Table 1, though, is still the dramatic and consistent increase in support for government policy with increased knowledge. One might argue that, where there has been no policy shift, as in our policy toward China, increased knowledge will bring equal defections from both poles; where policy has recently shifted (as it did with trade with the Soviet Union and to some degree with the arms race), increased knowledge will exert its *dominant* pull on those who advocate the old official policy. By this reasoning, those low in knowledge are, because of their diminished contact with mainstream influences, more likely to lag behind in policy shifts. In this instance, the shift represents a liberalization. This would suggest that, where administration policy shifts to the right, the move to the official alternative that accompanies increased knowledge will be greatest among those who favor the more liberal rather than the more conservative alternative. While we cannot test this hypothesis here, Table 1 does seem to offer some encouragement.

THE COGNITIVE CONSISTENCY MODEL

However, we must consider still another theory relating knowledge of foreign affairs to policy opinions, the cognitive consistency model. This final model contrasts with earlier consensus models in its implication that increasing

TABLE 1. Relation of Foreign Affairs Knowledge to Selected Policies
         (in per cent)

		Knowledge	
Policy	Low	Medium	High
China:[a]			
The United States should withdraw some of its support of the UN if other nations admit Communist China	24	16	12
The United States should oppose letting Communist China into the UN but should continue to support the UN if other nations admit Communist China	46	60	66
The United States should not oppose letting Communist China into the UN	30	24	22
	100	100	100
(N)	(152)	(202)	(159)
$x^2 = 13.9, p < .05$			
Trade:[b]			
The United States should not sell anything to Russia	29	16	14
The United States should only sell surplus food to Russia	33	45	50
The United States should be willing to sell anything except military weapons to Russia	38	39	35
	100	100	100
(N)	(159)	(203)	(161)
$x^2 = 19.9, p < .05$			
Military strength:[c]			
Should be built up	40	28	17
About right	55	65	70
Should be cut back	5	7	13
	100	100	100
(N)	(153)	(198)	(151)
$x^2 = 22.8, p < .05$			

[a]The question read: "Which do you think would be the best United States policy toward admitting Red China to the UN?"

[b]The question read: "Some discussion concerning trade with Russia has been in the news recently. Which of these positions is closest to what you think about the matter?"

[c]The question read: "There are a number of different opinions about how much military strength the U.S. should have. How do you feel? Do you think that the present military strength of the U.S. should be cut back, built up, or is it about right?

knowledge will change people in *different* directions leading to a greater polarization of opinion among the more knowledgeable. This model argues that endorsement of a specific policy position stems from more general attitudes and assumptions that are being applied to a specific case. Knowledge of foreign affairs is important not because it reflects enlightenment or exposure to mainstream influences but because it reflects conceptual sophistication. Such sophistication reflects the ability to integrate specific policies with more general attitudes and assumptions one holds.

Clearly, the cognitive consistency model implies a polarization of opinion among the more knowledgeable. Poorly informed individuals, even with different ideological orientations, will have difficulty relating their orientation to specific policies. The result is a good deal of randomness and inconsistency in the choices of such individuals and no clear differentiation among those members with different predispositions. However, among the sophisticated, those with different predispositions will rally around different specific policies, creating sharper differentiation among those with different ideological orientations. This model is summarized in Chart 2.

CHART 2

Summary of the Cognitive Consistency Model

Independent variable: One's general political orientation, ideology, and beliefs. For example, assumptions about the nature of the Soviet Union and the nature of the Cold War.
Intervening variable: One's conceptual sophistication and the ability to integrate general attitudes and assumptions with specific policy opinions. Such sophistication is likely to be a product of education and will be reflected in knowledge of foreign affairs.
Dependent variable: The degree of relationship between one's specific foreign policy opinions and one's general attitudes and assumptions.
Central hypothesis: The greater the conceptual sophistication, the greater the relationship between general assumptions and specific policy opinions.

To explore the cognitive consistency model, we need some measure of general attitudes and assumptions; since we are considering policies relevant to the Cold War, attitudes and assumptions about the Soviet Union seem appropriate. In a separate study, the authors have been attempting to evaluate three coherent sets of assumptions or "belief systems" about the Soviet Union by examining, through an analysis of historical data, the predictions they imply about Soviet-Western interaction. The assumptions these belief systems make about long-range Soviet goals, Soviet risk-taking behavior, and the Soviet view of the West have been outlined elsewhere.[7] Using this earlier formulation as a guideline, we wrote three

[7] See William A. Gamson, "Evaluating Beliefs about International Conflict," in Roger Fisher, ed., *International Conflict and Behavioral Science,* New York, Basic Books, 1964, pp. 27-40; William A. Gamson and Andre Modigliani, "Tensions and Concessions: The Empirical Confirmation of Beliefs about Soviet Behavior," *Social Problems,* Vol. 11, 1963, pp. 34-48; and William A. Gamson and Andre Modigliani, "The Carrot and/or the Stick: Soviet Responses to Western Foreign Policy, 1946-1953." Center for Research on Conflict Resolution, Carnegie Project No. 4, Working Document 10, paper presented at meetings of International Peace Research Society, Chicago, November 1964, mimeographed.

items to assess each respondent's assumptions about these aspects of the Soviet Union.

Each respondent was classified into one of three belief systems, which we shall refer to as Positions A, B, and C. Briefly, Position A states that the Soviet Union is actively pursuing the goal of world domination and is willing to incur high risks to achieve this goal. It views Western resistance as so sporadic that the Soviet Union can achieve its goals through continual pressure short of war. Position B states that the Soviet Union is actively interested in achieving a *limited* expansion of influence and is willing to incur only moderate risks in the achievement of its goals. It views the West as both susceptible to limited encroachments and as attempting such encroachments on the Soviet Union—much like an opponent in a game. Position C states that the Soviet Union is actively interested only in holding on to what it has and is unwilling to incur risks except in self-defense. The West is viewed as actively seeking to undermine Soviet influence and control in the world.

Each respondent was asked to make a first and a second choice among the following sets of statements:

I. *On Soviet goals:* Many people are concerned about what the Russian government is really trying to do. Which of these do you think is closest to what their aims really are?
    a. When all is said and done, Russia is determined to conquer the United States. (Position A)
    b. Russia is trying to get the most it can from the United States but it isn't really trying to conquer us. (Position B)
    c. Russia is more interested in increasing its own security and standard of living than it is in getting the most it can from the United States. (Position C)

II. *On Soviet risk-taking behavior:* How willing do you think the Russians are to take chances to get what they want?
    a. Russia is cautious and will try to avoid starting any trouble which could lead to a serious crisis. (Position C)
    b. Russia is even willing to risk starting a serious crisis in order to get what it wants. (Position A)
    c. Russia is willing to stir up quite a bit of trouble to get what it wants, but it will try to avoid causing any really serious crisis. (Position B)

III. *On Soviet view of the West:* Which of these best describes what the Russians believe about the United States—even if they are wrong in what they believe:
    a. Russia almost always seems to believe that they can take advantage of us and get away with it. (Position A)

b. Russia almost always seems to be afraid that we are tying to take advantage of them. (Position C)

c. Russia seems to believe both that they can take advantage of us and that we try to take advantage of them. (Position B)

We neither expected nor found a consistency across items that matched our ideal or a priori statement of the three belief systems. However, there was sufficient relationship among answers to the three items to identify each respondent with the belief system he most nearly approximated.

It is a central premise of the cognitive consistency model that specific policy opinions flow from more general attitudes and assumptions. If this is correct, then we should expect some relation between assumptions about the Soviet Union and the sort of policy items included in Table 1. Table 2 indicates that the expected relationship exists.

TABLE 2. Belief Systems by Selected Policies
   (in per cent)

	Belief System		
Policy	A	B	C
China: [a]			
Withdraw from the UN if China enters	24	16	16
Oppose entry but don't withdraw from the UN	56	62	48
Do not oppose Chinese entry to the UN	20	22	36
	100	100	100
(N)	(114)	(293)	(107)
x^2 = 13.1 p < .05, C = .19			
Trade: [a]			
Trade nothing with Russia	32	17	11
Trade surplus food only	39	47	36
Trade anything but weapons	29	36	54
	100	100	100
(N)	(117)	(297)	(109)
x^2 = 20.5, p < .05, C = .24			
Military strength: [a]			
Should be built up more	38	29	17
About right	57	64	70
Should be cut back	5	7	13
	100	100	100
(N)	(111)	(287)	(105)
x^2 = 14.5, p < .05, C = .21			

[a]See Table 1 for the exact wording of the items and alternative answers.

On policy toward China, Position A people are the most likely of the three groups to be for withdrawing from the UN; Position B people to oppose Chinese entry but not withdraw; and Position C people not to oppose Chinese entry into the UN. The other two items show a similar pattern. However, the degree of relationship is quite small. Using as a measure of degree the contingency coefficient, corrected so that it has an upper limit of 1, the three items show C's of only .19, .24, and .21 respectively.

The slimness of the relation between belief system and specific policy opinion is easily accounted for by the cognitive consistency model. Such a relationship, it suggests, will be pronounced only among respondents high in conceptual sophistication and knowledge. Those low in knowledge will be unable to relate their general assumptions to the specific situation in a consistent manner. By controlling for knowledge of foreign affairs in Table 3, we see that the predicted pattern emerges. The relationship between belief system and policy for those high in knowledge has coefficients of .46, .51, and .31 as against coefficients of .14, .19, and .14 for those low in knowledge. Clearly, belief systems are connected with policy opinions primarily for the knowledgeable.

One of the striking implications of the cognitive consistency model is that increases in knowledge should have a polarizing effect on the opinions of a set of persons. Knowledge has the effect of allowing one to understand more clearly the policy most consistent with his predispositions. This means that subsets of persons who share different belief systems will tend to deviate from one another with increases in knowledge, each moving toward the policy most consistent with its underlying assumptions. Thus, Position A advocates, with more knowledge, will be more sharply in favor of withdrawing from the UN, trading nothing with Russia, and building up arms. Position C people will move in exactly the opposite direction, becoming *less* favorable on all these alternatives, while Position B people will show larger percentages for the official government policy on all these items.

Note how such an interpretation is possible in the results of Table 1. If Position A and Position C people are moving[8] in opposite and offsetting directions and Position B people are moving toward the center from the more extreme alternatives, then the over-all effect will be an increase in the support for the official policy. Combining advocates of all three positions may conceal the fact that knowledge has a different relationship for those with different images of the Soviet Union.

[8]We ask the reader's indulgence in the use of such process language to describe differences among individuals with different knowledge. Our data, of course, show nothing about process, but since the models we are contrasting are talking about the effects of knowledge on opinion formation, it is stultifying to make use of elaborate circumlocutions whenever we discuss interpretations of this data. We hope that this general reminder will be sufficient to allow us the convenience of such language in interpreting static results.

TABLE 3. Belief Systems by Selected Policies, Controlling for Knowledge (in per cent)

| | Knowledge/Belief System | | | | | | | | |
| | Low | | | Medium | | | High | | |
Policy	A	B	C	A	B	C	A	B	C
China:[a]									
Withdraw	25	22	32	16	17	15	28	8	3
Oppose	45	50	35	58	63	51	67	71	54
Do not oppose	30	28	32	26	20	33	5	21	43
	100	100	100	100	100	100	100	100	100
(N)	(44)	(78)	(31)	(31)	(132)	(39)	(39)	(83)	(37)
		C = .14			C = .15			C = .46	
Trade:[a]									
Nothing	34	29	18	28	14	13	31	12	3
Surplus food	33	34	30	34	46	46	51	60	30
Anything	33	37	52	38	39	41	18	28	67
	100	100	100	100	100	100	100	100	100
(N)	(46)	(80)	(33)	(32)	(132)	(39)	(39)	(85)	(37)
		C = .19			C = .18			C = .51	
Military strength:[a]									
Build up	48	38	36	36	31	10	27	16	8
About right	48	57	61	61	61	80	65	75	66
Cut back	4	5	3	4	8	10	8	9	26
	100	100	100	100	100	100	100	100	100
(N)	(46)	(77)	(31)	(28)	(131)	(39)	(37)	(79)	(35)
		C = .14			C = .24			C = .31	

[a]See Table 1 for the exact wording of the items and alternative answers.

Table 4 (which is simply a rearrangement of Table 3, controlling for belief systems) shows the polarizing effect we have been discussing.[9] While the pattern is least clear with Position A people, by and large increases in knowledge tend to increase agreement with the policy that Table 2 showed to be associated with the belief system in question. Thus, Position A people are less likely to favor admitting China to the United Nations as knowledge increases, while Position C people are more likely to favor this alternative as knowledge increases. Similarly, on the question of trade with Russia, increasing knowledge moves Position A people away from freer trade, Position C people toward more liberal trade, and Position B people away from the extremes of trading nothing or anything.

[9]Our belief systems show only the slightest relationship to our measure of knowledge of foreign relations. Advocates of Position C are equally represented in all three knowledge groups; however, Position A people are slightly overrepresented at the expense of Position B people in the highest and in the lowest knowledge groups. The over-all relationship, however, is so slight and irregular that we will treat the two measures as independent.

TABLE 4. Knowledge by Selected Policies, Controlling for Belief Systems (in per cent)

	Belief System/Knowledge								
	A			B			C		
Policy	Low	Med.	High	Low	Med.	High	Low	Med.	High
China:[a]									
Withdraw	25	16	28	22	17	8	32	15	3
Oppose	45	58	67	50	63	71	35	51	54
Do not oppose	30	26	5	28	20	21	32	33	43
	100	100	100	100	100	100	100	100	100
(N)	(44)	(31)	(39)	(78)	(132)	(83)	(31)	(39)	(37)
		C = .34			C = .22			C = .38	
Trade:[a]									
Nothing	34	28	31	29	14	12	18	13	3
Surplus food	33	34	51	34	46	60	30	46	30
Anything	33	38	18	37	39	28	52	41	67
	100	100	100	100	100	100	100	100	100
(N)	(46)	(32)	(39)	(80)	(132)	(85)	(33)	(39)	(37)
		C = .25			C = .28			C = .33	
Military strength:[a]									
Build up	48	36	27	38	31	16	36	10	9
About right	48	61	65	57	61	75	61	80	66
Cut back	4	4	8	5	8	9	3	10	26
	100	100	100	100	100	100	100	100	100
(N)	(46)	(28)	(37)	(77)	(131)	(79)	(31)	(39)	(35)
		C = .24			C = .22			C = .45	

[a]See Table 1 for the exact wording of the items and alternative answers.

CONCLUSION

The over-all pattern of results in Table 4 is not without its aberrations. We are inclined to feel that they are best illuminated by a combination of the mainstream and cognitive consistency models. We would suggest that two primary forces are operating, both of which tend to correlate with education and knowledge. On the one hand, *there is a strain toward attitudinal consistency that increases with knowledge;* this produces a higher relationship between belief system and policy among the more knowledgeable and an increasing polarization around different policy alternatives for those who start with different premises. At the same time, *there is greater attachment to society and susceptibility to social influences*—a force that produces support for official government policies.

If we can interpret our measure of knowledge as reflecting both these forces, then some of the aberrations in Table 4 make sense. Let us consider the question concerning policy toward UN admittance of China. Among advocates of Position A, the strain toward consistency would impel them toward the extreme right,[10] or "withdrawal from the UN," position with increased knowledge, while the strain toward conformity would impel them toward the middle, or "opposition without withdrawal," position. Hence, with increasing knowledge there are two forces pushing Position A advocates away from the left, or "acceptance of China," position, but only one force pushing them into the extreme right position. The data, in fact, show that defection from the left position is much more pronounced than increased endorsement of the right position (see Table 4, China question, under Position A: endorsement of the "withdrawal" position increases only from 25 to 28 per cent, while endorsement of the "do not oppose" position drops from 30 to 5 per cent).

Conversely, for advocates of Position C we have two forces pushing them away from the extreme right position and only one pushing them into the extreme left position. Again the data show that increased knowledge brings greater defection from the right position than increased endorsement of the left position (see Table 4, China question, under Position C: endorsement of the "do not oppose" position increases only from 32 to 43 per cent, while endorsement of the "withdrawal" position drops from 32 to 3 per cent).

For Position B advocates *both* forces act to push them out of the extreme right *and* left positions and into the middle, and the data show defections from both extremes with increasing knowledge (see Table 4, China question, under Position B: endorsement of the "do not oppose" position decreases from 28 to 21 per cent, and endorsement of the "withdrawal" position also decreases from 22 to 8 per cent).

As a final complication, we would suggest that in cases where government policy has recently shifted, the pure direction of such a shift may be an important variable. Specifically, a shift to the left in government policy (as had recently occurred on trade with the Soviet Union and perhaps on arms build-up) may act as added reinforcement for leftward shifts, and deterrent to rightward shifts. And, indeed, on these two policy questions the data show that increased knowledge brings a much greater increase for the left alternative among Position C advocates than increase for the right alternative among Position A advocates.

---

[10]Our use of the terms "extreme right" and "extreme left" does not represent any judgment on our part about the true place of such alternatives in the political spectrum. We do not wish to imply, for example, that agreement with the proposition, "The United States should not oppose letting Communist China into the UN," reflects any kind of extremist position as that term is sometimes used; this opinion clearly may be held by moderates. We use the term "extreme left" *only* to refer to its position in the set of three alternatives offered. In fact, we attempted to word the items so that none of the policy alternatives would appear extreme in the absolute sense—that is, we wished to ensure some variance in our respondents' choices.

We cannot disentangle the contribution of these hypothesized forces in our own results. But with a careful selection of policy questions and with independent measures of conceptual sophistication and conformity to official doctrine, it should be possible to parcel out the effects of each.

5. NATIONAL STEREOTYPES AND FOREIGN CONTACTS

*Erich Reigrotski and Nels Anderson**

Since 1948 UNESCO has initiated several studies of common ideas about people in other countries.[1] The project reported here is an attempt to identify and examine the national stereotypes of the Germans and the French as held by other peoples and by themselves. It is the 1956-1957 follow-up of a somewhat similar study done in 1948 by UNESCO in Australia, Britain, France, Germany, Holland, Italy, Mexico, Norway, and the United States. In spite of shortcomings, the 1948 study illustrated the possibilities of this kind of cross-border research. Buchanan and Cantril, in their summary report of that study, called attention to these deficiencies, and they were taken into account in the plan of the present project.[2] Perhaps the most important suggestions made by them were that the questionnaire should be well-coordinated in advance and the cards should later be processed at a central point. Accordingly, a coordinated questionnaire was used to interview people in Belgium (482 Flemish and 597 Walloons), France (2,006), Germany (2,041), and Holland (1,000).

FINDING THE COMMON IDEAS

In this study three approaches were made to obtain the views of respondents about peoples of four other countries. In each approach they were asked to rate the people of specific countries, and their own people.

SOURCE: Erich Reigrotski and Nels Anderson, "National Stereotypes and Foreign Contacts," in *Public Opinion Quarterly*, XXIII (Winter, 1959-60), pp. 515-528. Reprinted by permission of the authors and Princeton University Press. Copyright 1960 by Princeton University Press.

*Credit for much of the basic work goes to Heidi Sauer.

[1] For a summary of these studies see "The UNESCO Tensions Project," *The Nature of Conflict*, Paris, France, UNESCO, 1957, pp. 9-32.

[2] William Buchanan and Hadley Cantril, *How Nations See Each Other*, Urbana, Ill., University of Illinois Press, 1953.

1. Respondents were given twelve descriptive terms and asked which of these terms (or none) in their opinion seemed to describe each of the four specified peoples, and their own people.

2. Respondents were asked to describe in their own words each of the four specified peoples, and their own people as well.

3. Respondents were asked which of the four peoples being rated they considered: (a) easiest and (b) most difficult to get along with.

Only the first of these approaches related to the 1948 project, using the same group of twelve stereotypes (Hardworking, Intelligent, Practical, Conceited, Generous, Cruel, Backward, Brave, Self-controlled, Domineering, Progressive, Peace-loving). Instead of the term "Backward" it was decided to use "Unprogressive." By each of the three approaches respondents rated four other peoples. Thus a Frenchman rated Belgians, Germans, Dutch and Italians, and then rated his own people. While the Italians were not interviewed, they were rated by the four peoples included in the study. The word list was translated into Dutch, Flemish, French, and German. For the Belgians there were a Flemish questionnaire and a French one.

THE PREDESIGNATED TERMS

The twelve terms mentioned above were used because they formed the main link between this study and that of 1948. Seven of these (Hardworking, Intelligent, Practical, Conceited, Cruel, Brave, Progressive) had been used in 1942 by the Office of Public Opinion Research.[3] Six of the twelve were among the eighty-four characteristics used by Katz and Braly on Princeton students in 1932.[4] Thus this technique may be regarded as an American importation.

Table 1 gives the ratings by French and Germans of each other and of their own people. As might be expected, the gap between self-ratings and other-ratings is considerable, both for the totals and for specific characteristics. For the French ratings the gap is greatest for the two negative qualities, Cruel (0.6 to 37.1 per cent) and Domineering (3.6 to 59.6 per cent), and the positive item, Generous, 52.9 per cent for themselves and 1.5 per cent for the

---

[3]Hadley Cantril and Mildred Strunk, *Public Opinion, 1935-1946,* Princeton, N.J., Princeton University Press, 1951, p. 502.

[4]Daniel Katz and Kenneth Braly, "Racial Stereotypes of One Hundred College Students," *Journal of Abnormal and Social Psychology,* Vol. 28, 1933, p. 283. These terms were used again at Princeton in 1950 by G. M. Gilbert, "Stereotype Persistence and Change among College Students," *Journal of Abnormal and Social Psychology,* Vol. 46, 1951, pp. 245-254. Gilbert found that students in 1950 were highly critical of the test, and the ratings they gave were more tolerant than those of 1932.

TABLE 1. What the French and Germans Think about Each Other and Themselves (in per cent)

	French Opinions		German Opinions	
Characteristics	About Themselves	About Germans	About Themselves	About French
+ 1. Hardworking	37.3	50.3	80.0	3.2
+ 2. Intelligent	58.0	24.7	54.0	30.3
+ 3. Practical	30.5	19.9	54.0	7.9
- 4. Conceited	13.2	13.8	13.3	31.4
+ 5. Generous	52.9	1.5	15.4	11.1
- 6. Cruel	0.6	37.1	1.5	11.8
- 7. Unprogressive	3.5	1.2	1.5	8.8
+ 8. Brave	39.8	32.1	60.2	9.2
+ 9. Self-controlled	7.7	12.8	16.6	4.9
-10. Domineering	3.6	59.6	11.6	24.4
+11. Progressive	36.1	35.8	51.8	12.0
+12. Peace-loving	38.4	2.5	38.5	7.3
No opinion	2.5	5.4	5.2	34.7
Ratio of positive to negative answers	144:10	16:10	132:10	11:10

Germans. The wide gaps for the Germans are for Hardworking, Practical, and Brave, on which they rate the French much lower than themselves.

Although space does not permit the inclusion of the ratings of the French and the Germans by the Belgians and Dutch, it should be mentioned that there was a high degree of agreement with the opinions of the French about the Germans and those of the Germans about the French. This agreement relates more to specific items; for example, the Germans are more Hardworking and more Practical, but also more Domineering. When the positive and negative opinions are balanced, we get the result shown in Table 2.

TABLE 2. Ratio of Positive to Negative Opinions of the French and Germans by Flemish, Walloons, Dutch, and the French and Germans

Opinions about the	Opinions Expressed by the				
	Flemish	Walloons	Dutch	French	Germans
French	14:10	45:10	36:10		11:10
Germans	28:10	22:10	16:10	16:10	

Here we find a division between the more German-oriented Flemish Belgians and the French-speaking Walloon Belgians. The Flemish are twice as favorable to the Germans as to the French (28:10, 14:10). The Walloons show a rating of 45:10 for the French and 22:10 for the Germans.

NATIONAL STEREOTYPES AS IMAGES

The word list used here has been selected by an international group of experts for the 1948 UNESCO study, and it was approved for this study by another international group of experts. The terms were called "stereotypes," although some prefer the term "image."[5]

A stereotype to Allport is not a category of persons or things, but a mark that is put on persons or things.[6] Different marks or labels may be used to characterize groups of persons or things. Here we are looking at European national groups and confining ourselves mainly to the French and Germans. What sort of people is each in the minds of the other? The word list provides some information, and it can be supplemented.

The stereotype of the Frenchman, for example, can be delineated by calling out certain descriptive words. Each word helps to give character and form to the image, which tends to become fixed in a stereotype. It is composed of innumerable elements, some clearly evident, some less evident, and still others recessive. Any or all of these may change, becoming stronger or weaker, and the composite changes with changes in its parts. The form and intensity of the stereotype is revealed in part by such a device as a word list. Thus from Table 1 we get the following stereotype "German" as seen by the French (in percentages):

Domineering	60	Brave	32	Self-controlled	13
Hardworking	50	Intelligent	25	Peace-loving	3
Cruel	37	Practical	20	Generous	2
Progressive	36	Conceited	14	Unprogressive	1

If a still longer list of words were used, the stereotype might be revealed in more detail, although the general image would remain the same. But if the same word list were presented to the same respondents later (assuming they have had new experiences with the rated people), there is no doubt that the percentages would change.

[5]Marten Brouwer, University of Amsterdam, in an unpublished manuscript dealing with opinion polls, proposes the use of "image" because "stereotype" has become too much a *loaded* word. But "image" is also a loaded word. It is probably not important which word is used so long as the meaning as used is made clear.

[6]Gordon W. Allport, *The Nature of Prejudice,* Cambridge, Mass., Addison-Wesley, 1954, p. 191.

While stereotypes may change, certain elements in the stereotype may appear to be more fixed or basic than others. Thus some hold the view that since stereotypes change, they can be *treated*, assuming that we know what they are to be treated for. This urge to treat stereotypes not infrequently reflects the idea that thinking in terms of stereotypes is socially bad.[7] This may or may not be true. Ichheiser sees utility in stereotypes, or images: "The whole process of classifying could not function as it does if we did not have prepared in our minds a whole system of well-defined images which we apply in the particular cases as they come along."[8] They are the Dewey Decimal System of the mind. This process of stereotyping, says Albig, "is psychologically inevitable in thinking and in memory. The stereotypes provide the symbols of discourse."[9]

THE SPONTANEOUS RATINGS

Albig's observation is illustrated by the second question in the interview, which asked respondents to describe other peoples. This was often done with single meaningful words or phrases, which were often loaded words from limited vocabularies. Unfortunately, the variety of terms used by each people was too great for classification into the limited number of categories needed for machine processing.

In Table 3 we see such terms as could be classified expressing the views of the French about the Germans and those of the Germans about the French. A point to be noted is that only a few of the terms (or their equivalents) used in our word list appeared among spontaneous words or terms used by the respondents. This is not surprising, since the word list is American. Efforts were made to square the translations with folk usages, but we now see that the meanings are not so easily transferred with the translation. To the German or Hollander "hardworking" conveys the idea of serious and continuous endeavor. It is a positive rating if Germans speak of another people as hardworking, but it may not have the same meaning if the Frenchman describes Germans as hardworking, especially when he adds the word "domineering." "Progressive" is a term that has different meanings as between countries and in some countries, apparently, as between social classes.

Another weakness of the word list is that it contains eight positive and only four negative terms, which may have influenced the number of positive to

[7]Otto Klineberg, "The Scientific Study of National Stereotypes," *International Social Science Bulletin,* Vol. 3, 1951, pp. 511-512.

[8]Gustav Ichheiser, "Misunderstandings in Human Relations," *American Journal of Sociology,* Vol. 55, No. 2, Part 2, 1949, p. 34.

[9]William Albig, *Modern Public Opinion,* New York, McGraw-Hill, 1956, pp. 80, 83.

TABLE 3. Spontaneous Opinions of the French and Germans about Each Other

French Opinions about the Germans	Per Cent	German Opinions about the French	Per Cent
Positive:		Positive:	
Hardworking	22	Light-hearted, contented, gay,	
Disciplined, orderly,		enjoyers of life	16
methodical	16	Friendly, ready to help,	
Brave, courageous	4	sociable	15
Organizers, technical, prac-		Intelligent	3
tical	4	Industrious, hardworking,	
		businesslike	2
Negative:		Negative:	
Authoritative, cruel, brutal	16	Lazy	9
Militaristic, domineering	12	Impulsive, temperamental,	
Querulous but submissive	6	quarrelsome	6
Vain, haughty, arrogant	5	Careless, hateful, false	6
Hypocritical, false, unreliable	5	Boastful, haughty, arrogant	5
Nationalistic	2	Chauvinistic, nationalistic	4
		German-haters	4
		Sloppy, dirty	2
Other characteristics	30	Other characteristics	8
No opinion	21	No opinion	40
Ratio of positive to negative answers	10:10	Ratio of positive to negative answers	10:10

negative ratings shown in Table 2. In Table 3 the positive to negative ratings tend to be more in balance.[10]

If prejudice is thought of as something negative, it may be seen in both the French stereotype of the Germans and the German stereotype of the French. Apparently, there are different types and intensities of negative attitude shown here, and the same holds for the positive terms.

[10]The Institut für Sozialforschung, University of Frankfurt, in 1952 interviewed 1,792 Germans, asking their opinion about their own people and the French. Twelve positive and twelve negative terms were used, and the ratio of positive to negative was 8:10. Percentages for the top six positive terms were Charming, 56; Intelligent, 31; Generous, 29; Technically progressive, 9; Clean, 9; Industrious, 8. The top six negative ratings were Easygoing, 51; Nationalistic, 43; Frivolous, 32; Revengeful, 25; Sloppy, 20; Fickle, 14. Twenty-three per cent of the respondents checked no positive terms and 18 per cent checked none of the negative terms. (Christoph Oehler, "Vorurteile im Bild der Deutschen von Frankreich [Prejudices in the Picture of the Germans by France]," *Kölner Zeitschrift für Soziologie [Cologne Sociological Journal]*, Vol. 10, 1958, pp. 254 ff.

Spontaneous descriptions applied by the French and Germans to each other are confirmed in the spontaneous ratings by the Flemish, Walloons, and Dutch. The Germans are called hardworking, businesslike, authoritative, brutal, militaristic. The French, among other characteristics, are called gay, friendly, charming, lazy, and light-hearted, but not hardworking.

INDEX OF CONTACT AND ACQUAINTANCE

In the expressed attitudes toward other peoples, no significant trends were found with respect to the age, sex, marital status, or other personal characteristics of the respondents. This observation seems to be less true for education. Persons of higher education tend to be more tolerant as well as more critical in their ratings. By more critical we mean that they are more likely to modify a negative rating with a positive one or a positive with a negative.

Foreign acquaintance and contact apparently also contribute to tolerance and critical judgment. Data on contact and acquaintance were secured by the following types of information: (1) whether or not the respondent had visited the specified countries, (2) whether or not the respondent spoke the language of one or more of the specified countries, (3) whether or not the respondent had friends or relatives from one or more of the specified countries.

In order to reduce such information to measurable terms, it was necessary to assign a weight to each type of contact. Thus, for travel in a designated country, 1 point; for knowing the language of a specified country, 1 point; and for having friends or relatives of a specified country, 2 points.

Each respondent would score from 0 for no contact to 4 if he reported all the contacts—travel language, and friends or relatives of a country. In Table 4 we see how this index of contact serves to group Germans and French into categories. The great majority are in the 0 group, and groups 2, 3, and 4 show more foreign contact for the French than the Germans. The index in this table is bilateral, concerning contacts between French and Germans only.

TABLE 4. Index of Contact Distribution of French and Germans (in per cent)

Index Groups	French Contacts with Germans	German Contacts with French
0	70	75
1	14	18
2	9	4
3	4	1
4	3	2

A full index of contact score for one country would be 4, and for two countries 8, while the maximum would be 16 for four countries. An extra point is given for each additional country (1, 2, or 3) with which the respondent has had contact, making the maximum score 16 plus 3. Table 5 shows how the Germans and French compare by such a multinational index of contact. Because the numbers in the upper groups are small, 1 to 9 and 10 to 19 have been combined.

TABLE 5. Multinational Index of Contact Distribution for French and Germans (in per cent)

Index Groups	Multinational Contacts of the	
	French	Germans
0	42	57
1-9	53	41
10-19	5	2

When we divide German and French respondents into the three index groups for the two types of self-image answer, we get the following distribution of positive to negative ratios:

	0	1-9	10-19
French self-image:			
Word-list answers	154:10	140:10	134:10
Spontaneous answers	18:10	10:10	11:10
German self-image:			
Word-list answers	166:10	141:10	95:10
Spontaneous answers	75:10	43:10	28:10

As international contact increases, the number of positive answers decreases in relation to the number of negative answers. We see an opposite trend in Table 6, showing positive and negative ratings of French and Germans by each other for both types of answer on the basis of foreign contact and acquaintance and on the basis of educational level. We note that, as positive opinions rise directly in relation to negative with foreign contact, they also rise with the level of education. This provides measured evidence of what many believe to be true.

LINKAGE OF SELF-IMAGE AND OTHER-IMAGE

We have already noted the gap between self-image and other-image ratings, especially for the word-list answers. We note that the gap is not so wide for the spontaneous answers as for the word-list answers:

Ratings	Self-Image	Other-Image
French:		
Word-list answers	144:10	16:10
Spontaneous answers	13:10	10:10
German:		
Word-list answers	132:10	11:10
Spontaneous answers	56:10	10:10

The answers for the self-image and other-image are not unrelated. What the Germans and French think about themselves is influenced in different ways by the opinions of other peoples. This was demonstrated by Hofstätter in his analysis of the ratings of the 1948 UNESCO study.[11] He used the Bravais correlation coefficient in which the values are distributed from +1 for complete agreement to −1 for complete divergence. For our use these values are elevated to +100 and −100. In terms of this formula, the self-ratings of a people are squared with the opinions other people have about them. We find that the French judgment of the Germans shows a higher degree of coincidence with the German self-image (+33) than does the German judgment of the French with the French self-image (+6). If we remove from the German self-image and from the French stereotype of the Germans the most mentioned term, "Hardworking," the measure of coincidence changes to $r = +11$.

TABLE 6. **Ratio of Positive to Negative Word-List and Spontaneous Answers of the French and Germans Describing Each Other**

Index Group and Level of Education	Word-List Answers		Spontaneous Answers	
	French Rate the Germans	Germans Rate the French	French Rate the Germans	Germans Rate the French
Index Group:				
0	14:10	10:10	8:10	8:10
1 + 2	21:10	15:10	13:10	12:10
3 + 4	27:10	18:10	19:10	22:10
Level of education:				
Common school	14:10	10:10	8:10	9:10
Higher school	22:10	14:10	16:10	14:10
University	23:10	18:10	19:10	13:10

[11]Peter R. Hofstätter, *Gruppendynamik, Kritik der Massenpsychologie [Group Dynamics: Critique of Mass Psychology]*, Hamburg, Germany, Rowalt Taschenbuchverlag, 1957, pp. 104 ff.

In Table 7 we see how the self-images of the French and Germans square with the opinions about the French and Germans expressed by other peoples in this study, and how the results appear when the rating peoples are divided into international contact groups. In each instance the coincidence coefficient for the group having no foreign contact or acquaintance is lower than for the 10-19 group, which has most foreign contact and acquaintance. This is seen notably for the Walloons, who are very friendly to the French but less so to the Germans,

TABLE 7. Measure of Coincidence for the Self-Images of the French and Germans, by Extreme International Contact Groups

Self-Images to Other Images	International Contact Groups	
	0	10-19
French self-image and:		
Opinions of Flemish	− 21	+57
Opinions of Walloons	+ 75	+85
Opinions of Germans	− 4	+50
Opinions of Dutch	+ 38	+91
Total	+ 88	+283
Average	+ 22	+71
German self-image and:		
Opinions of Flemish	+ 47	+73
Opinions of Walloons	+ 42	+60
Opinions of French	+ 15	+66
Opinions of Dutch	+ 9	+46
Total	+ 113	+245
Average	+ 28	+61

and for the Flemish, who think differently about the French and the Germans. The Flemish of the 0 group show a negative measure of −21 toward the French, but those of most contact with the other peoples show a positive measure of +57, a difference of 78 points. It must be assumed that respondents in the 10-19 groups tend to have higher education levels than those in the 0 groups.

The figures in Table 7 are derived from the word-list question. Respondents are grouped according to their index of contact with one or more of the foreign peoples in the study. In Table 8 respondents are grouped only on the basis of their index of contact with the French in one phase of the table and with the Germans in the other. Again, only the extremes are used, the 1-2 group being omitted. Here the rating peoples are paired: Dutch-Germans, Dutch-Flemish,

TABLE 8. Measure of Coincidence in Opinions about the French and Germans Expressed by Other Peoples, by Index of Contact

Ratings by Pairs	Index of Contact	
	0	3-4
Ratings of the French by the:		
Dutch and Germans	+61	+56
Flemish and Germans	+74	+74
Walloons and Germans	+11	+70
Walloons and Dutch	+62	+76
Walloons and Flemish	− 8	+66
Flemish and Dutch	+52	+60
Total	+252	+402
Average	+42	+68
Ratings of the Germans by the:		
Dutch and French	+95	+89
Flemish and French	+86	+89
Walloons and French	+92	+90
Walloons and Dutch	+89	+89
Walloons and Flemish	+94	+88
Flemish and Dutch	+88	+89
Total	+544	+534
Average	+91	+89

Dutch-Walloons, and so on. By this method we secure a measure of agreement about the French and about the Germans.

Table 8 confirms the existence in the minds of Belgians, Germans, and Dutch of a French national stereotype, although a diffused one. It confirms with greater emphasis the existence of a German national stereotype in the minds of Belgians, French, and Dutch. This was brought out by the word list, which is perhaps more suitable for rating the Germans than the French. But another list of words, equally suitable for both French and Germans, would probably not greatly change the pattern. Note that for the French there is more agreement and uniformity among the 3-4 contact groups than among the 0 contact groups; the average for the first is +68 and for the latter +42, but in the ratings of the Germans the averages are only two points apart, +91 for the 0 groups and +89 for the 3-4 groups.

SYMPATHY-ANTIPATHY CONTINUUM

In the third of the three rating questions respondents were asked to indicate which of the specified peoples they considered easiest to get along with and which the most difficult. Table 9 gives the answers of the Belgians, French, Germans, and Dutch. Since only one people is named for each category, the columns in each case conveniently add to a total of 100 per cent, which facilitates comparisons between the rated peoples. The Italians have been included, and their ratings serve a useful comparative purpose. Only in France did more people consider the Italians rather than the Germans easiest to get along with; for all except the Flemish higher percentages said the Germans are most difficult to get along with than said the Italians are. One shortcoming of this table is the high percentage in some cases of no answers, especially for the Germans, with 57 per cent for "most difficult" and 48 per cent for "easiest."

TABLE 9. Opinions of Belgians, French, Germans, and Dutch on Their Ability to Get Along Well or Not with Other Specified Peoples (in per cent)

Opinions about the	Opinions Expressed by the				
	Flemish	Walloons	French	Germans	Dutch
Easiest to Get Along With					
Belgians			44.0	5.8	37.4
French	32.3	67.5		7.9	12.1
Germans	18.7	8.0	9.7		21.3
Dutch	26.7	9.3	10.9	30.0	
Italians	2.3	5.5	20.6	8.3	2.8
No answer	20.0	9.7	14.8	48.0	26.4
Most Difficult to Get Along With					
Belgians			2.2	4.9	6.2
French	8.6	3.5		23.3	11.4
Germans	17.9	35.4	42.9		22.8
Dutch	20.3	20.8	7.2	3.9	
Italians	19.7	14.0	16.3	10.4	21.9
No answer	33.5	26.3	31.4	57.5	37.7

This idea of social distance was also brought out in a questionnaire given to French respondents in 1951. They were asked to rate ten peoples in rank order from 1 to 10. In Table 10 only the ratings for the Belgians, Dutch, Italians, and Germans are shown. For simplification the ten groups of ratings have been reduced to five, which does not damage the comparative worth of the table. These figures confirm the attitudes of the French shown in Table 9.

TABLE 10.   Rank Order Rating by the French of the Belgians, Dutch, Italians and Germans in Terms of Sympathy-Antipathy Opinions about Each (in per cent)

Rated Peoples	Rank Order of Ratings				
	1	2	3	4	5
Belgians	76	18	4	2	0
Italians	17	31	22	16	14
Dutch	12	40	28	15	5
Germans	2	5	8	13	72

SOURCE. Alain Girard and Jean Stoetzel, "Francais et immigrés [French and Immigrants]," *Travaux et Documents [Works and Documents]*, Section 19, Paris, France, Presses Universitaires de France, 1951, pp. 127 ff.

CONTACT AND THE SYMPATHY-ANTIPATHY CONTINUUM

When we add the percentages for opinions about people as shown in Table 9 (Example: Total for Belgians on "easiest" is 87 per cent), we get the percentages seen in the first panel of Table 11. Panel 2 shows the results when respondents are divided according to the multinational index of contact. In each panel of the table the countries are arrayed in descending order for "easiest to get along with." For each pairing, the figure for "most difficult" is subtracted from that for "easiest," which gives the "margin." Note that for each national group except the Belgians the figures for "easiest" of the 10-19 ratings are higher than for the corresponding index group 0 ratings. It should also be noted that for "easiest" the rank order of the rated peoples shows a different arrangement for the index 0 group than for index 10-19 groups. It should be remembered that the number of respondents in the 10-19 index groups are a minority of the total. We can think of these groups as representing the elite opinion, which is opinion-forming in its influence.

According to the index of contact, what of the French who described the Germans as easiest to get along with, and vice versa? In Table 12 we see that of the 1,521 Germans who have had no contact with the French, only 4 per cent rated the French as easiest to get along with. At the bottom of the table are 59 Germans in the 3-4 index group, of whom 37 per cent rated the French as easiest to get along with. Of the 1,409 French in the index 0 group, 6 per cent expressed this favorable opinion of the Germans, but of the 135 French in the 3-4 index group, 45 per cent thought the Germans were easiest to get along with.

TABLE 11.   Rank Order Rating of French, Belgians, Dutch, Germans, and Italians by the
Four Interviewed Peoples Regarding Easiest or Most Difficult to Get Along
With

Opinions about the	Easiest	Most Difficult	Margin
Sum of Percentages for All Responses			
French	120	47	+73
Belgians	87	13	+74
Dutch	77	52	+25
Germans	58	119	−61
Italians	40	82	−42
Responses Arranged According to Multinational Index of Contact			
Index Group 0:			
Belgians	102	8	+94
French	75	31	+44
Dutch	62	20	+42
Italians	32	62	−30
Germans	23	137	−114
Index groups 10-19:			
French	147	46	+101
Germans	102	99	+3
Belgians	95	21	+74
Italians	76	96	−20
Dutch	68	117	−49

TABLE 12.   French Rating Germans and Germans Rating French as Easiest to Get Along
With, by Index of Contact

Index Group	Number in Index Group		Percentage of French Who Thought Germans Easiest to Get Along With	Percentage of Germans Who Thought French Easiest to Get Along With
	French	Germans		
0	1,409	1,521	6	4
1	283	373	22	14
2	179	88	22	27
3-4	135	59	45	37

SUMMARY

These materials revolve about an effort to identify and examine two national stereotypes, those of the Germans and the French, as held by other peoples and by themselves. Germans are pictured as hardworking, practical, self-disciplined, and submissive to discipline; severely intent on objectives; domineering in their relations with other peoples; and sometimes brutal. In their self-image the Germans accept the more pragmatic positive labels, but reject almost completely the moral negative ones.

The French are pictured as friendly and easygoing, enjoyers of life, generous although not always practical, artistic, light-hearted, and socially facile. On the negative side, they are called lazy or avoiders of hard work. They are described as impulsive, temperamental, or fastidious, or as quarrelsome, disorderly, and not always neat. In their self-image the French accept most of these positive terms and some of the negative ones.

More important than the identification of stereotype traits, this study lends support to the idea that stereotypes tend to be modified through education and through foreign contact and acquaintance.

1. Increasing foreign contact tends to increase favorable opinion about other peoples and to render more critical one's opinions about his own people.

2. The self-image of a people may be influenced by the national stereotypes held by other peoples. For example, the French self-image may be in part an assimilation of the national stereotype of the French held by the Germans, and vice versa.

3. Favorable opinions of other peoples seem to increase directly with education.

Exceptions appear with respect to each generalization. For example, it should be said that, while attitudes of antipathy may be diminished by contact, so contact may diminish extreme attitudes of sympathy, such as that of the French-speaking Walloons for the French. Contact may be having some influence in the changing attitudes of Germans toward Dutch.

Foreign contact and education seem to be interrelated, and yet each factor is autonomous as well. The education factor is the weaker of the two. Moreover, the education factor seems to be ambivalent. Thus negative as well as positive attitudes may increase or diminish for either respondents of higher education or those of lower education. This means that education may be more closely integrated than foreign contact with the cultural controls of the country or locality.

One surprising outcome of this study is that it seems to make little difference whether the foreign acquaintance and contact was gained before or since 1945. Foreign contact before the war, during the war, or since 1945 in similar degree tends to encourage a favorable opinion of another people and more critical opinion of one's own people. This is true even in the present instance, where the self-images and the national stereotypes being examined are those of the French and the Germans.

6. INTERNATIONAL COMMUNICATION AND LEGISLATIVE BEHAVIOR: THE SENATE AND THE HOUSE OF COMMONS

Bruce M. Russett

THE ALLEGED EFFECT OF COMMUNICATIONS

According to the view well stated by David Truman, "The politician-legislator is not equivalent to the steel ball in a pinball game, bumping passively from post to post down an inclined plane" (Truman, 1951, p. 332). Political figures bring to their jobs a set of attitudes, predispositions, ways of looking at the world which, along with such traditionally recognized influences as party, executive leadership, and lobby pressures, affect the way they speak and act. Any explanation of legislative behavior which hopes to be complete must account for variables of personality and personal background.

Various kinds of international transactions contribute to decision-makers' perspectives. One of these, long recognized but seldom analyzed with care, is trade in goods and services. Few writers hold that trade necessarily improves relations between two countries, but some have come perilously close. Richard Cobden told his followers, "I believed Free Trade would have the tendency to unite mankind in the bonds of peace, and it was that, more than any pecuniary consideration, which sustained and actuated me" (Cobden, 1870, p. 421). One finds this sentiment in the most unlikely places. William McKinley, author of the MacKinley Tariff, declared, "Good trade insures good will. It should be our settled purpose to open trade wherever we can, making our ships and our commerce messengers of peace and amity" (Leech, 1959, p. 142). Even Nikita Khrushchev,

SOURCE. Bruce M. Russett, "International Communication and Legislative Behavior," in *The Journal of Conflict Resolution,* VI (December, 1962), pp. 219-307. Reprinted by permission of the author and the Center for Research in Conflict Resolution. Copyright 1962 by the University of Michigan.

[1]This article stems from a forthcoming larger study of Anglo-American relations and the theory of international integration (Russett, 1963).

inverting the economic determinist position, stated, "Trade is like a barometer; it shows the direction of policy" (*New York Times,* September 17, 1959, p. 18).

Most authors, of course, are more moderate, though very rarely do they state their qualifications in detail. To be specific, financial crises and debt defaults can seriously embitter international relations. If two countries are highly interdependent and one suffers from severe economic instability, the other will share the instability. Depression spreads from its origin by cutting other countries' exports. Irritation may also arise when one nation is the world's major exporter of a commodity, for the importing state may feel exploited if the supply is controlled by a monopoly or oligopoly. Even government price supports or production controls, though adopted merely to sustain the income of domestic producers rather than deliberately to exploit the buyers, may nevertheless cause hard feelings.

But if these difficulties are absent, trade becomes an important bond of mutual interest between two nations. Karl Deutsch et al. insist that a wide range of mutual transactions is necessary to the growth of a security community. These need not be commercial transactions, for strong economic ties are a helpful but not an essential condition for integration. But they are important, and if not present must be replaced by other transactions. The statement, "The helpfulness of economic ties may lie largely in the extent to which they function as a form of communication and as visible sources of reward," hits the crux of the problem (Deutsch et al., 1957, pp. 157, 169).

Economic interests may be important on matters which do not affect them in any immediate sense. An exporter is likely to have a general interest in the well-being of his market, an interest that transcends the marketing conditions, narrowly defined, for his product. He may become attuned to the needs of the importing country over a great range of noneconomic matters. Daniel Lerner found that, in a sample of French business leaders, support for EDC as opposed to the maintenance of a French national army varied directly with the importance of export trade to the businessman's firm (Lerner, 1956, p. 220). Only in a few cases could any of these businessmen be said to have a direct "economic interest" in the decision.

Commerce thus becomes important as a means of communication, exposing the trader to a wide variety of messages that would not otherwise reach him; he must listen to viewpoints he otherwise would never hear. Trade is a capability by which the needs of one country can be made known to another. It may serve as a direct or an indirect means of communication for a lawmaker. Though he may not be associated with the interest, the constituents, editors, fellow-legislators, lobbyists, and others from whom he gets most of his ideas and information may be. In addition, economic interests tends to bias decisions, and persons who are predisposed to particular decisions will try to mobilize available economic interest groups for the support of that decision. That is, economic interests may "determine" political decisions, or they may merely be used to support those decisions. The question of "priority" is for our purpose irrelevant: interdependence, not determinism, is the concern of the study.

Trade is not the only channel for mutual attention and communication. Contacts between two cultures are likely to be varied and continuing, and include, among many others, migration, tourism, student exchange, telegraph and telephone, newspaper attention, and the exchange of cultural products like books, magazines, and motion pictures. Four of Deutsch's helpful conditions for a pluralistic security-community were related to this matter: unbroken links of social communication, mobility of persons, a multiplicity of ranges of communications, and a compensation of flows of communications and transactions (Deutsch et al., 1957, p. 58). There are of course exceptions, especially when the cultures in question—as of Indian students in the United States—are particularly alien to each other. Communication by itself does not produce understanding or responsiveness; it may merely communicate grievances or difference of outlook. Yet communication is a *necessary* if not a *sufficient* condition for amicable relations between two nations who are affected by the consequences of each other's actions.[2]

The precise effect of international communication has seldom been studied systematically, and never on formal political decision-makers. This paper will examine some of its effects on legislators in Great Britain and the United States. We shall want to know: (1) whether international contacts make much difference in the way legislators behave, or whether such factors as personality and party loyalty overwhelm international influences, (2) which kinds of contacts are most effective, and (3) whether a legislator with many contacts is likely to behave differently from one who has some personal contacts, but fewer.

ANALYTICAL METHOD

The effect of many means of communication, especially the mass media, is difficult to evaluate with respect to individual decision-makers, but quite a number of others can be examined. In analyzing the attitudes of Members of Parliament, I investigated the business and personal connections of a sample of Members in each of three years.[3] Standard biographical sources such as *Who's*

[2]Homans reports that in small-group experiments there is a strong positive relationship between the frequency of interaction and favorable attitudes towards members of the group (Homans, 1950, ch. 5; Homans and Riecken, 1954).

[3]In each case the sample was composed of about 130 M.P.s (over 20 per cent of the total membership of the House of Commons) selected at random. Of the years selected, 1890 and 1954 were chosen because they were near the extremes of the timespan covered by the larger study. Since there were so few expressions of opinion on matters of Anglo-American relations in 1890 (see below), a third year, 1938, was added with reference to the needs of the complete study.

Who provided the basic material. Members with economic bonds included those who were officers or directors of firms engaged in exporting to the United States, firms with American subsidiaries, or businesses which were themselves subsidiaries of American companies. Others were M.P.s who owned businesses in the United States, whose firms imported American goods, who were engaged in foreign banking, merchant bankers, and owners of shipping lines with vessels that sailed to American ports.[4]

In addition to economic bonds, it seemed essential to identify as many men with personal ties as possible. Into this category fell M.P.s who were born or educated in the United States, who worked there for a while, or who married Americans. Men with this kind of link were said to have "strong" personal ties. There was also a group with bonds that seemed intrinsically weaker; ties which should not be included with the others yet ought not to be ignored. They included people who had received honorary degrees from American universities or American medals for war service in joint causes, who had worked on joint Anglo-American agencies during the World Wars, or who had traveled in the United States. While the influence of their experiences was unlikely to have been as great as that of marriage or education, the fact that they often took the form of rewards might well predispose the men in question to be responsive. In addition, I had data on membership in the Pilgrims of Great Britain in 1938 and 1954 and in the English-Speaking Union in 1954.[5] These associations have the specific aim of promoting closer Anglo-American relations. Unavoidably there must also have been a number of men with ties which could not be identified. The reader will be aware that the class of M.P.s without ties means, in the following tables, merely those with no known links. But even so, we shall see that there is a significant difference between the attitudes of M.P.s whom we know had ties and of those for whom there is no evidence of bonds to America.

I followed a similar procedure with members of the Senate in 1890 and 1954, though in this case it was possible to include the entire membership rather than just a sample. Thanks to the United States Census, which gives figures on agricultural, mining, and manufacturing production by state, I was able to add a dimension not possible for the House of Commons—legislators with "constituency ties." This term was applied to Senators whose home states gained at least 5 per cent of their gross income from any commodity of which at least 5 per cent of total production was exported to Britain. It seemed likely that producers of this

---

[4]The sources and procedures of identification are described in detail in the longer study (Russett, 1963, ch. 9).

[5]From correspondence with the secretary of the Pilgrims and conversation with the secretary of the English-Speaking Union. In the latter case the records of membership in 1954 had been destroyed, and the secretary gave me the names only of those he was certain were members then. That list is therefore accurate as far as it goes, but is not all-inclusive.

commodity might have a substantial source of influence over their Senators. The cut-off points chosen are unavoidably arbitrary, but I believe the procedure to be justified by the results presented below. I tried various higher cut-off points without significantly changing the findings.[6]

Except for the constituency data, membership in Anglo-American organizations, and travel information (where some supplementary sources were used) all information on legislators' backgrounds was derived from the biographical sketches. Some additional intelligence which might have been interesting was not to be found. Parents' birth, ancestry, and business connections were largely ignored—not universally, but generally enough that any attempt to draw conclusions from the isolated references found would require subjecting the analysis to too many unknown biases. Touring was also often unreported.

The task then was to test the role of these influences in affecting legislators' attitudes. For the House of Commons I chose to analyze public statements on policy rather than voting patterns. A Member of Parliament virtually *never* votes against his party, and almost all votes, certainly all on issues even remotely associated with foreign affairs, are those on which the party takes a partisan stand. If he does defy the whips, he risks expulsion from the parliamentary party, abandonment by his constituency organization, and defeat in the next election. A single lapse may be overlooked, but repeated violations of discipline will almost certainly end his political career. Even "crossing the floor" to the other party offers little hope—no member has done so, and been returned at the next election, since 1945. This is not to imply that British parties are dictatorial and can march M.P.s into their lobbies at will. There may be much pushing and hauling before a policy is settled, and the leadership must always beware of antagonizing the rank-and-file too seriously. But once policy is set and made a matter of public record, the Member who attacked it would do so at his great peril. Thus, an examination of voting records would provide little information about an M.P.'s true feelings or about the pressures he put on his party chiefs before the votes.

If an M.P. seldom votes against his leaders, he may abstain from voting somewhat more freely. Abstention is a recognized way of showing disagreement, and is unlikely to be punished by the leadership unless done repeatedly. Unfortunately the recording of abstentions (or better, absences) at divisions shows no significant pattern. Abstention can show those who are really interested how one feels on a matter—constituents, interest groups, or fellow Members can note one's abstention, and the leaders against whom one wants to protest will surely notice it. But even on an important measure there usually are many involuntary absences due to illness and business or personal demands for M.P.s' presence

---

[6]It would have been useful also to have identified M.P.s from constituencies where goods for export to America were manufactured, but there is no information on production by constituency in the United Kingdom.

elsewhere. One who merely reads the report of a division years after the event, without knowing the reasons for a particular M.P.'s failure to be recorded, can rarely discern a significant pattern.

But it is not unusual for a Member, even though he may vote as directed in the end, to criticize a policy during debate, to ask a hostile question during question time, or to oppose the policy in a speech to his constituents or another group. He feels particularly free to do so during the period before an official party position is adopted. For example, the Labour Party directed its members to abstain on ratification of the 1954 London and Paris Agreements to rearm a sovereign West Germany. Yet by the time the vote was taken almost half the Labour M.P.s had expressed opinions in Parliament, in letters to newspapers, or in outside speeches reported by a London or major provincial paper. In addition to providing information on Members' real feelings about matters which come up for division in the House, this kind of analysis also gives their views on a great number of issues that are never made a matter of record vote.

Much of this material, and practically all of it for the earlier years analyzed, came from the parliamentary debates themselves. For 1938 and 1954 this could be supplemented by reports of debates at the annual party conferences, and by party publications which cull newspapers and private speeches for statements— particularly those which might embarrass the opposition. These include the Tory *Hints for Speakers* and the *Liberal Magazine*. For 1954 there was also a superb collection of clippings at the Conservative and Unionist Central Office in London, containing a complete file of all reports of M.P.s' statements in the London daily and Sunday press, the most important country papers, and periodicals like the *New Statesman*. Though the files for a few deceased M.P.s had been disposed of, there were still, in 1960, clippings on over 90 per cent of the 1954 members of the Commons. Because these supplementary sources were not available for 1890, and only in part for 1938, the following tables record far more expressions of opinion in 1954 than in the two earlier years combined.

A major flaw in this kind of analysis is its implicit assumption that all topics on which an opinion might be expressed are of equal importance, both to the speaker and to the other government in question. Thus an M.P. might criticize the United States for its shipping subsidies, aid to Franco Spain, and lack of civil liberties, but support the American-backed program of German rearmament. Quite possibly the United States government would value the support on German rearmament highly enough to offset the other criticisms, and in an important sense the M.P. would be more "pro-American" than another Member whose attitudes on all four issues were reversed. There might be a serious fallacy in simply counting the number of issues on which the Member supported or criticized American policy. Yet in practice there is no thoroughly satisfactory way to weight the issues. No two observers could agree whether a statement on German rearmament was worth two statements on other policies, or worth four pronouncements, and so on down a list of 20 additional issues.

In the particular case this was not too serious a handicap. For the three years under study, nearly three quarters of the M.P.s expressing opinions did so uniformly—they were either always responsive to the United States or always unresponsive—thus substantially eliminating the weighting difficulty.[7] Still a more systematic method of solving this problem would be desirable, and it is offered by Guttman scale analysis. The essential principle of scale analysis is that,

> The items can be arranged in an order so that an individual who agrees with, or responds to, any particular item also responds positively to all items of lower rank order. The rank order of items is the scale of items; the scale of persons is very similar, people being arranged in order according to the highest rank order of items checked, which is equivalent to the number of positive responses in a perfect scale [Green, 1954, p. 353].

The classic illustration is a group of questions regarding height. If you ask a man if he is over 6' tall, and he responds affirmatively, you know that he would also answer yes to questions asking if he were over 5'10" in height, and over 5'8".

By finding that the issues in Anglo-American relations could be scaled we would side-step the "weight problem." That is, we might find that with regard to responsiveness to the United States, the four issues—Spain, civil liberties, subsidies, and German rearmament—ranked in that order. A man who opposed American aid to Spain would be unresponsive on all other issues. Similarly, if he defended the state of American civil liberties but criticized American shipping subsidies, he would also support assistance to Spain but oppose arming the Germans. We have not solved the weight problem in the sense of saying which issue is more "important," but we have avoided the necessity of worrying about it. We will not have to decide whether support on German rearmament is "worth" opposition on the other three matters, for such a situation will never occur. The procedure gives us a method of ordering legislators from most responsive to least responsive in a meaningful and consistent way.

The result is that we can describe the pattern of responses as "unidimensional" in scale-analysis terms, for the items in the scale measure related attitudes on a particular topic. We cannot be sure what basic feelings are responsible for the statements by the various M.P.s making those pronouncements, but we can be reasonably sure that all the particular measures were regarded as aspects of one general policy by the Members. A man normally highly responsive will not have been unresponsive on one issue because of extraneous factors.

The discussion in the last two paragraphs is, of course, an oversimplification. Hardly ever is unidimensionality so perfect that there are no variations within the

---

[7]In the interests of economy and of providing a large enough sample to test for statistical significance I have not here discussed attitude patterns on individual issues. Nevertheless the relationships identified do hold for most of the particular issues as well as for the group.

scale, no "errors" where a man is responsive when we would expect him to be unresponsive. Other factors do operate to some extent, but the amount of variation must be very limited if we still are to treat the list of issues as forming a scale. By convention, the response of no more than one man in ten may be in "error" on any item, and the total number of "errors" for all items may not exceed ten per cent of the number of items times the number of men. Since in fact no one item may have more than ten per cent error, and many items show less, this "coefficient of reproducibility" (total nonerrors divided by number of men times number of items) is almost always about .95 or higher. Thus the effect of extraneous variables is kept to a minimum.

The creation of a scale does not eliminate the need for sound judgment on the part of the researcher. One might indeed be measuring a single dimension, but it need not be the dimension which one is really trying to measure. In deciding what issues to try to put into the scale, and in interpreting the meaning of that scale when completed, one must know what the issues signified and have a set of independent criteria for picking them out. In this case I used the following criteria for issues involved in Anglo-American relations. No issues which did not meet these criteria were proposed, and it was essential that at least most of those items which did meet the criteria be capable of incorporation into the scale. (For further information and a list of votes see the appendix.)

1. Explicit criticism or approval of the other government or nation. (Criticism of individuals was not included unless it appeared that the speaker meant it to apply to the government itself or to all or most members of the other nationality. Criticism of President Eisenhower would probably be recorded as an attack on the United States, but remarks about Senator McCarthy might not be.)

2. A call for weaker or stronger ties with the other country.

3. Policies intended to increase mutual capabilities for responsiveness (whether by the creation of common institutions or by such means as eliminating restrictions on travel).

4. Ratification of a treaty signed by both governments.

5. A direct economic interest of the other country (tariffs or foreign aid).

6. Restrictions on the freedom of the government to conclude international agreements (the Bricker Amendment).

7. An expressed desire by the other government.

Much of the evidence needed to apply these criteria was contained in the debates. Outside checks nevertheless seemed necessary, particularly in the last class, to be sure that nothing was missed or inappropriately included. To fill this need I used diplomatic histories and memoirs, editorials in *The Times* of London and *New York Times*, and, for the two later years, the annual volumes by the Council of Foreign Relations *(The United States in World Affairs)* and the Royal Institute of International Affairs *(Survey of International Affairs)*.

These criteria do not produce a list merely of matters of direct economic interest—issues on which one would not be surprised that legislators linked with firms exporting to the other country would be responsive. The concerns are far wider and more indirect. Nor does the list include only major matters where the prestige of a government or a significant element of the other nation's welfare was at stake, but a great number of minor matters as well. Responsiveness is necessary not only at great crises, but in smaller everyday affairs. Many crises or dramatic displays of responsiveness can be avoided by quiet everyday awareness of and, where appropriate, acquiescence to another nation's needs or demands. Thus, I made no effort to choose years in which the most obvious, crucial, and immediate demands were made. Cooperative international relations are dependent on more common stuff.

This procedure made it possible to rank legislators from most responsive to least responsive, and I have applied it to the United States Senate.[8] In most of the following analysis it will be necessary to simplify the results, merely classifying lawmakers into three groups—responsive, moderate, and unresponsive—of as nearly equal size as possible. But the reader should remember that the information was made available through a complete ordering.

Like any other quantitative tool which imposes a certain amount of simplification on a complex reality, this procedure has its faults. It cannot tell us whether a particular legislator holds an opinion firmly or with little intensity. His action may result from deep conviction or strong interest-group pressure, or he may simply be "log-rolling" for support on issues of more importance to him. Perhaps an influential legislator determines the votes of a number of "satellites" on an issue.

These refinements can be made only with such other approaches as interviewing and examination of legislative debates and other public statements. But if these two methods (analysis of votes and analysis of statements) are used in tandem, one can get the benefits of both while avoiding most of the pitfalls which either alone sets. The analysis of public statements is peculiarly suited to the House of Commons, where roll call votes are relatively rare and a Member seldom votes against his party, and the examination of voting patterns is peculiarly suited to the Senate, where the opposite conditions prevail. If, using the two techniques, one in each body, we find that similar variables have similar effects on lawmakers' attitudes, we will have very strong evidence of the validity of the relationships so identified.

---

[8]Guttman scaling requires nearly complete information on attitudes. It therefore could not be applied to the data on Commons, which include expressions of opinion by only a minority of M.P.s on any given issue.

TIES AND RESPONSIVENESS

The information on Commons is analyzed in two ways. First, every M.P. is classified either as responsive, unresponsive, or "neutral"; i.e., no policy statement on any of these issues was recorded. Second, it was useful to record the number of statements on separate issues made by each M.P. Thus, if a member is recorded as responsive on one issue and unresponsive on two others, he is treated as, on balance, unresponsive, and a one is entered in the appropriate cell on the *left*-hand side of the following table. But on the *right*-hand side of the table we list individual statements on issues, so a one is recorded under "responsive" and a two under "unresponsive." Tables do not always add to 100 per cent because of rounding.

TABLE 1.   Per Cent of M.P.s With and Without U.S. Ties Who Were Responsive, Unresponsive, and Neutral, and of Responsive and Unresponsive Statements

			1890			
			Un-	Statements by		Un-
M.P.s With	Res.	Neut.	Res.	M.P.s With	Res.	Res.
U.S. Ties (N = 24)	8	88	4	U.S. Ties (N = 4)	50	50
No U.S. Ties (N = 118)	0	96	4	No U.S. Ties (N = 5)	0	100
			1938			
			Un-	Statements by		Un-
M.P.s With	Res.	Neut.	Res.	M.P.s With	Res.	Res.
U.S. Ties (N = 31)	16	81	3	U.S. Ties (N = 8)	88	12
No U.S. Ties (N = 101)	8	88	4	No U.S. Ties (N = 19)	79	21
			1954			
			Un-	Statements by		Un-
M.P.s With	Res.	Neut.	Res.	M.P.s With	Res.	Res.
U.S. Ties (N = 40)	20	60	20	U.S. Ties (N = 56)	48	52
No U.S. Ties (N = 89)	16	52	33	No U.S. Ties (N = 125)	26	74
			All Years Combined			
			Un-	Statements by		Un-
M.P.s With	Res.	Neut.	Res.	M.P.s With	Res.	Res.
U.S. Ties (N = 95)	16	74	10	U.S. Ties (N = 68)	53	47
No U.S. Ties (N = 308)	7	81	12	No U.S. Ties (N = 149)	32	68

In every subsection of Table 1 the same pattern holds. M.P.s with ties of any sort to the United States are more likely to speak up on matters affecting Anglo-American relations than are M.P.s without ties. And when they speak, they are more likely to be responsive. This is true whether each particular M.P. is characterized as responsive or unresponsive, or whether the statements are examined individually. In many of the above subtables there are not enough cases for the results to be statistically significant even at the .10 level, but they are so in the three with the greatest number of cases. For M.P.s the relationship between ties and responsiveness is significant at the .02 level in the table for all years combined. And for statements, the relationship is significant at well above the .01 level both for 1954 and for all years combined.

TABLE 2.   Per Cent of M.P.s With and Without U. S. Ties Who Were Responsive, Unresponsive, and Neutral, and Per Cent of Responsive and Unresponsive Statements, With Party Affiliation Controlled, 1954*

M.P.s With	Res.	Neut.	Un-Res.	Statements by M.P.s With	Res.	Un-Res.
Conservative (N = 64)	(16)	(67)	(17)	Conservative (N = 44)	(50)	(50)
U.S. Ties (N = 26)	19	65	16	U.S. Ties (N = 20)	70	30
No U.S. Ties (N = 38)	13	68	19	No U.S. Ties (N = 24)	33	67
Labour (N = 62)	(18)	(40)	(42)	Labour (N = 132)	(26)	(74)
U.S. Ties (N = 14)	21	50	29	U.S. Ties (N = 36)	36	64
No U.S. Ties (N = 48)	17	37	46	No U.S. Ties (N = 96)	22	78

*Three M.P.s—two Liberals and one Irish Nationalist—are not included.

For 1954 there are enough cases to control for party affiliation and the results are the same. For individual M.P.s the association of ties and responsiveness is as hypothesized, but not to a statistically significant degree. For the analysis by statements, however, the association is significant at the .01 level. The uniformity of direction identified in these two tables, and the high significance often found, form as persuasive a proof as could be expected with these data.

Note that the association between party and responsiveness is also quite strong, as Conservatives are much more likely to be responsive than are Labourites. In the "M.P.s" half of the table, the relationship is significant at the .02 level; in the "Statements" half it is significant at .001, an extremely high level. The relationship between party and responsiveness, in fact, is stronger on both sides of the table than is that between ties to the United States and responsiveness.[9] A Labour M.P. *with* a tie to America is less likely to indicate responsiveness

[9]For "M.P.s" the contingency coefficient for party and responsiveness is .29 and that for ties and responsiveness just .04. For "Statements" the comparable figures are .25 and .18. Certainly there is no attempt to claim that international contacts are the only variables affecting attitudes on foreign policy, but merely that such contacts are sufficiently important that no adequate explanation can ignore them.

than is a Conservative M.P. *without* an identifiable tie. We can only speculate on the reasons. Much of the difference is surely traceable to differences in ideology and interest-group support. But part of the explanation undoubtedly is that Conservatives tend to get most of their ideas from other Conservatives, and the same with Labourites. Since almost twice as many Conservatives as Labourites have known ties with America, their views probably carry a heavier "weight" in the informal opinion-forming processes of their party. Similarly, the greater "weight" of men with ties in the Conservative Party must give them a better chance of invoking party discipline in their favor. Although discipline is not enforced nearly as stringently in speeches as in voting, it is nevertheless a factor. Possibly a major element lies in ties to America of which we have no knowledge. It seems very probable that Conservatives, having on the whole more money, are more likely to have traveled to the United States than Labourites, and having more business connections, are more likely to have an economic link with the United States that was not caught in the rather wide-meshed net used to find M.P.s with commercial ties.

We can analyze the same influences on Senators' attitudes. In Tables 3–5 each Senator is classified as responsive, moderate, or unresponsive according to his position on the Responsiveness to Britain scale.

TABLE 3.   Per Cent of Senators With and Without U.K. Ties Who Were Responsive, Moderate, and Unresponsive

	1890		
Senators With	Responsive	Moderate	Unresponsive
U.K. Ties (N = 49)	37	33	31
No U.K. Ties (N = 35)	9	46	46
	1954		
Senators With	Responsive	Moderate	Unresponsive
U.K. Ties (N = 23)	48	22	30
No U.K. Ties (N = 73)	27	33	40
	Both Years Combined		
Senators With	Responsive	Moderate	Unresponsive
U.K. Ties (N = 72)	40	29	31
No U.K. Ties (N = 108)	21	37	42

Just as with M.P.s, we find a consistent relationship between the possession of personal or economic ties and responsiveness. For 1890 the relationship is significant at the .01 level; for 1954 and for the two years combined it is significant at the .10 level. A similar pattern emerges when we control for party affiliation.

TABLE 4.   Per Cent of Senators With and Without U.K. Ties Who Were Responsive,
Moderate, and Unresponsive, With Party Affiliation Controlled

Senators	Responsive	Moderate	Unresponsive
	1890		
Democratic (N = 37)	(57)	(43)	(0)
U.K. Ties (N = 27)	67	33	0
No U.K. Ties (N = 10)	30	70	0
Republican (N = 47)	(0)	(34)	(66)
U.K. Ties (N = 22)	0	32	68
No U.K. Ties (N = 25)	0	36	64
	1954*		
Democratic (N = 48)	(40)	(25)	(35)
U.K. Ties (N = 15)	40	20	40
No U.K. Ties (N = 33)	39	27	33
Republican (N = 47)	(23)	(36)	(40)
U.K. Ties (N = 8)	63	25	13
No U.K. Ties (N = 39)	15	38	46

*Excludes one Independent.

In two of the cases below the control for party affiliation emphasizes the importance of personal and economic bonds. For Democrats in 1890 and Republicans in 1954 the relationship is marked and highly significant (.01 level). For Republicans in 1890 and Democrats in 1954, however, there is no such relationship. But as we shall show below, the latter finding is due to the fact that in 1954, constituency ties were entirely without effect in promoting responsiveness. If only direct ties, economic and personal, are considered, those 1954 Democrats with them prove highly responsive.

As can be seen from the most cursory examination of these tables, party affiliation was an important variable. Particularly in 1890 party discipline (or perhaps likemindedness, we cannot tell which), was extremely powerful in matters of foreign affairs. We cannot be sure why, but an explanation would undoubtedly include much the same factors as were offered regarding the difference in responsiveness between the Conservative and Labour Parties in Britain. This sheds light on the political situation of the late nineteenth century when the Democratic Party was often accused of being pro-British, despite its dependence on the votes of Irish-Americans. Here is evidence that the Democrats were, in an important sense, much more "pro-British" than their partisan opponents. On every issue affecting Anglo-American relations a majority of Democrats was ranged on the responsive side against a majority of Republicans. Exactly 62 per cent of the Senators never voted against their party on these issues—21 Democrats and 31

Republicans. The "moderate" section includes *all* who ever voted against their party.

We can use this information to illustrate the influence of ties in another way. In 24 instances a Democrat voted against his party in an unresponsive manner; in 31 cases a Republican went against his party in order to be responsive. If we distinguish between those Senators with and without ties, and make a ratio of the number of votes against party over the number of Senators in each class, we have the following figures:

TABLE 5.   Votes Cast Against Party Per Senator, Senators With and Without Ties to U.K., 1890

Senators With	Responsive Votes	Unresponsive Votes
Ties to U.K.	.73	.33
No Ties to U.K.	.60	1.50

Note that the existence of a tie with Britain has a greater effect in moderating opposition to British wishes (column 2) than as a positive force in promoting responsiveness (column 1).

KINDS OF TIES

We also wish to know whether two or more links per lawmaker would be more effective than a single tie. The following table gives data for the House of Commons, with M.P.s possessing two or more links analyzed separately from those with only one.

TABLE 6.   Per Cent of M.P.s With and Without U.S. Ties Who Were Responsive, Unresponsive, and Neutral and Per Cent of Responsive and Unresponsive Statements, With Number of Ties Controlled, All Years Combined

M.P.s With	Res.	Neut.	Un-Res.	Statements by M.P.s With	Res.	Un-Res.
Two or More (N = 28)	21	61	18	Two or More (N = 28)	64	36
One U.S. Tie (N = 67)	13	79	7	One U.S. Tie (N = 40)	45	55
No U.S. Ties (N = 308)	7	81	12	No U.S. Ties (N = 149)	32	68

In the left-hand side of the table we see that Members with two ties were actually *less* likely to be responsive than M.P.s with only a single tie. On the other hand, Members with two or more links tended to speak out somewhat more often, whatever the content of their remarks. In the right-hand half of the table there is a slight tendency, significant at the .10 level, for responsiveness to be more frequent where there is more than one tie.

Examination of the Senate was also inconclusive on this point. In 1954 only two Senators had more than one discernible bond with the British, and both of them were highly responsive, but the cases were obviously too few to give any satisfactory indication. For 1890, however, the results were just the opposite of what one would expect. Though not to a statistically significant degree, Senators with two or more ties tended to be *less* responsive than those with only one. On this evidence, then, we must conclude that the fact of any link at all is far more effective than the reinforcement of that link by one or two additional ones.

In addition it seemed necessary to see whether the kind of tie made any difference; whether either economic or personal ties were more efficacious than the other. The following table lists separately all M.P.s with economic ties, all with no economic but "strong" personal ties, those with only "weak" personal ties, those whose only connection with the United States was through the English-Speaking Union or the Pilgrims, and finally those with no known link at all.

TABLE 7.   Per Cent of M.P.s With and Without U.S. Ties Who Were Responsive, Unresponsive, and Neutral, and Per Cent of Responsive and Unresponsive Statements, With Type of Tie Controlled; All Years Combined

M.P.s With	Res.	Neut.	Un-Res.	Statements by M.P.s With	Res.	Un-Res.
Econ. Ties (N = 53)	11	83	6	Econ. Ties (N = 22)	73	27
Strong Ties (N = 15)	20	60	20	Strong Ties (N = 27)	48	52
Weak Ties (N = 19)	21	63	16	Weak Ties (N = 19)	63	37
ESU-Pilgrim (N = 8)	25	63	13	ESU-Pilgrim (N = 10)	50	50
No U.S. Ties (N = 308)	7	81	12	No U.S. Ties (N = 149)	32	68

The association of responsiveness with economic ties is evident on both sides of the table, and is significant at the .01 level in each case. Among those with various kinds of personal ties to the United States, it makes little difference whether the bonds are weak, strong, or merely of membership in an organization like the Pilgrims. Possibly some differences would show up in a larger sample, but they are not evident here. But there is a *slight* difference, significant (at the .10 level) only in the right-hand half of the table, between all those with just personal ties and those with commercial bonds. Possibly economic self-interest plays a part. More likely, however, the difference is due to the fact that the ties of commerce are current ones: the legislator has a continuing channel of information and opinion from the United States. Most personal ties, on the other hand, were formed in the past, and it may have been many years since the individual talked to many Americans. As most of the American policies in question, such as German rearmament and China policy, were of relatively recent vintage, it is not surprising that men with past but not current contacts with the United States should fail to perceive American wishes or their justification. Of all the personal ties the only current one applicable to many M.P.s was membership in the Pilgrims or the English-Speaking Union, and one would not expect that to be a particularly high-capacity communications channel.

Notice that men with personal ties to America of any kind are more likely to speak up on matters affecting Anglo-American relations. Only 62 per cent of those with personal ties said nothing, whereas 81 per cent of those with no ties are unrecorded. They are even somewhat more likely to record unresponsiveness than are those without ties (17 per cent to 12 per cent). Perhaps this is because men who have been abroad or who have personal contacts with foreigners naturally have more interest in foreign affairs (whether contacts cause interest, vice versa, or it is a mutually reinforcing process is not relevant here). But it may also be that the experiences of these men have in some instances made them "anti-American." Clearly it is a danger to be considered. If a wider experience of foreign contact in a population is likely, in general, to increase responsiveness, it may also result in a certain concomitant increase in the level of hostility as well.

We cannot reproduce the analysis of Table 7 for the Senate, as in the two years under study a total of only five Senators had personal ties of any nature without also having economic ties to the United Kingdom, and this is too few to produce interesting results. But it is possible to compare the effects of all kinds of direct ties, personal or economic, with that of constituency ties. The following table lists all Senators with constituency economic ties, those with only direct bonds, and those with none at all.

TABLE 8.   Per Cent of Senators With Constituency Economic Ties, Direct Ties Only, and No U.K. Ties, Who Were Responsive, Moderate, and Unresponsive

	1890		
Senators With	Responsive	Moderate	Unresponsive
Constituency Ties (N = 46)	39	30	30
Direct Ties Only (N = 3)	0	67	33
No U.K. Ties (N = 35)	9	46	46
	1954		
Senators With	Responsive	Moderate	Unresponsive
Constituency Ties (N = 12)	25	25	50
Direct Ties Only (N = 11–	73	18	9
No U.K. Ties (N = 73)	27	33	40

The number of Senators who have only direct ties to Britain is too small for us to talk of statistical significance, but the figures are interesting nevertheless. They suggest that whereas constituency ties were once very powerful forces in producing responsiveness, they are no longer very important. In fact, in 1954 Senators with no links at all were more likely to be responsive than were those whose links passed through their constituencies. This apparent shift is not surprising when one examines the changes in America's economic structure since the turn of the century. In 1954 no state derived more than 12 per cent of its income from a commodity important in Anglo-American trade. But in 1890, no less than seven states—Texas (55 per cent), Mississippi (46 per cent), South Carolina (41 per cent), Arkansas (33 per cent), Alabama (32 per cent), Georgia (31 per cent), and Louisiana (19 per cent)—gained more than 12 per cent of their income from cotton, and wheat contributed at least that much to three other states—North Dakota (55 per cent), South Dakota (29 per cent), and Minnesota (17 per cent). No wonder, then, that the economic nature of his constituency made so much less difference in the way a Senator voted in 1954 than it did in 1890. Anglo-American commerce has diminished greatly both as a power base and as a means of communication to legislators who are not themselves directly tied in with it. In 1954 the British government deliberately discriminated, for balance of payments reasons, against imports from the dollar area. Possibly its action alienated some Senators from states which produced goods whose export to Britain continued, but in limited quantities. In any case, the above figures provide dramatic evidence of the South's diminished "internationalism," which many writers have noted.

This conclusion, that the effectiveness of constituency ties in promoting responsiveness is directly proportional to the weight of the economic interest in the constituency, rests on scanty evidence, but it can be buttressed with another set of data. For both years I ranked the states involved in Anglo-American trade according to the amount of income derived from goods important in that trade, and then ranked their Senators by degree of responsiveness. For 1954 (when no state derived more than 12 per cent of its income from such products), the correlation between the two rank orders[10] was only .14, and not statistically significant. But for 1890 the same procedure produced a correlation of .34 (significant at the .05 level), for Democratic Senators and the astonishingly high correlation of .86 (significant at the .001 level) for Republican Senators. With this evidence it is hard to imagine how the precipitous decline in Anglo-American commerce over the past 70 years could fail to work to the detriment of continued responsiveness from American policy-makers.

To summarize, we have found that: (1) Legislators with economic or personal ties to the other country are more likely to be responsive to the needs of the other country than are legislators lacking those ties. (2) This holds true when party

---

[10]Using the Kendall Rank Correlation Coefficient.

affiliation is controlled, though party is itself an extremely important variable. (3) It makes little difference whether an individual legislator has a number of ties to the other country, or only one. (4) There is some evidence, though not enough to be conclusive, that economic ties are more likely to be effective than personal ones. (5) The importance of a constituency tie in influencing a Senator is directly proportional to the weight of the economic interest in the constituency.

At this point we may consider two possible criticisms of the above findings. One is that we have reversed the chain of causality—people who already look favorably on another country are then willing to develop ties with it, not the reverse, though the association shows up equally in the analysis. With regard to bonds of education, travel, business, and particularly membership in Anglo-American organizations, this objection obviously carries some weight, but with many other ties self-selection is not a factor. A man has no influence over where he is born, and is unlikely to have much more over where or with whom he does military service in wartime. Many of the business firms in question—Lloyds, Macmillan's, Simmons—have international ties that long antedated the M.P.s' or Senators' association with them. Nor are they companies whose ties with the other country would be a major factor in attracting the legislator.

Another potential objection concerns the degree to which these findings can be generalized. Although these influences may be important for ordinary legislators, they may not be effective on such others as members of the executive, who must take a wider view and who are subject to immensely more varied pressures. Especially in Britain fifty or more years ago, cabinet members were likely to be rather wealthy landowners, and perhaps were less affected by narrow economic concerns. Joseph Chamberlain in the 1890's, for example, heartily championed an Anglo-American rapprochement, but he may well have had no strong economic interest in the United States. He wanted friendship with America to counterbalance the new threat of German power. The point, however, is that other men also feared Germany's might, but were not necessarily led to embrace the republic across the seas. But Chamberlain did, and it is perhaps no coincidence that he had an American-born wife. There is no attempt to argue cause in this particular case—he may have married an American because he already liked Americans generically; his marriage may have only reinforced an initial liking for Americans; or it may in fact have been no more than a coincidence. Yet since the association of links with responsiveness is so notable for M.P.s and Senators, it may affect cabinet members similarly. This seems particularly plausible because we are *not* arguing that one becomes responsive in any simple, direct way to one's economic stake in another country's welfare, but rather than the existence of an economic or personal link opens a man to messages he would otherwise never hear.

Appendix

I. List of issues in Anglo-American relations on which sampled members of the House of Commons made public statements, with the number of members speaking on each.

1890:
1. The American tariff (3)
2. British restrictions on import of American cattle (3)
3. American adherence to International Sugar Convention (1)
4. The American copyright law (1)
5. American import restrictions other than the tariff (1)

1938:
1. The Anglo-American Trade Agreement (9)
2. Calls for cooperation with America in specific areas (5)
3. General calls for cooperation with America (3)
4. Settlement of British debt to U.S. (2)
5. Imperial Preference (2)
6. U.S. gold policy (1)
7. Restrictions on the import of U.S. films (1)
8. Dismissals of British nationals by American firms (1)
9. U.S. disarmament proposals (1)
10. Visa requirements for travel between Britain and U.S. (1)
11. Exchange of aircraft landing rights in the Pacific (1)

1954:
1. German rearmament (30)
2. Withdrawal from British military base at Suez Canal (20)
3. Trade with Communist countries (19)
4. Alleged U.S. intervention in Guatemala (14)
5. SEATO (12)
6. Policy toward Communist China (10)
7. Actions of U.S. servicemen in Britain (9)
8. Commonwealth Preference and trade with America (8)
9. British defense spending and length of national service (8)
10. Possible intervention in Indo-Chinese war (7)
11. Friendship and cooperation with U.S., general (6)
12. Civil liberties in the U.S. (6)
13. Adoption of standard NATO Belgian-designed rifle (5)
14. U.S. military bases in Britain (5)
15. Anglo-Iranian oil agreement (5)
16. Amount of consultation and information from U.S. (5)
17. NATO (4)
18. American foreign policy, general (3)
19. U.S. activities in British Honduras and British Guiana (2)
20. Call for Summit meeting without U.S. (1)
21. American aid to Spain (1)
22. American shipping subsidies (1)

II. List of roll-call votes used to form Responsiveness to Britain scale in 1890, in the order in which they appear in the scale (high responsiveness votes first). Numbers are page references to *Congressional Record* Vol. 29, Washington, p. 890. When a vote for the measure is considered responsive, a (+) follows, where responsiveness is indicated by a vote against, a (−) follows.

1. Naval Appropriation Bill. Amendment to strike out appropriation for three long-range battleships. During the debate fears of antagonizing Britain were expressed. (p. 5297) (+)
2. Revenue Bill (Tariff). Conference Report. (p. 10740) (−)
3. Bill to classify worsted cloths as woolens, pay higher duty. (p. 4300) (−)
4. Customs Administration Bill. Evarts amendment regarding importers' rights of appeal on decisions of Customs. (p. 4128) (+)
5. Revenue Bill. Amendment to reduce duty on tinplate. (p. 4128) (+)
6. Revenue Bill. Amendment to reduce duty on band and hoop iron. (p. 8393) (+)
7. Revenue Bill. Plumb amendment to allow free import where domestic supply is controlled by a monopoly. (p. 9911) (+)
8. Customs Administration Bill. Vest amendment regarding importers' rights of appeal. (p. 4121) (+)
9. Customs Administration Bill. Evarts amendment regarding importers' rights of appeal. (p. 4121) (+)
10. Revenue Bill. Amendment to reduce duty on band and hoop iron. (p. 8370) (+)
11. Revenue Bill. Final vote. (p. 9943) (−)
12. Merchant Marine Subsidy Bill. (p. 7188) (−)
13. Customs Administration Bill. Final vote. (p. 4132) (−)

Coefficient of Reproducibility of scale = .962. Where a Senator was absent but either was paired or put his opinion on record, that expression of opinion was counted as a vote. Complete absences were counted neither as errors nor as item responses in calculating the Coefficient of Reproducibility.

At least a score of other roll-call votes, mostly on the Revenue Bill, scaled with these items and could have been included, but as they added no information (the voting pattern, except for absences, was just the same as on one of the votes that was included) there was no point in adding them.

Note that although most of these votes were on tariff questions, a wider range is covered, including the Maritime Subsidy Bill (an Ocean Mail Bill showed exactly the same pattern and so was not included) and the Naval Appropriation Bill. There were a number of other tariff votes that might possibly have been included, but in the interest of keeping to votes which would most seriously affect British manufacturers I decided to include votes only on measures which *The Times* of London listed as likely to injure British producers. These goods were linen, hoops and hoop iron, cutlery, tinplate, and woolens. (See *The Times,* June 2, 1890; p. 11; June 23, 1890; p. 11; and September 29, 1890; p. 9.)

II. List of roll-call votes used to form Responsiveness to Britain scale in 1954, in the order in which they appear in the scale. Numbers are page references to *Congressional Record,* Vol. 100, Washington, 1954.

1. International Sugar Agreement. Ratification. (p. 5662) Final vote. (+)
2. Mutual Security Authorization. (p. 13052) (+)

3. Mutual Security Authorization. Long amendment to reduce authorization by $1 billion. (p. 13038) (−)
4. Mutual Security Authorization. Long amendment to reduce authorization by $500 million. (p. 13039) (−)
5. Bricker Amendment. George amendment providing that nontreaty agreements may not take effect as internal law unless implemented by Congressional action. (p. 1358) (−)
6. Bricker Amendment. Final vote. (p. 2374) (−)
7. Bricker Amendment. Ferguson amendment that any provision of an international agreement which conflicts with the Constitution shall not take effect. (p. 1740) (−)
8. Bricker Amendment. Morse motion to recommit. (p. 2267) (+)
9. Atomic Energy Act. Lehman amendment to delete provision that the AEC should give maximum effect to policies contained in international agreements made after enactment of the bill. Lehman said the provision implied that the U.S. would treat "less seriously" agreements (i.e., with Britain) previously entered into. (p. 11954) (+)
10. Bricker Amendment. Knowland amendment to require that the Senate consent to ratification of treaties by roll-call vote. (p. 1782) (−)
    Coefficient of Reproducibility = .952.

Although many of these votes were on the Bricker Amendment, a wide range of other matters is also covered. The vote on the Lehman amendment is very particularly related to policy toward Britain. There were no other foreign affairs votes that would have scaled with these items, but there were five other votes that met the criteria set up in the main body of the article. One of these, however, was on reconsideration of the Universal Copyright Convention (p. 9133) which was of little interest to the British Government but of great importance to American printers. A number of liberal and otherwise responsive Senators voted to reconsider this measure because of its effect on labor. The other four votes—one on Mutual Security Appropriations (p. 14507), two on the Bricker amendment (pp. 1916, 2262), and one on extension of the Reciprocal Trade Act (p. 8886)—showed just too many errors (slightly over 10 per cent) to allow their inclusion in the scale, indicating that some other variable or variables affected voting behavior. One of the major values of scale analysis is just this, that it enables us to identify and concentrate on those votes where the variable of interest (responsiveness) is of overwhelming importance.

The Senators located at the two extremes of responsiveness are largely those whom the "common sense" observer would put near the same extremes from an independent knowledge of their opinions. The four highest-scoring Senators were "internationalist-liberals": Hayden, Hennings, Lehman, and Morse; at the bottom of the range were "isolationist-conservatives": Bricker, Butler (Nebraska), Frear, Malone, McCarthy, and Russell.

REFERENCES

Cobden, Richard. *Speeches on Questions of Public Policy*. John Bright and James E. T. Rogers (ed.). London: Macmillan, 1870, II.

Deutsch, Karl W. et al. *Political Community and the North Atlantic Area*. Princeton, N.J.: Princeton University Press, 1957.

Green, Bert F. "Attitude Measurement." In Gardner Lindzey (ed.). *Handbook of Social Psychology*. Cambridge, Mass.: Addison-Wesley, 1954, I, 335–66.

Homans, George. *The Human Group*. New York: Harcourt, Brace, 1950.

Homans, George and Riecken, H. W. "Psychological Aspects of Social Structure." In Gardner Lindzey (ed.). *Handbook of Social Psychology*. Cambridge, Mass.: Addison-Wesley, 1954, II, 786–832.

Leech, Margaret. *In the Days of McKinley*. New York: Harper and Bros., 1959.

Lerner, Daniel. "French Business Leaders Look at EDC," *Public Opinion Quarterly*, **20** (1956), 212–21.

Russett, Bruce M. *Community and Contention: Britain and America in the Twentieth Century*. Cambridge, Mass.: Massachusetts Institute of Technology Press, 1963.

Truman, David B. *The Governmental Process*. New York: Knopf, 1951.

CHAPTER THREE

Agents of Foreign Affairs and Formation of Foreign Policy

7. THE PROFESSIONAL SOLDIER, POLITICAL BEHAVIOR, AND COALITION WARFARE

Morris Janowitz

Inevitably, a gap exists between doctrine and practice in politico-military affairs. The political behavior of military leaders is a reaction to actual and immediate military experience, as well as an expression of explicit doctrine. The impact of conducting a war of coalition on a world-wide basis against the Axis "matured" the American military elite as much as did years of professional training. If, by 1950, key military managers could be judged either as absolutists or as pragmatists* in

SOURCE. Morris Janowitz, *The Professional Soldier,* New York: The Free Press of Glencoe, 1960, pp. 283–302. Reprinted by permission of the author and The Macmillan Company. Copyright © The Free Press, A Corporation, 1960.

*The absolutist doctrine entails the U.S. goal of total supremacy and a military strategy of Gibralter defense and massive deterrence; while the pragmatist doctrine entails the U.S. goal of active competition and a strategy of mutual security and graduated deterrence. [Ed.]

their thinking, the career experiences of World War II had much to do with molding their outlook.

An understanding of contemporary military politics must take into account the judgments which officers have come to hold about the conduct of World War II. Most officers who served either in Europe or in the Far East became convinced that the United States did not fully exploit the political potentials of the military resources mobilized during World War II. An important theme in contemporary military thinking centers precisely on the necessity of preventing such a repetition of events in international relations.

Considerable thought has been devoted by military staff officers and by study groups at higher military schools as to how military resources available to the United States could have been used for more satisfactory political settlements in central Europe and in China after 1945. Although the intellectual clarity of such studies varies considerably, on the whole, they are not characterized by political realism. One such study, Project Control, sponsored by the Air War College under the direction of Colonel Raymond Sleeper, went so far as to conclude that air power alone could have prevented the rise of Nazi expansionism and simultaneously contained the Soviet Union. These war games in retrospect generally fail to take into consideration the domestic political factors which placed limitations on United States foreign policy, and which produced such rapid demobilization of military resources after 1945.

While, in general, the military profession feels that the United States could have been more successful politically, its ranks are sharply divided in assessing the role of military strategy in the final political outcome. Did the United States employ correct military strategy for defeating the Axis? Would a different strategy have produced greater political returns? These questions have developed into polemics almost equivalent to the arguments that plagued the German general staff as to why Germany lost World War I. The issue is debated by means of the rhetoric of military operations—namely, the relative priority of the theaters of war: Europe versus the Far East. In its baldest form, the question is: What would have been the political outcome of the war if the Far East had been given first priority instead of Europe? In more sophisticated form the question is posed: Did the United States place an imbalance of emphasis on Europe as against the Far East?

An officer's participation in the Far East or in Europe strongly conditioned his views on this question of strategy. Consequently, World War II produced two groups of leaders, who by experience, or by conviction, or both, were either Europe-oriented or Asia-oriented. While neither group was oblivious of the global dimensions of modern warfare, in retrospect each reflected a different concept of the struggle, and each placed a different emphasis on post-war problems. For more than a decade, as new members entered the military elite, they still could be classified in terms of theater affiliations.

One source of these differences was a system of personal alliances, centering around loyalties to strong leaders. The military establishment, like any large-scale organization, produces personal alliances which play a role in fashioning attitudes and influencing decisions. In the military these pre-war alliances were essentially unpolitical in origin, since they arose out of personal associations during peace-time. But the hypothesis is offered that in the course of World War II, and there-after, these personal alliances became the focal points of politico-military think-ing.

Although personal and career experiences in time of war influence their politi-cal behavior, military leaders are also profoundly concerned with maintaining the prerogatives of their organization and their branch of service. From this point of view, doctrine is irrelevant, or at best a rationale for the pursuit of personal glory or organizational success. For example, when during the defense of the Phillip-pines, General Douglas MacArthur asked General Wainwright what command he wanted, Wainwright answered, without reference to the complexities of military stretegy: "The place where some distinction can be gained."[1] Often, a military operation can be viewed as both contributing to the stretegy for victory and en-hancing the future of a particular service. Secretary of the Navy Forrestal, a civilian with a deep understanding of military affairs, was aboard a naval vessel off Iwo Jima when the island was being assaulted. Surrounded by a group of rank-ing officers, he is reported to have said while the American flag was being raised: "The raising of the flag on Suribachi means a Marine Corps for the next 500 years."[2]

Clearly, the political behavior of the military, like that of any large organiza-tion, is grounded in strong elements of personal and organizational self-interest; this can be taken for granted. What invites analysis is the way these interests and sporadic rivalries have influenced military policy and political behavior.

STRATEGIC PRIORITIES

Before 1939, military planners in both the Army and the Navy were more con-cerned professionally with the Far East than with Europe, if only because the United States had important military installations in the Far East. When the Navy thought of military operations, it envisioned its organizational commitments in the Far East, where it believed it would have major responsibility. The geopoliti-cal writings of Captain Alfred Thayer Mahan were used to supply an intellectual basis for such an orientation. Naval conflict would conform to the classic pattern of a struggle between opposing fleets, and would involve prestigeful weapons—the

[1]Wainwright, Jonathan, *General Wainwright's Story*. Garden City: Doubleday, 1946, p. 11.
[2]Smith, Holland, *Coral and Brass*. New York: Scribner's 1949, p. 261.

battleship and the heavy cruiser. After World War I, the navy ruled out the possibility of operations against the British fleet, and came to assume that, for the Navy, to fight in Europe would be a secondary operation of escorting convoys and engaging in anti-submarine warfare, activities hardly suited to strategic planning.

Officers involved in Army planning, perhaps the majority, also looked toward the Far East. These included men who had been stationed in Hawaii, the Phillippines, and China. The troops stationed in the far East provided at least some basis for planning during a period in which all other military elements were imponderable and continuously in flux. As part of the mechanics of a peacetime army, alternate plans, including operations in Europe were prepared for the files, but few officers foresaw a global conflict. Even after the rise of national socialism, Army thinking was limited to passive defense and, up to 1938, to hemispheric resistance. Officers working on the development of air power were involved almost exclusively with the technology of their weapons, rather than the theaters of war.

Beyond these service commitments, the implicit cultural bias defined Japan as the traditional enemy of the United States. As for political interests, Europe had had its centuries of national wars, which seemed merely to shift the balance of power back and forth. American intervention would not be likely to alter drastically the course of events.* Even though the United States had, in effect, renounced territorial aspirations, the Far East provided the more likely arena for war and a locale for enhancing the prestige and influence of the country.

Yet, if there was a Far East orientation in the military before 1939, it was at best a vague and generalized feeling rather than an explicit doctrine. When World War I ended, the military did not prepare requirements as to what might be considered strategic positions for national security. During the inter-war years, War Plan Orange—military operations in the event of an attack by Japan—was repeatedly revised and with much more concern than were the Blue plans for Europe. Nevertheless, Louis Morton, the military historian, has concluded that the available military resources were so limited as to reduce these plans to fragile exercises.[3]

The military leaders, like the elected political leaders, lagged in the development of political expertise and confidence to deal with the vastly increased foreign responsibilities of the United States since the turn of the century. However, it is misleading to claim that the source of the difficulty was an unpolitical attitude on the part of the military; it is more accurate to point out that their political horizons were limited, and reflected the interests of civilian society. The

---

*And, indeed, why should military leaders have anticipated the consequences of totalitarian movements on international relations before civilian political leaders did?

[3]Morton, Louis, "War Plan Orange: Evolution of a Strategy." *World Politics,* 1959, **11**, 221-50.

armed forces, especially the Army, had been so constrained by Congressional action and by their self-imposed professional isolation, that even the elite members hardly thought in strategic terms. Mark S. Watson has characterized the period as one in which "Army chiefs, discouraged by rejections of their recommendations year after year, were reduced to asking not for what was needed but for what they thought they could get."[4]

However, once confronted with global war, professional expertise over-ruled service preferences, and military leaders unanimously endorsed priority for the European theater. Apparently, the military necessity of first defeating Germany, the more powerful enemy, was so basic and so obvious that, at the time, the question of military strategy could not produce professional differences.

Because of the immense scale of military operations, the residue of autonomous power in each service, as well as the power of each regional commander to redirect policy, was considerable. An excerpt from General Truscott's memoirs, recounting the lack of cooperation between the Navy and the Army in the use of landing craft for the European theater, helps to recall that military coordination had to cope with a strong element of service preference which weakened command decisions:

> Our Navy, General Eisenhower went on to say, was cold toward this plan. They favored operations in the Pacific where the Navy would have the dominant role. Our naval authorities thought that commitments in the Pacific would absorb all of their resources, and they were unwilling to undertake to provide the landing craft and to organize and train the crews to operate the craft which would be required in large number. There, Army Ground Forces itself would organize special engineer units to operate and maintain landing craft, establish bases and the like. . . .[5]

The strategic decision of Europe first had to face the "human fact that no general in his right mind wants to be downgraded to a secondary role."[6] Every general and admiral operating outside of the number-one target pushed continuously

---

[4]Watson, Mark S., *Chief of Staff: Prewar Plans and Preparations.* Washington: Historical Division, Department of the Army, 1950, p. 37. Watson points out that once the planning machinery of the War Department was geared to plan for a global war, it produced a vastly overexpanded set of military requirements. The victory program in which General Albert Wedemeyer was centrally involved was "far from the actual composition of the 1945 Army— a conspicuous variation being the conjectured total of 215 divisions, including 61 armored, which compared with the ultimate 91 divisions, of which 16 were armored" p. 344).

[5]Truscott, Lieutenant General L. K., Jr., *Comman Missions: A Personal Story.* New York: E. P. Dutton, 1954, p. 20.

[6]Marshall, S. L. A., *"Memoirs of a Military Meteor." Saturday Review,* December 12, 1958, p. 21.

for a greater share of available military resources. And, in the end, the defeat of Japan followed very shortly after the destruction of Nazi Germany.

Ten years after the end of World War II, professional officers who had participated in military operations had had time to reflect on their war-time experiences and the outcome of the post-war settlement. On the basis of their expressed attitudes, either in interviews or in public pronouncements, it was still possible to classify the more articulate ones as either Europe-oriented or Asia-oriented. Social scientists have long pointed out that a person's political attitudes and behavior are not composed of separate and disparate elements, but, instead, fall into some sort of consistent pattern. The theater-orientation distinction, while admittedly oversimplified, nevertheless is a partial key to an officer's attitude toward such questions as responsibility for the Pearl Harbor disaster, the reliability of the British as allies, and a host of other policy issues. In other words, the distinction is one that seems to keynote fundamental differences between military managers.

The "Europeans" not only accept the priority of war against the Nazis as having been correct, although they pressed for an early opening of a second front in Northwest Europe, in retrospect, they believe that shortages of ground troops and anti-submarine devices, and especially a shortage of landing craft, probably precluded an earlier invasion of the continent. They believe that the strategy employed was essentially sound, and that a quicker defeat of Germany, which would have placed the Allies in a stronger bargaining position vis-à-vis the Russians in central Europe, was most doubtful because of military limitations. Some might argue that there was an over-allocation of resources to the strategic air offensive, or that General Eisenhower's command direction after the breakthrough at Normandy was defective, but they agree that these factors could have altered the course of the war only by some few months at most. In their opinion, if Allied military power was not used effectively to contain the Soviet Union in Central Europe, this was the result of decisions made in the closing weeks of the war, not of basic strategy. These were decisions in which the military participated, influenced to some degree by their concern for avoiding casualties rather than solely for the exploitation of political objectives in Central Europe. Moreover, the "Europeans" do not believe that the war in Europe was fought to weaken United States efforts in China.

If the "Far Easterns" accept the wisdom of first priority in Europe, in retrospect they believe it was implemented in such fashion as to weaken or prevent the achievement of United States objectives in both Europe and the Far East, particularly in China. General Albert C. Wedemeyer, a truly unconventional military manager, has become the most articulate exponent of the Asia theory of World War II, as revealed in his memoirs.[7]

[7]Wedemeyer, Albert C., *Wedemeyer Reports.* New York: Henry Holt, 1958.

Wedemeyer holds that it would have been to the advantage of the United States not to have entered the war, or at least to have waited until Germany and Russia had exhausted each other. Once in the war, the strategy of the United States played into the hands of the Communists. Although the correct strategy was to fight the war in Europe first, it should have been done more quickly and directly, so as to deny the Communists access to central Europe. In his view, this could have been accomplished if, according to the strategy which he and General Marshall had developed, a direct cross-Channel assault had been launched in 1943. Instead, he feels, the peripheral campaigns in North Africa and Italy actually weakened the Allied effort, and permitted the Russians to take over central Europe.

Similarly, the "Far Easterners" argue that, once the Axis had been defeated in Western Europe, it was still within the power of the United States to prosecute the war in the Far East in such a way as not to have assisted the Chinese Communists. The "intrigue" of General Stilwell; the limitations of Department of State representatives in China; plus the actions of President Roosevelt and his civilian advisers, particularly Harry Hopkins, were to blame, not the professional military. An all-out strategy could have been developed which would have assisted in the reconstruction of the Chinese Nationalist Army. General Marshall, in his role as President Truman's special envoy to China in 1947, seeking a coalition between the Communists and the Nationalists, was responsible for blocking a military aid policy which would have permitted the Chinese Nationalists to defeat the Communists.[8]

The question as to how the war started and who was responsible for Pearl Harbor helps clarify the different political orientations of the two groups. Among those officers with extreme commitments to the "Far Eastern" point of view, some believe that the politicians, especially Franklin D. Roosevelt, were responsible. This point of view is embodied in a book by Admiral Robert A. Theobald.[9] Theobald, who was directly involved in the disaster as commander of the destroyer forces, asserts that President Roosevelt forced Japan into war by unrelenting diplomatic and economic pressure, and enticed it to initiate hostilities with a surprise attack by holding the Pacific fleet in Hawaiian waters as an invitation to attack.

[8]Our analysis is concerned with the patterns of political behavior among military leaders that resulted from World War II, and not with the activities and responsibilities of specific officers during hostilities. Nevertheless, it is historically important to note that General Wedemeyer, while commander of United States forces in China, repeatedly recommended military assistance to the Chinese Communists, and as late as January 27, 1945, suggested to General Marshall that United States policy regarding China should coerce the Nationalists and the Communists into a coalition. (See Sunderland, Riley, *Army*, February 1959, pp. 94–95.) The retrospective estimates and claims of Wedemeyer are crucial aspects in analyzing the post-war political behavior of the military.

[9]Theobald, Rear Admiral Robert A., *The Final Secret of Pearl Harbor: The Washington Contribution to the Japanese Attack*. New York: Devin-Adair, 1954.

Admiral "Bull" Halsey's introduction to the volume, which endorses these conclusions, reflects the appeal of this argument to a number of military officers.[10]

A similar pattern of differences emerges on a variety of other political-military issues. The "Far Easteners" are prone to see the British as unreliable allies,
reluctant to fight, except in defense of narrow self-interest. The "Europeans,"
although critical of British procedures, are more sympathetic to their contributions and their intentions.

Over-all, the Asia-oriented group is convinced, in retrospect, that even within
the framework of a "Europe first" strategy, a strong anti-Communist China
could have been created. As professional officers, they tend to place the bulk of
the blame for political losses on the civilian direction of war, rather than the
military establishment. They consider the outcome of World War II a failure,
mainly because of strategic political decisions. The Europe-oriented group, while
admitting the shortcomings of both the military establishment and civilians in
World War II, considers the strategy and its implementation to have been basically sound, and a measured success, in the sense that other outcomes could have
been disastrous.

Moreover, our interviews revealed a strong continuity between an officer's
estimate of the conduct of World War II and his contemporary adherence to
pragmatic or absolute doctrine. Those officers who believe that the coalition
warfare against the Axis was an unsuccessful war expressed an absolutist conception of warfare. They are not inclined to acknowledge any limitations in the pursuit of total victory. By contrast, the Europe-oriented group, who hold that
World War II was a measured success, tends to adhere to a pragmatic doctrine.
In the politics of the cold war there is a line of continuity, ranging from the
issues of Asia versus Europe to those of massive, versus graduated, deterrence.
The link is supplied by the activities of the leading spokesmen of each group.
This continuity is so powerful that, for example, Army officers of the Asia orientation, such as General Albert Wedemeyer, who hold the extreme absolutist view,
have emerged as advocates of massive and strategic air power at the expense of
reliance on ground forces.

Year by year, the military elite recruits new officers whose direct involvement
in World War II came at an earlier stage in their military career. For these officers, especially those in the Air Force, concern with the strategic issues of World
War II has declined. But for all members of the military elite who were studied,
including those interviewed as a sample of the future, a pattern could be found
which linked their views of World War II and their contemporary conceptions of

[10]The more typical concept accepts a measure of military responsibility, and is devoid of
belief in political conspiracy. In particular, self-critical naval officers emphasize that
"battleship-minded officers little appreciated the terrible destructive power of a mass air
attack." Sherman, Admiral Frederick C., *Combat Command: The American Aircraft Carriers in the Pacific War*. New York: E. P. Dutton, 1950, pp. 29–30.

the military operational code. Young officers, although less concerned with the details of the strategy of World War II, were concerned with its political outcome. Almost invariably, the stronger the criticism of the political outcome, the greater the commitment to absolutist doctrine for the cold war.

THE EMERGENCE OF PERSONAL ALLIANCES

No simple explanations can account for the evolution of a military leader's attitude toward the strategic questions of World War II. The data that were assembled permit analysis of only the elite nucleus, and mainly of those officers who were involved in politico-military assignments. But there are precisely the key decision-makers in each service and in each theater of operations.

The analytical task is parallel to that involved in investigating the split between the Nazi and the anti-Nazi factions in the German *Wehrmacht*. Which dimensions of the military profession influenced these political perspectives? In a detailed study of the top eighty-five *Wehrmacht* generals of World War II, Kurt Lang found that social background, as well as military experiences, were at work in giving rise to the twentieth *Putsch* against Hitler.[11] Lang divided the group of officers in his sample into the pro-Nazi praetorians, the uncommitted, and the anti-Nazi conspirators, on the basis of their demonstrated opposition to Hitler. The pro-Nazi praetorians tended to display those social traits which generally identified Nazi party leaders. More of them came from southern Germany, and from lower middle-class backgrounds. On the other hand, the opposition was not a monopoly of the aristocratic Junker group. While the anti-Nazi conspirators tended to come somewhat disproportionately from upper middle-class backgrounds, they could not be distinguished from the uncommitted on the basis of social background. Instead, their military careers, personal alliances, and civilian contacts were more important. Both conspirators and praetorians had many more quasi-political assignments than had the uncommitted, and their careers more often deviated from institutionalized army patterns. In all military organizations the most politically conscious are often characterized by unconventional career lines. The uncommitted officers were older, had the most traditional careers. conformed to the ideals of the purely technical officer, and were most isolated from the larger society.

In the United States, to an even greater extent, differences in political behavior between services or within services cannot be accounted for by social background. In the past, the military profession has recruited those whose social backgrounds have inclined them toward conservative commitments. Yet, analysis of social origins of the military elite demonstrates that there has been a progressive decline in

[11]Lang, Kurt, "Tradition, Skill, and Politics in the German Army." Unpublished manuscript.

the importance of social heritage and a rise in the importance of organizational experiences. The general or admiral who conforms to the heroic model demonstrates real or acquired ties to the "upper class," while the modern military manager is a more representative social type.

Undoubtedly, the political behavior of a military leader reflects his personality and his underlying motives to some degree. The efforts of social research to link political behavior to personality are revealing, but hardly definitive. In the study of any elite group, personality and motivational factors remain remote, and are available only from inference. On *a priori* grounds, it could be argued that the most "authoritarian" personality would be the most inclined to adopt an absolutist conception of warfare. While this assertion remains an untested hypothesis, personality factors clearly seem to re-enforce career experiences.

The following analysis focuses on the combined impact of the service and the theater in which an officer fought, and the elite alliance into which he was recruited. As already shown, each general and admiral displayed an obvious tendency to judge the outcome of the war from the point of view of his own service and theater. Those who had fought in the Far East, particularly in China, came to believe that their theater had been neglected.* They came to believe that a more decisive political victory could have been achieved by a higher priority to their own operations. This pattern applies most strongly to the ground force, which was involved in both theaters; to a lesser extent to the Navy, whose prestigeful operations were mostly in the Far East; and least to the Air Force, whose officers revealed the least identification with a particular theater of war.

In the military, as in any organization, the "big issues" are personified by outstanding men and the factions that develop around them. Within the elite nucleus the hypothesis is also relevant that an officer's perspectives are influenced by his network of personal alliances and contacts. Many an officer has served in a particular command without developing the point of view of the commander. More often he has found himself directly involved and personally committed to leading personalities and their points of view.

Intimate alliances are essential aspects of career success in a closed institution which places high emphasis on personal characteristics. The hierarchical structure of the military establishment, and the fact that organized factions are not permitted within the military bureaucracy, require that factionalism in doctrine and political behavior be expressed in the clash of alliances around outstanding personalities. In time of war, because of the pressures and strains of responsibility,

---

*The same feeling was apparent among those officers who had fought on the Italian front.

intense interpersonal loyalties and antipathies develop within the nucleus of leaders.[12]

It is neither feasible nor necessary to inventory all the personal networks within the military establishment during World War II. But it is possible to speak of the natural history of leadership groupings which persist over long periods of time and which mold the orientation of its members, and which in the long run, have important political consequences. Of the variety of personal networks that existed in the military establishment during World War II, alliances centering around George C. Marshall and Douglas MacArthur and their followers were the most dramatic, and in the end could be linked most clearly to differences between pragmatic and absolute conceptions of warfare, respectively. Like all organizational alliances their boundaries are difficult to determine, and their importance and pervasiveness can be overstated by the outsider. Because all organizational factions are amorphous, many officers remained indifferent, some shifted their attachments, while others sought to remain in contact with both leaders.

During World War II, this personality-doctrinal struggle originated in the Army, but at the very highest echelons it cut across service lines. The Marshall group was centered in the War Department and among those leaders involved in the war in Western Europe, although there were Marshall associates in important commands in the Far East. The MacArthur alliance, on the other hand, was based among those who fought against the Japanese in the Far East and in China. In fact, the rivalry has been described as a clash of opinion between MacArthur, as commander in the Far East, and the War Department in Washington. Moreover, during the decade after 1945 the pragmatic group recruited many of its leaders from among those who had managed the European theater of operations, while some of the most vocal exponents of the absolutist group came from the Far Eastern theater.

The factional divide between the Europe-first and the Asia-first groups was primarily a difference between managerial perspectives. The military careers of MacArthur and Marshall, the two key opinion leaders, were intertwined for more than forty years. Both served as junior officers in the Philippines before World War I, and both achieved prominence in France in 1917. Douglas MacArthur became a brigade commander; George Marshall was a staff operations officer. During the inter-war years, MacArthur, although only a year older, was Marshall's senior in rank and close to the center of power.

---

[12]The clash of personalities in the high command of the French Army at the time of the fall of France is brilliantly portrayed by the British general, Sir Edward Spears. Spears, who served as Churchill's personal representative to Paul Reynaud, French defense minister, explicitly states that "female" intrigue made its contribution to the tensions and rivalries among top French generals. Spears, Edward L., *Assignment to Catastrophe*. New York: A. A. Wyn, 1954, Vol. I, *Prelude to Dunkirk, July 1939–May 1940*.

As Superintendent of the United States Military Academy, and later as Chief of Staff under Herbert Hoover, MacArthur had the widest network of personal contacts. But the leading members of the MacArthur group were not recruited from among the important associates who had served under him while he was Chief of Staff. Older-type officers who dominated the Army, such as Generals Hugh Drum and Ben Lear, were friends of MacArthur, but not his associates. The core of the MacArthur group were loyal and devoted staff officers whom he recruited while in the Far East. In the service these officers were known as the "Bataan crowd," since some had served continuously with MacArthur from Pearl Harbor through the occupation of Japan. Among the most conspicuous were Major General Charles A. Willoughby, chief intelligence officer, Bonner F. Fellers, public relations officer, and Courtney Whitney, legal officer and chief of civil affairs matters. Whitney was a Minila lawyer, who had been acquainted with MacArthur since the early 1920's. This closely knit staff nucleus reflected Mac-Arthur's thinking and operated to extend his influence.

Secondly, the MacArthur group included operational and field officers whom he retained in his command. Because MacArthur was such a strong personality, some of his subordinate commanders became close associates; others did not. One of his chief ground force commanders, General Robert L. Eichelberger, had served in Washington while MacArthur was Chief of Staff, but his more personal attachment was to General Marshall and others of the Marshall group. By contrast, General George Kenney, MacArthur's air commander, became one of his most vocal supporters.

The Korean conflict brought additional officers into direct contact with Mac-Arthur. Of special note was General Edward M. Almond, who had served on MacArthur's staff since 1946, and who held the crucial 20th Corp command during the Chinese intervention in Korea. Equally important was the enlargement of the MacArthur circle in Korea by other Far Easterners who had served in China during World War II. Among such officers was, for example, General George D. Stratemeyer, Commander of Army air forces in the India-Burma sector in 1943 and in the China theater in 1945. General Albert Wedemeyer was another; Wedemeyer had served in the Far East before 1941 and, ultimately, as Army commander in China during World War II. Although he had not been under MacArthur's command in World War II, the issues of Korea put the men into close political contact.

Until he went to the Far East, MacArthur had been a leading figure in Army affairs. But the entourage which he created during World War II was regional in scope and, in fact, limited to the Far East. His "discipleship" was much less clear-cut than that created by the leadership of Marshall. With the events of Korea, MacArthur's policy demands had ramifications throughout the entire military establishment. However, by that time, the Air Force had become the ascendant arm. Many followers of MacArthur had retired without leaving a direct line of descent, and the main advocates of an absolutist doctrine came to be found in the Air Force.

By contrast, although Marshall occupied a more marginal position for part of his career, during World War II his influence became central, and it continued to have consequences in the ground forces in the post-war period. At one point during the inter-war years while MacArthur was Chief of Staff, Marshall was given a minor National Guard training assignment in Illinois. His appointment as brigadier general, as preparation for the Chief of Staff appointment was in part the work of civilian political leaders, who were searching for vigorous leadership which could modernize the Army. In 1936 Secretary of War George H. Dern was surveying potential officers for higher command. Dern was advised by General Frank McCoy, a close associate of General Pershing, who had known Marshall personally since World War I. Mrs. Marshall reports in her autobiography that General and Mrs. McCoy arranged a dinner in Chicago for Secretary of War Dern and Marshall during his period of "exile" to National Guard training duty.[13] Dern discovered that in many Army quarters Marshall had a reputation as an outstanding organizer and a man of considerable energy. Many individuals take credit for, and, indeed, were probably involved, in bringing Marshall to the attention of President Roosevelt; the influence of General Pershing was no doubt highly relevant. However, his appointment represents the efforts of civilian leaders to select from among the widest list of eligibles, rather than from among the most senior in rank and position.

Just as Marshall's appointment represented a departure from seniority appointment, so he, in turn, was vigorous in recruiting officers for higher command. His personnel appointments filled central staff positions in Washington and manned key posts in the military structure for the European theater, which it was presumed he might command one day. Many of these officers were deeply influenced by Marshall's leadership, and came to reflect his sentiments. For years, Marshall, like other aspiring officers, had been keeping lists of officers whose talents had impressed him, and whom he intended to select as commanders, if he were appointed Chief of Staff, or in a position to influence the selection of commanders. Being an innovator, he selected for his list men who were energetic and who had demonstrated ability at problem-solving by his standards.

Many of the key Marshall appointments were men who had come to his personal attention while he was commanding officer of the Infantry School at Fort Benning, Georgia. For Marshall, the assignment at Fort Benning was not a routine one, but provided an opportunity to develop infantry tactics and to continue the talent search. While there, he first became acquainted with Omar Bradley in 1929, and in 1931 he met Walter Bedell Smith, two men who were to become key

[13]Marshall, Katherine Tupper, *Together, Annals of an Army Wife.* New York: Tupper and Love, 1946, p. 20.

figures in Europe. The central figure in the European command, Dwight Eisenhower, although he did not have a history of long personal acquaintance with General Marshall, considered himself a disciple. Eisenhower was probably known to Marshall as a result of his service on the American Battle Monuments Commission with General Pershing. (A competent officer who came to the attention of Pershing, was usually known by Marshall, in turn.) After his successful participation in the Louisiana field exercises in 1940 Eisenhower came into more direct contact with Marshall. Prior to that time, Eisenhower had served under MacArthur, first in Washington and later as a personal assistant on public relations and political matters when MacArthur went to the Phillippines in 1935.

The men Omar Bradley had as his key commanders—Courtney Hodges, Lawton Collins, and Leonard Gerow—had also become personally acquainted with either Marshall or Bradley at the Fort Benning Infantry School. The same was true for Jacob Devers, the other Army group commander in the campaign in France. General George Patton was not a close personal associate of Marshall. Patton was the commandant at Fort Myer when General Marshall was assigned to Washington in 1938–39. However, by reputation, he was high on General Marshall's personal list, even before he went to North Africa. In addition, Patton had a personal link to Eisenhower which dated back to their association in the tank corps in 1919.

Marshall's professional "family tree" can be traced in various directions. H. H. Arnold, Chief of the Air Force, was a close associate, and their personal relation expedited the arrangement by which Marshall gave the Air Force organizational autonomy within the Army command structure. Marshall was generally recognized by air officers as inclined to support the development of air power. MacArthur did not have this reputation while he served as Chief of Staff; indeed he was resented for his alleged role in the courtmartial of Billy Mitchell. The inner core of top planners and logistical specialists included Lesley McNair, commander of the United States Army Field Forces, and Brehon Somervell, in charge of supply services, who were Marshall's associates, but did not serve in Europe.

The striking aspect of the Marshall alliance is its direct and indirect line of descent, because each field commander is permitted wide discretion in the selection of his subordinates. One of the most conspicuous example is General Alfred Gruenther, who had an extensive war-time career in Europe, who rose to be Eisenhower's Chief of Staff at SHAPE, and, later, commander of SHAPE. The line of second-generation descendants includes Generals Matthew Ridgway, Maxwell Taylor, and James M. Gavin. All of these officers, who served in the same division in Europe, were deeply influenced by Marshall and his direct followers, such as Omar Bradley. Ridgway, for example, served with Marshall at Fort Benning, accompanied him on a mission to Brazil, and was secretary of the general staff in 1940–41, while Marshall was Chief of Staff. The third level of association, where the link begins to run out, is with officers such as General

Lemnitzer. Lemnitzer served under Eisenhower in North Africa, and became Chief of Staff after having served as Commander of United States and United Nations forces in the Far East.

Personal alliances can break down under pressure and defections can occur. General Joseph W. Stilwell served with Marshall in China in the 1930's and was vigorously supported by him. Marshall esteemed Stilwell because he did not take the Army for granted. Stilwell also was the recognized expert on China in the War Department. The reversals of the China theater and the political demands of the Chinese Nationalists dissolved this association.

General Mark Clark was marked for higher command by Marshall when they both served in the 3rd Division at Vancouver Barracks in Washington in 1937. In 1944–45 he found himself in the isolated Italian theater of war. He was embittered by public attacks on his handling of American troops at the Rapido River crossing, and disappointed by the collapse of President Truman's efforts to make him ambassador to the Vatican. After his duty in Korea, he became critical of General Marshall, and began to associate himself ideologically with the Wedemeyer conception of World War II. Another outspoken figure was General James A. Van Fleet. Apparently, Van Fleet was not known to Marshall before 1941 as an officer with potentials for strategic command.[14] He distinguished himself as a regimental and divisional commander in combat, and was given higher commands on the recommendations of Eisenhower and Bradley. Ultimately, he became associated with MacArthur during the Korean conflict and found expression for his politico-military sympathies in the outlook of MacArthur.

But military operations influence military leaders in turn. The war in Europe, far more costly in lives and material, was cast more in terms of liberation than were operations in the Far East. From the top general to the lowest private, the end of hostilities brought more than a sense of personal relief. Americans sensed that their military efforts had produced some positive accomplishment, along with the destruction of the enemy. Because of relatively limited cultural and social differences, American forces were able to develop some sense of community, rudimentary though it may have been, with Western Europe.

By contrast, in military operations in the Far East, the enemy was satanized to a greater degree. Conflicts between isolated American and Japanese units were often fought to a bitter end. With the exception of the Phillippines, there was no sense of liberation on the part of the native population of the occupied southwest Pacific islands. While Japan acquiesced with formal ritualism, a deep gulf remained

---

[14]It is widely believed in Army circles that General Van Fleet was held back for promotion by General Marshall because Marshall had confused him with another officer—Van Vliet (also pronounced Van Fleet). Van Vliet was on Marshall's list as an officer who had earned a reputation that he should not be promoted. Apparently, it was not until Van Fleet showed great ability as a regimental commander on D-Day that Marshall learned of his mistake; thereafter, Van Fleet was promoted with suitable rapidity.

between the population and the occupying military forces, who found themselves in a completely alien world.

Military leaders in Europe who were charged with military government and occupational duties, recognized the powerful impulses of Western Europe to remain part of the non-communist world as the pressure of Soviet forces increased. American forces developed a real attachment to their immediate surroundings. The task of military defense seemed geo-politically feasible, even though the mechanics remained problematic. American military leaders, because of their experiences as "liberators," and because of their sense of community, became convinced that Western Europe had to be defended, and not used merely as a base of military operations. By contrast, as the cold war developed, the military forces in the Far East felt themselves in a much more isolated social setting. In addition to bitterness over the loss of China, an awareness of the immensity of the geo-political task was ever present. If, after 1945, military forces in Europe became fused into the social structure to some extent, in the Far East they remained relatively detached. Asia seemed more of an outpost than part of a political community.

Thus, in summary, professional experiences and personal attachments become deeply intertwined in fashioning an officer's outlook. To point out that policy orientations are conditioned by personal factors does not mean that officers are insincere in their beliefs about military policy, but that they are human beings. If historians broaden their efforts beyond the analysis of official records and collect essential data by the techniques of oral history, they will be able to document in greater and greater detail the interpersonal relations generated by two such strong leaders as Marshall and MacArthur, among others. The political behavior of the military elite, like that of any leadership group, cannot be understood without reference to the natural history of these rivalries and loyalties. In the case of the military, these personal attachments were tied, during World War II, to the issues of the European versus the Far Eastern theater.

After 1945, the importance of air power shifted the world-wide dimensions of the military establishment. Strategic questions were less theater-based and more concerned with the preparation for total versus limited warfare. With military unification and the creation of three services, the politico-military issues were no longer anchored within the War Department. New strategic issues submerged the personal associations created by World War II, although these associations persisted. The Korean conflict tended to perpetuate and transform them, especially within the ground forces. American military policy has come to be formulated at the political center of the nation. But, clearly, the military and personal experiences of World War II in the different theaters of war contributed to the strategic outlook—pragmatic or absolute—of the ranking officers.

8. DIPLOMACY AND COMMUNICATION

*Suzanne Keller**

This brief paper attempts to examine those aspects of diplomatic communication which derive not from conscious operational codes but from social factors of which the individual diplomat is either unaware or over which he has no control. In the past, diplomacy has generally been studied as it is practiced by individual negotiators or as it is influenced, if not determined, by the foreign policy of a country. Our interest is, for the moment, not in the psychological characteristics of the individual negotiator but in the social groups from which he stems and whose values he is seen to represent.

At the outset we must distinguish between two aspects of communication that are often confused. One refers to the technical side of knowing the symbols used by others so that cognitive contact can be established. As is well known, great stress is laid on this in the training of diplomats. The other refers to the emotional reaction to what has been said or written, to agreement not on what the symbols are but on what feelings they evoke. While equally great stress is laid on this aspect of communication, much less is known about it. It is the second aspect that mainly concerns us.

THE DATA

The ambassadors (and ministers where embassies did not exist) of Great Britain and of the United States to the most important countries of the world

SOURCE. Suzanne Keller, "Diplomacy and Communication," in *Public Opinion Quarterly,* XX (Spring, 1956), pp. 176–182. Reprinted by permission of the author and Princeton University Press. Copyright 1956 by Princeton University.

*When this article was written, the author was with the Program on International Communications at the Center for International Studies, M.I.T. The study was begun when the writer was a Visiting Fellow at the Center of International Studies, Princeton, New Jersey, from 1953–1954. The interest and support of the members of the Center, particularly of Dr. Frederick S. Dunn, Director, and Professor Gabriel A. Almond, as well as of Professor Gordon A. Craig, Department of History, Princeton University, is gratefully acknowledged.

during the first half of the twentieth century are the subjects of this study. The distribution of the sample is shown in Table 1. Information about the social backgrounds, family environments, education and careers of these men was obtained from a variety of sources including memoirs, newspaper clippings, Dictionaries of Biography and Foreign Service Lists. Only a fraction of the data is reported here.

TABLE 1. **British and American Ambassadors and Ministers,
1900–1950**

Country of Assignment	American	British
Great Britain	14	–
United States	–	13
France	13	10
U.S.S.R. (Russia)	15	11
Germany	12	6
Italy	16	10
Spain	11	12
Turkey	11	11
Iran	17	14
Japan	16	9
China	12	9
Total	137	105

FUNCTIONS OF A DIPLOMAT

Diplomats, it is generally agreed, must do at least three things: (1) represent their countries in foreign countries; (2) negotiate international agreements; and (3) inform their home offices about trends and conditions in the countries to which they are assigned. All of these depend on communication as this term is used to denote the transmission of messages, impressions and interpretations from one human source to another. The diplomat is a key link in this human network and the communication required of him is largely interpersonal communication in a formally specified setting.

REPRESENTATION

"I am not surprised," replied the Venetian Ambassador to the Duke of Tuscany when the latter complained about a particular Venetian resident at his court, "we have many fools in Venice." Whereupon the Grand Duke retorted:

"We also have fools in Florence but we take care not to export them."[1] Surely all countries are equally vigilant, but whom *do* they export? What is the collective self-image which one society presents to the world by way of its official national representatives? This, too, is communication. It serves to transmit the ideal national image by which that society would like to be known and recognized. Often it indicates what that society would like to be and to live up to, and as such, it touches on and conveys some of its fundamental values. In turn, participants in negotiation appraise each other not only as individual personalities but also as representatives of specific social groups. This stereotyping is unfortunate since it may lead to a too rigid perception of current personalities, but it is essential because it is economical.

THE COLLECTIVE MESSENGERS

Only a limited number of variables will be discussed and of these only the modal pattern will be revealed. Our main interest lies in the typical profile, those characteristics most frequently exhibited.

The British	Proportion of All Ambassadors
Father's Occupation: Landed Gentry	59%
Foreign Service Career Man	87
Schooling	
Leading Public School	56
Eton-bred	36
Oxford or Cambridge	53
Start in Foreign Service	
At the top	9
Number of countries assigned to*	
Only one	9
Ten or more	33
Number of geographical areas assigned to	
Three or more**	77
Age at first becoming Ambassador	
45–49 years	48

* This means the number of countries assigned to throughout career, not merely those to which a man was sent as Ambassador or Minister.
** The areas were divided as follows: Northern and Western Europe, Southern and Eastern Europe, Middle East, Far East, North America, South America.

[1] de Callieres, M., *On the Manner of Negotiating with Princes,* A. F. Whyte, trans., Boston and New York: Houghton Mifflin Co., 1919, p. 59.

| | Proportion of |
The Americans	All Ambassadors
Father's Occupation: Business and Law	51%
Career prior to Ambassadorship	
Business and Law	58
Region of Birth	
Northeast and North Central States	64
College or University	
Ivy League	45
Big Three	40
Start in Foreign Service	
At the top	64
Number of Countries assigned to	
Only one	45
Ten or more	6
Number of geographical areas assigned to	
Three or more	25
Age at first becoming Ambassador	
50 years and older	62
55 years and older	37

According to some of their cumulative characteristics, American and British ideal types differ sharply from each other but are each clearly recognizable. The ideal-type Britisher turns out to be in his late forties, born into the landed gentry and bred in one of Britain's leading public schools. Oxford and Cambridge were the universities he most frequently selected if he decided to continue with his studies. He generally entered the diplomatic service at the bottom rung and reached the height of his profession only after years of service in many parts of the world and in a wide variety of countries. Besides his native tongue he knew at least one foreign language before he joined the service and acquired a number of others afterward. His slow ascent in the service exposed him to the eyes of his peers in other foreign services and enabled them to observe his individual habits and preferences well in advance of his appearance as chief negotiator for his government.

The American national ideal typically would be in his fifties, often close to sixty, when he assumed the top post in the diplomatic service. Usually he came to this post from a successful career in business or in law, the areas where his father had also been most prominently active. It was likely that his college years were spent in one of the Ivy League schools, particularly in one of the Big Three, and that he had been raised and educated in the Northeast and North Central states (Pennsylvania, New York and Massachusetts alone account for 40 per cent of all ambassadors and ministers). Most of his life was spent in his own country speaking his native tongue and his first assignment in the foreign service is likely to have been his only one. There was little opportunity for others in the profession, either for peers in other foreign services or for subordinates in his own, to build up a personal impression of him which might be of use in later contact with him.

The collective image communicated by the Americans thus is even more likely to be the sole criterion upon which an estimate of national beliefs and intentions is based, since the system for selecting key negotiators prevents their becoming known in advance through most of the usual channels.

The role played by anticipatory models in diplomatic negotiation should not be underestimated.

The average decision-maker tends to operate on the basis of a speculative model of the general type of decision-makers from other communities he expects to meet in international negotiations. The accuracy of this model determines in a large degree his success in achieving his objectives.[2]

Diplomats must take their model where they find it. All bits of information are utilized in their continual speculation about real or inferred intentions.[3] The more one-sided and essentially incomplete the stereotype, the less accurate the inferences.

THE COLLECTIVE MESSAGE

It is not only in diplomacy that the assumption is made that if you know where a man comes from you can tell what he stands for and how he will behave in given situations. But in diplomacy it is doubly important because the objective characteristics of negotiators play a powerful role in diplomatic communication. The fact that a man attended Eton is important not only because of what it actually reveals about him but also because of what it, rightly or wrongly, suggests. The facts of a man's life and the interpretation of them influence the appraisals made by other diplomats. They also, however, influence the thinking of those who must select specific individuals for diplomatic negotiation from the start.

---

[2]Dunn, Frederick S., "The Scope of International Relations, " in *World Politics,* Vol. 1, No. 1 (Oct. 1948), p. 145.

[3]Upon being informed of the death of Talleyrand, one diplomat is supposed to have asked: "But what were Talleyrand's real intentions?" Quoted by Lindsay Rogers, "The Wonders of Diplomacy," in *Foreign Affairs,* (Jan. 1955), p. 316.

"My perfect diplomatist," reveals a man highly placed in the British Foreign Service, "need not be an Apollo; but he has to represent Great Britain, and the undersized, crab-like, scruffy type simply will not do. . . ."[4]

Foreigners don't expect British diplomats to talk like bus conductors or dress like bandleaders. . . .[5]

He must be representative of all that is best in our manner of life and endeavor to make known British policy, British institutions and the British way of life. . . .[6]

The list could be extended but it would add little more to the main point made: it is not accidental that the top level diplomats of Great Britain show such uniformity in social origins and training. The assumption governing their selection is that they are either most favorably endowed by virtue of these origins or most easily trained as a result of them to give expression to the ideals that the influential and articulate elements in their society consider most desirable.

At the same time that the diplomat is supposed to meet these criteria, he is also supposed to "register an interest in everything in the whole kaleidoscope of human experience, so that he can get something out of a visit to a factory or a coal mine, a picture gallery, a ballet, a church service, a political gathering, a race meeting, or an evening's talk in a village pub."[7]

Americans write in a similar vein. "How shall we represent America abroad? How can we best serve the interests—the highest interests of our people?" asks Joseph C. Grew. And he answers:

It has been a tradition and an age-old principle of the Foreign Service of our Government that we can present America best by presenting it truthfully. But I think it is not always fully realized that in order to do that you must *know* America: not just the State or region in which we have lived; not just the segment of society in which we have been raised, but the broad sweep of the land and the complex of human beings who live and work in it.[8]

[4]Ashton-Gwatkins, Frank T., *The British Foreign Service,* Syracuse University Press, n.d., p. 64.

[5]Middleton, Drew, "Notes on Diplomats and Diplomacy," *New York Times Magazine* (Oct. 30, 1955), p. 58.

[6]*Foreign Service Handbook* (London, Jan. 1948), p. 6.

[7]Ashton-Gwatkins, *op. cit.*

[8]Grew, Joseph C., *Turbulent Era,* ed. Walter Johnson, 2 vols., Boston: Houghton Mifflin Co., 1952, p. 1495.

The reality of the matter is that few of either the British or of the American negotiators do in fact know the broad sweep of their respective countries in any but a geographical sense or have had sustained contact with segments of society other than those in which they were born and bred. This is not automatically a result of their being recruited largely from the high status elements of the population, as critics of diplomatic performance have frequently supposed. The problem is that while social cohesion or *esprit de corps* enhances the security of individuals it limits their perspectives. This is so whether the members are recruited from paupers or from princes.[9]

The confusion between ideal and reality may be as harmful to successful negotiation as are bias or excessive caution, characteristics which have frequently been singled out as undesirable. Diplomats are expected to live up to the real demands of the political situation and to the ideal demands of their societies' self-images. These demands are often incompatible and therefore impossible to fulfill and it falls to the individual diplomat to settle this in his own way.

NEGOTIATION

Negotiation is usually discussed in terms of the desirable qualities in the negotiator and of useful tactics in negotiation. Generally omitted is the fact that negotiation requires of each participant the ability not only to persuade but to be persuaded. In order to persuade, a diplomat must be accorded the powers and prerogatives of his role and he must be familiar with the technical skills of his trade. In order to be persuaded, he must grant his opponents the same powers and prerogatives, and he must know who he is and what he stands for. Ignorance or insecurity in regard to his identity, which includes both knowing the way of life of only a limited social segment and knowing the ways of life of too many, is likely to result in excessive optimism or in excessive suspiciousness and distrust.

. . .it was difficult to convince . . . Sir Edward Grey that the envoy of some Balkan country did not possess the same sort of traditions, intuitions and principles, as he had inherited himself; he was inclined to regard them, if not perhaps as old Wykehamists, then at least as old Marlburians. If subsequent developments led him to revise this opinion, he would feel that a gross

---

[9]See, for example, the remarks made about wealthy men by a former American Ambassador to Germany. "Personal distrust got the better of me . . . I would not sit down to lunch with a Morgan except possibly to learn something of his motives and attitudes." In *Ambassador Dodd's Diary,* ed. by William E. Dodd, Jr., and Martha Dodd, New York: Harcourt Brace and Co., 1941, p. 100. The book has many such examples.

deception had been practiced upon him, and would regard the foreign statesman who had failed to live up to Old Marlburian standards as a man of irre-
deemable iniquity.[10]
The Americans . . . are convinced that all diplomatists are determined to en-
snare, entangle and humiliate all those with whom they negotiate. They enter
a conference as Daniel entered the den of lions. . . . An American diplomatist
will, in the presence of continental diplomatists, become overwhelmed with
diffidence and suspicion.[11]

This is where excessive uniformity in social backgrounds and training, despite its
advantages for developing a corporate identity, is potentially harmful. By being
immersed in the values and orientations of only one social group one can neither
negotiate with nor represent a great variety. A world in change demands of diplomats, no less than of policy, the ability to perceive and to meet this change.
No longer is it feasible to depend solely on the diplomats themselves to create
commonly accepted values by virtue of their social contacts in the service. This
professional freemasonry has long been considered an important component of
successful negotiation, even though it also helped to widen the gap between the
men who designed the policy and those who carried it out. When one reads today
what these career-borne standards depended on, it reminds one of an age that has
passed.

These officials representing their Governments in foreign capitals possessed
similar standards of education, similar experience, and a similar aim. *They desired the same sort of world,* . . . They had often known each other for years,
having served in some post together in their early youth; and they all believed,
whatever their government might believe, that the purpose of diplomacy was
the preservation of peace.[12]

Even here, the implicit assumption is that a knowledge of the group ties, the
values and the aims of one another is indispensable to the men facing each other
in negotiation.
    In this brief paper only a few of the sociological elements in diplomatic com-
munication have been highlighted. The official messengers of a society, taken together, are themselves a communication between nations. The meaning attached
to this cumulative image is a factor in negotiation.

[10]Nicolson, Harold, *Diplomacy,* London: Thornton Butterworth Ltd., 1939, p. 128.
[11]*Ibid.,* p. 129.
[12]Nicolson, Harold, *Evolution of Diplomatic Method,* London: Constable, 1954, p. 75.
Italics supplied.

9. WHERE THE ELEPHANT FEARS TO DANCE AMONG THE CHICKENS: BUSINESS IN POLITICS? THE CASE OF DU PONT

*Lewis Anthony Dexter**

Business response to political challenge or possibility has been the subject of much speculation and some recent exhortation. "Populist" and starkly "realist" elements in American political thought have tended to assume that powerful firms directly and unequivocally influence politicians.

Here, as elsewhere, simplistic political generalizations can probably be modified or discredited by the diversity of events. Westinghouse was probably more aggressive in its response to the actual or alleged threat of foreign imports than du Pont could have dreamed of being, just as the attitude of Republic Steel or Inland Steel toward the current enthusiasm for political education differs from that, say, of Allied Paper or Wilson and Company. So, the report we are about to

SOURCE. Lewis Anthony Dexter, "Where the Elephant Fears to Dance Among the Chickens: Business in Politics? The Case of du Pont," in *Human Organization,* 19 (Winter, 1960–1961), pp. 188–194. Also, Raymond Bauer, Ithiel Pool, and Lewis Anthony Dexter, *American Business and Public Policy,* New York: Atherton Press, 1963, pp. 265–276. Reprinted by permission of the author and the publisher, Atherton Press. Copyright © 1963, Atherton Press, New York. All rights reserved.

*The report here presented is part of a longer study, "Congressmen and the People They Listen To," Center for International Studies, Massachusetts Institute of Technology (dittoed), Parts I and II, 1955, available from the University Microfilms, Ann Arbor, Michigan. (This study is copyrighted by MIT and permission to use any part of it must be obtained through Lewis Dexter, 536 Pleasant Street, Belmont 78, Massachusetts.) An abstract of the entire study, called "The Representative and His District," appeared in *Human Organization,* XVI, No. 1 (Spring, 1957), 11–16. Participation as consultant to the Research Professor of Government, Harvard, 1960, in a study of business-in-politics movement led the writer to develop his views in this field; as did also participation in political campaigns.

The author is grateful to his colleagues, Raymond Bauer, Harvard University Business School, and Ithiel Pool, Massachusetts Institute of Technology, for guidance and advice in this analysis but the responsibility is, of course, entirely his own. He is also grateful to his patient informants, without whom no such study could be made.

present on du Pont and Delaware *applies* unequivocally only there.[1] Its significance, however, *extends* to a fairly considerable number of businessmen and business firms in contemporary American society; and, indeed, the current enthusiasm about "getting businessmen into politics," represents a (probably temporary) revolt[2] against an attitude which many firms, probably the majority, have held since 1937 and in essence hold today. Du Pont probably serves as a fairly good type of this attitude.

As a part of a study of reciprocal trade legislation,[3] and communications from and within the industrial community about it, we conducted a series of interviews in several different industries and Congressional districts in 1953, 1954, and 1955, when the reciprocal trade extension acts were debated in Congress. We chose to study Delaware chiefly because of du Pont.

Du Pont is huge, du Pont is colossal, du Pont is almost legendary. Du Pont is a $2,000,000,000 corporation which has grown up in a state with only one Congressional district. And du Pont is traditionally protectionist. Some State Department employees, with experience in commercial policy, *regarded* du Pont, in 1955, as one of their most serious enemies, just as some protectionists regard the State Department as their most serious enemy.

It happens that *both* senators from Delaware were on the Senate Finance Committee, the committee which handles tariff matters. This is quite unusual. Both of them leaned toward reciprocal trade; as did the Delaware congressman (when we started our study he was Herbert Warburton, R., who was succeeded in 1955 by Harris McDowell, D.). If there were a knock-down, drag-out fight on reciprocal trade extension, would not these two senators be under considerable pressure? Would not Delaware business and farming interests be stimulated to try to influence them? And would not du Pont, as unquestionably the greatest of these interest, exert the most pressure?

The answer to all these questions, as it turned out, was "No." And this answer raises some very interesting problems for the student of business and politics; problems such as this:

---

[1]It is believed that the findings are still pertinent to du Pont in 1960, but that the development of the attitude here reported occurred at du Pont between 1933 and 1947, more or less, and that it was not characteristic of the company prior to 1933.

[2]A revolt which will probably win over a few firms to follow the General Electric-type emphasis on the business climate, a good many more firms to stress political education as part of a management development program far more than has been customary, but which in all likelihood, will, in essentials, be beaten back by the limited sort of "partial incorporation" of a "revolutionary" ideology which the management development approach suggests also.

[3]An extensive report on this study is to be published as R. Bauer, I. Pool, and L. Dexter, *American Business and Public Policy* in 1961. A dozen or more articles arising out of the study have already been published.

Can a business be too big to be politically effective along some lines? That is what is meant by the title of this essay. "'Every man for himself' said the elephant as he danced among the chickens," may well have described the attitude and outlook of big business in the days of Rockefeller and Carnegie and the railroad "robber barons." But nowadays some really big corporations do not care to "dance among the chickens" any more—the consequences are, or may be, too unpleasant.

Du Pont, because it is located in the very small state of Delaware, is more of an elephant among chickens than most of the other great corporations; Anaconda is the only parallel that comes to mind. A. T. and T., for instance, although great on a nationwide basis is not locally preeminent anywhere; General Electric is in New York State; Ford and General Motors are cheek-by-jowl in Detroit; the Mellon interests are in Pennsylvania and, in any event, are scattered among a number of different companies; Standard Oil has been cut up into different companies.

But to the average outsider, du Pont is Delaware, Delaware du Pont. Thirty-odd years ago, *The Nation*, in a very serious (although superficial) evaluation, described the state as "the Ward of a Feudal Family"; and the notion persists. And it persists in part because du Pont, willy-nilly, is so much more in Delaware than any other corporation in any other state.

Add to this the fact that there are probably more than 100 du Pont households scattered throughout Greater Wilmington, and that the great majority of these households originally drew their influence and their wealth from the company; that they together control an extraordinarily high proportion of the total personal wealth of the state, a much larger proportion, presumably, than any other family in any other state. Not surprisingly, therefore, many of the great charities of the state are du Pont-planned, du Pont-directed, du Pont-named.

It might follow from all this that whatever the stand du Pont takes, Delaware senators and congressmen would fall into line. *But*, du Pont has been through many unpleasant experiences because of its size, its uniqueness, its success. In 1912, it was required by court order in effect to set up two separate and competing companies, Atlas and Hercules (of which more later); but, nevertheless, it has been under continuous supervision and attack for alleged violation of the anti-trust laws ever since.

In fact, one of the reasons, perhaps, why, during the 1953–1955 period, the central management of du Pont did not focus on such matters as the tariff was that, throughout the period, it was under assault in two very ambitious anti-trust suits. Even more important in the development of the company's public relations attitude and point of view was the great Nye committee (Munitions) Investigation of the mid-thirties. Du Pont, perhaps more than any other corporation, was pilloried as the satanic munitions-maker which gleefully piled up profits and created wars. One du Pont, remote from the company's management said:

I think that that investigation made them [the company] feel they should be very cautions and lean over backwards.

And there is a certain local suspicion of the du Ponts. For instance, Francis V. du Pont was for some years the leading Republican in the state[4] and he was *not* connected with the company. One of the most skillful local political analysts says,

There is only one reason he is not U.S. Senator: his name is du Pont and that would hurt him.[5]

The situation is not only one where a senator does not now dare be for du Pont but where du Pont does not dare have a senator (and particularly a Delaware senator) "in its pocket" and would go a long way to avoid creating this impression.

Of course, du Pont is continually involved in relationships with the United States Government, but, like most *big* corporations, it tends to deal directly with the agency in question. In the case of most corporations, this arises as much as anything out of the fact that business bureaucrats would rather deal with government bureaucrats, without being bothered by the temperamentally different politician as an intermediary; but, in the case of du Pont, this tendency is probably added to by the fear of appearing "to pick on somebody not its own size." The executive arm of the government can stand up to it; a Delaware senator looks as though he cannot.

Du Pont *may* work with great quietness to get Delaware senators or congressmen to follow its lead; after all, until 1948, a Delaware senator was a conservative du Pont in-law. But if it influences them on such matters as the tariff it is by stealthy maneuver, *not* by any overt pressure. *And we do not believe it does.* In any event, on the protectionist issue it was not successful if it did make any such effort in 1955; the senators and congressman supported reciprocal trade.

Of course, while du Pont may be on the whole protectionist, tariff protection probably is not the A-Number 1 issue in its table of priorities; there are a lot of things it cares about more. But if du Pont had the unquestioned dominance in Delaware that "Ward of a Feudal Family" suggests, of course that would make no difference; du Pont could treat the political officials of the state as its agents— in the way that the New England railroads at the turn of the century, according to tradition, treated their state officials. Du Pont does not, and could not, do

---

[4]From 1953 to 1955, Mr. du Pont was U.S. Commissioner of Roads.

[5]However, Alexis du Pont Bayard, New Deal candidate for the Senate in 1952, uses his middle name.

this; it must make choices in its access to public officials, the same as any other petitioner.

Du Pont, in some respects, is in the same position as some of the great overseas investors: Standard Oil and its subsidiaries, for example. Because everybody suspects Standard Oil of being an agent of imperialism, because for this reason, the United States Government will be more reluctant to intervene on its behalf than on behalf of some two-by-four hat manufacturer, such a corporation, in some ways, on political issues which are minor to it has less power than any other aggregation of wealth. And yet it will be held responsible for what it cannot—or does not—take any part in. So also with du Pont in Delaware.

Very probably this is *not* the only corporate reaction to the position of great power which du Pont and Standard Oil possess. Quite likely Anaconda in Montana or the tin companies in Bolivia behave very differently. But the point is that, within du Pont and Standard Oil and some other great companies, there has grown up a tradition of restraint, restraint based upon a calculation (or a myth?) of long-run welfare. This restraint may be compared to the doctrine of judicial restraint as developed, for instance, by Justice Jackson. It is a real social fact, having important political consequences, just as the attitude of some of the White House staff (coming incidentally from business) under President Eisenhower "we can't take part in 'propaganda' " had important political consequences for the Reciprocal Trade program. Obviously this attitude is not the only possible one for the White House to take; it rarely hampered similar operators in President Roosevelt's time. Of course, like the notion of judicial restraint, this corporate restraint unquestionably breaks down from time to time and is differently interpreted by different officers and divisions; nevertheless, it makes a difference, on the whole, between du Pont and Standard Oil, on the one hand, and Westinghouse or General Electric or Pittsburgh Plate Glass or Republic Steel on the other.

What has just been said does not bear on the question of whether du Pont is or is not protectionist. It may be that the issue of protection matters little to du Pont; but the best guess we can make is that du Pont would align itself considerably more actively than it has with those other chemical companies, Dow and Monsanto (two of the four firms which campaigned most energetically for protection), if it were not for the general preference for corporate restraint. Reversely, we suspect that Standard Oil and/or some of the other big international oil companies would have been more *directly* active than they were in fighting the Neely Amendment and similar proposals to bar Venezuelan oil if it were not for the notion of corporate restraint.

There is another aspect of the matter which has some bearing: du Pont, Standard Oil, and some big companies are far more likely to have on their staffs a *number* of people who have held significant governmental decision-making positions than have the cherry growers trade association or a woolen-worsted manufacturer. They will, consequently, be far more aware of the general fact that legislation is put into practice through a series of administrative steps and that, at each stage in the administrative process, an interested party may have the right to ask adaptation of the decision in such a way as to avoid injury to him. Big companies have the legal resources and administrative contacts to take advantage of such rights; small companies do not.[6] And, for big companies, this activity in the administrative sphere is far more attractive; it usually avoids the publicity which may spotlight the attempt to participate in the legislative process and is less apt to demand the time of top management; government administrators would often prefer to deal with the specialist in the corporation who knows the most about the topic, whereas senators or legislative committees are often believed to be more accessible to prominent people.

"Restraint" may also arise from the actual experience of du Pont officials. A company such as du Pont has to pay the cost of having lent top officials to government; although some government agencies may see things a little bit more as du Pont does, plenty of du Pont officials may see things somewhat more from the government agency's standpoint; and, in particular instances, even though they may disagree with the government standpoint, du Pont officials, because of their own government background, will be more hesitant to embarrass a government man for whom they have a fellow feeling by pressing a matter unduly than will a manufacturer of toy marbles or a garlic grower who has never had any reason to acquire such a fellow feeling.[7]

And officials of big corporations come to realize that their relationships with government are continuous, and that, if they press too hard for victory on one particular problem, even if they win, it may jeopardize their chances of success in some future, and more important, problem. That is to say, the relationship of such officials with government is the same as the relationship of members of Congress with each other; a congressman who presses one particular issue too hard may convince or get the better of his colleagues but the price may be a considerable loss of credit and potential support on future issues.

The acceptance of the notion that du Pont will not push too hard too far occurred in several of our Delaware interviews. Two examples will suffice:

1. A politician, who believes du Pont to be protectionist for the excellent reason that a du Pont officer[8] waited upon him to present arguments against the

---

[6]For this reason, the campaign against give-percenters hurt small business as compared with big business.

[7]There have been various accounts by businessmen (such as Clarence Randall) of what they have learned from government service, but presumably those who spontaneously write on such topics are *not* typical.

[8]Actually, the du Pont officer undoubtedly identified himself as representing a trade association; but the politician had forgotten this.

Reciprocal Trade Extension Act, was later discussing with us the vast volume of mail sent to congressmen and senators *against* the act by Monsanto and Westinghouse. One of us inquired as to whether du Pont did anything of the sort. An expression of great surprise crossed his face.

Oh, no; the company would not allow that sort of thing. [Bulk mail.] Two or three letters, that would be the most.

And other politicians expressed similar views.

2. In effect, through a holding company, du Pont owns the Wilmington papers. These papers, however, we were told by the editorial staff, have always supported reciprocal trade, and the company has never raised the issue nor had it crossed the editors' minds that it would. To be sure, Fred Singer, a du Pont officer, has written the editors several times and we believe discussed the issue with them; but the editors felt themselves under no more pressure from him than a college professor in one branch of a university would if a scholar in another branch criticized the way he organized his courses.

DU PONT IS NOT A UNIT

Both the du Pont family and the du Pont company have a wide variety of interests and orientations; there is no one point of view to which everybody adheres. Presumably, outside Delaware, the public picture of a du Pont is of a rather conservative right-wing businessman. Actually, the founder of du Pont, E. I. du Pont, was a close friend and correspondent of Jefferson's, and, in every generation since, including the present, there have been several du Ponts whose views and attitudes have been definitely Jeffersonian, and who would, therefore, tend to oppose the protectionist viewpoint which the interests of the company might be supposed to dictate.

Aside from this, there have been several family schisms among the du Ponts which means that some of the most prominent local du Ponts might not see eye-to-eye with the company at all. Finally, among those du Ponts who particularly built the company to its present eminence, there seems to have been a very amicable difference of opinion on the tariff. Three brothers followed each other as president in building the company; it is generally reported that Pierre, the first to be president, opposed the protectionist viewpoint, in contrast to his brothers.

It may not be accidental that Pierre, serving as president at one time, was more closely involved with General Motors than the other two. For General Motors, presumably, is the type of company which profits from export. In any case, the du Pont company owned about one-fifth of all GM stock and, in the first half of 1955, for instance, 85 cents per share of du Pont's earnings of $3.98 per share came from General Motors. This certainly might offset du Pont's concern as a chemical company with protection; on the other hand, as a report on Detroit[9] will suggest, GM's interest in expanding foreign trade is fairly general and unspecific. No one can really say how close the ties between General Motors and du Pont were; we were told in both Wilmington and Detroit that these made little difference. However, in view of the fact that the bigger of the anti-trust suits against du Pont (then before the Supreme Court) was directed toward ordering it to get rid of its General Motors' interests, management would naturally tend to play down the appearance of any community of interest even if it existed.

There is very real difficulty in discovering what "du Pont's interest" is because du Pont produces so many things and has so many irons in the fire. A du Pont economist at Wilmington said:

Don't ever talk of du Pont as being *an* industry; it is a lot of industries.

However, this same economist estimated that, altogether for all products, exports constitute only about six percent of sales, so he doubted that anybody in du Pont would get much interested in expanding foreign markets. But he added:

It might well be that a man in one division would decide that he wanted to join the Henry Ford [*sic*] group [meaning the Taft Committee to support reciprocal trade], hypothetically [although we do not think it would happen], the sales manager for foreign finishes, [selling a fair amount of paint abroad] might want to support all this reciprocal trade, whereas the rayon yarn people who are very alarmed about foreign imports would be on the other side. This whole problem is pretty academic to the people in nylon; they just would not care. So far as we know [and he is one of the twenty men in the company who would be expected to have reason to know], there is no overall company policy on trade and tariffs; it is left up to the individual divisions.

Now, du Pont is divided into ten separate operating divisions, making different kinds of products, with different general managers who, in theory, and apparently in practice, have a great deal of autonomy. For many purposes they act as separate companies. Each division has or may have its own "tariff representative," an officer charged with analyzing the foreign economic policy situation of the division. One tariff representative said:

[9]To be published in Bauer, Pool, and Dexter, *op. cit.*

The tariff representatives are the working stiffs. They do the leg work. The assistant general manager makes the decisions. Sometimes for months on end, I don't do any tariff work. At the moment [January, 1954] it is quite active because of customs simplification.

Another tariff representative said:

I cannot speak for other divisions. Different departments have varying interests. For instance, the textile fibers division never opened its trap about a tariff on nylon and I would think polychemicals would have a different [less protectionist] view on such things than organic chemicals.

We went through various major products with different officials and repeatedly heard the theme:

Each division has a different focus.

One man, for instance, continued:

Explosives are primarily concerned with quick service, shipping, and timing; foreign competition would not matter. Film and cellophane—they don't get into export much and are not adversely affected by imports.

Another middle echelon official added:

On balance, I think our paint department would gain more than it would lose by a reduction of tariffs. But at the other extreme is the dyestuff business which requires a combination of labor and technological skill, dependent on plodding, ordinary Ph.D.'s—who in Germany get 25 percent less salary than here, so that alone gives the Germans a substantial advantage.

Other men from other departments or with other orientations developed fully the argument that du Pont's "bread and butter," certain kinds of chemicals, can and will be produced more cheaply abroad than in this country—so du Pont needs protection. When we raised a question about some of these points, we were told:

Top management has been debating this whole area; they don't wish their position to be interpreted as extreme protectionist; they are trying for a middle-of-the road position.

SINGER CREATES AN IMPRESSION OF DU PONT

Mr. Fred Singer was chairman of the Tariff Committee under the Executive Committee of du Pont; this is the tariff committee for the (in essence) central staff, as distinguished from the tariff representatives who work for the operating divisions (described above). A tariff representative said:

Oh, the tariff representatives of the different divisions may see each other occasionally but they act quite independently; when they get together it is usually just to hear Singer [express his viewpoint]. But that central committee of his *cannot* tell any of the ten divisional managers anything; if the manager wants to do anything, he can; he is the kingpin.

But Mr. Singer can and does devote a good deal of time and effort to the cause of protection. He has been a stalwart supporter of the American Tariff League; he also serves on the trade association policy committees of *eight* different trade associations; he is, or has been, chairman of several of them. In this capacity, he makes statements and writes reports; and, since few people know or recognize the trade association name, and everybody has heard of du Pont, he is usually identified as a spokesman for du Pont rather than for whichever trade association he is at the moment speaking. For example, he testified before the House Ways and Means Committee in 1955 in opposition to the Reciprocal Trade Extension Act, as chairman of the International Trade and Tariff Committee, Manufacturing Chemists Association. At no point in his testimony did he mention or refer to du Pont in any way (although the representatives of Monsanto, Allied, Dow, and American Cyanamid testified presumably for their firms along the same lines).[10]

The question as to whether he does, in fact, speak for du Pont's top management or not is an interesting one. On the one hand, it may be that this indirect approach through trade associations is a tactical matter, designed to avoid controversy within du Pont. On the other hand, Mr. Singer may hold the same position as a university professor who testifies. When Seymour Harris, Harvard economist, testified, in effect, "in opposition" to reciprocal trade at the same hearings, no one (presumably) supposed that he was speaking for Harvard and everyone recognized his right to academic freedom. Du Pont may also give Mr. Singer a similar freedom without endorsing his views.

---

[10]Nor did du Pont testify as such on the customs simplification act in which some people say it is especially interested.

HISTORIC BACKGROUND OF THE NOTION DU PONT IS PROTECTIONIST; AMERICAN ASSOCIATION OF UNIVERSITY WOMEN, WILMINGTON

Historically, the vast development of the United States' chemical industry took place during and immediately after World War I. It appears to have taken place because of the protection against German competition and the seizure of German patents, etc., which resulted from the war. The chemical industry, therefore, has been regarded and has, on the whole, regarded itself as a beneficiary of protection.

In the interwar years, several du Pont economists, for example Edmund Lincoln, were particularly articulate spokesmen of protectionist views. It is generally believed that they played an influential part in the behind-the-scenes planning of the post-war tariff acts. These men were dead or retired at the time of our study but they were remembered in Wilmington and throughout the chemical industry.

We heard one interesting sidelight about the effect of du Pont on the community; The Wilmington chapter of the American Association of University Women is naturally composed, to a considerable degree, of wives of men in du Pont. A prominent member of the Wilmington group told us that the chapter

. . . disagrees with the stand of national AAUW on several matters, such as the tariff.

She then told me about a visit of a national officer of the AAUW to Wilmington to present the national's legislative program. The visitor, we were told, was "simply shocked" at the way the Wilmington group "tore her platform to pieces."

The two other big Delaware chemical companies, Atlas and Hercules, were separated from du Pont as a result of anti-trust action in 1912. We were told in several interviews that the president of one of these companies has privately expressed considerable support for freer trade, and we got the impression that the other company does not care much about the issue but might lean toward reciprocal trade. But neither of them would want to take a policy stand opposite to du Pont on such an issue. Both are willing to let the trade associations to which they belong (there are several in the chemical industry) speak for them, but evidently none of the company officials most likely to know has great interest in, or a clear impression as to what the trade associations actually do say. Communications from the associations to the firms on foreign economic policy receive little circulation within the companies.

It is not, of course, only du Pont's influence which keeps such firms as these from supporting reciprocal trade; it is the cumulative weight of the numerous protectionist firms in the chemical industry. One official of one of these firms said, in effect, that the firm is neutral on reciprocal trade because:

. . . the whole chemical industry buys and sells from each other; [so] we have important customers who definitely are for protection and these things make a difference. Personally I think the customers are making a mountain out of a molehill.

Both Atlas and Hercules are often confused with du Pont despite the fact that they have been forty years separated. Both firms showed a strong desire to *differentiate* themselves from du Pont without *differing* on policy from the latter. One reason is that they believe du Pont is unpopular in downstate Delaware.

OTHER DELAWARE BUSINESSES

Two Wilmington firms which might have had some industry associations which would lead them to be protectionist—although apparently neither of them themselves suffer from foreign competition—are managed and owned by old Quaker families. The managers possess the "concerns" which good Quakers are supposed to have, hence, in principle, both firms would support reciprocal trade.

One firm in another industry intended to oppose reciprocal trade because the trade association had asked it to do so. The export manager had not been abroad for many years; nevertheless exports run to seven percent or so of gross; but the export manager was delighted to oppose reciprocal trade because he is so irritated at foreign restrictions on trade. Other firms in the area, on the whole, had less interest even than these in the issue.

Dover is the state capital and second city. An informed person told us he had heard

. . . no complaints [there] about and no discussion of foreign trade or imports.

In 1954, the community was absorbed in tremendous expansion due to a newly established air base.

International Latex, which has since been sold, had done nothing and had been exposed to no pressures or requests on foreign economic policy.

Outside Wilmington, Delaware's population is predominantly agriculture-based. The poultry business is large; broilers and the like are processed as well as raised. The poultry processors or growers face a lot of direct political problems in the state and area—stream pollution, general nuisances, etc., and any political concerns they have go into these issues. Whether much of the poultry is ultimately exported, we have no way of telling; figures and records which would enable one to tell are not kept.

There is a good deal of processing also of sweet corn and lima beans, etc. There are apple people who, according to a state agricultural authority, are on an export basis, and wheat people. Most of the wheat growers, as part of a diversification program, are also in dairying (and dairying is generally protectionist although wheat is export-minded). We were told that thirty percent of the wheat acreage goes abroad.

At the instigation of Farm Bureau officers, because,

> Secretary of Agriculture Benson said he wanted to know how farmers felt in regard to issues on foreign trade,

a series of discussion meetings on the subject were held by farmers throughout the state. They took raised-hand votes afterwards which showed a considerable margin in favor of lower tariffs. About 500 people took part in these discussions. The senators and congressman are supposed to have heard about the results; but, in fact, remembered them only extremely vaguely or not at all.

We asked a farm leader if he knew how du Pont, etc. felt as to tariffs. He replied:

> No! I have often wondered about these matters and would like to know whether industry feels it would gain or lose by a tariff. I just don't know how they feel. No doubt agriculture would benefit more than industry would lose from more exports. . . . Of course some industries like watchmaking (not a Delaware area industry at all) would lose.

This is typical!

WHAT THE CONGRESSMEN HEARD AND DID NOT HEAR

Substantially, the congressman and senators in 1954 appear to have heard very little from the state about the reciprocal trade extension act. One of them said:

> On the Randall Commission, I am sure I did get some letters or calls but I cannot even recall them. No doubt somebody did [call].

Since all three are alert, attentive men, this means that the calls were probably not too important.

> No, I don't hear much at all on this issue . . . there is such a vacuum in our markets and the foreign markets there is no problem. [This at the time the coal, pottery, glass, chemical, textile, and many other industries were

complaining rather bitterly about foreign competition and unemployment.] Our farm commodities aren't too exportable; Farm Bureau meetings on foreign trade might not mean too much.

There aren't any real problems of voting on reciprocal trade. I have always voted for it and I just don't hear much on that; so far as any particular complaint or gripes or so forth on that, there just haven't been very many.

Another said:

> I've talked directly with the chemical companies about problems of interest, and I have received no particular specifications as to their views on the Randall Commission and the tariff; certainly they would be the most concerned; at the present time [April, 1954] , therefore, we have no special reason to expect to hear much when any legislation is introduced.

The third thought the chemical industry might have a predominant interest, had heard something from farmers, and:

> . . . pretty heavily from the leather industry. [He was not sure whether in or out of the state.] The greatest interest may well reflect the views of the Farm Bureau. It is rare that we have a person of unlimited means make a demand on us.

He then commented on the self-restraint of wealthy Delawareans. He had also heard from machine tools outside the state.

None of them had heard from labor on the issue, *in the state,* in 1954 or 1955. A few apparently randomly directed letters were received from outside textile or electrical workers against H.R.1 in 1955 (some of these workers may have lived in the state and worked outside).

In 1955, the three received considerably more mail. The League of Women Voters was noticeable as supporting reciprocal trade. Apparently all three received more pro- than anti-reciprocal trade mail from the state, although a good deal of anti-mail from outside. But, in the pressure of business on members of the Finance Committee, as a staff member put it:

> So many people have come in on all these things . . . we just haven't been able to bear in mind which was which.

That, again, indicates that the mail and visits on H.R.1 either were not impressive or the senators and congressman were immune to noticing that sort of pressure. One person close to a senator told me:

Oh, these pressure campaigns don't happen in Delaware. Never on any issue.

There is awareness in the congressional delegations that different divisions of du Pont might have different views on H.R.1. They know du Pont employees personally. The Northern Newcastle Young Democrats Club, composed according to the congressman, "largely of du Pont chemists, young businessmen, etc.," approached Congressman McDowell *in favor of* reciprocal trade. This is the only instance we encountered of a local political organization taking a definite stand with the congressman or senator *for* reciprocal trade; in Midland, Michigan, where Dow Chemical is located, the local Republican organization passed a resolution which it sent to the senators *against* reciprocal trade; but, in general, party organizations everywhere stay out of political issues such as this.

PROFESSIONAL EMPLOYEES: A BRAKE ON DU PONT?

In interviews with some business firms, the writer has been struck by the degree to which calculation about employee reactions affects them. One firm hesitates to take part in the current business-in-politics program because it is not unionized and fears anything which would "stir" the workers up; another is unionized but fears "jeopardizing a very amicable relationship with the union," which might conceivably interpret such a program as a threat.

Du Pont has this problem in a different and exaggerated form. Wilmington is du Pont headquarters; it depends for its very existence upon skillful and educated scientists, with educated wives. These men and women may, to be sure, influence the AAUW to drop one or another plank in its platform—locally! But, more significantly, they are part of and respond to the climate of opinion which the League of Women Voters, the AAUW, and other such internationally oriented groups express. They would object strenuously to any company program which sounded like economic nationalism; or, if not, a rational calculation by management would be that it is far more risky to chance losing their goodwill than to chance losing some sales to foreign competitors. In any company, this might be true; but du Pont depends on professionals to a singularly high degree. Wilmington to a like high degree has communities of like-minded scientists, and, with the history of the munitions investigation and FDR's attacks on "economic royalists," employees of du Pont may well be more sensitive to the possibility of being stigmatized as working for reactionaries than employees of, say, General Electric or Dow.

CONCLUSION

In general, Delaware congressmen and senators appeared to be free to choose for themselves, without much pressure, on foreign economic policy issues. No interest in the state is vociferously opposing reciprocal trade; and, although du Pont may lean in that direction, senators and congressmen in a state as small as Delaware know the rifts and cross-pressures within du Pont on such an issue as this, if they are at all "hep" and know du Pont will have issues on which it feels much more strongly. Nor is any interest in the state vigorously supporting reciprocal trade. The issue apparently stirred up less excitement than, say, the St. Lawrence Seaway. Although both senators are on the Finance Committee, and Delaware is economically part of the Philadelphia-Maryland area, they do not seem to have been expected by anyone to do anything for the firms in that area outside the state in this connection. Such instances as there were of possible injury due to foreign competition created no stir; Wilmington had then a situation of approximately full employment.

A Delaware senator or congressman could, if he were so minded and chose to dramatize it, probably get some following and attention by speaking up for old-fashioned protectionism; the vulcanized fibre plants, some of the textile plants, conceivably du Pont and the traditional conservatism of several areas, provide soil within which applause, votes, and some sympathy might be given to a man who tried to defend American industry against "cheap foreign labor." Particularly, if he made a good deal of the national-defense, preservation-of-skill argument, he might find financial support from some members of the du Pont family.

On the other hand, a Delaware senator or congressman who chose to dramatize the issue might also crystallize the latent freer trade concern in Atlas, Hercules, and International Latex, and among some of the farmers. Either way, protectionist or reciprocal trade, he could make an issue for himself which would attract some favorable attention and support.

As it was, none of the four men, Senators Frear or Williams, Congressmen Warburton or McDowell, focused on trade or the tariff, nor was there any particular reason why they should. So far as the record shows, all four supported reciprocal trade as requested by the Administration.[11]

---

[11] The only deviation we know of is that, in committee, Senator Frear voted for a two-year instead of a three-year extension of the 1955 Reciprocal Trade Act. We do not know why.

A 1967 POSTSCRIPT BY LEWIS ANTHONY DEXTER

I have probably not stressed enough in this article the issue of priorities. Although Du Pont has interests in Delaware, and although it had interests in reciprocal trade legislation generally, quite specific issues of business, research, etc., bulked larger in the *attention* of its managers. In large part, this may no doubt be due to the historic factors I postulate in the text; in larger part, probably, to the "organizational climate" within which Du Pont selects and socializes key executives.[1] But a factor may well have been simply this: the specific aspect of protection of greatest importance to Du Pont is generally said to have been the so-called American Selling Price provision. While not directly jeopardized, substantially at least, by any proposals of 1953–55, it appears that under the outgrowth of the Kennedy Round discussions, this particular advantage is jeopardized in 1967–68; it is also believed (although I have made no such intensive study as I made in 1953–55) that Du Pont is more active in the loose coalition of opponents to some of the Kennedy Round proposals than it was a dozen years ago. Obviously, the historic situation does not permit a neat separation of factors; although it may be that there is more rational economic interest in 1967–68, it is also true that there are fewer executives around who have undergone the traumas of the merchants of death accusations and the economic royalists' attacks and possible that the organizational climate of top Du Pont management has changed.[2]

---

[1] In this connection, two papers of mine on the notion of "Organizational Climate," read at Wayne State University and at the Midwest Political Science Association, April, 1967, hopefully to be published are relevant.

[2] Those interested in the theoretical aspects of this article should also read R. Bauer, I. Pool, and L. Dexter, *American Business and Public Policy*, Atherton, 1963, two sections on decision-making as a social process, pp. 475–83, and the section on self-interest, pp. 472–5, and also at the discussion of attention as the key variable in determining and defining "pressures" on political matters in my forthcoming book on Congress (Rand-McNally, probably 1969).

10. THE ROLE OF THE SCIENTIFIC ELITE IN THE DECISION TO USE THE ATOMIC BOMB

Joan W. Moore and Burton M. Moore

In his recent book, *The Power Elite*, C. Wright Mills makes important use of the concept "pivotal moment"—the moment at which important and far-reaching decisions are made by the small in-group of the power elite, institutional leaders of the military, corporations, and the state. (8) If Mills wants to clarify the governmental decision-making process by this concept, it seems to us that he succeeds only in oversimplifying the process to the point of serious distortion. Political decisions have histories: the history of any given decision is a series of prior decisions, which, depending on the matter dealt with, are often made by individuals entirely outside of the institutional network Mills considers. It may well be that many significant decisions *concern* only the big corporations, the state, and the army. To rule out consideration of other groups, institutionalized or not, that affect the political order, on such an implicit, quasi-statistical basis, however, does no service to the conceptual problems confronting the developing field of political sociology.

This point can be made clear by an analysis of one of Mill's own illustrations of a pivotal moment—the decision to drop the atomic bomb on Hiroshima. The implication of Mills' cursory, dramatic treatment of this decision is that the decision was self-contained. Once the resource—the atomic bomb—became available, the decision about whether and when to drop it was *the* significant political decision, and one in which only members of the power elite participated. An examination of the history of this decision, however, reveals a complex series of prior, consciously political decisions, made by men who were by no means members of Mills' power elite. These decisions relate not only to the final use of the bomb, but also to the early mobilization of the primary resource, the creative capacities of physicists, and their organization to produce the bomb.

SOURCE. Joan W. Moore and Burton M. Moore, "The Role of the Scientific Elite in the Decision to Use the Atomic Bomb," in *Social Problems*, 6 (Summer, 1958), pp. 78–85. Reprinted by permission of the authors and The Society for the Study of Social Problems. Copyright 1958 by the Society for the Study of Social Problems.

There was a series of "pivotal moments," at any one of which the final availability of the resource was placed in serious jeopardy. Analysis of this case and comparison of it with the development of nuclear physics in other countries could also provide a rich source of hypotheses about the ways in which the social composition and organization of the "scientific community," one of many nonelite political groups, can affect high-level national policy-making, although a systematic attempt to make this comparison will not be attempted here.

$$*\quad*\quad*$$

At the beginning, the fact of fission—or rather the special case of fission in the uranium nucleus—was known only by a very small group of scientists. Fission itself had been accomplished in 1935 by Otto Hahn and Fritz Strassmann. The fission products, however, could not be identified. When barium was definitely identified, only those persons closely following nuclear physics were able to make the critical necessary inference: i.e., that matter can artificially be converted into energy. These few nuclear physicists were working in several countries during the late '30's.

Hahn and Strassman, working at the Kaiser Wilhelm Institute in Berlin, announced the presence of barium in January of 1939. Otto Frisch passed the news on to his aunt, Lise Meitner, then in Stockholm. Almost immediately she interpreted the results correctly, as experimental verification of the Einstein matterenergy formula. For a time, she alone understood the theoretical significance of what had happened, and we can pinpoint the information at the beginning of this chronicle to a single physicist. Frisch immediately rushed to catch Niels Bohr, the Danish physicist, before he left on a lecture tour in America and succeeded in telling him, in rough outline, their conclusion. (4, p. 19) For a while, then, only these three people knew the correct implications of the Hahn and Strassmann observations. Niels Bohr was forced to spend a week on a transatlantic liner unable to pass on the single most important conclusion of modern physics. Once in the United States, Bohr lost no time. He arrived, greatly excited, at the physics laboratories at Columbia University. Enrico Fermi, then a refugee of four years' standing, happened to be away that day, and Bohr, "trembling with excitement," could talk only with Fermi's student, a certain Herbert Anderson, who immediately suggested verification on the Columbia cyclotron for his Ph.D. dissertation.* Four separate experiments, all of them in academic physics laboratories, soon established Meitner's conclusions. By February of 1939, confirmations were published by small groups at Columbia, Johns Hopkins, Carnegie Institute of Washington, and the University of California. (9, p. 25)

The implications of this discovery, and most especially of the heavy pulse of ionization that would accompany fission of the uranium nucleus, were recognized

*Personal interview with Herbert Anderson, Chicago, 1958.

almost at once by American, British, and German scientists. In the United States, a small supper-table group at Columbia (including Fermi, V. F. Weisskopf, Leo Szilard, Eugene Wigner, and Edward Teller—the latter three all recent Hungarian refugees) decided within three months of the confirmation that the "pulse" was of great military importance. The quick release of a large amount of energy was interpreted as having important potentialities for the development of a destructive weapon. Credit is ordinarily given to Fermi and Szilard, but at this date it is impossible to determine from whom the impetus came. Nevertheless Fermi made an immediate attempt to enlist the help of the U.S. Navy and was gently turned down. (6) Szilard refused to be discouraged and suggested that Albert Einstein might have enough influence to reach the President directly. Still not trusting Einstein's prestige, Szilard suggested that a close friend of both the President and Einstein be used. He was Alexander Sachs, a New York economist and investment banker, and on October 11, 1939, the now-famous Einstein letter was delivered. (9, p. 47)

Roosevelt was impressed and immediately appointed a three-man "Uranium Committee," with representatives from the Army, the Navy and a physicist from the Bureau of Standards. A small immediate grant was made to buy uranium for the group. The Committee made a favorable report and in June of the following year was itself merged into the National Defense Research Committee with $300,000 eventually spent for a small exploratory program. In the meantime, the group at Columbia decided that the military possibilities of fission should be kept out of the scientific journals, which, during 1939, had disseminated considerable information about the research to the scientific community.* Accordingly, in the spring of 1939 the Columbia group enlisted the support of Bohr in stopping, voluntarily, all research publication on the subject. Only one physicist disagreed, Joliot of France, and publication continued until April of 1940 when he concurred. In that month the "Reference Committee," composed of nuclear physicists, became part of a larger scientific organization, the National Research Council, and the editors of scientific journals agreed to send all papers of possible military interest to the Committee for review. This arrangement worked well and actually continued until June of 1945. (9, pp. 45–46)

Scientific communication was thereby confined—by consensus of the group—to the physicists working on this kind of project and the relevant governmental committee. These physicists were then at Columbia, the University of California, Johns Hopkins, the Bureau of Standards and a few other academic research centers. Full knowledge of the direction and possibilities of the research, however, was confined to about 20 scientists.** As the research expanded, 16 organizations subcontracted for specific aspects, without being admitted to formal knowledge of the military import of the research.

*During 1939 nearly 100 papers had been published. (9, pp. 25–6)
**Actually a year later, May, 1941. (9, p. 51)

During the next few years, research on the projects continued without the raising of important political issues. Until the spring of 1945 the atomic bomb remained only a possibility; it was far from certain that such a weapon could be produced. Between 1941 and 1945, then, the physicists were working. An examination of communication patterns established during this period (both within and between projects) casts considerable light on the general nature of the social relationships existing in the group. These relationships are of interest in part because they reflect, on a grand scale, the kind of communication pattern that maximizes productivity by permitting criticism and dissent (and were thus, perhaps, a precondition for the rapid development of the bomb). Of most direct interest to us here, however, is their relevance for the attaining of political consensus within the scientific community.

The basic mechanism of communication in academic research groups is the colloquium, or seminar. Here a researcher presents his evidence and conclusions for the information and criticism of his colleagues, and in time his work is printed in accessible form and/or verbally carried to other meetings and other lectures. The "machinery of advice" set up in 1941 and 1942 to advise the government of important scientific conslusions followed this pattern closely. At the top of this formal machinery sat a Top Policy Group, consisting of the Vice-President of the United States, the Secretary of War, the Chief of the Army Ground Forces, Dr. Vannevar Bush, director of the Office of Scientific Research and Development, and Dr. James Conant. Bush acted as liaison with the S-1 Section of this Office, which was directed by Conant and included 13 scientists, each of them working directly on the "uranium problem." (9, p. 76) Contracts were let directly by the Section. (These contracts were actually research funds for small, informally organized research teams in universities.)

The S-1 Section seldom met formally, the members preferring to discuss their work informally with Conant (Bush's representative) and with Dr. Briggs, the chairman. (9, pp. 77, 81) By May of 1942 this arrangement had clearly become unwieldy, and a new committee, much larger than the first, complete with Planning Board and Executive Committee, was set up, with Conant as chairman, including five of the original atomic scientists. (9, p. 81) Either directly or through Dr. Conant's membership in a series of scientific policy groups, the recommendations of this Executive Committee went to the Top Policy Group. The task of the men on this committee was research; as problems of policy came up they were bucked upstairs. Questions of production and procurement went to the Planning Board, to a special "district" of the Corp of Engineers.

Results and suggestions were sometimes discussed by the body of the Committee; sometimes they were simply given to Conant, Briggs, or Bush. While decisions were supposedly to be made by majority vote, the Committee seldom voted and while its decisions were not binding on any of the member scientists, they were usually followed. The Committee has never been dissolved; in time it ceased to have any functions and was forgotten. (9, p. 84)

In effect, while formal channels existed, the working organization and medium of communication was still the informal meeting. The scientist-members of the Executive Committee, nearly all Program Chiefs, continued to work loosely inside channels. Bush, Conant, and Compton quite casually decided to investigate plutonium as an "afterthought" during a luncheon after a meeting of the S-1 Section (the early committee). (4, p. 71) The vital early work at Columbia and Princeton was arranged informally during the Christmas holidays, Compton simply hearing from his colleagues what ought to be done and then asking them to do it—again outside the S-1 Section. The decision to concentrate plutonium production at Chicago was made in Compton's bedroom with the advice of men not even on the Committee. (9, p. 80) Even when the Chicago "Metallurgical Laboratory" had seventy separate research groups with a staff of 5,000 workers, Compton (their director) acted on the premise that his real authority was professional, that the workers followed his instructions because the executives under his direction respected him and knew about his research work. (9, p. 84) Norman Hilberry, his administrative director, was a former student, and therefore reasonably certain to work with Compton in harmony. (9, p. 85) The closer associates were all known to Compton personally. (9, pp. 84–85) Reports to the Committee were discussed with a "laboratory council" before they were sent out. Consensus was so highly valued—and deemed so necessary to the maintenance of working relations—that when Dr. Harold Urey wished to concentrate all effort on an alternative plutonium-producing method, even after the Committee's decision had been taken, Compton embarked on a long "discussion of the points" until Urey was satisfied. (9, p. 99) When Compton was forced to push a decision through the laboratory council, he was quite disturbed. He cited the Biblical story of Gideon and invited those who could not agree with the decision to leave the project without prejudice because "a large group divided" could not accomplish as much as a "small group of united, earnest men." (9, pp. 109–110) To him, consensus on these internal political matters was of prime importance. (This community crisis, incidentally, was simply the question of whether production aspects of the giant atomic bomb production should be given to private industrial firms.)

To recapitulate, during the years between 1941 and 1945 there was an enormous expansion in the number of people working on the research projects, with continued advances both in basic knowledge and techniques. The basic means of communication between (and apparently within) projects continued to be a modification of the academic seminar. Typically a situation that maximizes dissensus, because it is seldom connected with collective action, the seminar-type meeting served a dual function for the nuclear physicists. It both permitted the kind of expression of dissensus that is essential to the advance of knowledge—free flow of communication—and gradually became a sort of "town-meeting" situation, to be used to gain consensus whenever policy issues did arise. The persistence of this pattern of communication among the physicists was facilitated not only by habit and preference but also because secrecy requirements of the research inhibited written communication.

By contrast, the German nuclear physicists' failure to make the essential basic advances in scientific knowledge despite an equal amount of scientific "talent" and a "head start" can be seen largely as the effect of a failure in communication engendered in large part by the Nazi government. Disruption of academic communities by Nazi purges probably enhanced the cohesiveness of existing cliques among the physicists, which was further enhanced by differential support of the cliques by a government insensitive to scientific canons. It is probable that the general insecurity engendered by governmental policies not only strengthened barriers to communication between cliques but also reinforced the basic authoritarian structure of the German cliques, further restricting communication and the expression of the kind of dissensus so essential to scientific advance. (7)

Among the American scientists the political potentialities of their kind of habitual social relationship became evident when they had achieved success in their research and were faced with a significant political issue. From the "town meeting" the scientists evolved political factions, which agitated for a time, and which finally resolved their differences by resorting to the vote. This issue was whether the bomb should be dropped on the Japanese.

The President had appointed an Interim Committee to advise him on "the various questions raised by the imminent readiness of an atomic bomb." On May 31, 1945, Secretary of War Stimson put the question directly to the Committee: "Gentlemen, it is our responsibility to recommend action that may turn the course of civilization." (4, p. 219) The membership was Secretary Stimson, a special consultant to Stimson, a representative of the President, the Under-Secretary of the Navy, the Assistant Secretary of State, and three scientists. A Scientific Panel of four more scientists was established to advise the Committee. In brief, the committee was advised by the scientists in unanimity that dropping the bomb on a Japanese city was advisable; the Committee in unanimity so advised the President, and after suitable consultation with other heads of states, the deed was done. Consensus among the scientists leading to the decision of the Scientific Panel, however, was not easy to obtain.

The Interim Committee itself had been organized by suggestion from the scientists. Within the Metallurgical Project at the University of Chicago, a subcommittee on social and political consequences had long been in action. It was headed by James Franck, a distinguished scientist. A. H. Compton told General Groves about the work of the Franck group, and Groves suggested the Interim Committee to Stimson. On Stimson's advice the Committee was organized. For the scientists the moral problem became acute when it became obvious that

Germany would not stay in the war much longer. "Volney Wilson, now doubly troubled in mind, came to me in the earnest hope that we might avoid atomic attack on Japan. His reason was the straightforward one of Christian compassion. Could not some way be found to bring the war to a quick close without the ghastly destruction that we knew the bomb would cause?" (4, p. 223) Knowing of the report and of the imminence of the decision, the Franck subcommittee finished its report, which urged demonstration, not actual use of the bomb. Compton, on Franck's request, took the report to Stimson, who immediately presented it for study to the Interim Committee. The Committee considered it for two weeks and then answered the report in definite terms: "We can propose no technical demonstration likely to bring an end to the war; we see no acceptable alternative to direct military use."*

But the struggle for a clear-cut decision continued. One majority opinion had been rejected by the Scientific Panel; another was on the way. Leo Szilard wrote directly to the President opposing the use of the bomb on the Japanese. (He had approved of its use against Germans.) In addition, Dr. Szilard circulated a series of petitions among the laboratory groups at Los Alamos and Oak Ridge calling for "outlawing" of the bomb altogether. He got 67 signatures and turned it over to Compton for transmission. Two other petitions circulated at the same time: one urged unrestrained use of the bomb against the Japanese and the other asked for use, but with certain minor restrictions. "It was difficult," Compton says, "to get a balanced view of how our men were thinking." (4, p. 243) Accordingly, at General Groves' suggestion, Compton set up an elaborate opinion pool for the "leading scientists" at Chicago, Los Alamos, and Berkeley. The results of this poll clearly showed that this group favored military use—at least if, after other means were tried, this was found necessary to bring surrender.**

The results of this poll were ready before the Scientific Panel when the Interim Committee recommended use of the bomb. Thus they could reject a

---

* Full text is given by Stimson. (10) The Committee's reasons were those governing the use of any untried weapon with limited availability (only two bombs were available). First, the device might not go off and the demonstration would be ridiculous. Second, it *would* go off but only strengthen the hand of a determined military party, who could easily concentrate the remaining Japanese aircraft against high-level bombing attacks. Third, the Committee hoped there would be no more wars and that its use would prevent war. Fourth, the projected American casualties for the November invasion were staggeringly high. It should be noted that General George Marshall, Chief of Staff for the Army, initially opposed the use of the bomb because its secret possession would greatly enhance the future military position of the United States—in short, he disapproved of early disclosure of the weapon. The second bomb was dropped as the climax of a campaign by radio and leaflet to persuade the Japanese people to accept the terms of a settlement worked out at Potsdam. The leaflets warned of dire consequences unless the Emperor ended the war; obviously the second bomb would have to be dropped. Standard sources on the Japanese surrender should be consulted.
**Text given in Daniels and Compton. (5)

minority opinion of the Franck and Szilard variety with assurance that they were expressing a majority opinion. In effect, by the second week in June, 1945, the scientists knew that "they" wanted the bomb to be dropped. (Curiously, the executives—both military and civil—who still held the residue of the decision had serious qualms and referred back again to the scientists at least twice more for confirmation of the mood of the scientific community.) President Truman informed the allies at Potsdam of the bomb's availability and then, back in Washington, asked to see the results of the Compton poll. Compton delivered it to Truman, and then, to his amazement, was asked for his personal opinion. He gave it as follows: "My vote is with the majority. It seems to me that as the war stands the bomb should be used, but no more drastically than needed to bring surrender." (4, p. 247)*

There were no more inquiries from Washington and two weeks later the bomb was dropped.

*   *   *

If we regard a significant political decision as one which determines the use of major resources in terms of a set of values which relate to important aspects of national welfare, we can see that the scientists made one crucial major political decision by themselves—the decision to exploit an esoteric scientific discovery and their own talents to produce a powerful destructive weapon. The relation of the decision to the social backgrounds of the scientists—predominantly recent refugees—is obvious. A more significant point for our purposes is that this group could (as "normal" members of the "power elite" could *not*) recognize the existence of a resource of national value. From this early decision until 1945, the government served almost exclusively to facilitate the development of this resource. The significance of the particular way it functioned vis-a-vis the national scientific community can be seen clearly in the light of the experience of the German physicists. When the resource had been developed, it became a different resource—the atomic bomb.

If our government were fully rationalized, the disposition of this new weapon should properly have become the exclusive concern of the military. If Mills' general hypothesis about the ubiquity of the power elite were valid, members of the power elite alone would have participated in decisions about its disposition in a "pivotal moment." In fact, scientists were called upon not only to assist in technical decisions, such as the topographical features which would maximize the bomb's effect, but in the moral issue of whether or not to use the bomb against human beings. (That this decision related to strategic issues—details of the scheduling of the war—adds to the weight of the scientists in this decision.) In effect,

*There is an extensive literature on the rationale of the military and diplomatic decisions
  made on the Japanese war. (1, 2, 3, 11)

the scientists in this case seemed to represent an especially well-informed segment of the population, and their opinions were used as such by the political and military officials. This instance is one of many in which only the professionals—scientists or others—working on the development of a resource are capable of or privy to the understanding of the implications of the use of that resource. In the case of the dropping of the atomic bomb, the scientific community functioned much as the legislature would (although, of course, the scientists were not elected) in a less urgent, less secret, and less technical matter. Since 1945, the discoveries and opinions of scientists have continued to play a role in national policy-making.

In conclusion, this close examination of one of Mills' illustrations of a pivotal moment reveals not only the inadquacy of the concept of pivotal moment as either an empirical or theoretical concept, but also casts serious doubt on the utility of the concept of the power elite in the understanding of complex national policy-making. The addition of the "scientific community" or one of its sub-communities to the power elite compels consideration of the nature of the political issues as such—a task not achieved by Mills. Simplicity is not the only criterion of the adequacy of a theoretical orientation; it is our opinion that in this case the simplicity of Mills' constructs is an indication of grave theoretical weakness.

REFERENCES

1. Butow, Robert J. C., *Japan's Decision to Surrender* (Stanford: Stanford University Press, 1954).
2. Byrnes, James F., *Speaking Frankly* (New York: Harper, 1947).
3. Churchill, Winston S., *The Second World War*, v.6, *Triumph and Tragedy* (London: Cassell, 1954).
4. Compton, Arthur H., *Atomic Quest* (New York: Oxford University Press, 1956).
5. Compton, Arthur H., and Farrington Daniels, "A Poll of Scientists at Chicago," *Bulletin of the Atomic Scientists*, 4 (February, 1948), 44.
6. Fermi, Laura, *Atoms in the Family* (Chicago: University of Chicago Press, 1954), p. 162.
7. Goudsmit, Samuel, *ALSOS* (New York: H. Schuman, 1947).
8. Mills, C. Wright, *The Power Elite* (New York: Oxford University Press, 1956).
9. Smyth, Henry D., *Atomic Energy for Military Purposes* (Princeton: Princeton University Press, 1945).
10. Stimson, Henry L., "The Decision to Use the Atomic Bomb," *Harpers Magazine*, 194 (February, 1947), 101.
11. Stimson, Henry L., and McGeorge Bundy, *On Active Service in Peace and War* (New York: Harper, 1948).

CHAPTER FOUR
Social Characteristics and Foreign Relations

11. THE INTELLECTUALS IN THE POLITICAL DEVELOPMENT OF THE NEW STATES

Edward Shils

I. THE POLITICAL SIGNIFICANCE OF INTELLECTUALS IN UNDER-DEVELOPED COUNTRIES

The gestation, birth, and continuing life of the new states of Asia and Africa, through all their vicissitudes, are in large measure the work of intellectuals. In no state-formations in all of human history have intellectuals played such a role as they have in these events of the present century.

SOURCE. Edward Shils, "The Intellectuals in the Political Development of the New States," in *World Politics*, XII (April, 1960), pp. 329–368. Reprinted by permission of the author and The Center of International Studies, Princeton, New Jersey. Copyright 1960 by Princeton University Press.
*This article is a revised version of a paper presented at a conference on political modernization held under the auspices of the Committee on Comparative Politics of the Social Science Research Council at Dobbs Ferry in June 1959.

In the past, new states were founded by military conquest, by the secession of ethnic groups led by traditional tribal and warrior chiefs, by the gradual extension of the power of the prince through intermarriage, agreement, and conquest, or by separation through military rebellion. In antiquity, the demand that subjects acknowledge the divinity of the Emperor was no more than a requirement that the legitimacy of the existing order be recognized.[1] The interests of dynasty and kinship group, the lure of majesty, considerations of power, aspirations for office, and calculations of economic advantage have been the components of political decisions and the grounds for pursuit of power in the state. It is only in modern times in the West that beliefs about man's nature, his past, and his place in the universe, and about the ethical and metaphysical rightness of particular forms of political order—the concerns of intellectuals—have played an important part in public life.

In the West in modern times, however, politics—particularly civil politics—have never been a preserve of the intellectuals. Well-established aristocrats and landed gentry with ample leisure have provided much of the personnel of politics, both oligarchical and democratic; clergymen and high ecclesiastical officials and, above all, businessmen—the former earlier, the latter more recently—have likewise added to the pool. Retired army officers, trade unionists and, of course, mere professional politicians of diverse occupational backgrounds have also been among the incumbents of or contenders for political office and the leaders in the agitation surrounding selection and decision. Intellectuals, too—professors and teachers, scientists, journalists, authors, etc.—have had a substantial share in all these activities. Radical, much more than conservative, politics have been their province, but there too they have had to share the territory with politicians and trade unionists who were not intellectuals. Modern revolutionary politics have been a domain very much reserved for intellectuals; even those who were not intellectuals by training or profession have been almost forced into becoming so by the ideological nature of modern revolutionary politics.

The prominence of intellectuals in the politics of the new states of Asia and Africa arises in part from the special affinity which exists between the modern intellectual orientation and the practice of revolutionary or unconstitutional politics, of politics which are uncivil in their nature. But even in the small space allotted to civil politics before the new states' acquisition of sovereignty and in its larger area since then, intellectuals have had a prominent position. They have

---

[1]The maxim of the Peace of Augsburg: *Cuius regiò, eius religio,* was the beginning of the specifically modern view that a political order must be based on articulately affirmed beliefs. It too, however, was more concerned with the protection of dynastic interests and the guarantee of public order. The substance of the religion was less important than its acceptance, and in this way it differed from the more intrinsically ideological orientation toward politics that is characteristic of the modern intellectual.

not had to share their political role to the usual extent with the other participants in the building and ruling of states.

It was the intellectuals on whom, in the first instance, devolved the task of
contending for their nations' right to exist, even to the extent of promulgating
the very idea of the nation. The erosion of the conscience and self-confidence of
the colonial powers was in considerable measure the product of agitational movements under intellectual leadership. The impregnation of their fellow-countrymen with some incipient sense of nationality and of national self-esteem was to a
large extent the achievement of intellectuals, both secular and religious. The intellectuals have created the political life of the underdeveloped countries; they
have been its instigators, its leaders, and its executants. Until Gandhi's emergence
at the end of the First World War, they were its main followers as well, but this
changed when the nationalist movement began to arouse the sentiments of the
mass of the population.

One of the reasons for the political pre-eminence of the intellectuals of the
underdeveloped countries is a negative one. There was practically no one else. In
so many of the colonial countries, the princely dynasties were in decay, their
powers and their capacities withered, even before the foreigners appeared. Chiefs
and princes squirmed under foreign rule; they intrigued and schemed, and at
times even resorted to arms, but they organized no political movements and they
espoused no ideology. They sought only, when they protested, to retain or re-
gain their own prerogatives. There were no great noble families producing, in
generation after generation, courtiers and ministers who with the emergence of
modern forms of public politics moved over into that sphere as of right, as they
did in Great Britain from the seventeenth to the nineteenth century. The traditional intellectuals, the custodians of sacred texts, usually—with a few great exceptions like al-Afghani—had no political concerns. They were interested in keeping their traditional culture alive, and this traditional culture had little political
content other than to recommend leaving authority to those who already had it.
They were ready to adapt themselves to any ruler, native or foreign, who left
them alone to carry on their scriptural studies, their traditional teaching, and
their observances.[2]

Moreover, there was generally no military force either to fight against the
foreign ruler once he was established or to supply the educated personnel for a
modern political movement.[3] There was no military officer class except for a

---

[2]The religious reform movements like the Brahmo Samaj, Arya Samaj, the Ramakrishna
Mission, and the Muslim Brotherhood which contributed so much to national consciousness were primarily movements for the purification of religious life, and for the reform of
social institutions. Their political significance was either indirect or an afterthought.

[3]The practitioners of the guerrilla warfare and terrorism which have been carried on in various parts of Asia and Africa against the European rulers have always included a significant
admixture of intellectuals.

few subalterns in the jealously guarded army of the foreign ruler. There were many professional soldiers, but they were non-commissioned officers and other ranks and had no political interest whatsoever. The movement instigated in 1881 by the Egyptian Colonel Ahmed Orabi Pasha[4] had no counterparts until the tremors and tribulations of independence began to be felt. There was no profession of politics which men entered early, usually from some other profession, and remained in until final and crushing defeat or the end of their lives. There were very few merchants and industrialists who out of civic and "material" interest took a part in politics on a full or part-time scale—although many of them contributed substantially to the financial support of the nationalist and even the revolutionary movements. Prudence and the narrowness of their concerns kept businessmen out of politics. The "foreignness" of many business enterprisers in underdeveloped countries has further diminished the significance of this class as a reservoir of political personnel. There was and there still is scarcely any endogenous trade union movement which produces its own leaders from within the laboring class, and there have been practically none of those self-educated workingmen who helped to give an intellectual tone to the European and American socialist and revolutionary movements in their early years. There was no citizenry, no reservoir of civility, to provide not only the audience and following of politics but the personnel of middle and higher leadership. In short, if politics were to exist at all in underdeveloped countries under colonial rule, they had to be the politics of the intellectuals.

The intellectuals did not, however, enter into the political sphere merely because other sections of the population forswore or abdicated their responsibilities. They entered because they had a special calling from within, a positive impetus from without.

II. THE INTELLECTUAL CLASS IN UNDERDEVELOPED COUNTRIES

What Is an Intellectual?

We deal here with the modern intellectuals of the new states—not with traditional intellectuals. Whom do we regard as modern intellectuals in the new states? The answer, in a first approximation, is: all persons with an *advanced modern education*[5] and the intellectual concerns and skills ordinarily associated

---

[4] It was, in any case, more of a protest against unsatisfactory service conditions than a political movement.

[5] This definition is ceasing to be adequate because the extension of opportunities for higher education is changing the composition and outlook of the group of persons who have availed themselves of these opportunities. Furthermore, the increase of those with an advanced technical or scientific and specialized education is creating a body of persons whose

with it. For a variety of reasons, the present definition of the intellectuals is a less selective or discriminating one than we would use to designate the intellectuals in the more advanced countries. This is in no way condescension toward the new states. It is only an acknowledgement of the smaller degree of internal differentiation which has until now prevailed within the educated class in the new states, and the greater disjunction which marks that class off from the other sections of the society. It is also a recognition of a means of identification employed in the new states by the intellectuals themselves and by others.

In the new states, and in colonies which are shortly to achieve independence, the intellectuals are those persons who have become modern not by immersing themselves in the ways of modern commerce or administration, but by being exposed to the set course of modern intellectual culture in a college or university. Passage through this course of study is the qualification for being regarded as an intellectual, just as the possession of the diploma is regarded as a qualification for practicing a profession which is the prerogative of the intellectual. The "diplomatization" of society to which Max Weber referred, although it exists on a smaller scale than in Germany or Great Britain because there are fewer posts available, is as impressive in underdeveloped countries as in the advanced ones. It is not, however, the diploma which makes the intellectual. It is his prolonged contact with modern culture[6] which does so. The diploma is only an emblem, however valuable, of a part of his outlook which he and others regard as vitally important. The possession of a *modern intellectual culture* is vital because it carries with it a partial transformation of the self and a changed relationship to the authority of the dead and the living.

The Occupational Structure of the Intellectuals

The professions of the intellectuals in underdeveloped countries are civil service, journalism, law, teaching (particularly college and unidersity, but also secondary-school teaching), and medicine. These are the professions in which

---

5 *(Cont.)* interests are narrower than their predecessors' in their own countries, and whose contact with the humanistic and political tradition of the hitherto prevailing higher education is becoming more attenuated. They themselves will not merely be different from the conventional political intellectuals of the colonial or recently colonial countries, but will also less frequently identify themselves as "intellectuals." This will make a considerable difference. In this respect, the underdeveloped countries will begin to approximate the more advanced countries.

This definition is not intended to deny the existence of a class of traditional intellectuals, largely religious in their concerns. Nor does it seek to obscure the influence of traditional intellectuals in political life (like the Muslim Brotherhood, the Darul Islam, etc.) or of traditional ideas on modern intellectuals.

6 This does not mean that all intellectuals in underdeveloped countries who possess diplomas are intellectually equal, or that all intellectuals possess diplomas. There are a few who do not.

intellectuals are to be found and which require either intellectual certification or intellectual skill. (There are other professions with similar qualifications of certification and skill, such as engineering and accounting, which have usually been regarded as marginal to the circle within which the intellectuals dwell.)

The occupational structure which intellectuals enter in the underdeveloped countries is notably different from that of the more advanced countries. The occupational distribution of the intellectuals in underdeveloped countries is a function of the level of economic development and of their having only recently been colonial territories. Because they were impoverished countries, they lacked a fully differentiated middle class. They lacked and still lack a stratum of authors who could live from the sale of their literary products.[7] They have only a very meager class of technical intellectuals (electrical engineers, technologists, industrial chemists, statisticians, accountants). They have lacked the higher levels of scientific and humanistic personnel, the physicists, biologists, geneticists, historians, and philosophers who carry on the intellectual work which is the specific manifestation of the modern intellectual outlook.[8]

They lacked nearly all of these latter professions under colonial conditions, and most of the underdeveloped countries still lack most of them today under conditions of independence. In the colonial era, they lacked them because poverty and the absence of a significant development of industry prevented the emergence of demand for technical intellectuals, because illiteracy prevented the emergence of a market for literary products, and because the higher levels of modern intellectual creation and enquiry received no indigenous impulse and were too costly for poor countries to maintain. As a result, persons trained in those subjects found little opportunity for employment in their own country, and few therefore attempted to acquire these skills.[9]

Under colonial conditions, the underdeveloped countries lacked the effective demand which permits a modern intellectual class, in its full variety, to come into existence. Persons who acquired intellectual qualifications had only a few markets for their skills. The higher civil service was by all odds the most attractive of

---

[7] By very rough methods I estimated that there might be as many as one hundred professional literary men in India who are able to maintain themselves by their writings. The Director of the *Sahitya Akademi* thinks that there are only about fifty. Think then of the size of this stratum in Ghana, Nigeria, Egypt, or the Sudan!

[8] India is a very partial exception. It is practically alone in its possession of a large corps of intellectuals, a fair number of whom work at a very high level. This is partly a function of the much longer period that modern intellectual life has existed in India. The British stayed longer in India and exercised greater influence there than any other European power did in its colonial territory, and as a result many more modern intellectual institutions came into being.

[9] There are other important reasons, growing out of the culture of these countries, which precluded interest in these fields. We do not deal with them here since our interest lies primarily in the political sphere.

these, but opportunities were restricted because it was small in size and the posts were mainly preempted by foreigners. (In India in the last decade of the British Raj, there were only about 1,200 such posts in the Indian Civil Service and, of these, a little less than half were filled by Indians. In other countries, the number of posts was smaller and the proportion held by persons of indigenous origin was also much smaller.)

Journalism, as a result of generally widespread illiteracy, was a stunted growth and provided only a few opportunities, which were not at all remunerative. Journalism under colonial conditions was much more of an unprofitable political mission than a commercially attractive investment, and most of it was on a rather miniscule scale.

The medical profession was kept small by the costliness of the course of study, the absence of an effective demand for medical services, and the pre-emption of much of the senior level of the medical service by the government and its consequent reservation for foreigners.

Teaching at its lower levels was unattractive to intellectuals because it involved living in villages away from the lights and interests of the larger towns, and because it was extremely unremunerative. Nor were there many opportunities in it. On the secondary and higher levels, opportunities were also meager. Of all the underdeveloped countries, only India had an extensive modern college and university system before 1920; after that date, the additions to the Indian system of higher education came very slowly until the eve of the Second World War and the chaos which accompanied it. Outside of India there were at most only a few thousand posts available in institutions of higher learning in all of colonial Asia and Africa, and some of these were reserved for Europeans (and Americans, in the two American colleges of the Middle East). Thus opportunities for teaching on the upper levels of an extremely lean educational system were few. Where the authorities sought to maintain a high standard, they were very particular about whom they chose to employ. (It should be added that political considerations, at this time of nationalistic, anti-colonialist effervescence, likewise restricted the chances of entry, since many able young men disqualified themselves by the high jinks of adolescent politics during their student days.)

The Legal Profession

For these reasons, many of the intellectually gifted and interested who also had to gain their own livelihood entered the course of legal study and then the practice of the profession of the law. Entry to the legal profession was not restricted on ethnic grounds, the course of study was short and inexpensive and could be easily undertaken. There was, moreover, a considerable effective demand for legal services.

The colonial powers were concerned with order and justice and, in their various ways, had attempted to establish the rule of law in the colonial territories.

The wealthy landowning classes and the newer wealthy merchants were frequently engaged in litigations in which huge sums were involved and the possibility for lawyers to earn handsome fees gave an éclat to the legal profession which only the higher civil service otherwise possessed.

Furthermore, in countries like India, Egypt, or Nigeria, for example, what else could a university or college graduate do with his qualifications if he did not wish to settle for a clerkship in the government or in a foreign commercial firm? The law schools were therefore able to attract throngs of students. Once the legal qualification had been obtained, the young lawyer went into the nether regions of the bar, where he had much time for other interests. The leisure time of the young lawyer was a fertile field in which much political activity grew.

This existence of a stratum of underemployed young lawyers was made possible by their kinship connections. The aspirants to the intellectual professions in the underdeveloped countries almost always came from the more prosperous sections of society. They were the sons of chiefs, noblemen, and landowners, of ministers and officials of territories in which indirect rule existed, and of civil servants and teachers in countries under direct rule. In some countries, they occasionally came from prosperous mercantile families, though seldom in large numbers.

These social origins, against the background of the diffuse obligations accepted by members of an extended kinship system, meant that even where the income gained from a profession was inadequate to maintain a man and his immediate family, he could still continue to associate himself with the profession. The deficiencies in his earnings were made up by his kinsmen. Unlike teaching, the civil service, and most journalism, where membership in the profession is defined not merely by qualification and intermittent practice but by actual employment, a person need not earn a living by legal practice in order to be a lawyer. This is why the legal profession in nearly all the underdeveloped countries has been, before and since independence, crowded by a few very successful lawyers and a great number of very unsuccessful ones.

These are also some of the reasons why the legal profession supplied so many of the oustanding leaders of the nationalist movements during colonial times, and why the lawyer-intellectuals form such a vital part of the political elites of the new states.

Students

No consideration of the intellectual class in underdeveloped countries can disregard the university students. In advanced countries, students are not regarded as *ex officio* intellectuals; in underdeveloped countries, they are. Students in modern colleges and universities in underdeveloped countries have been treated as part of the intellectual class—or at least were before independence—and they have regarded themselves as such. Perhaps the mere commencement of an adult form of contact with modern intellectual traditions and the anticipation—however insecure—that acquisition of those traditions would qualify one for the *modern* intellectual professions conferred that status on university and college students and, derivatively, on secondary-school students.

The student enjoyed double favor in the eyes of his fellow-countryman. As one of the tiny minority gaining a modern education, he was becoming qualified for a respected, secure, and well-paid position close to the center of society, as a civil servant, teacher, or lawyer. As a bearer of the spirit of revolt against the foreign ruler, he gained the admiration and confidence of those of his seniors who were imbued with the national idea. ˈ

Formally, the student movements in the colonial countries began their careers only in the 1920's, but long before that the secondary schools, colleges, and universities had been a source of personnel for the more ebullient and aggressive nationalistic movements. Since the beginning of the present century, students have been in a state of turbulence. This turbulence flowed more and more into politics, until the students became vital foci of the national independence movements. The secondary schools, colleges, and universities attended by the students of underdeveloped countries became academies of national revolution. It was not the intention of the administrators and teachers that they should become such; rather, the contrary. Nonetheless they did, both in their own countries and in the metropolitan centers of London and Paris, where many of the most important architects of independence were trained, and where they found the intellectual resonance and moral support which sustained them in lean years.

The London School of Economics in particular has probably contributed much more to the excitation of nationalistic sentiment than any other educational institution in the world. At the School of Economics, the late Professor Harold Laski did more than any other single individual to hearten the colonial students and to make them feel that the great weight of liberal Western learning supported their political enthusiasm.

However, it was not only in the universities of London and Paris, but in shabby clubs and cafés, cheap hotels and restaurants, dingy rooming houses and the tiny cluttered offices of their nationalist organizations that the colonial students were educated in nationalism, acquired some degree of national consciousness, and came to feel how retrograde their own countries were and what they might be if only they became their own masters and modernized themselves. Personalities like Mr. Krishna Menon, Dr. Nkrumah, and Dr. Banda were themselves formed in these milieux, and in turn formed many of those who were to play an active part in the movement in their own countries.

The political propensities of the students have been, in part, products of adolescent rebelliousness. This has been especially pronounced in those who were brought up in a traditionally oppressive environment and were indulged with a spell of freedom from that environment—above all, freedom from the control of their elders and kinsmen. Once, however, the new tradition of rebellion was established among students, it became self-reproducing. Moreover, the vocational prospectlessness of their post-university situation has also stirred the restiveness of the students.

The Unemployed Intellectual

In most underdeveloped countries during the colonial period, the unemployed intellectual was always a worry to the foreign rulers and to constitutional politicians, and a grievance of the leaders of the independence movement. He still remains a problem in the underdeveloped countries which have had a higher educational system for some length of time and which are not rapidly expanding their governmental staffs. In Ghana or Nigeria, there is a shortage of intellectuals and all graduates can find posts; in Pakistan, which inherited only a very small part of the higher educational system of British India, the government has tried to restrict entrance to the universities, especially in "arts" subjects. In India and Egypt, however, despite rapid expansion of opportunities for the employment of intellectuals in government, there has been a more than proportionate expansion in the number of university graduates and the problem remains as acute as ever.

Yet the difficulty is not so much "intellectual unemployment" as under- and mal-employment. Most of the graduates, sooner or later, do find posts of one sort or another, but they are not posts which conform with expectations. They are ill-paid, unsatisfying in status and tenure, and leave their incumbents in the state of restlessness which they experienced as students.

III. THE POLITICAL OUTLOOK OF THE INTELLECTUALS

Intense Politicization

The nature of the political movements which preceded independence and the indigenous traditions of the underdeveloped countries both forced political life into charismatic channels. Charismatic politics demand the utmost from their devotees.

When the intellectuals of the colonial countries were ready to engage in politics at all, they were willing to give everything to them. Politics became the be-all and end-all of their existence. Those who were not restrained by fear of the loss of their posts in government schools and colleges or by the material and psychological advantages of their jobs became highly politicized. Some of the intellectuals who graduated in the years of nationalistic fervor did not even attempt seriously to enter upon a professional career but went directly into agitational and conspiratorial politics. Their middle-class origins and the economy of the extended family system, together with the relatively few needs of charismatically sensitive intellectuals, helped to make possible this consecration to politics. For these reasons and because an autonomous intellectual life in the modern sense had scarcely taken root in any of the underdeveloped colonial countries, politics of a very intense sort had the intellectual field largely to itself.

The high degree of political involvement of the intellectual in underdeveloped countries is a complex phenomenon. It has a threefold root. The primary source is a deep preoccupation with authority. Even though he seeks and seems actually to break away from the authority of the powerful traditions in which he was brought up, the intellectual of underdeveloped countries, still more than his confrere in more advanced countries, retains the need for incorporation into some self-transcending, authoritative entity. Indeed, the greater his struggle for emancipation from the traditional collectivity, the greater his need for incorporation into a new, alternative collectivity. Intense politicization meets this need. The second source of political involvement is the scarcity of opportunities to acquire an even temporary sense of vocational achievement; there have been few counterattractions to the appeal of charismatic politics. Finally, there has been a deficient tradition of civility in the underdeveloped countries which affects the intellectuals as much as it does the non-intellectuals. Let us consider each of these aspects.

The intellectual everywhere is concerned with his relations to authority. In underdeveloped countries, where authorities have tended on the whole to be more unitary, and where alternative authorities, and the authority of alternative traditions, have not yet emerged because of the small size of the primordial community and its relatively low degree of internal differentiation, the preoccupation of the intellectual with authority is all the greater. It is difficult for him to escape from a sense of its presence and a feeling of dependence on it. Such continuous presence, and the unindulgent attitude of traditional indigenous authority, once childhood has passed, breed resentment and antipathy which are submerged but not dissolved in the obedience required for the continuance of daily existence in the primordial community.

The external air of submission hides a deeper and unceasing enmity. Distant authority which has force at its disposal, which is impersonal, as bureaucratic authority must be, and which is not suffused with any immediately apprehensible charisma, provides an easy target for this enmity.

When one shares in authority, when one "is" authority, as a leading politician of the ruling party or as a civil servant, the antagonism toward authority is curbed by the counterbalancing need to be absorbed into it. For an intellectual in an underdeveloped country, authority is usually something into which he must be absorbed or against which he must be in opposition. It is seldom something about which he can be neutral while he goes about his business. The very structure of the underdeveloped countries, both in their primordial and in their wider aspects, both during the colonial period and during independence, is such that one can never be indifferent about authority. It cannot be overlooked, one's "business" cannot be carried on without regard to it.

Distant authority carries with it none of the compensations and urgencies of immediately present and permeative authority. Distance does not make for indifference among the politicized, among those whose passions are strong and no longer bound down by the weight of primordiality and tradition. The distance of authority renders revolt against it psychologically more practicable. Distant authority is "alien" authority. Even when it is ethnically "identical" with those over whom it rules, this "alienation" exists in those societies which are used to being ruled by visible and proximate authorities. (When distant authority is also ethnically alien, whether it be of the same general racial and cultural stock or as alien in color, cultural tradition, provenience, and physical appearance as the colonial authorities were, the impulse to revolt is all the stronger.)

The revolt against authority cannot, however, be complete and unequivocal. The need, from which no human being can ever wholly liberate himself, to be a member of an authoritative, transcendent collectivity remains. The individual, striving to emancipate himself from his primordial collectivity, must feel himself a part of some other more congenial, alternative collectivity. It must, moreover, be an authoritative one, a charismatically authoritative one. Where, in an underdeveloped society, with its relative churchlessness, its still feeble professional and civil traditions, and in the face of persisting particularistic loyalties, both subjective and objective, can the modern intellectual find such an authoritative collectivity? It is really only the "nation" which is at hand, and that organized body which represents the "nation"—namely, the "party of national independence."

This is one reason why the intellectual immerses himself, at least for a time, in intense political activities; it is why he seeks a "cause," an encompassing ideal. It is also the reason for the oppositional character of the politics of the intellectuals who themselves do not share in the authority. The belief in the efficacy of political action and in the political sources of evil and the remedies of evil also finds some of its explanation here. This is why the relatively unpolitical intellectual, or the intellectual who is indirectly connected with political affairs, the more specialized intellectual who wishes to work within his own professional tradition and to exercise his influence in the public sphere over the longer run and beyond the immediate disputes of the parties, is regarded as not being a "genuine intellectual" and even as a traitor to the ideals which the intellectual is properly called to serve.

The intense politicization of the intellectual is accentuated by the provision, through politics, of opportunities for individual effectiveness and achievement. In a society where status is traditionally determined by such primordial qualities as kinship connection, age, sex, and rank order within the family, the possibility of achievement, of making a mark on events by one's own actions, is minimal. In the larger society of the underdeveloped countries, although the narrower primordial determinants of status are to some extent transcended, the possibilities of achievement remain small. The opportunities for the satisfactory employment of an educated person under conditions of colonial rule were meager as long as the most authoritative positions in the civil service and in commerce were reserved to foreigners. They remain small under conditions of sovereignty as long as the economy is backward and posts integral to the modern part of the economy are relatively few, and as long as opportunities for specifically intellectual employment or the sale of the products of creative intellectual work are restricted.

The educated person acquires some degree of emancipation from the predominantly primordial tradition of status-determination. The content of this modern education, and its dissolution of the hold of traditional cultural standards and the traditional patterns of life, arouse in him the need to determine his status and his self-esteem by his own achievements. Where can such a person make his mark in a society which gives him little room to do so?

The political movement with its demands and challenges is almost the only arena open to him. A political movement, unlike a business firm or a university or a government department, can absorb as many people as apply to it. It can give him tasks to perform and it can thereby offer him the possibility of seeing the effects of his actions. By shooting, demonstrating, marching, agitating, threatening and bullying, fighting, destroying, obstructing, helping to organize, running errands, distributing handbills and canvassing, he can see some effects and can believe in the importance of his deeds in thwarting or coercing a distant impersonal bureaucratic authority, or in serving the will of the new charismatic authority to which he gives himself.

Especially during the period of late adolescence and youth, when the impulses of self-assertion and the striving for individuality and creativity are at their height, and before the traditional system of status has reasserted its empire over him, politics seem to be the only field in which he can act with some expectation of satisfying effectiveness.

Once independence has been attained, the need for effectiveness and achievement does not die away. Politics remain a major alternative to apathetic idiocy or regression into the acceptance of the traditional pattern of life. Politics will in fact remain a major alternative open to the intellectuals for achievement and for absorption into a wider, no longer primordial collectivity as long as the underdeveloped socieites remain underdeveloped. Only when they have become more differentiated occupationally, and when they have developed a sufficiently large and self-esteeming corps of professional intellectuals, carrying on the specifically intellectual professions with their own corporate traditions and corporate forms of organization, will the passionate sentiment and energy flow into channels other than the political.

Nationalism

The nationalism of the intellectuals usually made its first appearance alone, free from the complications of socialist and populist ideas. Only in those under-developed countries where the nationalist movement has come more lately on the scene has it been involved in other ideological currents which are not necessarily integral to it.

The nationalism of the intellectuals of the underdeveloped countries emerged at a time when there was little sense of nationality among the peoples whose nationality the intellectuals were proclaiming. Its first impetus seems to have come from a deepening of the feeling of distance between ruler and ruled, arising from the spatial and ethnic remoteness of the foreign rulers, and the dissolution of the particularistic tie which holds ethnically homogeneous rulers and ruled together. The identification of oneself as a subject of an unloved (however feared and respected) ruler with others who shared that subjection was one phase of the process. The discovery of the glories of the past, of cultural traditions, was usually but not always an action, *ex post facto,* which legitimated the claims asserted on behalf of that newly imagined collectivity.[10]

The assimilation of modern culture, which, historically, was a foreign culture, was an essential element in this process. The first generation of constitutional politicians in most underdeveloped countries were relatively highly "Westernized." The usual antagonism toward the older generation made the next, younger generation more antagonistic toward Western culture, and encouraged their rudimentary attachment to the indigenous traditional culture to come forward a little more in their minds. This provided a matrix for the idea of a deeper national culture and, therewith, of the nation which had only to be aroused to self-awareness. It was neither a simple attachment to their indigenous culture nor a concretely experienced love of their fellow-countrymen which made the intellectuals so fervently nationalistic. These would have presupposed a prior sense of affinity, which for many reasons was lacking and often still is. In fact, however, "fellow-countrymen" became so to the modern intellectuals primarily by virtue of their common differentiation from the foreign ruler. Fierce resentment against the powerful, fear-inspiring foreign ruler was probably a much more significant factor than either a sense of affinity or a conscious appreciation of the traditional culture.

The resentment of the modern intellectual grew from several seeds: one of the most important was the derogation implied in the barrier against entry into or advancement in the civil service. The other, closely related to this, was the feeling of injury from insults, experienced or heard about, explicit or implicit, which

---

[10]The stirrings of religious reform and the effort to rehabilitate the dignity of the traditional religious culture became political only when there was an alliance of religious leaders with a politicized modern intelligentsia.

the foreign rulers and their businessmen fellow-nationals inflicted on the indigenous modern intellectuals. Lord Curzon's derogatory remarks about the educated Bengali in his famous Calcutta University Convocation Address were only among the more egregious of an infinite multitude of such slights, injuries, and denigrations. The belittlement extended into every sphere of life, cultural, intellectual, religious, economic, political, and personal. A sense of distress and of anticipated insult became part of the indigenous intellectuals' relationship with foreigners for a long time. Even now in independence, the alertness to insult and the readiness to perceive it persist. They were at their height in the early period of nationalism.

The situation was rendered all the more insufferable by the genuine and positive appreciation which the native intellectuals often felt for the foreign culture, and their feeling of the inferiority of their own in comparison with it. Nationalism, of an extremely assertive sort was an effort to find self-respect, and to overcome the inferiority of the self in the face of the superiority of the culture and power of the foreign metropolis.

It was therefore logical that prior to independence the politics of the intellectuals, once the movement for constitutional reform had waned, should have been concerned with one end above all others: national independence. It was generally assumed by most politicized intellectuals that any other desiderata would be automatically realized with the attainment of that condition. The actual attainment of independence and of a condition in which the tasks of political life have become as demanding and as diversified as they must inevitably become in a polity where the state takes unto itself so many powers and aspires to so much, has not greatly altered the situation. Nationalism still remains one of the greatest of all motive forces;[11] it underlies many policies to which it is not really germane and serves as a touchstone of nearly every action and policy.

The socialistic and the populistic elements in the politics of the intellectuals of underdeveloped countries are secondary to and derivative from their nationalistic preoccupations and aspirations. Economic policies have their legitimation in their capacity to raise the country on the scale of the nations of the world. The populace is transfigured in order to demonstrate the uniqueness of its "collective personality." The ancient culture is exhumed and renewed in order to demonstrate, especially to those who once denied it, the high value of the nation. Foreign policy is primarily a policy of "public relations" designed not, as in the advanced countries, to sustain the security of the state or enhance its power among other states, but to improve the reputation of the nation, to make others heed its voice, to make them pay attention to it and to respect it. The "world," the

---

[11]Although it is by no means the chief reason, this nationalistic concentration is a significant factor in accounting for the poverty and uniformity of intellectual life of the underdeveloped countries.

"imperialist world," remains very much on the minds of the intellectuals of the new states. It remains the audience and the jury of the accomplishments of the nation which the intellectuals have done so much to create.

Nonetheless, despite the pre-eminence of the nationalistic sensibility, it does not rest upon a *tabula rasa,* cleared of all other attachments. The intellectuals of underdeveloped countries are not as "uprooted," as "detribalized," as they themselves sometimes assert with so much melancholy, or as, with more spite, their foreign and domestic detractors often allege. They have remained attached in many ways to their traditional patterns of social life and culture. These deeper attachments include parochial attachments to their own tribes and ethnic and caste communities, and almost inevitably seek expression in public policies and in domestic political alignments. The presence of these attachments is a supplementary generator of nationalistic sentiment. It is against them, and in an effort to overcome them—within themselves and in their fellow-countrymen—that many intellectuals in underdeveloped countries commit themselves so fervently to intense nationalism.

By a similar process, the extensive use of a foreign language in daily intellectual life also feeds the force of nationalism. The intellectuals' very large amount of reading in French and English and their feeling of continued dependence on these cultures, their continuing and still necessary employment of French or English for their own cultural creations and even for political, administrative, and judicial purposes, and their awareness of the slow and painful course through which their nation must pass before its own language becomes adequate to the requirements of modern life cannot avoid touching their sensibilities. The constant reaffirmation of their nationalistic attachment is an effort to assuage this wound.

Socialism

The socialism of the intellectuals of the underdeveloped countries grows, fundamentally, from their feeling for charismatic authority, from their common humanity, and from the anti-chrematistic traditions of their indigenous culture. More immediately, it is a product of the conditions and substance of their education, and of their nationalistic sensibility.

The intellectuals of underdeveloped countries are, in general, devotees of authority, even though they may be inflamed against some particular authority. They regard the existing distribution of authority as the source of present economic and social inequities and they seek a new distribution of authority as the instrument to abolish them. Their critical view of the state as it exists at present in their own country is partly a manifestation of their distrust of impersonal authority and of their faith in a more charismatic alternative.[12] They do not

[12]*Vide* the Gandhian socialists and the Bhoodan movement in India.

believe in the capacities of businessmen to increase the well-being of the nation. They have little sympathy, conscious or unconscious, with the man who is engaged in the pursuit of wealth.

None of the great traditional cultures gives a high rank to the merchant; even when they revolt against the traditional culture, or slip away from it unwittingly, the intellectuals usually retain that part of it which allots no high place to the businessman. In their mind, the life of the businessman is unheroic; it is untouched by sacredness and they will have none of it. Intellectuals very seldom seek careers in private business; when necessity forces them into it, they are ill at ease and restless. The intellectual who works for a private business firm lays himself open to the charge of having deserted his calling, even though he has deserted it no more than a civil servant or a lawyer. The notion of an economic system ruled by the decisions of businessmen, out to make a profit for themselves, is repugnant to the intellectuals of underdeveloped countries—even more than it is in advanced countries, where the businessman does not fare very well either at the hands of the intellectuals.

As long as the intellectuals of underdeveloped countries pursued the paths of constitutional reform and confined their attention to administration and representation, these deeper dispositions whose source was the traditional indigenous culture did not enter into their politics. They accepted most of the existing regime. When, however, they began to direct their attention to the society and the nation, when they ceased being politically "superficial" and began to touch on politically "sacred" things, the socialist potentiality of their fundamental orientation became more manifest.

These inner developments within the intelligentsia of underdeveloped countries coincided with the upsurge of socialist thought among the European intellectuals. To these, the intelligentsia of the underdeveloped countries felt drawn. The attractive power of the metropolis was enhanced by the congeniality of intellectual socialism. From the 1920's to the 1940's, the example of the late Professor Harold Laski elicited and fortified the socialistic disposition of many young intellectuals of the English-speaking underdeveloped countries; Jean-Paul Sartre has played a parallel role among the French-speaking intellectuals from 1945 onward.

The spread of socialistic ideas was aided by the large-scale migration of Asian and African intellectuals to Europe for further study and professional training. The great stream of Asians to European educational centers began in the 1890's; their intensive politicization, in the 1920's. The stream of the African students began in the 1920's and became much wider after 1945. From the end of the First World War and the Russian Revolution, the young Asians and Africans, impelled by events in the world and at home, found themselves in an atmosphere which gave the encouragement of a nearly universal assent to their socialist aspirations.

The association between socialism as a domestic policy and hostility toward an imperialistic foreign policy—a connection which is inherent in the postulates of socialist thought and its Leninist variant, although not all socialists have at all times shared it—made European, and especially British and French, socialism even more acceptable to the Asian and African students who came to the intellectual capitals of the European metropolis.

To these factors which made socialism appear such a bright ideal should be joined the nature of large-scale business enterprise in their own countries. In practically all instances, large-scale business enterprise in the underdeveloped countries was owned and controlled by foreign capitalists. Not just the Europeans, and latterly the Americans, owned large forms in Africa and Asia, but Chinese, Syrians, Lebanese, Parsees, Armenians, Greeks, and Italians, away from their own countries, showed exceptional enterprise. Encountering few indigenous competitors, they built up extensive organizations and ample fortunes in underdeveloped countries. The ethnic diversity and separateness of the peoples, even within large, centrally governed countries, often brought about a situation in which private businessmen who were of the same "nationality" as those in the midst of whom they lived and conducted their affairs, but who were of a different "community," were regarded as outsiders who had no moral claims on the loyalty of the intellectuals. Businessmen, by the nature of their calling, could never be part of the "people"; their ethnic distinctness was a further justification for treating them as alien to the "people."

On the other side, a socialistic economic system conducted in accordance with principles which are of intellectual origin, guided by persons who are imbued with these "principles," seems to be the only conceivable alternative to a privately operated economy. The intellectuals who dare to differ from such obvious conclusions constitute a small fraction of the intellectual classes in most of the underdeveloped countries, both colonial and sovereign.

The socialism of the intellectuals of underdeveloped countries, it should also be stressed, is a product of their pained awareness of the poverty of their own countries. The heightening of national sensibility led perforce to the discovery of the "people." Agitational activities brought them into contact with the "people"; the vague doctrine of nationalism, even in its liberal form, brought the idea of the "people" into the consciousness of the intellectuals. Often, too, on return from a period of foreign study where they had encountered socialist ideas and experienced a heightened national consciousness, the sight of their impoverished fellow-countrymen had a traumatic force. Confrontation with the poverty of their country evoked anguish and desperation in many intellectuals. They have been humiliated by their sense of the backwardness of their country. They have learned how gradually the advancement of the Western countries has moved, and they have heard of the speedy progress of the Soviet Union from a backward country to the status of one of the most powerful industrial nations in the world. What could be more harmonious with their present perceptions, their aspirations, and their background than to espouse a socialist solution to their unhappy problem? And if to this is added the fact that their countries have been held in subjection by capitalistic countries and the socialist countries proclaim their hostility to imperialism, the disposition toward socialism receives another impulsion.

Populism

The populism of intellectual politics in underdeveloped countries has a familial affinity to the populism of the intellectuals of more advanced countries during the past century and a half. It is a part of a universal process consequent on the emergence of an incipient and fragmentary world-wide intellectual community. It is a phenomenon of the tension between metropolis and province which arises from the trend toward that world-wide intellectual community.

The populism of the intellectuals is German in origin. It was a critique of the pretensions of a worldly, urban, and urbane authority. It was a critique of the feebleness of the petty elites of the system of *Kleinstaaterei*, alongside the grandeur of the Holy Roman Empire, and of the Germany which could emerge if the regime of the princelings could be abolished and all of Germany unified. It was a critique of the central institutional system, and particularly of the claims of the state, of the universities, and of the ecclesiastical authorities to embody what was essential in their society and of their insistence, on that basis, on their right to rule over it. It was a rejection of the urban bourgeoisie. It was a denial that the "nation" could be found in existing authoritative institutions and an assertion that the root of the future lay in the "folk."

In Russia, populism was a product of a similar situation, aggravated by resentment against a prevailing enchantment by the West, which was more pronounced than the Francophilia of the princely courts against which the first generations of romantic German populism had been a reaction. In Russia, the intellectuals had carried on a passionate love affair with Western Europe and many had been disappointed and had even come to feel guilty for deserting their "own" for foreign idols. Alienated from their own authorities of state, church, and university, hostile to their own mercantile bourgeoisie, disillusioned with Western European socialism after its failures in the revolutions of 1848, it had nowhere to turn except to the "people," whom it glorified as a repository of widsom and as the source of Russia's salvation.

American populism was not very different in its general origins. It, too, was the product of a reaction against the Anglophile intellectual elite of the Eastern seaboard and the political and industrial elites who ruled the country from the Eastern cities. In America, too, therefore, it was an effort to find a firm foundation for intellectuals who were alienated from the authorities of their society and from their xenophilic fellow-intellectuals. In America also it was a phase of the struggle of province against metropolis.

In the underdeveloped countries, the process has been essentially the same. Alienated from the indigenous authorities of their own traditional society—chiefs, sultans, princes, landlords, and priests—and from the rulers of their modern society—the foreign rulers and the "Westernized" constitutional politicians (and since independence, politicians of the governing party)—the intellectuals have had only the "people," the "African personality," the "Indian peasant," etc., as supports in the search for the salvation of their own souls and their own society.

The "people" are a model and a standard; contact with them is a good. Esteem and disesteem are meted out on the basis of "closeness to the people" or distance from them. It is a common worry of and an accusation against the intellectuals of the underdeveloped countries that they are "out of touch with the people," uprooted, *déraciné*, "brown" or "black" (as the case may be) "Englishmen" or "Frenchmen," etc. Many make the accusation against themselves, most make it against their fellow-intellectuals.

Factually it is usually quite untruthful. Most intellectuals in underdeveloped countries are not as "cut off" from their own culture as they and their detractors suggest. They live in the middle of it, their wives and mothers are its constant representatives in their midst, they retain close contact with their families, which are normally steeped in traditional beliefs and practices. The possession of a modern intellectual culture does remove them, to some extent, from the culture of their ancestors, but much of the latter remains and lives on in them.[13]

The experience to which the allegation of being "cut off" from the "people" refers is not to any serious extent a real result of the intellectuals' acceptance of the "foreign," modern culture. It rests rather on their own feeling of distance from the rest of their fellow-nationals, which is a product of the ethnic, tribal, kinship, and caste particularism of these underdeveloped societies and of the consequent lack of a true sense of civil affinity with the rest of their fellow-countrymen. It is the resultant of the superimposition of a nationalistic ideology, which demands fellow-feeling, on a narrower particularism, inharmonious with it and psychologically contradictory to it. There is a genuine feeling of strain; all the burden of this strain is put upon the fact that they possess some elements of an exogenous culture.

The frequent reiteration of the charge testifies to an awareness of this tension, and the choice of the foreign culture as its focus is a manifestation of a desire to find a way out which will conform to the requirements of ideological nationalism. Because the intellectuals assert it and, to some extent, believe it, they often try

---

[13]Much of the intellectuals' self-accusation rests on the populistic assumption that the "people," not being distracted or corrupted by modern culture, are the bearers of the traditional culture in its fullness and its glory. This assumption is probably an error; the "people" are quite unlikely to be in more than fragmentary possession of the corpus of traditional culture.

to make amends for it by some form of nativism, which extols the traditional ways of the people and juxtaposes them with modern and thus "foreign" ways.

This nativistic reaction accentuates demagogic political tendencies, and fosters a race among contenders for the distinction of being more "for" the "people" or more "akin" to them. It accentuates prejudice against the educated and a hostility against the modern education which the intellectuals of the new states need if they are to perform intellectual functions in a productive way, and without which they would not be intellectuals and their countries would flounder and sink.

Nonetheless, despite this preoccupation with the "people," the populism of the intellectuals of underdeveloped countries does not necessarily bring with it either intimacy with the ordinary people, a concrete attachment to them, or even a democratic attitude. It is compatible with them but it does not require them. It is equally compatible with a dictatorial regime which treats the people as instruments to be employed in the transformation of the social and economic order, and their culture and outlook as a hindrance to progress.

Populism can be the legitimating principle of oligarchical regimes, as well as of democratic regimes and of all the intermediate types. The "people" constitute the prospective good to be served by government policy, and they serve as the emblem of the traditional culture which is thus glorified even while it is being eroded and its traditional custodians disregarded or disparaged.

Oppositionalism

The populism of the intellectual is a product of opposition to the authorities who rule at home and to the foreign culture which fascinates him and his fellow-intellectuals in his own country. It is one facet of an oppositional syndrome.

The origins of this inclination to oppose constituted authority seem, at first glance, easy to locate. Practically all politics in the colonial period, once the constitutional phase had passed, consisted and still consist of root and branch opposition. Whether they took the form of conspiracy, sabotage, riots, assassination, clandestine or open journalism, public meetings, boycotts, demonstrations and processions, civil disobedience or unco-operative participation in representative institutions, opposition and obstruction of the foreign ruler were the main aims. Where it was impossible to share in the responsible exercise of authority, opposition was in fact the only alternative.

The degree of alienation from the constituted authority varied but it was almost always deeper and more drastic than the opposition which exists in advanced pluralistic societies.[14] It was the opposition of politicians excluded or withdrawn

[14]Its only parallel in the West is the conduct of the Irish members in the House of Commons in the latter part of the last century and of Communistic members of European parliaments when they were a small minority and did not seek a popular front. The "Irish members" had considerable resonance in India and their influence still survives, even where its origin has been forgotten.

from the constitutional order, who accepted neither the rules nor the ends of the prevailing system. It was, therefore, the opposition of politicians who refused in principle to consider the problems of the government as real tasks needing resolution. It was an opposition which was convinced by situation, temperament, and principle that it would never share authority with the foreign ruler. The only authority to which it aspired was complete and exclusive control of the entire machinery of state. Until that point was reached, its only policy was opposition.

The oppositional attitude of the intellectuals has another point of origin far removed from the political experience of a colonial situation. In most underdeveloped countries the traditional character of the culture sustains diffuseness in the exercise of authority. Diffuse authority, omnicompetent in the tasks facing the society, at least according to legendary beliefs, derives its legitimacy in part from its comprehensive effectiveness. Even though the substantive actions performed by such diffuse traditional authorities are no longer respected by intellectuals, the older pattern of expectation persists. Specific, delimited, impersonal, constitutional authority gives the appearance of being a weak authority, an unloving one which possesses no inner relationship with the ruled. The diffuseness of a charismatic authority is desired, and the bureaucratic rule of the foreign power or of its sovereign indigenous successor arouses little enthusiasm or even willing acknowledgment of any deeper legitimacy. The intellectuals of underdeveloped countries, despite their immersion in modern culture and their overt acceptance of modern political principles, are at bottom averse to a relatively weak, self-limiting government, even when that government is their own, bound to them by common ethnic ties, a common culture, and comradeship in the struggle for independence.

This is one of the underlying grounds for the widespread disillusionment which overcomes so many intellectuals in underdeveloped countries after independence. It must be remembered that, whatever has happened since, practically every new state of the postwar world began as a modern constitutional regime of representative institutions and public liberties. They have all had to employ modern bureaucratic methods of administration, even when they lacked the requisite personnel. They have tried to operate the rule of law. They all began as remote impersonal machines, exercising authority without the diffuseness of charisma or tradition. Their equilibrium has depended on a great charismatic personality who, at the peak of the governmental mountain, offset the distaste for bureaucratic-legal rule.

Thus, the establishment of a tradition of opposition in political life has, as has happened so often in almost every sphere of life in underdeveloped countries, coincided with a fundamental disposition resting on an indigenous cultural tradition.

It would be wrong perhaps to claim a universal validity for a generalization which could be drawn from Max Weber's criticism of Bismarck and the paralyzing influence which his autocracy in the Reichstag exerted on the opposition parties of that body. It was Max Weber's view that the irresponsible opposition which the Bismarckian regime and its Wilhelmine successor evoked would make the opposition parties incapable of responsible, efficient rule when they were given the opportunity to govern. He also asserted—and this is more important for our present discussion—that they would become incapable of conducting themselves as a responsible opposition, working within the rules of the parliamentary game. In certain of the underdeveloped countries, this generalization does not seem to be applicable. In India, for example, certain of the intellectual politicians, and above all the Prime Minister, have shown great adaptability in turning from a condition of complete and irreconcilable opposition to a responsible hard-headed exercise of authority, and some of the socialists and independents conduct their opposition in a most intelligent and responsible manner. The same obtains in varying degrees in Ghana and in Tunisia. Certain intellectual politicians have shown considerable capacity to rule, even though they have not been as democratic or liberal as they once aspired to be or as Mr. Nehru has succeeded in being. Not a few firebrands of the days of the independence movement have turned out to be responsible parliamentarians of the highest order.

Nonetheless, much truth remains in Max Weber's proposition. The intellectuals of the underdeveloped countries since they acquired independence, insofar as they are not in authority, do incline toward an anti-political, oppositional attitude. They are disgruntled. The form of the constitution does not please them and they are reluctant to play the constitutional game. Many of them desire to obstruct the government or give up the game of politics altogether, retiring into a negative state of mind about all institutional politics or at least about any political regime which does not promise a "clean sweep" of the inherited order.

Incivility

Although the intellectuals of the underdeveloped countries have created the idea of the nation within their own countries, they have not been able to create a nation. They are themselves the victim of that condition, since nationalism does not necessarily become citizenship. Membership in a nation which is sovereign entails a sense of affinity with the other human beings who make up the nation. It entails a sense of "partness" in a whole, a sense of sharing a common substance. This feeling of being part of the whole is the basis of a sense of concern for its well-being, and a sense of responsibility to it and for it. It transcends ineluctable divisions, softening them and rendering them tolerable to civil order, regarding them as less significant than the underlying community of those who form the nation. In political life, these dispositions form the virtue of civility.

Civility has hitherto not been one of the major features of the politicized intelligentsia of the underdeveloped countries. An intense politicization is difficult to bring into harmony with civility. Intense politicization is accompanied by the conviction that only those who share one's principles and positions are wholly legitimate members of the polity and that those who do not share them are separated by a steep barrier. The governing party in many sovereign underdeveloped states, and those intellectuals who make it up or are associated with it, tend to believe that those who are in opposition are separated from them by fundamental and irreconcilable differences. They feel that they *are* the state and the nation, and that those who do not go along with them are not just political rivals but *total* enemies. The sentiments of the opposition are, *mutatis mutandis,* scarcely different. These are the fruits of intense politicization.

The incivility of the politicized intellectuals has a history which precedes their birth. Traditional societies, based on kinship and hierarchy, are not civil societies. They do not know the phenomenon of citizenship, since rights and obligations are not functions of membership in a polity determined by territorial boundaries. The primordial qualities of traditional societies—kinship, age, sex, locality, etc.— are not qualities which define the citizen. In a pluralistic society they are not by any means incompatible with citizenship. In the more unitary, traditional society, they suffocate incipient civility.

The moral structure of the independence movement has enabled this uncivil tradition to persist. The independence movement conceived of itself as the embodiment of the nation, and after its victory it became and conceived of itself as identical with the state. Given the oppositional dispositions which come to the surface in parliamentary and journalistic circles not attached to the government party, there often appears to be a semblance of justification for the belief of an impatient and hypersensitive government that the opposition is subversive of the state and cannot be reconciled to it.

This does not imply that there are not civil intellectuals in every underdeveloped country, some of them in the government, some of them in opposition, and some in journalism, the universities, and the other liberal professions. They are, however, in a marked minority. The traditions by which they are sustained, although they do exist in some of the states, are frail.

IV. THREE STAGES IN THE POLITICS OF THE INTELLECTUALS IN UNDERDEVELOPED COUNTRIES

The First Stage

(a) *Constitutional liberalism.* The first efflorescence of the modern intellectual in the underdeveloped countries occurred roughly between the years when India was recovering from the trauma of the Mutiny and its repression and the First World War. In the few countries where there was anything of a class with a modern education and a certain amount of political stirring, these were the years of constitutional liberalism, eloquently and courteously argued. This first stage came considerably later to Black Africa and lasted a shorter time than it did in British India and the Middle East. In Southeast Asia, too, the course of development was greatly telescoped. The backwardness of Southeast Asia and Black Africa in the the construction of modern cultural and legal institutions, and the smaller numbers of persons who went abroad for higher studies, resulted in a much smaller intellectual class than in India, and a later, briefer, and feebler life of constitutional liberalism. Where the intellectual class scarcely existed, politics could only be embryonic.

This was the stage of the politics of lawyers and journalists. Their politics were the politics of *honoratiores*. They were well-educated men, many of whom had studied in the metropolitan countries; they had absorbed and appreciated something of the metropolitan culture and the liberal constitutional political outlook, which, in the circles in which they moved in the France and Great Britain of that period, appeared to be almost unchallenged.

They were not revolutionaries and they did not always aspire to independence, at least, not in the immediate future. One of their main grievances in this earliest phase was the restriction of the right of entry of their fellow-countrymen into the civil service which ruled their country on behalf of the foreign sovereign. They also desired that legislative institutions should be a little more representative of persons like themselves. These two concerns could be interpreted crudely as a manifestation of a narrow class interest, but they were actually broader and better than that.[15] There were serious grounds, in their own self-image, for their claim to share in the administration of the country and for a vote in the determination of the budget.

They had been brought up in a hierarchical tradition in which the landowning classes and the learned, in their own view and that of others, were the possessors of a "stake in the country." Insofar as it was a country, they felt it to be "theirs," and "theirs" almost exclusively. Many came from families which had in the past exercised great influence and which, in the countryside, still continued to do so. It was therefore part of their conception of the right order of things that they should share in the ruling of their own country, under a sovereign whom they were not in the main inclined to challenge in principle.

[15]Nor were these their only interests. They proposed the liberalization of the legal system, greater equity in its administration, and certain liberal social reforms such as the improvement of the legal position of women, the provision of more ample educational facilities, etc.

Obviously, there was some element of "class" and "self-interest" in some of their demands, such as the insistence that imported foreign manufacturers should not be allowed to enjoy any advantages over indigenously produced industrial goods. The interest of the whole society, the interest of a class and of an individual might all coincide on particular issues. This is probably the most that can be credited to the charge against the first generation made by the actors who came on the political stage a little later.

The liberal constitutional ideas which they acquired in the course of their mainly legal studies fitted in with their conceptions. Europe was boiling with democratic agitation—the labor and socialist movements were in process of formation. In the main, however, the very small trickle of Africans and the larger numbers of Asians who before the First World War went to the metropolis for advanced studies did not, on the whole, come into contact with these circles. They wanted a liberal governmental and legal order in the administration of which they could share.

Since they were largely lawyers, they developed the rhetorical skills and the self-confidence in dealing with authority which are an indispensable part of the equipment of the modern politician.[16] The structure of legal practice also gave them the time and the resources to absent themselves from their professional activities. As the occasion demanded, they were able, while still continuing to practice their professions, to devote themselves to public agitation, to attend and address meetings, to write books, pamphlets, and articles for the press, to meet representatives of their rulers from time to time in order to argue their claims, and to participate in consultative and representative bodies.

Side by side with this form of lawyers' politics, a daily and periodical press struggled to come into existence, largely in the metropolitan language but also in the indigenous languages. The journalists were not professionals. They were often political lawyers who had either left their profession or practiced it alongside of journalism; there were also among them men who had been teachers, or who had aspired to join the government service, or had actually been in governmental employ. They were usually well-educated men, with the gravity of the Victorian and Continental bourgeois liberals whom they admired. All this gave dignity and decorum to the political life of that stage of political development.

As journalists, they were not following a career in the material sense of the word. They were not trying to become rich. They were not interested in being purveyors of news and diversion. They were not seeking a livelihood in journalism. Where they could not gain their livelihood from journalism or from their auxiliary professions, they unquestioningly relied on the support of their kinsmen and patrons. They were journalists because there was a small literate public which could be reached and rendered coherent and articulate on behalf of the ideal of constitutional government in which the best-qualified of the ruled would have some hand.

These journalists and lawyer-politicians had few followers other than themselves, i.e., like-minded men in similar stations of life, such as liberal businessmen or princes, chiefs, and landowners. Leaders and followers together constituted no more than a small group. Only in India were the absolute numbers fairly large. In

---

[16]It seems to me not accidental that even now the highest flights of Indo-Anglian prose have the rhetorical quality of high-grade lawyers addressing a court or a parliamentary body.

the Middle East they were fewer, and in the rest of Africa and in Southeast Asia their numbers were negligible. Nonetheless they created, by their activity, the foundations of a still surviving tradition of the modern intellectuals in politics.

They did not have the field to themselves, even at the time of their greatest pre-eminence. They were being challenged by a more aggressive group, less complaisant toward their Western rulers and toward Western culture. These new rivals claimed that constitutional tactics led nowhere. They were the forerunners of the political type which came to the center of the political arena in the second stage. During the first stage, however, there was also another trend of intellectual activity which profoundly affected subsequent political developments, though it was not in itself primarily political or even political at all.

(b) Moral renewal. An impassioned effort of religious and moral self-renewal accompanied the development of political life of the underdeveloped countries during their colonial period. It was at first a feature of the countries which possessed conspicuous evidence of great indigenous achievements in the past—i.e., of the countries with a literary and architectural inheritance which in the midst of present degradation could remind contemporaries that their country had once been great. It was therefore also a characteristic of countries with an indigenous traditional intelligentsia made up of the custodians of sacred writings. Thus it was that in India and in the Middle East, through much of the nineteenth century, protagonists of the traditional cultures, and particularly of the religions of Hinduism and Islam, sought to purify their inheritance, to restore it to its pristine greatness or to fuse it with modern elements. Both in India and in the Middle East, the aim was to reinstate the dignity of the traditional religious culture, and the society which was based on it, and thereby to establish its worth in the face of the encroachment of Western culture and religion.[17]

This movement to evoke a national self-consciousness, through the renewal of cultural traditions which had been allowed to decay, was not directly political. There was not much contact between the modern men who represented constitutional liberalism, and the energetic, pious traditionalists.[18] The two movements seemed to run almost indepednently of each other; there was no antagonism between them, often little mutual awareness.

The agents of moral renewal were not secular social reformers. They were not modern intellectuals in the sense of the word used here. They were men of the traditional culture who were sufficiently sensitive to the impact of modern culture to feel the need to reaffirm their own.[19] Their task was the cleansing of the

---

[17]Movements to "re-establish" the glory of African civilization are a much later product.

[18]There were of course exceptions like al-Afghani, Mohammed Abdou, and M. G. Ranade.

[19]Their influence made itself felt, however, in both India and the Middle East, primarily among modern intellectuals. They exerted little effect on their fellow traditional intellectuals, who persisted in their torpor.

cultural—and this meant largely religious—inheritance of their society from what they claimed were historically accidental accretions which had brought it into disrepute among modern men and allowed their country to sink in the world's esteem and in its own and, particularly, to appear enfeebled and unworthy in comparison with Western achievements. They claimed that what was essential in their religious traditions could—by restoration and cleansing or by syncretism—be reformulated in an idiom more appropriate to the modern situation, and that if this were done, it would recommend itself to their fellow-countrymen who were needlessly and even perniciously enamored of Western culture. They were not unqualifiedly fanatical enemies of Western culture. They claimed that much of what it had to offer—particularly science, technology, and forms of organization—were necessary for the improvement of their countries and the re-establishment of their greatness among the nations. They insisted, however, that their countrymen must not lose their own souls to the West. They must instead rediscover their own essential being by the acceptance of a new and purer version of their own cultural tradition.

The older generation of modern "Victorian" intellectuals did not pay much heed to these preachments, although they were not hostile. In the next stage of political development, this effort of moral rediscovery and self-renewal had very profound repercussions. When, in the second stage, constitutional liberalism seemed to disappear or to be confined in a very narrow space, the movement of moral and religious reform was taken up and developed into a passionate nationalism. Now, even where the religious element in the traditional culture is passed over, praise of the essence of the traditional culture has become a plank in the platform of every movement for independence and of every new state.

The Second Stage

From constitutional liberalism and religious-moral renewal, the intellectuals of the colonial countries passed to a fervently politicized nationalism. With this shift, there also occurred a shift in the mode of political action and its audience.

India was the first of all the underdeveloped colonial countries to execute this movement; it was the one in which the traditional indigenous culture was richest and most elaborate and in which that culture had developed most systematically and comprehensively. It was also the country where the foreign rulers had been longest established in a thoroughgoing way and where the contact of the indigenous intellectuals with a metropolitan Western culture had given birth to a longer and richer modern tradition than was possessed by any other country of Asia or Africa. It was the country with the largest and most differentiated modern intelligentsia. The first long phase of fascination with the West had already begun, in the India of the 1880's, to produce from within itself a reaction in favor of more purely Indian things.

This was also the time of growing strength in the socialist movement in Europe and of the gorwth of anarchism. Terrorism was in the ascendancy in Russia and Ireland. Tales of the Russian underground spread in Asia, together with the repute and glory of the deeds of the "Nihilists" in Russia, the Sinn Fein in Ireland, and the Carbonari in Italy. Mazzini, Stepnyak, and Kropotkin were names well known among the younger generation of Indian intellectuals. Yeats was becoming a figure of weight among the literary intelligentsia and along with this went a feeling for the Irish Renaissance and a belief in the possibilities of a comparable Indian Renaissance. The writings of these *rishis* became known in India, imported from England; some of them appeared in Bengali translations.

The new generation which came to the surface of public life around the turn of the century was no longer content with constitutional agitation, or with such limited goals as more places in the Indian Civil Service and more consultative and deliberative institutions in which Indians would be amply represented. Indian traditional culture was being revived through the Ramakrishna Mission and the Arya Samaj, and a new Indian self-consciousness took hold of young men who, while not deeming themselves religious, were possessed by a profound resonance toward traditional Indian symbols. The Maharashtrian and Bengali terrorists gave no thought to the kind of social or political order which they wished to see established. They wished only to have India free of foreign rule, free to be itself, in its own Indian way.

Parallel developments a third of a century later could be seen in areas as far apart as the Gold Coast and Egypt. A half-century later, they began to appear in East Africa. The same pattern was visible in more foreshortened form in Syria and Iraq. The proportions and the tone of the movements in these smaller countries, with much smaller intelligentsias, have been roughly what they were in India.

In these smaller countries, too, there was a tendency to regard the older generation of liberal constitutionalists and piecemeal reformers as excessively subservient to the foreign rulers and as excessively bemused by their foreign culture and their foreign forms of government. The later, populistic phase of intellectual politics, which in a variety of forms continues into the present, only intensified and made more complex and luminous an already established pattern. The generally socialistic orientation of the politics of the Asian and African intellectuals, which took form after the First World War and became preponderant after the Second World War, in a similar fashion only elaborated the inherent potentiality of intense nationalism.

The intensification of political concerns was the outgrowth of the earlier political interest, in fusion with the more acute sense of nationality which the heightened awareness of the traditional indigenous culture had helped to arouse. The politics of the "second generation" touched a very much deeper chord than that which the earlier generation had reached; it is a chord which still vibrates. The greater depth of the new political movement meant also that it was more passionate, more in the complete possession of politics. The fundamental politicization of the intelligentsia of Asia and Africa led to the discrediting of the first liberal generation. The politics of cultured and urbane gentlemen, speaking French or English to perfection, interested in much else besides politics, was not for this generation.

The politics of the second generation received a further powerful impetus from its participation in a cosmopolitan movement, in which *foreign*, Western countries were involved. The intellectuals of the second generation, like those who preceded and those who have followed, were also held by their attachment to Western culture. The extremist nationalist movements in Asia and subsequently in Africa had a Western legitimation for their strivings. They drew inspiration and comfort from abroad, they felt that their actions were one with a mighty surge all over the world, a surge toward a new order of freedom, with possibilities unknown and unregarded.[20] This sense of being a part of the larger world infused into the politics of the second generation the permanently bedeviling tension between province and metropolis, and added, as it always does, the heat which arises from conflicting loyalties.

When the second generation was still in its youth in India, and only in conception in other Asian and African colonial countries, the Russian Revolution took place. Only a little while thereafter M. K. Gandhi established his ascendancy over the political scene in India.[21] These two events precipitated the populistic consciousness, which had been only latent in the exacerbated nationalism which had preceded them.

The early leaders of the second generation had been deferential to "ancient traditions," in contrast to the liberal, moderate, and progressive attitude of the earlier constitutional politicians, who had not given political significance to indigenous cultural traditions. The "people" had, however, not yet acquired the eminence which was later to be their due in the political outlook of the

---

[20]The role of exiles and expatriates living in the metropolitan centers of Great Britain, France, Germany, and Switzerland helped to maintain a continuous link between the revolutionary and radical tendencies in the metropolis and those in the underdeveloped countries. These exiles and expatriates provided a sort of training school for young Asians and Africans who had gone abroad to study, and they constituted a continuous representation of the interests of their countries before the public opinion of the ruling metropolis.

Like exiles and expatriates everywhere, they also were more "uprooted" than their countrymen who either stayed at home or returned home after a few years. This "uprootedness" did not, however, diminish the intensity of their politics. Rather, the contrary.

[21]And with it, he began his march toward ascendancy over the Western colonialist conscience. A skeptical attitude about the rightfulness of imperialism had already existed in the West for a long time, but it was Gandhi more than anyone else outside the European Socialist and the Communist movements who impressed it on the consciousness of the Western educated classes. As a result, a body of Western allies was formed and its existence was a reassurance and a stimulus to the politicized intellectuals who continued to stand in need of a sustaining tie with modern "Western" culture.

intellectuals. Now, under the guidance of Gandhi and an attenuated Leninism, they ascended to a central position.

Socialism was no further away than a step of the imagination. The preceding generation had been neither socialist nor anti-socialist. The issue had never arisen, as long as civil-service personnel policies, the extension of representative institutions, and criticism of the "drain" had been the main objects of political debate.[22] Politics now became "total politics" and its claims on those who gave themselves to it became all-embracing. Politics in colonial countries became a vocation, without becoming professionalized. Many came to live "for" politics, but few lived "from" politics in the way in which professional politicians live from it. The politics of the colonial intelligentsia became in a sense more profound; that is, they came into contact with the deeper layers of the intelligentsia's existence. The politics of the intellectuals became charismatic politics.

As one might expect from charismatic politics, a tremendous pull was exerted on the youth. Leadership still lay with the lawyers and a few who had once served the government as officials and clerks[23] or had been tempted sufficiently to prepare themselves to do so. A large and important part of the following, however, consisted of students—college and university students in countries with colleges and universities and high school students where these were absent. A great deal of the clamor and volatility of the politics of the second generation of the intellectuals came from the students.

The Third Stage

The third stage of intellectual politics sees the intellectuals in power in a sovereign state, ruled by an indigenous elite.

With this stage the intellectuals who have reaped the fruits of the struggle become dissociated from the intellectual class. A schism occurs in the corps of intellectual-politicians. One sector comes into power and takes to it like a fish to water. The exercise of authority—which is not identical with the efficient exercise of authority—seems to be almost as natural as breathing to those intellectuals who are in power. To an increasing extent, they see themselves as different from the intellectuals who do not share their power, and whom they chide as naggers, unreasonable critics, backsliders from the great national cause. The intellectuals in power feel themselves less continuous with the intellectual class than they did during the struggle for independence. As the burdens and challenges of office

---

[22]In Africa after the Second World War, nationalism, intense politics, socialism, and populism came into life almost simultaneously, as if they were inseparably involved with each other.

[23]Where there were few indigenous lawyers or others with higher education, leadership was exercised by clerks with secondary or elementary education. The educated, the *evolues*—intellectuals—have kept the lead, the highly educated when they have been available, the less well-educated where the former were lacking.

preoccupy them, and as they spend so much of their time with party bosses and machine-men who have never been or who long since ceased to be intellectuals, their own image of themselves as intellectuals wanes and they become more sensitive to the anti-political dispositions of their old companions.

This drift toward schism is aggravated by the fact that the opposition becomes the magnet which draws the intellectuals. Although within the political elite, at the peak of government there are many who were once intellectuals by education, vocation, or disposition and who have now become hardened politicians, no longer paying any attention to things of intellectual interest. Those who remain intellectuals in vocation and disposition seem to find their natural habitat on the opposite benches. There—and in common rooms and cafés—gather the intellectuals who in their outlook, in their studies and their self-identification, remain intellectuals.

The transformation of the intellectuals in power discloses the duality of the oppositional mentality. The hatred of authority is often no more than a facet of the fascination and love that it evokes. When they come to power, intellectuals who have hated it quickly allow the identification with it, against which they struggled previously, to come into full bloom. They attach to themselves the regalia of authority and feel that they and the state are now identical. Whereas during the struggle for independence, they felt that they represented the nation and that all who disagreed with them were outside the national community and had allowed their souls to be possessed by the foreigner, now when they are in power, they regard themselves and the state as identical and all those who disagree with them as enemies of the state.[24]

On the other side of the floor, where it is allowed to exist, the oppositional mentality retains all of its old forms. Bureaucratic administration is criticized as too remote and too impersonal. The government is charged with corruption; it is alleged to be "too distant" from the people, and to be the betrayer of the national idea. It is accused of damaging the reputation of the country in the world, or of turning the country over to a new form of foreign control.

The oppositional mentality of the third stage, however, possesses one feature which the second did not possess—i.e., disillusionment. Whereas the opposition of the second generation imagined an amorphously happy condition once their antagonists were removed, the oppositional mentality of the post-colonial period has no such utopian euphoria to assuage its present melancholy.

Oppositionalism, which was so involved in an intense politicization, tends among some of those who are out of power to shrivel into an anti-political

[24]Mr. Nehru is something of an exception, although he too regards the opposition as an unavoidable pestilence, as an inconvenient part of the community which remains, notwithstanding, as much a part of the community as he himself is. At the other extreme is that other intellectual in politics, Dr. Nkrumah, who regards any criticism or disagreement as *staatsfeindlich*.

passivity. It is not that politics no longer engages the attention. It still does, but among many intellectuals it has become a source of despondent inaction.

Among others, a quite substantial bloc, it flows into a more rigid form of activistic extremism. In some instances, this extremist alternative to passivity takes on a traditionalistic guise; in others, it assumes a Leninist visage. Both of these foster the intense and total rejection of the muddled, compromising, and often compromised, incumbent government, in the name of a higher ideal.

V. THE PROSPECTS OF THE INTELLECTUALS IN THE POLITICAL LIFE OF THE NEW STATES

Practically every new state has begun its career with a commitment to a regime of representative government and public liberties. Whatever might be the democratic and consultative elements in the indigenous tradition of government, the particular constitution which was actually chosen to give form to self-government is evidence of the role of intellectuals in the establishment of the new states. It was only through the influence of the intellectuals in contact with the modern political ideas which circulated in the larger world that this decision could have been made. This alone would be sufficient to testify to the still living inheritance of the notables who peopled the first stage of modern political life in the then colonial countries.

The fate of the new states, whether they persist and flourish as democracies, or whether they regress into more oligarchical forms of government, is as undeterminable as anything which lies in the future. As long, however, as they do not disintegrate into tribal and local territorial sovereignties, and as long as they at least aspire to be "modern," the intellectuals will go on playing a large role in the fulfillment of whatever possibilities fortune allots to their societies.

In most of the new states, the intellectuals still constitute a notable part of the ruling political elite, although their position is no longer as preponderant as when politics were a charismatic movement. Politics, as the new states were consolidated, became a profession and ceased to be a calling or a mission. The emerging professional politician, military or civilian in origin, is forced to be less of an intellectual in his outlook. The inevitability of the formation of a political machine has meant, and will continue even more to mean, that organizers with little intellectual disposition, interest, or sympathy will move into a more prominent position in the political elite. Back-benchers and party functionaries will include a very considerable proportion of place-holders, and the tasks they will have to perform will not be very attractive to intellectuals, living in the traditions of modern intellectuals.

Nonetheless, even on the government benches, if the regime continues to be more or less democratic there will remain some readiness of the professional party leaders to receive and sponsor intellectuals. The prestige of modern education will continue to be high and any political party and government will therefore wish to draw on its beneficiaries. Furthermore, the reservoir of persons available for political leadership will continue to be limited in the foreseeable future; this will force the party leaders to look in the intellectuals' direction, however reluctantly. At the same time, however, the oppositional tendencies of intellectuals and the hypersensitivity to criticism on the part of politicians of any sort—and of the politicians of new states in particular—will add to this reluctance.

Opposition parties, insofar as they are allowed to exist, will certainly draw on intellectuals for their critical ideas concerning the government and for leadership and following. Such parties are their natural home.

If the underdeveloped countries become completely oligarchical and are ruled by a military junta or a one-party state, the role of intellectuals in political life in the narrower sense will certainly decline. The diminution of public political life will tend to narrow the area permitted to intellectuals. Even then, single-party regimes are likely, because of their ideological nature, to find a place for some intellectuals within their leading circles.[25]

Regardless of the fate of democracy in underdeveloped countries, intellectuals will undoubtedly continue to be called upon for the civil service and for higher education. There will be increasing scope for intellectuals as the governments expand the range of their activities and as the demand grows for highly qualified persons for engineering, teaching, publicity and propaganda, health and social services, and research in social and natural sciences.

If the new states avoid the fate of the Latin American countries in the first century of their independence, and progress economically and socially, then indifferently of the political regime which rules them, the intellectual classes will become larger and more differentiated, and more fully incorporated into their own cultural institutional system in a variety of technological, administrative, educational, and therapeutic capacities.

This incorporation of the intellectuals into their own societies will depend to a large extent on the establishment of an equilibrium between the demand for and the supply of intellectuals. If there always is such a surplus of university and

[25]The professional army officer in the new states is to a certain extent an intellectual since he, especially in the technical branches, is the recipient of a modern education. In fact, the intrusion of the military into politics in the Middle East, at least, may be partly attributed to their attachment to modern ideas about order, efficiency, and probity in government, ideas which are not part of the indigenous tradition of government and which come to them through their modern training. The military *coups d'état* which have occurred in many of the new states may be interpreted as, at least in part, revolutions of the technological intelligentsia, acting on behalf of modern ideas of efficiency and progress.

college graduates that their salaries are low and many of them have to take posts which they regard as unsuitable, the process of incorporation will be obstructed. Instead the oppositional mentality will go on reproducing itself. Where a public political life is permitted, there they will be a perpetual source of unsettledness.[26]

Let us imagine that the economies of the new states develop toward greater productivity and that a measure of liberal political life survives the burdens under which the new states now labor. The intellectual classes will become more diversified than they are at present, as they find employment in applied science and technology, in governmental, industrial, and commercial administration, in scientific and scholarly research, and in the profession of letters. With this diversification, there will be less unity of sentiment, less sense of a common identity among them. The "intellectuals" will become only one part of the educated class and a situation which already exists in the advanced countries will emerge.

There will be more specialization, more philistinism, and a less general cultural sympathy in the new intelligentsia than in the old. The new intelligentsia will also be much less political in its outlook and more practical and professional. Each intellectual profession will, as it has long since done in the advanced countries, nurture its own traditions and ways of working. As in the past, these traditions will draw on the more differentiated and more elaborate intellectual traditions of the advanced countries. Creativity will come to be more appreciated and one necessary condition for its realization will thus be provided. The intellectuals of the underdeveloped countries will cease in the course of this process to be as dependent and provincial as they are now. They will become, as some already are, full citizens, with completely equal status, in the intellectual community of the world.

The opportunities for fruitful and satisfying employment of the skills of the intellectuals in the various spheres of civil and economic life and the establishment of absorbing and guiding traditions of an autonomous creativity in intellectual life proper will foster an attenuation of ideological dispositions. It can never eradicate them but it can reduce the commonness of their occurrence and mollify their asperity. Many with political interests will no longer feel the urgent obligation to participate directly in day-to-day political life. More of them will be

---

[26]This, in turn, would increase the demand for an ideological oligarchy, from outside the government, and would also impel the government itself to adopt oligarchical measures.

There is also the opposite danger of a disequilibrium in the relations between the intellectuals and the central institutional system arising from an excessive demand for intellectuals in technological and administrative roles. In countries which entered upon independence with an insufficient supply of qualified intellectuals and a very scanty complement of intellectual institutions, it is definitely possible to draw practically all of the best intellectuals into executive and technological roles, leaving too few for civil and intellectual functions. The rapid growth of the public services and the general trend toward the governmental pre-emption of so many diverse functions might well result in too small a proportion of the intellectual classes being left free for independent creative work and for vital activity in that publicistic borderland between the intellectual and the political.

content to play an equally vital but less immediate part in the formation of the life of their countries. They will concern themselves less than they do now with the issues of the here and now, and will deal with problems which are of longer-run significance, more remote from the immediate issues of party politics and of the prospects and favors of the incumbent political elite. The indirect influence on politics which comes from the cultivation of the matrix of opinion, and from the provision of the personnel and the institutional conditions of long-term development, will bring satisfaction to a larger proportion than it now does, and politicians will perhaps learn to appreciate the equal and perhaps even greater value to the community of this kind of activity on the part of intellectuals.

Their direct participation in politics will probably continue to have a radical bent. The traditions of the modern intellectual are too deeply rooted and the tendency is too intrinsic to the exercise of intellectual powers for this to be avoided—even if it were ever desirable. The radicalism of the intellectual's politics need not however be revolutionary or ideological; it can also work within the civil order. In the espousal of this standpoint at the center of political decision, in party councils, in parliaments and in cabinets, the intellectual will continue to have a unique and indispensable role, the abdication of which cannot be compensated by purely intellectual creativity or the efficient performance of executive, technological, and educational functions. In order, however, for this possibility to exist, the political society—the civil order itself—must first come into existence.

This brings us to one of the prototypical paradoxes of political development. For the intellectuals to inherit their true estate, they must live in a political society. But this civil order cannot be achieved unless the intellectuals, who would be among its greatest beneficiaries, help, against the greatest difficulties, to bring it about. Some of these difficulties reside within the intellectuals themselves, within the political and cultural traditions which enter into their constitution. The outcome then depends on whether those intellectuals who speak for civility in a modern society will by their talents, virtue, and good fortune be able to outweigh their own inhibitions, the dense incivility of their fellow-intellectuals, and the rocky obduracy of the traditional order.

12. DIMENSIONS ON CONFLICT BEHAVIOR WITHIN AND BETWEEN NATIONS, 1958-60

Raymond Tanter

This is a replication of a study by Rudolph J. Rummel (1963). The goals of that study were to determine the dimensions of variation in the domestic and foreign conflict behavior of nations, to locate nations on these dimensions, and to employ these dimensions in order to discover the relationship between both forms of conflict behavior. The goals of the replication are to obtain additional evidence relative to the dimensions of conflict behavior and the relationship between domestic and foreign conflict behavior. Data have been collected across eighty-three nations for 1958, 1959, and 1960 on the same twenty-two measures of conflict behavior used in the previous study. Similarly, these data are to be intercorrelated and factor analyzed, and multiple regression is to be used to examine the relationship between domestic and foreign conflict behavior.

SOURCE. Raymond Tanter, "Dimensions of Conflict Behavior Within and Between Nations, 1958-60," in *The Journal of Conflict Resolution,* X (March, 1966), pp. 41–64. (Slightly abridged.) Reprinted by permission of the author and The Center for Research on Conflict Resolution. Copyright 1965 by the University of Michigan.

[1]Prepared in connection with research supported by the National Science Foundation, Grant NSF-GS224. The data were collected as part of the Dimensionality of Nations Project supported by that foundation, the Carnegie Seminar supported by the Carnegie Corporation, and the International Development Research Center (IDRC) at Indiana University, supported by the Ford Foundation.

The author wishes to thank Fred Riggs, formerly acting director of the IDRC, and Rudolph Rummel, principal investigator of the Dimensionality of Nations Project, Yale University, for making this study possible. Professor Rummel has aided in the preparation of the research design phase of this study in order to assure continuity from his study (Rummel, 1963) to the present one. I am also quite grateful for his comments on my interpretation of the results, and in reading earlier drafts; any errors, however, are mine. In addition, I am grateful to Milton Hobbs, Harold Guetzkow, J. David Singer, and Dean Pruitt for their comments, and to the Indiana and Northwestern University Research Computing Centers for the generous provision of their facilities.

THEORY

Many of the generalizations about international conflict behavior have been discovered through the use of historical analysis. For example, Richard Rosecrance concludes that through time there is a tendency for international instability to be associated with the domestic insecurity of elites (Rosecrance, 1963, p. 304). Two other students of international relations, Ernst Haas and Allen Whiting, suggest an explanation for the relationship between internal and external conflict behavior. They contend that groups seeking self-preservation may be driven to a foreign policy of conflict. The authors reason that the elites become fearful of losing their domestic positions during periods of rapid industrialization and widespread social change; they then try to displace the attention of the disaffected population onto some outside target. But the authors suggest that this form of self-preservation rarely leads to war (Haas and Whiting, 1956, pp. 61–62).

In addition to Rosecrance and Haas and Whiting, Quincy Wright suggests that there is a general relationship between internal and external conflict behavior. Interspersed in his two volumes of *A Study of War* (1942) are propositions such as the following:

By creating and perpetuating in the community both a fear of invasion and a hope of expansion, obedience to a ruler may be guaranteed. A system of world politics resting upon a balance of power contributes to the integration of each power by maintaining among the peoples the fear of war as well as the hope of dominance [Vol. II, p. 1016]. Rulers have forestalled internal sedition by starting external wars [Vol. I, p. 140]. There is no nation in which war or preparations of war have not to some degree or at some time been used as an instrument of national stability and order [Vol. I, p. 254]. In later stages of the Napoleonic Wars, Napoleon began to appreciate the value of war as an instrument of internal solidarity [Vol. II, p. 725]. Governments have often started war because it appeared to them a necessary or convenient means of establishing, maintaining, or expanding the power of the government, party, or class within the nation [Vol. II, p. 727].

Hopefully, this study will provide a systematic examination of the propositions of such theorists as Rosecrance, Haas and Whiting, and Wright. From a systematic examination and a series of *replications,* it may be possible to construct a general theory of intra- and internation conflict behavior. (See below, pp. 209 ff., for a further discussion of such theories.)

REPLICATION

Increasing the number of observations or trials in a particular design is referred to in the literature on the logic of experimentation as increasing the replications. Increasing the replications generally increases the confidence that the findings are not the result of chance factors (Edwards, 1954, p. 273). One frequently comes across references to the need for replication in the literature on research methods. For example, Katz asserts that the history of social psychology shows the significance of the replication of findings in that many of the original propositions have not been confirmed by later studies (Katz, 1953, p. 64). Moreover, Sidman contends that the most appropriate empirical test of the reliability of data is provided by replication (Sidman, 1960, p. 70).

Replication is especially suggested when there is disagreement with a well-established finding, the number of replications warranted being a function of the extent to which the previous findings were firmly established (Sidman, 1960, p. 78). As regards quantitative studies, the finding that there is very little relationship between domestic and foreign conflict behavior (Sorokin, 1937; Rummel, 1963) contrasts with other findings of a negative relationship (Huntington, 1962) and a positive relationship (McKenna, 1962). On the other hand, most of the nonquantitative works support the hypothesis of a positive relationship (Haas and Whiting, 1956; Rosecrance, 1963).[2] The quantitative studies where the generalization was not based on the collected data (such as Wright, 1942) also support the finding of a positive relationship.

The quantitative studies where the generalization was based on the data meet a minimum criterion for replication, e.g., the standardization of the specifications for data. And as Katz points out, "Only when we attain the level of standardizing our specifications for data can we see the extent to which reported findings are true generalizations" (Katz, 1953, p. 64). Moreover, the ability to replicate scientific inquiry depends largely upon an explicit statement of the research design decisions such as data collection and analysis procedures.

POPULATION

To be included in this study, nations had to be sovereign for at least two years and have a population equal to or greater than 800,000 in 1958. As a result of more nations being able to meet these criteria for 1958 than for 1955, the

[2] The way some of these propositions are stated, however, it is almost possible to interpret them as suggesting a negative relationship. This interpretation, though, does not fit in with the context in which the propositions appear. With the introduction of a time lag between the occurrence of domestic and foreign conflict behavior, the theories of Coser (1956) and Simmel (1955) suggest a negative relationship.

population size increased to eighty-three from the seventy-seven in the 1955–57 study (see Appendix II for the list of nations). Intragroup replication would entail the use of the exact sample employed in the prior study. As with the Rummel study, however the total *population* is being used. Consequently, sampling restrictions of this sort are not applicable.[3]

DATA SOURCES AND CODING RELIABILITY

The New York Times Index, Deadline Data on World Affairs, Britannica Book of the Year, and *Facts on File* were used as sources of data for the twenty-two conflict behavior measures. The first two sources, however, proved to be far more productive of data than the others. Consequently, most of the data reported in this study were derived from *The New York Times Index* and *Deadline Data,* the others being consulted for an overview.

It may be argued that the cross-reference system of one of the primary data sources, *The New York Times Index,* is such that any reliability tests would have to be conducted over *all* the nations by two or more coders in order to test for the agreement between coders for a subset of nations. That position, however, is valid only as regards foreign conflict behavior measures. That is, when there is conflict between two countries, parts of the conflict behavior are recorded under each country involved as well as in other places. For example, as regards the United States, the bulk of its international activity is recorded under topic headings other than "United States." Although some of these cross-references are given in the *Index,* a large part of them are not. Consequently, only by going through all the nations can one be confident that he is obtaining most of the information on foreign conflict as regards a subset of the countries. For domestic conflict, however, the information is generally contained under the country heading. With these caveats in mind, reliability tests were conducted on the domestic measures. To assure maximum continuity in the codings for the 1955–57 and 1958–60 data, to discover the consistency of the author's codings at different points in time, and to ascertain the extent to which other coders would agree with the author's codings, three partial reliability tests were conducted.

A random sample of five nations from the 1955–57 data reported by Rummel were recorded by the author as regards the nine measures of internal conflict behavior. Agreement ranged from 85 to 100 percent, with purges and major government crises being the variables on which there was least agreement. Since the author did the large portion of the 1958–60 coding, he recorded a random sample of ten nations three months after the initial codings were made. In only two

---

[3]See Sidman (1960), p. 73, regarding intragroup and intergroup replication, and pp. 46 ff., as regards the concept of generality.

cases were there discrepancies. A third reliability test consists of the author re-coding the five nations for 1958–60 that were initially coded by two assistants. Perfect agreement was found for these five. Although these partial reliability tests indicate that *some* of the data are reliable, there may be coding errors in the data which might bias the conclusions.

SYSTEMATIC ERROR IN THE DATA SOURCES

Censorship may result in a systematic understatement of the conflict behavior of a given country in the sources. Accordingly, a three point censorship scale for 1958 is derived from the Inter-American Press Survey of 1958[4] and the Survey of the World's Press by the International Press Institute[5], and for 1959[6] and 1960[7] from Associated Press Surveys of World Press Freedom. Values for each year were then summed across the three years for each nation so that those with high censorship had low scores.

Lack of world interest in a country may also result in an understatement of its conflict behavior. World interest may be operationalized as the number of embassies or legations *in* each country for 1959. The assumption is that this value for each nation reflects world interest in that nation. Although there are obvious exceptions to this assumption, such as the values for East Germany and China, the assumption appears to be valid for most other nations. A second meas-ure of world interest is derived from one of the data sources–*Deadline Data on World Affairs*. It is the number of index cards per country in the card file itself.

These three error measures are included in the correlation and factor analysis. If censorship has no correlation with the conflict behavior measures, then syste-matic bias as tapped by the censorship measure does not distort the conclusions. Negative correlation of censorship and the conflict behavior measures is not cru-cial because one can assume the direction of systematic bias to be under- instead of overstatement. Aside from possible exaggeration by the press, one would not expect nations to overstate the number of riots and revolutions it has. So if censorship is negatively correlated with riots, it might be inferred that the corre-lations between riots and the other conflict behavior measures would undergo little change even if censorship were suppressing knowledge of such incidents. Positive correlations between the censorship and the conflict behavior measures indicate that censorship in a nation could be distorting the results; positive

[4]*New York Times,* March 29, 1959.
[5]*New York Times,* April 13, 1959.
[6]*New York Times,* January 3, 1960.
[7]*New York Times,* January 1, 1961.

correlation, however, is a necessary but not sufficient condition for such systematic error to distort the results of this study.

A high positive correlation between the world interest measures and the conflict behavior measures might mean that lack of world interest in some countries could be causing their conflict behavior to go unreported. Positive correlation, however, is a necessary but not sufficient condition for such systematic error to distort the conclusions. (In the Rummel study [1963] the direction of the correlation between the world interest measure and the conflict behavior measures was inadvertently stated as negative for systematic error to distort the results.)

RESULTS[8]

In order to determine how well the 1958–60 data reflect a longer period, the data were compared and correlated with Rummel's 1955–57 data.[9] Table 1 contains the correlations of the 22 measures of conflict behavior for both 1955–57 and 1958–60. In the upper left hand corner of the matrix the domestic variables are intercorrelated with themselves; the values to the left are the 1958–60 correlations. The fact that all the correlations for each period are positive indicates a remarkable degree of similarity in the direction of the relationships. Out of a total of 36 correlations for each period there are 10 which are greater than or equal to .50. In other words, 28 percent of the domestic correlations for each period are ≥.50.

This stability of the ratio of high correlations to the total for the domestic variables, however, is not found for the foreign variables. (The foreign variables for each period are located in the bottom right hand side of the matrix; the 1955–57 values are to the right of the diagonal while 1958–60 values are to the left). Out of a total of 78 correlations 23, or 29 percent, are ≥.50 for the 1955–57 period, while only nine, or 12 percent, are ≥.50 for the 1958–60 period. The direction of the relationships, however, argues for similarity between the periods. There are only two negatives for 1958–60 and three for 1955–57.

---

[8]Biomedical (BIMD) Computer Program 24 was used to test for outliers, and a visual test of linearity from the cross tabulation of each variable with every other. Outliers greater than three standard scores from the mean were "brought in" through transformation. No curvilinearity was found which might distort the conclusions.

[9]In addition, Richardson's data (1960) for thirty nations on war from 1825–1945 were correlated with 1958–60 data on war, war and military action, and number killed due to all foreign conflict; Harry Eckstein's data (Eckstein, 1962) for 1946–59 on total violence, internal warfare, and a coup are correlated with 1958–60 measures for seventy nations; and Raymond Cattell's correlations (Cattell, 1949) for five measures of conflict behavior were compared with similar correlations from 1958–60. The results indicate that the 1958–60 data are not unique to that period and appear to be moderately general to longer time periods.

TABLE 1. CORRELATION MATRIX, 1955-57 and 1958-60[a]

Measures[b]	1	2	3	4	5	6	7	8	9	10	11	12	13	14	15	16	17	18	19	20	21	22	23	24	25
1. Assass		28	45	35	31	45	19	(51)	33	23	28	01	03	16	-09	15	15	19	06	28	20	18	29	08	21
2. Strike	38		36	29	46	(56)	(50)	(57)	(51)	20	-01	-01	14	13	07	-04	01	-01	-10	-09	07	04	03	-03	00
3. Gu-War	49	36		09	17	13	33	20	(52)	00	00	-23	-08	17	-11	-10	-10	-10	-11	-11	-09	-04	06	05	-07
4. Gvters	43	42	(55)		30	36	38	41	20	21	29	10	28	-01	05	09	11	09	-05	05	11	13	12	05	22
5. Purges	29	04	25	24		42	49	36	(57)	24	13	08	32	18	24	26	30	17	24	13	27	34	12	-21	03
6. Riots	(51)	(55)	34	41	25		32	(69)	(53)	36	16	-19	18	26	08	15	08	12	13	02	21	19	29	05	19
7. Revolu	31	20	(65)	42	(51)	30		23	(62)	05	-04	-11	03	12	-11	-04	12	-04	07	-12	04	12	-02	-08	-06
8. Demons	46	(54)	32	42	19	(73)	19		45	38	26	29	14	26	28	36	16	20	23	21	35	21	47	-07	30
9. D-Kill	(51)	33	(67)	46	41	47	(69)	39		16	-04	00	-03	25	16	05	02	07	14	-06	12	22	18	-22	-01
10. F-Dmst	29	28	27	12	17	38	26	22	31		(53)	39	36	14	29	(50)	33	25	39	22	46	35	42	05	18
11. Negsan	23	00	20	14	20	17	10	13	13	21		47	33	05	33	(64)	35	24	45	38	48	30	(57)	03	33
12. Protst	04	15	05	-01	07	29	-01	24	04	27	39		19	09	47	(66)	39	(51)	(63)	46	(69)	(52)	(60)	-10	29
13. Sevdip	08	19	27	28	05	23	19	21	11	22	20	02		-08	12	38	(54)	07	15	23	39	31	04	-15	-08
14. Er-Amb	05	27	08	10	-03	16	-13	18	-08	19	36	(54)	09		25	12	-08	01	24	-10	11	02	24	-14	13
15. Er-Les	27	11	10	08	11	17	-01	15	04	16	32	20	13	25		(50)	13	33	43	14	45	32	42	-23	34
16. Threat	10	01	07	-08	06	20	-05	18	07	42	(55)	(59)	13	42	22		(62)	38	(68)	(55)	(81)	(63)	(72)	-19	25
17. Milact	05	03	05	06	19	12	06	10	12	17	30	39	05	28	07	47		45	45	(54)	(65)	(72)	19	-09	07
18. War	00	-06	-05	01	03	01	-02	02	07	-06	21	22	08	25	-09	24	(51)		32	37	(56)	(77)	(51)	-10	20
19. Trpmvt	14	01	01	-07	19	40	06	24	11	30	24	49	11	23	22	42	26	22		37	(62)	(53)	(74)	-13	33
20. Mobili	00	04	07	00	31	05	02	03	14	25	30	36	16	38	24	48	43	41	37		(46)	41	19	-17	07
21. Accusa	18	-07	17	07	32	19	16	18	12	25	47	(64)	12	40	29	(62)	49	38	39	44		(70)	(63)	-27	09
22. F-Kill	34	06	30	21	25	24	23	15	27	25	40	40	13	22	05	39	(60)	(52)	46	38	(51)		44	-16	08
23. Cards	03	10	05	-02	12	30	-05	31	09	28	35	(77)	-02	(53)	22	(67)	38	23	(55)	43	(63)	33		00	28
24. Censor	-03	19	-09	02	-28	17	-16	13	-13	21	-27	00	14	07	-18	-16	-37	-22	06	-09	-41	-26	00		39
25. D-Emby	01	34	04	06	-08	44	-17	40	-02	22	02	(52)	-02	37	21	21	06	01	34	15	14	-08	(57)	39	

[a] To the right of the principal diagonal of the matrix are the 1955-57 correlations, $N = 77$; to the left are the 1958-60 correlations, $N = 83$. Parenthesis indicates correlations $\geqslant .50$. Correlations are rounded off and multiplied by 100. Product moment coefficients of correlation are used throughout this study unless otherwise specified. No significance tests are given throughout this study because the entire universe under investigation is being analyzed.

[b] See Appendix I for full names of the variables as well as their definitions.

The other portions of the matrix, the correlations of domestic with foreign variables for both periods, are much more similar, although the negative range is greater in the earlier period. (The domestic-foreign intercorrelations for 1955–57 are in the upper right hand corner of the matrix, while those for 1958–60 are in the lower left hand corner.) An analysis of the percentage of correlations that fall within certain intervals argues for a similarity across both periods. This type of analysis does not tell one *which* variables have similar intercorrelations over both periods. An example of correlations between intra- and international characteristics that are similar across periods is furnished by "riots" and "anti-foreign demonstrations." The 1955–57 correlations is .36, and for 1958–60 it is .38. One of the most similar correlations across both periods, at the international level, is that between accusations and mobilizations, which is .46 for 1955–57 and .44 for 1958–60; one of the least stable is the correlation at the intranational level between purges and general strikes: .46 in 1955–57 and .04 in 1958–60.

The variability in Table 1 in the correlation of purges with general strikes might be partially explained by the very low correlation of 1955–57 purges with 1958–60 purges in Table 2. Out of 22 correlations, eight (36 percent) are ⩾.50. The variables which have the most similar intercorrelations generally appear to be those that happen most often, or those in which coding is not much of a problem (e.g., accusations, threats, riots).

DIMENSIONS OF FOREIGN CONFLICT BEHAVIOR

Table 3 gives the results of the factor analyses of the foreign conflict behavior measures for 1955–57 and 1958–60. The orthogonally rotated matrix is given.[10]

[10]Mesa 3 computer program is used for the factor analysis. Principal components technique is used with unities in the diagonal of the correlation matrix (see Rummel, 1963, ch. 3, for a detailed discussion of the research design decisions). Since the eigenvalue (sum of squares) of the unrotated fourth factor of the 1958–60 data is equal to only .95, only three factors are extracted and rotated orthogonally and obliquely. The criterion for the *number of significant factors* to extract and to which rotation is to be started is the same for the 1955–57 and 1958–60 studies. This criterion is the number of factors whose eigenvalues are ⩾ 1.00. An eigenvalue is the root of a characteristic equation.

Rotation is carried out in order to obtain a more stable solution, e.g., one that is not entirely dependent upon each particular variable in the analysis.

Orthogonal rotation is the fitting of factors to variables with the restriction that the correlation between the factors is zero. Hence, independence among the factors is forced on the data. The varimax criterion (Kaiser, 1958) is used to rotate orthogonally to simple structure, e.g., the maximization of low loadings.

Oblique rotation allows the factors to become correlated if such correlations actually exist among the factors.

The criterion for accepting either rotation is the extent to which simple structure is achieved. The number of variable loadings in the ±.10 hyperplane is used to indicate the degree of simple structure. Hence, the solution which has the largest number of near-zero loadings will be accepted.

TABLE 2. CORRELATIONS BETWEEN 1955–57
AND 1958–60 DATA[a]

Measures	Correlations[b]
1. Assass	24
2. Strike	33
3. Gu-War	(65)
4. Gvters	36
5. Purges	05
6. Riots	(69)
7. Revolu	(55)
8. Demons	44
9. D-Kill	(55)
10. F-Dmst	38
11. Negsan	47
12. Protst	(57)
13. Sevdip	08
14. Er-Amb	14
15. Er-Les	38
16. Threat	(66)
17. Milact	43
18. War	41
19. Trpmvt	(58)
20. Mobili	15
21. Accusa	(71)
22. F-Kill	48

[a]Each value for a 1955–57 measure is correlated with the corresponding values for 1958–60; $N = 74$. Parenthesis indicates correlations $\geqslant .50$.

[b]Egypt, Syria, and Yemen were originally included in the 1955–57 study but were excluded, along with the UAR for 1958–60, in the calculations of these correlations.

10 (Cont.) Loadings are correlations with factors for the unrotated and orthogonally rotated solutions. The values in the oblique matrices are pattern values which are coordinates rather than correlations.

The communality, h^2, of a variable is the sum of the squares of the loadings across the factors for the unrotated and orthogonally rotated solutions.

Percent of Total Variance under each column in the factor matrix is that portion of the variance in all the variables which that factor extracts. It is the sum of the squares in the factor column divided by the total number of variables.

Percent of Common Variance is the percent of variance that a factor has divided by the total number of variables.

TABLE 3.[d] FACTOR ANALYSIS OF FOREIGN CONFLICT MEASURES[a]: ORTHO-
GONALLY ROTATED FACTOR MATRIX, 1955-57 DATA WITH 1958-
60 DATA[b]

Measures	Diplomatic		War		Belligerency		Communality (h^2)	
	T_1	R_2	$T_2{}^c$	$R_1{}^c$	T_3	R_3	T	R
1. F-Dmst	34	42	03	13	(64)	(63)	52	60
2. Negsan	(58)	41	22	20	26	(64)	46	62
3. Protst	(79)	49	26	(62)	−06	22	70	67
4. Sevdip	−06	−17	09	13	(82)	(82)	68	71
5. Er-Amb	(67)	(66)	18	−16	−05	−08	49	47
6. Er-Les	(59)	(60)	−29	33	21	08	47	48
7. Threat	(70)	43	35	(65)	23	48	66	84
8. Milact	28	−14	(74)	(65)	02	(57)	63	77
9. War	02	15	(83)	(85)	−09	−10	70	75
10. Trpmvt	46	(59)	32	47	26	28	38	64
11. Mobili	34	−08	(58)	(60)	19	35	48	49
12. Accusa	(67)	35	46	(70)	09	41	66	79
13. F-Kill	21	10	(76)	(87)	23	19	67	80
% Common variance	43.3	24.6	37.7	46.2	18.9	29.1	100.0	100.0
% Total variance	25.2	16.3	21.8	30.7	10.1	19.3	57.9	66.4
Intraclass correlation coefficient	.68		.67		.67			

[a]Parenthesis indicates loadings $\geqslant$.50.

[b]Decimals omitted from all loadings.

[c]Signs reversed.

[d]Factors labelled "T" are Tanter's 1958–60 orthogonally rotated factors. Factors labelled
"R" are Rummel's 1955–57 orthogonally rotated factors (Rummel, 1963, p. 13).

In the orthogonally rotated solution of the 1958–60 data, a *diplomatic* dimension emerges first.[11] It is defined by the variables with high loadings, such as
protests, threats, and accusations. (The higher the loading, the more the variable
is associated with the factor, e.g., a set of highly related variables. The range of
the loading is from +1.00 to −1.00, as is the range for the product moment

[11]The orthogonally rotated solution is selected over the oblique because the former meets
more adequately the simple structure criterion. (The ±.10 hyperplane of the orthogonal
solution contains more low variable loadings than the oblique solution has low pattern
values.)

correlation coefficients if the univariate distributions are similar). This dimension represents a nonviolent type of foreign conflict behavior similar to that which emerged as the second factor in the 1955-57 study. The 1955-57 measures that are mainly correlated with the *diplomatic* dimension are expelling or recalling ambassadors, expulsion of lesser officials, and troop movements. The *diplomatic* dimensions from both periods pull together rationally calculated activities of a nonviolent nature, that is, diplomatic moves short of the use of force which are intended to influence other nations.

The second orthogonally rotated factor of the 1958-60 data is a *war* dimension. The variables with high loadings are war, military action, foreign killed, and mobilization. This dimension is comparable to the first factor which emerged from the 1955-57 data. Mobilization, war and number killed best define the 1955-57 *war* dimension. The *war* dimensions in both periods pull together activities which index the preparation for war, war itself, and its consequences.

The third rotated factor of the 1958-60 data has anti-foreign demonstrations and severance of diplomatic relations as the only high loadings. This factor might be labelled a *belligerency* dimension which is similar to the third factor of the earlier period. The 1955-57 *belligerency* dimension is defined by a cluster containing severance of diplomatic relations, anti-foreign demonstrations, military action of a limited nature, and negative sanctions. Some of the activities on the *belligerency* dimension in both periods are of an "emotional" nature as opposed to the "rational" nature characteristic of the activities on the *diplomatic* dimension.

Three dimensions of foreign conflict behavior describe both the 1955-57 and the 1958-60 data: *war, diplomatic,* and *belligerency* dimensions. (The degree of similarity—intraclass correlations—between the equivalent dimensions for each period is discussed in the section on *Comparisons of Dimensions from 1955-57 and 1958-60.)*

DIMENSIONS OF DOMESTIC CONFLICT BEHAVIOR

Table 4 gives the results of the factor analysis of the domestic conflict behavior measures for 1955-57 and 1958-60. The orthogonally rotated solution is given.[12] Upon orthogonally rotating the two factors for 1958-60 to a more stable solution, two distinct dimensions emerge, the first of which might be called a *turmoil* dimension. Demonstrations, riots, strikes, assassinations, and

---

[12]Since the eigenvalue of the third factor of the 1958-60 data is only .84, only two factors are extracted and rotated orthogonally and obliquely. The orthogonal solution is selected over the oblique because the number of loadings and pattern values in the $\pm$.10 hyperplane for each solution is the same (4). And since the orthogonal solution is the simplest, it is selected.

TABLE 4[d]. FACTOR ANALYSIS OF DOMESTIC CONFLICT MEASURES[a]: ORTHO-
GONALLY ROTATED FACTOR MATRIX, 1955-57 DATA WITH 1958-60
DATA[b]

Measures	Turmoil		Revolutionary	Internal War	Subversive	Communality (h^2)	
	T_1	R_1	$R_2{}^c$	T_2	$R_3{}^c$	T	R
1. Assass	(59)	(59)	−03	41	(66)	52	78
2. Strike	(79)	(52)	(60)	06	05	63	63
3. Gu-War	35	−04	28	(74)	(90)	66	90
4. Gvters	(53)	(60)	21	47	−04	50	41
5. Purges	01	32	(71)	(68)	03	46	60
6. Riots	(83)	(79)	31	21	09	73	73
7. Revolu	09	09	(85)	(89)	13	80	75
8. Demons	(86)	(85)	17	10	19	75	79
9. D-Kill	37	23	(75)	(78)	42	74	79
% Common variance	50.8	39.0	37.6	49.2	23.4	100.0	100.0
% Total variance	32.7	27.7	26.7	31.7	16.6	64.4	70.8
Intraclass correlation coefficient	.74		.45		.12		

[a]Parenthesis indicates loadings ⩾ .50.
[b]Decimals omitted from all loadings.
[c]Signs reversed.
[d]Factors labelled "T" are Tanter's 1958-60 orthogonally rotated factors. Factors labelled
"R" are Rummel's 1955-57 orthogonally rotated factors (Rummel, 1963, p. 12).

crises have high loadings and thus define the dimension. A similar dimension can be found in the rotated matrix of the 1955-57 data. The *turmoil* dimension for the earlier period is also defined by demonstrations, riots, crises, assassinations, and strikes.

The second 1958-60 orthogonally rotated factor pulls together a cluster of activities such as revolutions, domestic killed, guerrilla war, and purges. These activities are generally associated with organized conflict behavior of a highly violent nature. This factor might thus be labelled an *internal war* dimension. The *internal war* dimension of the 1958-60 data subsumes the *revolutionary* and *subversive* dimensions of 1955-57. The *revolutionary* dimension pulled together overt, organized conflict behavior, while the *subversive* dimension was defined by activities of a covert organized nature.

Domestic conflict behavior for 1958–60 may thus be separated into two independent scales—a disorganized spontaneous *turmoil* dimension and an organized violent *internal war* dimension. Since both dimensions account for almost equal amounts of the total variance in the rotated solution, they may be considered equally important in describing domestic conflict behavior during the 1958–60 period.[13]

* * *

RELATIONSHIP BETWEEN DOMESTIC AND FOREIGN CONFLICT BEHAVIOR

The relationship between domestic and foreign conflict behavior is discovered by first factor analyzing all the conflict behavior measures together and then by regressing upon one another the variables which best index both forms of conflict behavior. Table 5 contains the results of the merged factor analysis; the obliquely rotated solution is given.[14] Upon rotation to the more invariant oblique solution, domestic and foreign conflict behavior become clearly separate. In no case do any domestic measures have pattern values ≥.50 on the same factor on which a foreign measure is ≥.50.

The first factor in the oblique matrix is the *turmoil* dimension. The second factor is the *diplomatic* dimension and is defined by the communications variables as well as explusion of ambassadors. In addition to these measures of diplomatic activity, however, the two error measures of world interest also help to define this dimension.

As previously mentioned, negative correlation or lack of correlation between censorship and the conflict behavior measures is no cause for alarm. A second error measure—cards per nation in *Deadline Data*—has to be analyzed in a different manner. There is a high positive pattern value of cards (.82) on the *diplomatic* dimension, where protests also show a value of .82 and expulsion of ambassadors .72; and there are high positive correlations of cards with protests (.77) and cards with expulsion of ambassadors (.55). This indicates that the level of world interest in a nation is associated with the tendency for its protests and expulsions of ambassadors to be reported.

[13] The inference as to degree of organization was based upon an inspection of background information on the conflict events in question. This tentative distinction should not lead us to ignore such facts as that some of the riots were highly organized. A further study is planned where the degree of organization will be coded systematically to see whether organization varies with type of conflict behavior.

[14] Seven factors are extracted in contrast with the six-factor solution of the 1955–57 study because the eigenvalue of the seventh factor of the present work is 1.002 (see footnote 10). The oblique is selected over the orthogonal solution on the basis of simple structure criteria. The ±.10 hyperplane contains sixteen more loadings in the oblique than are found in the orthogonal solution.

TABLE 5.[c] FACTOR ANALYSIS OF DOMESTIC AND FOREIGN CONFLICT MEAS-
URES[a]: SEVEN FACTOR SOLUTION

| | | | Oblique Biquartimin Pattern Matrix[b] | | | | |
| | F_1 | F_2 | F_3 | F_4 | F_5 | F_6 | F_7 |
Measures	Turmoil	Diplomatic	Int. War	War			
1. Assass	(64)	−31	18	12	31	02	18
2. Strike	(70)	18	07	−02	−09	09	−23
3. Gu-War	28	01	(66)	−08	07	20	−24
4. Gvters	(53)	−03	37	08	03	11	−40
5. Purges	−05	09	(76)	−02	02	−19	06
6. Riots	(77)	09	14	07	−02	−01	28
7. Revolu	05	−07	(91)	−10	−12	06	−08
8. Demons	(81)	14	06	09	02	−09	05
9. D-Kill	35	−07	(76)	05	−13	−03	02
10. F-Dmst	04	11	22	−14	03	(53)	(52)
11. Negsan	−08	19	03	16	(62)	25	−01
12. Protst	05	(82)	03	09	14	−13	04
13. Sevdip	01	−15	−03	06	10	(83)	05
14. Er-Amb	08	(72)	−16	1	22	12	−34
15. Er-Les	13	14	−11	−27	(82)	01	−07
16. Threat	−14	46	−04	22	34	22	27
17. Milact	04	21	01	(74)	02	−08	01
18. War	06	06	−16	(91)	−21	−02	−04
19. Trpmvt	14	22	−06	25	01	05	(68)
20. Mobili	−27	47	22	36	−15	22	07
21. Accusa	−11	49	22	31	38	−09	02
22. F-Kill	17	−10	08	(79)	04	12	27
23. Cards	06	(82)	04	11	10	−17	13
24. Censor	20	09	−28	−33	−45	42	30
25. D-Emby	41	(73)	−15	−20	−13	17	03

[a]Parenthesis indicates pattern values ⩾ .50.

[b]Decimals omitted from all loadings. The oblique rotation is a part of the Mesa 3 computer program. It consists of the class of analytical solutions called *oblimin*, developed
by John B. Carroll at Harvard. The *biquartimin* solution is selected over the *quartimin* or
covarimin because the quartimin solution is generally biased toward factor axes which
are too highly correlated, while the covarimin is almost invariably biased toward factor
axes which are too orthogonal (cf. Harmon, pp. 324-34).

[c]Correlations between factors for oblique rotation are cosines of the angles between the
factors rather than the intraclass correlations based upon the pattern values. Correlations
> .25 are: $r_{F_1F_6}$ = .26; $r_{F_2F_7}$ = .28; $r_{F_3F_4}$ = .26; $r_{F_3F_5}$ = .26; $r_{F_4F_5}$ = .27.

The high correlation and mutually high pattern values of protests and the "cards" measure of world interest is likewise found for the other measure of world interest—the number of embassies or legations in a country. The latter measure has a .52 correlations with protests and a pattern value of .73 on the *diplomatic* dimension (see Tables 1 and 5).

The similar manner in which the world interest measures act with the protest variable indicates that the two world interest measures are tapping the same thing. The small difference between the two may come from the fact that the cards in *Deadline Data* measure the extent of interest that the *editors* manifest in particular nations, while the number of embassies or legations in a country may reflect the degree of interest other *nations* have in that country.

On the basis of the relationships between protests and expulsion of ambassadors on the one hand, and the world interest error measures on the other, propositions about these conflict measures should be qualified to this extent: the data of nations in which there is little interest *may not* be included in the correlations from which the propositions are inferred. But an alternative explanation is also plausible. The correlation of the cards measure of world interest with diplomatic behavior *may* be due to increased interest when there is diplomatic conflict. Also, the more important nations have more interactions with other nations, and this may give them more opportunities for protest as well as more foreign newspapers in which their activities are reported.

Besides the *turmoil* and *diplomatic* dimensions, other factors in the oblique matrix of Table 5 may be interpreted. These are *internal war* (factor 3) and *international war* (factor 4). The merged factor analysis seems to show a lack of relationship between domestic and foreign conflict behavior. This relationship may be investigated more precisely by using multiple regression.

MULTIPLE REGRESSION[15]

Both forms of conflict behavior for 1958–60 are regressed upon one another to discover the relationship between them at one cross section in time. In

---

[15]Multiple regression is a method by which the variation in a single dependent variable is related to the variation in several independent variables. Whereas factor analysis is the appropriate method for ascertaining the *interdependency* among variables, multiple *regression* is appropriate for discovering *independence-dependence* relationships. The rationale for factor analyzing prior to the regression analysis is to select conflict behavior variables for regression which best index the dimensions and which are relatively independent of one another. For example, one text asserts that "The more highly the independent variables are interrelated among themselves, the less reliably can the net regression of X_1 upon any of them be determined" (Ezekiel and Fox, 1959, pp. 283–84).

addition, the 1958–60 data are regressed on the 1955–57 data in order to discover the relationship between domestic and foreign conflict behavior with a time lag.

The independent foreign variables for the 1955–57 study are the *war, diplomatic,* and *belligerency* dimensions. The values of the variables used in regression in the Rummel study are the factor scores each nation has on each of the six factors extracted. These scores were estimated by adding together the standard scores of variables which have a loading ≥.50 on a particular dimension and no loading ≥.40 on another dimension within the matrix (Rummel, 1963, pp. 15–16).

The variables used in the prediction of domestic conflict behavior for 1958–60 are measures of conflict behavior which measure the dimensions, rather than the dimensions themselves. These measures are called representative variables. They are selected on the basis of having the highest loading on the orthogonally rotated dimensions, but no other high loadings in the matrix.

Thus the variables for the 1958–60 domestic dimensions are anti-government demonstrations and revolutions, which measure the *turmoil* and *internal war* dimensions respectively. The representative variables for the foreign dimensions are war, protests, and severance of diplomatic relations, which measure the *war, diplomatic,* and *belligerency* dimensions respectively.

In the time lag regressions of 1958–60 data on 1955–57 data, representative variables rather than factor scores for 1955–57 were employed as independent variables. Thus, the representative variables for the 1955–57 domestic dimensions are anti-government demonstrations, revolutions, and guerrilla warfare, which index the *turmoil, revolutionary,* and *subversive* dimensions respectively. The representative variables for the 1955–57 foreign dimensions are foreign killed, expulsion or recall of ambassadors, and severance of diplomatic relations, which measure the *war, diplomatic,* and *belligerency* dimensions respectively.

Representative variables were selected rather than factor scores because the substantive meaning of the variable is clear, whereas the meaning of factor scores is not so readily apparent. In addition, the theoretical significance of the representative variables can be readily discovered through a series of replications. But it is considerably more difficult to ascertain the theoretical significance of dimensions because the exact composition of the dimension is unique to each study.

Table 6 gives the results of the predictions of 1955–57 foreign from 1955–57 domestic conflict behavior dimensions carried out by Rummel (1963, p. 20). Only eight percent of the total variance in foreign conflict behavior is explained by domestic conflict behavior.[16] The small difference in the values for the

---

[16]The percent of total variance for the dependent variables is calculated by summing down the R^2 column, dividing the result by the number of dependent variables, and multiplying by 100 (Rummel, 1964, p. 20).

TABLE 6. PREDICTIONS OF 1955-57 FOREIGN CONFLICT BEHAVIOR[a]: INDE-
PENDENT VARIABLES–TURMOIL, REVOLUTIONARY, SUBVERSION

Dependent Variable	Year	Standard Deviation	Standard Error	Multiple R	R^2
War	1955-57	2.40	2.36	.26	.07
Diplomacy	1955-57	1.49	1.46	.26	.07
Belligerency	1955-57	1.00	.97	.31	.10

[a]N = 77(Rummel, 1963, p. 20).

standard deviation and the standard error indicates the failure of the domestic
dimensions to predict changes in the foreign dimensions.

Table 7 contains the results of the prediction of the 1958-60 foreign from the
1958-60 domestic conflict behavior variables. Only about four percent of the
total variance in foreign conflict behavior is explained by the domestic measures
for 1958-60, which is somewhat lower than the eight percent found for the
1955-57 data.

Results of the prediction of the 1955-57 domestic from the 1955-57 foreign
conflict behavior dimensions reveal that almost eight percent of the total variance in the domestic dimensions is explained by the foreign dimensions. This is
remarkably similar to the seven percent of the total variance in the 1958-60 domestic which is predicted by the 1958-60 foreign basic variables. . . .

From the two sets of regressions for the 1955-57 and 1958-60 cross sections,
there appears to be only a small relationship between domestic and foreign conflict behavior. This apparent lack of relationship at one point in time may be
investigated further by means of time lag regressions.

TABLE 7. PREDICTIONS OF 1958-60 FOREIGN CONFLICT BEHAVIOR[a]: INDE-
PENDENT VARIABLES–ANTI-GOVERNMENT DEMONSTRATIONS AND
REVOLUTIONS

Dependent Variable	Year	Standard Deviation	Standard Error	Multiple R	R^2
Wars	1958-60	.75	.76	.03	.00
Severance of diplomatic relations	1958-60	.15	.15	.26	.07
Protests	1958-60	.35	.35	.24	.06

[a]N = 83.

TIME LAG REGRESSIONS

The 1955–57 foreign predicts 22.3 percent of the variance in the foreign variables for 1958–60 (Table 8). But only half as much variance (11.7) percent) in the 1958–60 foreign is explained by the 1955–57 domestic (Table 9).

Table 10 contains the results of the prediction of 1958–60 domestic by 1955–57 domestic variables. The domestic conflict behavior of the 1955–57 period explains 27.5 percent of the total variance of the 1958–60 domestic.

TABLE 8. PREDICTIONS OF 1958–60 FOREIGN CONFLICT BEHAVIOR: INDEPENDENT VARIABLES– 1955–57 NUMBER KILLED IN FOREIGN CONFLICT BEHAVIOR, EXPLUSION OR RECALL OF AMBASSADORS, AND SEVERANCE OF DIPLOMATIC RELATIONS[a]

1958–60 Dependent Variable	Standard Deviation	Standard Error	Multiple R	R^2
Protest	.35	.33	.40	.16
War	.68	.52	.66	.43
Severence of diplomatic relations	.16	.15	.28	.08

[a]The independent variables are representative variables from the 1955–57 study (Rummel, 1963, p. 13). $N = 74$.

TABLE 9.   PREDICTIONS OF 1958–60 FOREIGN CONFLICT BEHAVIOR: INDEPENDENT VARIABLES– 1955–57 ANTI-GOVERNMENT DEMONSTRATIONS, REVOLUTIONS, AND GUERRILLA WARFARE[a]

1958–60 Dependent Variable	Standard Deviation	Standard Error	Multiple R	R^2
Protest	.35	.32	.42	.18
War	.68	.69	.12	.01
Severence of diplomatic relations	.16	.14	.40	.16

[a]These independent variables are representative variables from the 1955–57 study (Rummel, 1963, p. 13). $N = 74$.

TABLE 10. PREDICTIONS OF 1958-60 DOMESTIC CONFLICT BEHAVIOR: INDE-
PENDENT VARIABLES–1955-57 ANTI-GOVERNMENT DEMONSTRA-
TIONS, REVOLUTIONS, AND GUERRILLA WARFARE[a]

1958-60 Dependent Variable	Standard Deviation	Standard Error	Multiple R	R^2
Anti-government demonstrations	.38	.34	.44	.19
Revolutions	.26	.22	.60	.36

[a]These independent variables are representative variables from the 1955-57 study (Rummel, 1963, p. 12). $N = 74$.

The 1955-57 foreign, however, cannot predict the 1958-60 domestic variables. The results in Table 11 show that only 8.5 percent of the variance in the
1958-60 domestic is explained by the 1955-57 foreign variables.

TABLE 11. PREDICTIONS OF 1958-60 DOMESTIC CONFLICT BEHAVIOR: INDE-
PENDENT VARIABLES–1955-57 FOREIGN KILLED, EXPULSION OR
RECALL OF AMBASSADORS, AND SEVERANCE OF DIPLOMATIC
RELATIONS[a]

1958-60 Dependent Variable	Standard Deviation	Standard Error	Multiple R	R^2
Anti-government demonstrations	.38	.38	.16	.03
Revolutions	.26	.25	.37	.14

[a]These independent variables are representative variables from the 1955-57 study (Rummel, 1963, p. 12). $N = 74$.

From the time lag regressions one may conclude that there is a *moderate relationship* between domestic conflict behavior at one time and the same behavior
at a later point in time. Similarly, there is a *moderate relationship* between foreign conflict behavior at the two points in time. In the absence of the time lag,
only seven percent and 4.3 percent of the variance are explained by the 1958-60
foreign and domestic measures respectively. With the introduction of the lag, the
explained variance increases to 8.5 and 11.7 percent. Although this is still a very

small amount of variance on which to make a generalization, there seems to be some relationship between domestic and foreign conflict behavior with a time lag.[17]

DISCUSSION AND SUMMARY

Dimensions of Domestic Conflict Behavior

One finding that appears to emerge from the 1958-60 data is that the structure of domestic conflict behavior is slightly different from that found in 1955-57. The internal war dimension combines the 1955-57 *subversion* and *revolutionary* dimensions; the *turmoil* dimension, however, is found in both periods.

The correlation matrix of Table 1 illustrates the changes in shared variance that revolutions and guerrilla war have which may result in their separation in the 1955-57 study and their merger in this study. The correlation of the two for the 1955-57 data is only .33, while for 1958-60 it is .65. In addition to the fact of an increase in shared variance from the 1955-57 period, the absolute magnitudes and means for revolutions and guerrilla war have also increased. During 1955-57 *(N = 77)* there were 17 codings for the presence of guerrilla warfare and 44 revolutions with means of .21 and .57 respectively; on the other hand, during 1958-60 ($N = 83$), there were 58 codings for the presence of guerrilla warfare and 83 revolutions with means of .70 and 1.00 respectively.

Although 1958-60 domestic conflict behavior has a slightly different structure in comparison with the earlier period, foreign conflict behavior bears a remarkable similarity across the two points in time.

Dimensions of Foreign Conflict Behavior

The dimensions of 1958-60 foreign conflict behavior appear to reflect a strong similarity of structure with the 1955-57 dimensions with respect to the *type* of variables which define the clusters as well as to the magnitude and *pattern* of the loadings themselves. For example, the *war, diplomatic,* and *belligerency* dimensions do emerge from the 1958-60 data and the intraclass correlations are relatively high.

The previously mentioned change in the ratio of high to total correlations among the foreign measures in Table 1 might account for the slightly weaker loadings and consequent smaller amount of explained variance for the 1958-60 data. Not only are the correlations among the foreign variables lower than in the earlier

---

[17] The range of the multiple R is $\geqslant 0 \leqslant +1.0$. Thus R cannot be negative. In order to see whether the time lag resulted in any negative relationships between domestic and foreign conflict behavior, reference was made to the zero order correlations. None of the negative correlations was greater than $r = -.08$.

period; the intensity of conflict behavior appears to have decreased also. The most extreme change can be seen in one of the measures of intensity—number killed due to foreign conflict behavior. The total for 1955-57 is 51,123 with a mean value of 664, while for 1958-60 the total is 974 with a mean of 11.74.

Hence, foreign conflict behavior appears to be slightly less correlated and somewhat less intense during the 1958-60 period, but nonetheless is compares quite well with the earlier period as regards the dimensions of conflict behavior.

Relations between Domestic and Foreign Conflict Behavior

The merged factor analysis and the regression of both forms of conflict behavior on one another suggest only a small relationship between the two. A stronger relationship was expected on the basis of the theories of scholars such as Lewis Coser and Georg Simmel:

1. The unity of a group is frequently lost when it does not have an opponent (Simmel, 1955, p. 97).

2. Hostilities preclude the group boundaries from disappearing and they are frequently consciously cultivated to guarantee existing conditions (Simmel, 1955, p. 97).

3. If a group with basic consensus regarding its preservation engages in outside conflict, internal cohesion is likely to be increased (Coser, 1956, pp. 92-93).

4. Groups may look for enemies to help maintain and/or increase internal cohesion (Coser, 1956, p. 104).

5. Exaggeration of the danger of an enemy serves to maintain group structure when it is threatened by internal dissension (Coser, 1956, p. 106).

Whereas Simmel and Coser agree as to the tendency for between-group relations to be largely a result of within-group relations, the experimental data of Muzafer Sherif and his colleagues suggest otherwise. Their general thesis is that intergroup attitudes and behavior are determined *primarily* by the nature of relations between groups and *not primarily* by the pattern of relations and attitudes within groups themselves (Sherif et al., 1961, p. 38; italics in original). They conclude, however, that when friendliness already characterizes between-group relations, harmonious in-group relations probably contribute to solutions of mutual problems between groups (Sherif et al., 1961, p. 200).

The theories and findings of Coser, Simmel and Sherif are based upon small groups. Thus, expectations at the national and international levels on the basis of their propositions should be qualified. The finding in this study of a small relationship between domestic and foreign conflict behavior, expecially with a time lag, can be viewed more clearly in the perspective of other empirical studies at the national and international levels.

Another theorist, Samuel Huntington, contends that a decrease in the frequency of interstate conflict is likely to increase the frequency of domestic violence.[18] He thus admits that some relationship exists between the internal and external conflict behavior of nations, but he asserts that it does not follow that external peace stimulates internal conflict or that there is any *necessary* relationship between the two. Furthermore, he admits that in this century the data appear to suggest a general relation between the inhibition of external war and the prevalence of internal war (Huntington, 1962, pp. 40–41). This agrees with Rummel's cross-sectional finding of a small inverse relationship between subversion and foreign conflict behavior (Rummel, 1964, p. 47); but little evidence is provided for Huntington's hypothesis in the present study.

Rummel also found a consistently positive relationship between domestic conflict behavior other than subversion and the *diplomatic* and *belligerency* dimensions. In the cross sectional correlations of Table 1 the highest correlations between domestic and foreign variables are between riots and troop movements (.40), and riots and anti-foreign demonstrations (.38). Since anti-foreign demonstrations help to define the *belligerency* dimension, and the riots variable does not appear on the *internal war* dimension, this study provides evidence in favor of a small positive relationship between domestic conflict behavior other than *subversion* and one of the variables which helps to define the *belligerency* dimension.

Another facet of the relationship between the *diplomatic* dimension and domestic conflict behavior is suggested by Joseph McKenna (1962). McKenna suggests some internal effects of diplomatic behavior. He contends that diplomatic protests may function to assure domestic interests that the government is active on their problems and to provide propaganda for home consumption so that the general public may become aroused in support of the official policy toward the state to whom the protest is directed. More generally, he contends that the purpose of foreign policy is to influence external events so that domestic values are maintained and furthered (McKenna, 1962, p. 20; p. 26). Three of his findings bear directly on the theme of this study. He finds that the nations to whom United States protests were directed most frequently were characterized by revolution and other forms of domestic turmoil. Secondly, protest to major powers was less likely than to minor powers because the internal stability of the former probably minimized the number of offensive incidents directed at United States citizens. Thirdly, resistance to American demands was motivated by the domestic politics of the recipient (McKenna, 1962, p. 20; pp. 38–40; p. 201). The first two

---

[18]Although Huntington's hypotheses deal with the relationship between internal and external conflict behavior, he appears to have the international system as the unit of focus rather than the individual nations. In order for the propositions from the 1955–57 and 1958–60 studies to be comparable to Huntington's, one would have to sum each variable across all the nations and then examine the relationship between domestic and foreign conflict behavior at the *system* level. The design of this study, however, uses the *nation* as the unit, and examines the internal and external relationship across each nation.

propositions suggest a positive relationship between domestic and foreign conflict behavior. Thus, he suggests a positive relationship between protests, on the *diplomatic* dimension, and revolution and/or turmoil. But, in the present study, the highest correlation between protests and a domestic variable is that with riots (.29), and in the oblique biquartimin matrix of the merged factor analysis, riots and revolutions appear on factors different from protests (cf. Tables 1 and 5).

The studies of Sorokin (1937) and Richardson (1960) may also be relevant to interpreting the findings in the present study. Sorokin visually examines data through seventeen centuries, 525 A.D. to 1925, and finds a small association between unsuccessful external wars and internal disturbances. As with the present study, he concludes that the presence or absence of general war and internal disturbances are fairly independent of one another (Sorokin, 1937, p. 487; p. 492).

From 1820 to 1945, Richardson finds 112 mainly internal as compared with 137 mainly external fatal quarrels (Richardson, 1960, p. 186).[19] Even though he is primarily interested in the relationship between deadly quarrels and such variables as the rate of armaments increase, trade, language differences, contiguity, and other nonconflict variables, he does allude to the possible relationship between intranation solidarity and external threats (Richardson, 1960, p. 156). But a proposition about such a relationship does not emerge from his data, nor does he subject one to systematic test.

Implications of Findings for Theory Construction

The principal finding of a small relationship between domestic and foreign conflict behavior may have implications for theory-building. There may be no "simple" relationship between domestic and foreign conflict behavior, but there may be a causal relationship which is being obscured by other phenomena. That is, the relationship may be mediated by a third variable such as the personality characteristics of the national decision-makers as is suggested by Haas and Whiting (1956, pp. 61-62).

Evidence against the "third variable" interpretation for *aggregate* data, however, is provided by the Dimensionality of Nations Project of which the present work is a substudy. The 22 domestic and foreign conflict behavior measures were included in a factor analysis of 236 national and international characteristics across 82 nations. A domestic and a foreign conflict behavior dimension came out *separate* from one another as well as from economic development, political

---

[19]A fatal quarrel is a war in which a nation was involved which resulted in more than 3,163 deaths, e.g., more than $\log_{10}$ (deaths) = 3.5. Richardson contends that there is ambiguity as regards the classification of some forms of fatal quarrels; consequently, he categorizes them in three groups: mainly internal, mixed, and mainly external (1960, ch. 2; pp. 186-87).

orientation, and Catholic culture dimensions. The fact that domestic and foreign conflict behavior dimensions remain separate within the larger context adds evidence that they are unrelated to other aggregate data at one point in time. Thus, having *controlled* for such things as the level of development, political orientation, and Catholic culture, the domestic and foreign conflict behavior dimensions remain separated. (Cf. Rummel, Guetzkow, Sawyer, and Tanter, *Dimensions of Nations*, forthcoming, 1966.)

The "third variable" interpretation, however, may be valid for individual level characteristics as distinct from aggregate data. It may prove theoretically useful to inquire into the nature of the decision-maker's characteristics in order to see whether the relationship between domestic and foreign conflict behavior would increase. For example, the decision-making scheme presented by Richard Snyder and Glenn Paige (1958) might be relevant for suggesting third variables that mediate between the domestic and foreign conflict behavior relationship.

Summary

The goal of this study was to replicate an earlier work (Rummel, 1963) in order to obtain additional evidence relative to the dimensions of conflict behavior and the relationship between domestic and foreign conflict behavior. Data were collected across eighty-three nations on nine domestic and thirteen foreign measures of conflict behavior for 1958, 1959, and 1960. From a factor analysis of these data there emerged two domestic dimensions—*turmoil,* and *internal war*—and three foreign dimensions—*war, diplomatic,* and *belligerency.*

The *turmoil* dimension compares favorably with a similar dimension derived from the 1955–57 data, while the *internal war* dimension subsumes the *revolutionary* and *subversive* dimensions from the 1955–57 study. The three 1958–60 foreign dimensions are quite similar to the three derived from the 1955–57 foreign measures.

From a factor analysis of domestic and foreign conflict behavior, the domestic measures separated themselves from the foreign variables, implying only a small relationship between the two. This relationship was investigated still further with multiple regression. Representative variables were selected on the basis of high correlation with the dimensions. Representative variables which indexed domestic and foreign dimensions were regressed upon each other to discover the relationship between domestic and foreign conflict behavior. The regression yielded a small relationship between domestic and foreign conflict behavior that increased with a time lag.

Three error variables were used to discover the extent to which systematic bias might distort the conclusions. Two of these, number of cards per nation in *Deadline Data* and number of embassies or legations in a country, were found to correlate highly with the protest variable and also to have high pattern values on the *diplomatic* dimension. It was concluded that the level of world interest in a nation is related to the tendency for a nation's protests and (to a lesser extent) its expulsion of ambassadors to be reported. Hence, propositions about these two conflict measures should be qualified to the extent that the data of nations in which little interest is expressed *may not* be included in the correlations from which the propositions are inferred.

Propositions

The following generalizations are offered on the basis of an analysis of domestic and foreign conflict behavior for 1958-60:

1. The 1958-60 domestic conflict behavior of nations varies along two uncorrelated dimensions of equal importance—*turmoil* and *internal war*. The *turmoil* dimension is quite similar to the 1955-57 *turmoil* dimension, and the *internal war* dimension subsumes the 1955-57 *revolutionary* and *subversive* dimensions.

2. The 1958-60 foreign conflict behavior of nations varies along three uncorrelated dimensions of the following order of importance: *diplomatic, war,* and *belligerency,* which compares favorably with the 1955-57 foreign dimensions.

3. Acts or occurrences of 1958-60 domestic conflict behavior are generally highly related in a manner similar to that for 1955-57.

4. Acts or occurrences of 1958-60 foreign conflict behavior are generally highly related, but not as highly related as that for 1955-57.

5. There is a small relationship between 1958-60 domestic and foreign conflict behavior which increases with a time lag.

6. Five representative variables measure the dimensions of domestic and foreign conflict behavior for 1958-60: anti-government demonstrations (*turmoil*); revolutions (*internal war*); protest (*diplomatic*); war (*war*); and severance of diplomatic relations (*belligerency*). These compare favorably with the representative variables for 1955-57: anti-government demonstrations (*turmoil*); revolutions (*revolutionary*); guerrilla warfare (*subversion*); foreign killed (*war*); expulsion or recall of ambassadors (*diplomatic*); and severance of diplomatic relations (*belligerency*).

7. Level of world interest in a nation is associated with the tendency for its protests and expulsions of ambassadors to be reported.

Appendix I

DEFINITIONS OF CONFLICT BEHAVIOR MEASURES

The criteria by which the conflict behavior measures were chosen and brief definitions of the measures themselves are the same as those used in the 1955-57 study.

Measures of Conflict Behavior

With respect to the methods and goals of this study, any act or occurrence chosen to index conflict behavior must: (1) be capable of empirical delimitation; (2) be an act or occurrence of sufficient interest to be generally reported—that is, data must be available; (3) be applicable to all countries (e.g., "colonial violence," if made a measure, would not be applicable to those countries without colonies) if spurious factors are not to result; (4) be as diverse as possible to cover the greatest possible range of conflict behavior; and (5) be an act of or within, or an occurrence with respect to, seven or more countries (this is to prevent the correlations from being dependent on too few such happenings and, therefore, to reduce the role of aberrations on what are meant to be general conclusions).

On the basis of these criteria, nine measures of domestic and thirteen measures of foreign conflict were chosen for this study. The domestic conflict measures and a brief definition of the conflict aid or occurrence are as follows:

1. *Number of assassinations:* any politically motivated murder or attempted murder of a high government official or politician.

2. *Number of general strikes:* any strike of 1,000 or more industrial or service workers that involves more than one employer and that is aimed at national government policies or authority.

3. *Presence or absence of guerrilla warfare:* any armed activity, sabotage, or bombings carried on by independent bands of citizens or irregular forces and aimed at the overthrow of the present regime.

4. *Number of major government crises:* any rapidly developing situation that threatens to bring the downfall of the present regime—excluding situations of revolt aimed at such an overthrow.

5. *Number of purges:* any systematic elimination by jailing or execution of political opposition within the ranks of the regime or the opposition.

6. *Number of riots:* any violent demonstration or clash of more than 100 citizens involving the use of physical force.

7. *Number of revolutions:* any illegal or forced change in the top government elite, any attempt at such a change, or any successful or unsuccessful armed rebellion whose aim is independence from the central government.

8. *Number of anti-government demonstrations:* any peaceful public gathering of at least 100 people for the primary purpose of displaying or voicing their opposition to government policies or authority, excluding those demonstrations of a distinctly anti-foreign nature.

9. *Number of people killed in all forms of domestic violence:* any deaths resulting directly from violence of an intergroup nature, thus excluding deaths by murder and execution.

The measures of foreign conflict definitions are as follows:

1. *Number of anti-foreign demonstrations:* any demonstration or riot by more than 100 people directed at a particular foreign country (or group of countries) or its policies.

2. *Number of negative sanctions:* any nonviolent act against another country—such as boycott, withdrawal of aid—the purpose of which is to punish or threaten that country.

3. *Number of protests:* any official diplomatic communication or governmental statement, the purpose of which is to complain about or object to the policies of another country.

4. *Number of countries with which diplomatic relations severed:* the complete withdrawal from all official contact with a particular country.

5. *Number of ambassadors expelled or recalled:* any expelling of an ambassador from, or recalling for other than administrative reasons an ambassador to, a particular country – this does not involve expulsion or recall resulting from the severance of diplomatic relations.

6. *Number of diplomatic officials of less than ambassador's rank expelled or recalled:* replace "ambassador" by "officials of lesser . . . rank" in above definition.

7. *Number of threats:* any official diplomatic communication or governmental statement asserting that if a particular country does or does not do a particular thing it will incur negative sanctions.

8. *Presence or absence of military action:* any military clash of a particular country with another and involving gunfire, but short of war as defined below.

9. *Number of wars:* any military clash for a particular country with another and in which more than .02 percent of its population are militarily involved in the clash.

10. *Number of troop movements:* any rapid movement of large bodies of troops, naval units, or air squadrons to a particular area for the purpose of deterring the military action of another country, gaining concessions, or as a show of strength.

11. *Number of mobilizations:* any rapid increase in military strength through the calling up of reserves, activation of additional military units, or the de-mothballing of military equipment.

12. *Number of accusations:* any official diplomatic or governmental statement involving charges and allegations of a derogatory nature against another country.

13. *Number of people killed in all forms of foreign conflict behavior:* the total number of deaths resulting directly from any violent interchange between countries.

See Appendix I in the 1955–57 study (Rummel, 1963) for more extensive definitions.

Appendix II

LIST OF NATIONS

Afghanistan	Republic of China
Albania	Colombia
Argentina	Costa Rica
Australia	Cuba
Austria	Czechoslovakia
Belgium	Denmark
Bolivia	Dominican Republic
Brazil	Ecuador
Bulgaria	El Salvador
Burma	Ethiopia
Cambodia	Finland
Canada	France
Ceylon	Germany (DDR)
Chile	Germany (Fed. Rep.)
China	Greece

Guatemala	Paraguay
Haiti	Peru
Honduras	Philippines
Hungary	Poland
India	Portugal
Indonesia	Rumania
Iran	Saudi Arabia
Iraq	Spain
Irish Republic	Sweden
Israel	Switzerland
Italy	Thailand
Japan	Turkey
Jordan	Union of South Africa
Korea (Dem. Rep.)	USSR
Korea (Rep. of)	UK
Lebanon	USA
Liberia	Uruguay
Libya	Venezuela
Mexico	Yugoslavia
Nepal	Laos
Netherlands	N. Vietnam
New Zealand	S. Vietnam
Nicaragua	Morocco
Norway	Sudan
Outer Mongolia	Tunisia
Pakistan	UAR
Panama	

REFERENCES

Carroll, J. B. "Biquartimin Criterion for Rotation to Oblique Simple Structure in Factor Analysis," *Science,* 126, 3283 (Nov. 1957), 1114–15.

Cattell, R. "The Culture Patterns Discoverable in the Syntal Dimensions of Existing Nations," *Journal of Social Psychology,* 32 (1950), 215–53.

————. "The Dimensions of Culture Patterns of Factorization of National Characters," *Journal of Abnormal and Social Psychology,* 44 (1949), 443–69.

———— et al. "An Attempt at More Refined Definition of the Cultural Dimensions of Syntality in Modern Nations," *American Sociological Review,* 17 (1951), 408–21.

Coser, Lewis A. *The Functions of Social Conflict.* Glencoe, Ill.: Free Press, 1956.

Eckstein, H. "The Incidence of Internal Wars, 1946–59." Appendix I of *Internal War: The Problem of Anticipation,* report submitted to Research Group in Psychology and the Social Sciences, Smithsonian Institution, January 15, 1962.

———— (ed.). *Internal War.* New York: Free Press, 1964.

Edwards, A. L. "Experiments: Their Planning and Execution." In G. Lindzey (ed.), *Handbook of Social Psychology*. Cambridge, Mass.: Addison Wesley, 1954, 259-88.

Ezekiel, M., and K. A. Fox. *Methods of Correlation and Regression Analysis*. New York: Wiley, 1959.

Haas, E. R., and A. S. Whiting. *Dynamics of International Relations*. New York: McGraw-Hill, 1956.

Haggard, Ernest A. *Intraclass Correlation and the Analysis of Variance*. New York: Dryden Press, 1958.

Harmon, H. *Modern Factor Analysis*. Chicago: University of Chicago Press, 1960.

Huntington, S. P. "Patterns of Violence in World Politics." In S. P. Huntington (ed.), *Changing Patterns of Military Politics*. New York: Free Press, 1962, 17-50.

Kaiser, H. F. "The Applications of Electronic Computers to Factor Analysis," *Education and Psychological Measurement,* 19 (1959), 413-20.

————. "The Varimax Criterion for Analytic Rotation in Factor Analysis," *Psychometrika,* 23, 3 (Sept. 1958), 187-200.

Katz, D. "Field Studies." In H. Festinger and D. Katz (eds.), *Research Methods in the Behavioral Sciences*. New York: Dryden Press, 1953, 56-97.

McKenna, Joseph C. *Diplomatic Protest in Foreign Policy*. Chicago: Loyola University Press, 1962.

Richardson, Lewis F. *Statistics of Deadly Quarrels*. Pittsburgh, Pa.: Boxwood Press, 1960.

Rosecrance, Richard N. *Action and Reaction in World Politics*. Boston: Little, Brown, 1963.

Rummel, R. J. "The Dimensions of Conflict Behavior Within and Between Nations," *General Systems Yearbook,* 8 (1963), 1-50.

————. "Testing Some Possible Predictors of Conflict Behavior Within and Between Nations," Proceedings of the Peace Research Conference, Nov. 18-19, 1963.

————. "Dimensions of International Relations in the Mid-1950s." Forthcoming, 1966.

————, Harold Guetzkow, Jack Sawyer, and Raymond Tanter. *Dimensions of Nations*. Forthcoming, 1966.

Sherif, M., et al. *Intergroup Conflict and Cooperation: The Robbers Cave Experiment*. Norman: University of Oklahoma Institute of Group Relations, 1961.

Sidman, M. *Tactics of Scientific Research*. New York: Basic Books, 1960.

Simmel, Georg. *Conflict and the Web of Intergroup Affiliations*. Glencoe, Ill.: Free Press, 1955.

Snyder, R., and G. Paige. "The United States Decision to Resist Aggression in Korea: The Application of an Analytical Scheme," *Administrative Science Quarterly,* 3 (1958), 341-78.

Sorokin, P. *Social and Cultural Dynamics,* Vol. III. New York: American Book, 1937.

Wright, Quincy. *A Study of War*. Chicago: University of Chicago Press, 1942.

————. "The Nature of Conflict," *Western Political Quarterly,* 4 (June 1951), 193-209.

Part III

RELATIVELY NONINSTITUTIONALIZED INTERNATIONAL RELATIONS

Much human behavior can be predicted because people follow established patterns of conduct.[1] The patterns are adhered to and followed because there is normative consensus about them. The people involved know what the rules are, think adherence is proper, utilize sanctions to ensure conformity, and believe such sanctions are legitimate. Established procedures of this kind are institutionalized.[2]

Institutionalization, even within a society, is never total. Consensus is never complete; every group within a society has its own institutionalized patterns; all societal patterns do not fit together in an integrated fashion; and the patterns are never sufficiently specific to fully regulate conduct in any particular circumstance.

Clearly, much human behavior cannot be accounted for by institutionalization. People also act expressively—individually and collectively; they act expediently; and they are coerced and manipulated.[3] Certainly, even such conduct has some

---

[1]For a comprehensive discussion of the variety of norms and their relationship to conduct, see Judith Blake and Kingsley Davis, "Norms, Values, and Sanctions," *Handbook of Modern Sociology*, Robert E. L. Faris, ed. (Chicago: Rand-McNally, 1964), pp. 456–484.

[2]Although institutionalization is basic concept in sociological thought, definitions of it vary. See Peter M. Blau, *Exchange and Power in Social Life* (New York: John Wiley and Sons, 1964), esp. pp. 273–280; J. O. Hertzler, *American Social Institutions* (Boston: Allyn and Bacon, 1961), esp. pp. 92–119; and Talcott Parsons, *The Social System* (Glencoe, Ill.: The Free Press, 1951), esp. pp. 36–45.

[3]See, for example, Ralf Dahrendorf, *Class and Class Conflict in Industrial Society* (Stanford, Calif.: Stanford University Press, 1959); Everett C. Hughes, "Institutions," *New Outline of the Principles of Sociology*, Alfred McClung Lee, ed. (New York: Barnes and Noble, 1946), esp. pp. 236–247; Kurt Lang and Gladys E. Lang, *Collective Dynamics* (New York: Crowell and Co., 1961), pp. 489–542; and Neil Smelser, *Theory of Collective Behavior* (New York: The Free Press of Glencoe, 1963), pp. 270–381.

219

normative and consensual components, but we consider such conduct to be relatively noninstitutionalized.

Despite the complexity of the concept of institutionalization, it is useful in studying international relations and international conflict. The patterning of conduct by institutions represents a relatively high degree of integration and to some extent prevents the emergence of conflict. Even conflict based upon misunderstanding is less likely when parties can accurately predict each other's conduct, and institutionalization increases predictability. If there is conflict, institutionalized procedures for its regulation makes war a less probable means of resolving the conflict. The institutionalized procedures provide the means for reaching a collective decision.

In Part III of this book, the selections largely refer to relatively noninstitutionalized patterns of conduct. They are important in their own right: they are significant because so much of international relations is relatively noninstitutionalized. Lacking shared norms and agreement about sanctions, governmental and nongovernmental persons of different countries often interact expediently, calculatively, and expressively, without accurate knowledge of how the other party will respond. There still may be regularities in such relations whose patterns can be discerned. Knowledge of such regularities are essential to predict and understand international relations.[4]

Noninstitutionalized patterns of conduct are also important because they underlie the development and maintenance of institutionalized patterns. If certain patterns of conduct recur, expectations develop about their perpetuation and these expectations may begin to take on a normative character. In time, the patterns may become formally institutionalized. International law, in part, is an explicit codification of the recurrent international conduct of governments.[5]

Conversely, if conditions that shape the non-normative patterns of conduct alter, so will the conduct; this strains the institutionalized patterns that had emerged. Thus the rules of conduct embodied in the United Nations have been under strain and have been altered as the UN composition and the relations among the members have radically changed.

Finally, the movement of people and ideas across political boundaries are, in many essential ways, noninstitutionalized. They affect every society and thus affect every government's foreign policy. They tend to make societies more alike in technology, practices, values, and norms and this facilitates the development

---

[4]For discussions of bargaining and negotiations, see, for example Harold W. Kuhn, issue editor, "Game Theory, Bargaining, and International Relations," *The Journal of Conflict Resolution,* VI (March, 1962); and Thomas C. Schelling, *The Strategy of Conflict* (Cambridge, Mass.: Harvard University Press, 1960).

[5]William D. Coplin, "International Law and Assumptions about the State System," *World Politics,* 615–634 (July, 1965).

of shared understandings and the institutionalization of patterns of intergovernmental relations.[6] This is not a uniform process and relations between particular
pairs of sets of nations may become closer as, for example, ethnic or ideological
bonds are fashioned.[7] This, in turn, affects the relationship between such pairs
or sets of countries and other countries of the world.

The selections in Chapter Five deal particularly with nongovernmental international relations. They focus upon the movements and communications between
peoples as tourists, relatives, and students. Such movements and communications,
obviously, are regulated by governments to varying degrees. Each government, in
expressing domestic and international policies, exercises some control. That control is also affected by considerations of reciprocity between governments and
this is a basis for the development of some shared understandings about such control. The actual interaction of the people involved in the movement, however,
are not usually highly regulated, at least in their international aspects.

In Part II of the book, the selections indicated some of the consequences of
such transnational communications and interactions, particularly upon the participants. Hall and Whyte (in Selection 15) suggest some additional possible consequences; their emphasis upon the possible misunderstandings arising from
cross-cultural efforts at communication is important and should be compared to
the findings reported, for example, by Reigrotski and Anderson (Selection 5).

The papers by Angell (Selection 13), Deutsch (Selection 14), and Galtung
(Selection 16) examine the flow of transactions over time and among different
sets of political units. One deceptively simple and yet fundamental question is
whether or not the rate of interaction among the peoples of the world is increasing over time. The data presented by Angell and Deutsch seem to give different
answers to the question. But they are looking at different time periods, different
phenomena, and using different ways of measuring international transactions.
Deutsch utilizes the ratio of foreign to domestic transactions, whereas Angell
uses absolute figures. A ratio indicates the degree of international integration of
a country relative to the transactions within the country's own borders. It is possible that the volume of international transactions increases and the ratio declines because there is an even higher increase in the domestic transactions. Similarly, we may consider countries which vary in size: larger ones tend to have

---

[6]On the extent of similarities among societies of the world, due to mutual influence and to
independent covergence, see Pitrim A. Sorokin, "Mutual Convergence of the United States
and the U.S.S.R. to the Mixed Sociocultural Type," *International Journal of Comparative
Sociology*, 1, 143–176 (September, 1960); Irving Louis Horowitz, *Three Worlds of Development* (New York: Oxford University Press, 1966), esp. pp. 47–72; Robert C. Angell et al.,
"Social Values and Foreign Policy of Soviet and American Elites," *Journal of Conflict Resolution*, VIII (December, 1964); and Ernest Gellner, *Thought and Change*, (Chicago: The
University of Chicago Press, 1964.)

[7]For example, see Dudley Kirk and Earl Huck, "Overseas Migration from Europe since World
War II," *American Sociological Review*, 19, 447–455 (August, 1954).

much more foreign mail than do smaller nations, but the proportion of foreign mail to population or to domestic mail is less.[8] A large country then may appear to be less internationally integrated, but its role in the international network of mail transactions can still be relatively great.

One of the fundamental questions pertaining to the flow of international transactions is the extent to which they follow governmental ally and adversary ties or are affected by other factors such as size, wealth, geographical position, or relative ranking of the country in political blocs. The selections by Angell and Galtung and other studies indicate that each factor may play a role—but its significance varies for different kinds of transactions.[9] Galtung's paper presents much data on governmental transactions and should also be considered in the context of Chapter Seven. At present what is noteworthy is the evidence that interaction between the two major blocs in the world is largely chanelled through the leaders of the two blocs and that such patterning of interaction is much more evident for governmental than for nongovernmental transactions.

The selections in Chapter Six deal with governmental efforts to influence the peoples of other countries. This may be by agreement between the governments of the people, as in technical assistance and cultural exchange programs, or there may not be any agreement, as in psychological warfare and subversion. In either case, the effort is to influence, maintain, change, or overthrow the government in another country. This may be viewed, too, as a way of resolving a conflict. Changing another government or the domestic pressures influencing it can alter that government's pursuit of foreign objectives so that a conflict no longer exists. If a leader of one government believes that such changes are likely in an adversary, he may not risk direct organized violence as a means of attaining his objectives.

Gross (Selection 17) discusses some of the major ways in which one government may attempt to induce change in another country. Riley and Cottrell (Selection 18) summarize some of the findings regarding psychological warfare.[10]

---

[8]Jack Sawyer, "Dimensions of Nations: Size, Wealth, and Politics," *The American Journal of Sociology,* 73, 145–172 (September, 1967).

[9]Sawyer, *op. cit.,* Frank Thistlethwaite, "Migration from Europe Overseas in the Nineteenth and Twentieth Centuries," *Population Movements in Modern European History,* Herbert Moller, ed. (New York: Macmillan Co., 1964), pp. 73–92; and Karl W. Deutsch, "Communication Theory and Political Integration," *The Integration of Political Communities,* Philip E. Jacob and James V. Toscana, eds. (New York: J. B. Lippincott Co., 1964), pp. 46–74.

[10]For further material on psychological warfare and propaganda, see William E. Daughty in collaboration with Morris Janowitz, *A Psychological Warfare Casebook* (Baltimore, Md.: The Johns Hopkins Press, 1958); Daniel Lerner, ed., *Propaganda in War and Crisis* (New York: George W. Stewart, 1951); and Alexander L. George, *Propaganda Analysis* (Evanston, Ill.: Row, Peterson, and Co., 1959).

Wilson and Bonilla (Selection 19) report upon a series of studies of exchange of persons' programs.[11] Although all these papers indicate considerations and tactics which can make governmental efforts more or less successful, they also reveal the profound limitations to such efforts. For example, to be effective, appeals to the people of another country must be relevant and congenial to them. But this means that radical changes cannot be induced from the outside; internal conditions must have some congruence with the appeals. On the other hand, a government making appeals in its efforts to influence another people is constrained by its own objectives and commitments; thus Nazi Germany could not exploit the possibilities of anti-Soviet sentiments among Russians because of its own ideology and political objectives.[12] The studies reveal other dilemmas; for example, it may be possible to have greater influence upon young persons from another country, but the consequences upon the other society will be less than if leaders of the other country were influenced—yet doing this is much more difficult.

The selections in Chapter Seven pertain to governmental international relations. The papers by Lieberman (Selection 20) and by Raser and Crow (Selection 21) use experimental data to test and develop ideas about the international conduct of government officials. Such experiments can only examine certain aspects of the complex totality of intergovernmental relations, but those aspects can be examined under varying conditions while other aspects are held constant. Lieberman points out that persons acting expediently and calculating their own self-interest nevertheless will often act in a trustworthy fashion. In a series of interactions, honoring one's commitments, even if detrimental to one's immediate interests, will serve one's long run interests. This is the basic source of the self-enforcing character of much international law.[13] Normative elements may be

---

[11]On the Peace Corps, see, for example: Morris I. Stein, *Volunteers for Peace* (New York: John Wiley and Sons, 1966); and R. B. Textor, ed., *Cultural Frontiers and the Peace Corps* (Cambridge, Mass.: Massachusetts Institute of Technology Press, 1966); on student exchange, see, for example: John Useem and Ruth Hill Useem, *The Western Educated Man in India: A Study of His Social Roles and Influence* (New York: Dryden Press, 1955); Jeanne Watson and Ronald Lippitt, *Learning Across Cultures: A Study of Germans Visiting America* (Ann Arbor, Mich.: University of Michigan Press, 1955); and George V. Coelho, issue editor, "Impacts of Studying Abroad," *The Journal of Social Issues,* XVII(1) (1962).

[12]George Fischer, *Soviet Opposition to Stalin: A Case Study in World War II* (Cambridge, Mass.: Harvard University Press, 1952).

[13]For a comprehensive discussion of the extent to which international behavior is normatively oriented and of the constraints serving to maintain the international law, see Morton A. Kaplan and Nicholas deB. Katzenback, *The Political Foundations of International Law,* (New York: John Wiley and Sons, 1961).

added, but are not always necessary nor sufficient for the maintenance of international commitments.[14]

Self-interested, non-normative interaction is affected by a wide variety of conditions. The power of the interacting parties and the technology of the means of violence are certainly an important condition in international intergovernmental relations. Raser and Crow utilize Inter-Nation Simulation[15] to test some ideas about deterrence, given two weapon systems. In the experiments reported, persons simulate five countries divided into two blocs. Each bloc had one powerful country with nuclear weapons. The experimental variation was that one nation had an invulnerable nuclear weapons system during some runs of the experiment. As an invulnerable weapons system, consider a number of Polaris submarines deployed in the open seas; they could not be destroyed by a nuclear attack of an adversary.[16] Raser and Crow indicate the variety of consequences of one state, in a cold-war environment, attaining such a system.

Holsti, Brody, and North (Selection 22) and Etzioni (Selection 23) analyze an actual series of intergovernmental events. Holsti, Brody, and North use a variety of data to examine in detail the Cuban missile crisis of 1962 in order to understand why the crisis did not erupt into a nuclear exchange or other forms of warfare. In addition to the processes and conditions they analyze, we may consider others related to the findings from other selections in this book. The recurrent crises between the United States and the Soviet Union since the end of World War II have been resolved without direct open warfare. Experience with crises may have made them appear less encompassing and more amenable to at least a short-run solution. Thus Galtung (Selection 16) found that the number of diplomats between the NATO and the Warsaw Pact countries who were expelled rose with each major cold-war crisis, but the rise was smaller in each succeeding crisis. See, too, Smoker's observations about arms races and the integration of the international system (Selection 27). Finally, the working of deterrence in the full context of a concrete historical situation should be compared to the findings of Raser and Crow.

[14]For discussions of the normative and non-normative bases of reciprocity, see Alvin W. Gouldner, "The Norm of Reciprocity," *American Sociological Review*, 25, 161–178; (April, 1960); Louis Kriesberg, "Non-Normative Reciprocity: Critique of Gouldner's 'The Norm of Reciprocity,'" Clearing House for Sociological Literature, University of Wisconsin-Milwaukee, CFSL 66–10, ME-66/46; and Blau, *Exchange and Power in Social Life, op. cit.,* esp. 91–97.

[15]For detailed description and discussion of Inter-Nation Simulation, see Harold Guetzkow et al., *Simulation in International Relations: Developments for Research and Teaching* (Englewood Cliffs, N.J.: Prentice-Hall, 1963).

[16]The technology of weapons and social and political conditions also, of course, have implications for the possibility of arms control. See, for example, John R. Raser, "Weapons Design and Arms Control: The Polaris Example," *The Journal of Conflict Resolution*, 9, 450–462 (December, 1965); and Donald G. Brennan, ed., *Arms Control, Disarmament, and National Security* (New York: George Braziller, 1961).

Etzioni (Selection 23) analyzes the sequence of events in U.S. and U.S.S.R. relations following the Cuban missile crisis in order to test some ideas about unilateral initiatives. His discussion reveals some of the contributions that can be made by this form of interaction. When direct verbal communication and negotiation may be hampered by feelings and expectations of hostility, unilateral actions can be an effective means of communication. After some reciprocation, more formal negotiation is possible. The analysis also reveals the limits to such communication. Improved communication does not change the objective conditions and sets of interests in contention between parties, although it may permit mutual and complementary interests to become more visible.

Changes in the relative importance of various interests can alter the direction of policy and in this sense governmental objectives emerge from interaction with other governments and are affected by the mode of collective decision making utilized. Thus, once a government has proclaimed a particular objective and threatened use of force to attain it, that objective assumes higher priority than it had before. This is true because domestic support is mobilized and commitments made to it and because, once enunciated, it seems vital to be consistent toward the opposing side so that one's credibility is enhanced. In relatively noninstitutionalized relations, self-enforcement of patterns of conduct is crucial and consistency contributes to that. This is one reason for the rigidity in much foreign policy and for the unwillingness of government leaders to admit errors. Anticipating this, each side tends to credit the other with commitment to the objectives asserted to be so important.

Once one issue is given very high priority, other issues are relatively downgraded. This results in a polarization of issues. Even when at the outset both parties may have been aware of many common and complementary interests, in the course of increasingly hostile conflict, those other interests do become less salient. Nongovernmental ties may be broken reducing the costs of further escalation of the controversy (see Selection 26).

Threat and counterthreat also affect the international system within which the parties are contending. These changes may hasten the further movement of the collective decision making efforts toward the use of violence. Other parties may take sides and increase the polarization of the international system. Whatever rules there may be about other modes of decision making are discounted as the coercive threats increase.

CHAPTER FIVE

Nongovernmental Relations

13. THE GROWTH OF TRANSNATIONAL PARTICIPATION

Robert C. Angell

A fruitful concept is one subsuming data that need to be held together if one is to make valid generalizations. This does not mean that the bundle of data thus held together always has the same consequences. Take the concept of bureaucracy, for instance. There has been much dispute about the effects of what we call bureaucracy, and we now believe that under certain conditions it has one set of effects, under other conditions another set. But few would deny that it is a useful concept because it puts together a cluster of relationships that is central to modern complex societies.

SOURCE Robert C. Angell, "The Growth of Transnational Participation," in *Journal of Social Issues,* XXIII (January, 1967), pp. 108–129. (Slightly abridged.) Reprinted by permission of the author and The Society for the Psychological Study of Social Issues. Copyright 1966 by the Society for the Psychological Study of Social Issues. The ideas in this article will be more fully developed in Professor Angell's forthcoming book, *The Creeping Vine of Peace,* to be published by D. Van Nostrand and Company.

TRANSNATIONAL PARTICIPATION

Transnational participation is a concept that will probably have increasing fruitfulness as communication and transportation draw the world closer together. In trying to isolate the right set of phenomena to be conceptualized, the importance of the idea of crossing national borders is obvious; but it is not at all obvious what set of relationships among persons from different nations needs to be specified. The term participation is designed to draw upon the work of the social psychologists who have found that certain kinds of relationships have much more profound influence on the value-orientations of the actors than others. These relationships are of two sorts: (a) those in which there is necessary collaboration in achieving common objectives, and (b) those in which there is an intimate living together. In the former the participants have a specific, in the latter, a diffuse relationship. In both the interaction is close. If these relationships have been established voluntarily, the result is usually some convergence of the value-orientations of the participants. If, on the other hand, the participants find themselves together involuntarily, the consequence may be hostility and divergence. In either case the effect is profound. Thus, the concept of transnational participation draws together data on relationships across borders that are fateful one way or the other.

This definition of transnational participation excludes much that could be termed transnational experience. The brief and fleeting contacts of the tourist, for instance, are omitted. *A fortiori,* distance communication through the mass media or via school textbooks is not included. Even international trade is beyond the pale unless the traders are functioning in some non-contractual grouping. And if they are, it is that grouping, not their trade, that makes them transnational participants.

A concept is developed because it is useful in thinking about a problem—either practical or scientific. Transnational participation is useful for both reasons. It is relevant to the problem of attaining world peace, since it refers to the intimate connection for good or ill of citizens of the units that make war, the nation-states. It is significant scientifically because sociologists are becoming interested in intersystem relations at all levels—interinstitutional as well as intermetropolitan and intersocietal. Participation across system boundaries is therefore a phenomenon in need of conceptualization. Transnational participation can become a subconcept under the broader term, intersystem participation.

From the standpoint of intersystem conflict or cooperation there are two central questions to be asked about any form of intersystem participation: (a) What are the effects on the connected systems? and (b) Is the participation growing or shrinking? I am investigating both of these questions for the transnational case, but I am here presenting material only on the second question. These data are of course, inconclusive for both the practical problem of peace and the theoretical problem of intersystem accommodation without data on the first question, but as trend data they have interest because they describe what is going on in the world.

The six categories of transnational participation that follow are not the fruit of theoretical analysis but are simply those in which existing statistical series are gathered. One category that is important is not represented. This is residence abroad in military service. So far, we have been unable to unearth reliable figures on which trend analysis could be based. Since for several of the categories adequate statistics have only recently been tabulated, the trends are those of the last decade. The time span covered varies, but the figures for different categories are made comparable by computing the rate of increase compounded annually.

PARTICIPATION—BY RENEWING FAMILY TIES

Perhaps the oldest and the simplest form of transnational participation is the visiting of relatives and friends abroad. Human migration must always have been followed by the desire to renew old ties. With the explosion outward of European populations in the nineteenth century and the ability to pay for transportation in the twentieth this form of participation has mushroomed. The only adequate statistics on the subject, however, come from the United States. Fortunately they cover movement in both directions.

The Aviation Department of the Port of New York Authority made a study of all passengers departing for overseas from its international airport (then Idlewild) in 1956–57. The study was repeated in 1963–64. The data are broken down in two ways—by American or foreign residence of the passenger and by European or Bermuda-Latin American destination. We have chosen to utilize data on both American and foreign residents because transnational participation is a two-way street, but have utilized only the Europe-bound trips because we wished to adjust the figures to include those going by ship, and such figures are more reliable for transatlantic than for other voyages.

The adult passengers in a carefully designed sample of all out-bound trips filled out questionnaires about themselves and their trips. They were asked the reasons for their journey and these were coded into eleven categories. One was visiting relatives and friends.

Since roughly two-thirds of all transatlantic flights from the United States originate in New York, we assume that the proportions of all transatlantic air travelers going to or returning from visits to relatives and friends will be much the same as those given by the Port of New York Authority. It is, of course, much more risky to assume that the same proportions hold for transatlantic passengers going by sea. Since, however, there are no data on the reasons for the sea voyages, we make that assumption as better than any other. The number of air and sea passages to Europe are compiled annually by the United States Immigration and Naturalization Service. It is unimportant that the Service distinguishes between Americans and foreigners on the basis of citizenship rather than residence (which was used by the Port of New York Authority).

The proportion of New York transatlantic departures of American residents for the purpose of visiting relatives and friends in 1956–57 was 28%. Of foreign residents returning from visits in the United States it was 15%. In 1963–64 the corresponding figures were 29% and 27%. If these percentages are applied to all air and sea departures from the United States in the two years we get Table 1.

The 112.3% increase in seven years for American citizens amounts to a yearly rate of increase of 14% (compounded). The greater increase for aliens of 398.1% for the same period yields a rate of increase of 25.8% per year. This rapid rise undoubtedly reflects the fact that the economic recovery of Europe is allowing older Europeans to visit relatives and friends in the United States who migrated before the onset of the Great Depression. Americans have been able to afford the reverse journey since World War II. Though the numbers visiting in Europe are still almost twice the numbers visiting in the United States, the disproportion is decreasing rapidly. If the trends shown were to continue (which is unlikely) the two movements would balance in the year of 1967. A point that is interesting, but irrelevant for our purposes, is that foreigners continue to use sea travel more than citizens of the United States.

PARTICIPATION–BY CONDUCTING BUSINESS

The second category of transnational participation on which we have data is sojourn abroad for business reasons. These data too are drawn from the two studies of the Port of New York Authority. We have attempted to include only sojourns that involve organic ties with business enterprises or businessmen abroad by omitting those who were coded as traveling to attend a convention or fair or those traveling for business and pleasure combined.

As in the case of visiting relatives and friends abroad we have extrapolated the percentages for both Americans and foreigners leaving the New York International Airport to all those leaving by sea and air from the United States for Europe. These percentages were 19% for Americans and 30% for aliens in 1956–57. In 1963–64 the corresponding figures were 20.4% and 26.6%. . . .

In this case the rates of increase are quite similar in both directions, that for the United States citizens amounting to a compound increase of 11.9% a year and for the foreign citizens one of 13.5%. The volume of travel of the United States citizens is not very much greater than that of the foreigners. This is a little surprising in view of the much greater United States investments in Europe than of European countries in the United States. Perhaps it is explained in part, by

TABLE 1. Transatlantic Travel to Visit Relatives and Friends

| | American Citizens Going to Visit in Europe | | | | Foreign Citizens Returning from Visits in the United States | | | |
| | | | Increase or (Decrease) | | | | Increase or (Decrease) | |
Means	1956–57	1963–64	Number	Per Cent	1956–57	1963–64	Number	Per Cent
By air	93,481	276,790	183,309	196.1	16,291	141,416	125,125	768.1
By sea	66,793	63,453	(3,340)	(5.0)	19,651	36,601	16,950	86.3
Total	160,274	340,243	179,969	112.3	35,952	178,017	142,075	398.1

the employment of foreign nationals as managers by American companies operating abroad.

The term sojourn perhaps aptly describes what is involved in most business trips. The stays are short. The involvement in the other country may be minor. It, therefore, becomes important to ask what are the trends so far as long periods of residence are concerned. Since the duration of actual stay in the case of natives is recorded in the Port of New York Authority surveys, we have constructed Table 2 to show the trends in stays of less than and more than one year. Here we note that both types of stays for both United States and foreign citizens are increasing rapidly but that increase is most rapid for long-term stays of foreigners and least for long-term stays of Americans. If we call the long-term stays residence abroad in contrast to sojourn, the rates of increase per year are as follows:

Residence of Americans abroad:	11.6%
Sojourn of Americans abroad:	12.0%
Sojourn of foreigners in the United States:	13.2%
Residence of foreigners in the United States:	25.8%

Although the numbers involved in the residence of foreigners in the United States for business purposes are small, the rate of increase is surprisingly large. It is a curious fact that it is almost identical with the rate of increase of foreigners visiting relatives and friends in this country. It would seem to be true that transatlantic transnational participation is becoming a more balanced process than it has been in the past.

A word of caution is in order about extending the findings on transatlantic visiting and business to the whole globe. Both series would undoubtedly show sharp increases in many parts of the world, but whether the rates would be increasing in all parts of the world as fast as they are across the Atlantic seems doubtful. Per capita income is not increasing as rapidly in most other parts of the world. Nor are there as many ties of relationship and business enterprise.

PARTICIPATION–BY STUDY ABROAD

For our third category of transnational participation– residence abroad for study–we do not have to rely on data from the United States alone, but can turn to the world data set forth in the UNESCO Statistical Yearbook for 1963. Unfortunately the data there are quite incomplete. For many countries the data on foreign students either have not been collected or have not been reported to UNESCO. Table 15, for instance, shows the total number of students in the institutions of the third level (higher education) for 125 countries, but Table 17 which records the number of foreign students, gives data for only 75 countries. And for only 45 of these 75 can good trend data be obtained; that is, a comparison of 1955 with 1961 (or in a few cases 1960).

TABLE 2. Duration of Trips of Transatlantic Travelers for Business Purposes

Duration	American Citizens Going to Europe					Foreign Citizens Returning from the United States				
	1956–57	1963–64	Increase			1956–57	1963–64	Increase		
			Number	Per Cent				Number	Per Cent	
Less than one year	97,881	216,377	118,496	121.1		70,445	168,088	97,643	138.6	
More than one year	10,876	22,978	12,102	111.8		1,438	7,186	5,748	399.7	
Total	108,757	239,355	130,598	120.1		71,883	175,274	103,391	143.8	

Before looking at the trends for these 45 countries it is important to indicate to what degree they can be regarded as representative of the world trend. First, one can estimate roughly the percentage of all students studying abroad. From Table 15 we learn that in 1961 there were 13,012,996 students in the institutions of higher education of the 125 countries. More than 61% of these were in the 45 countries for which we have trend data. The other 80 countries in the table contributed under 39% of the total.

The most damaging omission from the standpoint of knowing the world picture is the Union of Soviet Socialist Republics. It had 2,639,900 students in its institutions of higher education in 1961, the second largest number for any country. Foreign students are perhaps 1% of this total, or 26,400. Other important omissions are the Chinese Peoples Republic and the Philippines, each with nearly 300,000 students in higher education, and Argentina with nearly 200,000. If the rate of increase in foreign students in these four countries is sharply different from that in the 45 countries for which we have trend data, the latter may be misleading. . . .

The increase for the 45 countries over the six-year period is 78.4%. This is a yearly rate of increase of 10.0%. Although we cannot have great confidence in this figure as reflecting the world situation, it probably is based upon some 70% of the students in foreign institutions. Although the 45 countries included in this tabulation have only 61.5% of the students in 125 countries, their institutions tend to be the larger and better known ones and hence more attractive to students wishing to study abroad. We might guess, then, that there are some 270,000 foreign students in all countries.

Though the world figures are the significant ones, it is interesting to compare them with the trends as shown by the departures from New York International Airport expanded to the total sea and air departures for Europe. Using the same techniques described for other forms of transnational participation, we find the compound yearly increase in travel for study and research is 16.6% for Americans leaving for Europe and 18.3% for foreign citizens returning home. These higher rates of increase shown for study abroad on the world level are somewhat surprising since one might have assumed that the United States, as a country long in the business of scholarly exchange, might not show as high rates of increase as more recently participating nations.

Beside data on trends in numbers, the UNESCO Statistical Yearbook gives, in Table 18, data on foreign students by country of origin, in fifteen countries for 1960, 1961 or 1962. Although we cannot derive trends from this table, it does make possible an analysis of the types of relationships that are being established—whether study abroad is mostly confined within ideological blocs, whether it is mostly a matter of students from developed countries going to other developed countries, or whether it is students from underdeveloped countries going to developed countries, and the like. Unfortunately again the fifteen countries are not well distributed over the several types. None of them is a Communist country. Eight of them are Western European, and 10 of them are in the Western camp. The 15 nations are: Australia, Austria, Belgium, France, West Germany, Ireland, Italy, Japan, Mexico, Senegal, Switzerland, Syria, United Arab Republic, United Kingdom, United States. In view of their unrepresentative character we shall supplement the pattern of linkages shown by the recorded data by estimating the pattern of linkages for the countries with large numbers of foreign students not included in the 15, and then combine the two sets of data into an estimated world pattern.

In order to analyze the pattern of transnational participation through study abroad we will classify nations on two bases. One is ideological, the other concerns the degree of development. There are three categories in each: Western, uncommitted and Communist; and developed, semi-developed and underdeveloped. The ideological classification is the conventional one, though some difficult choices had to be made. Finland, Israel and Japan, for instance, were included among the Western nations, Yugoslavia and all the Latin American Countries except Cuba were classified as uncommitted.[1]

The work of Harbison and Myers, *Education, Manpower and Economic Growth,* (1964) was drawn upon for the developmental classifications. Gross national product per capita and their Composite Index of Human Resource Development were used as follows:

Developed Nations: at least $400 gross national product per capita and at least 53 or more on the Composite Index.
There criteria bring in all the Western nations given above except Spain, Portugal, Greece, and Turkey plus the following: Argentina, Uruguay, Soviet Union, Poland, East Germany, Czechoslovakia and Hungary.
Semideveloped Nations: those not qualifying as Developed, but that are above $200 gross national product per capita and above 20 on the Composite Index. These criteria bring in the following nations: Mexico, Cuba, Costa Rica, Panama, Columbia, Venezuela, Brazil, Chile, Portugal, Spain, Yugoslavia, Romania, Bulgaria, Albania, Greece, Turkey, Cyprus, Lebanon, South Africa and Malaysia.
Underdeveloped Nations: those not qualifying as either Developed or Semideveloped.

[1]The Western camp has the following members: United States, Canada, United Kingdom, Ireland, Iceland, Norway, Sweden, Finland, Denmark, West Germany, Netherlands, Belgium, Luxemburg, Switzerland, France, Spain, Portugal, Italy, Austria, Greece, Turkey, Israel, Australia, New Zealand, Japan, Republic of China, South Korea, South Vietnam and Hong Kong. The Communist bloc embraces: Soviet Union, Poland, East Germany, Czechoslovakia, Hungary, Rumania, Bulgaria, Albania, Mongolia, Peoples Republic of China, North Vietnam, North Korea and Cuba. All the rest of the nations are classified as uncommitted.

The ideological and developmental classifications yield a nine-fold table. In such a table there are 45 sorts of linkages including linkages of a country of a particular type with another country of the same type. To simplify matters we have combined cases like the following: the linkage of a Western developed country with an uncommitted semideveloped one, and the linkage of an uncommitted developed country with a Western semideveloped one. This reduces the type of linkage to 36. The situation is most easily expressed in terms of barriers crossed. Table 3 is drawn up in this manner. It will be noted how few linkages there are across the Communist barrier. This, of course, is because only students from Communist countries going to other countries for study could gain entrance into this table, since there is no Communist nation among the 15 comprising it to catch the reverse flow. Hence this table is almost worthless for considering the world situation.

As a basis for estimating the world situation there are two sets of relevant data in the UNESCO volume. Table 17 gives the number of foreign students in 1960 or 1961 for 29 nations in addition to the 45 for which comparisons can be made with 1955. Of these 74, full data are available on 15. An estimate of the numbers in various categories of countries-of-origin for the remaining 59 could be made; however, it hardly seems worth the effort for those having less than 500 foreign students. This cuts out 39. Left are the 20 for which we have established the types of countries from which their foreign students come. This has been done by examining the distributions in the countries that are near them geographically, or like them in either ideology or level of development. It is obvious that there are inadequate analogues for many of them.[2]

The other set of relevant data is contained in the UNESCO Table 15 where the total number of students in 126 countries is given. By applying percentages of foreign students in countries known to be similar in certain respects, the percentage of all their students that are foreign can be estimated. Only 13 further countries were estimated to have more than 500 foreign students.[3] For these 13, distributions have been estimated by the country of origin as in the case of those countries the number of whose foreign students is known. Table 4 gives the linkages for these 33 countries. Whereas Table 3 showed a large proportion studying abroad within the Western orbit, Table 4 shows about   one-third studying abroad within the Communist bloc. This is only natural since the Communist countries of study did not appear in Table 3.

[2]The 20 countries are Morocco, Uganda, Canada, Colombia, Uruguay, Venezuela, Hong Kong, India, Israel, Lebanon, Turkey, Bulgaria, Czechoslovakia, Greece, Netherlands, Poland, Rumania, Spain, Yugoslavia and New Zealand.

[3]The 13 countries are: S. Africa, Cuba, Argentina, Brazil, Peru, Peoples Republic of China, Iran, Philippines, Singapore, West Berlin, East Germany, Sweden and Union of Soviet Socialist Republic.

TABLE 3. Number of Foreign Students in 15 Countries in Relation to Barriers

	Both Western	Both Uncommitted	Both Communist	One Western, One Uncommitted	One Western, One Communist	One Uncommitted, One Communist	Total
Both developed	46,446			903	2,329		49,678
Both semideveloped		331		14	27		372
Both underdeveloped		7,323					7,323
One developed, one semideveloped	14,232	14		12,489	1,349		28,084
One developed, one underdeveloped	11,656	66		70,578			82,300
One semideveloped, one underdeveloped		1,136		84		4	1,224
Total	72,334	8,870	0	84,068	3,678	31	168,981

TABLE 4. Number of Foreign Students (Estimated) in 33 Countries in Relation to Barriers

	Both Western	Both Un-committed	Both Com-munist	One Western One Uncommitted	One Western One Communist	One UnCom-mitted, One Communist	Total
Both developed	4,685	348	15,953	606	846	68	22,515
Both semideveloped	899	835	195	1,282	336	940	4,487
Both underdeveloped	74	6,530	2,494	632		2,787	12,517
One developed, one semideveloped	1,294	2,236	5,341	3,098	614	1,005	13,588
One developed, one underdeveloped	165	1,644	3,190	6,558	58	8,365	20,080
One semideveloped, one underdeveloped	37	5,209	310	5,563	84	837	12,040
Total	7,254	16,794	27,483	17,739	1,955	14,002	85,227

Table 5 is a composite of Tables 3 and 4. If any reliance can be placed at all on the estimates in Table 4, it would give some inkling of the world picture. Note first that it shows 254,000 students abroad, somewhat less than the 270,000 thought likely on the basis of world enrollments in higher education. Since, however, there are 78 of the 126 nations represented in UNESCO Table 15 that have not been included because they probably have less than 500 foreign students each, the original estimate may be not far from the truth. An average of 200 apiece would bring the total to 270,000.

It is no surprise to find the largest group of students are those linking the uncommitted, underdeveloped countries with the developed, Western countries. Next most important is the group from one Western developed country studying in another. At a much lower level is the Communist interchange of the same kind. If one looks at the columns that show the interchange with uncommitted countries it appears that there is a 7 to 1 advantage in favor of the Western as against the Communist nations.

Review of the data on study abroad indicates that this form of transnational participation is increasing steadily, though not so fast as visiting relatives and friends, and sojourn for business reasons. Study abroad, however, is linking nations of very different kinds and may well, therefore, have a more profound influence on future relationships in the world.

PARTICIPATION—BY OFFERING TECHNICAL ASSISTANCE

The fourth category of transnational participation is technical assistance. Both bilateral and multilateral assistance are included. For bilateral trends we have only United States data; for multilateral, the data from the United Nations.

The United States has had a succession of agencies in the technical assistance field—the Mutual Security Agency, The Technical Cooperation Administration and the Agency for International Development—but statistics on civilian personnel involved in foreign aid programs have been kept continuously. From 1958 to 1964 the statistics seem to have been gathered in identical categories. . . .Information on American nationals abroad and foreign nationals brought to this country or sent to other countries for training, for the three years—1958, 1961 and 1964— [shows] the former upward trend in personnel has been reversed of recent years. The figures for yearly increases in this situation are meaningless because they represent a combination of two trends. If the recent one persists the mean yearly increase will go to zero or even become negative. It is clear that United States Technical Assistance is not at present a source of increasing transnational participation.

The situation with respect to United Nations Technical Assistance is different. Both the regular programs of technical assistance of the several Specialized

TABLE 5. Number of Foreign Students (Estimated) in 48 Countries in Relation to Barriers

	Both Western	Both Un-committed	Both Com-munist	One Western One Uncommitted	One Western One Communist	One Uncom-mitted, One Communist	Total
Both developed	51,131	340	15,953	1,509	3,192	68	72,193
Both semideveloped	899	1,166	195	1,296	336	967	4,859
Both underdeveloped	74	13,853	2,494	632		2,787	19,840
One developed, one semideveloped	15,526	2,250	5,341	15,587	1,963	1,005	41,672
One developed, one underdeveloped	11,921	1,710	3,190	77,136	58	8,365	102,380
One semideveloped, one underdeveloped	37	6,345	310	5,647	84	841	13,264
Total	79,588	25,664	27,483	101,807	5,633	14,033	254,208

Agencies and the Expanded Program financed by the Economic and Social Council (often in cooperation with the Specialized Agencies) are steadily growing. Table 6 gives the figures. It is obvious that the Expanded Program, though growing slowly, is rapidly losing ground to the programs of the Specialized Agencies. This mirrors the fact that the Specialized Agencies, which originally performed mainly clearing-house functions in the field of technical assistance, have more lately been carrying out field projects. Thus, there is more decentralization of the programs.

The overall rates of increase of the number of experts and of the holders of fellowships for training are modest but significant. It is apparent that even if bilateral technical assistance declines, as that of the United States seems likely to do, the multilateral programs are likely to grow and take over a larger share of the total effort.

PARTICIPATION–BY WORKING FOR INTERNATIONAL ORGANIZATIONS

The fifth sort of transnational participation to be examined is that connected with international nongovernmental organizations. These bring people from different countries together in a multilateral fashion to achieve common objectives. For their study the *Yearbook of International Organizations* published by the Union of International Associations is essential. Here we will analyze the trends as shown in the 1956–57 and 1962–63 editions.

The *Yearbook* includes both intergovernmental and nongovernmental organizations. In the analysis to follow the 177 intergovernmental organizations in the 1962–63 edition are excluded. Such are the units of the United Nations, the official bodies of the European Community, those of the Communist bloc, and technical organizations resulting from treaties like the International Wheat Council. This leaves 1,570 nongovernmental organizations.

Table 7 shows the comparison of 1962–63 with 1956–57 in mere numbers of such organizations, classified according to whether they are regional in name or in fact, whether they have a religious, ideological or ethnic limitation though otherwise potentially world-wide in scope (particularistic), or whether they are potentially world-wide and actually more than regional. The much higher rate of increase for regional organizations is largely due to the great proliferation of groups formed within the Common Market after that was established in 1958. Almost two-thirds of the growth in this category is accounted for by the 223 such organizations. But this would have been the fastest growing category in any case. One reason for this may be the resentment by the less developed countries of the dominance of Europeans in world-wide international organizations. Of all the organizations in the 1962–63 *Yearbook,* more than 85% had their

TABLE 6. Transnational Participation in the United Nations Technical Assistance Programs

	Experts			Fellowships		
	Expanded Program	Regular Program of Specialized Agencies	Total	Expanded Program	Regular Program of Specialized Agencies	Total
1956	2,346	549	2,895	2,128	1,041	3,169
1963	2,817	1,866	4,683	2,545	3,437	5,982
Increase 1956–63	471	1,317	1,788	417	2,396	2,813
% Increase	20.1	240.0	61.3	19.3	230.2	88.6
Compound Yearly % Increase	2.7	19.1	7.1	2.6	18.6	9.5

TABLE 7. Number of International Nongovernmental Organizations

	World-Wide	Particularistic	Regional	Date Insufficient to Classify	Total
1956–57	503	246	191	13	953
1962–63	677	312	555	26	1,570
Increase	174	66	364		617
% Increase	34.6	26.8	190.6		64.7
Compound Yearly					
% Increase	5.1	4.1	19.5		8.7

headquarters in Europe and more than 75% of their directors and officers were from Europe.

The rate of growth for all types of organization of 8.77% certainly underrepresents the rate at which new people are becoming involved in this form of transnational participation, since the existing organizations are growing at the same time that new ones are being added. Although we cannot obtain any data on individual activity in connection with nongovernmental organizations we can obtain data on how many involvements of countries there are in particular organizations. For this purpose, involvement of Americans in the activities of any nongovernmental organization would count as one involvement for the United States. We have not analyzed this matter for all the organizations but we have done so for a selected group of "globally oriented" ones. These are of three types: those whose aim is to strengthen political ties among nations, those that are in fact participating in a nonpolitical world system, like organizations of meteorologists and those whose main purpose is international understanding. . . .

It is clear . . . that, not only is the number of these globally oriented organizations growing, but the number of countries involved in each is doing so. For those existing at the beginning and end of the six-year span the mean yearly increase is 6.3%.

We can show the increasing participation in these organizations in still another way: by analyzing involvement in relation to the barriers discussed in connection with study abroad. The same three classes of ideological position and the same three classes of development are used in reaching the conclusions set for in Table 8. Here we see that only 5 organizations have gone backward in coverage, either ideologically or in terms of the development spectrum; 31 have increased their coverage. . . . These organizations involved 44% more countries in 1962–63 than in 1956–57. It is evident that the net gain of 26 organizations with broader coverage among 150 organizations (17%) means that about two-fifths of the expansion in involvement carries these organizations across barriers.

Our discussion of nongovernmental organizations can be summed up in three statements: (a) the number of such organizations is growing at almost 9% per year; (b) their involvement of countries is growing at 6.3% per year; and (c) both ideological and developmental barriers are being progressively breached.

PARTICIPATION–BY BEING A MEMBER OF THE U.N.

The last kind of transnational participation to be considered is membership in United Nations secretariats. These consist of the headquarters in New York plus its branches in other parts of the world and the headquarters of the twelve Specialized Agencies and their branches. Members of delegations from member countries to these bodies are not here considered, both for practical and theoretical

TABLE 8. Coverage of Different Types of Countries by 150 Globally Oriented International Nongovernmental Organizations

	With Respect to Ideology			
With Respect to Development	Less in 1962–63 than in 1956–57	Same in 1962–63 as in 1956–57	More in 1962–63 than in 1956–57	Total
Less in 1962–63 than in 1956–57	1	1	0	2
Same in 1962–63 as in 1956–57	3	114	17	134
More in 1962–63 than in 1956–57	0	8	6	14
Total	4	123	23	150

TABLE 9. Established Posts in the United Nations and its Specialized Agencies

	All Established Posts	Established Posts not Related to Technical Assistance
1956	8,370	7,821
1963	13,165	11,299
Increase	4,795	3,478
% Increase	57.3	45.8
Compound Yearly % Increase	6.7	5.5

reasons. Information on the numbers who have served on delegations at different points in time is not easily available. More important, it is doubtful whether such service should be included under the concept of transnational participation. Instructed delegates hardly participate in the solution of common problems in a way that changes them fundamentally. They tend to interact on a formal level, and they do not live intimately together. It is for the same reason that we have excluded other intergovernmental organizations from consideration while including nongovernmental organizations.

The Annexes to the Official Records of the United Nations General Assembly gives figures each year on the number of established posts in the various agencies of the United Nations system. These are given in Table 9. Since these engaged on the Regular Programs in Technical Assistance as contrasted with the Expanded Program are holders of established posts, and we have shown in Table 9 the growth in United Nations Technical Assistance, we also show here the growth in established posts minus technical assistance personnel. The figures show that the technical assistance work has been growing somewhat faster than the other work of the several agencies, but both rates of increases are modest.

The six sorts of transnational participation that have been examined all show increases. Where we have some inkling of the world-wide situation, as in study abroad, multilateral technical assistance, international nongovernmental organizations and secretariats of the United Nations system, there seems to be a growth rate of between 5% and 10% a year. If this trend continues for a decade or more the results will almost certainly be important. But whether for good or ill will depend upon knowledge of the effects of the growing participation. Unfortunately, sociologists have carried out few studies of these effects.

REFERENCES

Harbison, Frederick H., and Myers, Charles A. *Education, Manpower, and Economic Growth.* New York: McGraw-Hill, 1964.

14. THE PROPENSITY TO INTERNATIONAL TRANSACTIONS

Karl W. Deutsch

In the thinking of some economic theorists, a "propensity" is the average share of efforts or resources allocated to a specific class of activities. Thus, the "propensity to save" is the average percentage of income which people allocate to saving. Such percentages can then be plotted against other variables which are believed to be relevant, in order to find out whether, and how, changes in each variable are correlated with changes in the proportions of resources allocated to the activities in question.

In this manner the average percentages of their incomes which the people of some country save can be plotted against the levels of their incomes, as found in different income groups. Very roughly put, it may then appear that those who are richer save a bigger share of their incomes; someone may infer from this that the "propensity to save" rises with the level of the income; and this inference may be tested by investigating whether, and to what extent, the same people, when and as they get richer, do in fact increase the proportions of their incomes which they save. Similar studies can be carried out for the behaviour of members of other social groups, so that one might speak of the "propensity to save" of farmers, or workers, or Protestants, or Negroes, or of more narrowly defined subgroups; and other types of behaviour can be studied in similar terms, such as the "propensity to invest," the "propensity to hoard," and so forth.[1]

It is impractical to go here beyond this extremely crude sketch of what is actually a considerably more complex field of economic theory and measurement.

SOURCE. Karl W. Deutsch, "The Propenisty to International Transactions," in *Political Studies*, VIII, No. 2, 1960, pp. 147–155. Reprinted by permission of the author and The Clarendon Press, Oxford. Copyright 1960 by Karl W. Deutsch.

[1]For an interesting attempt to extend the concept of propensities even further to aspects of economic and social behaviour that cannot be readily measured, see Walter W. Rostow, *The Theory of Economic Growth*, New York, Norton, 1950.

Yet the main points should be clear. A propensity is a quantitative concept; it is a proportion, derived from the measurement of some class of past activities of the members of some defined group, and applied to the tentative prediction of the future frequency of similar activities—and sometimes of related ones—within the same social group, or within similar ones. In its relation to other variables it can be depicted as a curve on a graph, and expected values can be read from it for various conditions. This concept and this technique have long been applied, successfully, in economics. They could be applied to other fields; and it is the purpose of the present paper to propose their application to the field of international relations.

In its broadest terms, a propensity to engage in international transactions would cover a considerable and ill-defined range of different activities. It might be better, therefore, to break it down into several more specifically defined propensities, referring in each case to a more narrowly definable class of activities, such as trade, postal communications, news reporting and readership, travel, migration, or the allocation of governmental expenditures. These propensities would have to refer in each case to the behaviour of the members of some defined group, such as the population of some country.

This approach would call, therefore, for measuring for at least one of these activities the volume of relevant transactions entered into by the members of this population, and for measuring further the proportions of such transactions which cross the boundaries of the country, as against those that remain entirely within it. Considerable statistical data are available in published sources—on national incomes and foreign trade, on the flow of domestic and foreign mail, on residence and migration, on governmental budgets, and on the content of newspapers and other media of mass communication—from which proportions of this kind could be computed.

From such computations propensities could be inferred. It could be supposed tentatively that such proportions should turn out to be fairly stable over longer periods of time; that they should be fairly similar for similar countries; that their variations should appear to be non-random and capable of being accounted for in an orderly manner; and that conspicuous changes or differences in these proportions should suggest interesting questions and potential insights, as to the underlying social and political structure of the countries and communities involved. These suppositions can be tested. In the course of several preliminary studies it has turned out thus far that the proportions discussed here do meet in fact, by and large, the qualifications just listed.

The collection and analysis of such data should be of interest to students of society and politics. The proportions found might be interpreted tentatively in terms of propensities, as defined above, and thus not necessarily in terms of any supposed psychological predispositions or national character traits. Such cultural or psychological assumptions would require additional and independent evidence to count as even strongly indicated. The empirical behaviour, measured by the propensities, might be caused simply by external arrangements or constraints, or by broad factors of geography, or industry, or occupation, or religion, or general type of culture, rather than by any peculiarities of inner group structure or individual decision. The study of propensities should start a process of more deep-probing analysis, not terminate it.

With these cautions, however, even tentative findings could serve as more general indicators of the levels and trends of international involvement on the part of groups or nations. In regard to the politics of each country, such findings might tell us something about the relative strength of those political and social interest groups that are directly involved in international transactions, as against those whose primary concerns are domestic. The relative strength of such internationally involved groups, and the share of economic resources involved in direct international transactions, have a direct bearing on the generation and distribution of political power in a country, and on the purposes to which it is applied. In addition to the power process, the processes of communication and decision-making are affected by the proportions of purely domestic messages which compete for the attention of social *élites,* political decision-makers, and the general population, as against the proportion of messages carrying some direct concern with matters abroad. Both the power process and the attention process are inseparably interlinked in politics; and both are significantly affected by the overall proportions of domestic to international transactions.

It is possible, of course, to deny in principle the significance of such quantitative data, by proposing something like a "vitamin theory" of the social and political importance of international transactions. Even though these were only present in small traces, it could be argued, their presence might still be essential to the functioning of the society or community concerned; and it might be asserted that any changes in the relative amounts of international transactions above this trace level should have next to no effect. Such a "vitamin theory" of politics, however, would require some evidence to sustain it; and it would clash with much that is known about interest-group politics, the importance of economic factors, and the quantitative aspects of mass communication.

If one grants, for the time being, the potential interest of such quantitative data and proportions, what actual ratios have been found and what do they suggest? From such data, would it be possible to construct a more general scale as a background and aid in their interpretation?

A TENTATIVE SCALE OF INTERNATIONAL AND INTERREGIONAL INTEGRATION

From a survey of the proportions of foreign to domestic mail-flows in a large number of countries, as well as of several other kinds of international and interregional transactions, a tentative scale for the integration or a relatively small community with its larger environment was proposed some years ago.[2]

The most convenient form for giving such a scale would be in terms of per cent. international transactions among the total volume of transactions of the relevant class. Such percentages are often given in the published sources, and their interpretation seems intuitively familiar to many social scientists. A somewhat more sensitive yardstick for changes, particularly in cases where international transactions form a small proportion of the total, is offered by the I/O ratio, that is, the proportion of internal transactions to outside ones. For the purposes of the present paper it seems best to give the scale in both kinds of units—percentages as well as I/O ratios. This scale might be most nearly applicable to countries or communities which are relatively small relative to their total outside environment—say, not above 10 percent. of the latter.

TABLE 1. A Tentative Scale of International Integration and National Autonomy (from sources given in footnote 2)

I/O ratio: Internal to Outside Transactions	Percentage of Outside Transactions among Total	Tentative Interpretation: Degree of	
		Integration to Outside World	Autonomy or Self-Preoccupation of Smaller Unit
1 or less .	50 +	High	Low
1–2 .	33–50	Fair to high	Low to fair
2–6 .	14–33	Fair	Fair
6–10 .	9–14	Low to fair	Fair to high
10–15 .	6–9	Low	High
15 or higher	6 or less	Extremely low	Extremely high

According to this scale, and in regard to the particular type of transactions studied, one might consider countries which show between two and six times as many internal as external transactions—corresponding to a share of 14 to 33 per cent. of the total for the latter—as fairly well intermediate between international integration and national autonomy, in so far as this particular type or range of transactions is concerned. Countries with more than ten times as many domestic as foreign transactions—i.e., with less than 9 per cent. of the total for the latter—might count as low in international integration and high in national autonomy or self-preoccupation; and they might be rated extremely so, in both regards, if domestic transactions were to outnumber foreign ones by more than

[2]Part of the data from this survey are published in K. W. Deutsch, "Shifts in the Balance of Communication Flows: A Problem of Measurement in International Relations," *Public Opinion Quarterly*, xx. 1, spring 1956, pp. 143–60; for the proposed scale, see *ibid.*, p. 160.

fifteen to one, reducing the international share of the total to about 6 per cent., or less. By contrast, international integration might be considered high, if domestic transactions should be equalled or outnumbered by foreign ones. Intermediate values between these "high," "fair," and "low" points on this scale might then receive appropriate "fair to high" and "low to fair" interpretations, as shown in Table 1.

SOME SPECIFIC FINDINGS

If one applies the tentative interpretations, suggested in this table, to the data about postal correspondence for a large number of countries, it appears that the mean share of international mail was less than 14 per cent. in 1880, indicating a low to fair level of international integration at that time. This average share of international mail then rose to a fair level of world integration, or at least interdependence, with almost 30 per cent. in 1913, but declined again to about 25 per cent. for the average of the years 1928–34, and further to about 18 per cent. for the period 1946–51, while still remaining above the lower limit of the "fair" category.[3]

International integration in regard to mail declined sharply with the area of a country, the size of its population, and the *per capita* number of letters. The last-named of these variables is correlated to some extent with literacy and *per capita* income, and apparently also with some characteristics of the general culture. Low levels of international postal integration, with less than 9 per cent. of foreign mail, were found after 1928 for such countries as the United Kingdom, France, Germany, and Italy. Extremely low values, well below 2 per cent., were found for the United States, and the bottom figures of just above 1 per cent. was that for the U.S.S.R. for 1936–the last year for which a figure for that country was given by the Universal Postal Union.[4]

The same scale can be applied to the results of a more recent survey of the proportions of foreign trade to national income for a large number of countries in the mid-1950's, and for a smaller number of countries at various earlier dates.[5]

---

[3]From data, *loc. cit.*, p. 156. Figures are for first-class mail. Between different periods, there is some variation among the countries with available data, but the overall trend seems large enough to be worth noting.

[4]For details see ibid., pp. 151–6.

[5]These percentage ratios of foreign trade to national income should differ conceptually somewhat from the I/O ratios, particularly in the case of countries with large import or export surpluses. If we call the domestic national product D – taking it as corresponding to the volume of domestic economic transactions – then the national income $Y = D + M - E$, where M and E stand for import and exports, respectively. The T/Y ratio then corresponds to $(M + E)$ divided by $/D + (M - E)/$, while the I/O ratio stands for D divided by $(M + E)$. For most countries, with the notable exception of the United States, this difference should be minor.

The first noteworthy fact here is that levels of international integration are significantly higher in regard to trade than they are in regard to mail. For a group of seventy-one countries in the mid-1950's, the median proportion of foreign trade, as compared to national income, was about 35 per cent. This is almost twice the average percentage of foreign mail found for a similar large group of countries in 1946–51, and it suggests a fair to high level of international trade integration for this group of seventy-one countries as a whole.[6] It should be borne in mind, of course, that the two periods and groups of countries are somewhat different, and that the mean value for one group is not strictly comparable to the median value for the other. The differences between the integration levels for trade and for mail seem too large, however, to be explained away by these discrepancies.

More nearly comparable figures for individual countries confirm the lagging of the share of foreign mail communications behind the levels of the shares of foreign trade. Thus France and Italy, which rated "low" in terms of international postal integration, rate "fair" in terms of international trade, which corresponded in 1957 to 26 and 32 per cent. of their national incomes, respectively. In the same year, the United Kingdom and the German Federal Republic rated "fair to high" in this respect, with foreign trade proportions at about 42 per cent. of national income for each country, and thus more than four times as high as their corresponding percentages of foreign mail. Even the United States and the Soviet Union were less self-preoccupied in their trade than they were in the letter-writing of their populations. The share of foreign trade in the United States was a little above 9 per cent. of national income in 1957, and a little below 9 per cent. in 1958, leaving that country's international integration rating in regard to trade just at the borderline between "low" and "low to fair," but still more than four times as high as the corresponding level of the share of foreign mails.[7] The Soviet Union, finally, with a foreign trade proportion of less than 5 per cent. in 1957, remained here, too, in the "extremely low" category of international integration— including, interestingly enough, the level of its trade integration with the countries of the Communist bloc.[8] The large share which these latter countries were getting of what Soviet foreign trade there was should not obscure the remarkably small proportion of all Soviet foreign trade when compared to the Soviet national income. It may be surmised, however, that even this low level of international trade integration in the case of the U.S.S.R. may still lie well above the corresponding level of its international integration in terms of the share of foreign mail, both to the world at large and within the circle of Communist countries.

[6]From data in K. W. Deutsch and Alexander Eckstein, *National Industrialization and the Declining Share of International Trade, 1890–1957*, Yale University multigraphed, 1959; publication forthcoming.

[7]Deutsch and Eckstein, *op. cit.*

[8]*Ibid.*

The level of international trade integration tends to drop sharply with the population size of countries. In the survey of seventy-one countries referred to earlier, the median proportion of foreign trade to national income for countries with populations of about 1 million was about 50 per cent., suggesting an integration rating of "high." For countries with populations near 10 million, the same foreign trade ratio was about 35 per cent., with an integration level "fair to high." For countries near 100 million, however, the theoretical value from the regression curve would have been about 12 per cent.; and for countries above 150 million, the share of foreign trade was below 10 per cent., with an apparent international integration level of "low," or "low to fair" at best.[9]

The fact of some decline in international integration with increasing country size should not be surprising, but the speed and extent of the decline are impressive. On the basis of these figures, any state uniting only as much as one-tenth of mankind would have to be expected to fall to a low level of international integration and to devote more than nine-tenths of its economic activities, and perhaps twice this proportion of its postal correspondence, to domestic activities. These figures might deserve the careful thought of proponents of such plans as Western European Federation, Atlantic Union, or Federal World Government, as well as that of students of integrative and disintegrative tendencies within the Soviet bloc. The trends suggested by the data need not have the inevitability of fate, but they seem to be clearly more than mere statistical artefacts, and they may well count at the very least as serious challenges to any integrative international policies or institutions.

Another type of international and interregional transactions relates to travel and migration. These processes are usually characterized by lower levels of international integration than are trade or mail, and they bring out strikingly the contrast between the high and still rising levels of integration among different regions within the same country, and the low, and sometimes even declining, levels of such integration among different countries. Thus, at censuses during the last hundred years, about 30 per cent. of the American people were found living outside their state of birth, showing a long-lasting "fair" level of interstate integration in the United States. For Switzerland, the analogous proportion in terms of Swiss citizens born outside their Cantons of residence rose from about 20 per cent. in 1860 to about 40 per cent. in 1950. In Bavaria the proportion of German residents born elsewhere was below 6 per cent. in the 1880's; it is well above 20 per cent. now, as it is in the entire Federal Republic, after the dislocations of World War II.[10] These processes may well have tended in all these countries to weaken regional separatism, and to increase the importance of national politics.

[9]*Ibid.,* "Statistical Appendix," in collaboration with C. I. Bliss.
[10]Data from standard statistical publications.

At the international level, however, developments in regard to migration have been different. Among most West European countries integration in terms of international migration must rate as "extremely low," with the proportion of foreign-born residents well below 6 per cent. Even in the overseas countries, migration levels during the last several decades have been far below those of the pre-1913 period, and they seem unlikely to recover without deliberate changes in national policies, as well as concerted international action.

International integration is somewhat higher, on the other hand, in terms of news coverage and news attention, devoted to subject-matters beyond one's national boundaries. Here, too, however, the proportion of news space devoted on the average to foreign developments may tend to decline with the size and power of countries. According to some preliminary surveys the proportion of foreign news in the average newspaper—as distinct from the *élite* papers—of such countries as the United States and the Soviet Union may be at or below 14 per cent. of total editorial content, suggesting a "low to fair" level of international integration, or at least involvement, while such countries as the United Kingdom, France, or the German Federal Republic are apt to have comparable proportions of foreign news in the "fair" or even "fair to high" ranges of international integration.

The picture of national self-preoccupation is somewhat strengthened if average-reader attention is taken into account; it tends to drop for foreign news. Thus the average share of foreign and international subjects in the news space of American newspapers was a little below 9 per cent., at a time when their share of reader attention was only about 7 per cent.—both figures suggesting a "low" level of international integration.[11]

A corrective is introduced, if one notes the much higher levels of attention to foreign news in the *élite* press of most countries. To cite just one example, about 40 per cent. of the editorials in both the London *Times* and the New York *Times* are devoted to international topics, and this proportion has persisted unchanged for about fifty years.[12] It is possible, therefore, that low or declining levels of international integration in the realm of material activities may be offset, to some limited extent, by a higher and conceivably even an increasing, proportion of attention to international matters in terms of news and symbols, particularly at the *élite* level.

---

[11]Cf. data in the excellent collection edited by Wilbur Schramm, *Mass Communications,* Urbana, Ill., University of Illinois Press.

[12]Cf. Ithiel Pool et al., *The Prestige Papers,* Stanford, Stanford University Press, 1951; and *Symbols of Internationalism,* Stanford, Stanford University Press, 1952. The results appear confirmed by more recent unpublished surveys at Yale University and The Fletcher School of Law and Diplomacy; cf. also unpublished survey data from the Center on Communications at Stanford University, collected under the direction of Professor Wilbur Schramm.

The process of "fundamental democratization" in the twentieth century—to recall a term of Karl Mannheim's here[13]—might then have quite different results at different stages, so far as international integration is concerned. During the first stage, mass politics might develop faster than mass acculturation to *élite* levels of international attention and interest. During the same period domestic economic development, communication, and migration might all develop faster than their international counterparts, and all these tendencies might be strengthened further through the ending of past colonial relationships. As a result of all these processes the propensities to international transactions might decline, and prolonged periods of increased parochialism and nationalism might occur in many countries just during the critical early decades of the nuclear age.

If these "dangerous decades"[14] could be surmounted without mass destruction, however, a second stage of development eventually might permit mass acculturation to catch up, just as it might permit substantial cumulative social learning and habit-changing on the part of old and new *élites.* In this event, international attention and concern in the major countries might attain and retain sufficiently high levels of quantitative strength and qualitative competence to permit mankind to live somewhat more safely with the vast new powers of physical destruction which it has acquired. At a still later stage, structural changes in technology, economics, and social institutions may then reach a point where the material processes of international integration will enable international and supranational communities, or even a world community, to attain and exceed the present-day integrative levels of the national state.

These last points are, of course, conjectural and connot be pursued here. The present paper will have served its purpose if it has managed to illustrate the intrinsic interest, as well as the practical possibility of using the aid of some measurable indicators in order to trace the rise and decline of some underlying processes of international or interregional integration, and if it should find some response in the research, analysis, and criticism of other students of society and politics.

[13]Cf. Karl Mannheim, *Man and Society in the Age of Reconstruction,* New York, Harcourt, Brace, 1940, 1947.

[14]Cf. Selig S. Harrison, *The Most Dangerous Decades,* New York, Columbia University Language Research Center, 1957 (multigraphed, with printed cover).

15. INTERCULTURAL COMMUNICATION: A GUIDE TO MEN OF ACTION

Edward T. Hall and William Foote Whyte

How can anthropological knowledge help the man of action in dealing with people of another culture? We shall seek to answer that question by examining the process of intercultural communication.

Anthropologists have long claimed that a knowledge of culture is valuable to the administrator. More and more people in business and government are willing to take this claim seriously, but they ask that we put culture to them in terms they can understand and act upon.

When the layman thinks of culture, he is likely to think in terms of (1) the way people dress, (2) the beliefs they hold, and (3) the customs they practice—with an accent upon the esoteric. Without undertaking any comprehensive definition, we can concede that all three are aspects of culture, and yet point out that they do not get us very far, either theoretically or practically.

Dress is misleading, if we assume that differences in dress indicate differences in belief and behavior. If that were the case, then we should expect to find people dressed like ourselves to be thinking and acting like ourselves. While there are still peoples wearing "colorful" apparel quite different from ours, we find in many industrializing societies that the people with whom we deal dress much as we do—and yet think and act quite differently.

Knowledge of beliefs may leave us up in the air because the connections between beliefs and behavior are seldom obvious. In the case of religious beliefs, we may know, for example, that the Mohammedan must pray to Allah a certain number of times a day and that therefore the working day must provide for praying time. This is important, to be sure, but the point is so obvious that it is unlikely to be overlooked by anyone. The administrator must also grasp the less dramatic aspects of everyday behavior, and here a knowledge of beliefs is a very imperfect guide.

SOURCE. Edward T. Hall and William Foote Whyte, "Intercultural Communication: A Guide to Men of Action," in *Human Organization,* 19 (Spring, 1960), pp. 5–12. Reprinted by permission of the authors and The Society for Applied Anthropology. Copyright 1960 by The Society for Applied Anthropology.

Customs provide more guidance, providing we do not limit ourselves to the esoteric and also search for the pattern of behavior into which a given custom fits. The anthropologist, in dealing with customary behavior, is not content with identifying individual items. To him, these items are not miscellaneous. They have meaning only as they are fitted together into a pattern.

But even assuming that the pattern can be communicated to the administrator, there is still something important lacking. The pattern shows how the people act— when among themselves. The administrator is not directly concerned with that situation. Whatever background information he has, he needs to interpret to himself how the people act *in relation to himself.* He is dealing with a cross-cultural situation. The link between the two cultures is provided by acts of communication between the administrator, representing one culture, and people representing another. If communication is effective, then understanding grows with collaborative action. If communication is faulty, then no book knowledge of culture can assure effective action.

This is not to devalue the knowledge of culture that can be provided by the anthropologist. It is only to suggest that the point of implementation of the knowledge must be in the communication process. Let us therefore examine the process of intercultural communication. By so doing we can accomplish two things: (A) Broaden knowledge of ourselves by revealing some of our own unconscious communicative acts. (B) Clear away heretofore almost insurmountable obstacles to understanding in the cross-cultural process. We also learn that communication, as it is used here, goes far beyond words and includes many other acts upon which judgments are based of what is transpiring and from which we draw conclusions as to what has occurred in the past.

Culture affects communication in various ways. It determines the time and timing of interpersonal events, the places where it is appropriate to discuss particular topics, the physical distance separating one speaker from another, the tone of voice that is appropriate to the subject matter. Culture, in this sense, delineates the amount and type of physical contact, if any, which convention permits or demands, and the intensity of emotion which goes with it. Culture includes the relationship of *what is said to what is meant*—as when "no" means "maybe" and "tomorrow" means "never." Culture, too, determines whether a given matter—say, a business contract—should be initially discussed between two persons or hacked out in a day-long conference which includes four or five senior officials from each side, with perhaps an assist from the little man who brings in the coffee.

These are important matters which the businessman who hopes to trade abroad ignores at his peril. They are also elusive, for every man takes his own culture for granted. Even a well-informed national of another country is hard put to explain why, in his own land, the custom is thus-and-so rather than so-and-thus; as hard put, indeed, as you would probably be if asked what is the "rule" which governs the precise time in a relationship that you begin using another man's first name. One "just knows." In other words, you do not know and cannot explain satisfactorily because you learn this sort of thing unconsciously in your upbringing, in your culture, and you take such knowledge for granted. Yet the impact of culture on communication can be observed and the lessons taught.

Since the most obvious form of communication is by language, we will first consider words, meanings, voice tones, emotions, and physical contact; then take up, in turn, the cultural impact of time, place, and social class relations on business situations in various lands. Finally, we will suggest what the individual administrator may do to increase his effectiveness abroad, and what students of culture may do to advance this application of anthropology.

BEYOND LANGUAGE

Americans are often accused of not being very good at language, or at least not very much interested in learning foreign languages. There is little evidence that any people are inherently "better" at languages than any other, given the opportunity and incentive to learn. The West and Central European who has since childhood been in daily contact with two or three languages learns to speak them all, and frequently to read and write them as well. Under similar conditions, American children do the same. Indeed, a not uncommon sight on the backroads of Western Europe is a mute, red-faced American military family lost on a Sunday drive while the youngest child, barely able to lisp his own English, leans from the window to interpret the directions of some gnarled farmer whose dialect is largely unintelligible to most of his own countrymen.

We should not underestimate the damage our lack of language facility as a nation has done to our relations all over the world. Obviously, if you cannot speak a man's language, you are terribly handicapped in communicating with him.

But languages can be learned and yet most, if not all, of the disabling errors described in this article could still be made. Vocabulary, grammar, even verbal facility are not enough. Unless a man understands the subtle cues that are implicit in language, tone, gestures and expression, he will not only consistently misinterpret what is said to him, but he may offend irretrievably without knowing how or why.

DO THEY MEAN WHAT THEY SAY?

Can't you believe what a man says? We all recognize that the basic honesty of the speaker is involved. What we often fail to recognize, however, is that the question involves cultural influences that have nothing to do with the honesty or dependability of the individual.

In the United States we put a premium on direct expression. The "good" American is supposed to say what he means and to mean what he says. If, on important matters, we discover that someone spoke deviously or evasively, we would be inclined to regard him thereafter as unreliable if not out-and-out dishonest.

In some other cultures, the words and their meanings do not have such a direct connection. People may be more concerned with the emotional context of the situation than with the meaning of particular words. This leads them to give an agreeable and pleasant answer to a question when a literal, factual answer might be unpleasant or embarrassing.

This situation is not unknown in our culture, of course. How many times have you muttered your delighted appreciation for a boring evening? We term this simple politeness and understand each other perfectly.

On the other hand, analogous "polite" behavior on a matter of factory production would be incomprehensible. An American businessman would be most unlikely to question another businessman's word if he were technically qualified and said that his plant could produce 1000 gross of widgets a month. We are "taught" that it is none of our business to inquire too deeply into the details of his production system. This would be prying and might be considered an attempt to steal his operational plans.

Yet this cultural pattern has trapped many an American into believing that when a Japanese manufacturer answered a direct question with the reply that he could produce 1000 gross of widgets, he meant what he said. If the American had been escorted through the factory and saw quite clearly that its capacity was, at the most, perhaps 500 gross of widgets per month, he would be likely to say to himself:

Well, this fellow probably has a brother-in-law who has a factory who can make up the difference. He isn't telling the whole story because he's afraid I might try to make a better deal with the brother-in-law. Besides, what business is it of mine, so long as he meets the schedule?

The cables begin to burn after the American returns home and only 500 gross of widgets arrive each month.

What the American did not know was that in Japanese culture one avoids the direct question unless the questioner is absolutely certain that the answer will not embarrass the Japanese businessman in any way whatsoever. In Japan for one to admit being unable to perform a given operation or measure up to a given standard means a bitter loss of face. Given a foreigner who is so stupid, ignorant, or intensive as to ask an embarrassing question, the Japanese is likely to choose what appears to him the lesser of two evils.

Americans caught in this cross-cultural communications trap are apt to feel doubly deceived because the Japanese manufacturer may well be an established and respected member of the business community.

EXCITABLE PEOPLE?

Man communicates not by words alone. His tone of voice, his facial expressions, his gestures all contribute to the infinitely varied calculus of meaning. But the confusion of tongues is more than matched by the confusion of gesture and other culture cues. One man's nod is another man's negative. Each culture has its own rich array of meaningful signs, symbols, gestures, emotional connotations, historical references, traditional responses and—equally significant—pointed silences. These have been built up over the millennia as (who can say?) snarls, growls, and love murmurs gathered meaning and dignity with long use, to end up perhaps as the worn coinage of trite expression.

Consider the Anglo-Saxon tradition of preserving one's calm. The American is taught by his culture to suppress his feelings. He is conditioned to regard emotion as generally bad (except in weak women who can't help themselves) and a stern self-control as good. The more important a matter, the more solemn and outwardly dispassionate he is likely to be. A cool head, granite visage, dispassionate logic—it is no accident that the Western story hero consistently displays these characteristics.

In the Middle East it is otherwise. From childhood, the Arab is permitted, even encouraged, to express his feelings without inhibition. Grown men can weep, shout, gesture expressively and violently, jump up and down—and be admired as sincere.

The modulated, controlled Anglo-Saxon is likely to be regarded with suspicion—he must be hiding something, practicing to deceive.

The exuberant and emotional Arab is likely to disturb the Anglo-Saxon, cause him to writhe inwardly with embarrassment—for isn't this childish behavior? And aren't things getting rather out of hand?

Then, again, there is the matter of how loudly one should talk.

In the Arab world, in discussions among equals, the men attain a decibel level that would be considered aggressive, objectionable, and obnoxious in the United States. Loudness connotes strength and sincerity among Arabs; a soft tone implies weakness, deviousness. This is so "right" in the Arab culture that several Arabs have told us they discounted anything heard over the "Voice of America" because the signal was so weak!

Personal status modulates voice tone, however, even in Arab society. The Saudi Arab shows respect to his superior—to a sheik, say—by lowering his voice and mumbling. The affluent American may also be addressed in this fashion, making almost impossible an already difficult situation. Since in the American culture one unconsciously "asks" another to raise his voice by raising one's own, the American speaks louder. This lowers the Arab's tone more and increases the mumble. This triggers a shouting response in the American—which cues the Arab into a frightened "I'm not being respectful enough" tone well below audibility.

They are not likely to part with much respect for each other.

TO TOUCH OR NOT TO TOUCH?

How much physical contact should appropriately accompany social or business conversation?

In the United States we discourage physical contact, particularly between adult males. The most common physical contact is the handshake and, compared to Europeans, we use it sparingly.

The handshake is the most detached and impersonal form of greeting or farewell in Latin America. Somewhat more friendly is the left hand placed on another man's shoulder during a handshake. Definitely more intimate and warm is the *"doble abrazo"* in which two men embrace by placing their arms around each other's shoulders.

These are not difficult conventions to live with, particularly since the North American can easily permit the Latin American to take the initiative in any form of contact more initimate than the handshake. Far more difficult for the North American to learn to live with comfortably are the less stylized forms of physical contact such as the hand on one's arm during conversation. To the North American this is edging toward what in his culture is an uncomfortable something— possibly sexual—which inhibits his own communication.

Yet there are cultures which restrict physical contact far more than we do. An American at a cocktail party in Java tripped over the invisible cultural ropes which mark the boundaries of acceptable behavior. He was seeking to develop a business relationship with a prominent Javanese and seemed to be doing very well. Yet, when the cocktail party ended, so apparently did a promising beginning. For the North American spent nearly six months trying to arrange a second meeting. He finally learned, through pitying intermediaries, that at the cocktail party he had momentarily placed his arm on the shoulder of the Javanese—and in the presence of other people. Humiliating! Almost unpardonable in traditional Javanese etiquette.

In this particular case, the unwitting breach was mended by a graceful apology. It is worth noting, however, that a truly cordial business relationship never did develop.

THE FIVE DIMENSIONS OF TIME

If we peel away a few layers of cultural clothing, we begin to reach almost totally unconscious reactions. Our ideas of time, for example, are deeply instilled in us when we are children. If they are contradicted by another's behavior, we react with anger, not knowing exactly why. For the businessman, five important temporal concepts are: appointment time, discussion time, acquaintance time, visiting time, and time schedules.

Anyone who has travelled abroad or dealt at all extensively with non-Americans learns that punctuality is variously interpreted. It is one thing to recognize this with the mind; to adjust to a different kind of *appointment time* is quite another.

In Latin America, you should expect to spend hours waiting in outer offices. If you bring your American interpretation of what constitutes punctuality to a Latin-American office, you will fray your temper and elevate your blood pressure. For a forty-five-minute wait is not unusual—no more unusual than a five-minute wait would be in the United States. No insult is intended, no arbitrary pecking order is being established. If, in the United States, you would not be outraged by a five-minute wait, you should not be outraged by the Latin-American's forty-five-minute delay in seeing you. The time pie is differently cut, that's all.

Further, the Latin American doesn't usually schedule individual appointments to the exclusion of other appointments. The informal clock of his upbringing ticks more slowly and he rather enjoys seeing several people on different matters at the same time. The three-ring circus atmosphere which results, if interpreted in the American's scale of time and propriety, seems to signal him to go away, to tell him that he is not being properly treated, to indicate that his dignity is under attack. Not so. The clock on the wall may look the same but it tells a different sort of time.

The cultural error may be compounded by a further miscalculation. In the United States, a consistently tardy man is likely to be considered undependable, and by our cultural clock this is a reasonable conclusion. For you to judge a Latin American by your scale of time values is to risk a major error.

Suppose you have waited forty-five minutes and there is a man in his office, by some miracle alone in the room with you. Do you now get down to business and stop "wasting time"?

If you are not forewarned by experience or a friendly advisor, you may try to do this. And it would usually be a mistake. For, in the American culture, *discussion* is a means to an end: the deal. You try to make your point quickly, efficiently, neatly. If your purpose is to arrange some major affairs, your instinct is probably to settle the major issues first, leave the details for later, possibly for the technical people to work out.

For the Latin American, the discussion is a part of the spice of life. Just as he tends not to be overly concerned about reserving you your specific segment of time, he tends not as rigidly to separate business from non-business. He runs it all together and wants to make something of a social event out of what you, in your culture, regard as strictly business.

The Latin American is not alone in this. The Greek businessman, partly for the same and partly for different reasons, does not lean toward the "hit-and-run" school of business behavior, either. The Greek businessman adds to the social element, however, a feeling about what length of discussion time constitutes good faith. In America, we show good faith by ignoring the details. "Let's agree on the main points. The details will take care of themselves.

Not so the Greek. He signifies good will and good faith by what may seem to you an interminable discussion which includes every conceivable detail. Otherwise, you see, he cannot help but feel that the other man might be trying to pull the wool over his eyes. Our habit, in what we feel to be our relaxed and friendly way, of postponing details until later smacks the Greek between the eyes as a maneuver to flank him. Even if you can somehow convince him that this is not the case, the meeting must still go on a certain indefinite—but, by our standards, long—time or he will feel disquieted.

The American desire to get down to business and on with other things works to our disadvantage in other parts of the world, too; and not only in business. The head of a large, successful Japanese firm commented: "You Americans have a terrible weakness. We Japanese know about it and exploit it every chance we get. You are impatient. We have learned that if we just make you wait long enough, you'll agree to anything."

Whether this is literally true or not, the Japanese executive singled out a trait of American culture which most of us share and which, one may assume from the newspapers, the Russians have not overlooked, either.

By *acquaintance time* we mean how long you must know a man before you are willing to do business with him.

In the United States, if we know that a salesman represents a well-known, reputable company, and if we need his product, he may walk away from the first meeting with an order in his pocket. A few minutes conversation to decide matters of price, delivery, payment, model of product—nothing more is involved. In Central America, local custom does not permit a salesman to land in town, call on the customer and walk away with an order, no matter how badly your prospect wants and needs your product. It is traditional there that you must see your man at least three times before you can discuss the nature of your business.

Does this mean that the South American businessman does not recognize the merits of one product over another? Of course it doesn't. It is just that the weight of tradition presses him to do business within a circle of friends. If a product he needs is not available within his circle, he does not go outside it so much as he enlarges the circle itself to include a new friend who can supply the want. Apart from his cultural need to "feel right" about a new relationship, there is the logic of his business system. One of the realities of his life is that it is dangerous to enter into business with someone over whom you have no more than formal, legal "control." In the past decades, his legal system has not always been as firm as ours and he has learned through experience that he needs the sanctions implicit in the informal system of friendship.

Visiting time involves the question of who sets the time for a visit. George Coelho, a social psychologist from India, gives an illustrative case. A U.S. business-man received this invitation from an Indian businessman: "Won't you and your family come and see us? Come anytime." Several weeks later, the Indian repeated the invitation in the same words. Each time the American replied that he would certainly like to drop in—but he never did. The reason is obvious in terms of our culture. Here "come any time" is just an expression of friendliness. You are not really expected to show up unless your host proposes a specific time. In India, on the contrary, the words are meant literally—that the host is putting himself at the disposal of his guest and really expects him to come. It is the essence of polite-ness to leave it to the guest to set a time at his convenience. If the guest never comes, the Indian naturally assumes that he does not want to come. Such a mis-understanding can lead to a serious rift between men who are trying to do busi-ness with each other.

Time schedules present Americans with another problem in many parts of the world. Without schedules, deadlines, priorities, and timetables, we tend to feel that our country could not run at all. Not only are they essential to getting work done, but they also play an important role in the informal communication process. Deadlines indicate priorities and priorities signal the relative importance of people and the processes they control. These are all so much a part of our lives that a day hardly passes without some reference to them. "I have to be there by 6:30." "If I don't have these plans out by 5:00 they'll be useless." "I told J. B. I'd be finished by noon tomorrow and now he tells me to drop everything and get hot on the McDermott account. What do I do now?"

In our system, there are severe penalties for not completing work on time and important rewards for holding to schedules. One's integrity and reputation are at stake.

You can imagine the fundamental conflicts that arise when we attempt to do business with people who are just as strongly oriented away from time schedules as we are toward them.

The Middle Eastern peoples are a case in point. Not only is our idea of time schedules no part of Arab life but the mere mention of a deadline to an Arab is like waving a red flag in front of a bull. In his culture, your emphasis on a dead-line has the emotional effect on him that his backing you into a corner and threatening you with a club would have on you.

One effect of this conflict of unconscious habit patterns is that hundreds of American-owned radio sets are lying on the shelves of Arab radio repair shops, untouched. The Americans made the serious cross-cultural error of asking to have the repair completed by a certain time.

How do you cope with this? How does the Arab get another Arab to do anything? Every culture has its own ways of bringing pressure to get results. The usual Arab way is one which Americans avoid as "bad manners" It is needling. An Arab businessman whose car broke down explained it this way:

First, I go to the garage and tell the mechanic what is wrong with my car. I wouldn't want to give him the idea that I didn't know. After that, I leave the car and walk around the block. When I come back to the garage, I ask him if he has started to work yet. On my way home from lunch I stop in and ask him how things are going. When I go back to the office I stop by again. In the evening, I return and peer over his shoulder for a while. If I didn't keep this up, he'd be off working on someone else's car.

If you haven't been needled by an Arab, you just haven't been needled.

A PLACE FOR EVERYTHING

We say that there is a time and place for everything, but compared to other countries and cultures we give very little emphasis to place distinctions. Business is almost a universal value with us; it can be discussed almost anywhere, except perhaps in church. One can even talk business on the church steps going to and from the service. Politics is only slightly more restricted in the places appropriate for its discussion.

In other parts of the world, there are decided place restrictions on the discussion of business and politics. The American who is not conscious of the unwritten laws will offend if he abides by his own rather than by the local rules.

In India, you should not talk business when visiting a man's home. If you do, you prejudice your chances of ever working out a satisfactory business relationship.

In Latin America, although university students take an active interest in politics, tradition decrees that a politician should avoid political subjects when speaking on university grounds. A Latin American politician commented to anthropologist Allan Holmberg that neither he nor his fellow politicians would have dared attempt a political speech on the grounds of the University of San Marcos in Peru—as did Vice-President Nixon.

To complicate matters further, the student body of San Marcos, anticipating the visit, had voted that Mr. Nixon would not be welcome. The University Rector had issued no invitation, presumably because he expected what did, in fact, happen.

As a final touch, Mr. Nixon's interpreter was a man in full military uniform. In Latin American countries, some of which had recently overthrown military dictators, the symbolism of the military uniform could hardly contribute to a cordial atmosphere. Latin Americans need no reminder that the United States is a great military power.

Mr. Nixon's efforts were planned in the best traditions of our own culture: he hoped to improve relations through a direct, frank, and face-to-face discussion with students—the future leaders of their country. Unfortunately, this approach did not fit in at all with the culture of the host country. Of course, elements hostile to the United States did their best to capitalize upon this cross-cultural misunderstanding. However, even Latin Americans friendly to us, while admiring the Vice President's courage, found themselves acutely embarassed by the behavior of their people and ours in the ensuing difficulties.

BEING COMFORTABLE IN SPACE

Like time and place, differing ideas of space hide traps for the uninformed. Without realizing it, almost any person raised in the United States is likely to give an unintended snub to a Latin American simply in the way we handle space relationships, particularly during conversations.

In North America, the "proper" distance to stand when talking to another adult male you do not know well is about two feet, at least in a formal business conversation. (Naturally at a cocktail party, the distance shrinks, but anything under eight to ten inches is likely to provoke an apology or an attempt to back up.)

To a Latin American, with his cultural traditions and habits, a distance of two feet seems to him approximately what five feet would to us. To him, we seem distant and cold. To us, he gives an impression of pushiness.

As soon as a Latin American moves close enough for him to feel comfortable, we feel uncomfortable and edge back. We once observed a conversation between a Latin and a North American which began at one end of a forty-foot hall. At intervals we noticed them again, finally at the other end of the hall. This rather amusing displacement had been accomplished by an almost continual series of small backward steps on the part of the American, trying unconsciously to reach a comfortable talking distance, and an equal closing of the gap by the Latin American as he attempted to reach his accustomed conversation space.

Americans in their offices in Latin America tend to keep their native acquaintances at our distance—not the Latin American's distance—by taking up a position behind a desk or typewriter. The barricade approach to communication is practiced even by old hands in Latin America who are completely unaware of its cultural significance. They know only that they are comfortable without realizing that the distance and equipment unconsciously make the Latin American uncomfortable.

HOW CLASS CHANNELS COMMUNICATION

We would be mistaken to regard the communication patterns which we observe around the world as no more than a miscellaneous collection of customs. The communication pattern of a given society is part of its total culture pattern and can only be understood in that context.

We cannot undertake here to relate many examples of communication behavior to the underlying culture of the country. For the businessman, it might be useful to mention the difficulties in the relationship between social levels and the problem of information feedback from lower to higher levels in industrial organizations abroad.

There is in Latin America a pattern of human relations and union-management relations quite different from that with which we are familiar in the United States. Everett Hagen of MIT has noted the heavier emphasis upon line authority and the lesser development of staff organizations in Latin-American plants when compared with North American counterparts. To a much greater extent than in the United States, the government becomes involved in the handling of all kinds of labor problems.

These differences seem to be clearly related to the culture and social organization of Latin America. We find there that society has been much more rigidly stratified than it has with us. As a corollary, we find a greater emphasis upon authority in family and the community.

This emphasis upon status and class distinction makes it very difficult for people of different status levels to express themselves freely and frankly in discussion and argument. In the past, the pattern has been for the man of lower status to express deference to his superior in any face-to-face contact. This is so even when everyone knows that the subordinate dislikes the superior. The culture of Latin America places a great premium upon keeping personal relations harmonious on the surface.

In the United States, we feel that it is not only desirable but natural to speak up to your superior, to tell the boss exactly what you think, even when you disagree with him. Of course, we do not always do this, but we think that we should, and we feel guilty if we fail to speak our minds frankly. When workers in our factories first get elected to local union office, they may find themselves quite self-conscious about speaking up to the boss and arguing grievances. Many of them, however, quickly learn to do it and enjoy the experience. American culture emphasizes the thrashing-out of differences in face-to-face contacts. It de-emphasizes the importance of status. As a result, we have built institutions for handling industrial disputes on the basis of the local situation, and we rely on direct discussion by the parties immediately involved.

In Latin America, where it is exceedingly difficult for people to express their differences face-to-face and where status differences and authority are much more strongly emphasized than here, the workers tend to look to a third party—the government—to take care of their problems. Though the workers have great difficulty in thrashing out their problems with management, they find no difficulty in telling government representatives their problems. And it is to their government that they look for an authority to settle their grievances with management.

Status and class also decide whether business will be done on an individual or a group basis.

In the United States, we are growing more and more accustomed to working as members of large organizations. Despite this, we still assume that there is no need to send a delegation to do a job that one capable man might well handle.

In some other parts of the world, the individual cannot expect to gain the respect necessary to accomplish this purpose, no matter how capable he is, unless he brings along an appropriate number of associates.

In the United States, we would rarely think it necessary or proper to call on a customer in a group. He might well be antagonized by the hard sell. In Japan—as an example—the importance of the occasion and of the man is measured by whom he takes along.

This practice goes far down in the business and government hierarchies. Even a university professor is likely to bring one or two retainers along on academic business. Otherwise people might think that he was a nobody and that his affairs were of little moment.

Even when a group is involved in the U.S., the head man is the spokesman and sets the tone. This is not always the case in Japan. Two young Japanese once requested an older American widely respected in Tokyo to accompany them so that they could "stand on his face." He was not expected to enter into the negotiation; his function was simply to be present as an indication that their intentions were serious.

ADJUSTMENT GOES BOTH WAYS

One need not have devoted his life to a study of various cultures to see that none of them is static. All are constantly changing and one element of change is the very fact that U.S. enterprise enters a foreign field. This is inevitable and may be constructive if we know how to utilize our knowledge. The problem is for us to be aware of our impact and to learn how to induce changes skillfully.

Rather than try to answer the general question of how two cultures interact, we will consider the key problem of personnel selection and development in two particular intercultural situations, both in Latin cultures.

One U.S. company had totally different experiences with "Smith" and "Jones" in the handling of its labor relations. The local union leaders were bitterly hostile to Smith, whereas they could not praise Jones enough. These were puzzling reactions to higher management. Smith seemed a fair-minded and understanding man; it was difficult to fathom how anyone could be bitter against him. At the same time, Jones did not appear to be currying favor by his generosity in giving away the firm's assets. To management, he seemed to be just as firm a negotiator as Smith.

The explanation was found in the two men's communication characteristics. When the union leaders came in to negotiate with Smith, he would let them state their case fully and freely—without interruption, but also without comment. When they had finished, he would say, "I'm sorry. We can't do it." He would follow this blunt statement with a brief and entirely cogent explanation of his reasons for refusal. If the union leaders persisted in their arguments, Smith would paraphrase his first statement, calmly and succinctly. In either case, the discussion was over in a few minutes. The union leaders would storm out of Smith's office complaining bitterly about the cold and heartless man with whom they had to deal.

Jones handled the situation differently. His final conclusion was the same as Smith's—but he would state it only after two or three hours of discussion. Furthermore, Jones participated actively in these discussions, questioning the union leaders for more information, relating the case in question to previous cases, philosophizing about labor relations and human rights and exchanging stories about work experience. When the discussion came to an end, the union leaders would leave the office, commenting on how warmhearted and understanding he was, and how confident they were that he would help them when it was possible for him to do so. They actually seemed more satisfied with a negative decision from Jones than they did with a hard-won concession from Smith.

This was clearly a case where the personality of Jones happened to match certain discernible requirements of the Latin American culture. It was happenstance in this case that Jones worked out and Smith did not, for by American standards both were top-flight men. Since a talent for the kind of negotiation that the Latin American considers graceful and acceptable can hardly be developed in a grown man (or perhaps even in a young one), the basic problem is one of personnel selection in terms of the culture where the candidate is to work.

The second case is more complicated because it involves much deeper intercultural adjustments. The management of the parent U.S. company concerned had learned—as have the directors of most large firms with good-sized installations overseas—that one cannot afford to have all of the top and middle-management positions manned by North Americans. It is necessary to advance nationals up the overseas-management ladder as rapidly as their abilities permit. So the nationals have to learn not only the technical aspects of their jobs but also how to function at higher levels in the organization.

Latin culture emphasizes authority in the home, church, and community. Within the organization this produces a built-in hesitancy about speaking up to one's superiors. The initiative, the acceptance of responsibility which we value in our organizations had to be stimulated. How could it be done?

We observed one management man who had done a remarkable job of building up these very qualities in his general foremen and foremen. To begin with, he stimulated informal contacts between himself and these men through social events to which the men and their wives came. He saw to it that his senior North American assistants and their wives were also present. Knowing the language, he mixed freely with all. At the plant, he circulated about, dropped in not to inspect or check up, but to joke and to break down the great barrier that existed in the local traditions between authority and the subordinates.

Next, he developed a pattern of three-level meetings. At the top, he himself, the superintendents, and the general foremen. At the middle level, the superintendents, general foremen, and foremen. Then the general foremen, foremen, and workers.

At the top level meeting, the American management chief set the pattern of encouraging his subordinates to challenge his own ideas, to come up with original thoughts. When his superintendents (also North Americans) disagreed with him, he made it clear that they were to state their objections fully. At first, the general foreman looked surprised and uneasy. They noted, however, that the senior men who argued with the boss were encouraged and praised. Timorously, with great hesitation, they began to add their own suggestions. As time went on, they more and more accepted the new convention and pitched in without inhibition.

The idea of challenging the boss with constructive new ideas gradually filtered down to the second and third level meetings. It took a lot of time and gentle handling, but out of this approach grew an extraordinary morale. The native general foremen and foremen developed new pride in themselves, accepted new responsibilities, even reached out for more. They began to work to improve their capacities and to look forward to moving up in the hierarchy.

CONFORMITY OR ADJUSTMENT?

To work with people, must we be just like them? Obviously not. If we try to conform completely, the Arab, the Latin American, the Italian, whoever he might be, finds our behavior confusing and insincere. He suspects our motive. We are expected to be different. But we are also expected to respect and accept the other people as they are. And we may, without doing violence to our own personalities, learn to communicate with them by observing the unwritten patterns they are accustomed to.

To be aware that there are pitfalls in cross-cultural dealings is the first big step forward. And to accept the fact that our convictions are in no respect more eternally "right" than someone else's is another constructive step.

Beyond these:

1. We can learn to control our so-called frankness in a culture which puts a high value on maintaining pleasant surface relations.

2. We can avoid expressing quick decisions when their utterance without a long period of polite preparation would show disrespect.

3. We can be on the lookout for the conversation patterns of nationals or whatever country we are in and accustom ourselves to closer quarters than we are used to. (This is uncomfortable at first but understanding the reason why it is important helps greatly.)

4. Where the situation demands it, we can learn to express our emotions more freely—most people find this rather exhilarating.

5. We can try to distinguish between the organizational practices which are really necessary to effectiveness and those that we employ from habit because they happen to be effective in the United States.

RESEARCH FOR ORGANIZATIONAL EFFECTIVENESS

We have outlined a point of view the individual can seek to apply in order to increase his own effectiveness. Valuable as that may be, we must recognize the limitations of an individual approach. Since each family transported overseas represents an investment of between $25,000 and $100,000 per year to the organization, the losses involved in poor selection or inadequate training can be enormous.

While no ready-made answers are now available, research can serve the organization both in *selection* and *training* of personnel.

It would be a mistake to assume that the ideal training program would fit just any administrator effectively into any given culture. We must assume that some personalities will fit more readily than others. By the time man reaches adulthood, his personality is rather solidly formed, and basic changes are difficult if not impossible to induce. It is therefore important to work to improve the selection process so that men with little chance of fitting into a foreign culture will not be sent where they are bound to fail.

Our Latin-American case of Smith and Jones is relevant here. One who had observed Smith in his native setting should have been able to predict that he would not be effective in handling labor relations in Latin America. However, that statement is based upon the hindsight observation that there was a very obvious lack of fit between Smith's personality and the cultural requirements of his job. It remains for research men to devise schemes of observation and testing which will enable personnel men to base their selections upon criteria of personality *and* culture.

To what extent can training improve the effectiveness of individuals in intercultural communication? Training of men in overseas operations is going on all the time. So far as we know, little of it currently deals with the considerations outlined in this article. Until organizations are prepared to develop training along these lines—and support research on the effects of such training—we shall not know to what extent intercultural communications can be improved through training.

We do not mean to give the impression that behavioral scientists already have the knowledge needed regarding intercultural communication. What we have presented here is only a demonstration of the importance of the topic. We have not presented a systematic analysis of the problems of communication from culture A to culture B. We have just said in effect: "These are some of the things that are important. Watch out for them."

What more is needed? In the first place, the problem calls for a new emphasis in anthropological research. In the past, anthropologists have been primarily concerned with the *internal* pattern of a given culture. In giving attention to intercultural problems, they have examined the impact of one culture upon another. Very little attention has been given to the actual communication process between representatives of different cultures.

Much could be learned, for example, if we observed North Americans in interaction with people of another culture. We would want also to be able to interview both parties to the interaction to study how A was interpreting B and how B was interpreting A. In this way we might discover points of friction and miscommunication whose existence we now do not even suspect. Such studies, furthermore, would provide systematic knowledge much more useful than the fragments provided in this article.

16. EAST-WEST INTERACTION PATTERNS

Johan Galtung

1. THE THEORY

The purpose of this paper is two fold: to explore the pattern of interaction of different kinds between the nations that are members of the NATO and the Warsaw treaty systems, and to explore the implications of some suggested changes in these interaction patterns.

Since we, in order to do this, need a perspective on international systems in general and the East-West system in particular, we shall make use of a recently-developed theoretical perspective.[1] According to this perspective, the world is conceived of as consisting of nations ranked according to a number of dimensions, such as size, wealth, military power, degree of development, etc.; in various degrees of interaction, negative and positive. However, in this complexity, two simple ordering principles appear:

1. The *rankings* have a tendency to be *concordant,* in the sense that a nation that ranks high on one dimension has a tendency also to rank high on other dimensions; and a nation that ranks low on one has a tendency to rank low on other dimensions as well. We shall refer to the former as topdog nations and to the latter as underdog nations.

SOURCE. Johan Galtung, "East-West Interaction Patterns," in *Journal of Peace Research,* No. 2, 1966, pp. 146-176. (Slightly abridged.) Reprinted by permission of the author and the International Peace Research Institute.

*This is a much revised and extended version of a paper originally presented at the Thirteenth Pugwash Conference on Science and World Affairs, Karlovy Vary, September 13–19, 1964, published in *Proceedings* pp. 133–139; here published as PRIO publication no. 21–4. Parts of the paper were also presented in a Lord Simon guest lecture, The University, Manchester, November 1964, and in the Quaker Seminar on European Security Problems, Gars am Kamp, Austria, April 22–30, 1966. I am very much indebted to Mr. Richard Edvardsen for imaginative assistance in the collection of data; to Pugwash friends and colleagues, particularly Professor Karol Lapter, for discussions and criticism of the ideas in the paper; and to the Norwegian Research Council for Science and the Humanities and to the Norwegian Council for Research on Conflict and Peace for financial support.

2. The *interaction* has a tendency to be *rank-dependent,* in the sense that there is much interaction between nations high in the ranking system, less between one nation that is high and another nation that is low, and much less between two nations low in the system. Thus, the degree of interaction is strongly dependent on the *total rank* of the pair.

An international system satisfying these two properties will be referred to as a *feudal system,* because the interaction patterns tie together the elements that are high up in the system—sew together the system at the top, so to speak—and split the system at the bottom, because the underdogs direct their interaction potential towards the top more than towards each other.[2]

But this system bears in it the seeds of its own destruction, because it permits more exploitation of the underdogs than the underdogs themselves will, in the long run, tolerate; because of the sub-utilization of human and national resources; and for other reasons. Thus, it can be destroyed if the underdogs unite and change the interaction pattern so that there is less rank dependence—and we get a *class system.* Or, it can be changed by breaking down the rank congruence, permitting all kinds of mixed rank patterns, and we get what can be referred to as a *mixed system.* Also, both processes may take place, in which case we arrive at an *egalitarian system.* However, according to our theory, the egalitarian system is not stable either, but will tend to relapse to the old dimensions defining the old feudal system, or some new dimensions will emerge defining a new feudal system. In this pendulum process between the feudal and egalitarian extremes there may be a dampening factor, so that the extremes are not really attained. Moreover, since the feudal end of this spectrum is more stable, we actually assume that the system will usually stay at that end.

In this article we shall discuss the case not of one system, but of two systems in various degrees of conflict with each other. In general, the units may be individuals or nations, and it helps theorizing in this field to draw on common-sense thinking and research from both levels of human organization. We shall call the two systems S_1 and S_2, where the first is split into a set of topdog nations T_1 and underdog nations U_1; and the latter, similarly into T_2 and U_2. Then, *within* each system we assume that there is most interaction between the T's, then between the T's and U's. and finally the lowest level of interaction between the U's. It may also be that the systems are less feudal, that they approach more the egalitarian model—but we assume that the topdogs can nevertheless be singled out (for instance the big powers in the NATO and Warsaw treaty systems). Table 1 gives this general picture.

TABLE 1. The General Scheme

System	S_1	S_2
Topdog	T_1	T_2
Underdog	U_1	U_2

As seen from Table 1, our total system has four types of actors: T_1, T_2, U_1 and U_2. It is fruitful to speculate what would happen if one strengthened the degree of interaction between the units, nations in our case, in all possible ways, and made it more positive. Thus, there may be more *within*-interaction in the sense that the T_1's start interacting more with each other, the T_2's more with each other, and so on—four cases altogether. And there may be more *between*-interaction, with T_1's interacting more with the U_1, or more with T_2—or more with the U_2, and similarly for T_2—six cases altogether. However, since there is complete symmetry between the two blocs we can reduce this to six cases; three within-bloc and three between-blocs:

1. *More T_1-T_1 interaction and more T_2-T_2 interaction.* This would make the blocs more feudal because of tighter integration between the topdog nations. In the NATO case, France has been pressing for a system of this kind, where decisions are virtually made by the three big powers in the bloc. In the world of individual relations, this would correspond to more upper class, capitalist, employer cohesion.

2. *More T_1-U_1 interaction and more T_2-U_2 interaction.* This would lead to a reinforcement of the blocs, which are then often referred to as *regions.* They would tend to become more self-sufficient; the smaller powers would look to the bigger powers for the solution to their internal and external problems. In the world of individual relations, this would correspond to employers carrying out welfare policies towards their employees, employer-employer associations and cooperation, etc.

3. *More U_1-U_1 interaction and more U_2-U_2 interaction.* This would lead the blocs into the class system phase, where the smaller powers would tend to coordinate their behavior towards the bigger powers, and start pressing for what they regard as more equitable prices for their exchange with the bigger powers. In the world of individual relations, this would correspond to local trade unions, and increased underdog cohesion would probably lead to increased topdog cohesion—i.e. to process no. 1 above.

4. *More T_1-T_2 interaction.* This would lead to a tendency for the big powers to regulate their conflicts over and above the heads of the smaller powers for instance by means of summit meetings. In the world of individual relations, this would correspond to covert and overt agreements between capitalists to coordinate economic activities.

5. *More T_1-U_2 interaction and more T_2-U_1 interaction.* This would lead to big power jealousy—T_2 would feel excluded in the first case and T_1 in the latter. In the world of individual relations, this would correspond to workers in one firm negotiating contracts with the employers of another enterprise.

6. *More U_1-U_2 interaction.* This would lead to some kind of class system for both systems. The process would be resented by both types of topdogs and may

force some type of cooperation between them, which means that it may induce a type 4 process. In the world of individual relations, this would correspond to the idea of horizontal, national trade unions whereby employers from different enterprises also are united.

Thus, these six processes are easily identifiable in the world of political and social behavior, at both levels of human organization. Can we now assume that they are completely unrelated, in the sense that a system consisting of two subsystems in conflict is free to do what it wants—or are there principles that regulate the processes relative to each other? Our answer lies, of course, in the latter direction. Although the tendencies towards a coupling of the processes may not be strong, it would be contrary to theory and data in the social sciences to postulate relative independence.

More concretely, we may offer three propositions with subpropositions which bring considerable theoretical order in this sytem of concepts and processes. We shall refer to these as the *homology* propositions, the *feudality* propositions and the *polarization* propositions respectively. The system of propositions is as follows:

1. *Homology propositions:* Systems that are comparable and in interaction will tend towards structural similarity (isomorphism, homology)
    1.1. *Vertical homology propositions*
        1.1.1.   Process 1 will lead to process 3, within each bloc, and v.v.
        1.1.2.   Process 4 will lead to process 6, between blocs and v.v.
    1.2. *Horizontal homology propositions*
        1.2.1. T_1-T_1 interaction will lead to T_2-T_2 interaction and v.v.
        1.2.2. U_1-U_1 interaction will lead to U_2-U_2 interaction and v.v.
        1.2.3. T_1-U_1 interaction will lead to T_2-U_2 interaction and v.v.
    1.3. *Diagonal homology propositions*
        1.3.1. T_1-U_2 interaction will lead to T_2-U_1 interaction
        1.3.2. T_2-U_1 interaction will lead to T_1-U_2 interaction.
2. *Feudality propositions:* The higher the total rank of the pair, the easier the interaction process.
    1. *Within bloc feudality propositions*
       Process 1 is easier than process 2, which is easier than process 3, within each bloc.
    2.2. *Between-blocs feudality propositions*
       Process 4 is easier than process 5, which is easier than process 6, between blocs.
3. *Polarization propositions:* The lower the total rank of the pair, the higher the tendency to break interaction in case of conflict.
    3.1. *Horizontal polarization propositions, between blocs*

3.1.1.   Process 6 will first be broken, then process 5 and then process 4.

3.1.2.   Processes 1, 2, and/or 3 will be strengthened.

3.2.   *Vertical polarization propositions, within blocs*

3.2.1.   Process 2 will be broken in case of class conflict.

3.2.2.   Processes 1 and 3 will be strengthened.

We shall make some brief comments on these propositions.

The homology propositions are all based on ideas of communication which leads to imitation, and the need for structural similarity, whether the relation between the two parties is positive or negative. Each party has to find its "opposite number" in the other party; each party will easily believe that a reorganization on the other side will strengthen that side relative to oneself, and that the best counter-tactic is to do the same. NATO was followed by a military supreme command in the East, and by the Warsaw treaty; EEC by Comecon, and so on.[3] Employers' unions and employees' unions are closely geared to each other.[4]

The feudality propositions have already been commented upon many times. Let it suffice only to say that these are nothing but efforts to put in proposition form the common-sense experience that topdogs draw more attention than underdogs, and that they control their systems and, hence, prefer interaction patterns consonant with this.

The polarization propositions can be seen as descriptions of conditions that precede destructive conflict behavior and/or result from them. The essence of the proposition is that the topdogs trust only themselves and consequently want to dominate interaction, and more so the more conflictuous they deem the situation to be. They do not rely on the underdogs for direct contact, but prefer the contact to go via the topdogs. Nor do they rely on their own underdogs for contacts with the topdogs of the other party—for fear that they will start negotiating special deals for themselves.[5] To avoid this, the topdogs have to pay for the decrease in interaction with the other party with increased interaction within the bloc, simply to provide for the needs of the underdogs. In general, the topdogs are forced all the time to convince their underdogs that they have more to gain by staying in the bloc than by attaching themselves to the other party—and if this cannot be done on the basis of bargaining, it has to be done by means of persuasion and/or force.

Thus, in a sense the topdogs will be most interested in breaking contacts of the type described in process 5, since contact with the topdog on the other side potentially is more rewarding to one's own underdogs. Nevertheless, in proposition 3.1.1. we have assumed that process 6 will be broken first, then process 5 and then process 4. This is because there may be cross-conflict topdog cooperation in preventing interactions of the type described in process 6—but not for the types described in process 5, where either side will enjoy underdog renegades from the other side.

It should be noticed that the polarization propositions are similar in form to the incest propositions, if we compare Table 1 with Table 2.

TABLE 2. Types of Incestuous Relations (broken lines)

	Male	Female
Topdog	Father	Mother
Underdog	Son	Daughter

The incest taboos are against relations structurally similar to relations outlawed by norms of polarization. This can be generalized to other types of small groups as well,[6] and probably contributes to learning generalized patterns of polarized behavior.[7]

However, the most remarkable feature of our set of propositions is the similarity between the feudality propositions and the polarization propositions: the former say that interaction at the top is favored in feudal systems; the latter, that interaction at the bottom is the first victim of polarization tendencies in a conflict. Concretely, this means that, *with a feudal relationship between two blocs or systems, polarization is already built into the system.* In other words, to the extent two systems have a relationship obeying the feudality propositions, to that extent are they already "stripped for conflict action," to use Coleman's excellent expression.[8]

At this point let us go straight to some conjectures for which we do not have sufficient data, although they are certainly testable:

1. Inter-nation relations tend to be more rank-dependent than intergroup relations within a nation,[9]

and

2. The more rank-dependent a relation between two systems (nations, groups), the more violent the conflicts between them.

These propositions are, no doubt, valid under some conditions, but since we know little or nothing about the conditions under which they are valid, we shall not use them as more than heuristic devices. For the obvious implications are (1) that international systems are more dangerous, which we generally hold to be true,[10] and (2) that they can probably be made less dangerous by counteracting rank-dependence in them.

Hence, our tasks in the following sections are these:

1. To explore with as good data as possible the exact nature of the interaction patterns between the two power blocs in order to see to what extent the degree of interaction, both positive and negative, is really rank-dependent; and how this varies with changing phases in the between-bloc conflict.

2. To explore in detail what the possibilities of decreased rank-dependence would be, to see whether the thesis above seems reasonable.

We now proceed to this.

2. THE DATA

To get data about East-West interaction patterns we sent a questionnaire to all Oslo embassies and the foreign ministries of GDR, Albania and Norway, of the 15 + 8 nations that were members of the two systems spring 1964, and asked for information about interaction with the other 22 nations. Only one embassy (the embassy of the German Federal Republic) refused to cooperate, whereas others were fairly late in their response and much direct correspondence with embassies and government offices had to be carried out. The responses were then checked and additional data were obtained through international yearbooks, particularly those of the United Nations, and *Keesing's Contemporary Archives.* The inter-action variables we wanted information on were the following fifteen:

1. *Diplomatic relations*
    1.1. Establishment of diplomatic relations
    1.2. Diplomat restrictions imposed and cancelled
    1.3. Expulsion of diplomats
2. *Political relations*
    2.1. State visits
    2.2. Notes exchanged
    2.3. UN interaction
3. *Economic relations*
    3.1. Trade agreements
    3.2. Trade restrictions imposed and cancelled
    3.3. Trade volume
4. *Cultural relations*
    4.1. Cultural agreements
    4.2. Cultural institutions closed
5. *Travel*
    5.1. Visa requirements
    5.2. Tourist restrictions imposed and cancelled
    5.3. Tourist volume
    5.4. Flight connections

Other types of interaction can certainly be imagined, but we felt that this was sufficient to test our hypothesis about the general pattern of interaction. Moreover, there are six negative types of interaction: 1.2, 1.3, 2.2, 3.2, 4.2, and 5.2. But in the period under discussion no directly belligerent activities took place between the present regimes in the nations belonging to the two systems—we do not count the wars against the Axis powers.

As *time variable* we shall use the phase variable for describing cold war relationships developed in an earlier article.[11] Thus, phase 1 is from June 22 1941 to December 31 1947, phase 2 from January 1 1948 to May 14 1955, phase 3 from May 15 1955 to June 5 1961, and phase 4 from then on to the end of 1965.

As *rank variable* we shall use the simple distinction between big powers and small powers mentioned above—where the big powers are the Security Council veto powers. But whether that distinction functions is an empirical question to be tested in the next section.

3. TESTING THE HYPOTHESIS ABOUT RANK CONCORDANCE

We shall now explore to what extent our model of the world as a feudal system is valid, and turn first to the problem of concordance for the ranks in the blocs. Table 3 summarizes some of the most important data about the big and small powers in the two alliances, and we have also added some information about (the People's Republic of) China. To add perspective to the comments on the Table we shall use the propositions about rank disequilibrium[13] and rank in congruence[14] as sources of change and (possible) conflict.

First of all, it should be noticed how remarkably concordant the eight dimensions dealing with *size* and *power* are, at least as long as we only deal with "big" versus "small" nations. For the Warsaw Pact nations the concordance is perfect, insofar as the Soviet Union ranks highest by a factor around 10 on the first four dimensions and is the only nation with nuclear arms, veto power, a world language and a sphere of interest. By and large this also applies to the NATO alliance, which means that the hypothesis is confirmed. *But there are some highly important exceptions in the NATO case:*

1. Germany ranks above two of the big powers in population, Italy ranks above one.
2. Canada ranks above all three in area, Italy and Germany above one each.
3. Germany ranks above France in GNP.
4. Germany comes very close to United Kingdom in armed forces.
5. Canada also speaks the world languages English and French.
6. Belgium speaks French (and Flemish).
7. Germany also has a "sphere of interest."

Thus, one would predict less rivalry and a higher degree of cohesion in general in the Warsaw Pact system than in the NATO system, because of the extreme rank dominance of the big power in the former, making for complete rank equilibrium and rank congruence. Of course, there may be important cases of rank

TABLE 3. A Comparison Between Big and Small Powers, West and East, and China[12]

| | | Size | | | | Power | | | | Nuclear Power Potential, Possible Bombs, year | Additional Information | | |
		Population (mill.)	Area, km² (thous.)	GNP US $, 1957 (bill.)	Armed forces (thous.)	Nuclear Power	Veto Power	World Language	Sphere of Interest		Defence Expenditure % of GNP	Defence Expenditure % of Central Gov't. Expenditure	Per Capita GNP, US $, 1957
Big powers	United States	194	9,363	443	2,660	yes	yes	yes	yes	–	8.9	53	2,577
	United Kingdom	54	244	61	440	yes	yes	yes	yes	–	6.7	26	1,189
North Atlantic Treaty Organization	France	49	551	42	557	yes	yes	yes	yes	–	5.1	22	943
Small powers	Average all 12	17	101	12	168	zero	zero	low	low	52	3.4	18	863
	Germ. Fed. Rep.	56	248	50	438	no	no	no	yes	187	5.0	34	927
	Italy	51	301	25	390	no	no	no	no	134	3.3	16	516
	Canada	19	9,974	32	120	no	no	yes	no	240	3.7	23	1,947
Big power	Soviet Union	228	22,403	122	3,150	yes	yes	yes	yes	–	5.7	16	600
Small powers	Average, all 7	15	145	7	160	zero	zero	zero	zero	4	3.0*	8.0**	492
	Poland	32	312	13	277	no	no	no	no	0	3.5	8.5	475
Warsaw Pact Nations	Czechoslovakia	14	128	9	235	no	no	no	no	30	3.9	9	680
	Germ. Dem. Rep.	17	107	10	112	no	no	no	no	0	2.5	–	600
Big power	China	650	9,761	46	2,486	yes	no	yes	yes	–	–	–	.73

* Albania not included
**GDR and Albania not included

disequilibrium or rank incongruence "in the small," among the small powers.
Thus, the German Democratic Republic ranks lower on area and on armed forces
than it should according to population and GNP, relative to Poland and Czechoslovakia.

In the NATO system each disequilibrium, and particularly the cases of incongruence with big powers, may lead to internal conflicts, potentially weakening the
alliance (in times of peace; one should of course not infer that these conflicts will
not lose in salience and even be forgotten in times of war or threats of war).
Germany, Canada and Italy have been singled out for attention in this connection.
Some years ago, the disequilibrium due to the "no" for France as to nuclear
power was a major source of conflict—and some of the conflicts centering around
France may still be attributed to the wounds created by this disequilibrium. Today the incongruence caused by Italy's population is of minor significance, particularly because of the low GNP per capita of that nation. But Germany and
Canada and Italy are, nevertheless, the nations that rank highest among the small
powers as to nuclear power potential, with Belgium (the only other country to be
mentioned in the disequilibrium list above) as a poor no. 4 (with 56 possible
bombs per year). Thus, the list serves as a very good predictor of nuclear power
potential, partly because size and economic potential permit this type of development—and partly, we presume, because of the motivation provided by the disequilibrium and/or incongruence itself. And this particular type of development,
under international supervision or not, is probably a key to present and future
power distributions.

Secondly, it should be noticed that it costs to be a big power, not only in absolute terms, but also relatively speaking. Big powers have to spend a much higher
fraction of their GNP than smaller powers on defence—even though Germany
comes very close to France. Grossly speaking, they also allocate a higher proportion of their total central government expenditure on the military sector, although
these figures are difficult to interpret because of the differences in political structure in the countries involved.

Thirdly, when we add one of the per capita variables, the GNP per capita, the
whole picture changes. The big are still big, but less so. In fact, whereas the five
nuclear powers in the world also are the five nations with the largest armies, with
veto power except for the anomaly where China's seat in the Security Council is
concerned, with world languages, etc., and are among the top 6 in GNP (West
Germany is no. 4), and among the top 12 in population (United Kingdom is no.
10, France is no. 12)—we find that they are only among the top 101 as to GNP
per capita. Thus, United States is no. 2 (after Kuwait!), United Kingdom no. 10,
France no. 13, Soviet Union no. 21 and China 101. This means that in a world
where the emphasis changes from absolute to per capita indicators—a world more
concerned with the status of the individual than with the status of the nation—the
small powers would mix very well with the big powers. But in a world where

military power is salient, this will not be the case for some time to come, for in a war absolute power counts more than power per capita. If military personnel as a percentage of population (aged 15–64) counted most, then the six leading nations would be Taiwan, North Korea, Israel, South Korea, Jordan and Albania—with France as no. 7, Soviet Union as no. 11, United States as no. 17, United Kingdom as no. 23 and China as no. 59.

Finally, there is China. She has suffered more from rank disequilibrium and rank incongruence than any other nation, having ranked low on nuclear power, veto power and GNP per capita. The first of these three sources of strain has been overcome; the US policy of refusing the People's Republic of China membership in the UN and a seat with veto power in the Security Council, has blocked equilibration at this point so far and probably contributed to withdrawal and extreme aggressiveness; and the lag in GNP per capita has led to extreme efforts to improve productivity.[15] At the same time a sphere of interest exists, the limitation of which is not well known; and, as long as the motivation produced by rank disequilibrium lasts, one will probably also have efforts to have the sphere of interest recognized.

It is interesting to compare the profiles for the Soviets and China. The Soviet Union is above China in area, GNP and GNP per capita, and China is above the Soviet Union in population—as to armed forces they are more equal. Thus, the rank incongruence theory is a good basis for predicting that the two would not join forces in an Eastern alliance; according to the theory they would live in isolation, in conflict or in both, and they seem to have chosen "both." Contributing to this rank incongruence is probably the Soviet self-definition as a young nation, at least compared to China. If the Soviet Union prefers to define itself as being in continuity with old Russia, she may claim up to 1000 years of existence, as compared with China's three millenia or more. From the Chinese point of view both the Soviet Union and the United States may both appear as *parvenus*.

That does, of course, not mean that China and the Soviet Union would necessarily have been friends, had they been of the same age. Thus both of the two superpowers today are newcomers on the international scene, filling the gaps of such powers as the United Kingdom, France, Germany, Italy and Austria (some of which earlier filled gaps left by Spain and Portugal). They are essentially struggling for the same goal, ascendancy over other nations, and, since the goal is scarce, the basis for conflict exists. And in this process they obtain rank incongruent positions relative to older nations and cultures—an incongruence the French seem to have felt particularly heavily.

China has now joined this struggle, and it is easy to see that she will have to build her own sphere of interest, since she is rank-incongruent with the other two superpowers. Moreover, she will probably mainly look for nations still lower in GNP per capita to avoid rank incongruence. That gives North Korea and North Vietnam, Burma, Laos, Mongolia and Nepal among her neighbors (and India,

Pakistan and Afghanistan among the more remote neighbors)—but not Thailand, Cambodia Ceylon and Indonesia.[16] Thus, the theory predicts instability in China—Indonesia relationships until China's GNP has surpassed Indonesia's, and predicts nations that would more easily attach themselves closely to China.

Thus, in general the essentially very simple theory put forward is both well confirmed and found to be fruitful. On the one hand, the predominant feature of the two blocs is rank-concordance; on the other hand, where rank-concordance does not occur the theory predicts conflicts and these conflicts seem to be easily identifiable empirically. More particularly, the difference in degree of overt external conflict in the NATO and Warsaw blocs is predicted by the theory. For instance, if one selects as rank dimensions the first four in Table 3, population, area, GNP and armed forces, the average degree of rank disequilibrium is 0.6 for the Warsaw powers as against 2.6, or more than four times as much, for the NATO powers.[17] In both blocs the highest (USA and Soviet Union powers) and the lowest (Luxembourg and Albania) powers are best equilibrated (perfectly so for the two Warsaw treaty powers), but then the differences in degree of internal disequilibrium emerge. However, it should of course be noticed that all this depends very much on which dimensions one selects for the calculation of degree of disequilibrium. On the other hand: the general finding is invariant of which set of the rank dimensions one uses.

And it should also be noticed that perfect rank-concordance with one power on top is not necessarily stable in the long run either: the smaller powers may unite against the big power. But this is unlikely to happen unless there is some measure of rank disequilibrium present in one or more of the smaller powers—preferably in one of the highest ranking of them—producing the kind of aggressiveness that can be easily converted into drive for change.[18]

4. TESTING THE HYPOTHESIS OF INTERACTION DEPENDENCE ON RANK.

We shall now investigate in detail how interaction between pairs of nations, one in the West and one in the East, depends on the total rank of the pair. By "total rank of the pair," then, we mean what we arrive at when we give a 0 to an underdog nation and 1 to a topdog nation, and then calculate the sum for the two nations in the pair. Thus, two big powers get a score of 2, one big and one small get a score of 1 and two small powers make 0—thus yielding three types of pairs. According to the hypothesis there should be more interaction the higher the total rank of the pair, and the differences should even be quite pronounced.

At this point one may object that this is trivial: that there is, for instance, more diplomatic activity between the big than between the small is a simple consequence of the circumstance that they are big. For that reason we are not simply trying to prove that there is more interaction, the higher the total rank of the pair, but also that there is more interaction relative to what one might expect, given the interaction potential. The precise meaning of this will be made clear for each case below, when types of interaction will be treated in the same order as they appear in the list in section 2 above. Since the NATO bloc is divided into three big and twelve small, and the Warsaw Pact bloc into one big and seven small, we get 3 pairs with total rank 2, 33 pairs with total rank 1 and 84 pairs with total rank 0—all together 120 pairs. Imagine now that we have an interaction phenomenon that is not measured in degrees, it either takes place or not, like the existence (or not) of diplomatic relations, state visits, flights, etc. To explore the degree of interaction dependence we calculate the percentage of pairs where the interaction is found, for each of the three groups, and compare these percentages. Examples of possible distributions are shown in Table 4.

TABLE 4. Some Examples of Types of Interaction Dependence (hypothetical) cal)

Type of pair	Big East-Big West	Big East/West-Small West/East	Small East-Small West	Percentage Difference
Total rank of pair	2	1	0	
Complete rank dependence	100%	50%	0%	100%
Partial rank dependence	80%	50%	20%	60%
Low rank dependence	60%	50%	40%	20%
No rank dependence	50%	50%	50%	0%
Inverse rank dependence	20%	50%	80%	−60%

In the first case, the case of complete rank dependence, the situation is very feudal indeed: the small do not interact directly, interaction goes via one or two of the big. Evidently, this is an extreme case, but well approximated by the rules of interaction in some bureaucratic organizations. It should be noticed that there are actually two dimensions at work here; not only degree of rank dependence but also average level of interaction. Thus, systems may be low on both (10-10-10), high on one but not on the other (50-30-0 or 80-80-80) and high on both (100-70-40). We expect most distributions to be of the "partial rank dependence" variety. Cases of no-rank dependence, not to mention the unlikely case of inverse rank dependence would be clear cases of disconfirmation, but even cases of low rank dependence do not confirm the hypothesis.

We then turn to the detailed examination of the relation between rank and interaction, using the fifteen types of interaction, using the fifteen types of interaction outlined in section 2 above.

4.1.1. Diplomatic relations

As the existence of diplomatic relations has long been regarded as an important indicator of the nature of the relations between two countries, we shall start with that kind of data. There are three values of the variable: embassy or legation exists, embassy or legation is not established, and the intermediate value of *accreditation*. In the latter case, diplomatic relations have been established, but for economic and/or political reasons the ambassador or minister resides in another capital, usually in a neighboring country.

The data are presented in Table 5.[19] The trend is as predicted. If we collapse the three types of diplomatic relation we get the following percentages for diplomatic relations: 100%–82%–58%, and a percentage difference of 42%, which is quite high. Thus, 41 pairs of the 120 pairs of nations did not have diplomatic relations. However, it should be noticed that the two Germanies accounted for a total of 21 or 51% of these gaps (the German Federal Republic has diplomatic relations with the Soviet Union) and if we add Portugal, which did not have diplomatic relation with any nation in the East, we account for a total of 28 of the pairs, or 68%. But this is no falsification of the hypothesis, only more detailed information about the mechanisms. The point is that the gaps in the diplomatic network matrix are not located at random, but concentrated on the lower levels—the tops of the system are completely sewn together in terms of diplomatic relations. Thus, accreditation is also found at the bottom: of the 26 cases of accreditation 21 or 81% stem from the three smallest NATO powers (Luxembourg, Iceland, Norway).

TABLE 5. East-West Diplomatic Relations, 1966, %

	Big East- Big West	Big East/West Small West/East	Small East- Small West	Total
Embassy or legation both ways	100	82	39	53
Accreditation one way	0	0	7	5
Accreditation both ways	0	0	12	8
No diplomatic relation	0	18	42	34
Sum	100	100	100	100
(N)	(3)	(33)	(84)	(120)

4.1.2. Diplomat restrictions imposed and cancelled

Restrictions on the freedom to move for diplomats were typical of the activities in phase 2—although some of them (mainly involving the United States and the Soviet Union) are still in force. The distribution is shown in Table 6.[20]

It will be seen that the hypothesis receives a very clear confirmation. And the interesting thing about this Table is that we are concerned with negative interaction, yet nevertheless find the same type of relationship. Thus, one might have imagined that diplomat restrictions would come more easily in relations between

TABLE 6. Restrictions Imposed on Diplomats, Phase 2

	Big-Big	Big-Small	Small-Small
No. of ordered pairs with diplomatic relations	6	58	64
No. of restrictions	6	29	16
% restrictions of total	100%	50%	25%
Percentage difference		75%	

small nations, since relations are already so meager—but the fact is as predicted by the theory, that *all* kinds of interaction are, if not monopolized, at least over-represented for the big powers. Interaction is between them, and between them and the smaller powers; the others are spectators and reflections.

4.1.3. Expulsion of diplomats

We perused *Keesing's* for material on the expulsion of diplomats. This relation is clearly not symmetric by definition, since country *A* can expel a diplomat from country *B*, without country *B* expelling a diplomat from country *A*. However, by and large the relation tends to be symmetric, *B* will have a tendency to find a pretext to reciprocate, and such pretexts are probably easily found. Nevertheless, we shall treat the data asymmetrically and calculate the percentages of cases of expulsion on the basis of diplomatic relations both ways. Moreover, as in Table 5 we shall use as a basis for the calculation not the total number of (ordered) pairs of nations (240 in phase 4), but the total number of ordered pairs with diplomatic relations—since expulsion cannot take place where there are no diplomatic relations.

. . . The hypothesis is confirmed for all three phases, especially phases 2 and 4. It may be objected that these percentages should have been calculated on the basis of the total number of diplomats, not on the basis of the total number of diplomatic relations. If this were done, the percentage differences would be re-duced, but the trend would still be there (except, possibly, for phase 3).

Let us then look at the total number of expulsions as a function of time, but in a more detailed manner [in Diagram 1]. In phase 1 we had the crises leading up to and including the formation of NATO, in phase 2 no particular crisis but con-tinuously bad relations, in phase 3 the Hungary-Suez crises and in phase 4 the Cuba crisis. How are they reflected in the curve for expulsion of diplomats?

If one should speculate on this meager basis, then one might read three hy-potheses out of this curve.

First of all, expulsions are concentrated, peaked and connected with impor-tant events. Thus, the three crises mentioned seem to account for about 50 per-cent of the total number of expulsions found in the period.

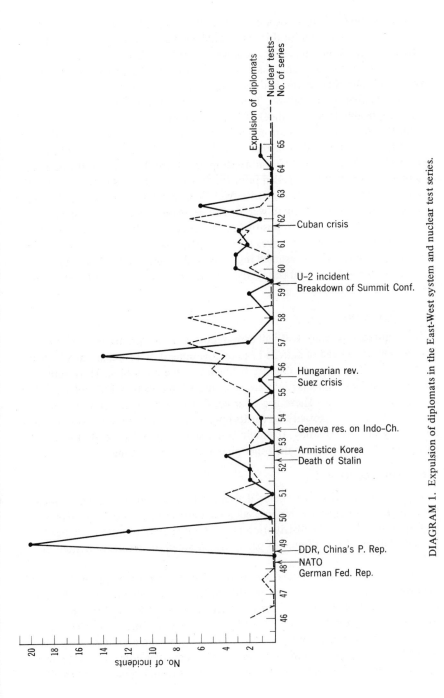

DIAGRAM 1. Expulsion of diplomats in the East-West system and nuclear test series.

Secondly, there seems to be a dampening in the system; the peaks become lower with time. To establish this, one would need an objective indicator of the relative severity of the three crises, and we do not have that. However, it does not seem reasonable to assume that the Cuba crisis was that much less severe than the Hungary-Suez crises, and that they in turn were that much less severe than what happened in 1948–49. Thus, the system has probably become more trained, more able to absorb shocks over a period of time.

Thirdly, the two intervals are equal, both equal to seven years. It would be foolhardy to see any kind of regularity in this and predict that the next East-West crisis would occur in 1970 (and extrapolate from the peaks to the number of diplomats that will be expelled prior to, during and after that crisis). Nevertheless, it does seem reasonable that crises will either increase in number and decrease in interval, eventually leading to war; or else decrease in number and increase in interval, eventually leading to positive peace—or else stabilize at a level that might well be every seventh year. It takes time to repair relations after a crisis, to enjoy the honeymoon feeling of resumed relations, and it takes time to build up a new crisis—so why not seven years altogether, provided the basic inter-bloc relations are the same?

4.2.1. State visits

We counted as a "state visit" all cases reported in the questionnaires and/or in *Keesing's* where a head of state, a head of government or a foreign minister had been on an official visit in a country belonging to the other bloc. Thus, summit meetings or private conversations are not counted, unless they fall under the definition given above.... There is a clear confirmation in phases 3 and 4. In phase 2 the state visit activity was at its lowest, just as we found for summit meeting activity in another study. It should be remembered that phase 4 only covers a period of 4 years, whereas the other phases are 6–8 years long.

4.2.2 Notes exchanged

Keesing's was perused for material about notes between governments. Since the number of notes very often exceeded the number of pairs of countries, we preferred to compare the distribution of the total activity of note exchange with the distribution of the number of pairs, and obtained the results presented in Table 7.

Here the confirmation is nearly extreme, since we get percentage differences in the neighborhood of 70. Thus, of the 407 notes we were able to locate, for the total period, 3% of the pairs of countries accounted for 51%, and the small-small pairs, 70% of the total, for only 7% of the note activity. This means that one or more big powers were involved in 93% of the activity, and even if *Keesing's* is biased towards big power reporting, this almost identifies notes with big powers. It also belongs to the picture that more notes went from big powers to small

TABLE 7. Distribution of Notes, and Pairs of Countries, Percentage

	Phase 1			Phase 2			Phase 3			Phase 4		
	Notes	Pairs	Diff.	Notes	Pairs	Diff.	Notes	Pairs	Diff.	Notes	Pairs	Diff.
Big-big	40	3	37	52	3	49	50	3	47	48	3	45
Big-small	60	30	30	40	27	13	46	27	19	52	27	25
Small-small	0	67	−67	8	70	−62	4	70	−66	0	70	−70
Sum	100	100	0	100	100	0	100	100	100	100	100	0
(N)	(5)	(98)		(266)	(120)		(113)	(120)		(23)	(120)	

powers than vice versa; 98 against 74 to be precise. Topdogs are trained in taking the initiative, and notes from the small to the big are most likely to be responses triggered by the stimulus given by a note from the top.[21]

The Table also gives a nice confirmation of the finding from an earlier article about summitry: phase 2, the bloc-formation phase, was also the phase highest on negative activity—and the content of the notes is almost always negative one way or the other. Thus, of the total period of close to 25 years, that particular 6 year period (less than one quarter of the time) accounted for two-thirds of the note output.

4.3.2 UN interaction

What is the contact network in the United Nations among the member nations of the two systems? Is the pattern the same or is it very different? To get an impression of this we examined data from Chadwick Alger's study of interaction in a committee (the fifth), of the United Nations General Assembly.[22] The methodology is simple: an observer located in the room where the meeting is held takes notes whenever informal communication takes place. These data are from the 17th session in 1962, where the committee held 70 meetings. Eighteen of these meetings were used to get to know the identity of the delegates, so the data are from the remaining 52 meetings. Since 94% of the interaction situations were bilateral, between two delegates, we can restrict ourselves to bilateral interaction. If we use the same division of countries as in Table 3—with the exception that the two Germanies do not appear since they are not members of the UN, and with Byelo-Russia and Ukraina joined with the Soviet Union we get interaction. . . [patterns which can be viewed] in many ways. One way is to focus on the very low frequencies. Thus, the NATO countries almost do not deal informally with the small Warsaw countries—the idea probably being that "they do not count." On the Warsaw side this is reciprocated only for the small Warsaw countries—the result being that from the very small in one bloc to the very small in the other there is no informal interaction at all. This comes as no surprise with the general hypothesis in mind, but is nevertheless interesting since the informal forces might be less strong. In fact, they are: . . . a lot of interaction does not correspond to the pattern for note exchange, for instance. But to study this we have to compare the interaction that takes place with the number of pairs in each category, and make use of the cruder distinction between big and small only. First of all, Table 8 shows that there is more interaction within bloc than between blocs, relative to what one might have expected. Secondly, the NATO system conforms better to the hypothesis than the Warsaw powers—there is more activity at the bottom. And the relation between blocs is interesting. Thus, the big powers in the West seem to avoid the Soviet Union, Ukraine and Byelo-Russia, and to prefer the smaller powers—for then, perhaps, to communicate the results to the small NATO-powers. The Warsaw powers seem to have different tactics: direct communication

TABLE 8. Ratio Between Number of Interactions and Numbers of Pairs, for Each
Category of Countries

FROM:	Big NATO (3)	Small NATO (11)	Big Warsaw (3)	Small Warsaw (6)
TO				
Big NATO (3)	1.9	3.0	0.8	1.1
Small NATO (11)	1.2	0.2	0.1	0.1
Big Warsaw (3)	1.2	0.1	1.3	1.8
Small Warsaw (6)	0.5	0.2	1.7	1.2

from big to big, and much discussion in the group. A more detailed inspection
seems to indicate that the West uses Netherlands in addition to the big powers as
a medium of communication with the East, and the East makes use of the Soviet
Union and Poland. Obviously, personality characteristics play a considerable role
here.

The picture is more refined than the predominantly feudal image we have obtained so far: the UN is an agency that gives more possibility for the smaller
powers, because the feudal structure of the international society is not mirrored
completely in the world of delegates; it gives more leeway. However, the interaction is still directed towards the big on the other side.

4.3.1. Trade agreements

We perused *Keesing's* and other sources for material on trade agreements,
starting with some data on the number of trade agreements in existence at different levels of total rank of the pair, and for different phases in East–West relations.
We also included phase 1 for comparisons. . . .

The hypothesis is confirmed in all cases. In phase 1 the two Germanies were
not included in the system. All percentages are higher than for all other phases,
reflecting some of the effects of the East–West polarization that took place later
on. But the strong dependence on interaction on total rank was as pronounced
as ever. On the other hand, one should not draw too many conclusions on the
basis of the relative sizes of the percentage differences, since they are extremely
vulnerable: one more big power trade agreement and the percentages as well as
the differences jump 33%.

We also investigated the average length of the trade agreements, but although
there was a tendency for agreements on the top to be concluded for a longer
period at the time, the correlations were unclear and unimpressive.

One reason why the rank-dependence is so pronounced for the first phase is
probably the influence of the war. World trade had to be reopened, and it was

natural, in a sense, that the big powers took a lead in this. It was their task, their responsibility in a world where the big powers play the role of the family fathers to provide for the small and the weak (not to mention for themselves) through a system of agreements. Later on the rank-dependence decreased, but the low rate of trade agreements among the small was maintained. We shall see later, in section 4.3.2 below, that this is clearly reflected in the data on trade volume.

Again one should be warned against taking these data too seriously. Much trade may go on without a trade agreement, and there may be trade agreements without much trade. Nevertheless, in the cold war system the trade agreement is tantamount to some kind of positive interaction and as such of interest in our context of analysis.

*   *   *

4.3.2. Trade volume

Trade data are problematic, but, since we are mainly concerned with gross characteristics of the trade in the East–West system, we have relied on the data given in the Europa Yearbook, and some United Nations statistics. For any pair of nations (excluding Luxembourg and Iceland) data have been obtained on the volume of (1) A exports to B, (2) B imports from A, (3) B exports to A, and (4) A imports from B. The difference between 1 and 4 is A's trade balance relative to B; the difference between 3 and 2, B's trade balance relative to A; there is no necessary reason why they should be 0. But 1 should be equal to 2, and 3 should be equal to 4, and where this is not the case we have used the arithmetic mean as the best estimate. Usually the discrepancies are of a small magnitude relative to the amount involved.

As trade is not exactly the same as power politics, we have chosen a different division where rank is concerned this time. The total export matrix for the East–West system was inspected and nations were ranked within each bloc according to the magnitude of their exports and their imports *in this system.* The rank order correlation for import and export was almost perfect (0.91 for NATO, 0.98 for Warsaw), so we used this rank order to divide the NATO powers into "high," "middle" and "low" as to trade volume, and the Warsaw powers into "high" and "low," as shown in Table 9. Thus, in the "high" classes are included not only the big powers but also the highest-ranking smaller powers according to the analysis made in 3 above. We have thereby reduced the complexity of the system from 21 nations to five categories of nations, four of them consisting of four nations each, and one consisting of five nations. In other words, the total trade in the system is divided into $5 \times 5 = 25$ categories of trade, and we are interested in the relative size of these trade volumes, measured in millions of US dollars.

One way of doing this is to set the total trade equal to 100, and calculate the 25 percentages. This gives [Table 10] :[23]

TABLE 9. Divisions of NATO and Warsaw Pact Nations
as to Trade

	NATO Nations	Warsaw Pact Nations
High	1. United States 2. German Fed. Rep. 3. United Kingdom 4. Canada 5. France	1. Soviet Union 2. German Dem. Rep. 3. Czechoslovakia 4. Poland
Middle	6. Netherlands 7. Belgium 8. Italy 9. Denmark	Category not used
Low	10. Norway 11. Turkey 12. Greece 13. Portugal	5. Hungary 6. Romania 7. Bulgaria 8. Albania

TABLE 10. The Relative Magnitude of Trade Within and Between East and West.
Percent, Based on Europa Yearbook, 1964

		To NATO Countries			To Warsaw Countries		
		High	Middle	Low	High	Low	Sum
From NATO countries	high	35.0	16.8	3.2	1.9	0.5	57.4
	middle	13.2	4.9	0.8	0.6	0.2	19.7
	low	1.7	0.5	0.0	0.1	0.0	2.3
From WARSAW countries	high	1.6	0.6	0.2	10.8	3.4	16.6
	low	0.5	0.2	0.0	3.1	0.2	4.0
Sum		52.0	23.0	4.2	16.5	4.3	100.0

One should be careful with interpretation of Table 10. Within each of the four blocs the Table is divided into there is a monotonic decrease in all percentages, from the upper left to the lower right hand corners of the subtables—as predicted by the theory. Trade is highly rank-dependent—but trade has also been used to determine the ranks. However, it is obvious that the results would be fairly much the same if we adhered to the criterion for dividing the nations into big and small used in Table 3 above.

Thus, we are not saying that it is in any sense strange that the data distribute as they do above: this is easily explained in terms of total capacity for import and export. The remarkable fact about the Table is rather how much of the total trade is in the hands of relatively few nations. Thus, if one looks at the exports one finds that the 9 countries classified as "high," or 43% of the total number of countries (39% if we include Luxembourg and Iceland) account for 74% of the export, whereas the countries classified as "low," 38% of the total number, account for as little as 6.3% of the export. If we look at the data from the point of view of imports, then the "high" group accounts for 68.5% and the "low" group for 8.5%. Thus, it also belongs to the picture that the "high" group has a positive and the "low" group a negative balance in the system. The consequence of all this is once more that the world interaction machinery is dominated by the big, far more than their number should warrant.

But most remarkable, in a sense, are the four cells indicating low-low trade relations: three of them are empty (very low trade levels). So, except for intra-East trade, where the distribution is less feudal, the tendency is to direct trade from "low" NATO countries away from other "low" countries, whether these countries are in the NATO or the Warsaw Pact systems. Thus, with the exception mentioned, there is underselection of the low by the low relative to what one would predict from import and export potentials.

4.4.1. Cultural agreements

The data on cultural and scientific agreements signed, according to the questionnaires and to *Keesing's* distribute as follows [Table 11].

TABLE 11. Percentage of Ordered Pairs with Cultural Agreements

	Phase 1	Phase 2	Phase 3	Phase 4
Big-big	0	0	100	100
Big-small	6.9	6.1	15.2	30.3
Small-small	1.5	0	0	1.2
Percentage difference	−1.5	0	100	100

The pattern is very parallel to the pattern we found for state visits, which is not strange since cultural agreements usually are on the agenda for such visits. And even if they were not, the two would be correlated since they are both aspects of the polarization-depolarization game between the big powers. Again, the general hypothesis is confirmed for two phases, but it should be noticed that phase 4 still is rather short, so the percentages have some more years to grow.

4.4.2. Cultural institutions closed

Seventeen cases of limitation of cultural freedom were found for the years 1950 (June) to 1953 (December); starting with United Kingdom and Czechoslovakia closing each other's information offices, and ending with USA and Rumania stopping publication activities. Big powers were involved in 16 of the 17 cases— but this must of course be evaluated relative to the distribution of information offices etc., which already shows a very heavy overselection of big powers. Nevertheless, the pattern is as predicted.

4.5.1. Visa requirements

"Is there a visa requirement for tourists?" was one of the questions we asked. At this point there is no simple hypothesis, since visa is not a form of interaction, but only a factor facilitating or impeding interaction. Actually, an hypothesis in this field of visa requirement might run the other way, predicting that big powers would impose more visa requirements than small powers, since it is compatible with their bigness—and still expect a disproportionately high quote of tourists and other visitors.

Actually, what we find is that the factor does not permit any test of any hypothesis of patterns between East and West, since all nations in East require tourist visas of all nations in West, and vice versa. Thus, the factor does not discriminate. But it does discriminate within the blocs. In the NATO alliance the United States is the only country consistently requiring visas of everybody (except its neighbor Canada) and unilaterally—the visa requirement is not reciprocated. Greece and Turkey also require visas of each other, since the Cyprus conflict, and Iceland requires visas of Portuguese tourists. With these exceptions tourist traffic is free, i.e. for 93% of the 210 possible (ordered) combinations. The corresponding figure for the countries belonging to the Warsaw Pact is 59%— to the best of our knowledge. Most of this is due to the visa policies of Albania and the German Democratic Republic.

4.5.2. Tourist restrictions imposed and cancelled

The major source of restriction in tourist volume is, of course, found in the visa regulations. But in addition one nation in the NATO system is known to have restricted travel for its citizen in the sense that the passports were not validated for such travel. . . . In the East travel restrictions are less explicit, and must be inferred from the extremely low level of tourists in the period referred to. The data have no clear relation to the basic hypothesis, however.

4.5.3. Tourist volume

Tourist statistics are rather unreliable, and we present our data with many warnings as to their quality; although the gross information that can be derived from the data probably is valid. We have used data supplied directly by embassies, foreign ministries or national tourist offices. Except for Albania, for which we have no information at all as a receiver of tourists, the Warsaw Pact nations seemed to have much more accurate information about incoming tourists than the NATO countries provide—partly because the tourist volumes handled by the NATO powers are enormous (in 1961 12.5 million tourists to Italy, in 1963 5.3 million to USA and 4.2 million to Germany, in 1962 3.8 million to Belgium, and so on), and partly because the tourist traffic is less centralized (the national tourist offices play a less dominant role in the tourist industry). Thus, we shall use the information on tourists from the NATO and Warsaw Pact countries received in the Warsaw Pact countries—since we do not have information from Belgium, Canada, France, Greece, Italy, Luxembourg and Norway as to tourists received from the Warsaw Pact countries.

In a sense, these data are interesting because they are so different from most of the other patterns we have found and which turned out as predicted by our hypothesis. And the immediate thought is that this is not strange: tourists travel to tourist-worthy countries within their reach geographically and economically speaking—and very often decide for themselves so that they can break with the pattern of the international system. The tendency to overselect big powers will probably be there, but it may be overridden by other tendencies. Thus, let us test the hypothesis that the Warsaw Pact countries attract tourists from the NATO countries proportionately to their (the WP countries) population. In that case, the rank correlation between population and tourists received should be 1.0. In fact it is only 0.18. But perhaps tourists from Warsaw Pact nations would select the nations that way, on the assumption that they would know more people and hence go most to the nations where there are most people to know? Even less so, the rank correlation is 0. And we get corresponding findings if instead of population we use any one of the other rank-dimensions; all correlations are rather low. This applies to tourists from either bloc, the rank correlation between their choices is 0.86 so there is little doubt that we are dealing not only with another factor, but also with a factor about which there is consensus across blocs. A look at the [data] tells one of the reasons immediately: countries famous for their tourist resorts like Bulgaria and Hungary are heavily overselected particularly by the Warsaw Pact nations. Less scenic countries like the German Democratic Republic and Poland get fewer tourists than they should, but this tendency is less pronounced for tourists from the NATO countries, who are probably also going to the East out of political curiosity and, consequently, choose the bigger countries.

In other words, a complete refutation of the hypothesis: but then it may be maintained that the hypothesis is about international relations and not so much about individual choices as they are reflected in the data on tourist traffic. So by and large it appears that when people are left to themselves, much of the feudal nature of the international system is countered. And this in turn means that to be a tourist nation has great potentialities as a compensatory dimension in the international ranking system.

Finally it should be noticed that a sizeable proportion of the total tourist volume, from East or West, in the Eastern countries is made up of people from the West. This is not reciprocated; the percentage of tourists from the East never exceeds 1% for the countries in the West.

4.5.4 Flight connections

Finally in this connection let us look at the number of flights per week between the most important cities in the NATO countries and the most important cities in the Warsaw Pact countries, as an indication of the travel possibilities between the countries. The *ABC World Airways Guide* (November 1965) was used for this purpose, and 173 weekly flights were found.[24]

We have omitted the data about within-bloc flights since they are less interesting for our purposes here. . . . The ordering of the countries is quite different from the ordering we obtained for trade-relations between blocs. In fact, the rank correlations between trade volume and flight volume to the other bloc was for the NATO countries .37 when based on import data and .43 when based on export data, and for the Warsaw Pact countries .90 when based on import data and .86 when based on export data. This indicates heavy correlation between a major rank variable and centrality in the communication structure for the Warsaw Pact countries and important discrepancies from this among the NATO countries.

There are several reasons for this low correlation.

First of all, there is a distance factor. United States ranks very low, but is also the country most removed from the scene together with Canada, which ranks even lower. United States has three flights with Czechoslovakia—that is all. However, we doubt that this can be explained in terms of geography alone. A direct flight New York—Moscow—New York is an important symbol that would be dissonant in many people's minds with norms governing behavior in a major conflict. For in a sense flights are among the most visible forms of interaction, in a sense even more visible than diplomacy and trade.

Secondly, there are all kinds of special factors that have to do with the air communication network in the world. For instance, Denmark ranks highest and Norway lowest in the Table, not because of any basic difference in their East–West philosophy but for the simple reason that Scandinavia's major airport is Kastrup, Copenhagen, from which transfer flights (and some direct flights) connect with Oslo and Stockholm. And many flights to Eastern Europe would stop in Praha and Warsaw—they are important cities, and on the way further South or East.

Nevertheless, in spite of all this, the major hypothesis is verified on the flight data (see Table 12). But the percentage differences are smaller than, for instance, for the diplomatic relations East-West—partly due to the factors mentioned above.

TABLE 12. East-West Weekly Flight Connections, 1965, %

	Big East- Big West	Big East/West- Small West/East	Small East- Small West	Total
No flights	33%	48%	62%	58%
1-6 flights	34%	45%	36%	38%
7* flights	33%	6%	2%	4%
Sum	100%	100%	100%	100%
(N)	(3)	(33)	(84)	(120)

4. DISCUSSION

What, then, does all this add up to? In one sentence: *that international politics (not non-governmental interaction) is big power politics, for good and for bad, between friends and (particularly) between enemies, in the past, at present and in the foreseeable future, probably to some extent as long as nations exist.* However, the circumstance that a structural arrangement is lasting does not necessarily make it laudable or unavoidable. To mention some of the less laudable consequences:

1. *Initiative is concentrated on the big and taken away from the small,* because "if you think it over, it's only the USA and the USSR that really count, the other countries are of little or no importance." This type of thinking stands in a positive feed-back relation to the kind of structure we have shown: the more people think like this, the more will they act accordingly and direct interaction upwards; and the more this happens, the more will they feel they are right and express themselves accordingly. This will stabilize the idea of letting everything important happen through the big powers, thereby reinforcing the structure of feudality and polarization. Another source of reinforcement is how dear this idea must be to many members of the biggest powers, the idea that they and they only count; and to decision-makers and others in smaller powers who seek pretexts and excuses for not taking independent initiatives.

2. *There is an over-exploitation of people in the big powers and an under-exploitation of people in the smaller powers.* Assuming that the human material is by and large of the same quality in all nations, big powers easily get into so central positions in the interaction networks that they will have difficulties staffing adequately all the programs they engage in internationally. After all, we have shown that there is an overlap in the size of populations, which would mean that it is, say, much easier for a Frenchman than for an Italian to get into an important job in some kind of international network. To the extent that this is the case, and we would like a direct verification of this hypothesis, the result is a waste of

manpower in the smaller countries, but also a reservoir that may serve to staff international organizations properly.

3. *The system is vulnerable in periods of conflict.* It follows from our findings that conflicts and negative interaction also will tend to concentrate on big powers, just as positive interaction will be concentrated there. But negative interaction, e.g. destructive behavior, will tend to lead to rupture of positive interaction—which means that even big power positive interaction will be reduced, perhaps down to zero. And, since there is little or no positive interaction at lower levels, this means that there is little or nothing to absorb the shock of a conflict in the two-bloc system. Since we have shown that the same type of relation applies between the representatives in the United Nations, the shock will not necessarily be absorbed through interaction in international organizations.

The last point can be made more clear by efforts to spell out what more independent small power interaction might imply for the capacity of the total system to absorb conflicts. More particularly, there seem to be four important mechanisms at work—although we do not claim to understand fully or know the conditions that would favor or impede their effective functioning:

1. *Improved communication*—if big power communication between the blocs breaks down, as it almost did during the Cuba crisis, there are still big to small, and small to small communication channels to rely upon, provided there is sufficient training in using them, provided they have a sufficient degree of autonomy, and provided intra-bloc communication has not broken down with member nations that have contact with the other side.

2. *Split loyalties*—if between-bloc communication is increased, the probability is strong that there will be some points in the total structure where split loyalties may accumulate. One reason for this is the simple circumstance that smaller powers are less self-sufficient and hence often have more needs that can be satisfied by the big power(s) on the other side (which, indeed, is a source of jealousy for the smaller powers' own big brother). With need-satisfaction some element of split loyalty may enter, and this will serve to subdue behavior in a conflict, reducing the escalation factor. Personal friendships between small power decisionmakers is probably particularly important here, for which reason one may assume that big power are very jealous of such contacts.

3. *The model factor*—the idea that small power interaction, if successful, may prove as a stimulus for the big powers. Thus, initiatives by small powers may become meaningful in terms of the present feudal structure through imitation. This is mirrored in

4. *The testing ground factor*—the idea that big powers may try out types of relationships, disarmament proposals, coexistence proposals, etc. at a lower level without committing themselves too much, and leaving to speculation whether what happens at a lower level has been learned at the top or not.

Thus, to the extent that these four factors are operative, one would probably be right in assuming that some benefits would derive from increased small power interaction in terms of making the system less vulnerable to conflicts. Essentially, increased small power interaction would reduce the degree of feudalism and polarization in the structure. But, according to the system of propositions presented in section 1 above increased small power interaction between the two blocs will also have the effect of increased big power interaction (proposition 1.1.2.). Thus, if this proposition is true, the result might well be a new division of the East-West system with the 19 small pitted against the four big in a class conflict instead of the East-West conflict we are accustomed to. The likelihood of this is perhaps not very high, but we nevertheless predict that in the years to come big powers will feel forced to cooperate in efforts to maintain their hegemony over smaller powers. The obvious countertactic would be for the small power to seek cooperation with the big power(s) on the other side in addition (and according to the diagonal homology propositions, some efforts in this direction would pay off with high dividends).

Thus, we assume, essentially, that the East-West system would be most stable if (1) interaction rates of all three kinds (big-big, big-small and small-small) are high and (2) interaction rates are relatively even, so that the system is not too vulnerable in case of big power conflict. However, it would be foolhardy to believe that interaction dependence on rank can be reduced down to zero—that would run against all ideas about what rank implies. Rather, there will always be some tendency for the high to interact more among themselves, partly because interaction with high rank units may be more rewarding, and partly because units with high rank often are more receptive to new types of interaction, are more innovators. Thus, we assume essentially the same theory as to how propagation of types of interaction will depend on total rank as we have developed for how attitude propagation depends on social position.

Hence, the problem is not to equalize completely the interaction frequencies but to make them more even, at the same time as the general level of positive interaction is increased. And the second problem is how to do this without transforming the system from an East-West conflict to a class conflict between nations. To discuss this let us look at some concrete policy implications.

5. SOME POLICY IMPLICATIONS

We shall now give specific content to these general ideas, and at this point it would have been useful to have a good typology of types of positive interaction between nations so that a theory could be developed, but no such typology exists to our knowledge. However, two basic axes in the set of types of positive interaction should be singled out for further attention.

The first axis is the distinction between bilateral and multilateral forms of interaction, depending on whether two or more nations take part. The multilateral forms may take place within or without a supernational organization. We shall, however, continue to limit ourselves to bilateral types of interaction, and postpone the analysis of multilateral interaction to later occasions.

The second axis is more important for our purpose.

Interaction is exchange of value; and positive interaction, hence, exchange of positive value. A trade relation is the typical example, or an exchange of exhibitions. In both cases exchange takes place, we assume, because of differences in utility: both parties "gain" because what they receive has more utility to them than what they send. This is the general principle behind *exchange* relations: no value is created in the process, but the utilities of both parties increase. But forms of interaction also exist whereby value is *created* so that the world as such contains more value than before. Norwegian and Polish scientists may cooperate in the field of disarmament research, Norwegian and Polish firms may enter agreements about co-production. This does not necessarily imply that the utilities to either party will increase: the Norwegian-Polish team of scientists may decide to keep their findings to themselves or give them to some formal supernational agency; and correspondingly for the co-production arrangement. Thus, we get these possibilities [Table 13].

TABLE 13. Different Types of Positive Interaction*

	total value constant	total value increased
both utilities constant	no basis for interaction	supernational interaction
both utilities increased	international exchange	international cooperation

* For simplicity we have assumed symmetry between the two parties.

If we assume that no interaction will take place unless both parties expect some kind of utility gain from it, only the bottom line has to be considered, and we can proceed with a dichotomy called *exchange vs. cooperation.* Thus, we assume that positive international exchange or cooperation always leads to some type of utility increase. But, we also assume that the best incentive for international exchange or cooperation is found when these types of interaction are not only sufficient but also necessary conditions for the utility increase. In other words, for exchange and cooperation to take place, they have to lead to some kind of gain, and if they are the only way of obtaining this gain, then they will take place particularly easily.

Let us then proceed to a short list of such forms of interaction,[25] some of the exchange type and some of the cooperation type, for instance 5 of each type, and examine them for their possible effects. We have not included in the list in Table 14 the typical war-horses (peace-horses?) of most cultural agreements, such

TABLE 14. A Short List of Proposed Types of Positive Interaction

Exchange items:	Cooperation items:
1. *Exchange of newspaper columns* in newspapers to provide for more local news, news that does not make headlines	1. *Cooperation in education,* by providing facilities for children and adolescents from East and West for summer courses and full year courses
2. *Exchanges between a maximum number of organizations,* trade unions, professional organizations, hobby organizations, etc., of persons and of objects	2. *Cooperation in science and culture,* by providing facilities so that scientists and artists can work together
3. *Roundtable discussions* between various members of the elite of the two countries to provide for maximum exchange of opinion and information	3. *Cooperation in peace research and peace proposals* by establishing permanent research and proposal groups on such problems as disarmament and peaceful coexistence.
4. *Exchange of heads of state and heads of government,* again to provide for maximum exchange of opinion and information at top level	4. *Co-production, i.e. economic cooperation,* by mixed staffing and investment in factories and other enterprises
5. *Establishment of a "hot line" between the foreign ministries,* to provide for exchange of information in periods of crisis and to facilitate direct communication	5. *Cooperation in the field of technical assistance,* by a. sending TA experts in pairs, one from a country in East, one from a country in West, to a country in "South."
Obviously, all of these five types of exchange will easily shade over into cooperation, in the sense that more comes out of the exchange than just transfer of values. Information will lead to new ideas that would otherwise not have arisen, etc.	b. having mixed East-West peace corps teams, with volunteers in "middle-level" manpower, sent to a country in "South." c. cooperation in a capital-requiring project (particularly for big power cooperation).

as exchange of exhibitions, scholars and artists, students, sports teams of different varieties, and tourist travels—in short, not the types discussed in the analysis above.

In this Table, no proposal is included that presupposes any change in domestic ideology or structure in any participant nation, or change in existing levels of armament. The proposals are value-free where these factors are concerned, not because status quo in these fields is considered desirable, but because proposals that do not touch these variables are more easily accepted, and nevertheless of considerable potential effect as sources of integration between the two blocs. However, there are other conditions that also have to be satisfied; we hypothesize:

1. that the exchange or the cooperation take place on an equal basis, i.e. that there is no exploitation,
2. that the exchange or cooperation take place over some time,
3. that the exchange or cooperation yield substantial utility increases, and
4. that these utility increases could not be obtained more easily by other means.

Thus, we do not assume that the utility of "peace" will be considered sufficient for engaging in such activities, for two simple reasons: first of all, the gains in terms of peace, if any at all, are long-term and not easily demonstrated; and secondly, since we have (negative) peace between the two blocs today, there is no immediate gain in positive utility, rather a stronger guarantee against negative utility. But this is hardly as strong a source of motivation as some gain in positive utility.

Thus, if in general we have two systems, S_1 and S_2 with m_1 and m_2 small power members, and n proposals for positive, bilateral interaction, then the total number of peace proposals is $m_1 \times m_2 \times n$—in our special case $12 \times 71 \times 0$, or 840, peace proposals. This is on the assumption that each pair of countries, one from East and one from West, carries out the whole gamut of positive interaction. A practical objection against this would probably be the lack of skilled manpower needed to staff all these schemes of cooperation; another objection, that not all of this is needed to obtain the positive effects described above. Where the latter is concerned, it is difficult to say what the minimum of cooperation is, and we do not even know whether the amalgamating effect is a continuous or discontinuous function of the degree of interaction.

Two reasonable minimum conditions might be

1. All nations in one system shall have at least one type of interaction with all nations in the other system

                              and

2. All nations shall have experience with all types of interaction.

Thus, a simple pattern would be for one nation in S_1 to distribute the patterns of interaction on all the nations in S_2. If $n = m_2$, this is easy; if $n < m_2$, some patterns will have to be repeated; if $n > m_2$, some ideas will not be used. This is also the case for the next nation in S_1, but it will have to distribute its pattern of interaction in such a way that the S_2 nations do not engage in the same type of interaction with the second nation as with the first. Again, if all S_2 nations shall engage in all n activities once and only once, then we must also have $n = m_1$. In other words, we get the simple case with $n = m_1 = m_2$. Imagine that they are all equal to 5, and that the forms of interaction are called A, B, C, D and E. We get, for instance, this pattern:

S_2 *nations*

	A	B	C	D	E
	A	B	C	D	E
	B	C	D	E	A
S_1 *nations*	C	D	E	A	B
	D	E	A	B	C
	E	A	B	C	D

This kind of square, where the symbols are distributed in such a way that there are never two equal symbols in the same row or the same column, is known as a Latin square. It has the desirable properties: All nations interact with all nations and all nations practice all types of interaction. But instead of the 125 interaction patterns a maximum scheme would presuppose, 25 are sufficient for this minimum scheme. In general, $m_1 \times m_2$ or m_2 (since we assume that they are equal) would do; we do not need m_3.

Of course, this scheme and this way of thinking do not belong to practical politics: we cannot assume two blocs to have the same number of small powers, or that human inventiveness shall produce exactly the same number of forms of interaction as there are small powers in the blocs. In the actual case with 12 and 7 small powers, respectively, and, say, 10 proposals, there would be some duplication; moreover, there is no law in human affairs saying that one nation shall choose only one form of interaction with any other nation. But what would be the minimum form of cooperation in this "rectangular" case? 84 would not do, for this would mean that the NATO nations would not be trained in all forms of interaction, since there would not be enough Warsaw treaty nations to practice them on. But 120 would do (12 NATO nations engage each in 10 forms of cooperation, and distribute them on the 7 Warsaw treaty nations) since they can always be distributed in such a way that all nations on either side get practice in all forms of interaction. In general, we get the minimum scheme by multiplying the two highest of the numbers m_1, m_2 and n, and the maximum scheme by multiplying all of them. This means that any existing arrangement can be evaluated in terms of how far it is on the road between minimum and maximum, using the coefficient:

$$\frac{N - \text{min}(N)}{\text{max}(N) - \text{min}(N)}$$

where N is the number of forms of interaction in the total system. Of course, $\text{min}(N)$ may be equal to 0, in the case of complete polarization, in which case the formula reduces to $N/\text{max}(N)$.

As mentioned, we have very little concrete information as to what will happen when this coefficient increases in value, or when more specified coefficients measuring types of interaction grow. But the general hypothesis, by no means tested by our data, that a system will become more resistant to violent conflict when the general level of positive interaction is higher and less dependent on rank (whether this is done by new initiatives of the type outlined above or by correcting the distributions in section 4) appears not only reasonable, but also highly plausible. To the extent this is true, increase and uniformity in positive interaction may appear as a very attractive road to peace because the process itself is so positive.

NOTES

[1] The most complete theoretical formulation is found in Johan Galtung, "International Relations and International Conflicts: A Sociological Approach," International Sociological Association, Plenary Session, September 4–11, 1966. A test of the theory on the Latin-American system of nations is found in: Johan Galtung, Manuel Mora y Araujo and Simon Schwartzman: "El Sistema Latino-Americano de Naciones: Un Analysis Estructural," *America Latina,* 1966; English version: "The Latin-American System of Nations: A Structural Analysis," *Journal of Social Research,* 1966, and Simon Schwartzman: "International Cooperation and International Feudalism: The Latin-American Case," First General Conference, International Peace Research Association, Groningen July 3–5 1965.

[2] For an extensive analysis of this phenomenon for the case of interpersonal interaction see: Johan Galtung: "Small Groups Theory and the Theory of International Relations," Lecture at the 75th Anniversary of the University of Chicago, June 1–4, 1966. However, we would like to illustrate the thesis with some cases from international relations. One clear example of how interaction is concentrated on the top in the international system is found in the article by J. David Singer and Melvin Small, "Formal Alliances, 1815–1939, A Quantitative Description," *Journal of Peace Research,* 1966, pp. 1–32. . . .

[3] The NATO treaty was signed on April 4 1949, the Warsaw Pact on May 14 1955. EEC may be said to have been founded on March 25 1957 and Comecon on January 25 1949, but perhaps as a reaction to the Marshall plan.

[4] For an analysis of this, see Coser, Lewis, *The Functions of Social Conflict* (Glencoe: The Free Press, 1956), p. 131: "In a number of instances, for example in the garment industry, unions have forced employers to form associations so that the union might avoid bargaining with many different small employers."

[5] We are thinking particularly of the feelings of the United States and the other Western big powers when the German Federal Republic makes overtures to the Soviet Union, and the feelings of the latter when Poland encourages interaction with the big powers in the West.

[6] For a generalization, see Parsons, T. and Bales, F.: *Family, Socialization and Interaction Processes,* (Glencoe: The Free Press, 1955) pp. 305–306.

[7] For a theory on the effect of congruent systems, see Eckstein, H., "A Theory of Stable Democracy," *Research Monograph No. 10,* Center of International Studies, Princeton University, 1961.

[8] For what is still the best discussion of polarization in sociological literature, see Coleman, J.: *Community Conflict* (Glencoe: The Free Press, 1957).

[9]One reason for this, according to the theory outlined in Galtung, Johan, "International Relations and International Conflicts" lies in the general lay in the structure of the international system of nations relative to at least many intranational systems of individuals or groups. Thus, in many intranational systems there is nothing quite corresponding to the idea of the "big power" after the abolition of nobility as a status with tremendous ramifications into economic and political life.

[10]There are of course exceptions to this. In Latin-America, for instance, intranational conflict is far more dangerous than international conflict. But one reason for this is precisely that Latin-American societies are so rank-dependent, within as well as between. As to the latter see Galtung, Mora and Schwartzman, 1966.

[11]See Galtung, Johan, "Summit Meetings and International Relations," *Journal of Peace Research,* 1964, pp. 36–54, particularly pp. 38–39. For a validation of the time-cuts introduced in that article and used here, see Smoker, Paul, "Trade, Defence and the Richardson Theory of Arms Races: A Seven Nation Study," *Journal of Peace Research,* 1966, p. 162, and also Table 8 in the text for validation in terms of note exchange.

[12]*The Military Balance 1965-1966* (London: Institute for Strategic Studies, 1965) for Population, Armed Forces, Nuclear Power Potential (table 7 parts A and B combined, p. 46) and defence expenditure (table 4, p. 43)

World Handbook of Political and Social Indicators (New Haven: Yale University Press, 1964) for area (table 40, p. 139), GNP (table 43, p. 152), GNP per capita (table 44, p. 155)

For "veto power" is used the "permanent member of the Security Council" definition (USA, UK, France, Soviet Union, "China")

For "world language" is used the UN definition (English, French, Spanish, Russian, Chinese). The "working languages" are English and French.

For "sphere of interest" is used a combination of "recognized sphere of interest" (as defined by the Monroe-Johnson doctrines, the Commonwealth and Communaute agreements, the Yalta agreement) and the refusal of the German Federal Republic to recognize borderlines in the East. It is difficult to lay down formal criteria in this field.

[13]The propositions are developed in Galtung, Johan: "International Relations and International Conflicts." The basic idea is simply that *one* unit, *in casu* a nation which is high on one rank-dimension and low on another, will tend to develop patterns of aggressive behavior if other sources of mobility are blocked, because it will try to equilibrate upwards.

[14]The propositions are developed in Galtung, Johan: "International Relations and International Conflicts." The basic idea is simply that *two* units, *in casu* two nations where one is high where the other is low and vice versa (a young nation with nuclear weapons vs. an old one without), will tend to develop patterns of either withdrawal or conflict towards each other, for many reasons (they are competitors for the top position they may arrive at if both of them are permitted to equilibrate upwards, for instance).

[15]It is difficult to find a better analysis of the relation between Chinese self-image and their perception of how others perceive them than the analysis given in Fitzgerald, C.P., *The Chinese View of their Place in the World* (London: Oxford University Press, 1964).

[16]*World Handbook of Social and Political Indicators,* pp. 155–157.

[17]For operationalization of the concept of rank disequilibrium, see Galtung, Johan, "International Relations and International Conflicts." The formulae developed there are used to calculate the average rank disequilibria referred to in the text.

[18]For a general theory of this see Galtung, Johan: "A Structural Theory of Aggression," *Journal of Peace Research*, 1964, pp. 95–119.

[19]Data from *Europa Year Book*, 1965, checked with embassies and foreign ministries.

[20]Data from *Keesing's Contemporary Archives*. *Keesing's* has excellent indices so that perusal of *Keesing's* for data is greatly facilitated. Another question is to what extent *Keesing's* covers what happens in the world well enough, and we are not prepared to comment on that since we have made no thorough check of what is reported in *Keesing's* relative to an objective baseline. It is obvious that *Keesing's* would be oriented towards United Kingdom and the Commonwealth more than, say, the *New York Times* would be–and it is quite conceivable that it is big power oriented so that data from *Keesing's* will have systematic bias in favor of our hypothesis of rank dependence. To check on this we selected *Keesing's* for 1963 and counted the number of relationships in which a nation occurred (bilateral or multilateral interaction with other nation, as listed in the index). UK appeared 54 times, then USA with 40, USSR with 32, South Africa with 28, Portugal and India with 22 each, France with 21, German Federal Republic with 17 and People's Republic of China and United Republic with 16 each–to take the top 10. There is nothing unreasonable in this list–and if we look at it from the other end (countries that are never mentioned or mentioned only once) there seems to be nothing unreasonable in that either. Later on this type research may be carried out on direct source material–where we only checked with the questionnaires. However, we doubt that this would change our conclusions.

I am indebted to Simon Schwartzman for his assistance with the data-collection.

[21]For more on this, see Galtung, Johan: "Small Group Theory and the Theory of International Relations." Lecture at the 75th Anniversary of the University of Chicago, June 1-4 1966.

[22]I am indebted to Dr Chadwick Alger for making data available to us and to Mr Kurt Jacobsen for assistance in the data analysis. A report on Alger's study is published in J. David Singer, ed., *International Yearbook of Political Behavior Research*, vol. VII (New York: The Free Press 1965). There is a correction for seat-mates vs. non seat-mates.

[23]The trade data are for 1962 in most cases, except 1963 for Netherlands and 1961 for USA and the German Democratic Republic. I am indebted to Dr Simon Schwartzman and Vigdis Vollset for assistance with the data-collection.

[24]I am indebted to Reidar Kvadsheim for assistance with the data-collection. Flights are counted in one direction only.

[25]These peace proposals are taken from Galtung, Johan, *Norske fredsinitiativ: 20 forslag* (Oslo: Pax, 1964) and Galtung, Johan, *100 forslag til fredsinitiativ* (Oslo: Pax, 1966), forthcoming. Also see proposal by the Norwegian Pugwash Group in *Proceedings* from the Fifteenth Pugwash Conference on Science and World Affairs, Addis Ababa, December 28 1965–January 4 1966. For an interesting Polish view see Josef Soldaczuk, "Regional Integration and East-West Trade," *Polish Perspectives*, January 1966, pp. 10–17.

CHAPTER SIX

Government to Subgovernment Relations

17. SEIZURE OF TENSION AREAS

Feliks Gross

THE THREE MAJOR PERIODS OF WESTERN ANTAGONISM

The history of great antagonisms in the Western world can be divided into three major periods: (1) religious, (2) national, and (3) ideological. In a sense, all are ideological and at certain stages also have a quality of class antagonism. The first period may be traced from the seventh through the seventeenth century. By the end of the ninth century the earlier dissensions within the Christian Church had developed into a great schism and culminated in the division of Christianity into the Western and Eastern churches. This division into the Roman Catholic, on the one hand, and the Greek Orthodox Church, on the other, was the beginning of agelong antagonisms and tensions that have resulted in religious wars, especially on the Polish, Russian, and Ukrainian borders. Religious wars were in a sense ideological. Both were frequently combined with or reflections of social-economic struggles. Often they were only rationalization of political conflicts, conflicts of wills contending for power.

SOURCE. Feliks Gross, *World Politics and Tension Areas,* New York: New York University Press, 1966, pp. 162–186. Reprinted by permission of the author and the publisher. Copyright 1966 by New York University.

Not all wars were of such nature. Cases and cases can be cited of nations and rulers belonging to the same church conducting long and devastating wars when dynastic or national political interests were dominant. Nonetheless, the "zone of great antagonisms" was persistent. Religious, national or ideological antagonisms supplied the accent and uncompromising style of the conflicts. Reduction of differences to a single ideology or religion does not guarantee peace. Conflicts are reduced when individuals and nations learn how to respect and cherish differences. What is suggested here is the great symbolic theme, the accent of persistent historical conflicts of the past, conflicts in the Western World or on the outskirts of Europe.

The second zone of tensions, between the Islamic and Christian worlds, lasted more than a thousand years. It began in Spain, perhaps with the conquest of Spain in the eighth century, intensified at the end of the eleventh century with the first Crusades, and ended almost in the twentieth century with the disintegration of the Ottoman Empire. The ethnic antagonisms of the Balkans in the nineteenth century also had religious overtones.

The third area of religious antagonisms was the European struggle between units within the Roman Catholic Church that resulted in the Protestant movement. This schism appeared very early. Arbitrarily we may choose the Albigensian-Waldensian Crusade of the thirteenth century as the beginning, after which the long period of religious revolutions and wars extended almost to the end of the seventeenth.

Ethnic tensions in their intensive form appeared in Europe by the end of the eighteenth century in the form of rising nationalism and the struggle for national independence. However, the roots of these antagonisms can be traced to times of early conquest; e.g., Cossack uprisings in Eastern Europe against the Poles and the Russians were in many respects an expression of social-economic class and ethnic and religious tensions.

Modern nationalism appeared in definite form as ideological and patriotic movements. At first, the religious identity was separated from the national identity. It was not until later that the issue of the establishment of a sovereign state through ethnic, national identity developed into a new concept of legitimacy of power: the will of the people ("general will") who belong to the same nation, who speak the same language, who have the same historical tradition and origin, should determine the legitimacy of power and the establishment of the state. The old dynastic, traditional legitimacy was displaced by the new legitimacy of the general will; the monarchic form of government, by the republican. Ethnic tensions combined with nationalism appeared throughout Europe and continued until the end of World War II. This period of national-ethnic antagonisms extended for more than one hundred and fifty years, and overlapped in the twentieth century with ideological tensions.

Ideological antagonisms as a source of international tensions first appeared during the French Revolution. With the defeat of Napoleon Bonaparte and the Congress of Vienna, they largely subsided as international antagonisms, and re-appeared only with the Russian Revolution of 1917. They touched the outer fringes of the three major camps: fascism, Communism, and democracy.

European ideologies have a tendency to split, a fact that appeared early in the religious movement. The splits (deviations) might be explained by social-eco-nomic conditions, but this is only a part of the total picture. Ideas by their very nature harbor the germs of future dissensions. Contradictions arise on the issues of means and ends. The problem of authenticity of ideologies and of their inter-pretation results in further deviation.

Two major tendencies are evident in both the religious and political movements: (a) the dogmatic and authoritarian and (b) the liberal or democratic. They appear in the French Revolution, reappear in the Social Democratic movement, and re-cur in other political forms with an elaborate philosophy and theory. Ideological schisms foster historical divisions and struggles, and are usually the starting point of basic contradictions and antagonisms. Almost every idea system results eventu-ally in contradictory and inconsistent interpretations. This is perhaps the very nature of the ideas, especially those rooted in dialectical philosophies such as grew in Europe.

The potentialities of international conflict arise when militant ideologies unite with control of the state, which has a monopoly of physical and economic power. When proselytizing and militant religions capture the power of the state; when aggressive nationalistic ideologies transform the state; when again proselytizing universal ideologies establish a monopoly of power—the danger of ideological war and conflict appears. At this moment, the intergroup tensions between ideo-logical groups within the state move into a stage of interpolitical tensions.

In a modern democratic system, with its complex value structure and myriad institutions, the power of the state is not under the permanent control of one ideology and one party. In consequence, the state does not become a submissive tool of a single political orientation, and cannot be sublimated to the role of a means to an end. The state is designed to serve many goal systems (objectives) and many ideologies. Political parties win and lose elections and while they are in power, the state machinery is not reduced to the role of an aggressive party ap-paratus. From the viewpoint of international relations, this is a major merit of the democratic system.

In reality, religious, ethnic-national, and ideological-political tensions and antagonisms are similar in nature. They are all ideological tensions arising from differences in idea systems. (Religion is an idea system.) Ethnicity and differences in ethnicity are expressed in nationalistic ideologies.

Today ideological differences are expressed in social-economic (class) and po-litical outlooks, and can often be creative in nature. In the continuous contest of ideologies, new tendencies emerge and society moves toward new goals. It is the nature of a creative social process to eliminate institutions, customs, and behavioral patterns that are harmful to large sections of the productive population and have a deleterious effect on changes necessary for the improvement of conditions. The institution of slavery can serve as an example.

In the history of the Western world, ideological differences and conflicts led to violent expressions. The idea systems were reflections of social-economic conditions of their times, and were more often than not rationalizations of interests of certain social classes. This relationship should not be underestimated. Nonetheless, by its very nature the incompatibility of values and ideas led to conflict.

It is sufficient to peruse the history of religious wars and study the issues involved in order to find the significance of ideas and concepts in human behavior. In medieval times, the prophesies and interpretations of sacred books had an impact on religious and social mass movements. Confused, mystical, sometimes unintelligible, they impressed not only the uneducated masses, but also the clergy. Unverified vision resulted in mass movements and collective, emotional phenomena. The mystical interpretation of the testament of Joachim of Fiore (1145–1202), with its prophesies of the coming of Antichrist and his overthrow, had an impact on church and politics. Reinterpreted later by a dissident Dominican, it had a wide appeal.[1] Of course, those movements were a reflection of deep, unknown needs. Nevertheless, they integrated multitudes into opposing camps.

Idea systems are incompatible when the basic tenets cannot be reconciled, especially in extreme cases where they are combined with a belief that survival of one precludes the existence (continuance) of others. There are degrees of incompatibility. Idea systems which are not proselytizing might be incompatible, but may not necessarily result in open conflicts. Here the coexistence of religious groups on the level of indifference is both possible and probable, and has occurred many times in history. Once the normative idea system postulates a monopoly of truth and absolute values, and combines these concepts with the duty or proselytizing "sinners," then incompatibility moves toward a militant stage. The "sin" and the "dogma" might be religious or political. Dogmatic absolute concepts do not tolerate deviations from the basic norms. Such idea systems, when combined with a concept of "mortal sin" for those who disagree, are prone to result in conflict.

The question of absolute values is not easy. . . . I do not intend to say here that all values, whatever their differences, are equal in significance and merit. What makes an idea system of strong absolute values a motivating force of aggressive and destructive action is not a belief in the validity of basic tenets, but the absence of respect for difference, for doubt, or for creative criticism and the refusal of a possibility of disagreement, even on minor issues. It was precisely disagreements on minor issues that led to strong schisms and mutual determination, to mention only one of the many issues that troubled the Christian religion.

History teaches us that incompatibility of religious idea systems led to long wars until the exhausted antagonists found that the problem could not be solved by force of arms. Religious wars ended with mutual accommodation (which we have called . . . "coordination"). None of the groups submitted wholly to the others. Certain countries became predominantly Catholic, others Protestant; and societies, influenced by political experience, civilization, and a philosophical spirit, introduced a concept of pluralism.

The incompatibility of ethnic, nationalistic ideologies ended in the holocaust of two world wars. In Western Europe during the twentieth century, nationalism led to extreme forms of conflict and to the temporary but total subordination of the militarily weaker nations to the stronger and more aggressive ones, led by Germany. Not before the defeat of Nazism and fascism was a solution possible. And, both were defeated, not by a revolution, but by an international war. Here, the massive change in idea systems was achieved through interpolitical coercive subordination of the violent forms of nationalism, and by repression of the aggressive nature of the proselytizing creed; by "ideological" changes, and a de facto or international agreement on noninterference or limited interference.

The further solution of nationalistic antagonism in Europe required new idea systems, new values, and new institutions that would permit the reintegration of European peoples. New loyalties appeared in the wider form of continental integration.

Germany might be a typical example. Here the regional and local values were strengthened, vis-à-vis loyalty toward Germany as a national entity. Now a German was also a Bavarian and a European. Emphasis on the universal and the regional values brought about the reintegration of the German population in the community of European nations.

The world today has moved into a period of ideological antagonism rooted in social, economic, and political outlooks for which solutions have not as yet been discovered. The past gives us a few lessons, but the future may require new answers. In the past, after a thousand years of struggle, solutions were found in noninterference and separation through a profound change in idea systems. This meant simply the end of the crusades, and in time, of inquisitions and persecutions. "Coordination," representing a consensus, was also achieved by the development of new ideas and institutions combined with the physical defeat of groups representing the most aggressive expression of ideological tendencies.

MODERN IDEOLOGIES' APPEAL TO SOCIAL-ECONOMIC, RELIGIOUS, OR RACIAL-ETHNIC IDENTITY

Man belongs to many groups, not only to one. Man also has many loyalties. In a modern society the religious loyalty may differ from the national or the social-economic. The same person belongs to a church and is a member of a nation and a trade union. In certain historical periods, the three loyalties were complementary, in others they might be contradictory or at least alien to the dominant policy of the state. An individual's identity, united with his social-economic position in society, is of fundamental significance. A person acts in defense of his livelihood if he sees that political change may deprive him of it.

In order to exist, a man must satisfy his basic biological needs, and his level of needs changes with the development of industrial culture. In a different situation or a different historical period, however, another aspect of man's identity may be emphasized. In medieval times the religious identification was generally regarded as a dominant one. In the eighteenth and nineteenth centuries ethnic identification played a similar role. In the middle of the nineteenth century, labor and peasant movements, the social-economic class identification, carried the dominant accent.

Accentuation of identification has an impact on individual and collective motivation. The individual discovers his "social, ethnic, or religious consciousness," or his group identification, his "reference group." His resultant "class consciousness" signifies that he has achieved group identity.

One function of ideologies is group identification, since they are "collective representations," a concept advanced more than a half-century ago by Emile Durkheim. Ideologies serve as instruments through which group identification is emphasized and accentuated. In consequence, they integrate individuals into social groups. Their appeal is strongest when they respond to urgent needs. Thus, the same individual can be integrated to one group through identification of his ethnicity, or to another, through identification of his class.

Various ideologies have different ranges of appeal. Racial ideologies may appeal to people having certain physical characteristics. Consequently, the range of appeal for them is narrowed to certain personality types within a "racial" group. Not all persons of the same race respond to racism. Subnational ideologies appealed to groups smaller than a nation; e.g., a tribe or a regional group. Supernational party appeals to universal ties, superior to the national and racial identity. (The broad proletarian ideologies: socialism, anarchism, syndicalism, and Communism, are universal in nature.) The supernational ideologies, frequently called international ideologies, represent a wide range of potential appeal.

The appeal of religious ideologies depends on the nature of the religions. The Orthodox Jewish religious movement appeals to a narrow group consisting of those who are Jewish or have an orthodox orientation toward the Jewish religion. However, a Catholic ideological movement appeals to people of different orientations, and because Catholicism is a universal religion, it has a wider range of appeal.

Contemporary ideologies appeal primarily to needs and interests related to social, economic, and political conditions. Such is the nature of the anarchist and social-democratic ideologies, syndicalism, trade unionism, cooperatives, and Communism. In Europe, the nationalist ideologies are now in a period of decline. The supernational ideologies, combined with social-economic ideologies, are dominant. This, of course, might constitute a temporary change. But it seems to me that the nationalistic racial identities are on the decline in the Western world, although they still flourish in lands distant from the germinating centers of philosophical idea systems and the social sciences.

Modern social, economic, and political ideologies, combined with the supernational, appeal to a wide range of groups and individuals. In this respect they are akin to the medieval religions, which accentuated the supernational and universal over the ethnic and the national. Nineteenth-century nationalistic ideologies limited their appeal to the ethnic or racial identification.

The range of appeal of an ideology is relevant for our discussion of tension areas. Social-economic ideologies, in which ethnic identity plays only an ancillary or tactical role, have a worldwide appeal. Proselytizing and aggressive ideological movements carrying such ideologies may control tension areas on a worldwide basis. Supernational ideologies complementary to or detached from ethnic identity have a similar appeal, and they contain potentialities for the reduction of tension on a worldwide scale. Thus the range of political operation of nationalistic movements in a definite tension area is geographically limited, while movements universal in nature or appealing to social-economic identity have a global range and lend themselves to centralized control.

When social-economic tensions appear in a zone as a result of economic conditions or oppression and exploitation, a universal ideology can supply a sense of direction, a social image for the future, and possible solutions. It acts as an integrating element, uniting the discontented classes and groups both internally and with a wider community. Such a universal ideology can offer a worldwide appeal, while an ethnic-racial ideology is limited in this respect.

Many social-economic tensions can be reduced by social-economic changes. Often, however, the firmly entrenched ruling classes refuse to yield their privileged positions and the government lacks the imagination and strength to embark on basic reforms and changes. Therefore, once an ideology appears, an outside state identified with the latter may use the movement in the tension area for its own strategic objectives. Here, the intergroup social tension changes to interpolitical tension. Since two or more states are eventually involved, such ideological political tensions may lead to more general conflict. There are moments in history when revolution is a necessary vehicle of change and a condition of peace.

STRATEGY OF CONQUEST

In our era of worldwide strategies of conquest and control, local ideological tensions change rapidly from intergroup to interpolitical tensions. A local tension may, through the intervention of outside powers or organizations, become an international issue, especially in strategic areas. Social disorganization as an "objective" revolutionary condition is created or escalated by external forces. The area has strategic significance, therefore the tension is escalated to a local war with the purpose of capturing the area, since it forms a stage in the strategy of conquest. Tensions can be "real" or "manipulated." We may call them "real" if the ideological tensions are strongly reflected in local social-economic discontent arising from social-economic relations, class structure, and the situation of the population. The tension is "manipulated" if the ideology is represented by only a small group and is not reflected in the "social base," in the mass of the population, but used and intensified for the purpose of transforming the conflict from local to interpolitical, and of furthering the objective of capturing the area.

There are only a few techniques in the seizure of areas. We shall limit our discussion to some principal models with many variations. A discovery of new tactics creates a new situation, since the state or political party exposed to the new tactical design is usually unable to cope with the new pattern of political attack.

ELEMENTS OF ANALYSIS

The leaders of a political movement oriented toward basic social changes have to consider the social-economic conditions within which the movement operates, its opponents or antagonists, and the strength and organization of the party. Social political movements are not created in a vacuum. They are the result of the conditions in which they operate. However, political movements change the social-economic situation.

I shall call the conditions within which a political movement operates, the social base; later, in my analysis of tension areas, the social-internal base. Organized or unorganized pressures from the discontented multitudes or social classes shall be identified as movements "from below," or of the base. The organized social-political movement which operated within a social base shall be called "the party." The party and the social-economic base form the two elements of an internal political analysis, particularly in times of crisis or of revolutionary changes.

These two concepts appear early in social and political theory. At the beginning of the nineteenth century, they were not formally classified. However, they can be traced in the *Essay on the Revolution in Naples* (1801) of Vincenzo Cuoco, an Italian historian and theoretician of the revolution.[2] The significance of the ideas, organization, and of the masses was also discussed a half a century later by men of action and theoreticians such as Giuseppe Ferrari[3] and Giuseppe Mazzini.

The Russian revolutionary theoreticians analyzed the problem of organization of the party and of social-economic conditions, particularly in the last quarter of the nineteenth century. Joseph Stalin and Lenin formulated these concepts. Stalin, in the lectures on strategy and tactics which he delivered in Svierdlow (and which were later published in *Pravda* in 1926 and reprinted many times later), distinguishes these two elements. He calls the party the subjective element and social-economic conditions the objective element, of a revolution. His theory of strategy and tactics is built on an analysis of those two elements.[4]

The seizure of political power in a tension area requires coordination of the social-economic base with the political movement of the party. Conditions can then be manipulated or created by outside interference. For example, a tactic of individual terror combined with indiscriminate terror may produce a planned disorganization of the society and weaken the institutional structure.

Roughly, three types of seizure of political power can be distinguished: from above, from below, and a combined seizure (an amalgam of the two). The capture of power from above is also called a coup d'état (*colpo di stato, golpo de estado*) or, by many theoreticians, a revolution from above.

A distinction must be made between social and political revolutions. The social revolution is concerned with essential and rapid changes of social-economic conditions, social structure, institutions, and values. A rapid change—peaceful or violent—of these elements reflects a social revolution in many other aspects also. The term "political revolution" is applied to violent transfer of political power, the capture or destruction of the state, or the violent destruction of political institutions, and the establishment of a new power structure or a new social and political organization. The political revolution does not necessarily coincide with a social revolution, or vice versa.

The revolution from above is a simple technique of the capture of basic instruments and symbols of power by a small group of armed men, frequently supported by the military force, the armies. The seizure of weapons is essential in a revolution from above, and the role the army plays in such a coup is frequently decisive.

This type of revolution appeared in Spain, Italy, and Russia in the first quarter of the nineteenth century, and was called a military revolution or uprising. Giuseppe Ferrari, in his book on Italian revolutions, writes that the revolutionary movement of 1820 in Italy was a military revolution (*sollevazione militare*) that collapsed while passing from the military barracks to the public piazza. The masses of the population were passive or indifferent. He wrote later that "the conspirators were the only means, the only force of Italy. On the one hand were the conspirators and on the other, the Inquisition and the brigands."[5]

Vincenzo Cuoco made a distinction between an active and a passive revolution: An active revolution is one that moves from the base; in which the masses participate. A passive revolution is one accomplished without, or in spite of, the people.

The passive revolution was for Cuoco one in which a small minority of progressive and enlightened revolutionaries seized power with the support of the invading army.[6] As we shall see, this pattern appears in more elaborate form in the twentieth century, and is sometimes called the external revolution. Cuoco's concern was the establishment of democracy and the victory of enlightenment in Italy. The pattern is, however, "neutral" and can also be used by those who plan authoritarian rule.

The seizure of weapons or other means of violence is typical of the first stage of a revolution from above. The action of the masses is the basic element in the first stage of a revolution from below. In the second stage, arms become paramount. The revolution from below is based on mass movements by ethnic groups or social classes that are dissatisfied with existing social, political or economic systems and revolt against them. The third type, "a combined seizure," is a union of a coup with a revolution from above and from below. The social discontent of the working class, of the peasantry, or of certain ethnic groups becomes an important element of the strategy of a well-organized revolutionary group. This party strikes at the opportune moment, and the seizure of the symbols and instruments of power coincides either with the passive indifference of the masses or with spontaneous revolutionary activities.[7]

The three major revolutionary techniques have an application in the capture and control of tension areas that are basically revolutionary in nature. The political tension in such cases reflects deeper social-economic unrest. The support of an outside government or party, however, modifies the revolutionary pattern. With external political and military pressure, the revolutionary tensions move from an intrapolitical to a complex and international, interpolitical stage, and change in nature. The outside government may now use the local tension and the local party for the capture of the tension area.

With the change of a tension from internal ideological to complex and interpolitical, new elements appear and the nature of the tension changes. Internal tension is reinforced by external pressure. In consequence, two fronts appear: the internal and the external. The external front is formed by the military force and all the other elements of power, such as mass communication, economic support, and the political and diplomatic support of an external government and party. The pressure may be expanded to areas in which the government involved is vulnerable.

All the resources of the outside state form the external base. The latter is well protected, since the internal government is already involved in its own tensions and usually avoids any direct attack against its ideological enemy. First, the domestic tension and unrest concentrate the attention of the home government on its own affairs; secondly, they reduce the government's potential to act effectively and to use its political power in the field of international relations to the full. The explosive ideological and political conflicts in the tension area absorb most of the government's resources.

From the external base the revolutionary party is supplied with money, weapons, propaganda, and trained personnel. This skillful use of the external base as a supply depot and for reinforcement of tension within the social internal base is a key element in the strategy of capture of a tension area.

Thus, we must distinguish between the external strategic base and the internal social base. The first forms a center of operation for the external front; the second, for the internal front. Both, however, are closely connected, since the operations of each are coordinated and reinforced. When the home government acts, exposing the "internal political party," the outside government is still able to reserve its own forces and its own strength for the ultimate coup.

Four "major models" for the capture of tension areas appear in modern history. One is the military internal revolution (coup) combined with external pressure; two, the military external revolution; three, infiltration combined with revolution from above or below and the external front; and four, revolution from below combined with the external front.

PROBLEMS OF TERMINOLOGY

The distinction between political and social revolution has been already made. At this time, we are primarily concerned with political revolution: the violent transfer of power in a state. In terms of values and ideology, "revolution" is associated with a progressive, enlightened movement that innovates improvements for the underprivileged in an extension of freedom. Such was the concept of revolution in the nineteenth century.

The term "counterrevolution" has been used in the nineteenth and twentieth centuries for the identification of movements that represent a return to the status quo, to conditions favoring the privileged classes. The term "counterrevolution" meant also the introduction of a centralistic versus a liberal and democratic government; a return to the old regime.

Freedom and order are not contradictory concepts. Nonetheless, the forces of counterrevolution stressed the contradiction. Theirs was basically an ideology of "order" versus "freedom," a promise of order and social peace instead of social change combined with democratic and liberal institutions. In such a context the terms "revolution" and "counterrevolution" carry definite values and are also political symbols which appear in proclamations and in theoretical, philosophical discussions. In this normative sense the Nazi revolution was a counterrevolution, as was the victory of Franco in Spain. In a sociological sense, however, the Nazi seizure of power was a revolutionary movement directed toward the violent seizure of a state. Thus, we must distinguish between the sociological and normative (social-philosophical) concepts of revolution, as well as the two concepts of social and political revolution. I.shall use the term "revolution" in its empirical, sociological sense, rather than in the normative sense.

In both Latin America and Continental Europe, the term "revolution" has frequently been abused in its normative sense since the nineteenth century, with "democracy" being used for dictatorship and "progress" for changes that moved mankind backward. Nonetheless, the term "revolution" has its attraction, and usage of the term "counterrevolution" results in hostility. In popular parlance, a "counterrevolutionary" is one who is against the people.

As I have said, the interpolitical tensions of our time are largely ideological. Therefore, the choice of symbols is of great significance. Nations that have recent revolutionary traditions are sensitive to the names applied to their actions. Since ideological tensions frequently reflect deeper social or economic unrest, the movements fostering rapid change have an appeal to the people, in contrast to those of the status quo.

The choice of political terminology in times of ideological struggle is not without significance.

TECHNIQUES OF CAPTURE

Various types and techniques of capture reflect relationships of the attacking political party or military group to the internal social base and external strategic base. A small dynamic party or internal front, with external assistance, has succeeded in capturing a strategic area many times in the past when social classes or nonorganized multitudes regarded by them as logical allies were either passive or passively and silently hostile.

Nations in the past have been conquered by foreign armies and also by their own military forces, who consolidated their power for many years. The internal military revolution combined with an external front is a simple technique, representing a coup d'etat, or a revolution from above. A military group, supported by regiments or battalions that blindly obey orders, captures the instruments and symbols of power and displaces the existing government. At the beginning of the nineteenth century, this technique was called a military revolution. In modern times it is frequently supported by an outside power or an external front. The revolutions in the Arab countries of the Near East follow this pattern. That in Iraq, which ended a royal dynasty, was a military revolution, related to a "combined seizure" (there was support from "below") and supported from outside by the might of the United Arab Republic. The external strategic base was in Egypt; the internal social base was in Iraq.

A military revolution is a technique that may serve a variety of objectives. In countries in which the democratic tradition has not yet developed, and where the masses are passive or indifferent under a strong despotic form of government, a military revolution frequently carries through progressive change and reforms. The Turkish Revolution of Kemal Pasha (Ataturk) was primarily a military revolution. The early Russian revolutionaries, the Decembrists, were also military in character, representing progressive ideologies, including the abolition of serfdom and the introduction of a constitution. A victory of the Decembrists would have marked the beginning of a fundamental social revolution in Russia, but it failed.

In our case, the external military revolution is of greater interest. The technique has been used frequently in modern times, yet its beginning can be traced back at least 150 years. This strategy was applied during and after the French Revolution. During the political revolutions in Italy in 1799, the multitudes, the people of the cities, supported the ruling classes, the aristocracy, the king, and the church. The liberation of Italy from the oppression of feudalism, autocracy, and Inquisition could come only from the outside. Inside Italy, the new ideas of freedom and enlightenment appealed only to the intellectual elites. (Here is the origin of the passive revolution described by Cuoco.)

The strategy of the passive revolution was a combination of a strong external front—the French army—with a weak internal front, represented by a handful of enlightened Republican intellectuals and Jacobins. Once the French army withdrew, the Lazzaroni and the lower classes took revenge on the unfortunate rebels. There was a real political hunt for Jacobins and Republicans in Tuscany.[8]

In modern times, the idea of an "exported revolution" was advanced by Marshal Tukhachevski, the leading Soviet military theoretician, and perhaps its most gifted military leader. Writing on the Polish-Soviet war of 1920, Tukhachevski suggested that the Red army, through a strategy of war, could bring the revolution to Western Europe. The defeat of the Bolshevik army at the gates of Warsaw arrested this advance.[9]

Tukhachevski's introduction of parachutist troops as a strategy of war was intended as external support for the internal revolutionary movements. (According to Adam Ciolkosz, a German military staff mission first witnessed a parachutist exercise in Russia, and adapted the tactic for Germany, which used it years later against the Russians.[10])

The tactics of infiltration are usually combined with a revolution from above or below. Two types of infiltration may be distinguished: (1) social-political and (2) geographical. The first type is primarily the tactic of penetrating political parties, the army, the police, and other strategic associations and groups. Geographical infiltration is connected with guerrilla warfare, and its purpose is to ignite a revolution from below. It was applied in Venezuela in 1963 by the followers of Fidel Castro. A similar tactic is being used by the anti-Castro Cuban revolutionaries who seek to launch a full-scale revolution from below.

The Nazis used political-social infiltration on a large scale to penetrate the state machinery of Austria before that country's capture. Infiltration was used by Stalin between 1945 and 1948, as a stage in a long-range strategy of control over Central and Eastern Europe. It combined an external revolution with social-political infiltration. Stalin exercised military, diplomatic, and economic pressure, and simultaneously infiltrated the military, the police, government apparatus, as well as non-Communist parties. Tension was created, and the area fell under Communist control with simultaneous pressure from outside.

Chinese strategy in Vietnam is an example of geographical infiltration of a territory. The Vietcong infiltrate villages and extend Communist influence through propaganda and terror. Communist China and Viet Minh form the external base from which the Vietcong are supported. The infiltration is intensified; so is the tension through continuous action. A Vietcong victory would mean the indirect extension of Communist Chinese influence over Vietnam. Through such a strategy of war by "proxy," or indirect war, Communist China extends its influence deep into Southeast Asia with relatively small expenditure of its own potential.

Finally, a strong social movement, a real revolution from below, can be assisted in a tension area by an external front. Here, the internal front is really supported by a mass movement, and assisted by external pressure. The combination of external military aid with a revolution from below as an interpolitical conflict is also not new. As early as 1808, Count Neithardt Gneisenau outlined a plan for a national mass uprising in Prussia against the French, with the simultaneous military support of the allies. As a good Prussian, Gneisenau first submitted his plan to the King of Prussia and received royal agreement. In his own way, Gneisenau understood the significance of an ideological appeal. He wrote: "It is cheap and statesmanlike to give the people a fatherland."[11] In other words, the appeal to patriotism is inexpensive.

Of course, the four patterns represent major types only. They also appear in a variety of combination, which can be used in a strategy of conquest or of revolution. These patterns represent techniques, and as such can be used for a variety of objectives by representatives of various ideologies and orientations.

The choice of technique for the capture of a tension area in a stage of interpolitical tension depends on a number of factors: (1) the nature of the social-economic internal base, the support which the party gets from below, and the attitude of the masses; (2) the size of the party's organization and its dynamism; (3) external support; (4) the time element set for capture of the tension zone. The paramount factors are (a) the relationship between the party and the social-economic base; (b) the relationship between the external and internal base.

THE PARTY AND THE SOCIAL BASE

I have already mentioned that social movements should be analyzed in their social-economic context; in other words, the party should be related to the social-economic conditions or social-internal base in which it operates. In itself, however, the party is a complex concept. Four elements are essential in its analysis, especially if it is a revolutionary party: (1) ideology: (2) structure (type of organization); (3) strategy and tactics or pattern of action; and (4) leadership. All are mutually interdependent.

The structure of the party is of paramount significance. A small, very well-organized, and dynamic group may conquer large, but passive and disorganized, multitudes.[12]

The pattern of party organization in the tension area depends to a great extent on the nature of the social, economic, and political base. When the movement of the "social base" ("from below") is strong, the party organization usually differs from those where the organized social groups and the multitudes are passive or hostile to the objectives of the party. In such a case, a small, well-organized party must rely on the external front and the external base.

THE IDEOLOGY

Today, ideological political tensions require ideological appeal. The attacking party in a tension area advances its ideas and appeals with symbols and ideas. The defending party must answer these appeals, since ideological attacks require ideological answers. Pragmatic reforms without vision or without symbols will not suffice. A purely military tactical action cannot solve the problems in a tension area. Ideological interpolitical tensions are of a specific nature and require specific action on the social-economic level and in the realm of ideas. Mazzini, in discussing the French Revolution, argued that ideas govern the world and events: "A revolution is a passage of an idea from a theory to practice. The French Revolution," he wrote, "cannot be considered as a program, but as the last formula of the epoch which is concluded. . . . Religion or a philosophy can be found at the base of every revolution." A new revolutionary movement makes new ideas, he argued.[13] Misery and oppression can produce "revolts" *(sommosse),* but a "revolution" needs an idea.

The French anarcho-syndicalist theoretician Georges Sorel, first in his famous book on *Reflections on Violence,*[14] and later in his essay *On the Decomposition of Marxism,*[15] indicated the significance of broad, symbolic visions. Ideas suggest both objectives and answers to vital problems. Not all "political cultures" appeal equally to visions and symbols. In England and America the emotional appeal to distant vision is less effective than in Continental Europe and Latin America, where the mass movements have been motivated by broad visions and symbols.

In ideological interpolitical tension areas, the appeal of ideas is relevant. Of course, the masses are not active in all tension areas. They are often passive and unresponsive. In such cases, the ideological appeal is ineffective, and direct action involving rapid social reform carries more weight.

ON CERTAIN ILLUSIONS AND ON QUANTITY

A few popular illusions have to be dispelled or at least clarified before we can advance our discussion and analysis of strategic-tactical patterns in ideological and interpolitical limited tensions.

When Hernán Cortés left Cuba on February 19, 1519, he had eleven ships, five hundred soldiers and slightly more than one hundred sailors. Of the soldiers, fewer than fifty had muskets or crossbows. They had ten small guns and four culverins.[16] With this small group, Cortés conquered an empire. Francisco Pizarro undertook the conquest of Peru with three brothers, one hundred and eighty-five soldiers, and thirty-seven horses.[17] On November 21, 1873, one hundred and twenty French soldiers took the citadel of Hanoi, marking the conquest of Tonkin.[18]

Small, well-organized groups conquered empires because the conquered were either passive and indifferent or divided and quarrelsome. They prevailed also because of a superiority of weapons. Their rule lasted for centuries, not because of the assent of the governed, but because of the indifference and passivity of the ruled.

In past history, small, oppressive minorities frequently dominated multitudes which hated them. Few governments in the not so distant past ruled by the consent and with the support of the majority, or a substantial minority, of the governed.

There is a persisting illusion to the effect that the aggressing party in a tension area is always on the side of social justice, and always has the massive support of the population. It is often true that discontent, social unrest, and the disorganization of the fabric of society provide favorable conditions for the development of a revolutionary movement, but this is not always so. The 1799 revolution in Naples and the rise and fall of the Parthenopean Republic are examples of social movements in which the mass support of the peasantry and the poorer classes for the cause of social equality and political freedom were lacking. Still, the combination of external and internal fronts resulted in the victory of the republican forces, at least for a time. Vincenzo Cuoco, a contemporary revolutionary author, writes that the "largest part of the nation was indifferent. . . . The immense population of the capital was more stupefied than active."[19]

The political behavioral patterns of the subordinated social classes are not the same in all cultures. The peasantry in Southeast Asia may react differently to political stimuli or exploitation than those in Brazil or Russia. In certain cultures, the peasants are more patient than the working class; in others, they are more responsive to political and social stimuli. The political passivity of the peasant class in Italy, even of the urban classes, in certain historical periods, impressed many Italian sociologists and political theoreticians and served as the basis for their theories of the revolutionary elite. Similar observations had already been recorded by revolutionary leaders of the past century.

A few decades after the defeat of Napoleon Bonaparte, Mazzini noticed the decline of revolutionary dynamism and initiative among the peoples of Europe. At the end of the nineteenth century and the turn of the twentieth, the leading Italian sociologists, Gaetano Mosca, Vilfredo Pareto, and Cesare Lombroso, discussed the passivity and submission of a large section of the population in their writings. Lombroso argued that inertia and resistance to change characterize the broad masses of the population and the general attitude of a society. He called it misoneism. In his view, a revolution was the act of a few that succeeded only in rare moments of history when a number of conditions favored its success.[20] This argument of Lombroso is not convincing, in spite of his maps and statistical data, and is not borne out by such recent experiences as the Russian Revolution of 1917 and the October revolutions in Poland and Hungary in 1956.

Mosca's theory of an elite was the result of observation and experience and, like other Italian sociologists and political scientists, he stressed the passive nature of the large sections of human society.[21] Their experience, however, was based on observation of the Italian scene at times when specific social conditions were present, conditions that differed from those in many other countries. Their generalizations were rooted in those experiences. Actually, there were many periods in Italian history when urban and rural populations and social classes were active or restive. In other periods, large sections of the population were passive.

Countries have been transformed into tension areas through infiltration and guerrilla warfare. Through terror, manipulation, and appeal, minor tensions in a countryside have been escalated to serious conflicts. Terror is cumulative in nature. To the terror of the government, the guerrillas respond with terror, which is, in turn, reciprocated by the terror of the government. Unfortunately, this was frequently the unwise practice of those seeking to defend a tension area. Through fear of terror or oppression, the passive population is compelled to action. An experienced guerrilla leader, Che Guevara of Cuba, argues that it is not necessary to delay a revolution until conditions for such a revolution exist. The revolutionary activity, he argues, may create such conditions.[22]

Another illusion is that the underprivileged represent the progressive element that always reacts to slogans of liberation, freedom, and social justice. In most cases, it is the organized working class and peasantry that react to the appeal of equality and freedom. Nonetheless, certain sections of the working class supported fascism and Nazism, and Juan Peron in Argentina was able to win large support among the underprivileged. Even in the glorious times of the Renaissance, in 1478, the crowds in Florence were aroused against those who attempted to weaken the tyrannical rule of the Medicis in the name of Freedom. The appeal "Liberty" was countered successfully with "Viva Lorenzo che ci da la pane" (Long live Lorenzo who gives bread).[23]

It is the combination of an external front with the internal front that forms the crux of operation in a tension area. A small group that is: (1) properly structured; (2) dynamic; (3) well-equipped, with efficient control of substantial means; (4) applies an effective pattern of action; and (5) has the strong support of an outside power—can successfully extend control in a tension area over large but passive or indifferent masses of population.

One hundred years ago Mazzini had already observed that the strength of a party is not in its numbers, but in its cohesion; in its union and composition.

THE INTERNAL BASE

While tension areas vary in nature, it is also true that the "classic pattern" prevails in many cases today. By this pattern we understand conditions of social discontent and disorganization that favor dynamic social revolutionary changes. Such conditions appear especially in areas of unequal distribution of property, low working-class salaries, and social, political, or national oppression. In consequence, the parties of rapid social change advocate changes in political institutions, transformation of the class structure, redistribution of land and higher wages, or a new social-economic system that will secure better economic conditions to the workers. Some advocate a dictatorship to administer rapid social-economic change; others propose democratic institutions and the extension of political freedom. When tension arises, social problems present a number of choices and solutions, and there is usually a number of parties offering a variety of answers.

The control of ideological, interpolitical tension areas, their capture or defense, is not purely a matter of military tactical action. The "internal front" is complex, and is primarily a social-political problem. Those sections of the population that demand change are won by new ideas and by rapid social, economic, and political changes, and become a strategic element of defense through efficient political organization and leadership. To consider the tension area solely as a military problem is to overlook its complex nature. As I have said, tension areas vary to a high degree. In one tension area the population may be active; in others, the area is infiltrated and the conflict escalated through guerrilla activities; in yet another, ethnic antagonism dominates; and in still another, the ideological tensions reflect profound social-economic problems. The last-mentioned, the subject of our discussion, required a broad policy on various levels.

The social base is the subject and the object of the strategic design in an ideological tension area. Action on this level requires imagination and political courage. When the tension is intense, it frequently reflects a serious social and economic unrest. If this is the case, the answers must come fast, and fundamental changes must be made. (We shall use the term "rapid change.") This type of social change is more of a peaceful social revolution than a slow reform movement, since it must be accomplished in a very short time and requires a fundamental change. Tensions of ethnic and political nature call frequently for a revolutionary change. Emancipation, national independence, and self-determination are often necessary stages toward social and political progress. Self-determination and national independence as such offer opportunities for progress but do not by themselves generate a better economy or increase production and the efficiency of a people. In order to give more to its citizens a nation must produce more. National independence is frequently a social myth, a promise of a new millennium. Programs of social change are also empty phrases unless accompanied by skills and capacity for better and more advanced forms of production. The simple fact that in order to improve conditions a nation must produce more and use more progressive techniques is so often forgotten, and foreigners are blamed as the cause of all evil.

A revolution, like any social process, moves in space and in time. In a social revolutionary change, the changes must be telescoped in a very short time span. The dissatisfied segments of the population look for immediate answers. The visible, immediate improvement of conditions has a direct effect and wins the people in the long run. But rapid social-economic reforms alone do not suffice. The strategy in an ideological tension area requires new and imaginative ideas. An ideology incorporating the status quo has little appeal in explosive situations. More than a hundred years ago, Mazzini argued that a revolution is a closing of an epoch rather than a beginning; that what he called the "revolutionary initiative" needed new ideas, in addition to those developed by the revolution.[24]

Perhaps one of the major factors in the success of Tito's partisan movement was his ideological appeal to the various nationalities of Yugoslavia. The partisans waged a three-way struggle: *against* Nazi and fascist occupation of Yugoslavia; *against* the status quo; and *for* a new social and political organization. The opposing Chetniks were identified with the status quo, and primarily with the Serbian nationality.

In a tension area, the ideological appeal of the aggressive party must be answered by the persuasive and efficient appeal of the defending party. The capture of a classic tension area requires well-organized groups, strong ideological appeal, and a program of rapid social, economic, and political changes. In consequence, the defense of the area and the easing of tension require a proper organization and structuring of the parties opposing the attackers. Rapid changes must occur in the tension area or there will be a silent conquest and establishment of a new oppressive regime.

Thus, social and political strategy within an ideological interpolitical tension area has three major components: (1) the party and the ideological appeal; (2) rapid social, economic, and political changes; (3) organization of the population.

THE SOCIAL-POLITICAL STRATEGY IN THE PHILIPPINES

The recent history of the Philippines may serve as an example of effective social-political strategy in a tension area. The Philippine army took a constructive part in this strategy of relatively rapid social reform. The strategy employed was imaginative and constructive. It was aimed to help the people, to stop the wave of terrorism, and to win over the revolutionary party by a humane policy. The techniques are instructive and point the way to ease certain types of tensions in the future.

Many elements contributed to the rise and development of the powerful revolutionary movement of the Huk (an abbreviation of the Hukbalahap, the local appellation of the movement). However, three major factors can be identified: (1) the early development of a labor movement in the Philippines, as well as later ideological developments and influences prior to the Japanese invasion; (2) the Japanese invasion and the struggle for independence; and (3) social-economic conditions in the Philippines, especially the land-tenure system and exploitation of the peasantry. The third factor comprises the essential element of the internal social-economic base, of which the land tenure is a part.

For the Philippine peasant, the land is not solely the economic base of his subsistence. The yearly, as well as the daily, rhythm of his life is built around agriculture and his land. His rituals and festivities are rooted in agriculture. However, large sections of the peasantry did not own any land at all.

The land-tenure system of the Philippines was inherited from Hispanic times. It involved two different and mostly antagonistic social groups: the peasant and his family; the *Tao* who works on the land; and the caciques, or landowners, and the church, which held claim to vast estates. This system continued under American rule. In certain areas of Central Luzon, only 12 percent of the farms were operated by owners. The remainder was divided between sharecroppers and part-owners.[25] Most of the peasant farms were very small, usually measuring less than 5 hectares (about 12 acres).[26] The haciendas of the church and of the caciques or of private companies ranged from 1,000 to 5,000 acres in size.

The relationship between the landowners and the Tao was highly exploitative. As late as the 1950's, a tenant farmer had to give about 70 percent of his crop to the owner. (The legal limit was 50 percent, but the law was circumvented.) Interest rates were extremely high, reaching 100 percent per year in 1952. The exploited Tao could turn only to the Chinese merchant, who gave him credit at a very high interest and served as his banker and sold his products.[27]

Large groups of the peasantry suffered from this exploitative system for centuries, but they did not always accept it patiently. Revolts against the church and the landowners were recorded as early as 1662.[28]

Socialist and labor ideology has an old tradition in the Philippines. After the Communist revolution and the Bolshevik coup in Russia, the Communist trend appeared in the Philippine labor movement. In the beginning, the Communist Party was legal and held meetings without difficulty. By 1931, the party was declared illegal, and it went underground and infiltrated other movements.

The Japanese invasion of the Philippines changed the political situation. With their coming, a number of underground organizations emerged—among which were the partisans—that harassed and fought the Japanese. The Communists joined forces with other groups in 1942 and formed the organization in Central Luzon known as the Huk.

The social-economic internal base of the tension was rooted in the discontented peasantry of the central Philippines, where the highly exploitative sharecropping practices prevailed. The Huks introduced new ideas and offered a vision of a new world, besides advancing a program of rapid social and economic reforms combined with guerrilla warfare.

The Huks did not disarm after the war. Led by skillful and able leaders, they retained their organization and continued fighting, this time against the Philippine government and the Philippine army. Communist-trained and Communist-led, they transformed the central Philippines into a true ideological tension area, which could have been escalated to the interpolitical level with very little additional effort. The struggle was ruthless and cruel on both sides. Many of the peasants were forced to join the Huks by fear of retaliation against their families. They also joined the Huks because of their fear of government action against the villages occupied by the Huks or as a reaction against the brutal action of the government troops.[29]

Filipino reports admit that the "general situation was bad enough. Even worse, there were . . . instances of officers involved in matters definitely unworthy of one who is by definition an officer and a gentleman by the act of our Congress. Instances, including demanding bribes for the performance or nonperformance of duty, occurred in all ranks. Each, of course was magnified by Huk propagandists and sympathizers. Few of the offenders were punished appropriately and publicly. We had a few big scandals in Central Luzon during this period. In a general statement, we can say that troop behavior was so low that it cultivated an antipathy by the masses for the man in uniform."[30]

Tactics of geographical and social infiltration was widely used by the Philippine government in counteracting the Huks, who numbered 34,000 men.[31] Such infiltration was used by both sides, and resulted in confusion. Terror was also applied on both sides. But it was humanity, not terror, that won back the sympathy of the population. We read in a report on the guerrilla warfare in the Philippines that "Justice and goodwill are keywords to success in any operation." The same report, however, gives a substantial account of tactics of deception.[32]

A fundamental change in social-political strategy was introduced by the secretary of Defense, Ramón Magsaysay, later elected president of the republic. At this time, the Huks were well rooted in Central Luzon, and had not only a great deal of military strength but also represented skills in administering the territory. They appointed administrators, controlled schools in the area, and acted as a formal government. Huk units were frequently more powerful and more numerous than the army.

The new defense secretary (Magsaysay) developed an imaginative social-economic strategy and substantially changed the military tactics. He embarked on a process of social-political reforms in the areas affected by peasant misery and exploitation. The army was recruited for this work, and a special section (Edcor) became the instrument of a wide social reform. Magsaysay immediately removed corrupt officers, and advanced those who were efficient. Small farms of six to ten hectares (about 15–25 acres) were distributed among the peasants; cottages and civic centers were built, and new villages and settlements emerged. The Edcor cleared the fields and built houses.

Simultaneously, the defense secretary sought to win the Huks by a policy of social reform and persuasion. Respect for human beings displaced former antagonistic attitudes. By 1954, splits within the Huk party had developed, as the policy of Magsaysay influenced the Huks and their leaders. On May 17, 1954, Luis Taruc, the Huk leader, surrendered and expressed his willingness to work for the government's social reforms. Magsaysay's humane attitude toward the peasant population, his reform movement, and an honest election won large sections of the peasantry to his camp.

Magsaysay was elected president, and under his administration a land reform law was introduced.[33]

The Philippine example was by no means an isolated case. An active policy of social reforms, attempts to win the friendship of the population by constructive action rather than by war, became an important strategy in tension areas. However, this type of action is not equally effective in every place.

THE ORGANIZATION OF THE POPULATION

An estimate of the situation in a tension area requires a careful evaluation of the attitude of the population toward the attacking party as well as toward the formal power centers in the territory. During the war in French Indochina, the French were unable to win the support of the population. They operated as in a vacuum, or as in a foreign territory. Without the support of the population, the political action of the formal government was brought to nothing.[34] The support of the population or in many cases its active participation is of primary significance.

The third element of the general pattern is the organization of the population and its structuring into groups. (In this respect, the Viet Minh in French Indochina [now Cambodia, Laos, and Vietnam] may serve as an example.)[35]

A totalitarian system may organize a village population in "parallel hierarchies." On the one hand is the party; on the other, the administrative institutions: the youth and women's organizations, and trade unions that absorb the active element in a system of parallel, mutually interdependent lines of command and organization, dependent on the decision of one central power. Those who are not in the hierarchy have no power whatsoever. Freedom of movement is frequently limited, except by special permission. All other organizations are absorbed or disbanded. Only one central line of command and one powerful structure, built around the party, survives, reducing the other elements of the population to a subordinate position.

The civil organization is of paramount significance in any revolutionary action and in any consolidation of power. However, a democratic libertarian movement cannot apply structures of organization similar to those of authoritarian movements. And, in certain times of crisis, a command structure may act more effectively, since it is under a single command.

The sociology of antagonism and conflict in an ideological tension area is complex, as are the techniques for the reduction of those tensions. In many typical areas, the easing of such tension or even the maintenance of control requires broad action of a sociological-economic, rather than military, nature. An ideological tension has positive results also. It forces change, making man reconsider his present existence and the condition of his neighbors. Violent and dangerous as it is, it challenges both camps continuously and forces them to change.

AGAIN, SOCIAL CAUSATION

An analysis of an ideological tension area revolves around the problems of that area. It is directed toward the understanding and explanation of the reasons for the unrest. The causes explain the nature of the antagonisms. Should we then reduce the causal analysis of a complete social conflict in a tension area to two or three major variables: psychological, ideological, and social-economic, as was once suggested in this volume?

I have already repeatedly indicated that tension areas differ. One tension area may be entirely dissimilar from another in the same country but on a different border. Every single ideological tension area requires a careful consideration and listing of the interacting variables.

What, then, should be the procedure in an analysis of tension areas? A causal analysis requires an inventory of causal factors or variables in order of perception, without attributing any specific weight or priority to them. After the preparation of this inventory, we may proceed to the . . . . evaluation of causal variables. In this second step, the variables are evaluated according to their relevance, or weight.

Perhaps methods could be devised to assign ranking or weight to various variables, but by the very nature of the process, such arbitrary ranking would serve only for a general orientation. However, after evaluation, the less significant could be reduced. The proper analysis of an ideological tension area implies a pluralistic causal approach.

THE ANTAGONISTIC SEQUENCE IN IDEOLOGICAL-INTERPOLITICAL TENSION AREAS

Ideological tensions may also move through an antagonistic sequence. Such a sequence may start "below," because of social-economic and ideological unrest. From there, it may move to an intrapolitical stage. At this stage, the government, representing the formal power center in the area, intervenes to ease the tension or force the movement into submission. The moment another government intervenes to support one of the parties, the tension changes to the complex and interpolitical. But such a tension can also be manipulated from above, and a government may infiltrate the area from an external base and escalate the tension to an interpolitical status, involving two or more governments or states. Furthermore, as in the case of Berlin, an interpolitical tension can be treated by the decision of an outside government.

The type of tension prevailing in Berlin is decided in the capitals of the external powers. The internal base has little significance. The decisions and the policy are determined by the strength of the external base of the decision makers; by their power, strategy, and tactics. Reduction of such tension cannot be accomplished by changes within the social-economic base of the local areas. Easement will not be achieved by improving the social conditions or providing a strong appeal. The tension is purely interpolitical, and its easing requires direct negotiations between the external parties. The psychological devices and techniques of easing tensions developed in interethnic intergroup tensions will be of no use in this case.

An interpolitical ideological tension is settled by negotiation and, in times when the ideologies are incompatible, by an evaluation of the strength of the contending powers and the risks and dangers involved. The reduction of tensions is accomplished by factors outside the tension areas.

The nature of tension areas differs in different cases. The social and political processes are different; the causation is different. In consequence, stalemating or reduction of such tensions requires different means. It is an error indeed to attempt to apply the techniques used in the reduction of an interethnic tension to a purely interpolitical tension of the nature of Berlin. Of course psychological analysis and techniques could be applied in negotiation to create conditions for mediation, but this is a different matter. A purely psychological approach, without the support of the political elements, will not suffice in stalemating or in a reduction.

TENSION AREAS AND STRATEGIC STAGES

Certain areas that are affected by ideological or ethnic tensions have as much strategic significance in a policy of expansion and conquest as they have in a policy of maintaining peace. Such areas can be selected by an aggressive government as stages in a strategy of expansion. In that way a government and a state expands through indirect war, or in a war by substitution from one area to the other, from one stage to the next, in a local strategy of expansion. The utilization of geographical areas as stages in an expansionist policy is also "thrifty politics" for the expanding and aggressive state in terms of economic expenditures and human losses. The war is waged by foreign guerrillas and foreign nationals. The damages, misfortunes, and tragedies are suffered in distant lands, while the aggressing nation remains untouched, supplying weapons, money, ideological appeal, and expert personnel.

The ideological tension is initiated in an inconspicuous manner. Infiltration follows, and then the ideological tension is escalated, utilizing the social-economic condition of the area. In consequence, the capture is advanced in a silent war.

A political observer of Communist Chinese strategy and tactics—and Mao Tse-tung is a prominent tactician—may readily notice China's strategy of advance from one area to another. The June 14, 1963, letter of the Central Committee of the Chinese Communist Party to its counterpart in the Soviet Communist Party indicates clearly that peace is not Mao Tse-tung's goal at present. His concept of a protracted war is primarily the idea of a war through stages, in which a variety of means and devices are utilized.[36] The capture of strategic tension areas closely follows Mao Tse-tung's strategy and tactics. Wishful thinking cannot change the hard facts, nor save the peace.

The presence of Communist China in the U.N. may help to break the isolation and modify diplomatic behavior. This may create conditions for negotiations and for at least a "cold peace" at the "point of indifference."

NOTES

1. See Norman Cohn, *The Pursuit of the Millennium* (Fairlawn, N.J.: Essential Books, 1957), pp. 99 ff.

2. Vincenzo Cuoco, *Saggio Storico Sulla Rivoluzione di Napoli* (Milano: Universale Economica, 1st ed. 1801), Vol. 1.

3. Giuseppe Ferrari, *La Rivoluzione e i Rivoluzionari in Italia* (Milano: Universale Economica, n.d., first published in *Revue des Deux Mondes*, 1844-1845; in Italian, 1852).

4. J. V. Stalin, *Collected Works,* Volume V, 1921–1923 (Moscow: Foreign Languages Publishing House, 1953). See also, Feliks Gross, *Seizure of Political Power* (New York, 1958), Chaps. 2 and 3, pp. 65 ff. and pp. 241 ff.
5. *Op. cit.,* p. 22.
6. *Op. cit.,* pp. 9, 12, 18.
7. Gross, *op. cit.,* pp. 27, 39 ff., 47, 52 ff.
8. Ferrari, *op. cit.,* p. 21.
9. Tukhachevski presented his views at the Military Academy of Moscow on February 7–10, 1923. His lecture was reprinted in Joseph Pilsudski, *L'Année 1920* (Paris, 1920).
10. Adam Ciolkosz, "Tajemnica Tuchaczewskiego" (The Secret of Tukhachevski), *Polemiki,* I, No. 1 (Fall, 1963, London), 103.
11. "Uber die Idee des Volksaufstandes," in *Historische Zeitschrift,* Neue Folge, Vol. 50 (Munchen-Liepzig, 1901), pp. 78 ff. Reprinted in: Neihardt von Gneisenau, *Schriften Uber Gneisenau* (Berlin, 1954), pp. 230 ff.
12. See Appendix I [in Gross, *World Politics and Tension Areas*].
13. Giuseppe Mazzini, "Sulla Rivoluzione Francese del 1789," in *Scritti* (Milano: Casa Editrice Sonzogno; n.d.), II, 138 and 154.
14. Georges Sorel, *Reflexions sur la violence* (Paris: Riviere, 1925 edition).
15. Georges Sorel, "Decomposition of Marxism," in Irving L. Horowitz, *Radicalism and Revolt against Reason* (New York: The Humanities Press, 1961).
16. "Hernán Cortés," *Enciclopedia Barsa (Encyclopaedia Britannica)* Buenos Aires, Chicago, Mexico, 1957), V, 173.
17. "Francisco Pizarro," *Enciclopedia Barsa (op. cit.),* XII, 150.
18. "Francis Garnier," *Larousse du Vingtième Siècle* (Paris, 1930), III, 719.
19. Cuoco, *op. cit.,* Ch. XVI, "The State of the Nation of Naples," pp. 79 ff. and 82 ff. See also Constance A. Diglioli, *Naples in 1799, An Account of the Revolution of 1799* (London: John Murray, 1903).
20. C. Lombroso and R. Laschi, *Il Delitto Politico e le Rivoluzioni* (Torino: Fratelli Bocca, 1890).
21. Gaetano Mosca, *Elementi di Scienca Politica,* ed. Laterza (Bari, 1953).
22. Che (Ernesto) Guevara, *Guerrilla Warfare* (New York: M. R. Press, 1961).
23. Eugenio Garin, *L'Umanesimo Italiano,* Laterza, Bari 1964, p. 94.
24. Mazzini, *op. cit.,* p. 211.
25. Reginald G. Hainworth and Raymond T. Moyer, *Agricultural Geography of the Philippine Islands* (U. S. Department of Agriculture, Office of Foreign Agricultural Relations, Washington, D. C., December, 1945), quoted in: Gerald D. Berreman, *The Philippines: A Survey of Current Social, Economic and Political Conditions,* No. 19, Southeast Asia Program, Department of Far Eastern Studies (Cornell University, 1956), p. 27.
26. Robert A. Polson and Agaton P. Pal, *The Status of Rural Life in the Dumaguete City Trade Area* (Philippines, 1952; Ithaca: Cornell University, 1956; mimeo.), Table 34, P. RAP 56: 103–150 ff.
27. Berreman, *op. cit.,* pp. 27 ff. See also Bernard Seerman and Laurence Salisbury, *Cross-Currents in the Philippines* (New York-San Francisco: Institute of Pacific Relations, Far Eastern Pamphlets, No. 13, 1946).

28. Alvin H. Scaff, *The Philippine Answer to Communism* (Stanford University Press, 1955), p. 6.

29. *Ibid.,* pp. 36 ff., pp. 118–134.

30. Napoleon D. Valeriano, Colonel AFP, "Military Operations," in *Anthology of Related Topics on Counterinsurgency* (Fort Bragg, North Carolina, June 15, 1961), pp. 144–150.

31. Valeriano, *op. cit.,* p. 147.

32. Some of the cases and tactics described indicate the ruthless nature of this struggle, which may alienate and discourage friends and the non-committed and challenge the very principle of democracy. Here appears again the problem of moral imperatives imposed on a democratic system, while the others may disregard the principles.

33. Frances Lucille Starner, *Magsaysay and the Philippine Peasantry: The Agricultural Impact on Philippine Politics, 1953–1956* (University of California Press, 1961), University of California Political Science Publications, Vol. X. On the role of the army in social and political reform in the Philippines and the effect of those actions on the reduction of friction, see also "Civic Activities of the Military in Southeast Asia," by Col. E. G. Lansdale. Lansdale gives an interesting and general survey of military civil assistance as a policy of easing tensions. The American, French, and Indonesian armies were helping local populations in Southeast Asia, distributing food, giving assistance in agriculture, public works, medical aid, even legal defense. He gives a general account of aid and civil administration in the Philippines, Vietnam, Cambodia, Burma, Indonesia. The general rehabilitation plan, the Edcor Plan, for the Philippines is included. (Anderson, Southeast Asia Subcommittee of the Draper Committee, *Anthology of Related Topics on Counterinsurgency* (Lackland Air Force Base), III, 282–291.

34. N. E. Geneste, "Danger from Below," in *United States Naval Institute Proceedings* (November, 1960), Vol. 86, pp. 33–46.

35. On group structures and organization of the civil population of the Viet Minh during the war in Indochina, 1949 and 1951, see Geneste, as quoted above, and Colonel Lacheroy, "Guerre Revolutionnaire," in *Marine* (September, 1958), No. 21 (Paris), pp. 41 ff.

36. The full text of the letter was published in the New York *Times* on July 5, 1963.

18. RESEARCH FOR PSYCHOLOGICAL WARFARE

John W. Riley, Jr., and Leonard S. Cottrell, Jr.

Shortly after D-day, in June 1944, the first rounds of leaflet shells were fired from artillery positions on the still insecure Normandy beachhead. Within a few hours, six German soldiers, each carrying a surrender leaflet, crossed the fluid battle line to surrender to the American forces. With the interrogation of these first German POW's in France there began one of the little known but highly useful research operations of World War II.

The typical research design followed in these operations called for data which would permit the correlation of leaflets with number of prisoners, and provided information on prisoner comments concerning the leaflets themselves. Here was an operational research problem in its simplest form. Here was one way to cope with the query of the hard-bitten field commander who asked: "Can you come up with some real evidence that these paper shells of yours do anything but clutter up the landscape?"

Here, however, is illustrated one of the great dilemmas of psychological warfare research. On the one hand, it is highly necessary to develop readily applicable research techniques which will provide some immediate answers to the commander's problems as he understands it. On the other hand, it is equally important that the research not be left at such a superficial level. Sooner or later the commander needs to know why and under what conditions psychological warfare produces actual surrenders. The simple inference of causation, whenever leaflets are found on prisoners, is no substitute for such insights as those of the British psychiatrist, Colonel H. V. Dicks, who, later in the war, on the basis of systematic analysis of POW interrogations, identified the "hard-core" Nazi as "idealistic zealots" who lived on unrealistic and metaphysical arguments; or as "party toughs" who were held in line by "a sense of comradeship in guilt, excitement

SOURCE. John W. Riley, Jr., and Leonard S. Cottrell, Jr., "Research for Psychological Warfare," in *Public Opinion Quarterly,* 21 (Spring, 1957), pp. 147–158. Reprinted by permission of the authors and Princeton University Press. Copyright 1957 by Princeton University.

and adventure;" or as "concealed fanatics" whose "private fantasy world [and] the Nazi ideology and practice of brutality fit as a perfect expression of a . . . distorted mentality."[1]

Nor is the evidence of consistently favorable prisoner comment on leaflets any substitute for the more sophisticated research approaches which, during the Korean War, began to yield conceptualizations of surrender as a much more complex process than appears on the surface. As Linebarger has put it, "surrending does not depend upon the disposition of the individual enemy soldier to say yes or no to the war as a whole. . . . The actual physical process of surrender is an elaborate one. . . ."[2]

Another illustration also begins on the Normandy beachhead. Air strikes against German posts in various French villages had been ordered as part of the softening-up process just after D-day; and while general warning leaflets, designed to protect French civilians, had been dropped prior to each attack, it was soon evident that the message on the leaflet was frequently not heeded. A small research team was consequently detached to find a quick answer. The project didn't take long. French civilians, even while seeking kin and possessions in the smoking rubble, were asked if they had noticed any leaflets prior to the bombing. The answer was invariably in the affirmative. They were then shown a copy of the actual warning leaflet which had been dropped and asked if they had happened to see this particular one. The answers continued in the affirmative. Next they were asked to give the sense of the message and, in most cases, their answers showed that its meaning was comprehended. They were finally asked why they had not acted on the message and moved out of the village, and their answers were quite straightforward. They simply had not supposed the leaflets were meant for them. They thought that possibly the wind had carried them from some other battle area.

While the research came up with a perfectly satisfactory operational answer to the immediate problem—that is was impossible to communicate with French civilians in villages which were about to be bombed unless the actual target was clearly indicated on the leaflet—it did not throw much light on the more basic question of why the French perceived the leaflets as they did.

Later in the war, there were several cases of more elaborate research findings demonstrating, among other things, that the acceptance, rejection, or distortion of any communicated message depends in no small measure upon the nature of the group relationships of the recipients of the message. One interesting example of this was the Shils-Janowitz analysis of the disintegration of the German

---

[1] As reported in "Psychological Foundations of the Wehrmacht" and summarized in Daniel Lerner, *Sykewar,* New York: George L. Stewart, 1949, p. 139.

[2] P. M. A. Linebarger, *Psychological Warfare,* Second Edition, Washington, D. C.: Combat Forces Press, 1954, p. 288.

Wehrmacht, in which it was pointed out that the most receptive targets for Allied messages "were groups where solidarity and ability to function as a unit were largely destroyed.[3]

During World War II, and later in Korea, research in support of psychological warfare operations played a significant role. Yet no systematic account of this effort, comparable to the story of research on soldier reaction to training and combat described in *The American Soldier* will probably ever be written, despite the fact that the research problems put to the Psychological Warfare Division were no less significant for military effectiveness than those which were put to the Research Branch of the Information and Education Division.[4]

Perhaps the absence of such a systematic summary of psychological warfare research may be explained partly in terms of widely varying types of problems which were posed for research. At one extreme were the simple operational problems of the nose-counting variety: "What proportion of prisoners carried leaflets?", "Were the French civilians warned to move?" Such questions as these could usually be dealt with successfully, since appropriate research techniques were at hand. At the other extreme, global and far-reaching questions of psychological warfare strategy were asked. These questions led directly to the bases of human motivation, communication, and social structure. Not only were the research techniques inadequate; the necessary theory was lacking as well. Research on these broad questions, with a few exceptions such as the projects of Dicks, or Shils and Janowitz, did not thrive.

THE NEED FOR MIDDLE-RANGE RESEARCH

One might well inquire why research has tended to fluctuate between these two extremes and disregard the important middle-range problems. It is our contention that this is in part reflective of the varying moral and financial support accorded to psychological warfare research. Whenever, at the simple level, a few projects have succeeded in finding reasonably satisfactory answers, an atmosphere favorable to research was created. The increased research activity, however, has

---

[3]Edward Shils and Morris Janowitz, "Cohesion and Disintegration in the Wehrmacht in World War II," *Public Opinion Quarterly,* Vol. XII (1948) No. 2.

[4]Several excellent accounts have of course appeared, notably: Daniel Lerner, *Sykewar;* Edward Barrett, *Truth is Our Weapon;* Paul Linebarger, *Psychological Warfare;* Charles Thomson, *Overseas Information Services of the United States Government;* Wallace Carroll, *Persuade or Perish.* Interested readers will also look forward to Murray Dyer's forthcoming work on this subject which, incidentally, has been helpful in the preparation of this essay. An overview of the literature as a whole is given by the new bibliography prepared by Bruce L. Smith and Chitra M. Smith, *International Communication and Political Opinion,* Princeton University Press, 1956.

invariably led to the raising of basic questions and, at this point, disillusionment has quickly followed. The hard-headed user of research has little patience with the defining of abstract types, or with mathematical models of interaction, despite the researcher's need of all such tools before he is ready to come up with solutions applicable to complex problems. What seems to be required, therefore is a realistic research program on a level which is intermediate between the simple and the complex. Answers at the simple level are not enough. Answers at the complex level await the development of requisite techniques and an appropriate body of theory.

Conventionally, propagandists tend to think in terms of the formula: *Who* says *what* to *whom,* and with *what effect.* Thus, a basis is provided not only for a division of labor in an operational sense, e.g., leaflet or script writers who produce the communicated "what," the research personnel who report on the "what effect," and so on; but also implicit in the scheme are the elements of a theory of communication. This is not to say, however, that any unified theory of communication is actually at hand. It is, rather, to point out that most of the work has centered in a somewhat disjointed fashion upon one or more of these elements:

1. The audience (the *whom* element), i.e., classificatory or descriptive analyses of target audiences.

2. The message content (the *what* element), i.e., content analyses and policy considerations as to what is communicated.

3. Response and evaluation (the *effect* element), i.e., research on the extent to which the message has produced the desired effect.

The fourth element—the communicator or the information source—has received very little attention in the development of research for psychological warfare, despite its obvious importance. Results of basic research on this element, such as that being conducted by Carl Hovland and his associates at Yale,[5] remains to be codified for psychological warfare purposes. Ultimately, any full-fledged theory of communication must deal with both communicator and audience as participants in an interactive process.

For the present, this essay follows the three-fold outline mentioned above, mainly because this provides a convenient scheme for listing some operating guides which might well serve as starting points in planning a realistic psychological warfare research program. These points, scattered as they are and not entirely cognate with one another, have grown out of research experience at the operational level. Our review will consist of statements of some of these points, discussions of the contexts from which they emerge, and consideration from a

---

[5]Carl I. Hovland, Irving L. Janis, and Harold H. Kelley, *Communication and Persuasion,* New Haven: Yale University Press, 1953.

sociological point of view of some of the possibilities for research. In the effort to redress the balance of certain earlier emphases, our emphasis is essentially sociological, with the main focus on the relationship between communications and group structures. No claim is made that what we propose constitutes all or even the most important problems. However, our suggestions are realistic both from the point of view of the practical needs of the field and as a move toward a more adequate research program.

We shall necessarily be limited in the scope and number of our examples. For reasons of security and of space, we shall not discuss or refer to the postwar research programs of such organizations and offices as the former Human Resources Research Institute of the Air Force; the RAND Corporation; or the Operations Research Office, the Human Resources Research Office, and the Special Operations Research Office, all of the Army; or any of the research operations of the Department of State, the Central Intelligence Agency, or the United States Information Agency. Suffice it to say that in our opinion the field of research in psychological warfare would greatly benefit from a more adequate theoretical structuring and practical implementation. Our present discussion will be concerned with psychological warfare in the restricted military sense of utilizing propaganda and other communicative acts against an enemy. We view psychological warfare as a relatively limited aspect of the broader area of political communication.[6]

THE TARGET AUDIENCE

On the problem of audience definition, two points are of special interest:

1. *For purposes of propaganda the internal differences in the target audience cannot be disregarded.*

To be sure, this is the exact opposite of the thesis announced by R. B. Lockhart, who, as director of the English Political Warfare Executive, had a good deal to say about Allied propaganda policy during World War II in Europe. The dictum was, at least as far as strategic propaganda was concerned, "it should be addressed to the masses;[7] the implication being clear that it was hardly worthwhile for a large scale effort to seek out special target audiences. Lerner, in *Sykewar,* gives a supporting judgment:

[6]This distinction has been suggested in a paper by Leonard S. Cottrell, Jr., "Social Research and Psychological Warfare," which was delivered at the Washington meeting of the American Sociological Society, September, 1955.

[7]See his *Comes the Reckoning,* Putnam and Company, London, 1948. See also Wilbur Schramm, et al., *Four Working Papers on Propaganda Theory,* Urbana: University of Illinois, 1955.

. . . strategic propaganda concerns itself with the longer-term causes, conduct, and consequences of the war. With such an approach the interests of larger and more varied publics could be reached, and the lines of political differences among Germans could be crossed by Sykewar.[8]

This view is, however, not without its critics. Among them, Hans Speier is perhaps the most articulate. In his essay "Psychological Warfare Reconsidered" he suggests two types of fallacies. On the one hand, it is fallacious to think of the individual as being greatly involved personally in the weighty issues of the state, and on the other hand, it is equally fallacious to assume that individuals are equally powerful in the influence which they can bring to bear.

"Since in modern societies the mass of the population cannot overthrow, or actively influence the policies of despotic regimes . . . *the population at large is no rewarding target of conversion propaganda* from abroad. Any notion to the contrary may be called the democratic fallacy. . . ."[9]

Similarly, our own view is that, while much communication will of necessity be beamed to an undifferentiated mass audience, all possible research should be conducted on ways and means of identifying and reaching crucial subgroups and categories of individuals within a total population. In this connection, a number of lines of inquiry might well be pursued.

In the first place, the studies of voting in the United States[10] have, for example, suggested that individuals under "cross-pressures," those whose loyalties are divided between groups with conflicting norms, are those most ready to shift their political views. The possible implications for psychological warfare of such a finding might well be investigated further.

Second, the disaffected segments of an enemy population certainly represent a critical target. These include the openly rebellious, as well as those ambivalent persons who fear to admit their rebellion, even to themselves, and who cling compulsively to the established ways. Research is needed on the conditions under which such ambivalent persons can be won away from loyalty to the enemy.

Third, the long-run objective of psychological warfare is sometimes not merely to win over segments of a population, but to change certain values within a given society. Here, too, the propagandist must work with one segment at a time. Each segment or sub-group may play a different role in the re-formulation

[8]Daniel Lerner, *Sykewar,* New York: George W. Stewart, Inc., 1949 p. 148.

[9]Published in Daniel Lerner and Harold Lasswell, eds., *The Policy Sciences,* Stanford: Stanford University Press, 1951, p. 259. Italics ours.

[10]See especially Bernard R. Berelson, Paul F. Lazarsfeld, and William H. McPhee, *Voting,* Chicago: University of Chicago Press, 1954. pp. 129 ff.

of group opinion, and techniques are needed to identify and analyze such inter-action processes. What can be learned through research about which population elements are crucial in bringing about such changes?

If psychological warfare, following such lines as these, is to take account of the internal differences in its audiences, this will require a shift in the basic con-ceptual model on which much media research has been conducted in the past. Earlier studies "have, on the whole, tended to conceive of the audience as a series of discrete individuals. . . . But this conception is oversimplified [since] any given person in the audience reacts not merely as an isolated personality but also as a member of the various groups to which he belongs. . . ."[11] This may involve changes in sampling and other research procedures, so as to take into account the structural aspects of the society. Beyond this, mass media techniques them-selves may well require various extensions and changes, if sub-groups within the audience are to be given special treatment.[12]

2. *The most promising method of distinguishing critical "special audiences" within the target audience is in terms of objective criteria.*

During World War II, some of the special problems posed for psychological war-fare before the collapse of Germany centered around the possibilities presented by readily recognizable groups within the total target area. For example, the in-mates of concentration camps or the members of involuntary labor units were considered to be audiences deserving special psychological warfare attention. As contrasted with such relatively obvious targets, many less obvious but important specific targets may require highly sophisticated and detailed psychological war-fare intelligence for their identification. Research is needed to determine what objective criteria are correlated with important variables of the social structuring of the audience.

THE MESSAGE CONTENT

It is, of course, basic to any theory of the communication process that con-tent cannot, save for descriptive purposes, be separated from either the audience or its response. But to pursue the conventional distinctions, the following sug-gestions refer mainly to the operational problem of what goes into a psychologi-cal warfare message.

[11]Matilda White Riley and Samuel Flowerman, "Group Relations as a Variable in Communi-cations Research," *American Sociological Review,* April, 1951, p. 174.

[12]For an account of the Communists' utilization of this type of information in Korea, see John W. Riley, Jr., and Wilbur Schramm, *The Reds Take a City,* New Brunswick, New Jersey: Rutgers University Press, 1951, pp. 103–127.

3. *Varying interpretations will be placed upon psychological warfare messages regardless of the objective truth of such messages.*

One of the keenest arguments with psychological warfare circles during World War II had to do with the so-called strategy of truth, although this was consistently the central element of the official policies of the United States.[13] Crossman, one of the major World War II psychological warfare policy makers, saw this strategy as demanding an extremely high degree of empathy on the part of the sender of psychological warfare messages.

> In every occupied territory we had two audiences, motivated by precisely opposite emotions—our friends, whose hopes made them intensely credulous of good news; and our enemies, ready to dismiss as 'enemy propaganda,' even the most sober statement of an allied success. Whether on the radio or in leaflet form, the same news had to be selected and presented so as to appear objective to both these audiences, the credulous friend and the skeptical enemy.[14]

Stated in its simplest terms, the import of this point is that even if we want to tell only the objective truth, we must have some basis for predicting how and to what extent it may be distorted. This view is not unlike that which W. I. Thomas prescribed for social science in general. Thomas insisted that the relationship between an objective situation and any behavior could never be regarded as a simple cause and effect relationship. Rather it is always mediated by the subjects' definition of the situation. Thus in his famous "Methodological Note" we find this statement:

> . . . the effect of *a* social phenomenon depends in addition [to its empirical content] on the subjective standpoint taken by the individual or the group toward this phenomenon and can be calculated only if we know, not only the objective content of the assumed cause, but also the meaning which it has at the given moment for the given conscious beings.[15]

This is tantamount to saying that there are two kinds of reality: objective reality; and that which a person "sees," i.e., his subjective reality. Obviously, if the latter serves to *interpret*, to *select* from, or to *distort* the former, the two may

---

[13]See, for example, Edward W. Barrett, *Truth is Our Weapon*, New York: Funk and Wagnalls Company, 1953.

[14]Quoted in Daniel Lerner *Propaganda, in War and Crisis*, New York: George W. Stewart, 1951, p. 336.

[15]E. H. Volkart, *Social Behavior and Personality, Contribution of W. I. Thomas*, New York: Social Science Research Council, 1951, pp. 54–55.

frequently, and usually do, fail to coincide. It is this proposition which research for psychological warfare operations must take fully into account.

What constitutes this subjective reality undoubtedly varies from one segment of the enemy population to another. This is the sort of thing which Speier apparently had in mind when he pointed out that psychological warfare objectives cannot be conceived simply in terms of reducing the enemy's "will to fight," for actually there are many "wills." In short, we are led to believe that strategic messages, regardless of their generality, will carry quite different meanings to different segments of the audience, depending upon their reference systems and relationships. In order to throw further light upon the specific workings of this hypothesis, research might be conducted in various settings to test such propositions as:

1. In respect to media behavior, any member of the audience will react not merely as an individual, but also as a member of the various groups to which he belongs (or aspires) and with which he communicates.

2. The values of the media messages will be accepted, rejected, or distorted in line with the values of the significant reference groups to which the recipient belongs, or to which he aspires.[16]

The dynamics of this relationship between group membership and perception of the message rests upon the ease or difficulty with which the communicated norms or values can be harmonized with the relevant group norms or values characteristic of the target group.

4. *The more salient the content of a message is to an audience, the greater the probability of its effect.*

This operating guide is included here simply because so much of the actual psychological warfare effort of the last war failed to heed it. The typical conception (at least in the case of Germany) was that strategic propaganda which attacked the doctrinal basis of Nazism would eventually defeat the enemy. Shils and Janowitz, however, have pointed out that "propaganda attacks on Nazi ideology seem to have been of little avail." They go on to conclude that:

> ... attempts to modify behavior by means of symbols referring to events or values outside the focus of attention and concern would be given indifferent response by the vast majority of the German soldiers.[17]

---

[16]See, e.g., Matilda White Riley and John W. Riley, Jr., "A Sociological Approach to Communications Research, *Public Opinion Quarterly,* Vol. XV, No. 4, (1951), pp. 445–460.

[17]Shils and Janowitz, *op. cit.*

Further research is obviously needed here. Much experimental work remains to be done by way of greater development of the appropriate instruments for testing hypotheses in this area. We need, for example, to know more about the relationship between the status of recipients and the salience of content. This leads to the next point, which is larger than, and subsumes, this matter of salience from the point of view of the receiver of the message.

5. *Psychological warfare messages must be cast within the frame of reference of the intended recipients.*

This statement is almost tautological, since there can be no communication without shared meanings. It is included in this listing because the self-evidence of such an assertion is often overlooked in psychological warfare practice. While the words may be accurately translated into the recipient's native tongue, the importance of his native symbols and values is often forgotten. Indeed, there is frequently a strong temptation for the psychological warrior simply to play games with his counterpart in the enemy camp, to outwit a mock opponent without regard to the impact of his message upon the real target audience.

In one of the better essays[18] on the theory of propaganda, it is shown that the essential nature of all propaganda involves a set of relevant values. Talcott Parsons, following W. I. Thomas, says, "a selection is made of those aspects which are functionally related to the particular orientations, values . . . of the person." In the design of research, therefore, the exhortation of Paul Linebarger and others must be constantly kept in mind that "the propagandist must tell the enemy those things the enemy will heed."[19]

Yet, in times of great stress, the relevant values of the recipient are often difficult to uncover. Even if the receivers of the message are right at hand where they can be readily studied, they may be unaware of their own values and unable to report them. A case in point arose in connection with a periodic study of general magazine audiences which was conducted during the past war.[20] Readers from the general public repeatedly told interviewers, "We are sick of the war. Therefore, we won't read or listen to anything which reminds us of it." Observations of actual reading behavior, however, when analyzed so as to focus analysis on the specific symbols which either encouraged or discouraged decisions to read particular articles or stories, demonstrated overwhelmingly that no subject matter

---

[18]Talcott Parsons "Propaganda and Social Control," in *Essays in Sociological Theory,* The Free Press, 1949. Pp. 275–309.

[19]See his *Psychological Warfare,* Second Edition, Combat Forces Press, Washington, 1954, for a full discussion of this point.

[20]For a discussion of the method used see Matilda White Riley and Hans Zeisel, "Reading Indices," *Journal of Marketing,* October, 1941.

was acceptable which was not explicitly couched in wartime terms and surrounded by symbols of a military culture.

Far more complex is the problem of ascertaining the values of an enemy population in wartime, particularly those of its disaffected members. Of crucial significance may be those who are under strain, ambivalent, at once torn between loyalty to patriotic values and to the new values being offered by the communicator. Such a segment may be a critically important target, and it is necessary to understand the nature of its ambivalence and the implications for psychological warfare possibilities. While such a segment is drawn to the new values, its allegiance to the old is made more compulsive by guilt feeling evoked by its attraction to the new. Among such a population we should expect strong ritualistic conformity which would serve to deny evidences of hospitality to the alien values. Beneath this ritualism, however, we should also expect to find the repressed side of the ambivalence, the side which represents a disposition to espouse the new values.

Research is now needed on the readiness of individuals under strain to accept communications which represent both the expressed and the repressed sides of their ambivalence. It has been suggested that such individuals will reject any overt statement of the repressed side; but that they may pay attention if the repressed value is expressed in fictional form, so that it may be received on the level of fantasy, thus protecting the receiver from the need to decide whether or not he believes, or is willing to accept, such a conflicting value. It is our belief that research along such lines as these would have far-reaching operational usefulness for psychological warfare.

THE EFFECT OF THE MESSAGE

While in practical terms communication is frequently conceived simply as a transfer of information from one person (or source) to another, the most intriguing, and at the same time the most perplexing, aspect of the problem is properly seen in terms of effect. The ultimate purpose of any communicated message is to influence human conduct.[21] Certainly any operation in psychological warfare has, in the long run, to be designed to influence behavior, yet it is precisely the attempt to evaluate influence which has yielded so little solid and convincing information. For this reason, therefore, it seems worth noting in the present context several suggestions which may be valuable in providing additional perspective on this problem.

[21] See Claude Shannon and W. Weaver, *The Mathematical Theory of Communications*, Urbana: University of Illinois Press, 1950.

6. *The degree of effectiveness of psychological warfare messages is measured by the degree of change in the values of the recipients brought about by the messages.*

This point simply means that, short of observations of the behavior actually resulting from a communication, the effectiveness problem should center upon the study of values and their changes. As Lasswell expresses it: "The most fundamental way to examine any response is in terms of values—does it modify or conserve values?"[22]

What seems to be needed at this juncture is the development of techniques for measuring value changes, for indicating both consensus and cleavage in values within groups and subcultures, and, equally important, for determining which values are perceived and selected out of media messages. The general approach to these problems has been to work with relatively small groups and by successive approximation to obtain measures which will replicate and produce internally consistent results in the hope that such measures may ultimately be applicable to psychological warfare problems.

7. *The closer a psychological warfare message comes to meeting an existing predisposition or need in the target audience, the more effective the message.*

This point emphasizes the reinforcement aspect of learning theory as it applies to communications.[23] On the other hand, it is a proposition of great practical significance for psychological warfare, since, assuming first-rate intelligence reports, some workable rules could be derived from the theory. Lerner, in writing of the conditions necessary for effective propaganda, lists four points; (1) Secure the attention of the audience; (2) Secure the credence of the audience; (3) Work within the predispositions of the audience; and (4) Don't expect the audience to do the impossible (the environment should make the proposed action feasible). He goes on to say:

> What we wish to emphasize here is that . . . predispositions define the limits within which audiences can be effectively persuaded to modify their experiences. . . .[24]

This statement comes very close to the type of research which would seem to be most productive. Attention must be paid to the function of the messages for the

---

[22]Bruce Lannes Smith, Harold Lasswell, and Ralph Casey, *Propaganda, Communication, and Public Opinion.*

[23]See Carl I. Hovland, et al., *op. cit.*

[24]Lerner, *Propaganda, in War and Crisis,* op. cit., p. 347.

recipient. One important set of needs is assumed to derive from the recipient's group relationships and it might be hypothesized that those could be classified as of two kinds: (1) The need to reinforce group identification, i.e., what meaning does the message have for the recipient's acceptance by group members or loyalties to group members, and (2) the need to escape from group frustration, i.e., what answers are provided by the message for the recipient to adjust to strains deriving from his group relations.

IN SUMMARY

This paper has suggested that the uneven development of research for psychological warfare is in part a reflection of the tendency for research questions to be posed either at the very simple level of operations, or as extremely complex and basic problems in the broad areas of human motivation and interaction. A consideration, in the light of current sociological knowledge, of some of the important operational guides to emerge from psychological warfare research experience during World War II, has convinced us of the feasibility of a realistically conceived program somewhere between these two extremes. More particularly, it is our belief that human actors both give and receive communications stimuli not as discrete individuals but as individuals who are identified with, and a·e in personal relationship with, other individuals in groups. Moreover, the individual's participation and integration in larger, more complex social systems is accomplished and made meaningful largely through his membership in smaller groups. Finally, we maintain that interactional models must replace the conventional stimulus-response concepts if we wish to understand communication phenomena and to use this understanding in psychological warfare. If social science research is to make its proper contribution to the solution of problems of psychological warfare, or any other type of communication effort, it must move promptly to theoretical formulations and implementing methodologies which are capable of dealing with the dimensions of the field we have indicated.

19. EVALUATING EXCHANGE OF PERSONS PROGRAMS

Elmo C. Wilson and Frank Bonilla

When one is in America, one realizes what immense advantages there are in having the boundaries separating countries disappear. In international relations, if only the spiritual boundaries would disappear. That's something I worked out for myself over there. . . I didn't realize that before at all, but there one sees people together who come from many different countries and everyone speaks a different language. But I felt so at home there. Then I realized that boundaries are unreasonable.

Previously, I did not care a whit about any nation. Today—and this is something which resulted from my trip to the United States—I see that a nation consists of individual people who have their personal problems, ambitions, and each his own life. I have seen that any person as an individual has his own worth and can contribute something to the general welfare. When one believes this and acts accordingly, one will always find other people who believe in the same ideas and with whom one can come to an understanding and cooperate.

These are the words of two from among several thousand young Western Europeans brought to this country during the last three years to study, work and visit in American schools and American homes. Nor are they simply polite flatteries, offered to American friends here or to officials who helped to arrange their trips; they are statements made by young exchangees to total strangers of their own nationality, who were in no way identified with the exchange-of-persons programs which brought them to America.

SOURCE. Elmo C. Wilson and Frank Bonilla, "Evaluating Exchange of Persons Programs," in *Public Opinion Quarterly,* 19 (Spring, 1955), pp. 20–30. Reprinted by permission of the authors and Princeton University Press. Copyright 1955 by Princeton University.

Today there are literally hundreds of organizations in the United States and other countries which sponsor or participate in exchange programs of different kinds. Communities, clubs, foundations, corporations, schools and individuals, as well as national governments, support the foreign exchange-of-persons movement. Most of those who come to the United States under these programs are students, although visits are also arranged for persons who come to teach, lecture, do research, and gain work experience. At the present time, for instance, the program carried on in Europe by the United States Department of State, with the support of both public and private funds, includes teen-agers (from Germany and Austria) who come to the United States to attend school and live with an American family; college students; specialists who come for advanced training or research; university professors who come to lecture; and civic and political leaders who come as individuals or as teams. Students, professors, and research specialists usually remain here the better part of a year, but some specialists and most of the leader groups stay only a three to four month period.

The largest private agency in the field of international education, the Institute of International Education, administers exchange programs between the United States and 74 countries. This organization conducts exchanges under numerous programs for the Department of State, including exchanges under the Fulbright and Smith-Mundt Acts, as well as special German-Austrian programs. The stated objectives of the Institute throughout its 34 years of operation have been:

- To increase understanding between the United States and other nations through the exchange of promising college students and of advanced specialists in many fields.
- Through these educational exchanges to help develop leadership to deal with basic problems of worlds' people.[1]

These, with varying emphases, are the objectives of almost all the organizations engaged in exchange programs. For some, the major objective may be the transmission of specific skills and techniques to help other countries relieve economic misery at home and to raise the cultural and material levels of life around the world. Others view exchange programs primarily as a means of increasing international understanding and achieving world peace. The Department of State, as the agency charged with the regulation of the United States' relations with other peoples, looks on the programs as an instrument for increasing understanding, respect, and friendship toward the United States and Americans, as well as a means of bolstering democracy abroad, cementing ties with allies, and securing cooperation for U. S. policy.

---

[1] *The World at Your Door,* Special Publications Series, No. 2, Institute of International Education, November, 1952. See also *34th Annual Report,* Institute of International Education, January, 1954.

THE PROBLEM OF EVALUATION

The problem of evaluating the effectiveness of almost any exchange program reduces itself to two fundamental questions:

1. Has the exchange experience succeeded in implanting, broadening, or reinforcing the skills, information, or attitudes which the program is designed to promote among exchangees?
2. Are returned exchangees effective in influencing people and events in their home countries in accordance with the objectives of the exchange program?

These are questions which deal with problems of learning, opinion change, and attitude formation. We wish to know whether the exchangee, during his sojourn in the United States, has incorporated into his intellectual and emotional stockpile the facts, ideas, or postures which will strengthen the free world; and whether, having returned to his own country, he is successful in leading others of his people to accept and act upon these principles. Research into these questions requires not only measures of opinion and attitude change in relevant areas among exchangees and their associates, but consideration of the entire range of problems associated with studies of interpersonal communications and the ways in which the influence of individuals mediates opinion change and action in others.

Formal evaluations of exchange programs utilizing modern techniques of social research are a fairly recent innovation.[2] There was, nevertheless, substantial evidence of the successes achieved by exchange programs with particular participants, and in particular countries even before scientific methods were applied to evaluations. The scholastic achievements, professional competence, and work proficiency of students and specialist trainees were ample evidence that certain information and techniques had been effectively communicated.

In many countries material progress directly attributable to the activity of American-trained nationals and the diffusion of American "know-how" left little doubt about the value of technical aid programs and the exchange-of-persons in this regard. There was also little doubt in the minds of administrators of exchange programs, who were in close contact with participants, that many friends were being won for the United States by the sizeable two-way traffic of exchanges between the United States and other nations. There was, and there still is, less

---

[2]The growing importance of such research was highlighted by the appointment in 1952 of a Committee on Cross-Cultural Education by the Social Science Research Council. This Committee has undertaken a three-year program of research into the impact of American educational experience on students from other nations. Members of the Committee met in conference at Cornell University in August, 1953, to assess their preliminary experience and to make recommendations for subsequent research. A report of that conference, as well as several monographs reporting specific studies carried out under Committee auspices have been published by SSRC.

understanding and consensus about the factors which make for success in some cases and for dismal failure in others, of the exact processes involved in bringing about changes in attitude among exchangees, and of the roles actually played in their home countries by returned exchangees.

AN EVALUATION IN LATIN AMERICA

One of the early evaluation studies undertaken by INRA[*] was initiated late in 1951. The country selected for study was one in Latin America, where exchanges had been conducted under the Buenos Aires Convention since about 1940. A total of 60 exchangees who had visited the United States between 1941 and 1952 was interviewed along with a matched group of persons who had applied for grants but had not visited the United States.[3] In addition, a number of persons who were designated by grantees as close personal associates were included in the study. In none of these interviews were the respondents aware of the basis for their selection for interview. They were approached ostensibly as randomly selected members of an "opinion leader" sample in their country. In all cases, interviews were carried out by nationals of the country concerned.

The study thus attempted to cut across the entire exchange experience and, in a single operation, both to gauge overall effects and to disclose the factors contributing to the effects. As such, it aimed at an overall assessment of the impact on the grantee of his stay in the United States. This was an important first step in evaluation (particularly from the point of view of the administrator) and it served to guide subsequent research into specific problems of selection, programming and follow-up work with exchangees in their home countries. The research produced such evidence of impact as the following:

1. Most exchangees who had visited the United States testified that they had left with a more favorable opinion of America and our style of life than when they arrived;

2. This was confirmed by comparing their answers to certain questions about America with those of similar individuals who had not travelled in the United States;

---

[3]Whenever possible, grantees were matched with "eligibles"—persons who had been awarded grants but had been unable, for personal reasons, to make the trip. When this was not possible, persons were selected who had been turned down, not for reasons of character of lack of competence, but because of the limited number of grants available. The two groups were matched for place of residence, field of specialization, type of grant applied for, and year in which application was made. They were also very similar in regard to sex, age and socio-economic status.

[*][International Research Associates, Inc.]

3. Their increased professional competence and the prestige of travel to the United States seemed to augment their influence among their colleagues on professional questions as well as questions related to the United States.

A REPETITION IN WESTERN EUROPE

In a subsequent study, the same research design served to document the basic findings of the Latin American evaluation for the program in West Germany. More rigorous sampling and matching procedures, and interviews with larger numbers of exchangees in the different categories, (leaders and students) permitted more reliable measures of the differences in opinion and attitude; and enabled study of differences not only between exchangees and "eligible" nonexchangees, but between exchangees in the different categories, as well. In contrast to the qualitative interview used in the earlier study, a highly structured interview facilitated quantification of the results and comparability of the responses. Elaborate precautions were taken to mask the sponsorship of the research, and no direct questions about the exchange program appeared in the questionnaire.

This second study confirmed the overall finding of the Latin American survey that exchangees are in general better informed about the U. S. and more favorably disposed toward America and Americans than are similar individuals who have never visited the United States. In addition, it was possible to distinguish areas in which some classes of exchangees seemed to have changed more than others. The exchange trip seemed more effective in arousing the political interest of teen-agers and in bringing them to accept democratic ideals than was the case among students at the college level of among visiting specialists. The latter, on the other hand, were considerably more impressed with the accomplishments of the United States in such fields as labor-management relations and political organization. The ideological plasticity of the teen-age group might single them out as an ideal point of entry for introducing democratic ideas. At the same time, their apparent susceptibility to change suggested that this group would require closer follow-up attention than would more mature exchangees.

A FOLLOW-UP STUDY OF TEEN-AGERS

This problem was accordingly more thoroughly investigated in a follow-up study carried out among returned German teen-agers. These young people, mostly between the ages of 16 and 18, had spent a year in the United States attending school and living with foster families carefully selected by various American private organizations. The data of the study consisted of intensive and detailed

information, from a relatively small number of these teen-age exchangees, regarding:

  a. The impressions that remained with them of their experiences in America;
  b. The kinds of adjustment problems they had experienced on their return
home and how these had been resolved;
  c. The kinds of changes, if any, that the exchange experience had made in
their life plans.

Some of the interviews with the young exchangees lasted as long as 12 hours
and were conducted over several sessions. A minimum of two other persons who
knew each teen-ager with varying degrees of intimacy were also interviewed.[4]
The material offered by the teen-ager about himself was thereby checked against
observations made by persons of different outlook and, in some respects, better
able than the teen-ager to gauge and describe the changes brought about in him
by his trip abroad.

On the basis of detailed and rounded histories that were compiled of each
teen-age exchangee's experience, a large number of specific recommendations
with regard to selection and screening procedures, orientation and programming,
and the extent and nature of follow-up procedures considered advisable were
made. Considerable related data of theoretical sociological interest also emerged.

It became clear that the program objectives could not be achieved simply by
working a unilateral change in exchangees and returning them to the old milieu.
The American values which the exchangees had assimilated could not be transferred whole cloth into their lives at home. The returnees had to be forewarned
and prepared for these problems. It was found, for example, that some of the
teen-agers who returned bursting with news and ideas for innovations found themselves in frustrated isolation because there were no other pro-democratic elements
in their environment, or simply no interest whatever in hearing about their experiences. It was suggested, therefore, that teen-agers be selected in groups from
the same school or community or from schools and communities where former
exchangees were present rather than from isolated institutions.

During the year away from home some of the young people had even lost
some of their facility in their native tongue. These lapses of grammer or pronun-
ciation were not infrequently qualified by critics at home as affectations or evidences of "Americanization." It was felt that extravagances in haberdashery,
gum-chewing, and other instances of behavior often criticized in Americans ought
also to be discouraged.

Returnees were also to be cautioned to avoid describing in two glowing terms
what they had observed in America and especially to avoid harshly invidious

---

[4] About a third of these interviews were made with mothers and fathers of the teen-agers, another third with teachers, ministers, employers and other adult friends of the youngsters,
and the final third with siblings, schoolmates and other friends of their own age.

comparisons with conditions at home. A moderate approach with regard to reforms was suggested. In short, the recommendation was made that returnees be impressed with the need for giving initial priority to re-establishing themselves as members of their families and communities rather than embarking on a wholesale Americanization of their country.

A BEFORE-AFTER COMPARISON

Answers to some of the problems arising from the evident impotence of those returnees who had found themselves isolated in communities hostile to the ideas and attitudes they had acquired in America, have been sought in a new program, which concentrates on civic, educational and, political *leaders*. Groups consisting of directors or leaders of political parties, civic organizations, labor unions, municipal government, educational and religions institutions, women's clubs and other organizations are brought to the United States and are given the opportunity to observe and study the operation of citizens' groups in American cities. This approach envisions that the teams (which generally number from 8 to 10 members), will, upon their return, stimulate their communities to solve, through democratic action, civic problems in fields such as housing, public welfare, public health, education, and city government.

Efforts are made to have team members represent all the important action organizations common to the country concerned. Persons who are leaders in more than one type of organization are especially sought after, since much multiple representation can be expected to magnify the impact of single individuals upon their return. Most importantly, this arrangement fosters change-inducing effort on a group level; acting in concert, these leaders may together find the courage and practical means for implementing new ideas that they might fail to find as individuals.

An elaborate experimental design was set up to test the effectiveness of this program in action. The basic elements of this experimental design were "before" and "after" interviews,

a. with a total of 16 such groups of leaders,
b. with close friends and associates of the members of these groups, and
c. with the general population of the communities they represented.

The essentially quantitative terms of the study design were supplemented by a special set of qualitative materials, systematically collected and organized: one group was accompanied by a trained social scientist who was able to record a wealth of observational details and pertinent comment from the participants during their American experience. This participant observer was with the group from morning to night, was in a position to be informed about all the experiences of each team member, and was a spectator to the reactions of exchangees to the personalities they encountered and the events they witnessed.

This design afforded numerous advantages over the research which had previously been carried out; although it owed much, obviously, to the experience gained in earlier studies. First, the researchers had a measure of attitudes prior to visiting the United States which was based on something more solid than the exchangees' recollections of what their state of mind had been at some time in the past. Second, the re-test, using nearly identical interview schedules on the second wave of interviewing some months after their return made it possible to *measure*, rather than *infer*, attitude change. Third, interviews with cross-sections of the local populations provided a means of determining to what extent, if any, the attitude changes observed in the exchangees and their contacts could be attributed simply to variations in the general climate of opinion.

Of particular interest, for similar studies in the future, are modifications of the conventional panel technique which had to be devised in order to retain its patent advantages and, at the same time, to overcome certain disadvantages it held for this research, in particular. To have interviewed *all* the exchangees before their departure might have aroused suspicion among them as to the purpose of the investigation. Conversations among the team members during the course of their three months together could easily bring to light that each of them had talked to an interviewer—and about the same topics—before his departure. Such a discovery might have seriously hampered the administration of the second wave or even have invalidated its results. The possibility of "sensitization effects" and "consistency reactions," common to panel studies, was also especially to be feared in such a situation.[5]

The design finally adopted combined interviews with a panel and interviews among carefully matched groups. In addition to offsetting the difficulties just discussed, this approach facilitated a measure of the re-test effect on the panel respondents.[6] Table I indicates the scheme of interviews and the number obtained in each group. The initial comparisons made it clear that the exchangees were a unique group to begin with, particularly as regards the areas in which possible changes were being investigated. Even before their trip, this group was substantially more interested in public affairs and substantially better informed than either their associates or the general public. They were more favorably disposed to the United States and were generally more democratic in their views on a number of subjects. The changes produced among exchangees as a result of their

[5]The problems of sensitization and consistency reactions were conceptualized by Carl Hovland. See Studies in Social Psychology in World War II, Vol. III: *Experiments on Mass Communication* by Carl I. Hovland, et al., Princeton University Press, Princeton 1949, Chapter 2, p. 21ff., for a discussion of measurement problems encountered in before-and-after studies.

[6]The effects of re-test were found to be negligible, even on information items.

TABLE 1

	First-Wave Interviews	Second-Wave Interviews Repeat	Non-Repeat	Total Interviews
Exchanges	62	46	65	173
Contacts	192	144	187	523
Cross-section	800	–	767	1587

trip were thus not evidenced by ideological shifts on abstract issues. On the whole, they did not become markedly more democratic in outlook. There were, however, changes (favorable) in their evaluation of the American character and a revision (also favorable) of their ideas about those aspects of life in America that they could readily observe during their stay.

Among their associates, changes that could be attributed to the influence of exchangees were likewise most marked in these same areas. For example, a quite favorable change was observed in the conception which both exchangees and their associates had of race relations in America. Not only the exchangees, who had witnessed at first-hand relations between white and Negro Americans, but also their friends at home, expressed views on race problems in the United States more in keeping with the facts, when interviewed after the exchange trip. Among exchangees as well as among their contacts, the proportion who had a more authentic notion of the Negro's situation in America was approximately doubled by the time of their second interview. The fact that this is an issue which is mercilessly exploited in anti-U.S. propaganda underscores the importance of the change accomplished.

The participant observer's account of the three-month visit of one group of these exchangees reports numerous incidents that aroused comment among the group because they involved experiences which either did not fit in with their preconception of life in America, or were startlingly different from what was customary at home. A middle-aged woman's remarks after a visit to a Police Athletic League center typify such reactions.

Don't the police have an aura about them that makes this type of work difficult for them? In C——, one wants to have as little as possible to do with the police; the appearance of the police at someone's home is greeted with apprehension.

Despite its complex design and the stringent measures taken to ensure the reliability of its results, a single study such as this could hardly constitute a definite evaluation of the program for exchange of community leaders. One would, of

TABLE 2. Proportion Who Responded "Favorably"
on Two Items on Race Relations*

Among Exchangees

"Before"   20%

"After"   52%

Among Contacts

"Before"   13%

"After"   21%

*Respondents were asked whether they believed that the position of the Negro in the
United States has improved during the past ten years and, secondly, to estimate the number
of Negroes who had died by lynching in the last two years.

course, except that some change in their views (on issues relevant to the program's objectives) would be apparent within three to four months after their return to their homeland; but it is also quite possible that in some cases, or on some
issues, opinion might not have crystallized fully within so short a period. By the
same token, it would not be surprising if some of the exchangees who indicated
change on the second interview should revert to their original points of view with
the passage of time.

More importantly, this study did not undertake to measure *intensity* of attitude. This means that it is possible for the exchange experience to have reinforced
an exchangee in his originally favorable attitudes without this effect being mani-
fested in the study results. It may well be that some of the exchangees who will
in the long run do most to realize the objectives of this program are those whose
attitudes were initially so favorable that their reinforcement could not register as
"more favorable" in the second interview, but whose conviction, motivation,
and capacity to act in accordance with the viewpoint fostered by the program
were intensified by the exchange experience.

In subsequent evaluation studies, attempts should be made to meet this last
problem by the use of scaling techniques for investigating attitudes and their components. Such studies, like those described above, would be designed to evaluate
program effectiveness as evidenced by the diffusion of program-supported values

from the participants to others in their home country. They would, however, undertake to do much more than document the fact of favorable change due to the program in a particular country. They would seek to measure *the degree of conviction* with which program-sponsored attitudes are held by participants, by matched standby candidates who did not come to the United States, and by associated of both these groups. The application of scaling techniques would permit the ranking of respondents in relation to relevant attitude areas and to such attitude components as intensity, closure, and involution, resulting in the distinction of invariant groups who are "positive" or "negative" for the attitude under study.[7]

A LOOK FORWARD

This has been a brief resume of exchange evaluation studies by International Research Associates. These studies have concentrated solely on determining whether certain of the exchange programs have, in fact, succeeded in inducing change among individuals who, in turn, disseminate newly acquired information and ideas in their native lands. Little attention could be given, except in the most informal way, to many related questions which bear both theoretical and practical interest, but which did not have the operational urgency of the primary mission.

One might note, for example, that the not inconsiderable impact of foreign nationals on Americans here at home has been largely ignored, as have the reciprocal effects on Americans, and on the participating countries, of the visits of American students and specialists outside our shores. Only minimal use has been made of existing records and standard report forms, as well as of the rich but unorganized information available from administrators and others who have had years of intimate contact with exchangees; much remains to be done to systematize such record-keeping and observation in a way that would make them more useful to scientific evaluations. The influence of personality factors, the expectations and motivations of selectees, different approaches in pre-trip and post-trip orientation, variations in programming and length of stay all remain largely unexplored. Students concerned with the role of personal influence and group loyalties as factors affecting information and the change of stability of opinion might find valuable opportunities here.

---

[7]Cf. Louis Guttman: "The Principal Components of Scalable Attitudes", Chapter V of *Mathematical Thinking in the Social Sciences,* Paul F. Lazarsfeld, Ed. The Free Press, Glencoe, Ill., 1954.

CHAPTER SEVEN

Intergovernmental Relations

20. *i*-TRUST: A NOTION OF TRUST IN THREE-PERSON GAMES AND INTERNATIONAL AFFAIRS

Bernhardt Lieberman

INTRODUCTION

In the many debates about the conduct of international affairs, though not necessarily in the actual conduct of such affairs, there is considerable concern with the notion of trust.[2] A number of questions are often debated. Among them are the following: should we trust another nation or group of nations? Is it important, possible, or sensible to trust a nation, or group of nations, in the conduct of international affairs? Once a treaty is signed to limit arms, to refrain from arming, or to take or refrain from some action, can or should a nation or group of nations be trusted?

SOURCE. Bernhardt Lieberman, "*i*-Trust: A Notion of Trust in Three-Person Games and International Affairs," in *Journal of Conflict Resolution,* 7 (September, 1964), pp. 271–280. Reprinted by permission of the author and the Center for Research on Conflict Resolution. Copyright 1964 by the University of Michigan.

Without doing lethal damage to the essence of the arguments, it is possible to dichotomize the various views about these questions. One group argues it is irrelevant, and possibly dangerous, to consider the notion of trust in the conduct of international relations. Nations, it is said, will act in their own self-interest and abrogate treaties, agreements, or their word informally given, whenever it is believed to be necessary to do so. It is said that a nation that does not act in its own self-interest is difficult to deal with; trustworthy behavior contrary to national interests is irresponsible and dangerous. Therefore there is no point in concerning oneself with such a value-laden notion as trust. Trust is irrelevant in the conduct of international affairs, it is said, and if we seek to resolve conflicts among nations rationally, before they become harmful and mutually destructive, we must not trust our opponents at all; we must not even consider such a notion seriously.

A second group believes that at the root of the difficulty in international affairs is the fact that nations cannot and do not trust each other. Aggressive behavior and conflicts arise not so much from genuinely irreconcilable conflicts, but more from mistrust, suspicion, and untrustworthy acts. They believe that one should impress upon one's opponent one's good intentions. One should take actions that do not endanger one's own security, but that promote trust and demonstrate good will. One should sign arms control and disarmament agreements, small ones at first, but agreements that will build mutual trust and positive feeling.[3]

For the sake of contrast, the varying views have been dichotomized. But even those who do not hold such extreme, gross views, those who hold more sophisticated and delicate opinions, have overlooked what appears to be an essential ingredient in the analysis of the notion of trust. We do trust other nations, but this trust is not based primarily on moral considerations or on any notion of the building of positive feelings; it is based on a sophisticated notion of self-interest.

When an act in fulfillment of an international agreement is clearly contrary to the important interests of a nation, and when this act requires the nations to be

[1]An earlier version of this paper was delivered on March 7, 1963 at the fortieth annual meeting of the American Orthopsychiatric Association in Washington, D.C.

Work on this research was supported in part by the Public Health Service, when the author was a postdoctoral research fellow (MF8534) of the National Institute of Mental Health, and by the Center for International Affairs, Harvard University, when the author was a research associate of that Center. Support from the State University of New York at Stony Brook and a grant from the National Institute of Mental Health (MH-07666) facilitated the completion of the work.

The following people made helpful criticisms of an earlier version of this paper: W. Bennis, L. Finkelstein, J. Harsanyi, R. Levine, M. Mandelker, R. Meyersohn, E. Moot, J. Richardson, and R. Richman.

[2]For another recent analysis of the notion of trust, see Deutsch (1958).

[3]Advocates of both positions probably agree that where there are significant conflicts, as between the United States and the Soviet Union, the parties do not trust each other.

trustworthy, the nations will, in all likelihood, abrogate the agreement. But it is often in the interest of a nation or group of nations to keep an agreement, not for immediate gain—even contrary to this consideration—but in the interest of its coalition structure. A nation may take an action contrary to its immediate self-interest, or when its own self-interest is unclear, in order to promote the stability of its coalition structure. It has long been obvious to statesmen and it was demonstrated in the particular laboratory experiment reported here that rewards and payoffs often come to the stable alliance, and that an alliance has stability when its members can be reasonably certain that their partners will not desert them for some temporary gain. No matter how amoral the conduct of international affairs may appear to some, a notion of trust, or some similar notion, is involved. We can consider an example of trustworthy behavior between nations.

We rarely have the opportunity to see the actual, intimate behavior of national leaders when they are considering the trustworthiness or untrustworthiness of others; but early in 1961 such an apportunity arose. On a television program the Kennedy administration showed excerpts from the activities of the President on a single day. The program revealed a case in which our national leaders did trust the Russians and they trusted in turn. It showed Kennedy with his advisers, discussing the course and future of disarmament negotiations. It was early in 1961; the administration had recently taken office and wanted time to review what had occurred and to prepare its disarmament policy and programs. One of his advisers indicated to Kennedy that the Soviet Ambassador had agreed that the Soviets would make no major disarmament proposal until the fall; the Russians would not, in the coming months, exploit the fact that the United States did not have its disarmament policies ready. Both representatives had agreed that neither side would engage in any extensive pro-disarmament propaganda for a number of months. As far as can be discerned both countries trusted each other and kept the agreement. We could and did trust the Soviets successfully. We went about preparing our program for disarmament proposals. Our officials were probably not overly concerned about any sudden Soviet propaganda offensive. The Soviets, had they chosen to, could have mounted a serious propaganda campaign for immediate disarmament at that time, and perhaps have gained from such a campaign. However, both sides believed that it was advantageous to refrain from taking some action that might bring immediate gain. In a sense, we and the Soviets had formed a coalition for these limited purposes.[4]

The notion of trust that is being developed here is somewhat different from the notion that we use in ordinary conversation. Usually when we use the word it remains only vaguely defined, but if we think about it generally, some consideration of morality and personal feelings are involved. When we say "a person has

[4]For an account of the negotiations of this period see *The New York Times Index* (1961), p. 68.

pledged his word" to do or not to do something, we imply a consensus among the parties that it would be improper or wrong not to keep the pledge. We believe the person will fulfill the commitment—we trust the person. If the person fails to do as he agreed, he is untrustworthy and hence reprehensible. If he behaves as agreed, he is believed to be trustworthy and is more likely to be trusted in the future. His behavior is not thought to be particularly virtuous, since trustworthy behavior is expected. It is a thesis of this paper that such a usage of the word trust does not describe the behavior of national leaders in the conduct of international affairs. In such affairs the personal–moral connotations of the term are often absent or suppressed.

The argument is sometimes made that we have international conflicts because statesmen are not trustworthy in the personal–moral sense, and that we will continue to have wars and destruction until national leaders either become personally more trustworthy or are induced to be so by some effective system of enforceable international agreements. Such an argument is answered by statements to the effect that questions of national interest must always outweigh attempts at personal morality, and that conflicts among nations are often provoked by genuine, irreconcilable conflicts.

This paper will not deal with that set of questions. Its purpose is not to argue the normative question but to examine behavior and see where some notion of trust is descriptive. The concept that will be developed in the remainder of this paper will be one involving the *interests* of the persons involved; hence the term *i*-Trust. This notion developed from the results of a laboratory experiment. The experiment examined interaction among three people in a game situation. The situation was such that the experimental task itself did not supply the players with standards of behavior; the game had no solution that would dictate a resolution of the conflict situation the subjects found themselves in. In the experimental situation, many of the players developed a notion of trust similar to the one being offered here. The puzzling situation the subjects found themselves in, the details of the experiment, will be presented. We will then consider the results of the experiment and see how this notion of *trust based on interest* helped some subjects resolve the conflict. We will conclude with a definition of the notion *i*-Trust.[5]

---

[5]Underlying this paper is the assumption that there are common principles involved in the interaction of three persons in a laboratory experiment and the interaction of nations in the conduct of international affairs; and that the laboratory experiment can, with some degree of success, model inter-nation relations and discover the common principles. Intuition, and the arguments of many, deny the assumption that essential or interesting elements of international bargaining can be simulated in the laboratory. This attempt and others are being made to determine the usefulness of the assumption. The question will be answered finally by the presence or absence of interesting results, not by *a priori* opinion.

A THREE-PERSON, ZERO-SUM, MATRIX GAME

The notion i-Trust arose in an experimental study of behavior in a three-person, zero-sum, majority game situation. The three-person game is intended to be a model of interaction among three persons where the parties involved are in a situation of simultaneous conflict and cooperation. When three people interact it is often possible and profitable for two to ally against the third, and many believe that this is one of the central problems involved in understanding the significant features of three-person interaction.

A small number of three-person, zero-sum games do have what we might consider generally accepted, unambiguous solutions; precise prescriptions that enable the participants to resolve a conflict in a way that seems reasonable. The larger number of three-person games do not have such solutions, although a variety of solution notions of varying types have been offered.[6]

Some of the questions the study was designed to answer were:

1. How do the subjects come to resolve the conflict situation which has no precise, unambiguous, mathematical solution?

2. Does the size of the payoff to the coalition influence the frequency of the formation of that coalition?

3. How will the subjects divide the payoffs they receive?

4. Are the various solution notions that have been offered descriptive of actual behavior?[7]

METHOD

The Game. In the three-person, zero-sum, majority game that was played, each player (designated 1,2,3), by a personal move, chose the number of one of the two other players. If two chose each other's number a couple or coalition was formed. Three distinct couples were possible; on any one play of the game only one couple or none at all could occur. The coalition that formed won an amount of money from the third player. The winning pairs had to decide, by the use of written communications, how to divide the winnings. The subjects played 40 repetitions of the game described by the following payoff function:

If coalition (1,2) formed, the coalition received 10 cents from player 3.

If coalition (1,3) formed, the coalition received 8 cents from player 2.

If coalition (2,3) formed, the coalition received 6 cents from player 1.

[6]For a discussion of three-person solution theory, see Luce and Raiffa (1957, pp. 189–204) and von Neumann and Morgenstern (1953, pp. 220–33).

[7]This study is described more fully in Lieberman (1962). The relationship of the observed behavior to solution theory is discussed there.

Procedure. Three players and the experimenter were seated around a table. Written communications among the players were permitted between moves. At the moment of decision each player did not know the choices of the others. Choices were made by placing a card with a player's number face down on a table. The cards were then turned over simultaneously to determine the outcome of each of the 40 plays of the game.

Subjects. Twenty-four Harvard College undergraduates were the subjects of the study. Eight groups of three players participated.

Materials. The materials used consisted of the following items: instruction sheets for each player; red, white, and blue chips; red, white, and blue choice cards which contained the players' numbers; blank cards for communications; scrap paper and pencils for each subject; and three dollars for each player.

Results

The relationships among the three players are quite intricate. One might think that a simple way of resolving the conflict would be for players 1 and 2 to form a permanent coalition and divide their winnings equally. When this does occur, however, it immediately becomes obvious to player 3 that it is advantageous for him to form a coalition with one of the two others. He can make an offer to player 1 to form a coalition with him, from which player 1 can receive more than the 5 cents he can receive together with player 2. It is even advantageous for player 3 to offer 7 cents or even 8 cents to player 1. Thus, player 1 is tempted to break his coalition with player 2 and take the full 8 cents from player 3. Seeing this, player 2 can then make a more attractive offer to 3 or 1. The process can be repeated.

The three players quickly learned to see the complexities of the situation. What occurred was instability, offer and counteroffer, acceptance, rejection, deception, and the "double cross." Coalitions formed and were changed; in not one of the eight groups did a coalition form on the first trial and remain constant through all the forty plays of the game.

Data obtained in the study are presented in the tables below. Table 1 presents the percentages of occurrence of the possible outcomes in blocks of five trials—five plays of the game.[8] The no-coalition outcome occurred on 7.2 percent of the plays; outcome 1 occurred on 35.3 percent of the plays of the game; outcome 2 on 18.1 percent of the plays; and outcome 3 on 39.4 percent of the plays. The

---

[8]After each subject made a choice an outcome occurred, and after the subjects divided the payoff, a play of the game was completed. A single play of the game is also called a trial in the experiment—the complete experimental session consisted of forty plays of the game or forty trials. In this paper the term game is used in two ways: to describe a single occurrence of play, and also to refer to the forty plays by a group of three subjects. For the latter usage the term "super-game" might have been used.

TABLE 1. Data Obtained from the Forty Plays of the Game

	Percentage of Occurrence of Outcome			
	0	1	2	3
Trials	No Coalition	(1,2)[a]	(1,3)	(2,3)
1–5	10.0	47.5	22.5	20.0
6–10	0	32.5	17.5	50.0
11–15	10.0	37.5	10.0	42.5
16–20	12.5	22.5	22.5	42.5
21–25	7.5	27.5	30.0	35.0
26–30	7.5	40.0	17.5	35.0
31–35	2.5	40.0	17.5	40.0
36–40	7.5	35.0	7.5	50.0
Mean	7.2	35.3	18.1	39.4

[a](1,2) indicates that players 1 and 2 chose each other's numbers and formed the winning coalition.

outcome that occurred most frequently was thus the one that yielded the smallest payoff to the winning coalition. Evidence from this and a similar study indicates that player 1 was seen as the strongest or most exploitative individual; this may have led players 2 and 3 to unite against him to form their coalition with greater frequency.

Table 2 presents the frequency of the divisions of the payoffs the subjects agreed upon. An equal division of the winnings was the most frequent settlement. On 297 of the plays of the game some payoff occurred; on 23 no coalition formed. Of the 297 payoffs, a total of 182 or 61.3 percent of the settlements were equal divisions. The common notion that winnings should be divided evenly is descriptive of much of the obtained behavior.

The way in which some of the subjects came to resolve the tangled situation facing them is the point of major interest here. The formal situation, the structure of the game, offered no obvious, readily understandable solution. Table 3, which shows the number of coalition changes for each of the eight groups of three subjects who played the forty repetitions of the game, reflects this. There was not one group which did not have at least one coalition change. Five had fewer than ten changes; the remaining three had more than twenty changes; the largest number of changes was 33.

The situation the subjects found themselves in was perplexing. The structure of the game offered no way to resolve the conflict. Some behavioral standards or criteria for the resolution of the conflict had to develop. The nature of the game

TABLE 2. Division of Payoffs

Coalitions Formed	Division of Payoffs	Frequency
(1,2)	10–0[a]	0
	9–1	0
	8–2	4
	7–3	17
	6–4	20
	5–5	65
	4–6	3
	3–7	0
	2–8	2
	1–9	0
	0–10	2
(1,3)	8–0	0
	7–1	0
	6–2	10
	5–3	16
	4–4	24
	3–5	1
	2–6	1
	1–7	5
	0–8	1
(2,3)	6–0	5
	5–1	0
	4–2	2
	3–3	93
	2–4	23
	1–5	3
	0–6	0
0		23
Total		320

[a]When coalition (1,2) formed, this division indicates that player 1 received 10 cents and player 2 received 0 cents. Similarly, 0–10 indicates player 2 received 10 cents.

made complex negotiations inevitable. The agreements, breaking of agreements, and bargaining that occurred led to an interesting result. From observations of the subjects' behavior, and an analysis of their messages, it became obvious that in a number of games the players came to realize that a maximum return on one or

TABLE 3. Number of Coalition Changes in the
Forty Plays of the Game

Group Number	Number of Coalition Changes
1	2
2	33
3	22
4	5
5	24
6	2
7	9
8	2

two plays of the game was not important. It was far more profitable to enter into a stable, continuing agreement with one other player. Since defection was not an infrequent occurrence, *an intuitive notion of trust* was significant in determining which coalitions formed and held together. The subjects stated that they would enter into coalitions with the player they trusted, the one they believed would not be tempted to defect from their coalition for a more attractive offer on a subsequent play of the game.

In five of the eight groups that played the game a notion of trust similar to the one defined in this paper was developed. The notion of trust contained the element of the desire to maximize one's payoff, and this could be done best by entering into a stable coalition with one other player. The elements of giving a pledge, making a commitment, and fulfilling the pledge or commitment were present.

In three of the five groups that developed the notion, the actual word "trust," or some variation of it such as "trustworthy," was used. In the two games where the specific word "trust" was not used, obvious equivalents were present. For example, one player said: "I have found that I cannot take 1 at his word. Disappointed as I am, I would be willing to listen to any offer you make."

A particularly clear example of how the notion helped to resolve the conflict situation is illustrated by the following description of the play of one of the groups. Prior to the first play of the game, player 1 made an offer to 2, and 2 accepted. Then player 3 made an offer to 1, and player 2 made an offer to 3. Players 1 and 2 saw the complexities and the possible dangers, reinstated their initial agreement, and took the 10 cents from player 3, completing the first play of the game. This coalition occurred on the second play also. On the third play of the game, player 3 offered player 1 one cent more than he was receiving from 2 and formed a coalition with him. On the fourth play, players 2 and 3 decided to form a coalition and split the earnings in half. They pointed out to each other that player 1 had alternated between the two of them on the initial trials. Before the sixth play, in response to an offer, player 2 said to 1, "I cannot trust you." Before the eighth play, 3 said to 1 that he, 3, and 2 could trust each other. On the eleventh trial, player 1 was still trying to destroy the (2,3) coalition and made the statement, "If you don't trust me there is no use making further offers. You will note that I have played 2's every time since my last offer." This was an attempt on 1's part to have 2 trust him. Finally on the fourteenth trial, player 1 made a last attempt to separate the (2,3) coalition. He said to player 3, "If you trust me I will offer you a four-four split." Although this would have enabled player 3 to make more money than he was receiving with 2, 3 declined the more lucrative offer and continued his coalition with 2.

Another example illustrates the same point. In another of the groups, the notion of trust pervaded the entire bargaining process. By the tenth trial player 2 had broken an alliance with 1; players 2 and 3 were in a coalition. Player 1 said to 3: "Two broke an alliance. Want the 6–2 now?" Player 3 responded: "If I broke my alliance with him [meaning player 2] I'd be no better than him. I owe him one hand. Next time around I'll consider it." The subjects, sensing the importance of the stable alliance, but not wishing to commit themselves for all the remaining plays of the game, discovered the technique of making agreements for two, three, or a greater but limited number of moves. If a player defected after the agreement was completed he could still be trusted.

In this group the longest unbroken alliance (between players 3 and 1) lasted between trials 15 and 28 when player 3 said to 2: "A long time with you has been doubtful. I *must* trust 1 and he can trust me. If I leave him, you'll wonder if I might leave you. Then if you two team up, I'll have nowhere to turn." The alliance between 1 and 3 lasted through the 28th trial.

From the 29th to the 38th trial, the coalition (1,2) held together. Player 2 appealed to 1 by saying: "I broke no promises, I merely withdrew proposals." On the last two trials the (1,3) coalition again formed, 1 deserted 2, and 2 said, "I can no longer trust you but must offer 3 a deal." That threat was to no avail— player 3 accepted an offer from 1 and the game concluded. In this case the game concluded with all the players emphasizing the importance of trust, but each making deals with others. However, they did keep their limited agreements.

The notion of trust appeared to emerge inductively as the bargaining proceeded. The study was designed to answer the previously listed general questions about coalition formation in a three-person game situation; as the participants experienced offer, counter-offer, agreement, and deception, they came to realize the importance of being able to rely on a partner who would fulfill his commitments. The study was not designed to investigate the phenomenon of trust—the result was an unanticipated finding—and so it is difficult to say whether some subjects were aware of the importance of a trust notion from the very beginning of the bargaining, and that the notion just became more explicit as the negotiations proceeded, or whether the subjects were initially unaware of its importance. However, the notion did not appear immediately in the groups in which it was important, but occurred after the subjects had some experience with defection and came to realize that a reputation for unreliability was damaging. A more detailed study of the emergence of the concern with trust might yield information about the timing of its emergence and its relationship to the stability of coalition structure.

THE DEFINITION OF i-TRUST

Before specifying just what is meant by the term i-Trust, we can consider the connotations of the term which are *not* involved. These are the personal-moral connotations. Such elements are present and important when the term is used to describe personal relations, but they are much less important and often absent when we consider the relations among nations. We may say, "I trust my young son to tell me the truth about what he plans to do when he goes to visit a friend, even though he knows that, if I disapprove of his plans, I may prevent him from visiting that friend." But we do not expect to trust a prime minister to tell us the truth of what he plans to do about the Suez Canal, if this will defeat his purpose and be contrary to his nation's interests.

Yet the notion of trust cannot be dispensed with entirely, because certain expectations and obligations that have some striking similarity to the common usage of the term do arise among nations; and these expectations and obligations are often fulfilled. The notion i-Trust to be defined here may be descriptive not only of the behavior of the twenty-four college students who played a particular three-person game, but may also be descriptive of the behavior of statesmen in the conduct of international affairs.

The elements that comprise the concept are as follows: i-Trust is a belief or expectation about behavior in a situation in which the problem of forming a stable coalition structure is important. It is necessary to form a stable, continuing alliance, because such a situation often yields the greatest payoff to the members of the coalition. Without allies, players (and nations) will lose what they value and so they strive for the largest payoff to the coalition. The expectation which we have named i-Trust is the belief that the parties involved in an agreement will actually do what they have agreed to do; they will fulfill their commitment not only when it is obviously advantageous for them to do so, but even when it may be disadvantageous, when they must sacrifice some immediate gain.[9]

---

[9]J. Richardson and E. Moot have raised the point that in many situations it appears advantageous not to be part of a coalition, as in the case of India, Yugoslavia, and the nonaligned African countries. Such situations exist, of course, and the notions discussed here fail to

However, the belief does not require that the person take an action that is clearly contrary to an important self-interest. The person who sacrifices some immediate gain to fulfill a commitment believes he is acting in his own interest, because his interests transcend the increased immediate gain he might make if he defected from a coalition. His interests lie in preserving his alliance, which is what yields him his maximum gain. An attractive offer may be tempting but it also may be ephemeral and dangerous. He keeps agreements so that he will be trusted, so that his partner in turn will stay with him and the coalition will grow rich. Often the present situation is unclear; each person (or nation) cannot see plainly what he should do, what actions he should take, what behavior will best further his long-term interests. In such a situation, where one's interests are not clear, an unbreakable alliance which yields some gain is preferable to the uncertainty of a swiftly changing coalition structure, with the possibility that one may be left without allies. In such a situation, a large single gain is often not at all attractive.[10]

CONCLUSION

The particular notion of trust discussed here is based on a notion of interest, and is akin to the conception of maximizing gain in game theory. In the three-person, zero-sum game played, many subjects had no way of deciding which player to choose. The formal structure of the game offered clues but gave no answers. For some, the answer seemed obviously to choose the person who would

---

9 *(Cont.)* account for these processes. However, if the findings of this study are descriptive, we would expect that at some time in the future the United States and the Soviet Union will coordinate their foreign aid policies toward some of the nonaligned countries, i.e., form a coalition for these limited purposes. In the future it seems likely that the nonaligned countries will not have the freedom they now enjoy to accept aid as they choose from the two powers. Although it is likely that aid will continue to be given to advance the interests of each of the major powers at the other's expense, it is also likely that the Soviet Union and the United States will come to see their common interest in there particular three-person games, and plan their policies accordingly—that is, if their own conflicts are not repeatedly exacerbated. This seems to be one implication of the results and ideas presented here; should it occur it can be seen to be quite a usual occurrence in a three-person game.

10. This problem of fulfilling one's commitments is obviously a basic one and it is not surprising that writers of the past have considered it. Machiavelli (1940, p. 64) considered just this problem in *The Prince* when he said, "Therefore, a prudent ruler ought not to keep faith when by doing so it would be against his interests, and when the reasons which made him bind himself no longer exist. If men were all good, this precept would not be a good one; but as they are bad, and would not observe their faith with you, so you are not bound to keep faith with them." Machiavelli takes the simple position that one is not bound by a commitment when fulfilling the commitment would be contrary to one's interest. The present analysis goes further than this reasoning; it says that one's interest is often not clear and so individuals often fulfill commitments even when the commitments appear to be contrary to their immediate interest.

repeatedly choose him and not be tempted by attractive offers. Analogously, in international affairs, payoffs often come to stable alliances; and statesmen do much to maintain these alliances.

REFERENCES

Deutsch, M. "Trust and Suspicion," *Journal of Conflict Resolution,* II, 4 (December. 1958), 265–79.

Luce, R. D., and H. Raiffa. *Games and Decisions.* New York: Wiley and Sons, 1957.

Lieberman, B. "Experimental Studies of Conflict in Some Two-Person and Three-Person Games." In J. Criswell, H. Solomon, and P. Suppes (eds.), *Mathematical Methods in Small Group Processes.* Stanford: Stanford University Press, 1962.

Machiavelli, N. *The Prince and the Discourses.* New York: Modern Library, 1940.

The New York Times Index for the Published News of 1961. New York: The New York Times Company.

von Neumann, J., and O. Morgenstern. *Theory of Games and Economic Behavior.* Princeton: Princeton University Press, 1953.

21. A SIMULATION STUDY OF DETERRENCE THEORIES

John R. Raser and Wayman J. Crow

This paper reports a study on the impact of a specific weapons system characteristic on the structure of deterrence. It includes (1) a brief definition of deterrence, and (2) a short discussion of several nuclear deterrence strategies and their instabilities and hazards. (3) It describes a theoretical model based on hypotheses derived from the deterrence literature, as to how an invulnerable retaliatory force characterized by "capacity to delay response" might affect an international system. (4) It reports the results of tests of these hypotheses in an Inter-Nation Simulation.

DEFINITION OF DETERRENCE

Deterrence is a process which prevents unacceptable behavior in another by promising to *punish* him for unacceptable actions or to *deny* him success. Both methods have been used in international relations. For example, the custom of holding hostages and the Roman decimation policy guaranteed that unacceptable actions would result in the loss of something valued. The "balance of power" system in 19th century Europe, on the other hand, was an attempt to deter by *denial*; in essence, it promised to face any potential aggressor with a defensive coalition so strong as to *deny* him any possibilities of success.

DETERRENCE STRATEGIES

Prior to 1945, nations relied chiefly on deterrence-by-denial. Nuclear weapons have now rendered that policy obsolete, *if the act to be denied is a nuclear attack,*

SOURCE. John R. Raser and Wayman J. Crow, "A Simulation Study of Deterrence Theories," from the Western Behavioral Sciences Institute. Reprinted by permission of the authors. Copyright 1965 by John R. Raser and Wayman J. Crow.

for effective *defense* against attack by nuclear-armed supersonic bombers and missiles is all but impossible. However, *punishment* by nuclear retaliation is comparatively cheap and fairly certain of success.

Confronted by a world in which several nations possess nuclear weapons and at least minimum delivery capability, and by the likelihood that more nations will join the "club," the nuclear powers are of necessity committed to mutual deterrence by promise of punishment or, in Churchill's phrase, a "balance of terror." Peace is to be maintained by reciprocal threat, each nation promising the others that attack will bring retaliation of such magnitude as to offset any possible gains. Aggressions short of attack within the nation's boundaries are to be deterred by fear that *any* conflict can escalate into thermonuclear war; if that fails they are to be met with conventional or even nuclear tactical forces.[2]

Examination of this strategy, however, shows that it may not only fail to prevent war, but may even *increase* its possibility. Which nation is the deterrer, which the deterred? Each sees his own preparations as defensive and the other's as aggressive. The following illustration shows how war could be precipitated.

America considers herself to be on the defensive, but how might this posture be seen by a "defensive" antagonist? Not long ago, the United States retaliatory force was so vulnerable to surprise attack that it almost certainly could not have weathered one and carried out its mission. Knowing this, an opponent might logically conclude that since the United States' force was clearly useless for retaliation, it must be intended for a first strike. Had he not better pre-empt the initiative and himself strike first? But the United States, anticipating this chain of logic, might well decide that she should strike first in order to deny him the possibility of a first strike designed to prevent her first strike . . . and so on. . . . This is an unstable situation, unstable in the sense that the "defensive" system designed to prevent war might of itself actually precipitate it.[3]

In recognition of this possibility, a new deterrence strategy has been developed, based on the doctrine that it is not *gross* nuclear capability which effectively deters, but only that *portion* of it that can survive a surprise attack and effectively retaliate.[4] The United States implemented this strategy with SAC "alerts," designed to convince her opponents that she would not wait for impact, but would retaliate on *warning*. However, the possibilities for false interpretations of "warning" signs, the need for "hair trigger" responses, and the demand for instant decisions by local commanders, could, it is clear, result in accidental war. These inherent dangers are compounded when manned bombers are supplemented with vulnerable and unrecallable missiles.

A related approach to deterrence maintains that if intelligence reports seem to indicate that the opponent is *preparing* an attack the "defender" could then strike first (a "pre-emptive" first strike) and cripple the aggressor's forces. This is a new form of the old doctrine of deterrence-by-denial, and is one aspect of counterforce strategy. But this leads to mutual fear of mutual misapprehension—side *A* fears side *B* may *think* side *A* is about to launch a first strike, in fear of side *B*'s anticipated first strike . . . and so on. . . .

Even if these strategies should not lead to war, they create other difficulties; e.g., the constant *fear* of surprise attack or of accidental war; expensive arms races; the continuing necessity for a state of national "alert," and the necessity to act belligerently in order to convince an opponent of the nation's *will* to strike on warning. Foreign policy must be geared to maintaining those alliances and base-rights which insure the most advantageous strategic position. Continuing threats to kill *en masse,* and the continuing possibility of being killed *en masse,* may erode the nation's value system.

All of these problems have been frequently discussed; but the proposed solutions—preventive war, comprehensive arms control, unilateral or multilateral disarmament—seem to be either unacceptable or unachievable. Strategists are therefore searching for other ways to stabilize deterrence and eliminate some of its drawbacks.

Theorists of deterrence have proposed that stability is primarily a function of the *invulnerability* of the retaliatory system; that is, its capacity to survive and to retaliate overwhelmingly, after a surprise attack of any magnitude. It is thought that such invulnerability would both eradicate the first-strike premium and eliminate the probability of accidental war, inherent in the strategy of strike-back-on-warning. Possession of an invulnerable retaliatory force, however, provides a new strategic possibility—that of refraining from immediate strike-back, and delaying the retaliatory blow in order to deliver it later at a time and in a manner of the "defender's" choosing. Secretary of Defense McNamara advocated such a force and such a strategy when he testified before the House Committee on Armed Services, February 23, 1961:

> In this age of nuclear-armed intercontinental ballistic missiles, the ability to deter rests heavily on the existence of a force which can weather a massive nuclear attack, even with little or no warning, in sufficient strength to strike a decisive counter-blow. This force must be of a character which will permit its use, in event of attack, in a cool and deliberate fashion and always under the complete control of the constituted authority.

Such a capability has been termed "capacity to delay response" or for convenience, "CDR." Some theorists have reasoned that if one nation is known to possess this capacity, the stability of the deterrence situation will be increased.[5] Can this be confirmed?

From discussions of invulnerability in the literature, it becomes apparent that what invulnerability actually does is to create a "package" of options constituting a CDR; these options are enumerated below. In general it is presumed in the deterrence-literature that a CDR will change other nations' perceptions of the nation which acquires it, and affect the interactions within the international system. However, much of the literature is ambiguous and contradictory as to the *nature* of this effect. It therefore seemed worthwhile to codify the options arising from invulnerability, to develop a series of hypotheses as to the effect of these options in an international system, and to test the hypotheses in the Inter-Nation Simulation. In short, we have attempted to explicate and test that which is implicit and untested in the literature, in order to ascertain whether CDR would indeed increase the stability of the deterrence situation.

CAPACITY TO DELAY RESPONSE

The Capacity to Delay Response requires *(a)* a weapons-system capable of withstanding the most devastating blow or series of blows, and of retaliating decisively (*weapons-invulnerability*); *(b)* a command, communications, and information-gathering organization capable of surviving such a blow and, despite it, of gathering and evaluating information, and planning and executing a chosen retaliation *(command-and control-invulnerability)*; and *(c)* recognition of, and ability to accept, delay as a possible response strategy *(response-flexibility)*.

A nation achieving these three capabilities (a "CDR-nation") would acquire certain options, briefly stated as follows:

A. It need not retaliate immediately upon the occurrence of unexplained or ambiguous events, or upon *warning* that attack is on the way.

B. It need not retaliate immediately upon attack, the source of which is unknown.

C. Since it need not retaliate on warning of attack, it need not promise to do so.

D. It is not under pressure to strike first (pre-emptively) to avoid loss of its retaliatory force.

E. Since a CDR nation has more time to make the decision to retaliate it can better centralize and rationalize its decision-making process.

F. It need not retaliate on a pre-programmed basis, but can retarget its retaliatory forces after attack.

G. Since it can delay retaliation, a CDR-nation can establish responsibility for the initiation of nuclear war.

H. Since it can choose its time, it can retaliate when the attacker's defenses are weak.

I. Since it need not empty its arsenals, or lose them, it can retain deterrence-capability after attack.

J. Since the technical requirements for effective surprise attack may overlap those for CDR, a CDR-nation might be able to strike first more effectively.

K. Since it need not retaliate reflexively a CDR-nation can deliberate its response and thus might not retaliate at all.

The literature suggests that consequences for the international system will flow from the known possession of these options by one nuclear nation. That is: *Changes will be affected in an international system by the known existence of these options whether or not an occasion arises for exercising them.*

The remainder of this paper focuses on the interrelated effects for an international system arising simply from the knowledge that *one* nation has these options.

THEORETICAL MODEL

A detailed theoretical model was constructed, predicated on the options listed above and the hypotheses derived from them. The hypotheses, and the ways they are linked, were drawn from more than two hundred writings on deterrence strategy. There is also experimental evidence (to a certain extent contradictory) substantiating some of the linkages in the model diagrammed in Figure 1.

The reasoning in the deterrence-literature is, of course, much more detailed than is presented here.[6] What follows, however, should suffice to acquaint the reader with the background for the choice of the hypotheses and the development of the theoretical model.

Options *E, F, G, H, I,* and *J*—that is, those relating to more rational decision-making, post-attack retargeting, fixing responsibility for nuclear initiation, continued deterrence, and first-strike capability—may have the effect of making the CDR-nation appear stronger to others, while at least one Option, *K*—relating to the increased possibility that the nation may not respond at all—may make it appear weaker.

Some of the same options, specifically *F, H, I,* and *J* may also make the nation appear more threatening, while Options *A, B, C, D, E,* and *K*—that is, those relating to responses to ambiguous events, to attacks from unknown sources, to promises to retaliate on warning, to the temptation to pre-empt, to rational decision-making, and to the increased possibility that the nation might not retaliate at all—may make it less threatening to others. "Perceived strength" and "threat," then, constitute the first two dependent variables.

The knowledge that one nation possesses Options *A, B, C, D,* and *E*—those relating to responses to ambiguous events, to attacks from unknown sources, to promises to retaliate on warning, to temptations to pre-empt, and to rationalized decision-making—may cause changes in the system such that accidental, catalytic, and pre-emptive ("unintended") wars will become less probable, while Option *J,* giving the nation greater first-strike effectiveness, may make such wars more probable.

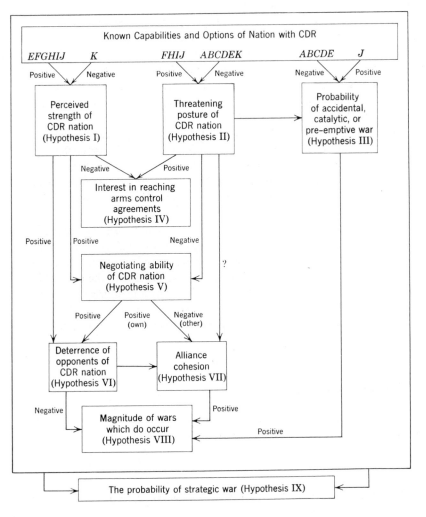

FIG. 1

I. A nation known to possess CDR will be perceived as stronger (weaker) than the same nation without such a capacity.

II. A nation known to possess CDR will be more (less) threatening than the same nation without such a capacity.

III. The probability of accidental, catelytic, and pre-emptive war will be less (greater) in a deterrence system where one of the nuclear powers is known to have CDR.

IV. Interest in arms control agreements will be less (greater) when one of the nuclear powers is known to have CDR.

Changes in the "strength" and "threat" variables should have a variety of related consequences for the system.

Thus, it is proposed, if the CDR-nation feels itself stronger it should be less interested in arms control agreements, if it feels weaker, its interest should increase; while interest of other nations is directly correlated with the CDR-nation's threat. The "strength" and "threat" variables should also effect the CDR-nation's ability to negotiate: if it is seen as stronger but less threatening, it should be better able to negotiate, and if it is seen as weaker but more threatening, it should be less able to negotiate.

Negotiating ability as well as perceived strength should affect a nation's deterrence-capability—i.e., better negotiating ability should better enable a nation to offer its opponents alternative courses of action, or to solve critical conflicts. In turn, the effectiveness with which a nation can deter its opponents, combined with its threat and negotiating ability, should influence the cohesion of all alliances in the system.

The CDR-nation's deterrence-capability, the cohesiveness of all alliances in the system, and the likelihood of "accident" or "pre-emption" should combine to influence the escalation, and thus the magnitude of any wars which do occur.

Finally, it is proposed, the perceived strength and threat, the probability of accidental, pre-emptive and catalytic war, the interest in arms control agreements, negotiating ability, deterrence-effectiveness, alliance cohesion, and likelihood of escalation, should all interact in such a way as to affect the probability of strategic war.

METHODOLOGY

Because of its flexibility and because it can provide a wealth of data, the Inter-Nation Simulation was chosen as the research tool with which to test the

FIG. 1 *(Continued)*

V. A nation will be able to negotiate more (less) adequately when it is known to possess CDR.

VI. A known CDR will increase (decrease) the deterrent capability of the possess nation.

VII. Alliance cohesion will be less (more) in a system in which one nuclear power is known to have a CDR.

VIII. Wars which occur when one of the nuclear nations is known to have CDR will be more (less) limited than when no CDR exists.

IX. The probability of strategic war will be decreased (increased) when one of the nuclear nations in the system is known to have CDR.

hypotheses contained in the theoretical CDR model. Since the INS has previously been described in detail,[7] only a brief outline will be presented here.

The INS is a laboratory "game," composed of a number of simulated "nations," each with different parameters, constituting an "international" system. Each nation includes a mathematical model of the major economic and political variables operating in a nation-state; human "decision-makers" (the participants) and "resources," which the participants allocate to accomplish their goals. The international system has itself certain resources and relationships with respect to trade, aid, communication, espionage, alliances, treaties, war, etc. To test the CDR hypotheses, the "world" was so structured that false warnings, accidental firings, surprise attacks, and attacks from unknown courses were possibilities. Strategy choices as to timing of responses, promises to retaliate for attacks on allies, promises to respond on warning or not to respond until after impact, were all available. In short, the possibilities and uncertainties confronting the players were as similar as possible to those faced by real world decision-makers.

In the present study, the "world" consisted of five nations divided, at the start, into two alliance-blocs. One consisted of UTRO, a rich and powerful nuclear nation, allied with two small non-nuclear nations, ALGO and INGO. The other consisted of a powerful nuclear nation, OMNE, and a somewhat smaller non-nuclear nation, ERGA. All nations except INGO were members of an international organization, the I.O.

At the start of play, the participants were given a history of their "world"—a long record of war and conflict, inter-bloc suspicion and hostility, unsuccessful efforts at arms control, unrest and revolution within some nations. In short, the aim was to create, as the starting condition, a bi-polar, Cold War world—a simplified version of the post-World War II situation.

The data were obtained from 12 replications, or "runs"; each run consisted of twelve 70-minute periods, and required three days of play.

Subjects, i.e., the national decision-makers, were recruits at the Naval Training Center in San Diego, California, awaiting transfer to special schools. For each run, 20 recruits (out of about 1600) were selected on the basis of educational level, General Classification Test scores, and "boot" camp performance. After two days' orientation, each subject was randomly assigned to one of the nations and to a role within his nation as Central Decision Maker, Aspiring Central Decision Maker, External Decision Maker, or Decision Maker for Force.

The level of involvement was intense. There were all-night sessions in the Base library, and statements such as, "this has been the most important experience of my life. . ."; perspiring palms and foreheads, nervous tics, tears of frustration, and two fights, testified to the sense of reality experienced by the participants.

The research-design contained two conditions—CDR and non-CDR. In the latter, all nuclear weapons-systems were vulnerable; in the CDR condition, *one* nation, OMNE, obtained invulnerability as a research-and-development payoff, and an editorial in the *World Times* (a dittoed newspaper issued each period) pointed out the options, to insure that their existence was known to all. The CDR condition ended when an R & D payoff gave UTRO a "detection system." The conditions were manipulated in the course of the study as follows:

PERIODS

	1–3	4–7	8–12
6 runs	Non-CDR	CDR	non-CDR
6 runs	CDR	non-CDR	CDR

The participants thus served as their own controls, reducing the variability arising from personality differences among decision-makers. Since this design gave equal importance to shifts from non-CDR to CDR, and from CDR to non-CDR, it was possible to examine what happened when the CDR-nation gained or lost its invulnerability.

RESULTS[8]

Hypothesis I

That Omne would be perceived as stronger (weaker) with CDR than without it. The perceived strength of the CDR nation was operationally defined as the combined ratings of all participants on the following periodically distributed questionnaire item:

Rate each of the *nuclear* nations (including your own if you are a nuclear nation) on the following scales. (Place the first letter of the name of the nuclear nation in the space in which it belongs. You may place more than one nation in the same space).

extremely	quite	slightly	neither	slightly	quite	extremely
weak						strong
militarily						militarily

The number of shifts in the direction of the hypothesis was compared with that of shifts toward the counter-hypothesis, and the statistical significance obtained with a sign test.[9] Omne was seen as stronger after gaining CDR ($p < .0001$), and weaker after its loss ($p < .0005$). It was decided, therefore, that: *when Omne had a known CDR she was perceived as stronger than when she did not.* Apparently Options *E, F, G, H, I,* and *J,* were more important in the minds of the participants than was Option *K.*

Analyses of the interactions on a nation-by-nation-basis yielded a highly interesting and unexpected result. When Utro's perceptions of Omne's strength were compared with Omne's own perceptions of her strength, it was found that while Omne saw herself as stronger when she gained CDR ($p < .0006$), she did not see herself as weakened by its loss, though all the other nations did. Generalizing from this result, it may be that a powerful nation readily sees a weapons breakthrough as increasing its strength, but does not see nullification of the breakthrough as decreasing its strength.

Why is this? Nothing was found in the literature of international politics to suggest such a phenomenon. Do nations readily see augmentations to their strength, but find it difficult to recognize losses? While the answer appears to be "yes," on the basis of the data, it is not intuitively obvious and certainly seems worth exploring.

This unexpected result raised an interesting second question. If a nation readily sees additions to its strength, but is reluctant to recognize losses, then might there not be a mirror-reaction in an opponent—that is, might not the opponent fail to perceive additions to the strength of another nation, but be quick to recognize any losses? Should this be the case, it would logically complement, and tend to verify, the first finding. It would be expected in our study, then, that Utro would fail to see Omne's gain of CDR as adding to her strength, but would clearly see its loss as decreasing her strength. And so it proved. Utro did not significantly change her rating of Omne when the latter obtained CDR, but did indeed see her as weaker upon its loss ($p < .009$). Thus the postdiction was confirmed. These results suggest that changes in national strength may give rise to three types of reactions:

1. The nation experiencing these changes tends to perceive only its gains in strength and not its losses.

2. The primary opponent fails to recognize additions to the other nation's strength, but readily perceives its losses.

3. The nations less directly involved are able to perceive changes in strength more accurately.

Hypothesis II

That Omne would be more (less) threatening with CDR than without it. Its threat was operationally defined as the combined ratings of all participants on four 7-point scale items: "extremely cautious—extremely rash"; "extremely belligerent—extremely peaceful"; "extremely threatening—extremely reassuring"; and "extremely likely—extremely unlikely to precipitate war." Data were gathered and treated as for Hypothesis I.

On gaining CDR, Omne was seen as *more* likely to precipitate war ($p < .02$), and on losing it, as *less likely* to do so ($p < .04$); as *less cautious* ($p < .03$), on gaining CDR, as *less rash* ($p = .007$) on losing it. On the peaceful—belligerent scale there was no shift when Omne gained CDR, but a strong trend (p = .1) toward seeing her as *more belligerent* when she lost it. There was a strong trend towards the threat-end of the threat—reassurance scale when Omne gained CDR ($p < .08$), but no shift when she lost it.

Summarizing the results of these four ratings, it was decided that: *Omne was more threatening with CDR than without it.*

It should be recalled from Figure 1 and from the list of CDR options that Hypothesis II was drawn from two sets of relationships between certain of the options and "threat." A nation possessing CDR could be seen as *more* threatening due to Options *F, H, I,* and *J,* all of which increase its ability to wage war effectively. Conversely, it was proposed that Options *A, B, C, D, E,* and *K* would serve to decrease the threat posed by the nation possessing CDR, since it would be seen as less apt to precipitate war by accident or design (*A,B,D*); it could have a more rationalized decision-making process (*E*); it need not act belligerently to maintain the credibility of its deterrent (*C*); and it might be seen as unlikely to use its nuclear force at all (*K*). On the basis of the results it was concluded that in the INS, the options which increased war-waging capability were dominant. It is of course, possible that the participants simply ignored the options, and that in a cold war system, if one belligerent is seen as gaining strength, it almost automatically becomes more threatening.

Hypothesis III

Accidental, pre-emptive, and catalytic war would be less (more) likely when Omne had CDR.

Data to test this hypothesis were obtained by comparing the participants' responses under CDR and non-CDR conditions, to two scenarios:

1. "If, as the situation now stands, a nuclear weapons impact occurred in the nuclear power of your bloc, it might mean several things. It might mean that some nuclear forces had exploded by accident, but if so, the opposing bloc might assume that you would believe it to have been the first wave of an attack from him and he might feel it wisest to hit you before you struck back at him. It might be a missile launched from one of the smaller powers who had obtained nuclear weapons secretly, and who hoped to make the great nuclear powers go to war with one another in order to enhance his own position. It might be the first wave of an attack from an opponent of which you had received no warning. If such an event did occur, *what would be your recommended response for your bloc?* Your recommendation should be made on the basis of how likely you feel that this would be an intentional strike rather than an accident, on how you feel the opponent would respond to such an event, on the basis of what your condition would be after accepting a first strike, and on your ability to prevent the opponent from hitting

you if you do strike immediately with an attempted disarming blow."
_____ a. No military response. _____ b. Military response.

2. "If, as the situation now stands, you received unverifiable but apparently well-founded intelligence reports that the other bloc was in the process of preparing to launch an all-out nuclear strike against you, what would be your recommended response for your bloc? Your recommendation should be made on the basis of how believable you would consider such information, given the current state of the world, on what your condition would be after accepting a first strike, and on your ability to prevent their hitting you by striking first with an attempted disarming blow."
_____ a. No military response. _____ b. Military response.

When Omne gained CDR, a significant number of participants ($p < .05$) shifted from "military" to "no military" response; when Omne lost CDR the shifts were in the opposite direction ($p < .01$ on the first scenario, and $p < .001$ on the second).[10] The decision was that: *accidental, pre-emptive, and catalytic wars were less likely when Omne had CDR than when she did not.*

This hypothesis was drawn from two sets of related options: since Options *A, B, C, D,* and *E* decrease the likelihood that the CDR-nation will act inappropriately, the probability of "unintended" wars will be decreased; however, Option *J* designating increased capability of waging pre-emptive war, may actually increase the probability of such wars, since the nation possessing this option might be more likely to exercise it; furthermore other nations' anxiety concerning this, might evoke behavior that itself would increase the probability of such wars. On the basis of the results, it was concluded that the Options *A* through *E* were dominant and that Option *J* did not importantly influence the situation.

Hypothesis IV

Interest in arms control agreements would be less (greater) when Omne has CDR than when she does not. To test this hypothesis data were drawn from subjects' responses on a 7-point scale ("extremely important—extremely unimportant") to the following item:

Indicate how important you feel it is, given the present state of the world, that arms control or disarmament agreements be reached.

Data were treated as for Hypothesis I and II. It was predicted in the model that the outcome would depend on changes in the "strength" and "threat" variables. Since Omne perceived herself as strengthened when she gained CDR, the model predicted that she would be less interested in arms control agreements. There was a weak trend in this direction ($p = .13$, one-tailed), but she did not shift toward greater interest when she lost CDR. This is as expected, since she did not see herself as weakened. The prediction that if other nations saw Omne as stronger and more threatening they would be more interested in arms control agreements was also partially confirmed: interest was significantly greater (p = .01) when Omne gained CDR, though scarcely changed (p = .25) when she lost it.

Hypothesis V

Omne's known possession of CDR would enable her to negotiate more (less) adequately. It was reasoned that perceptions of the CDR nation as stronger and less threatening would enchance its negotiating ability, and conversely. Because Omne was seen as both stronger and *more* threatening, no prediction could be made.

Bales Interaction Analysis[11] was carried out for all I.O. meetings and on a random sample of written messages. Indices of "task orientation," "difficulty of communication," and "expressive-malintegrative acts" were developed for interpreting the Bales scores on this communication flow, with respect to negotiating ability. The gain or loss of CDR did not significantly affect any of the indices, or result in any consistent trends. The hypothesis that there is a relation between CDR and negotiating ability was therefore rejected.

Hypothesis VI

Omne's known possession of CDR would increase (decrease) her deterrence capability. According to the model, if Omne is seen as stronger, and if she is better able to negotiate, her opponents will be more effectively deterred. Omne was indeed seen as stronger but since her negotiating ability was not affected, the prediction can be made, but with somewhat less confidence. Nevertheless, the results tend to indicate that CDR did increase Omne's deterrence-capacity. Responses to the following scenarios were gathered and treated as for Hypothesis I, II, and IV:

1. "If, as the situation now stands, the nuclear power of the other bloc should begin moves which threaten to result in a loss of prestige and power for your bloc, *how great would this threatened loss have to be* before you would recommend that your bloc respond with military action? Your recommendation should be made on the basis of what you feel may be accomplished at the present time through the use of military force; on the basis of comparative power positions and whether you think you could win a war; and on the basis of how successful you feel that negotiations might be in preventing such moves."

Extremely ___ ___ ___ ___ ___ Quite minor
great loss   loss

2. "If, as the situation now stands, waging war with the other bloc seems to you to be the best means for accomplishing military, political, economic, or moral ends, *how important would these ends have to be* before you would recommend

war as the course of action for your bloc? Your recommendation should be made on the basis of what you feel may be accomplished at the present time through the use of military force, on the basis of your comparative power positions and whether you think you could win a war, and on the basis of how successful you feel that negotiations might be in accomplishing such ends."

Extremely   Of minor
important   importance

There was a strong trend for Omne's opponents to be more deterred when she gained CDR (p = .08, one-tailed, on the first scenario and p = .07 on the second). There was a strong trend (p = .09) on the first scenario, and a significant shift (p = .02) on the second scenario, towards Omne's opponents' being less deterred when she lost CDR. It was concluded that *when Omne had CDR there was a strong trend for her opponents to be more deterred.*

Hypothesis VII

Omne's known possession of CDR would reduce (increase) alliance cohesion. The model predicted that alliance-cohesion would change as a function of changes in the threat of the CDR-nation, its negotiating ability, and/or its deterrent-capacity. However, evidence in the literature as to these linkages is contradictory. Brody's INS studies indicate that alliance cohesion is *positively* correlated with outside threat, while Pepitone and Keliner, in a small-group laboratory, found a *negative* correlation between "group cohesion and outgroup threat."[12] The consequences of deterrent effectiveness for alliance-cohesion are also in dispute; in some discussions of NATO it is assumed that more effective deterrence will increase alliance-cohesion, while in others it is assumed that the resulting sense of security might weaken alliances. Since in this study CDR did not effect Omne's negotiating ability, that factor had to be omitted. For all these reasons, it was impossible to predict how alliance-cohesion would change as a function of CDR.

Alliance-cohesion was measured in three ways. (1) Changes with the gain and loss of CDR in the ratio of inter-bloc to intra-bloc messages were calculated for each run to provide an "index of differentiation"; no significant results were obtained (sign test) for either alliance, and no consistent trends emerged. (2) Data were obtained from 7-point scales indicating how friendly the decision-makers felt toward their allies, and how friendly they believed their allies felt toward them; data were handled as for Hypothesis I. Results were not significant, though the level of friendliness among allies tended to decrease slightly when Omne had CDR. (3) Data on the ratio between the number of positive, supportive, and friendly messages exchanged within a bloc and the number of negative messages were obtained by Bales Interaction Analysis and an "index of solidarity" calculated for each run. CDR was not correlated with a change in the Omne alliance, but the opposing alliance was significantly *less* cohesive ($p < .05$, two-tailed; Wilcoxen Matched Pairs Signed-Ranks Test.)[13] Since significant results were obtained on only two of the three measures, it was decided to reject the hypothesis that CDR affects alliance-cohesion.

Hypothesis VIII

When Omne is known to have CDR, any wars that occur will be more (less) limited. It was predicted that as an outcome of Omne's increased deterrence-capacity, the slightly lessened alliance-cohesion, and the reduced likelihood of "unintended" wars following the advent of CDR, wars would be *more* limited.

This was not the case. Wars occurred in seven of the twelve runs; during non-CDR conditions the average conventional attack involved 755 FC's, and the average nuclear attack involved 7 FN's ("FC" and "FN" designate one unit of conventional and nuclear force, respectively). During CDR conditions, size of conventional attacks rose to 1000 FC's, while that of nuclear attacks rose to 66 FN's. Though the attack-*N* was too small for statistical treatment, the conclusion seems inescapable that in the INS, at least there was strong correlation between Omne's possession of CDR and *increased* magnitude of wars. This outcome directly contradicts that predicted by the model, and the assumptions in the deterrence-literature. Discussion of Hypothesis IX will elucidate this result.

Hypothesis IX

Omne's known possession of CDR would decrease (increase) the probability of strategic war. As was discussed earlier, it is the hope of deterrence strategists that the likelihood of strategic war will be *reduced* as a consequence of a nation's known possession of CDR. If it is assumed, however, that more frequent and heavier attacks and the replacement of conventional by nuclear fire-power indicate a greater likelihood of strategic war, then, in the INS at least, it must be concluded that strategic war was *more* likely when Omne had CDR.

During non-CDR conditions, Omne launched 4 attacks against others, while Utro launched 3. But when Omne had CDR, she launched 13 attacks and Utro launched 8, 5 of them against Omne, all but one retaliatory. It is clear that Omne was primarily responsible for the increase in number of sizeable nuclear wars. It was concluded that *strategic war was much more probable when Omne had CDR, primarily because Omne was more belligerent and aggressive and more ready to make war when she had CDR.* This conclusion is supported not only by the increase in number and size of wars during CDR conditions, but by others' perceptions of Omne, and her own self-perceptions, as measured on the "threat" scales. There is further evidence from Omne's responses to the scenario used to measure willingness to engage in military action to reach national goals: after obtaining CDR, Omne's willingness significantly ($p < .05$) increased.

CONCLUSIONS

The most important conclusion to be drawn from this study is that one whole aspect of the effect of a capacity-to-delay-response has been neglected by the theorists; *what is the effect of invulnerability and the consequent capacity-to-delay response on the nation's sense of its own strength, on its aggressiveness, and on its willingness to engage in war to achieve national goals?*

It may be that because most of the theorists are American, and are discussing *American* invulnerability, such speculations simply do not occur to them. But while one may generalize from *any* simulation to the real world only with great caution, the results from this INS study strongly suggest that this is an aspect of invulnerability which should not be ignored.

The unexpected and thought-provoking results obtained in this study vindicate the use of the experimental approach for investigating highly complex social phenomena. At the same time, they highlight the need for validity-studies, so that we may know to what extent such results can be generalized. Simulation models need to be made more isomorphic to the "reality" with which we are concerned; and we need to learn more about how age, experience, intelligence, personality, and cultural differences affect the participants' behavior. Work is steadily going forward with respect to both these questions at Northwestern University, at the Western Behavioral Sciences Institute, and at other centers for simulation study. The cultural factors are being examined in a variety of ways: for example, the study reported here has been replicated in Mexico City and in Tokyo.[14] Efforts are under way to develop an international scholarly community which can, through cooperative research with simulation and other techniques, furnish crucial insights into complex world problems.

NOTES

1. This is a much condensed version of a research report entitled: "WINSAFE II: An Internation Simulation Study of Deterrence Postures Embodying Capacity to Delay Response," Western Behavioral Sciences Institute, La Jolla, California, July 31, 1964. The research was supported in part by Naval Ordnance Test Station Contract N123(60530)35639A.

2. An exceptionally clear summary of the development of deterrence doctrine in the United States may be found in William Kaufmann, *The McNamara Strategy*, New York, Harper and Row, 1964, especially in chapters 1 and 2.

3. For discussions of this problem see Snyder, G., *Deterrence and Defense: Toward a Theory of National Security*, Princeton, New Jersey, Princeton U. Press, 1961; Schelling, T. C., *The Strategy of Conflict*. Mass.: Harvard U. Press, 1960; Brodie, B., *Strategy in the Missile Age*, New Jersey, Princeton, 1959, Morgenstern, O., *The Question of National Defense*, N. Y., Vintage Books, 1961.

4. Wohlstetter, A. "The Delicate Balance of Terror," *Foreign Affairs*, 1959, 37, 211–234, provided the first concise statement of this problem.
5. Those who have been closest to this terminology are: Richard C. Snyder, *Deterrence, Weapons Systems, and Decision-Making*, N.O.T.S. TP 2769, China Lake, Calif., Oct. 1961; T. E. Phipps, "Need for Staying Power of the FBM Submarine System, US N.O.T.S., Memo, Nov. 28, 1961; and T. W. Milburn, "Capacity to Delay Response," Memo to Authors, April, 1963.
6. The foregoing reasoning was drawn from more than 200 writings on deterrence, much of which had already been put in propositional form by Richard C. Snyder in his *Deterrence, Weapons Systems, and Decision-Making, op. cit.* A selected list of other writings which have been particularly important would include Amster, W., "Design for Deterrence," *Bull. Atomic Science*, 1956, 12, 164–165. Backus, Commander P. H., "Finite Deterrence, Controlled Retaliation." *U. S. Naval Institute Proceedings*, March 1959, 85, 323–31. Brodie, B., "The Anatomy of Deterrence," *World Politics*, 1959, 11, pp. 173–179. Brody, R. A., "Some Systemic Effects of the Spread of Nuclear Weapons Technology: A Study Through Simulation of a Multi-Nuclear Future," *J. Conflict Resolution*, December 1963, Vol. VII, Number 4, pp. 662–787. Brower, M., "Controlled Thermonuclear War," *New Republic*, July 30, 1962. Brower, M., "Nuclear Strategy of the Kennedy Administration," *Bull. Atomic Sci.* 18, pp. 34–41, 1962. Burns, A. L., "The International Consequences of Expecting Surprises," *World Politics*, 10, 1958, pp. 512–536. Buzzard, Rear Admiral Sir Anthony, "Massive Retaliation and Graduated Deterrence," *World Politics*, 1956, 8, pp. 228–237. Deutsch, M., "Some Considerations Relevant to National Security," *J. Soc. Issues*, 1961, 17, pp. 57–68. Gartoff, R. L., *Soviet Strategy in the Nuclear Age*, New York, Praeger, 1958. Halle, Louis J., "Peace in Our Time? Nuclear Weapons as a Stabilizer," *The New Republic*, Dec. 28, 1963, pp. 16–19. Halperin, M. H., "Nuclear Weapons and Limited War," *J. Confl. Resolution*, 1961, 5, pp. 27–29. Kahn, H., *On Thermonuclear War: Three Lectures and Several Suggestions*, Princeton, Princeton U. Press, 1961. Kaplan, M. A., "The Calculus of Nuclear Deterrence," *World Politics*, 1958, 11, pp. 20–43. Kaufmann, W. H., *The Requirements of Deterrence*, Memo No. 7, Princeton U., Center of International Studies, 1954. Kobe, D. H., "A Theory of Catalytic War," *J. Confl. Resolution*, 1962, 6, pp. 125–143. Leghorn, R. S., "The Problem of Accidental War," *Bull. Atomic Scientists*, 1958, 14, pp. 205–209. McClelland, C.A. (ed.), *Nuclear Weapons, Missiles, and Future War: Problem for the Sixties.* San Francisco, Chandler, 1960. McNaughton, J. T., *Arms Restraint in Military Decisions*, Speech prepared for delivery at Int. Arms Control Symposium, Univ. of Michigan, Ann Arbor, Dec. 19, 1962. Milburn, T. W., *Capacity to Delay Response*, April 1963, Typed Memorandum to the Authors. Milburn, T. W., "The Concept of Deterrence, Some Logical and Psychological Considerations," *J. Soc. Issues*, 1961, 17, pp. 3–12. Milburn, T. W., "What Constitutes Effective Deterrence?" *J. Confl. Resolution*, 1959, 3, pp. 138–145. Morgenstern, O., *op. cit.*, New York, Vintage Books, 1961. Pepitone, A., and Kleiner, R. "The Effects of Threat and Frustration on Group Cohesiveness," *J. Abnormal Psychol.*, 1957, 54, pp. 192–199. Pilisuk, M., "The Hostile Enemy: A Factor in Credible Deterrence," Ann Arbor, Univ. of Michigan, 1961, Ditto. Pruitt, Dean G., "Threat Perception, Trust and Responsiveness in International Behavior," Center for Research on Social Behavior, Univ. of Delaware, Newark, Delaware, Technical Report no. 11 for the Office of Naval Research, Washington, D. C., Contract No. Nonr-2285 (02), January 9, 1964. Russett, R. M., "The

Calculus of Deterrence," *J. Confl. Resolution,* 1963, 7, pp. 97–109. Schelling, T.C., "Bargaining, Communications, and Limited War," *J. Confl. Resolution,* 1957, 1, pp. 19–36. Schelling, T. C. *op. cit.* Sherwin, C. W. "Securing Peace Through Military Technology," *Bull. Atomic Sci.,* 1956, 12, pp. 159–164. Singer, J. D., "Threat Perception and the Armament-Tension Dilemma," *J. Confl. Resolution,* 1958, 2, pp. 90–105. Singer, J. D., *Deterrence; Arms Control, and Disarmament: Toward a Synthesis in National Security Policy,* Columbus, Ohio, Univ. of Ohio Press, 1962. Snyder, G. H., *op. cit.* Wohlstetter, A., *op. cit.*

7. Guetzkow, Alger, Brody, Noel and Snyder, *Simulation in International Relations,* Englewood Cliffs, N. J., Prentice-Hall, 1963. See also, Verba, Sidney, "Simulation, Reality, and Theory in International Relations," *World Politics,* XVI, No. 3, April, 1964, pp. 490–520.

8. The data reported here are only a small portion of the complete study which used content analysis, detailed studies of each world by observers, examination of world events, and player evaluations, in addition to the scale data reported here. The different types of data reinforce one another quite consistently.

9. See Siegel, S., *Non-Parametric Statistics for the Behavioral Sciences,* New York: McGraw-Hill, 1956 pp. 63–83. The .05 level (two-tailed) of rejection was used, with .1 considered a strong trend.

10. The McNemar test for the significance of changes was used for this dichotymous choice data. For a description see Siegel, *op. cit.* pp. 63–67.

11. Robert F. Bales, *Interaction Process Analysis,* Ann Arbor, Univ. Microfilms, Inc., 1962, gives a detailed description of the twelve categories to which message units may be assigned. We used comparisons among the number of message units assigned to different categories to arrive at the indices named.

12. Brody, R. A., *op. cit.,* and Pepitone, A., and Kleiner R., *op. cit.*

13. Pages 75–83 of Siegel, *op. cit.,* described this test.

14. The results of the Mexico City replications are reported in "A Cross-Cultural Simulation Study," by Wayman J. Crow and John R. Raser, La Jolla, Calif., Western Behavioral Sciences Institute, Oct. 31, 1964. In general, the results on the hypotheses were the same as with the American participants. The Mexicans, however, exchanged far more messages, concentrated much more energy on the international interaction, neglected their internal economies, did not engage in arms races, emphasized the importance of the International Organization, and shared power more with subordinates. The results of the Tokyo study are not yet available as of the time of writing.

22. MEASURING AFFECT AND ACTION IN INTERNATIONAL REACTION MODELS: EMPIRICAL MATERIALS FROM THE 1962 CUBAN CRISIS

Ole R. Holsti, Richard A. Brody, and Robert C. North

THE BACKGROUND—THE CUBAN CRISIS

In October, 1962 the first nuclear confrontation in history was precipitated by the establishment of Soviet missile sites in Cuba. For a period of approximately one week, the probability of a full-scale nuclear exchange between the United States and the Soviet Union was exceedingly high. Speaking of the events of the week of October 22, Attorney General Robert Kennedy recalled: "We all agreed in the end that if the Russians were ready to go to nuclear war over Cuba, they were ready to go to nuclear war, and that was that. So we might as well have the showdown then as six months later."[1]

An examination of the events immediately surrounding the crisis, analyzed in four rather distinct periods, offers the clear-cut case history of a conflict that escalated to the brink of war—and then de-escalated. This presents a useful contrast with another great crisis in history—which spiralled into major war. The two are almost classic patterns of international conflict.

During the 1962 pre-crisis period President Kennedy had been under considerable domestic pressure to take action against Cuba. In addition to attacks on Administration policy by Senators Capehart,[2] Bush, Goldwater, and Keating,[3] the Republican Senatorial and Congressional campaign committees had announced that Cuba would be "the dominant issue of the 1962 campaign. . . . Past mistakes toward Cuba could be forgotten if the Administration now showed itself willing

SOURCE. Ole R. Holsti, Richard A. Brody and Robert C. North, "Measuring Affect and Action in International Reaction Models," in *Journal of Peace Research*, Nos. 3–4, 1964, pp. 170–189. (Slightly abridged.) Reprinted by permission of the authors and the International Peace Research Institute.

to face reality. But there is little evidence of willingness to recognize the developing danger and to move resolutely to cope with it" [6, p. 35]. Public opinion polls revealed an increasing impatience with American policy toward Communist influence in the Caribbean [37, p. 184]. When the President arrived in Chicago on a campaign tour in mid-October, one "welcoming" sign read: "Less Profile—More Courage" [35, p. 186].

There had been a number of rumors regarding the emplacement of Soviet missiles and troops in Cuba, but "hard" evidence was lacking; those most critical of administration policy were not, in fact, willing to reveal their sources of information. Although Cuba had been under surveillance for some time, the first active phase of the crisis, from October 14 to October 21, began with the development of photographic evidence that Soviet missiles had indeed been located in Cuba. It was during this period that—according to President Kennedy—"15 people, more or less, who were directly consulted" developed "a general consensus" regarding the major decision to invoke a limited blockade [4, p. 2]. Unfortunately for the purposes of this analysis, there are no publicly-available documents from either Soviet or American decision-makers for the period.

The second and third periods—October 22–25 and October 26–31 respectively—might be described as the "period of greatest danger of escalation" and the "bargaining period." The present paper is confined to this time span, and is not concerned with the final period, during which the agreements reached between President Kennedy and Premier Khrushchev were assertedly carried out and in which further questions regarding verification were raised.

The period of most acute danger of escalation began with President Kennedy's address to the nation on October 22 regarding recent events in Cuba and announcing the institution of certain policies designed to compel the withdrawal of Soviet missiles from the Caribbean. The President announced:

> Within the past week unmistakable evidence has established the fact that a series of offensive missile sites is now in preparation on that imprisoned island. The purposes of these bases can be none other than to provide a nuclear strike capability against the Western Hemisphere.
>
> Additional sites not yet completed appear to be designed for intermediate-range ballistic missiles capable . . . of striking most of the major cities in the Western Hemisphere.
>
> This urgent transformation of Cuba into an important strategic base—by the presence of these large, long-range, and clearly offensive weapons of mass destruction—constitutes an explicit threat to the peace and security of all the Americas, in flagrant and deliberate defiance of the Rio Pact of 1947, the traditions of this nation and hemisphere, the Joint Resolution of the 87th Congress, the Charter of the United Nations, and my own public warning to the Soviets on September 4 and 13.

The United States would, according to the President: (1) impose a "strict quarantine" around Cuba to halt the offensive Soviet build-up; (2) continue and increase the close surveillance of Cuba; (3) answer any nuclear missile attack launched from Cuba against any nation in the Western Hemisphere with "a full retaliatory response upon the Soviet Union"; (4) reinforce the naval base at Guantanamo; (5) call for a meeting of the Organization of American States to invoke the Rio Treaty; and (6) call for an emergency meeting of the United Nations. At the same time he stated that additional military forces had been alerted for "any eventuality." James Reston reported 'on highest authority' that,

> Ships carrying additional offensive weapons to Cuba must either turn back or submit to search and seizure, or fight. If they try to run the blockade, a warning shot will be fired across their bows; if they still do not submit, they will be attacked. [21, p. 1:4]

In accordance with the Joint Congressional Resolution passed three weeks earlier, the President signed an executive order on October 23 mobilizing reserves. It has been reported that decision-makers in Washington also wanted the North Atlantic Treaty forces placed on a maximum missile alert, which meant putting American-controlled nuclear warheads on the NATO-controlled missiles aimed at the Soviet Union. This would prepare them for instant firing. General Lauris Norstad, Supreme Commander of NATO, is reported to have objected successfully, on the basis that in the absence of secrecy, such preparations could bring war when neither side wanted it, by way of "the self-fulfilling prophecy" [2, p. 6].

In its initial response the Soviet government denied the offensive character of the weapons, condemned the blockade as "piracy," and warned that Soviet ships would not honor it.[4] It was also reported that Defense Minister Malinovsky had been instructed to postpone planned demobilization, to cancel furloughs, and to alert all troops. Although the issue was immediately brought before the United Nations and the Organization of American States, the events of October 22–25 pointed to a possibly violent showdown in the Atlantic, in Cuba, or perhaps in other areas of the world. President Kennedy apparently expected some form of retaliation in Berlin. In his October 22 address he specifically warned the Soviet Union against any such move: "Any hostile move anywhere in the world against the safety and freedom of people to whom we are committed—including in particular the brave people of West Berlin—will be met by whatever action is needed."

The blockade went into effect at 10 a.m. Eastern Standard Time on October 24. At that time a fleet of 25 Soviet ships nearing Cuba was expected to test the American policy within hours. Statements from Moscow and Washington gave no immediate evidence that either side would retreat, although the Soviet Premier dispatched a latter to Bertrand Russell in which he called for a summit conference. The next day rumors of an American invasion of Cuba were strengthened by the announcement by Representative Hale Boggs that if the Soviet missiles were not removed the United States would destroy them: "if these missiles are not dismantled, the United States has the power to destroy them, and I assure you that this will be done" [21, Nov. 3, 1962, p. 6:1–2]. At the same time American intelligence sources revealed that work on the erection of missile sites was proceeding at full speed.

The first real break in the chain of events leading to an apparently imminent confrontation came on October 25 when twelve Soviet vessels turned back in mid-Atlantic. It was at this point that Secretary of State Dean Rusk remarked, "We're eyeball to eyeball, and I think the other fellow just blinked" [1, p. 16]. Shortly thereafter the first Soviet ship to reach the blockade area—the tanker *Bucharest*—was allowed to proceed to Cuba without boarding and search.

By the following day the crisis appeared to be receding somewhat from its most dangerous level. The Soviet-chartered freighter, *Marucla* (ironically, a former American Liberty ship now under Lebanese registry), was searched without incident and, when no contraband was discovered, allowed to proceed to Cuba. In answer to an appeal from Secretary General U Thant, Soviet Premier Khrushchev had agreed to keep Soviet ships away from the blockade area for the time being. President Kennedy's reply to the Secretary stated that he would try to avoid any direct confrontation at sea "in the next few days." At the same time, however, the White House issued a statement which said: "The development of ballistic missile sites in Cuba continued at a rapid pace. . . The activity at these sites apparently is directed at achieving a full operational capability as soon as possible." The State Department added that "further action would be justified" if work on the missiles sites continued. Photographic evidence revealed that such work was continuing at an increased rate and that the missile sites would be operational in five days.

The "bargaining phase" of the crisis opened later in the evening of October 26. A secret letter from Premier Khrushchev acknowledged the presence of Soviet missiles in Cuba for the first time.[5] He is reported to have argued they were defensive in nature but that he understood the President's feeling about them. According to one source, "Never explicitly stated, but embedded in the letter was an offer to withdraw the offensive weapons under United Nations supervision in return for a guarantee that the United States would not invade Cuba" [21, Nov. 3, 1962, p. 6:3]. A second message from Premier Khrushchev, dispatched twelve hours later, proposed a trade of Soviet missiles in Cuba for NATO missile bases in Turkey; the United Nations Security Council was to verify fulfillment of both operations, contingent upon the approval of the Cuban and Turkish governments.

In his reply to Khrushchev's secret letter of Friday evening, the President all but ignored the later proposal to trade bases in Turkey for those in Cuba. At the

Attorney General's suggestion, the President simply interpreted Premier Khrushchev's letter as a bid for an acceptable settlement [1, p. 18].

> As I read your letter, the key elements of your proposal—which seems generally acceptable as I understand them—are as follows:
> 1. You would agree to remove these weapons systems from Cuba under appropriate United Nations observation and supervision; and undertake, with suitable safeguards, to halt the further introduction of such weapons systems into Cuba.
> 2. We, on our part, would agree—upon the establishment of adequate arrangements through the United Nations to ensure the carrying out and continuation of these commitments—(a) to remove promptly the quarantine measures now in effect and (b) to give assurance against an invasion of Cuba.

He added, however, that,

> . . . the first ingredient, let me emphasize, . . . is the cessation of work on missile sites in Cuba and measures to render such weapons inoperable, under effective international guarantees. The continuation of this threat, or a prolonging of this discussion concerning Cuba by linking these problems to the broader questions of European and world security, would surely lead to an intensification of the Cuban crisis and a grave risk to the peace of the world.

In responding to Khrushchev's proposal to trade missile bases in Turkey for those in Cuba, a White House statement rejected that offer: "Several inconsistent and conflicting proposals have been made by the U.S.S.R. within the last 24 hours, including the one just made public in Moscow. . . . The first imperative must be to deal with this immediate threat, under which no sensible negotiation can proceed."

Despite the advent of negotiations, the probabilities of violence remained high. On October 27 an American U-2 reconnaissance plane had been shot down over Cuba, and several other planes had been fired upon. The Defense Department warned that measured would be taken to "insure that such missions are effective and protected." At the same time it was announced that twenty-four troop-carrier squadrons—14,000 men—were being recalled to active duty. The continued building of missile sites, which would be operational by the following Tuesday, was of even more concern. Theodore Sorensen, speaking of the events of October 27, said, "Obviously these developments could not be tolerated very long, and we were preparing for a meeting on Sunday [October 28] which would have been the most serious meeting ever to take place at the White House" [20, p. 42].

On the following morning, however, Moscow Radio stated that the Soviet Premier would shortly make an important announcement. The message was broadcast in the clear to shortcut the time required by normal channels of communication.[6] Premier Khrushchev declared that,

> I regard with great understanding your concern and the concern of the
> United States people in connection with the fact that the weapons you de-
> scribe as offensive are formidable indeed . . . The Soviet Government, in addi-
> tion to earlier instruction on the discontinuation of further work on weapons
> construction sites, has given a new order to dismantle the arms which you
> describe as offensive, and to crate and return them to the Soviet Union.

The statement made no reference to the withdrawal of American missiles from Turkey.

In reply, President Kennedy issued a statement welcoming Premier Khrushchev's "statesmanlike decision." He added that the Cuban blockade would be removed as soon as the United Nations had taken "necessary measures," and further, that the United States would not invade Cuba. Kennedy said that he attached great importance to a rapid settlement of the Cuban crisis, because "developments were approaching a point where events could have become unmanageable." According to one source, all agreed that the Soviet missiles had to be removed or destroyed before they were operational; thus, an air strike against the missile sites was planned by no later than Tuesday, October 30 [1, p. 18].

Although Khrushchev stated that the Soviet Union was prepared to reach an agreement on United Nations verification of the dismantling operation in Cuba, Fidel Castro announced on the same day that Cuba would not accept the Kennedy-Khrushchev agreement unless the United States accepted further conditions, including the abandonment of the naval base at Guantanamo. But the critical phases of the Soviet-American confrontation seemed to be over. Despite the inability to carry out on-site inspection, photographic surveillance of Cuba confirmed the dismantling of the missile sites. The quarantine was lifted on November 21, at which time the Pentagon announced that the missiles had indeed left Cuba aboard Soviet ships.

THE INTERACTION MODEL

What research questions does the Cuban crisis suggest? The crisis may be analyzed from several perspectives. From one point of view, it was a unique event, and not comparable to previous situations. In relation to either World War, the weapons systems of the adversaries were of incomparable magnitude. The nations, as well as their leaders, were different. And certainly in its potential consequences, the Cuban crisis surpassed all previous cold war confrontations and, for that matter, any previous crisis in history. Even the alerting and mobilization of armed forces, which were so crucial to the escalation into war in the summer of 1914, resulted in a different outcome in October 1962. From this perspective the investigator may focus his attention on the unique characteristics of the situation.

The analyst of international relations may, on the other hand, examine the events of October 1962 in such a manner as to permit relevant comparisons with other crisis situations, both those resolved by war and those eventually resolved by non-violent means. Are there, for example, patterns of behavior that distinguish the situation which escalates into general war—as in 1914—from those in which the process of escalation is reversed? This concern for comparable, replicable, and cumulative studies requires a model and research techniques which permit the student to investigate international transactions, examine how they were initiated and received, and compare those of October 1962 with others as widely separated in time and circumstance as the events leading to world war in 1914, and the continuing Arab-Israeli conflict.

A conceptual framework developed for such analysis is a two-step mediated stimulus-response model [26]; $S\text{-}r: s\text{-}R$. Within the model the acts of one nation are considered as inputs to other nations. The nations are information processing and decision-making units whose output behavior (responses), in turn, can become inputs to other nations (Figure 1). The basic problem is this: given some action by Nation B, what additional information is needed to account for Nation A's foreign policy response?

Within the model a stimulus (S) is an event in the environment which may or may not be perceived by a given actor and which two or more actors may perceive and evaluate differently. A stimulus may be a physical event or a verbal act.

A response (R) is an action of an actor without respect to his intent or how either he or other actors may perceive it. Both S's and R's are non-evaluative and non-affective. For example, during the early autumn of 1962, the Soviet Union

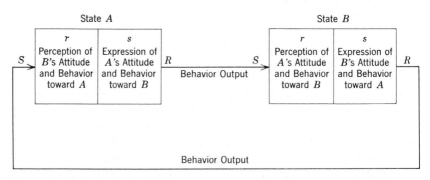

FIG. 1. The interaction model.

began erecting launching sites for medium range ballistic missiles in Cuba *(R)*. Regardless of the Soviet motives or intent behind this act, it served as an input or stimulus *(S)* to the United States, which responded by a series of steps, including the blockade of Cuba *(R)*.

In the model the perception (*r*) of the stimulus (*S*) within the national decision system corresponds to the "definition of the situation" in the decision-making literature [30] [18]. For example, the Soviet missile sites in Cuba (*S*) were perceived by President Kennedy as a threat to the security of the Americas (*r*). Finally, the *s* stage in the model represents the actor's expression of his own intentions, plans, actions or attitudes toward another actor, which becomes an action response (*R*) when carried out. Both *r* and *s* carry evaluative and affective loadings.[7] Thus, irrespective of Russian intent, the Cuban missiles were perceived as a threat (*r*) by President Kennedy, who expressed American intent *(s)* to remove them from Cuba. This plan was put into effect by the blockade (*r*), which then served as an input (*S*) to the Soviet decision-makers.

Operationally it would be much simpler, of course, to confine oneself to an analysis of actions (*S* and *R*) as do many classical formulations of international politics. In some situations the one nation's actions may be so unambiguous that there is little need to analyze perceptions in order to predict the response; consider, for example, the case of the Japanese attack on Pearl Harbor. Unfortunately, as Kenneth Boulding and others have pointed out, it is less clear that rewarding actions will lead to reciprocation.

In any case, not all—or even most—foreign policy behavior is consistent or unambiguous. For political behavior, what is "real" is what men perceive to be real. Boulding [3, p. 120] has summarized this point succinctly:

> We must recognize that the people whose decisions determine the policies and actions of nations do not respond to the "objective" facts of the situation, whatever that may mean, but to their "image" of the situation. It is what we think the world is like, not what it is really like, that determines our behavior.

At this point one might protest that surely well-trained statesmen will find little difficulty in interpreting the facts as they pertain to foreign policy. Yet one can cite example after example to the contrary. Consider, for example, the various interpretations—even among foreign policy professionals—which in the USA and other NATO countries almost inevitably follow nearly every turn in Soviet policy. Such problems of interpretations are encountered at every point in the stream of decisions which constitute foreign policy, and *mis*perceptions may have behavioral consequences as "real" as more accurate perceptions do.

If the real world for a President, Prime Minister or Foreign Secretary—and for their counterparts in friendly and hostile nations—is the world as they perceive it, perceptual variables are crucial in a conflict situation [22]. Thus, since all decision-making is rooted in the perceptions of individuals, our model attempts to assess both objective and subjective factors. Our research indicates the necessity of accounting for perceptual variables [23].

There have been serious doubts about the feasibility of quantifying perceptual and affective data, and the inclination, until recently, has been to emphasize "hard" variables and aggregate data; to measure gross national products and populations, or to count troops or planes or ships or megatons and assume that decision-makers respond to the "objective" value assigned to these capabilities by the investigator.

As important as these "objective" data are, they may fail to take into sufficient account how human beings react to these factors. Moreover, objective data are usually compiled on an annual, quarterly, or monthly basis. Thus, while these indices may well be relied upon to reveal the existence of an environment conducive to crisis [28] [8] such as Europe in 1914 or the Cold War since 1945—they may prove less useful for the intensive study of a short time period and for identifying human factors giving rise to conflict. Thus it is particularly important for the investigator who seeks to analyze short term changes in the international system—such as the crisis situation—to incorporate subjective data into his model.

Some objective indices—such as commodity futures, exchange rates and securities prices—are available on a day-to-day basis. A study of the 1914 data had revealed a striking correlation between fluctuations of the economic indices and such psycho-political variables as perceptions and expressions of hostility [10]. These indices are particularly useful as an independent check on the validity of one's techniques of measurement, and will be incorporated into this analysis of the Cuban crisis.

METHODOLOGY AND DATA

The premise that the analysis of political behavior is enriched by the incorporation of perceptual data poses special problems for the student of international relations. Clearly the standard method of attitude measurement—the personal interview, the questionnaire, or the direct observation of decision-makers in action—can rarely be used by the social scientist who seeks to study human behavior at the international level. What he needs are instruments for measuring attitudes and actions "at a distance." This is perhaps the primary rationale for settling upon the content analysis of the messages of key decision-makers—those who have the power to commit the resources of state to the pursuit of policy goals at the international level—as an important research tool.

Source materials used for the analysis of perceptions (s and r in the model) consist of 15 United States, 10 Soviet, and 10 Chinese documents, a total of approximately fifty thousand words, from the ten-day period opening on October

22—the day of President Kennedy's address on the Cuban crisis—and closing on October 31. Whereas all Soviet and American documents focus on the situation in Cuba, five of the Chinese documents are concerned solely with the border fighting in India. After relevant decision-makers had been selected, *all publicly-available documents* rather than a sample, were used. For example, President Kennedy, Secretaries Rusk and McNamara, Ambassador Stevenson, and Attorney General Kennedy were selected as the key American decision-makers. *The entire verbatim text of every available document* authored by these five persons during the ten-day period was included.

These documents were subjected to analysis by means of the General Inquirer system of automated content analysis via the IBM 7090 Computer [33]. The Stanford version of the General Inquirer includes a dictionary which can be used to measure changes in verbalized perceptions—the r and the s sectors in the basic model—in terms of both frequency and intensity [9] [11].

The scaling of action data (S and R in the model) resulted in the following ratings (1 is the highest level and 10 is the lowest level of violence or potential violence): [8]

TABLE 1. Scaling of Action Data

	October									
	22	23	24	25	26	27	28	29	30	31
United States	2	3	1	4	5	6	7	9	10	8
Soviet Union	3	1	2	5	6	4	7	8	9	10

The perceptual data generated by the General Inquirer are combined with the scaled action data into the $S-r$: $s-R$ model for the United States and the Soviet Union in Tables 2 and 3. It is apparent that Soviet and American actions during the period are closely correlated; that is, the actions for both sides are most violent or potentially violent in the first three days, followed by a relatively steady decline through October 31. The Spearman rank-order correlation between Soviet and American actions ($r = .89$) is significant at the .01 level. The correlation co-efficient should not be interpreted to indicate that the level of violence in the actions of each of the two parties was of equal magnitude; the separate scaling of Soviet and American actions precludes such an inference. Rather, it indicates that as the level of violence in the actions of one party increased or decreased, the actions of the other party tended to follow a similar pattern.

The input (S) and output (R) action may also be compared with the perceptual General Inquirer data (r and s). The pattern of perceptions was relatively consistent with the course of events surrounding the Cuban crisis.[9] In each case October

25–26–previously identified as the point dividing two phases of the crisis–was the point at which mutual perceptions appeared to change. The rigidly negative-strong-active perceptions of the period of highest danger became somewhat modi-fied at this point. Perceptions along the evaluative dimension became more neu-tral and, in some cases, actually became positive. As one would expect, during the latter days of the crisis there was also an increase in perceptions of passivity. The potency dimension, on the other hand, remained predominantly on the strong side throughout the crisis period.

Spearman rank-order correlation coefficients across various steps in the model are presented in Table 4.[10] The evaluative dimension is the most sensitive to be-havioral changes; the highest correlation coefficients are consistently those for positive affect (positive correlation with decreasing violence).

Table 4 also reveals that there is a relatively close correspondence between the actions of the other party (S) and perceptions of the adversary's actions (r). By themselves these findings are hardly conclusive. When compared with a similar analysis of the crisis which escalated into World War I [12], however, one interest-ing point emerges. The members of the Dual Alliance (Germany and Austria-Hungary) consistently reacted at a higher level of violence than did the members of the Triple Entente (Britain, France and Russia). At the same time, they also consistently overperceived (r) the level of violence in actions (S) taken by mem-bers of the Triple Entente. British, French and Russian decision-makers, on the other hand, underperceived (r) the level of violence in the actions of the Dual Alliance. In terms of the $S-r:s-R$ model, this relationship between one coali-tion's actions (S), the other coalition's perceptions of those actions (r), and the resulting policies (R) was apparently the crucial one.

In the Cuban crisis, however, both sides tended to perceive (r) rather accu-rately the nature of the adversary's actions (S), and then proceeded to act (R) at an "appropriate" level; that is, as the level of violence of potential violence in the adversary's actions (S) diminished, perceptions of those actions (r) increased in positive affect and decreased in negative affect, and the level of violence in the resulting policies (R) also decreased. Thus, unlike the situation in 1914, efforts by either party to delay or reverse the escalation were generally perceived as such, and responded to in a like manner. Whether the different patterns of action and perception found in the 1914 and Cuban cases will be found consistently to dis-tinguish crises that escalate and de-escalate, of course, can only be determined through continuing research.

Up to this point Chinese actions and attitudes have not been considered. As an observer rather than direct participant in the crisis, there are few, if any, Chinese actions with respect to the Cuban situation. Despite China's peripheral role, however, the analysis of its attitudes has considerable significance. The sug-gestion has often been made that while the antecedents of the Sino-Soviet schism predate the Cuban crisis, the gulf between Moscow and Peking widened considerabl

TABLE 2. Action and Perceptual Data—The United States

Oct. 1962	S	Positive	Nega-tive	Strong	Weak	Ac-tive	Pas-sive	Posi-tive	Nega-tive	Strong	Weak	Ac-tive	Pas-sive	R
22	3*	1.3*	33.5	37.2	5.5	16.2	6.3	11.9	11.2	29.5	4.4	31.8	11.2	2
23	1	0.3	30.3	26.1	3.6	32.3	7.4	11.6	9.7	35.7	2.0	35.7	5.3	3
24	2													1
25	5	17.8	15.6	31.1	0.0	24.4	11.1	16.0	9.0	21.0	5.0	32.0	17.0	4
26	6	13.5	8.1	21.6	2.7	35.2	18.9	30.3	0.0	30.3	3.0	12.1	24.3	5
27	4	10.7	16.1	21.4	8.9	19.6	23.3	24.3	1.7	28.6	6.7	22.7	16.0	6
28	7	25.3	13.4	33.3	2.7	18.6	6.7	16.4	21.7	23.1	3.7	21.7	13.4	7
29	8													9
30	9													10
31	10													8

S — Soviet action
r — U.S. perceptions of Soviet action
s — U.S. statements of intent
R — U.S. action

*The values for S and R are rank-order figures.
*The values for r and s are percentages of the total loading on the three dimensions.

TABLE 3. Action and Perceptual Data—The Soviet Union

Oct. 1962	S	Posi-tive	Nega-tive	Strong	Weak	Ac-tive	Pas-sive	Posi-tive	Nega-tive	Strong	Weak	Ac-tive	Pas-sive	R
22	2*													3
23	3	2.4x	27.2	28.8	1.6	34.0	5.0	17.7	13.6	31.2	6.4	22.8	8.3	1
24	1	5.9	19.6	21.6	3.9	31.4	17.6	24.5	10.5	27.8	3.5	15.1	18.6	2
25	4	0.0	16.7	22.2	2.8	30.5	27.8	22.2	7.4	22.2	3.7	7.4	37.1	5
26	5	0.0	29.7	21.6	0.0	48.7	0.0	21.2	1.9	26.9	0.0	32.7	17.3	6
27	6	15.9	12.9	22.1	9.8	27.0	12.3	24.7	6.9	20.1	9.2	20.7	18.4	4
28	7	12.6	16.6	23.4	4.0	30.3	13.0	24.6	8.1	25.9	4.5	21.4	15.5	7
29	9													8
30	10													9
31	8													10

S — U.S. action
r — Soviet perceptions of U.S. action
s — Soviet statements of intent
R — Soviet actions

*The values for S and R are rank-order figures.
*The values for r and s are percentages of the total loading on the three dimensions.

TABLE 4. Rank-Order Correlations Across $S-r:s-R$ Model

	Soviet Union ($n = 6$)		United States ($n = 7$)	
	U.S. Action (S)	Soviet Action (R)	Soviet Action (S)	U.S. Action (R)
Perceptions of Other State (r)				
Positive	+.70	−.07	+.93	+.71
Negative	−.43	−.20	−.82	−.79
Strong	−.13	−.13	+.11	−.25
Weak	+.54	+.09	−.24	+.17
Active	−.43	−.20	−.18	−.14
Passive	−.31	+.03	+.18	+.32
Self-Perceptions (s)				
Positive	+.66	+.32	+.79	+.71
Negative	−.31	−.60	−.11	−.11
Strong	−.31	−.49	+.46	+.21
Weak	+.20	−.32	+.29	+.29
Active	+.37	+.14	−.86	−.71
Passive	−.37	+.03	+.79	+.54

as a result of it. China, of course, was deeply involved in a concurrent crisis with India, but a number of Chinese documents during the period relate to the events in Cuba.

One immediate indication of differences is the seemingly calculated manner in which the Chinese ignored the role of the Soviet Union. A frequency count of the appearance of various nations in the documents (Table 5) reveals the extent to which Soviet and American decision-makers perceived the Cuban situation almost immediately as a Soviet-American issue, rather than one involving Cuba. The Chinese, on the other hand, referred constantly to Cuba as a primary actor in the crisis, and only rarely mentioned the Soviet Union. This, of course, renders impossible any direct analysis of Sino-Soviet attitudes, although there are occasional veiled references to the Soviet Union. After the Kennedy-Khrushchev agreement of October 28, for example, *Renmin Ribao* editorialized that, "The peoples of the world cannot under any circumstances lightly put their trust in the empty promises of United States aggressors," implying that Premier Khrushchev had done so. The same editorial went on to praise Fidel Castro for the "justified and absolutely necessary" opposition to the on-site inspection agreed to by the United States and the Soviet Union.

The data do not permit a direct comparison of Chinese and Soviet perceptions of each other, but some indirect analyses are possible. For the purposes of comparison, all documents have been divided into two periods—October 22-25 and

TABLE 5. Frequency of Appearance of Actors in Documents Relating to Cuban Crisis

	United States Documents			Soviet Documents			Chinese Documents		
Date	United States	Soviet Union	Cuba	United States	Soviet Union	Cuba	United States	Soviet Union	Cuba
Oct. 22	54.5%	37.2%	8.3%	–	–	–	–	–	–
Oct. 23	45.8%	34.6%	19.6%	59.6%	29.8%	10.5%	–	–	–
Oct. 24	–	–	–	27.5%	71.0%	1.5%	79.7%	0.0%	20.3%
Oct. 25	61.1%	38.9%	0.0%	60.5%	39.5%	0.0%	75.7%	2.0%	22.3%
Oct. 26	40.9%	59.1%	0.0%	53.9%	46.1%	0.0%	–	–	–
Oct. 27	41.0%	59.0%	0.0%	41.8%	48.2%	10.0%	–	–	–
Oct. 28	57.8%	41.4%	0.8%	30.8%	65.7%	3.5%	63.5%	1.0%	35.5%
Oct. 29	–	–	–	–	–	–	–	–	–
Oct. 30	–	–	–	–	–	–	–	–	–
Oct. 31	–	–	–	–	–	–	50.2%	0.9%	48.9%

October 26–31. The data are further divided to distinguish between perceptions of one's own actions toward others (s in the model), and the actions of others toward oneself (r in the model). From the General Inquirer output it was determined whether these actions were perceived as positive or negative, strong or weak, and active or passive, together with the intensity level of each. The results yielded a series of fourfold contingency Tables.[11] Tables 6a and 6b reinforce the earlier finding that both the United States and the Soviet Union regarded *each other* as significantly less negative during the latter stage of the crisis period. They also regarded *themselves* as less negative toward the adversary than during the first four days of the crisis.[12]

TABLE 6a. United States Perceptions in the Early and Late Periods of the Crisis

United States Perceptions of Soviet Actions								
	October 22–25	26–31		October 22–25	26–31		October 22–25	26–31
Positive Affect	13*	40	Strong	153	57	Active	153	47
Negative Affect	203	36	Weak	28	13	Passive	39	38
X^2 = 80.3	P = .001		X^2 = 0.1	P = n.s.		X^2 = 15.7	P = .001	

United States Perceptions of United States Actions								
	October 22–25	26–31		October 22–25	26–31		October 22–25	26–31
Positive Affect	106	61	Strong	149	75	Active	280	60
Negative Affect	90	31	Weak	31	14	Passive	79	45
X^2 = 4.2	P = .05		X^2 = 0.1	P = n.s.		X^2 = 15.9	P = .001	

*Figures are weighted (frequency x intensity) totals.

TABLE 6b. Soviet Perceptions in the Early and Late Periods of the Crisis

Soviet Perceptions of United States Actions

	October 22-25 26-31		October 22-25 26-31		October 22-25 26-31
Positive Affect	16* 50	Strong	176 85	Active	216 115
Negative Affect	163 61	Weak	12 23	Passive	46 43
$X^2 = 52.1$	$P = .001$	$X^2 = 14.4$	$P = .001$	$X^2 = 5.2$	$P = .05$

Soviet Perceptions of Soviet Actions

	October 22-25 26-31		October 22-25 26-31		October 22-25 26-31
Positive Affect	76 128	Strong	127 127	Active	92 117
Negative Affect	56 35	Weak	21 29	Passive	46 85
$X^2 = 18.5$	$P = .001$	$X^2 = 0.6$	$P\%$ n.s.	$X^2 = 2.6$	$P =$ n.s.

*Figures are weighted (frequency x intensity) total.

Chinese perceptions of the Cuban crisis, on the other hand, differ markedly from those of both the Soviet Union and the United States (Table 6c). There is no change (at the .05 level of statistical significance) in Chinese perceptions of American actions during the two periods; the proportion of negative affect to positive affect remains relatively constant. Nor is there any difference in perceptions of Chinese and Cuban actions toward the United States during the two periods in question. Thus, despite the lack of data for direct comparison, the available data do suggest a considerable difference in evaluation of the course of events in October 1962. Subsequent direct Chinese attacks on Soviet policy during the crisis have confirmed these differences.

TABLE 6c. Chinese Perceptions in the Early and Late Periods of the Crisis

Chinese Perceptions of United States Actions

	October 22-25 26-31		October 22-25 26-31		October 22-25 26-31
Positive Affect	3* 20	Strong	110 306	Active	120 413
Negative Affect	96 300	Weak	14 41	Passive	14 63
$X^2 = 1.5$	$P =$ n.s.	$X^2 = 0.0$	$P =$ n.s.	$X^2 = 0.9$	$P =$ n.s.

Chinese Perceptions of Chinese-Cuban Actions

	October 22-25 26-31		October 22-25 26-31		October 22-25 26-31
Positive Affect	11 88	Strong	39 291	Active	20 231
Negative Affect	35 129	Weak	13 22	Passive	8 48
$X^2 = 2.9$	$P =$ n.s.	$X^2 = 9.7$	$P = 0.1$	$X^2 = 1.8$	$P =$ n.s.

*Figures are weighted (frequency x intensity) total.

As indicated earlier, certain financial indications were used in a study of the 1914 crisis as a validity check against the measurement of other variables. A strictly analogous study—in which data are gathered from all nations involved in the crisis—is not possible for the Cuban crisis, owing to the absence of free markets in either Cuba or the Soviet Union. Data were gathered from major American markets, however, for a number of financial indices. . . . There is a significant correlation between Dow-Jones average of industrial securities and the level of violence or potential violence in both Soviet and American actions; as the crisis intensified, the value of stocks fell sharply, followed by an even greater rise in stock prices as the crisis receded. The pattern for wheat futures was the reverse, with a significant increase in prices corresponding with the heightened tensions. Although the value of the American dollar—in relation to the Swiss franc—fluctuated in the predicted direction, the correlation coefficient is quite low.

The relationship between the financial indices and decision-maker's perceptions are roughly similar to those for the action data, although not significant at the .05 level for $n = 6$.

While the movements of the financial indices *by themselves* cannot be used as indicators of international crisis—the stock market crash of 1962 is a good case in point—the results during the Cuban crisis add to the confidence with which the other quantified data may be employed.

DISCUSSION

Having utilized the $S-r: s-R$ model to examine the pattern of Soviet and American interaction, it may be useful to attempt at least a partial explanation for the patterns with some comparisons with the 1914 crisis. Such an analysis will be concerned primarily with what might be called "styles of decision-making," and must of necessity be based on incomplete data. Although there are several accounts of the process by which American policy was formulated, such data with respect to the Soviet Union are much more fragmentary and inferential [14] [13].

One major characteristic of Soviet policy during this period is clear. Unlike German leaders in 1914, Premier Khrushchev did not irrevocably tie his policy to that of a weaker—and perhaps less responsible—ally. The Cuban response to President Kennedy's address of October 22 was stronger and more unyielding than that of the Soviet Union. Premier Castro in fact ordered a general war mobilization *prior to* the delivery of the President's speech. The following day Premier Castro in effect left no room for either Cuba or the Soviet Union to maneuver: "Whoever tries to inspect Cuba must come in battle array! This is our final reply to illusions and proposals for carrying out inspections on our territory" [7, p. 42]. Premier Khrushchev, on the other hand, like President Kennedy, almost immediately chose to interpret the crisis as one involving the United States and the Soviet Union alone. In his correspondence with President Kennedy during October 26–28, it is also apparent that the Soviet Premier was unwilling to let the intransigence of Dr. Castro stand in the way of a possible solution of the crisis. In his letter of October 28, in which Khrushchev offered to withdraw the missiles, there was, in fact, no acknowledgement of the necessity to obtain Cuban agreement on the terms of the settlement.

American decision-making in regard to the missiles in Cuba was characterized by a concern for action based on adequate information. The resistance of the Administration against action—despite public pressure—until photographic evidence of the missile sites was available, has already been noted. As late as Thursday, October 18 a series of alternatives was being considered pending more accurate information, and while the decision to institute a blockade was being hammered out, open discussion of the alternatives was encouraged. The President recalled that "though at the beginning there was a much sharper division . . . this was very valuable, because the people involved had particular responsibilities of their own" [4, p. 4]. Another participant in the decision-making at the highest level wrote: "President Kennedy, learning on his return from a mid-week trip in October, 1962, that the deliberation of the NSC [National Security Council] executive committee had been more spirited and frank in his absence, asked the committee to hold other preliminary sessions without him" [31, p. 60]. Thus despite the very real pressure of time—the missile sites would be operational by the end of the month—the eventual decision was reached by relatively open discussion. Group decision-making does not ensure the emergence of sound policy, of course, but it does limit the probability of a decision performing a personality-oriented function [34, p. 103].[13]

Actually, it was not until Saturday, October 20—almost a week after the photographic evidence became available—that the general consensus developed. The President himself acknowledged that the interim period was crucial to the content of the final decision: "If we had had to act on Wednesday [October 17], in the first 24 hours, I don't think probably we would have chosen as prudently as we finally did, the quarantine against the use of offensive weapons" [4, pp. 2–3].[14]

Another characteristic of the decision process in October 1962 was the very conscious concern for action at the very lowest level of violence—or potential violence—necessary to achieve the goals. J. William Fulbright and Richard B. Russell, both Democratic policy leaders in the Senate, were among those who urged immediate invasion of Cuba, a suggestion against which the President stood firm [20, p. 30]. According to Kennedy, the decision to impose a blockade was based on the reasoning that: "the course we finally adopted had the advantage of permitting other steps, if this one was unsuccessful. In other words, we were starting, in a sense, at a minimum place. Then, if that were unsuccessful, we could have gradually stepped it up until we had gone into a much more massive action which might have become necessary if the first step had been unsuccessful" [4, p. 4]. By this step, no irrevocable decisions had been made—a number of options remained.

The concern of the President and his advisers with maintaining a number of options was based at least in part on an explicit differentiation between a violent "bid" or threat (such as the blockade), and a violent commission. The use of threats has become a more or less accepted tool of international politics in the nearly two decades of cold warring. The United States and the Soviet Union, on the other hand, had systematically abstained from direct violent action against each other. The desire to avoid killing Soviet troops was an important factor in the decision to refrain from an air strike against Cuba [20, p. 22]. Instead the blockade shifted the immediate burden of decision concerning the use of violence to Premier Khrushchev. Even if Soviet ships refused to honor the blockade, the initial American plan was to disable the rudders of the vessels, rather than to sink them [2, p. 6].

The flexibility provided by a number of plans requiring less than the use of unlimited violence stands in marked contrast to the situation in 1914. One factor in the rapid escalation in 1914 was the rigidity of various mobilization plans. The Russian attempt to mobilize against only Austria was anathema to the Russian generals because no such formal plan had been drawn up. According to General Dobrorolski, "The whole plan of mobilization is worked out ahead to its final conclusion and in all its detail . . . Once the moment is chosen, everything is settled; there is no going back; it determines mechanically the beginning of war" [5, p. 343].

Similarly the Kaiser's last-minute attempt to reverse the Schlieffen plan—to attack only in the east—shattered Moltke, who replied: "That is impossible, Your Majesty. An army of a million cannot be improvised. It would be nothing but a rabble of undisciplined armed men, without a commissariat. . . . It is utterly impossible to advance except according to plan; strong in the west, weak in the east" [5, pp. 348–9].

American decision-makers also displayed a considerable concern and sensitivity for the position and perspective of the adversary as a vital variable in the development of the crisis. Unlike some of the key decision-makers in the 1914 crisis, those in October 1962 thought in terms of linked interactions—closely tied reciprocations—rather than two sides, each acting independently, *in vacuo*. Theodore Sorensen described the deliberation as follows: "We discussed what the Soviet reaction would be to any possible move by the United States, what our reaction with them would have to be to that Soviet reaction and so on, trying to follow each of those roads to their ultimate conclusion" [20, p. 17].[15]

This sensitivity for the position of the adversary was apparent in a number of important areas. There was a concern that Premier Khrushchev should not be rushed into an irrevocable decision; it was agreed among members of the decision group that "we should slow down the escalation of the crisis to give Khrushchev time to consider his next move" [20, p. 19]. There was, in addition, a conscious effort not to reduce the alternatives of either side to two—total surrender or total war. According to one participant, "President Kennedy, aware of the enormous hazards in the confrontation with the Soviets over Cuba in October, 1962, made certain that his first move did not close out either all his options or all of theirs" [31, pp. 20–21].

Sorensen added that:

The air strike or an invasion automatically meant a military attack upon a communist power and required almost certainly either a military response to the Soviet Union or an even more humiliating surrender. . . . The blockade on the other hand had the advantage of giving Mr. Khrushchev a choice, an option, so to speak, he did not have to have his ships approach the blockade and be stopped and searched. He could turn them around. So that was the first obvious advantage it had. It left a way open to Mr. Khrushchev. In this age of nuclear weapons that is very important [20, p. 22].

Thus, unlike the 1914 situation, in which at least one ultimatum was worded so as to be incapable of execution, there was no demand which the Soviet Premier could not understand, none that he could not carry out, and none calculated to humiliate him unduly. During the summer of 1914, by way of contrast, there were numerous instances of failure on all three of these important points. The Austro-Hungarian ultimatum was deliberately worded in such a manner as to humiliate Serbia and to provoke rejection. The policy of the other powers, on the other hand, was hardly characterized by clarity. Russian decision-makers failed to communicate their initial desire to deter Vienna rather than to provoke Berlin. This was matched by England's inability to convey to German leaders their intention to intervene should the local conflict engulf the major continental powers.[16] And, in the culminating stages of the crisis, decision-makers in the various capitals of Europe made the very types of demands upon their adversaries—notably in regard to mobilizations—which they admitted they could not reciprocate.[17]

METHODOLOGICAL APPENDIX

The Stanford General Inquirer is programmed to measure perceptions—as found in written documents—along three dimensions: strength—weakness, activity—passivity, positive affect—negative affect. These dichotomized dimensions correspond to the evaluative, potency, and activity dimensions which have been found to be primary in human cognition in a variety of cultures [25] [33] [5] [24]. The dictionary thus reflects the assumption that when decision-makers perceive themselves, other nations, events—or any stimulus—the most relevant discriminations are made in a space defined by these three factors. The computer can be used to analyze perceptual units defined in terms of the following elements: the *perceiver*; the perceived *agent* of action; the *action* or *attitude*; and the *target* of action. The components may be illustrated in a statement by President Kennedy (perceiver): "Soviet missiles [agent] threaten [action] all the Americas [target]." For the present analysis the computer has been instructed to measure the *action-attitude* component within a specified set of agent-target relationships involving the United States, Soviet Union, China and Cuba.

The scaling of action data (S and R in the model) was accomplished by the following technique. Three judges were given a set of cards concerning Soviet and American actions for the ten-day period October 22–31—the same period which encompasses all the publicly-available documents by key Soviet and American decision-makers. Each action was typed on a separate card and these were then aggregated on a day-to-day basis. Thus each judge was given a set of cards for both United States and Soviet actions, each set being subdivided into ten periods. The judges were instructed to rank order the events—using the day as the unit of analysis—for the degree of violence or potential violence. The Soviet and American actions were scaled separately largely because of the disparity of available data; published chronologies of American actions during the crisis period are detailed to almost an hourly basis, whereas the action data for the Soviet Union are relatively sparse.

The level of agreement between each pair of judges for scaling both Soviet and American actions was:

Judge	A	B
C	.800	.883
	.891	.842
B	.967	
	.939	

The top figure is level of agreement for the scaling of Soviet action; the bottom figure is that for the scaling of United States action. All figures are significant at beyond the .01 level.

NOTES

*This study was supported by the United States Naval Ordnance Test Station, China Lake, California, Contract N60530–8929. The authors wish to express their gratitude to Mrs. Marian Payne for her research assistance in collecting the financial data analyzed in this paper.
1. 1, p. 16.
2. "He [President Kennedy] said to Mr. Khrushchev you go ahead and do whatever you want to in Cuba, you arm in any way to wish, and do anything you want to. We'll do nothing about it. . ." [20, p. 8].
3. "I am sure the administration must have been fully aware of what has been going on for the past month and yet they have reamined silent on the threat to our security now festering in Cuba" [20, p. 8].

4. William Knox, Chairman of Westinghouse Electric International, was told by Premier Khrushchev on October 24—the day the blockade went into effect—that "as the Soviet vessels were not armed the United States could undoubtedly stop one or two or more but then he, Chairman Khrushchev, would give instructions to the Soviet submarines to sink the American vessels" [20, p. 36].

5. This is apparently the only communication between the United States and the Soviet Union during the crisis period which is not publicly available (cf. Larson, 1964).

6. During the Cuban crisis, it took four hours, with luck, for a formal message to pass between Kennedy and Khrushchev. Any such message had to be carried physically from the head of state to the local embassy, translated, coded, transmitted, decoded on the other side, and carried to the other leader" [2, p. 6].

7. A number of factors—including those of personality, role, organization and system—will affect the perceptual variables in the model. A further elaboration may be found in [11, Chs. 1–2].

8. A more complete description of the research techniques may be found in the Methodological Appendix at the end of this paper.

9. The reader may wonder why, in Table 2, the highest level of negative affect in the s sector of the model is found on October 28, the day of the Kennedy-Khrushchev agreement. This result is due primarily to President Kennedy's expressions of regret about an American weather airplane straying over Soviet territory; many of the words used by the President are "tagged" for negative affect in the General Inquirer Dictionary.

10. Because there are no United States perceptual data for October 24, the average of the values of October 23 and 25 has been used for the purpose of calculating the correlation coefficients in Table 4.

11. The cell entries, which are based on a weighted (frequency x intensity) total, are independent of each other. The frequency and intensity of positive actions, for example, have no bearing on the number of actions which are rated negative. Nor can a single action word be entered in both the positive and negative cells; no dictionary entry is tagged for both ends of a single dimension.

12. The figures in Tables 6a and 6b support other studies which have found the evaluative dimension of cognition to be the most important (Osgood et al., 1957; Levy and Hefner, 1962). It is also true, however, that the activity dimension provides rather consistent discrimination between the early and later periods of the crisis. Inasmuch as there was little, if any, actual change in Soviet and American capabilities during the short period under investigation, it is not surprising that perceptions of potency show little variation.

13. In this respect the contrast to many of the crucial decisions made in 1914 is striking. That the German Kaiser underwent an almost total collapse at the time he made a series of key decisions—the night of July 29–30—is evident from a reading of his marginal notes [19].

14. Despite the relative lack of speed—with the possible exception of the German army—with which European weapons systems could be mobilized in 1914, decision-makers in the various capitals of Europe perceived that time was of crucial importance—and they acted on that assumption. The Kaiser, for example, immediately upon learning

of Russia's mobilization (which had been intended only to deter Austria-Hungary), ordered: "In view of the collossal war preparations of Russia now discovered, this is all too late, I fear. Begin! Now!" [19, p. 368]. One can only speculate on the outcome had there been some delay in the making of such decisions in 1914.

15. President Kennedy and others were aware of the possibility of mispreconception by their counterparts in the Kremlin, "Well now, if you look at the history of this century where World War I really came through a series of misjudgments of the intentions of others . . . it's very difficult to always make judgments here about what the effect will be of our decisions on other countries" [4, p. 3].

16. The failure of communication was not, of course, solely attributable to the sender. The Kaiser, for example, consistently dismissed the warnings of his able ambassador in London, Prince Lichnowsky.

17. For example, both the Kaiser and the Tsar demanded that the other stop mobilizing, Nicholas replied that, "it is technically impossible to stop our military preparations" [19, p. 402]. At the same time Wilhelm wrote: "On technical grounds my mobiliza-tion which has already been proclaimed this afternoon must proceed against two fronts, east and west" [19, p. 451].

REFERENCES

1. Alsop, Stewart and Charles Bartlett. "In time of Crisis," *The Saturday Evening Post,* Dec. 8, 1962, 15–20.

2. Bagdikian, Ben. H. "Press Independence and the Cuban Crisis," *Columbia Journalism Review,* (Winter, 1963) 5–11.

3. Boulding, Kenneth E. "National Images and International Systems," *The Journal of Conflict Resolution,* III (1959), 120–31.

4. C.B.S. News. "A Conversation with President Kennedy," Dec. 17, 1962. (Mimeograph transcript)

5. Cowles, Virginia. *The Kaiser.* (New York: Harper and Row, 1964)

6. Data Digest, *Cuban Crisis.* (New York: Keynote Publications, 1963)

7. Draper, Theodore. "Castro and Communism," *The Reporter,* Jan. 17, 1963, 35–40.

8. Holsti, K. J. "The Use of Objective Criteria for the Measurement of International Tension Levels," *Background,* VII (1963), 77–96.

9. Holsti, Ole R. "An Adaptation of the 'General Inquirer' for the Systematic Analysis of Political Documents," *Behavioral Science,* IX (October, 1964), in press.

10._____ and Robert C. North, "History as a 'Laboratory' of Conflict," in Elton B. McNeil (Ed.), *Social Science and Human Conflict.* (Englewood Cliffs, N. J.: Prentice-Hall, in press).

11. _____, Richard A. Brody and Robert C. North. *Theory and Measurement of Interstate Behavior: A Research Application of Automated Content Analysis.* (Stanford University: mimeo.) 1964 a.

12. _____, Richard A. Brody and Robert C. North. "Violence and Hostility: The Path to World War," Paper read at American Psychiatric Association Conference, Los Angeles, California (May, 1964 b).

13. Horelick, Arnold L. "The Cuban Missile Crisis: An Analysis of Soviet Calculation and Behavior," *World Politics*, XVI (1964), 363-89.

14. Kolkowicz, Roman. "Conflicts in Soviet Party-Military Relations: 1962-1963," RAND Corp. Memo., RN-3760-PR, 1963.

15. Kumata, H. and Wilbur Schramm. "A Pilot Study of Cross-Cultural Methodology," *Public Opinion Quarterly*, XX (1956), 229-37.

16. Larson, David L. *The "Cuban Crisis" of 1962*. (Boston: Houghton Mifflin Co., 1963)

17. Levy, Sheldon G. and Robert Hefner. "Multi-dimensional Scaling of International Attitudes" (unpublished: mimeo.), Center for Research on Conflict Resolution (November 1, 1962). Working paper no. 201.

18. March, J. G. and H. A. Simon. *Organizations*. (New York: John Wiley and Sons, Inc., 1958)

19. Montgelas, Max and Walther Schücking (Eds.). *Outbreak of the World War, German Documents Collected by Karl Kautsky*. (New York: Oxford University Press, 1924)

20. N.B.C. "Cuba: The Missile Crisis," Feb. 9, 1964.

21. *New York Times*. October-November 1962.

22. North, Robert C. "International Conflict and Integration: Problems of Research," in Muzafer Sherif (Ed.), *Intergroup Relations and Leadership*. (New York: John Wiley and Sons, 1962)

23. _____, Richard A. Brody and Ole R. Holsti. "Some Empirical Data on the Conflict Spiral," *Peace Research Society Papers*, (1964) 1-14.

24. Osgood, Charles E. "Studies on the Generality of Affective Meaning Systems," *American Psychologist*, XVII (1962), 10-28.

25. _____, George J. Suci and Percy H. Tannenbaum. *The Measurement of Meaning*. (Urbana, Ill.: University of Illinois Press, 1957)

26. _____ and Robert C. North, "From Individual to Nation: An Attempt to Make Explicit the Usually Implicit Process of Personifying International Relations," an unpublished manuscript. (Urbana and Stanford, 1963)

27. Rapoport, Anatol. *Fights, Games and Debates*. (Ann Arbor, Mich.: University of Michigan Press, 1960)

28. Richardson, Lewis F. *Arms and Insecurity*. ed. by Nicolas Rashevsky and Ernesto Trucco. (Pittsburgh, Pa.: The Boxwood Press, 1960)

29. Rosenau, James N. "Pre-Theories and Theories of Foreign Policy." Paper prepared for the Conference on Comparative and International Politics, Northwestern University, April 2-4, 1964.

30. Snyder, Richard C., et al. (Eds.). *Foreign Policy Decision Making*. (New York: The Free Press of Glencoe, 1962).

31. Sorensen, Theodore C. *Decision-Making in the White House*. (New York: Columbia) 1963.

32. Stone, Philip J., Robert F. Bales, J. Zvi Namenwirth and Daniel M. Ogilvie. "The General Inquirer: A Computer System for Content Analysis and Retrieval Based on the Sentence as a Unit of Information," *Behavioral Science*, VII (1962), 484-94.

33. Suci, George J. "An Investigation of the Similarity between the Semantic Space of Five Different Cultures." Report for the Southwest Project in Comparative Psycholinguistics, 1957.

34. Verba, Sidney. "Assumptions of Rationality in Models of the International System," *World Politics*, XIV (1961), 93-117.

35. Wright, Quincy. "The Cuban Quarantine of 1962," in John G. Stoessinger and Alan F. Westin (Eds.). *Power and Order.* (New York: Harcourt, Brace and World, Inc., 1964)

23. THE KENNEDY EXPERIMENT

Amitai Etzioni

The pattern of events between June 10 and November 22, 1963, provided a partial test of a theory of international relations. The essence of the theory is that psychological gestures initiated by one nation will be reciprocated by others with the effect of reducing international tensions. This tension reduction, in turn, will lessen the probability of international conflicts and wars.

Examining this theory in light of the 1963 experiment, I ask: (*a*) What are the main propositions of the theory? (*b*) What initiatives were actually taken by the United States in the experiment period, and how did the Union of Soviet Socialist Republics react? (*c*) What were the effects of these initiatives and responses on inter-bloc relations, and to what degree did these effects conform to the expectations of the theory? (*d*) What other factors, not accounted for by the theory, could have produced all or part of these effects? (*e*) What factors limited both the scope and the extent of the experiment, and under what conditions could it be replicated or extended?

A PSYCHOLOGICAL THEORY OF INTERNATIONAL RELATIONS

The theory views the behavior of nations basically as that of persons who have strong drives that motivate their pursuit of goals, influence their choice of means,

SOURCE. Amitai Etzioni, "The Kennedy Experiment," in *Western Political Quarterly*, XX (June, 1967), pp. 361-380. Reprinted by permission of the author and the University of Utah, copyright owner.

NOTE. This article grew out of my work at the Institute of War and Peace Studies at Columbia University. I am grateful for the research assistance of Sarajane Heidt and Robert McGheean. Since this article was written two books have appeared which provide additional documentation for the points made but seem not to affect the conclusions reached: See Theodore C. Sorensen, *Kennedy* (New York, Harper and Row, 1965), esp. chap. XXV. and Arthur M. Schlesinger, Jr., *A Thousand Days* (Boston, Houghton Mifflin, 1965), esp. pp. 888-923. Additional treatment of this subject will be included in my *The Active Society: A Theory of Societal and Political Process* (New York: Free Press of Glencoe, forthcoming).

and distort the communications they send and receive. It suggests that nations, when in conflict, tend to be caught in a spiral. The hostility of one as perceived by the other evokes his hostility, which in turn is perceived by the first side, further increasing *his* hostility. Arms races, in which the participant countries increase the level of their armaments because the other countries are doing so, are viewed as an expression of such upward spiraling of hostile reactions.

Psychological analysis of international behavior has been so discredited[1] that most political scientists and members of sister-disciplines might find their patience tried when asked to examine such a theory. It should therefore be stressed from the outset that the evidence provided below, although partial, provides some new support for some elements of the psychological approach. While the more extreme version of the theory remains unsupported, a moderate version is strengthened enough to stand among the major hypotheses on international behavior that are to be explored further. After a brief recapitulation of the theory and its two versions, the evidence speaks for itself.

According to both versions of the theory, a high level of hostility generates psychological blocks that prevent the sides from facing international reality. Various defense mechanisms are activated: for one, a high level of tension tends to produce a *rigid* adherence to a policy chosen under earlier conditions, e.g., the sides increase armaments and hold to a hostile posture ("cold war"), though armaments have been procured beyond military needs, and hostile feelings are no longer justified in view of changes in the character and intentions of the opponent.[2] These changes are *denied*, another mode of defensive behavior, to make the continuation of the earlier policy psychologically possible.

Further, fears of nuclear war, *repressed* since they are too threatening to be faced, express themselves in stereotyping and paranoia, indications of which advocates of the theory find in the conduct of nations locked in a state of international tensions. *Stereotyping* is represented by the divisions of the world into black and white, good and bad, nations,[3] and the manipulation of information by selecting among and distorting the content of communications, so that positive information about one's adversary is ignored and negative information about one's own side disregarded. Blocked or distorted communication between the sides thus prevents "reality-testing" and correction of false images.

---

[1] See, for example, Kenneth Waltz, *Man, the State, and War* (New York: Columbia U. Press, 1959), chap. III.

[2] Gabriel A. Almond, *The American People and Foreign Policy* (New York: Praeger, 1960), p. xvi.

[3] Urie Bronfenbrenner, a psychologist, found that when American school children were asked why the Russians planted trees alongside a road, they responded that the trees blocked vision and "made work for the prisoners," whereas *American* trees were planted "for shade." *Saturday Review,* January 5, 1963, p. 96.

Stereotyping is often accompanied by *paranoia*. Whatever the adversary offers is interpreted as seeking to advance his own goals and as a trap for us. If the Soviets favor complete and general disarmament, this in itself brings Americans to point to disarmament as a Communist ruse.[4] A possibility of a genuine give-and-take is ignored. The same repressed fear, the psychological analysis continues, causes even reasonable concessions to the other side, made as part of a give-and-take, to be seen as submission or, to use the political term, appeasement. The labeling of bargaining behavior as disloyal or treacherous impedes negotiations that require open-mindedness, flexibility, and willingness to make concessions even though not sacrificing basic positions and values.

What could a therapy be? How, the psychologists ask, can the vicious circle of hostile moves and counter-moves be broken? The answer is similar to psychoanalytic technique—increased and improved communication. Communication can be increased by visits of Americans to Russia and Russians to America, exchange of newspapers, publication of American columns in Soviet newspapers and vice versa, by summit conferences, and the like.[5] Communication will become less distorted and tensions will be reduced if one of the sides begins to indicate a friendly state of mind. While such indications will be initially mistrusted, if continued they will be reciprocated, reducing hostility which in turn will reduce the counter-hostility, thus reversing the cold war spiral. Once the level of tension is reduced, and more communication is received from the other side, there will be an increased ability to perceive the international reality as it is, which will further reduce tensions. Joint undertakings are also favored because psychological experiments with children have shown that the introduction of shared tasks helps to reduce hostility.[6] International cooperative research, joint exploration of the stars, oceans, and poles, joint rather than competitive development aid, are hence favored.[7]

There are significant differences in the extent to which this theory claims to explain international behavior. Strongly put, it suggests that "war starts in the minds of man" and "the situation is what we define it to be." In this interpretation, the causes of war are psychological and can be fully explained in

---

[4] On disarmament as political gamesmanship, bee John W. Spanier and Joseph L. Nogee, *The Politics of Disarmament* (New York: Praeger, 1962), chap. 2.

[5] These ideas are also held by non-psychologically oriented writers. For example, see C. Wright Mills, *The Causes of World War III* (New York: Simon and Schuster, 1958), pp. 103 ff.

[6] A study often cited in this context is Muzafer and Carolyn Sherif, *Groups in Harmony and Tension: An Integration of Studies on Intergroup Relations* (New York: Harper, 1953).

[7] See discussions of the International Cooperation Year—for instance, the *Washington Post*, March 7, 1965.

psychological terms. Arms are merely an expression of these attitudes of mind.[8] If attitudes are modified, arms will either not be produced or have no threatening impact. The people of New Jersey, it is pointed out, do not fear nuclear arms held by New Yorkers.

More moderate versions of the theory view psychological factors as one aspect of a situation that contains economic, political, and military dimensions as well. Just as triggers without hostilities do not make a war, so hostilities without arms cannot trigger battles. Moreover, even if armaments were initially ordered to serve a psychological motive, once available they generate motives of their own to propel hostile postures and wars. Thus one can hold the psychological theory with varying degrees of strength.[9] Osgood, in most of his writings on this subject, has advanced the stronger version,[10] while this author subscribes to the more moderate one.[11]

A second line of variation centers on where the blame for triggering the spiral is placed. Some writers tend to view the sides as equally at fault with no "real" reason for a cold war other than misunderstanding. For example, Stalin only wished to establish weak friendly governments on his Western borders, a desire which the West misperceived as expansionistic. Others tend to put more of the blame on the West or on the East. All of these interpretations can be coupled with the psychological analysis on the grounds that regardless of the initiator and whether the initial cause was real or imagined, the same process of psychological escalation is at work. The therapy, hence, remains the same. To insist that the side that triggered the process be the one to take the initiative to reverse it, is viewed as immature behavior.

---

[8]In a statement typical of this line of argument, Erich Fromm points out: "This time the choice between violent-irrational, or anticipatory-rational behavior is a choice which will affect the human race and its culture, if not its physical survival.

"Yet so far the chances that such rational-anticipatory action will occur are bleak. Not because there is no possibility for such an outcome in the realistic circumstances, but because on both sides there is a thought barrier built of clichés, ritualistic ideologies, and even a good deal of common craziness that prevents people—leaders and led—from seeing sanely and realistically what the facts are, from recognizing alternative solutions to violence. Such rational-anticipatory policy requires . . . a serious examination of our own biases, and of certain semipathological forms of thinking which govern our behavior." Erich Fromm, *May Man Prevail?* (Garden City: Anchor Books, 1961), p. 8.

[9]For a discussion of various versions of this approach, see Arthur I. Waskow, *The Worried Man's Guide to World Peace* (New York: Anchor Books, 1963), pp. 74–82.

[10]Charles E. Osgood, *An Alternative to War or Surrender* (Urbana: U. of Illinois Press, 1962), esp. chap. III. See also John H. Kautsky, "Myth, Self-Fulfilling Prophecy, and Symbolic Reassurance in the East-West Conflict," *Journal of Conflict Resolution,* 9 (March 1965), 1-17; Raymond A. Bauer, "Problems of Perception and the Relations Between the United States and the Soviet Union," *Journal of Conflict Resolution,* 5 (September 1961), 223–30.

[11]Amitai Etzioni, *The Hard Way to Peace* (New York: Collier Books, 1962), esp. chap. 4, and *Winning Without War* (Garden City: Anchor Books, 1964), esp. pp. 21–26, 62–68, 209–12.

Next, there are important differences in the steps suggested to break the cycle. It is generally agreed that measures which require multilateral negotiations are not appropriate for the initiation of tension reduction. The high level of hostility and mutual suspicions invariably disrupts the negotiations, and the mutual recriminations that follow increase rather than reduce the level of international tensions. Unilateral steps are therefore needed. The important differences between the two versions of the theory concern the nature of these steps. Jerome Frank, for instance, stresses that the initiatives must be clear, simple, and dramatic to overcome the psychological barriers,[12] for any minor concessions will be seen as a trap to encourage the opponent to lower his guard. Actually, in Frank's judgment, unilateral renunciation of nuclear weapons might well be the only sufficiently large step to break the vicious cycle.[13] More moderate interpretations call for significant reductions of arms as initiatives; still more moderate interpretations seek to restrict the unilateral steps to purely symbolic gestures not involving any weakening of the military strength of the initiator even though some arms reduction, such as the cutting of arms surpluses, might be recommended.[14]

Finally, there are those who believe that the transition from a "cold war" to a "stable peace" would be achieved by a chain of unilateral initiatives followed by reciprocations by the other side, while others believe that such exchanges would open the way to effective multilateral negotiations. The unilateral-reciprocal approach, it is suggested, is needed to create the atmosphere in which important international accommodations such as broad-based arms reduction schemes can be introduced, but those in themselves cannot be introduced in this way because the unilateral-reciprocation approach can carry only comparatively simple communications, and the sides are unlikely to make major arms reductions unless those of the other side are made simultaneously.[15]

[12] Jerome Frank, "Breaking the Thought Barrier: Psychological Challenges of the Nuclear Age," *Psychiatry,* 23 (1960), pp. 245–66;

[13] *Ibid.,* pp. 263–65.

[14] *The Hard Way to Peace, op. cit.,* esp. chap. 7.

[15] *Ibid.,* pp. 95–98. Others view unilateral reciprocation as a much more encompassing measure. Schelling points out another difference in the policy's use—as a communication method (which can convey hostility as well as good will) and as a treatment of international conflicts. His approach is that of a communication method. Thomas Schelling, "Signals and Feedback in the Arms Dialogue," *Bulletin of the Atomic Scientists,* January 1965, pp. 5–10.

Another major difference is among those who favor continuing unilateral concessions if the other side does not reciprocate and those who would stop after awhile. Sibley favors continuing, even if this would involve unilateral disarmament. See Mulford Sibley, *Unilateral Initiatives and Disarmament* (Philadelphia: American Friends Service Committee, 1962), pp. 19–28. Osgood (*op. cit.*) is not completely clear on this point.

See also Arthur Herzog, *The War and Peace Establishment* (New York: Harper and Row, 1965), pp. 144, 159. Etzioni favors stopping after several steps (the number depends on the scope of each step); See *The Hard Way to Peace, op. cit.,* pp. 99 ff. It is surprising to learn that Levine finds Etzioni unclear on this point on p. 56—Robert E. Levine, *The Armed Debate* (Cambridge: Harvard U. Press, 1963)—only to report the Etzioni position correctly on p. 228.

AMERICAN INITIATIVES

The Kennedy experiment can be viewed as a test of a moderate version of the psychological theory that seeks to use symbolic gestures as unilateral initiatives to reduce tension to get at other factors, leading toward multilateral negotiations.

The first step was a speech by President John F. Kennedy at the American University on June 10, 1963, in which he outlined "A Strategy of Peace." While it is not known to what degree the President or his advisors were moved by a psychological theory, the speech clearly met a condition of this theory—it set the *context* for the unilateral initiatives to follow. As any concrete measure can be interpreted in a variety of ways, it is necessary to spell out the general state of mind these steps attempt to communicate.[16]

The President called attention to the dangers of nuclear war and took a reconciliatory tone toward the Soviet Union in his address. He said that "constructive changes" in the Soviet Union "might bring within reach solutions which now seem beyond us." He stated that "our problems are man-made . . . and can be solved by man." Coming eight months after the 1962 Cuban crisis, when the United States and Russia stood "eyeball to eyeball," such statements marked a decisive change in American attitudes. United States policies, the President added, must be so constructed "that it becomes in the Communist interest to agree to a genuine peace," which was a long way from the prevailing sentiment that there was little the United States could do, so long as the Soviet Union did not change. Further, there was doubt that the Soviet Union was capable of a genuine interest in peace. Nor did the President imply that all the blame for the cold war rested with the other side; he called on Americans to "re-examine" their attitudes toward the cold war.

Beyond merely delivering a speech, the President announced the first unilateral initiative—the United States was stopping all nuclear tests in the atmosphere and would not resume them unless another country did. This, it should be noted, was basically a psychological gesture and not a unilateral arms limitation step. The United States at that time was believed to command about five times the means of delivery of the Soviet Union and to have them much better protected, and had conducted about twice as many nuclear tests including a recent large round of testing. American experts believed that it would take about one to two years before the information from these tests was finally digested, that in all likelihood little was to be gained from additional testing even after that date,[17] and that if

[16]Such a speech had been advocated, in 1961. *The Hard Way to Peace, op. cit.,* p. 96. The importance of the context is overlooked by Levine, *op. cit.,* p. 327. Levine, belittling the role of gestures, argues that they have taken place "for years." He refers, of course, to such isolated acts as the closing of a military base or reducing travel restrictions, which took place in a cold war context without the context provided by a "strategy for peace."

[17]Jerome B. Weisner and Herbert F. York, "The Test Ban," *Scientific American,* 211 (1964), 27.

testing proved to be necessary it could be conducted in other environments, particularly underground. Thus, in effect, the President used the termination of testing as a psychological gesture.

The steps that followed had much the same quality. Kennedy's speech, delivered on June 10, was published in full during the next few days in the Soviet government newspaper, *Izvestia*, as well as in *Pravda* with a combined circulation of 10,000,000, a degree of attention rarely accorded a Western leader. Radio jammers in Moscow were turned off to allow the Russian people to listen without interruption to the Voice of America's recording of the speech, a fact that was reported in the United States and, therefore, had some tension reduction effect on both sides. Premier Khrushchev followed on June 15 with a speech welcoming the Kennedy initiative. He stated that a world war was not inevitable and that the main danger of conflict stemmed from the arms race and the stockpiling of nuclear weapons. Khrushchev reciprocated on the psychological-military side by announcing he had ordered that the production of strategic bombers be halted. The psychological nature of this step is to be seen in that the bombers were probably about to be phased out anyway and that no verification was offered for cessation of production.

In the United Nations, the Soviet Union on June 11 removed its objection to a Western-backed proposal to send observers to war-torn Yemen. The United States reciprocated by removing, for the first time since 1956, its objection to the restoration of full status of the Hungarian delegation to the United Nations.

Although the United States had proposed a direct America-Russia communications link at Geneva in late 1962,[18] the Soviets finally agreed to this measure on June 20, 1963. Next, attention focused on the test ban. Following the United States' example, Russia reciprocated by not testing in the atmosphere, so that until the treaty was signed, both sides refrained from such testing under an understanding achieved without negotiation but rather through unilateral-reciprocal moves. This development, in line with the moderate version of the theory, led in July to multilateral negotiations and a treaty, signed on August 5, 1963. The signing of the treaty was followed by a number of new proposals for East-West agreements. Foreign Minister Gromyko, on September 19, 1963, called for a "non-aggression pact between the members of the Warsaw Treaty [*sic*] and the members of the North Atlantic bloc" and asked for a peace treaty with Germany. President Kennedy came before the United Nations and dramatically suggested, on September 20, 1963, that the United States and the Soviet Union explore the stars together. Also mentioned repeatedly in the front-page news in those weeks were the possible exchange of observer posts at key points to reduce the danger of surprise attack; expansion of the test treaty to include underground testing;

---

[18]Richard D. Stebbins, *The United States in World Affairs 1963* (New York and Evanston: Harper and Row for The Council on Foreign Relations, 1964), p. 84.

direct flights between Moscow and New York; and the opening of an American consulate in Leningrad and a Soviet one in Chicago.

The next step actually taken came in a different area—a symbolic reduction of the trade barriers between East and West. As part of the cold war, the United States and, following its guidance, other Western nations had sharply limited the trade between East and West. Not only was trading of a long list of strategic material forbidden, but trade in other materials required an export license that was difficult to obtain. Restrictions were also imposed on the credits Russia could obtain. There were occasional violations of these bans, especially by traders in Western countries other than the United States, but the total East-West trade remained very small.

On October 9, 1963, President Kennedy approved the sale of $250 million's worth of wheat to the Soviet Union. The almost purely psychological nature of this step is not always understood. As the test ban treaty had, for reasons mentioned above, a limited military significance, so the wheat deal had little commercial importance. The barriers to East-West trade were *not* removed; credit and license barriers were maintained. The President himself said that this decision did not initiate "a new Soviet-American trade policy,"[19] and such trade remained a small fraction of the total Soviet foreign trade. The total value of the wheat the United States actually sold was $65 million. The main values of the deal were, hence, as a gesture and in the educational effect of the public debate which preceded the Administration's approval of the deal.

October brought another transformation of a unilateral-reciprocal understanding into a binding, multilateral formal agreement. This time it concerned the orbiting of weapons of mass destruction and, once more, though it appeared to be a military measure, it was largely a psychological one. The United States had formerly decided, after considerable debate, that it was not interested in orbiting nuclear bombs.[20] The Soviet Union, as far as could be determined, had reached a similar conclusion. Neither side orbited such weapons while it was watching the other side. On September 19 Gromyko suggested such a pact, and Kennedy indicated that the United States was willing. An agreement in principle was announced on October 3, and the final resolution was passed in the General Assembly on October 19, with the approval of both powers. Its immediate effect was to publicize and formalize an area of agreement that had in effect existed in the preceding years. Another measure, psychological in nature, was an exchange of released

---

[19]*Documents on American Foreign Relations* (New York and Evanston: Harper and Row for the Council on Foreign Relations), 1962, pp. 182–93.

[20]Mainly because these bombs are more difficult to deliver on target than when carried by air or missile. See Donald G. Brennan, "Arms and Arms Control in Outer Space," in Lincoln P. Bloomfield (ed.), *Outer Space* (New York: The American Assembly, 1962), p. 129. See also Amitai Etzioni, *The Moon-Doggle* (Garden City: Doubleday, 1964), pp. 118 ff.

spies. While spies had been exchanged under a variety of circumstances in the past, the October 1963 exchange served the new policy.

In late October and in the first three weeks of November, there was a marked slow-down of American initiatives, and reciprocation to Soviet initiatives almost completely stopped. The reasons were many: the Administration felt that the psychological mood in the West was getting out of hand, with hopes and expectations for more Soviet-American measures running too high;[21] allies, especially West Germany, objected more and more bitterly;[22] and the pre-election year began, in which the Administration seemed not to desire additional accommodations. The present posture seemed best for domestic purposes. There had been some promising signs for those who favored disarmament, and no matters of grave enough importance were involved so that even if all went sour—if the Soviets resumed testing, orbited bombs, etc.—no credible "appeasement" charge could be made by Republicans. There was an expectation that moves would be renewed after the elections. For the election year, however, even such measures as air and consular treaties were delayed.[23] (The experiment was actually resumed after the election; the factors that prevented its success merit a study in their own right.[24])

SOVIET RESPONSES

One of the prevalent criticisms against the unilateral initiatives theory is that the Soviets might not respond to such initiatives.[25] The Soviets, it is said, are

[21]Max Frankel wrote on October 25, 1963, that "there is real concern here [in Washington] about the decay of the vigilance so carefully developed in the non-Communist world and about the erosion of barricades erected against the spread of Soviet influence." *New York Times,* October 25, 1963, p. 6.

[22]Adenauer, then still West German Chancellor, said of the *détente* that "only the stupidest calves choose their own butcher." *New York Times,* October 6, 1963, p. 6. For German objections to the treaty, see *Documents, op. cit.,* 1963, 26, 27; *Department of State Bulletin* (Washington, D.C.: G.P.O., September 2, 1963), pp. 353–55; United States Senate, *Executive Report 3* (on Executive M), 88th Cong., 1st Sess., September 3, 1963.

[23]*New York Times,* December 18, 1964, p. 1.

[24]On December 17, 1964, air and consular convention negotiations were reopened. Further, on January 3, 1965, the United States and the Soviet Union expanded their cultural exchange agreement. On February 2, 1965, the United States unilaterally announced a new cutback in production of enriched uranium for atomic weapons. On February 5, 1965, as a "symbolic step toward curbing the spread of atomic weapons," the United States placed one of its reactors under international inspection. Also on February 5, the liquidation of 129 missile sites was announced, following an earlier announcement of the closing of other bases. This sequence, however, was simultaneous with the American escalation of the war in Vietnam in early 1965.

[25]Robert A. Levine, "Unilateral Initiatives: A Cynic's View, *Bulletin of the Atomic Scientists,* 19 (January 1963), 22.

Marxists and quite aware of the difference between real and symbolic moves. A policy of symbolic gestures would appeal only to people who think in Madison Avenue terms and not in political, military, and economic ones. The evidence on this point is fairly clear. For each move that was made, the Soviets reciprocated. Kennedy's "Strategy for Peace" speech was matched by a conciliatory speech by Khrushchev; Kennedy's unilateral declaration of cessation of tests was followed by a cessation of the production of strategic bombers; spies were traded for spies, etc. The Russians showed no difficulties in understanding the gestures and in responding to psychological initiatives; and they participated in a "you move— I move" sequence rather than waiting for simultaneous, negotiated, agree-upon moves. Further, they shifted to multilateral-simultaneous arrangements once the appropriate mood was generated, as reflected in the test-ban treaty and outer space resolution.

Another "danger" critics of unilateral initiatives warned of was that the Soviets might reciprocate "below par" and thus accumulate an advantage. While these matters are not readily measurable, it seems that the Russian reciprocations were "proportional" to the American ones. Khrushchev's speech might have been somewhat less elegant than Kennedy's, but it would be difficult to defend the proposition that announcing a halt to the production of bombers is lower in value than the declaration of cessation of tests, both basically psychological gestures. Spies were exchanged for spies; the test treaty and the space ban involved substantively identical, strategically similar, commitments. In short, neither side seemed to have made a disproportionate gain.

While the warnings of the critics were not realized, a danger that seems not to have been anticipated by the United States Government did materialize: the Russians responded not just by reciprocating American initiatives but by offering some initiatives of their own, in the spirit of the *détente*. [26] Washington was put on the spot: it had to reciprocate if it were not to weaken the new spirit, but it could lose control of the experiment. The first test came at the very outset, when Russia took the initiative and suddenly removed its objection to the sending of United Nations observers to Yemen. The United States reciprocated, as previously mentioned, allowing the restoration of full status to the Hungarian delegation to the United Nations. The United States also responded handsomely to Russia's initiative on a space ban. If found it more difficult, however, to respond to the other Russian initiatives. The United States agreed to the wheat deal, but only after hesitation that was sufficient to reduce the gesture's value. It never quite succeeded in making a good case for its objection to a non-aggression pact between the North Atlantic Treaty Organization and the Warsaw Treaty Organization. (The argument that this would involve a recognition of East Germany was a

---

[26]This could have been anticipated on the basis of previous Soviet conduct. *The Hard Way to Peace, op. cit.,* p. 107. For Russian moves that were not reciprocated by the United States, see Stebbins, *op. cit.,* pp. 76–77.

thin one, for several wordings were suggested that would circumvent this difficulty.) It was felt that a non-aggression pact between these two was already covered within the United Nations charter, which would be weakened if the message were rearticulated in another document. In other cases the United States was unconcerned about such duplication, for instance, between the Organization of American States and the United Nations.[27] The United States hesitated in responding to the Soviet initiative on an air treaty, as well as on more encompassing moves regarding Germany and disarmament. Despite this reluctance, however, there were enough initiatives and reciprocations as well as multilateral measures within the three months to allow a partial testing of the theory. What was the effect of the gestures and counter-gestures?

THE PSYCHOLOGICAL IMPACT

The first steps in June 1963 did not produce what later became known as the Soviet-American *détente,* or the 1963–64 thaw in the cold war. In accord with the preceding psychological analysis, they were rather received with much ambivalence and suspicion. The *New York Times* seems to have reflected accurately the mood the author observed in Washington at the time, when it stated on June 16, 1963, that

> . . . there was a new threat of international peace in the air this week, the kind of threat that leaves sophisticates smirking and the rest of us just dumbfounded. The "accommodators," as outraged Republicans call them, were simply delighted. The "cold warriors," as the accommodators call them, regarded conciliation as a shrewd new tactic.[28]

Thus, even the initiating side was not convinced that there really was a new line, and, if we may assume that Russian authorities read the *New York Times,* they too could hardly have been immediately persuaded.

In line with the theory, Kennedy's initiation speech included recognition of Russia's achievements ("We can still hail the Russian people for their many achievements—in science and space, in economic and industrial growth, in culture and in acts of courage") and suffering ("And no nation in the history of battle ever suffered more than the Soviet Union suffered in the course of the Second World War"). These statements seemed to have weakened the rigid image that was typical of the cold war period.

[27]Monzales M. Minerva, *Aspectos Politicos Del Sistema Inter-americano* (Mexico City: National University, 1961).

[28]*New York Times,* June 16, 1963.

The impact of the speech was felt outside the seats of government. In the United States, "from around the country came a generous flow of messages echoing all these responses, but more approving than not. And from around the globe came new bursts of hope kept alive by quick signs of interest in Moscow."[29] A *New York Times* correspondent in Moscow reported that "the ready approval of its contents by ordinary Russians was evident in the reactions of Muscovites who lined up at kiosks to buy newspapers."[30] But the main turning point came when the test treaty—considered an important "breakthrough"—was successfully negotiated. That at first hopes for a treaty ran low, and that it took great effort to obtain it only increased the significance of its ratification.

The treaty to partially ban thermonuclear tests was the central gesture of the Kennedy experiment. Until it was reached, gestures and counter-gestures were met with caution, if not skepticism. When in early July Khrushchev offered a ban on tests in sea, air, and space (as was ultimately agreed), but coupled this offer with a suggestion of a non-aggression pact between the North Atlantic Treaty Organization and the Warsaw Treaty Organization, the *New York Times* referred to the offer as "Another Booby Trap?"[31] A week later, discussing the test treaty negotiations, the same source reflected the mood in the capital: "If these talks are successful, it is generally believed that a new chapter in East-West relations will open. But there are grave doubts on all sides that such a new chapter is indeed at hand."[32] Thus, a test ban was viewed as having major tension-reduction potential, but there was much doubt whether it would be achieved. A Washington reporter still refers to the *détente* at this point with a question mark and explores at length the possibility "that the Soviet Union did not really want an agreement"[33] (i.e., was negotiating in bad faith). An American report from Moscow indicated that "Mr. Khrushchev would also hope that conclusion of a partial test-ban treaty would create an atmosphere in which he could negotiate other advantageous agreements, especially on Germany."[34]

The treaty was negotiated in July, signed in August, and ratified in September. Thus, for more than two months, it served as the focus for discussions about Soviet intentions, the possibility of peaceful co-existence, and the dangers of nuclear war; and the Senate hearing helped to keep the debate alive. Its ratification was therefore not merely one more gesture in an international sequence of

[29]*Ibid.*
[30]*Ibid.*
[31]*Ibid.*, July 7, 1963, p. 1E.
[32]*Ibid.*, July 14, 1963, p. 1E.
[33]*Ibid.*, p. 5E.
[34]*Ibid.*

THE KENNEDY EXPERIMENT   427

pseudo-events,[35] but a major educational act. The American public that entered the period with ambivalent attitudes toward a test-ban treaty, remembering the arbitrary resumption of testing by the Soviet Union in 1961, after three years of voluntary moratorium, as well as the 1962 Cuban crisis, was now strongly in favor of the agreement. Louis Harris reports that a national poll taken in July, before the negotiations on the treaty had begun, found that 52 per cent of the population strongly supported a treaty. This percentage had risen to 81 by September when the treaty was ratified.[36] The tone of the press also changed; there was now an "official amity" between the United States and the Soviet Union.[37] While some newspapermen, accustomed to sudden shifts in international winds, continued to be cautious, a report from Moscow stated:

> As Secretary of State Rusk left the Soviet Union today, after six days of discussions with Soviet leaders, it appeared almost certain to Western observers here that a surface of calm would descend on East-West relations. . . . The prospect, it is believed, is for a long period of manifold negotiations at all levels and in many cities and countries on all sorts of issues. . . . The feeling is that the Russians are generally interested in maintaining the current state of improved relations with the West. They are believed to be hoping for a minimum of friction.[38]

The correspondent who had reported smirking and dumbfoundedness over any possible thaw in June now stated that "we have cleared the air and cleared the atmospheres and warmed the climate and calmed the winds."[39] The test-ban treaty had allayed many of the doubts about Russian intentions.

Following the signing of the treaty came a number of new proposals to improve East-West relations and further extend the *détente*. While none of these materialized in this period, the repeated and frequent offering of various tension-reduction measures had some effect in itself. Actually, hopes rose so quickly that late in August, Secretary of Defense McNamara warned that it was perilous to relax in a "euphoria," and Kennedy cautioned in September that the test ban was "not the millennium."

By late October, almost no new American initiatives were taken, and those of the Soviet Union were not reciprocated. The press referred to a "pause in the

[35]This concept was introduced by Daniel J. Boorstein in *The Image* (New York: Atheneum, 1962), esp. pp. 9–12. A pseudo-event has the following characteristics: it is not spontaneously initiated; it is manufactured largely for publicity purposes; and it is intended to be a self-fulfilling prophecy, to create its own consequences.

[36]*Washington Post,* September 16, 1963.

[37]*New York Times,* August 4, 1963, p. 1E.

[38]*Ibid.,* August 11, 1963, p. 3E.

[39]*Ibid.,* September 22, 1963, p. 8E.

thaw"; there was a marked slow-down in tension reduction though efforts continued, as we shall see, to preserve the measure of *détente* that had been achieved. The assassination of President Kennedy and the beginning of the election year ushered in a year of more or less stable semi-*détente.*

What are the conclusions from this brief and incomplete test of the theory? Certain of the central hypotheses were supported: (*a*) unilateral gestures were reciprocated; (*b*) reciprocations were proportional; (*c*) unilaterally reciprocated gestures reduced tensions; (*d*) unilaterally reciprocated gestures were followed by multilateral-simultaneous measures, which further reduced tensions; (*e*) initiatives were "suspected," but, when continued, they "got across"; (*f*) the gestures and responses created a psychological momentum that pressured for more measures, a reversal of the cold war or hostility spiral; (*g*) when measures were stopped, tension reduction ceased (we shall see the significance of this point below); (*h*) the relatively more consequential acts were initiated multilaterally or were transformed from an initially informal, unilaterally reciprocated basis to a formal, multilateral one.[40]

Not all the assumptions and derivations of the theory were as clearly supported. Most important, it is impossible to tell, without re-running history for "control" purposes, whether multilateral negotiations could have been successfully undertaken without the "atmosphere" first having been improved by unilateral steps. The fact, however, that both the test treaty and the space ban were first introduced on a unilateral-reciprocal basis and that even in the reduced tension condition these measures were hard to defend before Congress, suggests that, if not preceded by tension reduction, they either might have failed, or the risks of failure would have been sufficiently high for the Administration to refrain from introducing them. (Attempts to advance a test ban in earlier periods failed.)[41]

Also, the Kennedy experiment was only a partial application of the theory: the gestures were not the clear signals a full test of theory would require. Thus, for instance, to gain the Senate's consent for a test-ban treaty, its value for American security was stressed.[42] It would allow, it was said, stopping of testing while we were ahead both in number of tests and weapons technology. Further, President Kennedy made it clear that the United States would "vigorously and diligently" pursue its underground nuclear test program.[43] The wheat deal was interpreted in a similar fashion,[44] e.g., as a show of Russia's weakness. Further, during the

---

[40]*The Hard Way to Peace, op. cit.,* pp. 99 ff. That this was necessary was a point of some debate. See Waskow, *op. cit.,* pp. 75 ff.

[41]Spanier and Nogee, *op. cit.,* chap. VI.

[42]United States Senate, Committee on Foreign Relations, *Nuclear Test Ban Treaty: Hearings on Executive M, 88th Congress, 1st Session, August 12-17* (Washington, D.C.: G.P.O., 1963), pp. 97–109.

[43]*Documents . . . , op. cit.,* 1963, no. 27.

[44]*New York Times,* October 14, 1963, p. 1E.

whole period, American observers provided various interpretations of the gestures as other than efforts to communicate a desire for peaceful co-existence (e.g., the *détente* exacerbates the Soviet-Sino rift). While a policy if often supported by a large variety of arguments, and the self-serving ones are usually emphasized when facing Congress, their preponderance could not but have had negative side-effects on Soviet-American relations. Also, the same gestures would have been more effective had they been introduced with less hesitation, and if Soviet initiatives had been met with less ambivalence.

Above all, since the process was halted, one cannot tell whether psychological measures open the door to "real" give-and-take or are essentially meaningless in the absence of basic and lasting settlements of differences and conflicts. The fact remains, however, that gestures that were almost purely psychological in nature led to an American-Soviet semi-*détente* lasting from June 1963 until now. Whether more of the same could have brought about more fundamental changes cannot be learned from this case.

ALTERNATIVE EXPLANATIONS

Even though the adoption of the measures advocated by the theory yielded the expected psychological results, there still remains the possibility of spuriousness; i.e., that the result was produced by factors other than those specified by the theory. We need, then, to ask what other factors could account for the *détente*? Two alternative sources of tension reduction most often cited are examined below; we shall see that they do not invalidate the claim that the unilateral-initiatives approach deserves credit for the *détente*. It is, however, always possible to claim that still another factor was at work; there is no final test against spuriousness. But until it is actually shown that there was another factor that caused the specified effects, we are justified in holding that the theory has been strengthened by the Kennedy experiment. This is especially so, as we can trace directly the contribution of the unilateral initiatives to the *détente*.

The first alternative explanation is that of catharsis. According to this theory, the door was opened for a *détente* after the Cuban blockade discharged a large amount of frustration that Americans had accumulated over the cold war years. Traditionally, Americans have expected that wars will be short, end with an American victory, followed by the restoration of peace. In contrast, the cold war required a continual state of mobilization and prolonged tensions without the prospect of victory. The resulting frustration was deepened by the widely held belief that the Communists were more successful than the West in Asia, Latin America, and Africa. Under the pressure of these frustrations, it is often suggested, efforts to reach accommodation with Russia became viewed as showing weakness, and a "tough" *verbal* posture was popular. The establishment of a Communist government in Cuba, Soviet successes in space, the fiasco of the 1961 Bay of Pigs invasion, and the positioning of Soviet missiles in Cuba in 1962 all further deepened American frustration. While initially the 1962 blockade raised many fears, once it proved not to lead to war and to yield a Soviet retreat, it became the first American victory in a long time. While the blockade's successes were widely viewed as supporting the "tough" line, suggesting that power politics could be used in the nuclear age, the psychological effect was in the opposite direction, one of cathartic release. One of the values of the psychological line of analysis is to highlight such differences between verbal postures and underlying emotional commitments. Fierce posture on one level need not be accompanied with the same on the other. "Tough" words may cover a moderate feeling. In this case, it is said, the Cuban showdown increased the American public's emotional willingness to accept arms control negotiations with the Soviet Union.

The other interpretation associates the initiation of the *détente* with the unfolding of a different psychological process—the effects of the increased visibility of the disintegration of the blocs. In 1962 Communist China attacked the Soviet Union publicly, criticizing Soviet involvement in Cuba as "adventurism" and its retreat as "defeatism." Russia, like America, continued its economic and military support to India when it came under Chinese attack in 1962. About the same time, the American-French dispute forced itself on the public's attention.

Initially, the popular American press, apparently reflecting the opinion of the public at large, tended to ignore or regard as a "put-up job" the split in the East and to underplay the rift in the West. But the rifts finally gained recognition with the hostile rejection of Mao and of De Gaulle partially replacing that earlier focused on the Soviet Union. The Soviets now seemed "reasonable" and "responsible" compared to Communist China, for Russia appeared willing to share with us the concern over nuclear proliferation and dangers of war provoked by over-eager allies.

Some evidence to support the effect of this bifurcation of the bloc images in generating the *détente* can be seen in the press. A typical *New York Times* Sunday review-of-the-news section ran the following captions: "Conflict in East," "Russia vs. China," and "U.S. vs. France"; and last—"East vs. West."[45] Direct reporting of the relationship between changes in the intra-bloc situation and those which were inter-bloc was also common. For example:

> The answer seems to hinge on whether Premier Khrushchev really wants a test ban. One school of thought is that he does. The argument runs that Moscow's relations with Peking have reached the point virtually of open rupture. Consequently, Premier Khrushchev is thought to be willing to deal with the

[45]*Ibid.,* July 7, 1963, p. 1E.

West, especially if one result of such dealings might be increased difficulty for Peking in acquiring nuclear capability.[46]

It is not implied that the only effect of the decline in the solidarity of the blocs was to bring the two superpowers closer to each other. In reality, the Soviet Union was occasionally reluctant to agree to American proposals so as not to lose points in its fight with China over control of the Communist movement in third countries. Similarly, the United States was not always eager to agree to Soviet initiatives for fear of displeasing West Germany and thus playing into the hands of France. But the consciousness of deep differences of interest within the blocs, even when they agitated against agreement between the bloc leaders, had the psychological effect of reducing inter-bloc tensions. The recognition of the splits in the alliances undermined the prevailing simplistic image of the forces of light fighting the forces of darkness. As a result, it is suggested, the ideological fervor of the international atmosphere declined, tension was reduced, and *détente* was enhanced.

Such a weakening of ideological fervor is important for the initiation of negotiations which give and take, because otherwise politicians find it hard to face their voters with the outcomes of the negotiations. As long as any give and take, even when completely symmetrical, tends to be viewed as a concession, if not outright appeasement, ideological disarmament is needed to allow the public to see that some genuine bargaining is possible, and that certain kinds of accommodations serve both sides to the disadvantage of neither.

At the same time, bifurcation of the bloc images shifted the focus of the xenophobia. Regarding the Communist camp, China became, with considerable disregard of its actual foreign policy, the villain; in the West, the focus of American self-righteousness was now De Gaulle. These two replaced the previous preoccupation with Soviet Russia. Xenophobia, it is suggested, was rechanneled rather than reduced. (Or, more technically, a new object was substituted rather than the drive extinguished or significantly weakened.)

All these psychological processes might have been feeding into each other. Catharsis, bifurcation of images, and unilateral initiatives might all have contributed to the *détente* as well as to each other. For instance, catharsis might have eased the initiation of a policy of unilateral initiatives, and in turn the resultant reduction of inter-bloc tensions accelerated bifurcation of the bloc images, which made easier the further reduction of tensions through additional unilateral initiatives.

We still remain with the difficult question of the relative weight of the three processes in bringing about the *détente*. While it is impossible to answer this question with precision, it seems that while catharsis and bifurcation might have helped, they were not necessary prerequisites to the resultant situation; unilateral

[46]*Ibid.* See also August 14, 1963, p. 1E, and August 25, 1963, p. 4.

initiatives alone could have produced the effect. The best evidence for this is found in the examination of two other occasions in which a thaw was achieved— the 1959 Camp David spirit, and the 1955 Geneva spirit. These cannot be analyzed within the limits of this paper, but they seem to show the validity of the assertion that unilateral initiatives can bring about a *détente* without the support of the other two psychological processes.

It also should be noted that the 1963–64 thaw did not immediately follow the termination of the Cuban crisis, in the sense that no *détente* existed between November 1962 and June 1963 (though this still would not rule out the role of catharsis as a preparatory condition). Similarly, while the bifurcation of the bloc images was deepened in 1962, it existed before, and was as much caused by the *détente* as it effected the *détente*. Above all, the effect can be most directly traced to the unilateral initiatives; it started with them, grew as they grew, and slowed down only as they decreased.

THE EFFECTS OF SABOTAGE

Sabbotage is a traditional tool of foreign policy, going back at least to the ancient Greek states. In the age of mass democracies, one of its forms is that of creating international pseudo-events to affect the psychological atmosphere in a direction counter to that of the prevailing policy. In some formulations of the psychological theory, this problem is disregarded, for nations are conceived as analogous to individuals, thus being able to shift policies in the manner of one man changing his mind.[47] In formulations which take into account the existence of vested interests in the continuation of inter-bloc tensions, both overt opposition to tension reduction and sabotage are expected.[48] The lesson of the U-2 flight which triggered the termination of the 1959 thaw was analyzed before the 1963–64 *détente* took place. It showed the need of policymakers to realize that many governmental activities have a communicative value, and that if a government seeks to communicate that it has shifted to a new posture, measures are to be taken to ensure that no activities are undertaken or continued that conflict with the new posture. This point is to be emphasized, as some inconsistency is often deliberately introduced in the policy of most countries. For example, the U.S. position on M.L.F. for a while attempted to assure the Russians that there would be no proliferation of arms while at the same time encouraging the West Germans to hope for some control of nuclear weapons. But when one engages in

---

[47] Asked by a journalist if he believed that "nations act like people," Osgood is quoted as having answered, "I do." Herzog, *op. cit.*, p. 158.

[48] *The Hard Way to Peace, op. cit.*, p. 104.

psychological campaigns, consistency has a high value because "out-of-character" steps largely undermine the effect of the campaign on recipients who, the psychological theory suggests, are suspicious to begin with.

The foregoing discussion assumes that the U-2 flights were continued due to an oversight (neglecting to cancel this "hostile" activity as the change in posture took place), or were a planned attempt to reap the benefits of continued violations of Soviet territories on one level, while trying to reduce tensions on another. If, on the other hand, the flights were an act of sabotage by a service or group within it not concurring with the change in policy, then it would seem that if the American government is to follow a tension-reduction policy, a tightening of internal controls is necessary.[49]

The lesson of the U-2 incident is that it is necessary to anticipate both unwitting and deliberate sabotages and prepare a proper response. Several observers suggested that Premier Khrushchev was, for domestic reasons, looking for a way out of the 1959 *détente* and that the U-2 just provided an excuse. But the possibility that the Russian premier was really embarrassed before his fellow members of the powerful Presidium, some of whom objected to the *détente,* cannot be ruled out. That would suggest that he had not foreseen an act of sabotage and was not prepared to act in a way that would diffuse its chilling effect on the thaw. Further, Eisenhower's insistence that he personally ordered the flight and his refusal to make apologetic comments, behavior which is common in such circumstances, made Khrushchev's accommodation in favor of continuation of the *détente* more difficult—if he desired to continue. It also gave him a ready excuse if he were looking for one, although in this case he might sooner or later have found one anyway. The fact that Khrushchev was unwilling to terminate the Camp David atmosphere without such an excuse, suggests that he was not particularly anxious to terminate it at all. Moreover, had time been gained by not providing such an excuse, the pro-*détente* motives and forces might have prevailed. Drawing on all this, I suggested in 1962 that unilateral initiatives be guarded against sabotage, and, if it occurred anyway, the sabotage should be rapidly defused rather than allowed to damage the *détente.*[50]

We have already seen that domestic forces and politics as well as allies prevented the United States from giving a clear signal of a shift to a Strategy for Peace. Several leading Democratic senators and important representatives of the military objected to the test-ban treaty; the wheat deal was made with much hesitation and debate; and various tension-provoking interpretations were given to the *détente* policy. Direct acts of sabotage also occurred, but their effect on the

---

[49]Sabotage has been suggested as an explanation for the out-of-character "tailgate" incident outside Berlin in October 1963. See Jean E. Smith, "Berlin, the Erosion of a Principle," *Reporter,* November 21, 1963, pp. 32–37.

[50]*The Hard Way to Peace, op. cit.,* pp. 104–5.

détente was much more limited than the U-2 flight; they were treated more in accord with the theory.

An example of an "out-of-character" event is found in a note struck by President Kennedy himself, when, during a speech at West Berlin's City Hall on the twenty-sixth of June, he not only described himself as a Berliner and repeated the usual statements regarding America's commitment to Germany's defense but added, in tones familiar to the pre-*détente* period:

> There are many people in the world who really don't understand—or say they don't—what is the great issue between the free world and the Communist world. Let them come to Berlin.
>
> There are some who say that Communism is the wave of the future. Let them come to Berlin.
>
> And there are some who say in Europe and elsewhere—"We can work with the communists." Let them come to Berlin.
>
> And there are even a few who say it's true that Communism is an evil system but it permits us to make economic progress. Let them come to Berlin.

Khrushchev, giving a counter speech a few days later in East Berlin on the occasion of Ulbricht's birthday, chose not to reciprocate in kind, and thus the incident was soon forgotten.

The "tailgate" clash on the route to West Berlin on October 10–12 came closer to undermining the Kennedy experiment. Briefly, what happened was that the Americans riding in a convoy to West Berlin refused to dismount for a head count, and the Russians would not allow them to pass. The Russians claimed they usually were granted the right to count the passengers, but the West claimed this was the case only if more than thirty soldiers were involved, and there were fewer this time. (When fewer, the Russians looked over the tail-gate, hence the name of the incident.) When the Russians countered that there were more than thirty, the United States answered that the balance were civilian drivers who did not "count"; the Russians claimed that they did. The Americans tried to break through; the Russians blocked the route with armed carriers. Headlines around the world projected for two days an image of two sides standing "eyeball to eyeball," finger on the trigger, in a typical cold war test of will, lacking any *détente*-like spirit. Finally, the crisis was resolved, and the convoy was allowed to pass.

Although who was to blame for the incident is by no means clear, this is of little importance to the analysis of its effect on America-Russia relations: tensions mounted rather than declined, and to most American newspaper readers the fault was completely Russian, and the senselessness of the act amidst a *détente* heightened anew their suspicions of Russia's good faith. The *New York Times* declared that "the provocative Soviet behavior on this matter has set back the cause of the *détente,* reinforced Western suspicion of Moscow."[51] The *Herald Tribune's* editorial on October 12 was entitled, "The Soviet Mask Slips." It claimed that "the wholly unjustifiable display of Soviet pettifogging at the entrance of Berlin, then, will be taken by the American government and people as an indication that the protestations of Mr. Khrushchev and of Mr. Gromyko concerning Russia's desire for more friendly relations with the U.S. are just a mask."

But once the incident was settled, the explanation encouraged by Washington was that there was a "misunderstanding" about the rules and not a new Soviet pressure on the West or a shift in Russian policy away from *détente.*[52] Others attributed the incident to abuse of authority by low-ranking Soviet officers. One reliable American journal published an account that provided evidence suggesting the issue was largely caused by American army officers.[53] A second interpretation, seeking to defuse the effects of the incident, was that Berlin was an "abnormal" situation, excluded from the general *détente* the Russians otherwise did favor.[54] While the incident left the *détente* marred, especially as it was about to be slowed down anyway, these interpretations, encouraged by Washington and London, succeeded in restricting its damage. This was in sharp contrast to the impact of the U-2 flight.

A second incident, which occurred on October 31, 1963, had almost exactly the same pattern. An American scholar, Professor Frederick C. Barghoorn, was arrested in Moscow on espionage charges. President Kennedy stated that the charges were "unwarranted and unjustified" and that they "badly damaged" Soviet-American relations. Western newspapers again asked if Russia were shifting away from the conciliatory "Spirit of Moscow," and the conservative press sounded its "I told you so" horns. The professor was released, and it was almost immediately suggested that "the arrest might have been carried out by security officers . . . anxious to throw a monkey wrench into Premier Khrushchev's policy of 'coexistence' with the West."[55] Khrushchev chose not to identify with the arrest but let the Professor go because of the "personal concern" of President Kennedy.[56] Later, although the incident had left its mark, its impact was, once again, defused. American sources further helped to dissipate the resultant tensions by suggesting that "they still found it conceivable that something had occurred to arouse their [the Russians'] suspicions about the professor."[57] In each case, then, when a

[51] *New York Times,* October 13, 1963, p. 8E.
[52] *Ibid.,* October 20, 1963, p. 6E.
[53] *Reporter,* November 21, 1963, p. 36.
[54] *New York Times,* October 20, 1963, p. 6E.
[55] *Ibid.,* November 17, 1963, p. 1E.
[56] *Ibid.*
[57] *Ibid.,* November 16, 1963, p. 3.

dissonant note was sounded during the Kennedy experiment, it was soon softened and modified to protect the main theme. Thus, both the fragility of the *détente* and the mechanisms to safeguard it were demonstrated.

PSYCHOLOGICAL VS. "REAL" FACTORS

By far the most difficult question to answer is what gains can be achieved from a *détente* in other than psychological terms. The 1959 *détente* was the shortest and yielded nothing; the 1955 *détente* was longer and brought about the neutralization of Austria, the main instance since World War II in which territory held by the Red Army was released to a society with Western institutions. There is a widely held belief that the 1955 *détente* could have yielded much more, possibly an arrangement regarding Germany and Berlin, but this must remain speculation. The 1963 *détente* led to a partial test ban and a ban on the orbiting of weapons of mass destruction, both steps of largely psychological value. Whether or not it did prepare the ground for additional steps is yet unknown.

There remains a more general question which is of a different order from the analysis of any one period and its psychology: how important are psychological factors in affecting international behavior? Answers range from theories which imply these factors are all-important to those which view the determinants of international relations to be exclusively "real" factors. The correct view is probably somewhere between the extreme positions. Certainly factors other than psychology are relevant, and it can easily be demonstrated that psychological factors have "real" consequences. The question then is one of the *relative* importance of these factors.

While we are unable to provide a definite answer to this question, several comments can be made. First, the advent of nationalism and mass media has increased the importance of psychological forces. Second, the consequences of these forces seem to have increased with the introduction of nuclear deterrence forces, because deterrence is itself a psychological concept and is therefore affected by such factors as credibility, fear, and misperception.

In addition, the present study suggests that psychological forces are most important when the sides wish to *initiate* a change in policy but seem not to be strong enough to *sustain* the change when it is not supported by other factors. When other processes agitate for change (e.g., a new congruence in Soviet-American interests with regard to the spread of nuclear arms), a modification of psychological variables in the same direction makes the new policy easier to introduce. Moreover, the psychological forces might get somewhat "out-of-hand" and bring about changes in policy above and beyond what other considerations seem to suggest. (For example, in 1958 the United States sought to *negotiate* a moratorium on nuclear testing but not to bring about its initiation. When Russia suddenly declared a moratorium unilaterally, the United States felt it had no choice but to reciprocate. This did not, however, lead to additional arms control measures.) On the other hand, it seems that the psychological factors are basically well in hand; they cannot be used to bring about a policy that is a major departure from the policy other forces favor. Thus, in general, psychological factors have *significant auxiliary* and *limited independent* effects.

A study of the "actors" who are affected by psychological factors might in large part illuminate the reasons for the preceding statement. Most statements about "international tensions" are actually referring to states of mind of citizens rather than relations among nations or among the governing elites of the nations.[58] The kind and degree of influence of the citizenry on foreign policy is a complicated question that cannot be explored here. But it might be suggested that to a great extent *the effect of psychological factors on international behavior of a state is that of the citizens on foreign policy-making elites.* In the pre-nationalist stage, the mass of the citizens had little effect on foreign policy, and psychological factors were, therefore, relatively unimportant. In totalitarian societies, citizens have less influence on foreign policy than in democratic ones; hence psychological factors are relatively less consequential there.

In democratic societies, public opinion is determined through a complicated process in which the public, its local leaders, the mass media, the national elites, and various social and economic processes are working on each other. In the short run, one of the most outstanding features is that the national leadership is confronted with the public opinion it helped to crystallize at earlier points in time. Once a context (or *gestalt*) is established, there is a demand for consistency. Seeming inconsistency activates various psychological processes, such as the feeling of betrayal. Thus, at various points American Administrations have felt they could ill-afford politically to support the admission of Communist China to the United Nations, because the American public was educated against it, and the Administration believed that no amount of short-run explanation could change public opinion to make the political costs low enough. The Kennedy experiment, it seems, was much more oriented toward the American people than toward the Russians or any international "tensions." Its primary purpose, it seems, was not to affect international relations directly but to increase the range of options the Kennedy Administration could take up without running high political risks from a public steeped in cold war psychology. Thus the policy of unilateral initiatives can be said to have worked, and the experiment to have been successful. A wider range of foreign policy options was made politically feasible.

---

[58]For a study of psychological factors affecting international relations by affecting the interaction of national representatives, see Bryant Wedge and Cyril Muromcew, "Psychological Factors in Soviet Disarmament Negotiation," *Journal of Conflict Resolution,* 9 (March 1965), 18–37.

Part IV

RELATIVELY INSTITUTIONALIZED INTERNATIONAL RELATIONS

A new set of processes and conditions will now be added to those illustrated in the preceding selections. In this Part the focus of attention is upon regular patterns of interaction sustained by normative consensus and by legitimate sanctions. We will consider some aspects of such patterns, rudimentary as they may be; we wish to consider how they emerge, what forms they assume, and what some of their consequences are. This may be studied on the world level or within a group of countries, as in the case of a region or political alliance.

Fully developed institutionalized patterns entail rules of conduct, concrete organizations embodying and sanctioning the rules, and underlying social relations maintaining and reinforcing the patterns. These elements are respectively emphasized in studies of international law, international organizations, and international integration. These elements are all interdependent, but since analysis requires abstraction, each element may be the subject of special emphasis. With the selection of one or another emphasis, a different range of phenomena is given attention.

In the study of international law, attention is usually given to the rules of international conduct. But they are hardly institutionalized to the same degree as are the laws within a complex society.[1] There is no continuing legislative or other organization to make, modify, interpret, or enforce the rules. The rules are usually made by agreement among governments and are maintained by the requirements of reciprocity—the self-interest of the governments. The International Court of Justice is circumscribed in the cases presented to it and its success in making adjudications.[2] Yet the consensus represented by international law increases

[1]Morton A. Kaplan and Nicholas deB. Katzenbach, *The Political Foundations of International Law* (New York: John Wiley and Sons, 1961), Juris A. Lejnieks, "The Nomenclature of Treaties: A Quantitative Analysis," *The Texas International Law Forum,* II (Summer, 1966), pp. 175–188; and George Scharzenberger, *The Frontiers of International Law* (London: Stevens and Sons, 1962).

[2]See Selection 30 in this book and R. P. Anand, "Execution of International Judicial Awards: Experience Since 1945," *University of Pittsburgh Law Review,* 26 (June, 1965), pp. 671–703.

predictability and probably thus prevents minor controversies from escalating into major conflicts. In recent years the rules have become increasingly subjected to discussion and investigation through the perspectives of the social sciences.[3]

Institutionalized relations that are more than rudimentary require some concrete organizational expression. The ordering of relations within an organization specifies the rules and possible sanctions about which consensus exists. The literature on international organizations is vast, although much of it is descriptive—reporting upon the formal structure and activities of the organizations. Increasingly, however, attention is being given to the informal as well as formal processes within organizations, unintended as well as intended consequences, and the empirical analysis of the relationship between different organizational forms and the social relations among countries and their representatives participating in the organization.

The previous selections reported about characteristics of political units relevant to international relations and about the processes of interaction among different peoples and governments. Those conditions and processes both affect and are affected by institutionalization as expressed in international law, international organization, and unification. Repeated patterns of activity are expected to continue and such expectations become constraints. This is the beginning of institutionalization. Once institutionalization has occurred, the constraint upon conduct is great. But if the factors which determined the patterns are so changed that new patterns begin to occur frequently, the strain upon the institutionalized patterns may become too great, and the rules for conduct either break down or are altered.

All this obviously is related to international conflict as expressed in organized violence. Although a fully institutionalized political unit may still be disrupted by violence, as in civil war, this is less likely or of lesser magnitude than war between regimes. Even pairs of countries with relatively little formal institutionalized mechanisms, given a sufficiently high degree of integration and within the context of a given international system, are unlikely to become engaged in warfare—for example, the United States and Canada today. Nevertheless, in general, institutionalized relations makes intense conflict less likely and provides relatively effective means of resolution without resorting to war.

In Chapter Eight the selections pertain to the development and structure of international organizations and to integration at the world and regional levels. It

---

[3]Kaplan and Katzenbach, *op. cit.*; Schwarzenberger, *op. cit.*; Myres S. McDougal and Associates, *Studies in World Public Order* (New Haven, Conn.: Yale University Press, 1960); William D. Coplin, "International Law and Assumptions about the State System," *World Politics*, XVII (July, 1965), pp. 615–633; Michael Barkun, "International Norms: An Interdisciplinary Approach," *Background*, 8 (August, 1964), pp. 121–130; Vilhelm Aubert, "Competition and Dissensus: Two Types of Conflict and Conflict Resolution," *The Journal of Conflict Resolution,* 7 (March, 1963), pp. 26–42.

might seem a truism that cultural, political, social, and economic similarity among societies increases the likelihood of the societies and their representative successfully establishing joint institutions or a more embracing union. Yet this is not the case. It depends upon what is shared *and* what can be exchanged; it also depends upon the form and content of the organizations and unions; finally, it depends upon the pre-existing patterns of communication and exchange.[4] Presumably, a high ratio of common and complementary interests to conflicting ones, and homogeneity in cultural and political styles facilitating communication would make possible an organization or union to which much authority may be delegated; but with less conducive conditions, an organization or union with less centralized authority might also succeed.

The complexity of factors involved in the establishment of an organization or union means that the creation of an appropriate organizational form dealing with an appropriate area of concern is critical. It also means that the timing of each step in the establishment of an organization is equally crucial. This can be illustrated in the ups and downs of the general movement toward European union. The creation of the European Coal and Steel Community in 1952 depended upon many underlying social relations, but it also depended upon the particular world international system at the time, and the ingenuity of the organizational objectives and forms. The next major step in the movement toward union was the effort to establish the European Defense Community; in 1954 that effort failed.[5] Only in 1957, when the European Economic Community was fashioned, was a major forward step in the movement toward union successfully taken.

Etzioni (Selection 24) provides a general explanation for the emergence of new unions and their organizations. Note his attention to the relative power and resources among the units constituting a union. He then discusses the alternative ways in which a more embracing and centralized union may occur. These ideas are examined in more detail in his book examining four unions: The United Arab Republic, the Federation of the West Indies, the Nordic Council, and the European

---

[4]Louis Kriesberg, "Internal Differentiation and the Establishment of Organizations," *Institutions and the Person: Essays Presented to Everett Hughes,* Howard S. Becker, David Riesman, Blanche Geer, and Robert S. Weiss (eds.) (Chicago, Ill.: Aldine Press, 1968); Ernst B. Haas, *The Uniting of Europe,* (Stanford, Cal.: Stanford University Press, 1958); Karl W. Deutsch et. al., *Political Community and the North Atlantic Area* (Princeton, N.J.: Princeton University Press, 1957); Robert W. Gregg, "The UN Regional Commissions and Integration in the Underdeveloped Regions," *International Organization,* XX (Spring, 1966), pp. 208–232; and David Mitrany, *The Progress of International Organization* (New Haven, Conn.: Yale University Press, 1933).

[5]On the failure of EDC, see Daniel Lerner and Raymond Aron, *France Defeats EDC* (New York: Frederick A. Praeger, 1957); and F.S.C. Northrop, *European Union and United States Foreign Policy: A Study in Sociological Jurisprudence* (New York: The Macmillan Co., 1954). Also see Edward A. Shils, "The Failure of the UN Atomic Energy Commission: An Interpretation," *The University of Chicago Law Review,* XV (Summer, 1948), pp. 855–876.

Economic Community.[6] The establishment of an international organization or union does not ensure its growth or even survival. A viable and expanding union or organization provides payoffs to significant participating units and subunits. It creates conditions which give them some vested interest in the organization or union.[7]

Etzioni's analysis is concerned with regional unions. One may well ask whether such unions facilitate or inhibit integration at the world level. One may argue that the creation of successful new superunits simply draws clearer lines in dividing the world into potentially warring parties. It is also arguable that the channeling of interaction among leaders of such super units reduces the number of persons needed to agree upon still wider unions.[8] This suggests an implication of Galtung's findings (Selection 16) which he does not stress. If interaction between major power blocs is largely channeled through the leaders of the blocs, that regularity may facilitate the development of norms about the interaction.

In Kriesberg's paper (Selection 25) attention is drawn to nongovernmental international organizations. These have been increasing at a rapid rate and provide another set of integrating bonds (see Selections 13 and 26).[9] In addition to such nonprofit, nongovernmental relations, many business corporations operate at an international level and constitute another set of relations only partly influenced and controlled by political regimes.[10]

The analysis by Kriesberg focuses upon the relationship between structural arrangements of organizations as related to the membership composition and the activities of the organizations. The analysis reveals the dilemmas in structuring an organization that maximizes participation, diversity, and viability.

[6]Amitai Etzioni, *Political Unification* (New York: Holt, Rinehart and Winston, 1965).

[7]Haas, *The Uniting of Europe, op. cit.*; Etzioni, *Political Unification, op. cit.*; Louis Kriesberg, "German Public Opinion and the European Coal and Steel Community," *The Public Opinion Quarterly*, XXIII (Spring, 1959), pp. 28–42; Louis Kriesberg, "German Businessmen and Union Leaders and the Schuman Plan," *Social Science*, 35 (April, 1960), pp. 114–121; and Louis Kriesberg, "Die Europaische Gemeinschaft für Kohle und Stahl im Urteil der Deutschen," *Kölner Zeitschrift für Soziologie und Sozialpsycholigie*, 11 (1959), No. 3, pp. 496–516.

[8]See Selection 16. Also see Amitai Etzioni, "The Dialectics of Supranational Unification, *The American Political Science Review*, LVI (December, 1962), pp. 927–935; Louis Kriesberg, "Societal Coordination by Occupational Leaders," *PROD*, III (September, 1959), pp. 34–36.

[9]Paul Smoker, "A Preliminary Study of an International Integrative Subsystem," *International Associations*, 17 (June, 1965), pp. 638–646.

[10]Alvin W. Wolfe, "The African Mineral Industry: Evolution of a Supranational Level of Integration," *Social Problems*, 11 (Fall, 1963), pp. 153–164; Richard J. Barber, "Big, Bigger, Biggest: American Business Goes Global," *The New Republic*, 154 (April 30, 1966), pp. 14–18; and Raymond Vernon, "Multinational Enterprise and National Sovereignty," *Harvard Business Review*, 45 (March-April, 1967), pp. 156–172.

The UN and its affiliated international organizations constitute a major component of the international system. They provide a means for some resource allocation of money and personnel in meeting the health, educational, agricultural, and industrial requirements of the countries of the world.[11] They also provide the means for formal and informal communication with representatives from other countries. Most governments have a greater opportunity for direct contact with representatives of other governments through international organizations than through direct bilateral diplomatic relations.[12] Most visibly, of course, the UN provides mechanisms for the regulation of international conflict (see Selection 29). In the present context, it is noteworthy that the structure and operations of the UN and other international organizations are affected by informal processes as well as the formally enacted agreements. Thus studies have revealed that power differences among the members of the UN are expressed in the voting patterns and committee assignments of the UN Assembly, despite formal equality.[13] This is important, because if the structure of the organization diverged too greatly from the international reality, its effectiveness would be seriously impaired if not destroyed. In many international organizations therefore the formal structure has built in some recognition of the power differences, for example, by having some form of weighted voting. In the case of the UN, the Security Council and the veto power of some countries are such devices.[14]

Finally, Smoker (Selection 26) examines the growth of integration at the world level in relation to arms races and international wars. In discussing arms races, he uses Richardson's equations:

$$\frac{dx}{dt} = ky - ax + g$$

and

$$\frac{dy}{dt} = lx - by + h$$

[11] Walter R. Sharp, "International Bureaucracies and Political Development," *Bureaucracy and Political Development,* Joseph LaPalombara (ed.) (Princeton, N.J.: Princeton University Press, 1963), pp. 441–474.

[12] Chadwick F. Alger and Steven J. Brams, "Patterns of Representation in National Capitals and Intergovernmental Organizations," *World Politics,* XIX (July, 1967), pp. 646–663.

[13] See, for example, Marshal R. Singer and Barton Sensing III, "Elections within the United Nations," *International Organization,* XVII (Autumn, 1963) pp. 901–925; John G. Hadwen and Johan Kaufmann, *How United Nations Decisions Are Made* (New York: Oceana Publications, 1962); Thomas Hovet, Jr., *Bloc Politics in the United Nations* (Cambridge, Mass.: Harvard University Press, 1960); and Hayward R. Alker, Jr., "Dimensions of Conflict in the General Assembly," *American Political Science Review,* LVIII (September, 1964), pp. 642–657.

[14] For some of the possible consequences of representation by management and labor as well as governments in an international organization, see Ernst B. Haas, *World Politics,* XIV (January, 1962), pp. 322–352.

In addition to the explanation in the text, for these equations, the reader is referred to Richardson's own work and the summary by Rapoport.[15] Suffice it to say at this point, the equations state how the preparedness efforts of country x are related to the preparedness of the other country, y, and how y's preparedness efforts are related to x's defenses. Crudely worded, the defense expenditures of each, over time, are a function of the other's defense minus the costs of the defense efforts plus their grievances against the other. Smoker considers what other factors, including the nature of the international system, may constrain the tensions associated with arms races. By relating arms races and the growth of nongovernmental organizations, he attempts to show the mutual interaction between the level of integration of the international system and the escalation of conflict. Smoker also examines patterns of trade between pairs of countries and the countries' later adversary or allied relations in war.

In Chapter Nine, the selections illustrate some of the consequences of international organizations. Two major sets of consequences may be distinguished: (a) those that are related to the manifest objectives of the organization, for example, provision of technical assistance or mediation of conflict; and (b) those that are unintended or are by-products of the major purposes of the organizations, for example, the effects upon the attitudes of participants and changes in the international system.

One way international organizations alter the international system may be illustrated by the proliferation and expansion of the number of international nongovernmental organizations. To some extent international organizations stimulate the creation of additional ones. This occurs through several processes. In response to the creation of an international organization, new interest groups for which organizational expression seems appropriate are created; this may be as countervailing forces, as representatives in relation to the established organization, or as specialized organizations to fill in the gaps in the efforts of the established organization.[16] Established organizations also facilitate the creation of new organizations by providing channels for communication and the discovery of common and complementary interests. Finally, the existence of organizational solutions to problems makes such a solution seem more feasible. This may sometimes lead to the formation of organizations when the underlying conditions are not sufficiently supportive. In that case, organizational survival would be impaired. This may account for the finding that among nongovernmental organizations founded between

---

[15]Lewis F. Richardson, *Arms and Insecurity* (Chicago, Ill.: Quadrangle Books, 1960), and Anatol Rapoport, "Lewis F. Richardson's Mathematical Theory of War," *The Journal of Conflict Resolution*, 1 (September, 1957), pp. 249–304.

[16]For example, see Haas, *The Uniting of Europe, op. cit.*; Lewis L. Lorwin, *The International Labor Movement* (New York: Harper and Bros., 1953); and B. E. Matecki, *Establishment of the International Finance Corporation and United States Policy* (New York: Frederick A. Praeger, 1957.)

1900 and 1914, only about a third survived until 1954; of the organizations established between 1860 and 1899, about 50 percent survived; and of those established after 1914, about 60 percent survived.[17] The optimistic feelings about international relations at the turn of the century may have led to the rapid rate of establishment of organizations during that time as well as their relative lack of durability.

Alger (Selection 27) describes some of the consequences of participation in the UN General Assembly upon the perceptions and attitudes of representatives to the Assembly. For every member of an international organization, the experiences of participation should be a major influence upon their values and beliefs concerning other countries and regimes and the international system. (The processes and conditions discussed in Part II of this book may be reviewed in this light.) This is true for persons serving as delegates, bureaucrats, and experts on contract to provide special services.[18] It should not be assumed, however, that all experiences as participants in an international organization uniformly increase support for the organization or for other participants.

A matter of particular concern is the extent to which participation in an international organization may increase commitment to it, so that it assumes some supranational character. The analysis by Alker (Selection 28) seeks to discover whether or not there is any commitment to the UN as supranational organization. By analyzing the votes in special and emergency special session of the UN General Assembly, Alker concludes that supranationalism is a factor in Assembly decisions.[19]

Finally, Holsti (Selection 29) examines the role of international organizations and other institutionalized as well as noninstitutionalized procedures for resolving international conflicts. Examining the periods 1919-1939 and 1945-1965, he does not find that institutionalized procedures for attempting to settle conflicts are dominant nor that have they increased. Settlement attempts by international organizations have increased, but the percentage of international organizations attempts that were successful has not increased. These sobering findings should at least moderate any hopes that institutionalization and integration are already high and steadily advancing.

---

[17]The data are summarized in Selection 27 and presented in more detail in G. P. Speeckaert, "Introduction," *Les 1,978 Organisations Internationales Fondees depuis le Congres de Vienne* (Brussels: Union des Associations Internationales, 1957).

[18]Ingrid Eide Galtung, "The Status of the Technical Assistance Expert," *Journal of Peace Research* (1966), No. 4, pp. 359-378; and Gerard J. Mangone (ed.), *UN Administration of Economic and Social Programs* (New York: Columbia University Press, 1966).

[19]Also see Cromwell A. Riches, *Majority Rule in International Organization* (Baltimore, Md.: The Johns Hopkins Press, 1940).

CHAPTER EIGHT

Development and Structure

24. THE EPIGENESIS OF POLITICAL COMMUNITIES AT THE INTERNATIONAL LEVEL

Amitai Etzioni

A MODEL FOR THE STUDY OF POLITICAL UNIFICATION

Historical and Contemporary Unifications

So long as international relations are governed by highly calculative orientations, or by the exercise of force, there is relatively little that sociology can contribute to their study. However, during recent decades international relations seem to have changed: Ideology became a major force; non-rational ties among nations were more common; and, recently, institutional bridges became more numerous. Thus, international relations gradually have become more amenable to sociological analysis. Of these trends, probably the most interesting to the sociologist is the

SOURCE. Amitai Etzioni, "The Epigenesis of Political Communities at the International Level," in *American Journal of Sociology*, LXVIII (January, 1963), pp. 407–421. Reprinted by permission of the author and The University of Chicago Press. Copyright 1963 by The University of Chicago Press.

[1]This article was written while the author was on the staff of the Institute of War and Peace Studies at Columbia University.

formation of new unions whose members are nations [e.g., the European Economic Community (EEC)] .

The EEC is by no means an extreme case. There have been many "historical" unions in which units that were previously autonomous merged to such a degree that today they are considered as one unit (e.g., Switzerland, the United States, Italy, Germany); and there are quite a few contemporary unifications where the new community is just emerging and is far from complete (e.g., the Scandinavian community; East European one), exists as a treaty and formal organization rather than as a full-fledged sociological entity (e.g., the Ghana-Guinea-Mali union, the Latin American Free Trade Area), or is so tenuous that it is more likely to collapse than to reach fuller integration (e.g., the Federation of Nyasaland, Rhodesia).

The emerging communities are frequently referred to as supranational communities, a term that is misleading since it implies that the merging units are nations. Actually, many of the historical unifications occurred before the units were sanctified by nationalism (e.g., the Italian cities; the American colonies), and even contemporary unions are not necessarily unions of nations (e.g., the federation of Eritrea with Ethiopia, the formation of the Federation of Nigeria, and the merger of Southern Cameroons with the Cameroon Republic). Moreover, analytically the emergence of a nation state from several tribes, villages, or feudal states—let us say in contemporary Ghana, India, or late medieval France—is in many ways similar to supranational unification. Hence, our concern is with unification of political units that previously shared few or no political bonds. The degree to which these units have been foci of identification for their populations and the degree to which the normative substance of this identification was secular-historical of the kind that marks nationalism are two variables of our analysis, not part of the definition of the concept. Therefore, we refer to the emerging entities simply as political communities and to the process as one of unification. The term "unions" refers to entities that seem to develop in the direction of a political community but have not reached such a high level of integration.

Epigenesis Versus Preformism

A strategy often used in sociological studies of international relations is to draw on theories developed in the study of interaction among other social units, bearing in mind the special nature of the subject to which they are applied, and checking whether additional variables have to be introduced or whether the theories require revision in view of the new data. Here we draw on a sociological theory of change.

Most studies of social change presuppose the existence of a unit, and ask: How does it change, why, and in what direction? The analytical framework frequently used for this analysis of social dynamics is the *differentiation model,*[2] which assumes that the "primitive" social unit contains, in embryonic form, fused together, all the basic modes of social relations that later become structurally differentiated. While relations orginally fused gain their own subunits, no new functions are served or new modes of interaction are molded. There are, for instance, some universalistic relations in the most primitive tribe. According to this viewpoint, every social unit, if it is to exist, must fulfil a given set of functions, those of adaptation, allocation, social and normative integration. On the individual level, the evolution from infancy to maturity can be analyzed in terms of the differentiation of the personality.[3] On the societal level, the evolution of a primitive society, from a traditional into a modern one, is also seen as a differentiation process. All societal functions are fulfilled by the primitive tribe; they merely become structurally differentiated; that is, they gain personnel, social units, and organizational structures of their own. Religious institutions gain churches, educational institutions gain schools, economic institutions gain corporations, and so forth.

Philosophers and biologists have long pointed out that there is an alternative model for the study of change. While Bonnet, Haller, and Malpighi represented the differentiation (or preformism) approach, according to which the first unit or seed possesses in miniature all the patterns of the mature plant, Harvey, Wolff, and Goethe advanced the accumulation (or epigenesis) approach, according to which "adult" units emerge through a process in which parts that carry out new functions are added to existing ones, until the entire unit is assembled. Earlier parts do not include the "representation" of later ones.

The two processes are mutually exclusive in the sense that new units are either institutional "embodiments" of old functions or serve new ones. They may occur at different times in the same social unit: for example, a unit may first follow a preformistic model of development, then shift to an epigenetic model (or the other way around); or it may simultaneously develop some subunits following one model and some following the other. But unlike the particle and wave theories, which are used to explain the same light phenomena, the change pattern of all

---

[2]This model is applied to the study of small groups by Robert F. Bales and Philip E. Slater, "Role Differentiation in Small Decision-making Groups," in Talcott Parsons, Robert F. Bales, and Edward A. Shils, *Working Papers in the Theory of Action* (Glencoe, Ill.: Free Press, 1953); to socialization process by Parsons, Bales, et al., *Family, Socialization and Interaction Process* (Glencoe, Ill.: Free Press, 1953), chap. iv; to industrialization by Neil Smelser, *Social Change in the Industrial Revolution* (Chicago: University of Chicago Press, 1959); to the study of the family by Morris Zelditch, Jr., "Role Differentiation in the Nuclear Family: A Comparative Study," in *Family, Socialization . . . , op. cit.,* pp. 307–51, and by Smelser, *op. cit.,* chaps. viii–x; to the study of elites by Amitai Etzioni, "The Functional Differentiation of Elites in the *Kibbutz," American Journal of Sociology,* LXIX (1959), 476–87; and to the study of underdeveloped countries by Neil Smelser, "Toward a Theory of Modernization," in Amitai and Eva Etzioni (eds.), *Social Change: Sources, Patterns and Consequences* (New York: Harper and Row, 1963).

[3]*Family, Socialization . . . , op. cit.,* chap. iv.

sociological units of which we are aware follows at any given period either a differentiation *or* an accumulation model.

Until now sociology focused almost exclusively on differentiation models. There are, however, several social units whose development cannot be adequately accounted for by a preformistic model. This article presents an outline of an alternative model, drawing for illustration on the formation of various social units, in particular, international unions. The following questions are asked: (1) Where is the power located that controls the accumulation process? (2) What form does the process itself take? (3) What sector is introduced first? (4) How does this affect subsequent development of sectors? (5) What sequences does the entire process follow? (6) What kinds of "products" do different accumulation (or epigenesis) processes produce? It is essential to bear in mind constantly the peculiar system that does not exist but which the potential members are gradually building up. It is like studying the effect of social relations among students in their post-graduate life before they have graduated.

POWER AND EPIGENESIS

Locus of Power: Elitism and Internalization

The main distinction between performism and epigenesis is the function that new subunits serve; that is, old functions versus new ones. Determining the structural location of the power that controls the development of a social unit, especially that of new subunits, is essential both for distinguishing between units whose development follows one model and for differentiating between those of one model and those of the other. We need to know whether or not any one, two, or more elite units specialize in control functions; that is, whether or not control is equally distributed among all or most units. This will be called the *degree of elitism*. To the degree that there are elites, the question arises whether they operate from within or from without the emerging union. This dimension will be the *degree of internalization* (of control).[4]

1. *Degree of elitism.* Organizational analysis shows that there are two major ways of forming a new corporate body: An elite unit may construct the performance units, or several existing organizations that have both elite and performance units may merge. On the international level, a new community is formed in the first way when a nation more powerful than the other potential members "guides" the unification process. Prussia played such a role in the unification of Germany; Ghana, in the formation of the Ghana-Guinea-Mali union;

---

[4]I found this dimension of much value in analyzing the relationship between specialized units and parent organizations [see "Authority Structure and Organizational Effectiveness," *Administrative Science Quarterly,* IV (1959), 62-67].

Egypt, in the late UAR. The cases in which one nation played a central role are so numerous that Deutsch *et al.* suggest that unification requires the existence of one "core" unit.[5]

While many organizations and communities are established by one or a few elite units, the control center of others is formed through a merger of many units, each contributing a more or less equal part. The power center of the emerging community is a new unit rather than an existing unit subordinating the others. One might refer to the first as elitist, to the second as egalitarian, unification. A study of the Northern Baptist Convention in the United States provides a fine illustration of egalitarian unification.[6] The development of the Scandinavian union appears to follow an egalitarian pattern also. While Norway was initially less supportive of the union than Sweden and Denmark, the differences in their support to, and in their control of, the emerging union (and the Nordic Council, its formal instrument) comes close to the egalitarian ideal type.[7]

The degree of elitism (or egalitarianism) should be treated as a continuum. In some nation unions one unit clearly plays a superior role (England in the early Commonwealth); in some, two or more countries are superior (Brazil, Argentina, and to a degree Chile, of the seven members in the Latin America Free Trade Area); in others, participation, contribution, and power are almost evenly distributed among all participants (as in the Scandinavian union).

The degree to which one or more units control the unification process versus the degree to which it is an effort of all participants is closely related to the means of control used. At the elitist end of this continuum we find mergers in which one country coerces the others to "unify." It seems that on the international level cases of elitist and coerced unification are much more frequent than egalitarian, voluntary unions, especially if we regard the extensive use of economic sanctions, not just military force, as resulting in a non-voluntary unification.[8] At the egalitarian end, use of normative means, such as appeal to common sentiments, traditions, and symbols, plays a much more central role than coercive means or economic sanctions. Economic factors operate here more in the form of mutual benefits derived from increased intercountry trade than sanctions or rewards given by one country to the others.

---

[5]Karl W. Deutsch et al., *Political Community and the North Atlantic Area* (Princeton, N.J.: Princeton University Press, 1957), pp. 28, 38–39.

[6]Paul M. Harrison, *Authority and Power in the Free Church Tradition* (Princeton, N.J.: Princeton University Press, 1959).

[7]Frantz Wendt, *The Nordic Council and Cooperation in Scandinavia* (Copenhagen: Mumsgaard, 1959), pp. 98–100 [see also Norman J. Padelford, "Regional Cooperation in Scandinavia," *International Organization,* XI (1957), 597–614].

[8]The infrequency of voluntary unions is stressed in Crane Brinton, *From Many to One* (Cambridge, Mass.: Harvard University Press, 1949), pp. 44 ff.

This raises an empirical question: How effective are the various means of unification? One is inclined to expect that unification that begins with coercion ends with disintegration. But the Roman empire, despite its coercive techniques, lasted for about five centuries before it finally collapsed. Nor was the German union weak or ineffective because of the methods employed by Bismarck to bring it about. Quite possibly the line that distinguishes effective from ineffective unification efforts lies not between coercion and non-coercion but between high coercion (of the kind used to keep Hungary in the Communist bloc in 1956 or to hold the Federation of Rhodesia and Nyasaland together in 1961) and lesser coercion.[9] Effectiveness seems also to be highly determined by the degree to which coercion is coupled with other means—for instance, with propaganda.

2. *Degree of internalization.* Collectivities whose developments follow an epigenesis model can be effectively ordered by a second dimension, namely, the degree to which the elite unit (or units, if they exist) controls the emerging union from the outside or from the inside. This is not a dichotomous variable, for there are various degrees to which an elite unit can be "in" or "out." An elite might be completely "out," encouraging or forcing the merger of two or more units into a union which it does not join, sometimes relinquishing control once unification is initiated. Colonial powers brought together, frequently unwittingly, subordinated units, only to have to withdraw once their union was cemented: For example, resisting the British control was a major force in bringing together the thirteen American colonies, the various tribes in the Gold Coast that became Ghana, and the Jewish colonies in Palestine that formed the Israeli society. On the international level, the United States required some degree of intra-European economic co-operation as a condition for receiving funds under the Marshall Plan; it encouraged the union of the six countries that formed the European Economic Community, and is now encouraging the EEC to include Britain, without having joined these unions. Britain was the major force behind the efforts to launch a Federation of the West Indies and the formation of the Federation of Nigeria. In all these cases the center of power was with a non-member, external unit.

In other cases, the elites that initiate and support unification do not stay entirely out of the emerging community, nor are they a fully integral part of it. The United States, for instance, is an "informal but powerful" member of CENTO. It signed bilateral pacts with Iran, Turkey, and Pakistan, the three members of CENTO, which in 1961 showed signs of becoming more than just a treaty.[10]

[9]For an outstanding discussion of the Soviet bloc from this viewpoint see Zbigniew K. Brzenzski, *The Soviet Bloc* (Cambridge, Mass.: Harvard University Press, 1960), chap. xii, and his "The Organization of the Communist Camp," *World Politics*, XII (1961), 175–209.

[10]The Ministerial Council of CENTO decided in its meeting in Ankara in April, 1960, that a shared military command would be developed; intercountry roads and telecommunication improved; and economic and cultural ties increased (*New York Times*, April 29, 1961). Projects already completed include a new Turkish–Iranian railway, a new road linking the CENTO countries, as well as a microwave communication network [*International Organization*, XV (1961), 523].

Similarly France, while not a member of the Conseil de l'Entente (a loose West African custom, communication, and, to a degree, military union of Ivory Coast, Upper Volta, Niger, and Dahomey), still is an active participant in this union through various treaties.[11]

Finally, in still other cases, the elite is a full-fledged member of the union as Britain was in the European Free Trade Area and Prussia in the unification of Germany.

3. *Power, capability, and responsiveness.* The units that control the epigenesis of political communities differ not only in their degree of elitism and internalization but also in their communication capabilities and degree of responsiveness to the needs and demands of participant units.[12] Deutsch pointed out that when all other conditions are satisfactory a unification process might fail because the *communication capabilities* of an elite are underdeveloped. This was probably a major reason why empires in medieval Europe were doomed to fail; they were too large and complex to be run from one center given the existing communication facilities.[13] Sociologists have concerned themselves extensively with communication gaps, but studies frequently focus on the interpersonal and small-group level (even in many of the so-called organizational studies of communication). Sociologists are often concerned with the structure of communication networks (two-step communication systems,[14] as against chain systems[15]) rather than with the articulation of these networks with the power structure.[16] For students of political systems and of complex organization, ideas such as "overloading" of the elite (presenting it with more communication than it is able to digest; requiring more decisions per time unit than it is able to make) is an interesting new perspective that connects communication studies with power analysis much more closely than the widespread human-relations type of communication analysis.

The concept of *responsiveness* further ties communication analysis to the study of power by asking to what degree does the power center act upon communication

---

[11]Immanuel Wallerstein, "Background to Paga," *West Africa*, July 29, 1961, p. 819, and August 5, 1961, p. 861, and Walter Schwartz, "Varieties of African Nationalism," *Commentary*, XXXII (1961), 34.

[12]Karl W. Deutsch, *Nationalism and Social Communication* (New York: John Wiley and Sons, 1953), pp. 65, 142.

[13]Karl W. Deutsch, *Political Community at the International Level* (Garden City, N.Y.: Doubleday and Co., 1954), pp. 13–15.

[14]Elihu Katz and Paul Lazarsfeld, *Personal Influence* (Glencoe, Ill.: Free Press, 1955).

[15]Alex Bavelas, "Communication Patterns in Task-Oriented Groups," *Journal of the Acoustical Society of America*, XXII (1950' 725–30.

[16]For one of the few studies that successfully ties the two see R. H. McCleary, *Policy Change in Prison Management* (East Lansing: Michigan State University, 1957).

received and digested in terms of reallocating resources and rewarding the compliance of sectors.[17]

Thus to analyze epigenesis effectively, we must know not only who has how much power over the process but also what are the communication capabilities and what is the degree of responsiveness of the various power centers.

Performance and Control: A Dynamic Perspective

The performance, power, and communication elements of a social unit developing epigenetically do not always develop at the same rate. As the limbs of an infant develop before he has control over them so new performances might be taken over by the accumulating unit before its power center gains control over them. Frequently, part of the performances of an accumulating unit are controlled by another unit, at least temporarily. The industrial capacity of colonies often developed before they gained political control over industry.

New communities, whose development follows the pattern suggested by epigenesis rather than that of preformism, tend to develop new performance abilities first and to internalize control over these activities later.[18] Just as a child first learns to walk, then gains the right to decide when and where to walk, or as military units in basic training first learn to act as units under the control of the training ("parent") unit's instructors and sanction system before acquiring their own command, so some countries engage in some collective activity under the control of a superior, non-member power.[19] Later, control is internalized by the evolving supranational system, and a supranational authority is formed, which regulates collective activities previously controlled by the superior external power.

It is the existence of a supranational authority—at first limited, then more encompassing—that distinguishes *unions of nations* from *international organizations.* Unions have at least a limited power center of their own, whose decisions bind the members and are enforcible; they have internalized at least some control. International organizations, on the other hand, are run by intergovernmental bodies, whose "decisions" are merely recommendations to the members and are not enforcible.[20] They have, in this sense, no power of their own.

[17]Deutsch, *Nationalism and Social Communication*, p. 143 (see also his *Political Community at the International Level*, p. 37).

[18]"Internalize" means here the transfer of power from external elites to internal elites.

[19]It should be pointed out that on the international level the power of a new union is more often generalized from its constituent units—"pooling of sovereignty"—than internalized from superior power. From the present viewpoint this distinction is not relevant; the question is: Who controls the collective action—the unit itself or other units (without regard to whether they are outside or constituent units)?

[20]For an outstanding discussion of the differences between intergovernment and supranational decision-making bodies, see Ernst B. Haas, *Uniting of Europe* (Stanford, Calif.: Stanford University Press, 1958), chaps. xii, xiii. The following discussion of the High Authority draws on Haas's work.

The special importance of the High Authority, a governing body of the European Coal and Steel Community (ECSC) is that its decisions directly bind the steel and coal industries of the six member nations and it can levy fines on industries that do not conform to its rulings (though national police forces would have to collect the fines, if they were not paid). Moreover, individuals, corporations, and states have the same status before the Court of Justice of the ECSC; they all can sue each other, an individual suing a state, or the High Authority suing a member state.[21]

Until the ECSC was formed in 1952, almost all European co-operation, such as the Organization for European Economic Cooperation (OEEC) and NATO, was intergovernmental. In 1952 the High Authority was formed; this was the first major step toward self-control of the evolving supranational community. (Interestingly, this is also the year NATO developed a supranational authority with the formation of SHAPE, which provided a supranational headquarters for the multination armies.)[22] In the following years functions and powers of the High Authority gradually increased. In 1957 the more encompassing common market (EEC) was established, which has its equivalent of the High Authority, the Economic Commission, except that its supranational powers cover more "performances"—much of the intercountry economic actions—than does the High Authority, which is limited to matters related to steel and coal.[23]

Attempts to develop supranational control over shared political activities, in which the members of the EEC do engage, have not yet succeeded. Whatever collective political action the Six take is based on intergovernment consultations of these countries, not supranational direction. *Thus, in the development of this union of nations, as in the epigenesis of many other social units, collective performances expand more rapidly than collective control.* (It should be noted that while frequently performance accumulation occurs before power internalization, the reversed sequence might occur, too. Power *capabilities* can be built up before performance. Modern armies, for instance, train groups of officers in headquarters work before they are given command of military units.)

We saw that communities are built up by accumulation of *new* performances (e.g., military ones) and control over them. We now turn to the dynamics of

---

[21]In March, 1961, the Economic Commission—which is roughly, to the EEC what the High Authority is to the ECSC—brought the Italian government before the court of the EEC for violation of an article of the Treaty of Rome concerning a ban on subsidies for trade in pork. This was the first such action taken since the formation of the EEC (*New York Times,* March 27, 1961).

[22]See Andrew J. Godpaster, "The Development of SHAPE: 1950–1953," *International Organization,* IX (1955), 257–62, and William A. Knowlton, "Early Stages in the Organization of SHAPE," *International Organization,* XIII (1959), 1–18.

[23]William Diebold, Jr., "The Changed Economic Position of Western Europe," *International Organization,* XV (1960), 1–19, esp. p. 12.

accumulation, recognizing three problems as basic to the analysis of all accumulation processes: (*a*) Under what conditions does the process start? (*b*) What factors contribute to its expansion and pace? (*c*) What is the sequence in which the functional sectors that make a complete community are assembled? The rest of this article is devoted to these problems.

INITIATION, TAKE-OFF, AND SPILL-OVER

Between Initiation and Take-Off

The concept of take-off, borrowed from aerodynamics, is applied to the first stage of epigenesis to distinguish the initiation point from that where the continuation of the process becomes self-sustained. The image is one of a plane that first starts its engines and begins rolling, still supported by the runway, until it accumulates enough momentum to "take off," to continue in motion "on its own," generating the forces that carry it to higher altitudes an greater speeds. The analogue is that through accumulation, while relying on external support, the necessary condition for autonomous action is produced. Also during "take-off" the pilot, released from airport tower control, gains control of his plane. (This control take-off might occur before or after the performance take-off.)

Economists use this concept in the study of industrialization, especially in reference to foreign aid. An underdeveloped country requires a certain amount of investment before its economy reaches the level at which it produces a national income large enough to provide for current consumption and for increased investment which, in turn, provides for additional growth of the economy.[24] An economy has taken off when additional growth is self-sustained; when no external investment or externally induced changes in saving, spending, or work habits are needed.

The concept of take-off can also be used in studying political, communication, and other social processes. A group of leaders, some labor unions, or "reform" clubs, join to initiate a new political party. Again, "to initiate" has two meanings, to which the concept of take-off calls attention: There is the day the leaders decide to launch the new party, a day that, if the launching is successful, will be known as the party's birthday. However, the new party initially draws its funds, staff, and political power from the founding leaders and groups. Gradually, as the party grows, it accumulates followers and contributors directly committed to it, and if it is successful, it eventually reaches the stage at which it can do without the support of its initiators and continue growing "on its own." While this point is far

---

[24]W. W. Rostow, *The Stages of Economic Growth* (Cambridge: Cambridge University Press, 1960), pp. 4, 7–9, 36 ff.

from being sharply defined, obviously it rarely coincides with the actual birth date. Much insight can be gained by comparing different polities with regard to the lapse between their initiation and their take-off points. For instance, the greater the lapse the more difficult it is for small or new groups to gain political representation. On the other hand, if the lapse is very small, entering the political competition becomes too easy, and it will be difficult to find a majority to establish a stable government.

In many countries there is a formal barrier that has to be surmounted before political take-off. Parties that poll less than a certain percentage of the votes are denied parliamentary representation. Frequently founders' support is given until the election day; then the party either gains representation and becomes a political factor in its own right or it flounders; it either takes off or crashes. One of the special characteristics of the American political system is that the take-off point is remote from the initiation point. Many "third-party" movements that polled many hundreds of thousands of votes still could not continue to grow and to become permanent participants on the federal level.[25]

Take-off is especially important for the study of social units that are initiated by charter, enactment of a law, or signing of a treaty. While sometimes these "paper" units might be an expression of an already-existing social unit, often the formal structure precedes the development of a social one. While it has been often pointed out that an informal structure is likely to evolve, turning the formal one into a full-fledged social unit, we do not know under what conditions these informal processes take off, as against those conditions under which they never reach such a point. Clearly not all formal structures become functioning social units. This applies in particular to international relations where the supranational take-off, that is, the transition from a formal, intergovernmental structure to self-sustained growth toward a political community, is quite infrequent.[26] Under what conditions, then, does take-off occur?

While these problems still require much research, there appears to be one central factor bringing unification movements to take-off: the amount of decision-making called for by intercountry *flows* (e.g., of goods) and by *shared performance* (e.g., holding a common defense line) that, in turn, is determined by the scope of tasks carried out internationally. If the amount is large, intergovernment decision-making will prove cumbersome and inadequate and pressure will be generated either to reduce the need for international decision-making—by reducing the international tasks—or to build a supranational decision-making *structure,* which is a more effective decision-making body than are intergovernmental ones.

The central variable for the "take-off" of supranational authority is the amount of international decision-making required. This, in turn, is determined largely by

[25]Daniel Bell (ed.), *The New American Right* (New York: Criterion Books, 1955).

[26]See Deutsch et al., *op. cit.,* pp. 85–87, on supranational take-off.

the amounts and kinds of flows that cross the international borders (e.g., tourists, mail) and the amounts and kinds of shared international activities (e.g., maintaining an early-warning system). It should be stressed, however, that each flow or shared activity has its own decision-making logarithm. Some flows can increase a great deal and still require only a little increase in international decision-making; others require much more.[27] Moreover, the relationship seems not to be linear; that is, some increases in a particular flow (or shared activity) can be handled by the old decision-making system, but once a certain threshold is passed, some supranational authority is almost inevitable.

It seems also that expanding the power and scope of a supranational authority is easier than to form the first element of such an authority. Initially a supranational authority is often accepted on the grounds that it will limit itself strictly to technical, bureaucratic, or secondary matters, and that the major policy decisions will be left in the hands of a superior, intergovernment body. This was the initial relationship between the High Authority and the Council of Ministers of the ECSC; between the Economic Commission and the Council of Ministers of the EEC; and between NATO's SHAPE and NATO's conferences of ministers.

Once such a bureaucratic structure is established, a process often sets in whereby full-time, professional bureaucrats tend to usurp functions and authority from the part-time, political, "amateur" superior bodies, thereby expanding the scope of the supranational authority. At the same time, the very existence of supranational control in one area tends to promote such control in others. The concept of spill-over, or secondary priming, which is used here to study the epigenesis of nation unions, is applicable to the study of accumulation processes in general.

Secondary Priming of Change

"Spill-over" refers to expansion of supranational performances and control from one sphere of international behavior to another. It was introduced by Haas to refer to expansions within the sector in which unification originally started (e.g., from coal and steel industries to transportation) and from sector to sector (e.g., from the economic to the political).[28] Spill-over refers only to secondary priming; that is, to processes—in our case, unifications—that have been initiated or have taken off because of epigenesis in *other* social sectors. NATO, for instance, unifies the military organizations of fifteen nations, and the EEC integrates the economies of six of the NATO countries. While these processes probably support each other, only a little spill-over has taken place. Basically the military unification

---

[27]Hence the fact that a mere increase in flows is not related to increase in supranationalism does not reject the hypothesis that these variables are positively related. Cf. I. Richard Savage and Karl Deutsch, "A Statistical Model of the Gross Analysis of Transaction Flows," *Econometrica*, XXVIII (1960), 551–72; Deutsch, "Shifts in the Balance of Communication Flows," *Public Opinion Quarterly*, XX (1956), 143–60.

[28]*Uniting of Europe, op. cit.*, chap. viii.

did not initiate the economic one or vice versa.[29] There was original priming in each area. Both unifications may have had certain common sources (e.g., the conflicts between the United States and Soviet Russia) and may be mutually supportive, but they did not trigger each other. On the other hand, the integration of the economies of the Six generates pressures toward integration of their governments, though so far political unification is mainly a "grand design."[30]

It follows that one can hardly understand supranational spill-over without studying the internal structure and dynamics of the participating societies. This must be done from a dynamic perspective, for spill-over raises the following questions: Under what conditions and at what level of change does unification of one sector lead to the exhausting of its "degrees of freedom" and trigger unification in other sectors?[31] Which sector is likely to be affected first, second, and nth? Which sector will be affected most, second, and nth?

THE SEQUENCE OF EPIGENESIS

Clockwise and Counterclockwise Sequences

The concept of take-off suggests that epigenesis has to gain a certain momentum before it becomes self-sustaining. However, it does not suggest in what sector accumulation takes off, or what the effects of the selection of a particular take-off sector are on the probability that general unification will ensue. Similarly, the study of spill-over traces the relation between sectors once take-off in one sector has occurred, but it does not specify either in which sector accumulation is likely to start or in what order other supranational sectors are likely to be built up (since it does not account for primary, simultaneous, or successive priming). To put it in terms of the accumulation model, we still have to determine: Which part is assembled first, which ones later?[32]

A hypothesis defining the sequences most functional for the epigenesis of nation unions can be derived from an application of the Parsonian phase model.[33]

---

[29]Diebold (op. cit.) points to the reasons why efforts to base economic integration on NATO have been unsuccessful. Kissinger, on the other hand, believes that NATO could serve as the basis of an Atlantic confederacy (Reporter, February 2, 1961, pp.15–21). Deutsch et al. pointed out that where the initial unification efforts were based on military integration half of these efforts failed (op. cit., p. 28).

[30]On spill-over from the economic to the political area see essays by Paul Delouvrier and by Pierre Uri in C. Grove Haines (ed.), European Integration (Baltimore: Johns Hopkins Press, 1957).

[31]In other words, up to a point each institutional realm changes independently, but, once that point has been reached, further change affects another institutional realm.

[32]Note that though sector spill-over occurs in the member societies, it leads to expansion in the scope of the supranational community.

[33]Parsons et al., Working Papers . . . , op. cit., pp. 182 ff.

Parsons suggests that the most functional cyclical fluctuations in the investment of resources, personnel, and time follow one of two patterns: either a clockwise sequence (adaptive, allocative, socially integrative, and normative integrative), or a counterclockwise sequence.[34] The two patterns can be applied to the study of epigenesis. They suggest that it is most functional for a new community to assemble its subunits and its self-control from the adaptive to the normative, or the other way around; and that all other sequences are less functional.[35]

Before we turn to express this hypothesis in more substantive terms the difference between the application of the Parsonian phase model to preformism and its application to epigenesis should be pointed out. The phase model, as such, concerns the movement of an existing system, not its pattern of growth or change in its structure. Unless other processes take place, after a full round of the phase movement the system is the same as it started. Moreover, while each system is once accumulated or differentiated, the phase movement can continue ad libitum.[36]

Parsons also suggested a pattern for the analysis of social change, that of differentiation, according to which fused units bifurcate first into expressive and instrumental elements; then, each of these splits. Expressive elements are divided into social and normative ones; instrumental into adaptive and allocative ones. This, like all performism models, is a pattern a ccording to which functions that were served by one, fused structure, become structurally differentiated; that is, they gain their own subunits.[37] The accumulation model, on the other hand, knows no bifurcation, but suggests an order in which new structures serving new functions are conjoined. For example, countries that shared only a common market also establish a common defense line; that is, the union acquires a new function, not just a structural wing. The order we expect to be functional for unification

---

[34] Here, as well as in an earlier work, I found it fruitful to apply Parsons' concepts with a certain amount of liberty. A long conceptual quibble seems unnecessary. The use of allocation instead of "goal attainment" and of normative integration instead of "pattern maintenance and tension-management" may serve as a reminder to the reader concerned with such conceptual subtleties that Parsons is not responsible for my way of using his scheme.

[35] This is one of those statements that sounds tautological but is not. Since there are four phases in the system, the statement suggests that two modes of movement are more functional than twenty-two possible other ones. The first pattern–adaptive to normative–is referred to as clockwise because the convention is to present the four phases in a fourfold table in which the adaptive is in the upper left-hand box, the allocative in the upper right-hand box, the social-integrative in the lower right-hand box, and the normative in the lower left-hand box.

[36] Note also that there is no one-to-one relationship between the pattern in which a system is built up (whether accumulated or differentiated) and the pattern in which it is maintained; e.g., the epigenesis of a system might be counterclockwise and the system will "click" clockwise once its epigenesis is completed.

[37] For a later development of this model see Talcott Parsons, "A Functional Theory of Change," in Amitai and Eva Etzioni (eds.), op. cit.

movements to follow is either from the adaptive to the normative or the other way around.

In more substantive terms, the major question raised by the hypothesis concerning the sequence of accumulation is this: Is unification initiated in a particular sector more likely to lead to complete unification (to a political community)? If so, which is it: the military, economic, political, or ideological? Is the probability of success higher if accumulation follows a certain sequence? Which sequence (if any)? And is the most effective sequence the same for all types of unifications? (See below.)

On the basis of the study of ten historical cases Deutsch and his associates reached the following conclusion:

> It appears to us from our cases that they [conditions of integration] may be assembled in almost any sequence, so long only as all of them come into being and take effect. Toward this end, almost any pathway will suffice.[38]

They added, however, that:

> In this assembly-line process of history, and particularly in the transition between background and process, timing is important. Generally speaking, we found that substantial rewards for cooperation or progress toward amalgamation had to be timed so as to come before the imposition of burdens resulting from such progress toward amalgamation (union). We found that, as with rewards before burdens, consent has to come before compliance if the amalgamation is to have lasting success.[39]

Deutsch's distinction between sequence and order in time seems unnecessary for our purposes. Especially after examining his important book, *Backgrounds for Community*, in which his historical material is analyzed in great detail and potency, we conclude that Detusch suggests—if we push the freedom of interpretation to its limit—that the allocative phase tends to come before the adaptive one (rewards before burdens); and that the normative phase (consent) tends to come before the social-integrative phase (compliance). In other words, interpreting liberally, we find Deutsch suggesting that a counterclockwise sequence from normative to adaptive is most common.

Haas compares the findings of his study of a modern unification with the findings of Deutsch et al. on historical cases from this viewpoint.[40] He distinguishes

---

[38]*Op. cit.,* p. 70.

[39]*Ibid.,* p. 71.

[40]Haas, "The Challenge of Regionalism," in Stanley Hoffman (ed.), *Contemporary Theory in International Relations* (Englewood Cliffs, N.J.: Prentice-Hall, Inc., 1960), pp. 230–31.

between identical expectations (or aims) and converging expectations that make actors co-operate in pursuing their non-identical aims. The distinction comes close to Durkheim's dichotomy of mechanic and organic solidarity and is similar to the dichotomy of expressive and instrumental elements.[41] Haas reports that the ECSC has followed a clockwise sequence in which convergent (or instrumental) expectations preceded the identical (or expressive) ones.[42] Interpreting Haas liberally, one could state that in the case of the ECSC adaptive integration (custom union) came first, followed by allocative integration of economic policies (regarding coal and steel and later the formation of a common market). The union is now on the verge of political integration (election of a European parliament; planning group for federal or confederal institutions) and at the beginning of normative integration. Actually by the time Haas completed his study in 1957, there was hardly any supranational merger of normative institutions, and even attitudes only started to change from convergent to identical.

Any effort to codify Deutsch's and Haas's findings for the benefit of further research on the question of the relative effectiveness of various sequences will have to take into account (1) the nature of the merging units, (2) the nature of the emerging unit (i.e., the kind of union established), and (3) the nature of functional statements.

Merging Units

One might expect that supranational unification of societies that differ in their internal structure will proceed in a different sequence. If, for instance, the merging units are three newly independent states such as Ghana, Guinea, and Mali— states that in themselves are still in the process of building up their "expressive" foundations—the emphasis on normative and social integration on the supranational level might well be higher than when long-established and well-integrated states unify, as in the Scandinavian union, where the instrumental elements of the unification are stressed. These observations support the far from earth-shaking hypothesis that sector integration most responsive to the functional needs of the individual societies that are merging will come first in the unification sequence. After take-off, however, unification is expected to *proceed more and more in accord with the intrinsic needs of the emerging political union, less and less in accord with the internal needs of the merging units.*

The preceding statements should not be read to imply that "political communities develop differently in different historical context"; that, for instance, one can account for the difference between Deutsch's findings and those of Haas by pointing to the fact that Deutsch deals with historical cases while Haas is concerned

---

[41]*Ibid.*, p. 229. In Haas's own words: "Converging expectations make for regional unity instrumental in nature rather than based on principle."

[42]*Ibid.*, p. 230.

with a contemporary one. Such statements are frequently made by historians who believe that each context is unique, hence what needs explanation is not diversity but uniformity—if ever found. For the sociologist the "historical context" is a shorthand phrase referring to the values of a myriad variable; unless these are specified, little is explained by the statement that "the context is different." In our case the question is: Which contextual variables account for the difference in sequences and for how much of the difference? (Often numerous factors have an effect but a small number accounts for most of the variance.)

"Historical cases," for instance, are often preindustrial societies; hence it comes to mind that the level of industrialization might account for part of the difference; industrialized societies might tend to merge in an adaptive-first, normative-last sequence; non-industrial ones, in a normative-first, adaptive-last sequence. This formulation seems suggestive because, if valid, it points to the direction in which these findings can be generalized. We would expect, for instance, contemporary non-industrialized societies to unify in the "historical," not in the "contemporary," fashion. The hypothesis also calls attention to the special importance of historical cases in which unification came after industrialization. If these unifications followed a "contemporary" sequence, the hypothesis on the relation of industrialization to the sequence of unification would be strengthened.

Another variable to be teased out of the undifferentiated phrase, "historical context," is the degree of nationalism. There seem to be three major kinds of unions: pre-nationalist (e.g., the Roman Empire); post-nationalist (e.g., the EEC); and unions that are themselves an expression of rising nationalism (e.g., the unification of Italy). All other things being equal, we would expect the initial phases of pre- and post-nationalist unions to stress the adaptive aspect and follow the clockwise pattern; and those unions that express nationalism to be initiated on the normative side, following the counterclockwise sequence.

Kinds of Union

The sequence of unification is determined not only by the *initial* needs of the merging units (e.g., industrialization) and the "period" (e.g., advent of nationalism) but also by the function the union fulfils for the various participant units as it is *completed.* Unions of nations differ greatly on this score. The most familiar type is that of custom unions, which keep up the level of international trade among member countries. The new Central American Union, formed in 1959, and the Latin America Free Trade Area, ratified in 1961,[43] are actually oriented at economic development, international division of labor, sharing of information, and even of capital rather than increased regional trade.[44] Wallerstein points to still a

---

[43] See "The Emerging Common Markets in Latin America," *Monthly Review* (Federal Reserve Bank of New York), September, 1960, pp. 154 ff.

[44] This point was made by Lincoln Gordon in "Economic Regionalism Reconsidered," *World Politics,* XIII (1961), 231–53.

different function of unions: Some serve as instruments of subordination, while others serve to bolster independence.[45] Thus the white, who are stronger in Southern Rhodesia than in Northern Rhodesia and Nyasaland, use the federation of the three regions to hold the regions in which they are weak.

Functional analysis of social units that develop epigenetically is more complex than such an analysis of existing social units, for here we deal with functional analysis of change where the system itself is changing. Thus, as unification evolves, it comes to fulfil different (either additional or substitute) functions for the participant units and the emerging union. The West European unification might have been initiated in 1947 as a way to gain capital aid from the United States to reconstruct the postwar economies; soon it acquired the additional function of countering Soviet military expansion; then it came to serve economic welfare and, with the "rebellion" of France since De Gaulle has returned to office, it even serves, to a degree, to countervail United States influence in the Western bloc.[46] (It should be mentioned in passing that at a given stage of development the same union may have different functions for different participants. Thus, Germany supported the EEC partially to overcome its "second" citizen status in the community of nations; allied control of German steel industry, for instance, was abolished when Germany entered the ECSC.[47] France supported the formation of NATO in part to gain some control over a rebuilt and rearmed Germany.)

All functional needs—those of individual members, those common to all members, and those of the evolving community—vary with the various stages of the unification process; and they all seem to affect the sequence in which the "parts" are assembled. It remains for future studies to relate differences in sequence to these functional variations, to validate two hypotheses: (a) the higher the degree of unification the more its pattern of accumulation can be accounted for by common (identical or complementary) needs, rather than by the individual needs of member states, and by needs of the union rather than by common needs of the members, (b) accumulation sequences, whatever their take-off sector, are most likely to complete the process of unification if they follow the clockwise or counterclockwise sequence than any other.

Functional and "Real" Sequences

An important difference between the statements about sequences made, on the one hand, by Deutsch and by Haas and the statements made, on the other, by Parsons, his associates, and in the preceding discussion is that the former refer to

---

[45] On these unions see Immanuel Wallerstein, *Africa* (New York: Random House, 1962), chap. vii.

[46] Edgar S. Furniss, Jr., "De Gaulle's France and NATO: An Interpretation," *International Organization*, XV (1961), 349–65.

[47] *Uniting of Europe, op. cit.*, pp. 247–48.

actual occurrences (the ECSC followed this and that pattern) and empirical frequencies (nine out of ten historical cases followed this sequence), while the latter refer to functional sequences. Functional statements suggest that if epigenesis proceeds in a certain sequence, it will be most effectively completed; if it follows another sequence, certain dysfunctions will occur. The nature of the dysfunctions can be derived from the nature of the stages which are skipped (e.g., high social strain is expected if the expressive elements are not introduced), or incorporated in a "wrong" order (e.g., high strain is expected when allocation of resources is attempted before adaptation has been built up). The fact that a particular unification follows a sequence other than the one suggested by the epigenesis model does not invalidate the latter so long as it is demonstrated that the "deviation" from the model caused dysfunctions. In short, the test of the model lies in its ability to predict which course of action is functional and which one is not, rather than to predict the course of action likely to be followed.[48]

In the construction of epigenesis models for the various kinds of nation unions, the use of two types of functional models must be distinguished: The crude *survival* model and the more sophisticated and demanding *effectiveness* model. The first specifies the conditions under which a structure exists or ceases to exist; the second also takes into account differences in the degree of success. In the case of nation unions, then, while many are likely to continue in existence, some will stagnate on a low level of integration while others will continue to grow in scope, function, and authority.

CONCLUSION

Sociological theories of change tend to be preformist; they provide differentiation models for the analysis of the structural development of existing social units. We presented some elements of an alternative, epigenesis model, which suggests that some social units acquire new subunits that fulfil new functions, do not just provide new subunits for functions served before in a less specialized manner. Since these new elements are incorporated from the environment, epigenesis (or accumulation) models are much more concerned with input from, and articulation with, external units than preformism (or differentiated) models. Hence the first question we asked was: Where does the power lie that controls the process—is it evenly distributed among the participant units or is it concentrated in the hands of elites? Are the power-holders members of the new emerging communities or outsiders? Does increase in self-control of the union precede, follow, or coincide with the growth in its performances?

[48]Note that the system this statement refers to is not the existing one but a future state—that of a complete unification—of a community. The use of a future-system reference might prove useful for the general development of the functional analysis of change.

Turning from the powers that control accumulation to the pattern of accumulation itself, we asked: Where does the process start, what subunit is built up first? Which follows? What effect does the construction of one part have on that of the others? The concepts of take-off and secondary priming proved to be useful in understanding the initiation and progress of accumulating processes. An application of Parsons' phase model served us in formulating a hypothesis concerning the functional sequence of accumulation.

The distinctness of accumulation models should be emphasized: While differentiation models focus our attention on internal processes, accumulation models are concerned with boundary processes; while differentiation models are interested in internal elites, accumulation models ask about the changing power distribution between external and internal ones and their respective impacts on accumulation. Analytically speaking, preformist models see their subject units—even when undifferentiated—as functionally complete, whereas epigenesis models view their units as either partial (to varying degrees) or complete.

We emphasized the need to treat social units and their change as multilayer phenomena, including at least a performance, a power (or control), and a communication layer.[49] If we deal with a phase, differentiation, or accumulation model, we need not assume that changes on one layer are automatically concomitant with changes on the others.

Although the epigenesis model can be applied to many social phenomena, we are interested here primarily in using it to study international unification. There is hardly a subject less frequently studied by sociologists and more given to sociological analysis than the development of political communities whose members are nations. Since the evolution of these communities is likely to be supportive of both the short-run armed truce and the development of the social conditions for lasting peace,[50] and since the processes of social change involved in forming supranational communities are comparatively highly planned, deliberately and frequently drawing on expert advice, the study of supranational unification carries the extra reward of not just better understanding of human society but also of understanding how to better it.

---

[49]See my *A Comparative Analysis of Complex Organizations* (Glencoe, Ill.: Free Press, 1961), chaps. v and vii.

[50]These functions of nation unions are discussed in chap. viii of my *The Hard Way to Peace* (New York: Collier Books, 1962).

25. U. S. AND U. S. S. R. PARTICIPATION IN INTERNATIONAL NON-GOVERNMENTAL ORGANIZATIONS

Louis Kriesberg

The study of international non-governmental organizations can be useful for the understanding of the conditions for international peace[2] and for the sociology of organizations. International non-governmental organizations, hereafter called NGO's, typically are associations of voluntary organizations from several nations. At present, there are about 1,500 NGO's in existence.[3] The names of some of the NGO's indicate their diversity: the International Chamber of Commerce, the International Confederation of Free Trade Unions, the Women's International Cycling Association, the Scandinavian Society of Anethesiologists, and the International Union of Health Education.

Analyses of NGO's can indicate the extent to which a world society exists and cast light upon the actual and potential role of NGO's in the development of a world society. NGO's may contribute to the conditions that underlie world political institutions and their effective functioning in several ways. Members of NGO's may develop perspectives that are broader than national ones.[4] NGO activities may ameliorate the material and social conditions that underlie certain international conflicts. They may foster the development of international interest groups which cross-cut national boundaries. Formulas for settling international conflicts may be developed in NGO's and then used in governmental organizations or international law. NGO's may develop structural arrangements for handling conflicts among their own members that can be utilized by governmental organizations. On the other hand, NGO's may simply reflect and reinforce international divisions as they are expressed in regional and other alliances and political groupings. More fundamentally, NGO's may be essentially trivial, transitory,

SOURCE. This paper is being published for the first time in this form in this book. A shorter version was published under the title, "How a Plowing Contest May Ease World Tensions," in *Trans-action*, 5 (December, 1967), pp. 36–39.

epiphenomena with little impact upon the conditions relevant for the effective operation of world organizations. Or they may simply reflect the governmental conditions and have little independent effect upon the governmental order or the social conditions underlying the political structure.

In any case, the study of NGO's can be useful for the understanding of the conditions related to international peace. In addition, since NGO's are voluntary organizations which differ in many ways from national voluntary organizations, their inclusion in the realm of sociological analysis can aid our understanding of voluntary associations and formal organizations in general. A comprehensive analysis of NGO's would require an immense research effort. Nevertheless, considerable information about NGO's has been collected by the Union of International Associations and is published in the *Yearbook of International Organizations*. The data for the present analysis has been drawn largely from the 1962–1963 edition of the *Yearbook*.

THE QUESTION AND SOME HYPOTHESES

In this paper I will consider one important question pertaining to NGO's and the world community. To what extent do particular national differences affect the membership, structure, and activities of NGO's? The answer to the question will suggest some of the limits of the role which NGO's can play in fostering a world community.

Several ideas from the study of voluntary associations are pertinent in seeking an answer to the question. We may begin with the premise that among potential members of an organization, it is those whose common, like, or complementary interests overweigh their conflicting interests who will join together in an organization.[5] On the basis of that premise, we would expect that nations which have few like, common, or complementary interests and have many conflicting interests are least likely to be represented in many of the same organizations. Furthermore, the organizations in which they do participate will be those which involve like, common, or complementary interests rather than conflicting ones.

Actually, of course, nations are not members of NGO's. Since national associations or even individuals may be members, the selection may not be representative of the nation. Particular religious, political, or economic groups join together because they perceive certain common or complementary interests with similarly situated or oriented persons in other nations. An analysis of national differences in terms of the nationality of members of the NGO's therefore is a crude indicator of actual national differences in interests among members. Nevertheless, most NGO's are concerned with activities that have relevance for occupational roles.[6] This sets some limits to the self-selection of national members and makes economic differences among nations a relevant national characteristic. Significantly, too, the fact that most NGO's are formed in terms of members' occupational roles indicates that such roles involve experiences and interests which can be shared and even collectively aided across national boundaries. These ties are among the most fundamental in the development of a world community.

The interests of the members are only one side of the equation. Membership depends upon the characteristics of the organization as well as upon the interests of potential members. We must consider what it is that participation in the organization requires of its members and what benefits they may derive. Several plausible hypotheses about the consequences of different balances of interests among members upon organizational structure and activities can be suggested. First, it may be hypothesized that if members have many conflicting as well as some like, common, or complementary interests and yet are members of the same organization, the organization will operate in a fashion which minimizes demands upon the members even if this means that little is received by the members. On the other hand, it may be hypothesized that participation for such members must yield a great deal of benefits to them, making membership attractive, even if this entails making relatively high demands. A third hypothesis is that special structural arrangements will be developed to insulate possible conflict while maximizing possible benefits. Finally, one may hypothesize that organizational requirements are so dominant that if members with many conflicting interests do share membership, this will have little effect upon the structure and activities of the organization. Since the balance of interests may differ in different types of organizations, testing these hypotheses among different types of NGO's will permit further specification of the hypotheses.

THE FINDINGS

Membership of associations from the United States and from the Union of Soviet Socialist Republics in the same NGO's is used to indicate a high ratio of conflicting interests to common, like, or complementary ones.[7] The use of this indicator has particular political significance, but in the context of the present analysis, it is the set of like, common, complementary, and conflicting interests that is important. Thus the differences in the organization of the economies of the two societies limit the similarity and commonness of interests in the economic sphere. The similarities in scientific activities, on the other hand, make probable some like and complementary interests, if not common ones. Differences in political ideologies and international power positions entail conflicting interests; the extent to which this colors other spheres of potential NGO members' interests is problematical. In general, it would seem that common interests are not as probable as are like or complementary ones. This is indicated by the stated objectives of NGO's with and without joint U.S. and U.S.S.R. representation. One NGO objective is the promotion of social or material status of the members or representing the members in relations with other organizations. Among NGO's in which the U.S. and U.S.S.R. both participate, only 7 percent claim this objective; among NGO's in which the U.S. but not U.S.S.R. participates, 20 percent make this claim; among NGO's in which the U.S.S.R. but not the U.S. is represented, 54 percent state this objective; and among NGO's in which neither the U.S. nor the U.S.S.R. participate, 37 percent state this objective.

The first expectation we will examine concerns the likelihood that the U.S. and the U.S.S.R. will tend not to participate in the same NGO's. Among the NGO's for which information is available, about one-third restrict membership to some geographic area. Among the remaining NGO's, 21 percent have members from both the U.S. and U.S.S.R., 50 percent from the U.S. but not the U.S.S.R., 3 percent from the U.S.S.R. but not the U.S., and 26 percent have members who are from neither the U.S. nor the U.S.S.R. This does not support of the first expectation. It is true that only one out of five of the organizations which are not regionally restricted have U.S. and U.S.S.R. members and that the U.S. is more often represented in NGO's without the U.S.S.R. than ones with U.S.S.R. members.[8] But if the generally high U.S. level of participation in NGO's and the very low U.S.S.R. level are considered, the U.S. and U.S.S.R. are each more likely to be in NGO's with the other country than in NGO's in which the other is not represented.

These findings can be interpreted in several ways. First, the relative proliferation of associations in the United States must be considered. The number and variety of American associations means that there are more potential members of NGO's in the U.S. than in the U.S.S.R. Furthermore, the relative freedom of association in the U.S. facilitates the self-selective quality of membership which in turn facilitates associational membership in NGO's.[9] Moreover, in addition to the fact that there are fewer Soviet associations, their international participation is affected by Soviet governmental policy.[10] Furthermore, potential members within the Soviet bloc are fewer than in the non-Soviet bloc. Nevertheless, these findings suggest that even if there are conflicting interests among potential Soviet and American members, at least in certain spheres of activity, there are also common, like, and complementary interests. Indeed, they suggest that for potential Soviet members, membership with American associations offers particular attractions.[11]

The issue is clarified when we consider the types of NGO's in which the U.S. and U.S.S.R. are represented. Joint membership varies with the type of organization. One can compare the proportion a given type of organization constitutes in the various categories of national representation. For example, NGO's which are made up of workers, as in trade union organizations, are a major type of NGO. There are few such NGO's, however, in which both the U.S. and the

U.S.S.R. are represented.[12] Professional and trade union organizations constitute about 10 percent of the NGO's in which the U.S. but not the U.S.S.R. is represented, 14 percent of the ones in which the U.S.S.R. but not the U.S. participates, and 17 percent of the NGO's in which neither the U.S. nor the U.S.S.R. is represented; but such NGO's constitute only 1 percent of all the NGO's in which both the U.S. and the U.S.S.R. participate. The pattern for NGO's in the area of commerce and industry is similar: 11, 4, 18, and 2 percent, respectively. On the other hand, in science and scientific research, the percentages are quite different: 4, 0, 2, and 18 percent, respectively.

On the basis of the framework outlined earlier and in order to permit detailed analysis, the NGO's were divided into three types in terms of their potentiality for consensus. The types are intended to reflect varying degrees to which the international community, and particularly the U.S. and U.S.S.R., share goals and beliefs about the means to reach the goals. Thus Type 1 includes NGO's concerned with technology, science, medicine, or sports; consensus is presumably relatively high in these areas. Type 2 consists of the social or economic NGO's such as employer or profession, trade union, commerce and industry, social and political science, law and administration, or bibliographic NGO's; in these, consensus is presumably moderate. Type 3 includes NGO's dealing with matters about which consensus is presumably low; NGO's concerned with philosophy or religion, international relations, social welfare, education and youth, and the arts are included. In classifying NGO's, their categorization in the *Yearbook of International Organizations* was utilized; see note 2 of Table 1.

It is likely that in areas in which consensus is high, issues are viewed as technical matters. Where consensus is low, value differences are likely to be prominent. In the latter case, the mode of handling the issues is likely to involve bargaining, log-rolling, and other political methods rather than the means used in technical matters. Nevertheless, as will be discussed later in the paper, the extent to which an issue is viewed as a technical or as a value matter is not inherent in the issue. It depends, in part, upon the context and handling of the issue. Organizational arrangements may affect the context and style of handling issues; they may even be structured so that the issues are viewed as relatively technical matters. This mode of adaptation may be used particularly in organizations which have members with many conflicting interests relative to like, complementary or common interests. Consequently, the level of consensus and the degree to which organizations deal with technical or value issues, although empirically related, may be analytically distinguished.

One of the previously mentioned features of NGO's can mitigate the significance of an area of interest having low consensus. National representation in an NGO can consist of self-selected associations or associations with specially selected individuals. This is particularly likely in organizations involved in highly value-related activities. In the case of Types 1 and 2 NGO's, however comprehensive national associations are likely to pre-date and be formed independently of the NGO so that such self-selection is less likely.[13] Nevertheless, even in such NGO's self-selection of various kinds can occur. For example, during the immediate post World War II period when the World Federation of Trade Unions included Communist and non-Communist trade unions, the American Federation of Labor was not a member; the Congress of Industrial Organizations, however, was a member. Even within NGO's without Communist representation, self-selection of membership can occur which reduces potential dissensus and conflict among members. Thus the U.S. Farm Bureau withdrew from the International Federation of Agricultural Producers, largely because of policy differences over the role of governments in agriculture; other U.S. farm organizations remained members.[14] In the case of the International Chamber of Commerce, instead of the U.S. Chamber of Commerce, the American member is the U.S. Council of the International Chamber of Commerce. The U.S. Council was established at the close of World War II and consists of members who are heavily involved in international trade.

On the whole, the findings presented in Table 1 are consistent with the expectation that the U.S. and U.S.S.R. are most likely to be represented in organizations concerned with matters of presumably high consensus. About half of the NGO's in which they both participate are in the science, health, etc., category, while among the organizations in which they both do not participate, only about one-fifth are concerned with such matters. The lack of any real difference in the participation of American and Soviet associations in NGO's of presumably low consensus compared to those of moderate consensus may be due to the self-selective factor discussed above. In any case, it does appear that joint U.S. and U.S.S.R. representation is most likely in NGO's engaged in areas of activity in which American and Soviet associations are particularly likely to share similar goals and beliefs about reaching them. In such organizations, representatives of the U.S. and U.S.S.R. would tend to have like, complementary, and even common interests, while conflicting interests would be relatively few.

The second set of issues to be explored in this paper is the possible effect of joint U.S. and U.S.S.R. participation upon the structure and activities of NGO's. Actually, these issues are not independent of the likelihood of both the U.S. and U.S.S.R. being represented in the same organizations. Certain organizational arrangements or levels of activity may be conducive to American and Soviet joint representation. As a matter of fact, it is true that Type 1 NGO's, compared to other types, are less likely to have their own paid staff or a large staff, to have more than two levels in the organizational structure, or to have frequent meetings of the general membership. Do these characteristics of Type 1 organizations contribute to the attractiveness of such organizations for joint U.S. and U.S.S.R. representation? Or does the joint participation of the U.S. and U.S.S.R. induce such modifications in NGO's and the concentration of U.S. and U.S.S.R. membership in Type 1 organizations help account for such characteristics of Type 1 NGO's?

TABLE 1. Type of NGO by Type of National Participation[1]

Type of NGO[2]	Type of National Participation			
	U.S. and U.S.S.R.	U.S. but not U.S.S.R.	U.S.S.R. but not U.S.	Neither U.S. nor U.S.S.R.
Science, health, etc.	53	22	18	18
Economic, social, etc.	28	41	43	56
Religion, art, international relations, etc.	19	36	39	26
Totals (%)	100	99	100	100
(N)	(192)	(451)	(28)	(241)

[1] In this table, and in all the following tables, NGO's which restrict membership to any geographic area are excluded.

[2] The science, health, etc. type includes NGO's classified in the *Yearbook of International Organizations* under: technology; science, scientific research; medicine and health; sport, touring recreation. In the economic, social, etc. type are included NGO's classified in the following fields of activity: employers, profession; trade unions; commerce and industry; economics and finance; agriculture; transport, communications; law and administration; social and political sciences; and bibliography, press. In the religion, art, international relations, etc. type are NGO's classified in the following categories: philosophy, religion; international relations; politics; social welfare; education and youth; and arts, literature, cinema.

First we will examine the kind of activities which the organizations report conducting. Nearly all organizations report the facilitation of the members' activities as an organizational aim. We coded several ways in which this was reported to be done. One way is the exchange of information and establishment of personal relations through congresses, institutes, and exchange visits. Since nearly all organizations report these activities, they are of little relevance to our purposes here. Three other kinds of activities are of more pertinence: (1) engaging in joint efforts such as coordinating research or other work of members, (2) providing services for members such as libraries, abstracting services, and training programs, and (3) developing common standards or agreements about nomenclature and uniform codes. Obviously, these activities vary in frequency among the different types of organizations. But more pertinent to our present interest, within each type of NGO, those in which both the U.S. and the U.S.S.R. are represented are more likely to report such activities than are organizations in which either or both countries are not represented (see Table 2). However, among the Type 1 organizations, there is no difference in reports of joint efforts of service to members between NGO's with both U.S. and U.S.S.R. participation and NGO's in which either or both countries are not represented. Presumably, the organizational requirements

TABLE 2. Percent of NGO's Reported to Engage in Specified Activities by Type of
National Participation, and by Type of NGO

Activity	Science, Health, etc.		Economic, Social, etc.		Religion, Art, International Relations, etc.	
	U.S. and U.S.S.R.	Not U.S. and U.S.S.R.	U.S. and U.S.S.R.	Not U.S. and U.S.S.R.	U.S. and U.S.S.R.	Not U.S. and U.S.S.R.
Engage in joint efforts	46	44	72	58	56	38
Provide services for members	14	16	42	25	47	27
Develop common standards or agreements	40	22	34	23	12	4
(N)	(101)	(147)	(53)	(328)	(34)	(233)

are more important for these matters than whether or not the U.S. and U.S.S.R.
are both represented in the same Type 1 organization. Since the organizations in
which the U.S. and U.S.S.R. are both represented tend to be ones with a large
number of members and such organizations tend to report engaging in these
activities more than do NGO's with few nations represented, it is necessary
to control for number of nations represented. Holding constant the number of nations represented, we find that in some kinds of activities, among the small organizations, there is no longer any difference between NGO's with and without
joint participation of the U.S. and U.S.S.R. Nevertheless, on the whole, it appears
that their joint participation is not accompanied by a lessening of activity, but
often by a higher level of activity.

Other information from the *Yearbook of International Organizations* can be
used to test this inference. The level of organizational activity is in part indicated
by the size of the organization's staff and this is reflected in the size of the budget. The size of the staff in voluntary associations has significance in addition to
the level of organizational activity. A large staff is likely to mean that staff persons
or the executive secretary of the organization has relatively great power in the
organization's policy formation.[15] The delegation of such power to staff persons
is not likely in organizations which have few common and many conflicting interests. Therefore it is to be expected that in NGO's with both the U.S. and
U.S.S.R. participating, the staff and budget will tend to be small or nonexistent.
On the other hand, we have already noted some evidence that NGO's with both
the U.S. and U.S.S.R. represented tend to have higher levels of organizational

activity than other NGO's—or at least no lower levels. Consequently, we have discrepant expectations about the relationships between national representation in NGO's and the size of the organizations' budget and staffs.

Budgetary information is lacking for many NGO's. Among the NGO's for which information is available, NGO's with and without joint representation of the U.S. and U.S.S.R. do not appear to differ in the size of their budgets. If we hold constant the number of nations represented in the organizations, a suggestive difference is revealed. The comparison can only be made among the larger NGO's because of the small number of cases for which information is available among the smaller NGO's. Among the large NGO's there is a tendency for those with joint U.S. and U.S.S.R. representation to have medium-sized budgets (between $10,000 and $49,000) rather than very large or very small budgets. The pattern for staff size is similar. Overall, staff size also does not differ markedly among NGO's with and without U.S. and U.S.S.R. participation. When the number of nations represented in the NGO's is held constant, however, some suggestive differences are again revealed (see Table 3). Among the NGO's of presumably high or moderate consensus, those with joint U.S. and U.S.S.R. representation are slightly less likely than other NGO's to have very large staffs. Among the large NGO's with presumably low consensus, those with or without joint U.S. and U.S.S.R. representation are equally likely to have large staffs. First of all, it is clear that the sphere of organizational activity would affect the size of the staff: staffs are relatively small in NGO's concerned with science, health, etc. Whether or not there is joint U.S. and U.S.S.R. representation is not a major determinant. This may be due to what is in this context conflicting implications of staff size: a high level of activity and delegation of decision-making. Before making any concluding references, it is necessary to examine other findings.

The preceding discussion was based upon the supposition that NGO's with joint U.S. and U.S.S.R. participation will not have centralized decision-making. One indicator of this characteristic available from the *Yearbook* is the number of levels in the organization. Presumably, the larger the number of levels, the more centralized is decision-making and the greater is the delegation of authority by the members. In the case of voluntary associations, the argument is that rank and file direct participation in decision-making is less where several levels exist than where few exist, except that a general membership and only an executive committee may also indicate relatively high delegation of authority by the rank and file members.[16]

Within each type of NGO, organizations with or without U.S. and U.S.S.R. joint representation are equally likely to have three or more levels (see Table 4). Holding the number of nations constant, there is still no difference except among small Type 2 NGO's and large Type 3 NGO's; in these types, NGO's with U.S. and U.S.S.R. participation tend to have only one or two levels (there are too few cases to permit comparison among small Type 3 NGO's). There is a slight tendency, moreover, for NGO's without both the U.S. and U.S.S.R. as participants to have

TABLE 3. Size of NGO Staff by Number of Nations in NGO, by Type of National Participation, and by Type of NGO

Size of Staff	Twenty-Five or More Nations Represented						Twenty-Four or Fewer Nations Represented					
	Science, Health, etc.		Economic, Social, etc.		Religion, Art, International Relations, etc.		Science, Health, etc.		Economic, Social, etc.		Religion, Art, International Relations, etc.	
	U.S. and U.S.S.R.	Not U.S. and U.S.S.R.	U.S. and U.S.S.R.	Not U.S. and U.S.S.R.	U.S. and U.S.S.R.	Not U.S. and U.S.S.R.	U.S. and U.S.S.R.	Not U.S. and U.S.S.R.	U.S. and U.S.S.R.	Not U.S. and U.S.S.R.	U.S. and U.S.S.R.	Not U.S. and U.S.S.R.
None	59	46	27	31	31	35	67	61	56	47	–	45
Volunteers or use other organizations'	13	20	20	8	19	8	13	21	22	15	–	24
1-2	17	22	20	15	9	11	20	7	11	19	–	15
3-9	9	8	18	16	19	19	0	4	11	9	–	9
10 or more	0	3	9	24	22	21	0	2	0	4	–	3
Some, but number not given	1	1	5	6	0	6	0	5	0	6	–	5
Totals (%)	99	100	99	100	100	100	100	100	100	99	–	101
(N)	(86)	(65)	(44)	(93)	(32)	(105)	(15)	(84)	(9)	(235)	(4)	(129)

TABLE 4. Number of Levels in Organization by Type of National Participation, and by Type of NGO

Number of Levels	Science, Health, etc.		Economic, Social, etc.		Religion, Art, International Relations, etc.	
	U.S. and U.S.S.R.	Not U.S. and U.S.S.R.	U.S. and U.S.S.R.	Not U.S. and U.S.S.R.	U.S. and U.S.S.R.	Not U.S. and U.S.S.R.
Only general membership	7	7	0	6	3	5
2 levels	67	62	65	61	60	57
3 levels	20	25	35	27	37	30
4 or more levels	3	1	0	2	0	3
Executive committee only	3	5	0	4	0	6
Totals (%)	100	100	100	100	100	101
(N)	(99)	(146)	(52)	(325)	(35)	(233)

four levels or to have only an executive committee, except among NGO's with potentially high consensus.

If delegation of authority is somewhat less likely in NGO's with both U.S. and U.S.S.R. participation, then general membership meetings might be expected to be substituted. Yet frequent general membership meetings may be relatively difficult if the members have few common, like, or complementary interests and many conflicting ones. As a matter of fact, we find that NGO's with both the U.S. and U.S.S.R. represented have less frequent general membership meetings than do other NGO's (see Table 5). Among the NGO's with potentially low consensus, surprisingly, this pattern does not hold. Presumably, the self-selection of constituent organizations is an important factor here. Among these NGO's, those with U.S. and U.S.S.R. participation are particularly likely to either have few or many general membership meetings. Holding constant the size of the NGO's does not alter these relationships.

The findings thus far, taken together, have some puzzling inconsistencies. Joint U.S. and U.S.S.R. participation does not seem to decrease the activities conducted, but the development of a large staff to implement the activities may be inhibited. In part, this may be due to the avoidance of delegating authority to a staff and a secretary-general. Similarly, an elaborated number of organizational levels may be inhibited; but frequent general membership meetings are not substituted to compensate for this structural arrangement. These inconsistencies in the findings

TABLE 5. Frequency of General Membership Meetings by Type of National Participation, and by Type of NGO

Frequency of General Membership Meeting	Science, Health, etc.		Economic, Social etc.		Religion, Art, International Relations, etc.	
	U.S. and U.S.S.R.	Not U.S. and U.S.S.R.	U.S. and U.S.S.R.	Not U.S. and U.S.S.R.	U.S. and U.S.S.R.	Not U.S. and U.S.S.R.
No general meetings	5	8	0	5	3	6
1 every 5 years or less often	3	4	14	5	18	6
1 every 4 years	23	11	14	5	12	10
1 every 3 years	24	20	23	17	3	19
1 every 2 years	20	20	27	21	26	23
1 a year or more often	24	37	22	46	38	35
Totals (%)	99	100	100	99	100	99
(N)	(95)	(143)	(49)	(311)	(34)	(217)

are partially resolved when we consider one other organizational characteristic: the number of committees in the NGO's.

Despite the jokes and satire about committees and their proliferation, committees can be a useful device for organizations. In the context of the present analysis, an important utility lies in the possibility that they tend to transform problems from issues to be decided by political bargaining and negotiation to technical matters to be decided by consensus among experts. This can be made clearer if we consider what the differences are between technical and nontechnical issues. As noted earlier in the discussion of consensus and dissensus, the distinction, in large measure, depends upon the persons trying to solve the issue and how they try to handle it. The distinction is not inherent in the issue or content area. If the mode of reaching a decision involves log-rolling and bargaining and the style of the discussion involves polemical debate, the issue will be seen as nontechnical and political in a fundamental sense. Certain conditions makes such elements more or less prominent. If the participants have clear constituencies who can hear the discussion, if there are many constituencies represented, and if the issues are phrased in such broad terms that, at least for the participants, basic value differences are connected to the substantive issue, then the issue is not likely to be viewed as a technical one.

The establishment of committees can affect these conditions. Thus committees meet in relative privacy and all phases of the discussion are not heard by the constituents. Members of a committee may be selected because of their specialized knowledge—their "expert" qualities; this enhances the likelihood that they will discuss the issue in technical terms and feel independent of a definite constituency. A small committee limits the number of constituencies involved in the discussion. Handing problems to a committee usually means first dividing the problem into some of its components and this makes each component seem relatively technical. Most fundamentally, the processes in a committee meeting regularly can help transform an issue. A few persons, meeting regularly and frequently, can develop rules of discussion and common understanding. The shared understandings diminish value differences.[17]

The number of committees NGO's have is highly associated with whether or not the U.S. and the U.S.S.R. both participate in them. Within each type of NGO, if the U.S. and U.S.S.R. both participate, the NGO is much more likely to have committees and many of them compared to other NGO's (see Table 6). Furthermore, it should be noted, this organizational characteristic does not vary among the different types of organizations; it is true that large NGO's tend to have committees and more of them than do small NGO's. Nevertheless, even holding constant the size of the NGO, those with joint U.S. and U.S.S.R. participation tend to have committees and many of them. The establishment and proliferation of committees, then, may be an important organizational device to minimize and channel potentially disruptive consequences of joint U.S. and U.S.S.R. participation in NGO's.

TABLE 6. Number of NGO Committees by Type of National Participation, and by Type of NGO

Number of Committees	Science, Health, etc.		Economic, Social, etc.		Religion, Art, International Relations, etc.	
	U.S. and U.S.S.R.	Not U.S. and U.S.S.R.	U.S. and U.S.S.R.	Not U.S. and U.S.S.R.	U.S. and U.S.S.R.	Not U.S. and U.S.S.R.
None	52	75	47	64	50	69
1–6	14	5	9	10	11	8
7–10	7	1	4	4	3	2
11 or more	9	1	11	3	6	2
Some, but number not given	18	18	28	19	31	19
Totals (%)	100	100	99	100	101	100
(N)	(101)	(148)	(53)	(328)	(36)	(237)

CONCLUSIONS

The political and economic characteristics of a nation affect the extent to which its voluntary associations join the same NGO's as do associations from particular other nations. In the cases examined in this paper, the similarities and differences between the U.S. and the U.S.S.R. do seem to have affected the type of NGO in which they both are represented. NGO's pertaining to substantive issues about which members of the two countries are likely to have consensus are most likely to have joint representation. Even in NGO's concerned with issues of relatively low consensus, the self-selection which freedom of association makes possible presumably facilitates joint participation. In addition, complementarity of interests may be of great significance in joint representation when consensus is low.

The NGO's concerned with science, technology, medicine, and sports are considered to deal with matters about which the U.S. and U.S.S.R. have relatively high consensus. Significantly these NGO's tend to have a lower level of activity and less centralized decision-making than do NGO's concerned with social or economic or with moral or political matters. Effectiveness in the latter spheres would seem to require more concerted action than in the former spheres. Such requirements may be an additional factor encouraging joint U.S. and U.S.S.R. participation. These findings indicate some of the limits which national differences set to the role that NGO's can play in the development of a world community.

On the other hand, these same findings have another meaning. For many aspects of the organizations under study, whether or not the U.S. and the U.S.S.R. are both represented in the same NGO has relatively little consequence. Any given aspect or characteristic of an organization is affected by, and itself affects, a multitude of other organizational characteristics and environmental conditions. Herein, of course, lie some of the hopes attached to the joint participation of associations from different nations. If organizational processes unrelated to the conflicting interests of sets of organization members have relatively great importance, then the possibility of forming stable and effective organizations cross-cutting national political boundaries is increased.

In this paper, the analysis has focused upon the consequences of joint U.S. and U.S.S.R. participation in NGO's. We noted that such joint participation seems to be associated with an increased probability of NGO's reporting engaging in a variety of activities. The inference was drawn that in order for members with many conflicting interests relative to common, like, or complementary interests to participate in the same NGO, the NGO must provide attractive benefits. This inference is supported by the indication that among NGO's concerned with issues about which the U.S. and U.S.S.R. are most likely to have consensus, whether or not the U.S. and U.S.S.R. jointly participate has the least consequence.

In order for an organization, at least a voluntary association, to provide many benefits to the members, the members must make high contributions to the organization. One such contribution may be delegation of authority to the leadership or staff of the organization. Presumably, if both the U.S. and U.S.S.R. are represented in the same NGO, there would be some reluctance to do this. Indeed, we found some evidence of this in regard to the number of levels in the organization, size of staff, and size of budget.

The implied inconsistencies in the above findings were resolved by the findings in regard to the structural elaboration of NGO's. The implementation of activities does not seem to be accomplished by an increased frequency of general membership meetings which might compensate for limiting staff size or hierarchal differentiation. This form of adaptation, indeed, may be the source of additional strains with both the U.S. and U.S.S.R. represented. The analysis revealed that joint U.S. and U.S.S.R. representation is usually associated with infrequent general membership meetings. The proliferation of committees appears to be an important organizational arrangement which resolves many of the inconsistencies and dilemmas discussed. Committees can help de-politicize issues and help transform them into technical matters. Committees can also provide a basis for organizational integration different from hierarchal differentiation, federalism, or collective union of sentimental attachments or like interests. The proliferation of committees can be a kind of *functional differentiation.* Just as many NGO's embody a functional differentiation within the world community, cross-cutting national boundaries, so can divisions based upon particular sets of problems within an organization cross-cut national differences among the membership. This kind of differentiation provides an alternative basis for organizational integration.

These findings have implications for the study of organizations in general and of the role of NGO's in the building of world community. Attention to organizational arrangements such as functional differentiation points to the ways in which organizations can be integrated and maintain their activities to some extent independently of the characteristics of individual members of the organization. The empirical findings also indicate that the international exchange which participation in NGO's can provide may be limited by some of the adaptive arrangements that may help to preserve and perhaps promote the life and effectiveness of NGO's.

In short, characteristics of potential members of an NGO affect whether or not they will belong to an NGO and whether or not they belong is affected by certain characteristics of the NGO. Some of the organizational characteristics, moreover, are affected by the composition of the organization's membership. The impact of the membership composition upon the NGO, in turn, is also dependent upon many other aspects of the NGO and its environment. Some of these mutual relationships are further illustrated in Table 7. Clearly, in each type of NGO, those which report engaging in some joint activities by the members are much more likely to have committees than are other NGO's. Furthermore, among NGO's engaging in joint membership activities, those with both the U.S. and U.S.S.R. represented

TABLE 7. Percent of NGO's Having Committees by Engaging in Joint Activities, by Type of National Participation, and by Type of NGO

Type of NGO	Engage in Joint Activities		Do Not Engage in Joint Activities	
	U.S. and U.S.S.R.	Not U.S. and U.S.S.R.	U.S. and U.S.S.R.	Not U.S. and U.S.S.R.
Science, health, etc.	89 (44)	52 (63)	16 (51)	5 (77)
Economic, social, etc.	68 (38)	50 (189)	13 (15)	17 (138)
Religion, art, international relations, etc.	78 (18)	53 (87)	25 (16)	19 (144)

are more likely than other NGO's to have committees. This pattern is particularly marked among NGO's concerned with science, health, etc. Committees, then, do seem to be a way of getting organizational tasks done. This way is particularly appropriate when members have many conflicting interests relative to common, like, and complementary ones. This adaptive arrangement is particularly likely in organizations in which members tend to view issues as technical matters.

Despite the crudity of the measures used, some clear findings have emerged from the analysis. The implications of the findings, both for the study of organizations and for the role of NGO's in a world community appear significant enough to warrant further research. Such additional research is needed to specify and test the findings and interpretations presented in this paper.

NOTES

1. The research reported upon here was made possible by a grant from the Syracuse University International Organization Research Program, funded by the Ford Foundation. Alphonse J. Sallett assisted in the coding of the necessary information.

    An abridged version of this paper was presented at the American Sociological Association meetings, 1966.

2. For example, see William M. Evan, "Transnational Forums for Peace," in Quincy Wright, William M. Evan, and Morton Deutsch (eds.), *Preventing World War III: Some Proposals* (New York: Simon and Schuster, 1962); Lyman C. White, *International Non-Governmental*

Organizations (New Brunswick, N. J.: Rutgers University Press, 1951); Ernst B. Haas, *The Uniting of Europe* (Stanford: University of California Press, 1958); Louis Kriesberg, "German Businessmen and Union Leaders and the Schuman Plan," *Social Science,* **34** (April, 1960), pp. 114–121; Peter H. Rohn, *Relations Between the Council of Europe and International Non-Governmental Organizations* (Brussels: Union of International Associations, 1957); J. J. Lador-Lederer, *International Non-Governmental Organizations and Economic Entities* (Leyden, Netherlands: A. W. Sythoff-Leyden, 1962). Also see G. P. Speeckaert, *Select Bibliography on International Organization 1885–1964* (Bruxelles: Union of International Associations, 1965).

3. In the 1962–1963 edition of the *Yearbook of International Organizations,* published by the Union of International Associations, Brussels, Belgium, more than 1700 international organizations are listed and over 1500 are non-governmental. In order to be listed, the organization must (1) have members (with voting powers and who are active) from at least three countries; (2) be nonprofit; (3) be active within the preceding two years; and (4) derive financial support from more than one country.

    Certain types of organizations are excluded: movements without any definite structure, international institutes whose activities are primarily limited to teaching or training, fan clubs, fraternity and university clubs, and trusts or foundations. In addition, if there is insufficient information, the organization is not listed. (From personal communication by A. Judge, Research Secretary, and G. P. Speeckaert, Secretary General, Union of International Association, June 8, 1964).

    For purposes of the analysis reported upon here, other international non-governmental organizations were excluded: NGO's which are confederations of other NGO's, or sections of other NGO's, or whose membership consists only of exile groups. The number of NGO's remaining is 1470. Furthermore, NGO's for which information about the nations which participate is not given are excluded from much of the analysis reported in this paper.

4. For an analysis of the consequences of interaction within international governmental organizations, see Chadwick F. Alger, "Personal Contact in Intergovernmental Organizations," in Herbert C. Kelman (ed.), *International Behavior* (New York: Holt, Rinehart and Winston, 1965), pp. 523–547; for a discussion of the contributions of international non-governmental sociological associations, see Paul F. Lazarsfeld and Ruth Leeds, "International Sociology as a Sociological Problem," *American Sociological Review,* **27** (October, 1962), pp. 732–741.

5. This premise is consistent with the point of view of MacIver and Page, when they write: "An association is likely to be formed wherever people recognize a like, complementary, or common interest sufficiently enduring and sufficiently distinct to be capable of more effective promotion through collective action, provided their differences outside the field of this interest are not so strong as to prevent the partial agreement involved in its formation." Robert MacIver and Charles H. Page, *Society* (New York: Rinehart and Co., 1949), p. 437.

    Like interests exist when persons have similar goals and the attainment of those goals by some persons does not necessarily diminish their attainment by others. *Common* interests exist when persons have goals whose attainment is shared so that some persons cannot approach that goal without the others doing so. *Complementary* interests exist when two or more persons each have resources which the other values sufficiently to make possible a mutually satisfactory exchange. *Conflicting* interests exist when two or more persons have goals such that as one attains his, the other's attainment is diminished. This may be the case if they have the same or different goals. What is critical is that one or both parties is unable to exchange compensating resources with the other party or is unwilling and finds it unnecessary to do so. My use of these terms is similar to that of MacIver and Page, *op. cit.,* p. 440.

For an important discussion of the ambiguities in the relationship between national similarities and differences as a basis for the formation of international organizations, see Amitai Etzioni, *Political Unification,* (New York: Holt, Rinehart and Winston, 1965), esp. pp. 19–27.

6. Within the United States, voluntary associations are even more overwhelmingly organized in relationship to occupational activities. The distribution of types of organizations at the national level, since they in large measure constitute the market of potential members in NGO's, sets some limit to the distribution of types of NGO's. For data on types of voluntary associations in the United States, see *Encyclopedia of American Associations* (Detroit, Michigan: Gale Research Company) and Sherwood Dean Fox, "Voluntary Associations and Social Structure," unpublished Ph.D. dissertation, Department of Social Relations, Harvard University, 1952. An accurate comparison of the types of national and of international associations is impossible without a common set of categories and coding of the associations. Nevertheless, the rank order of the percentage of various types of organizations in the U.S. and among the NGO's is probably similar.

7. A more precise measure of the balance of interests among members would require information about the associations which actually belong to the NGO's. Such a measure, however, would obviate the possible significance arising from national differences in general.

Even using national representation as a measure could be variously done. Instead of the joint participation of two particular nations, nations could be grouped in terms of many different criteria and the relative proportion of each type of nation represented in the NGO could be used as a measure.

8. The People's Republic of China (Communist China) is represented in very few NGO's, probably about 3 percent of those which are not regionally restricted. This probably reflects the Chinese government's policy, but also the level of associational proliferation and contact with voluntary associations in other countries.

9. Recent disclosures of support for international activities by the Central Intelligence Agency of the United States testifies to the importance of NGO's. Such financial aid also indicates that in many cases it is difficult to make a perfectly clear distinction between governmental and non-governmental organizations, even in the United States. See, for example, Sol Stern, "A Short Account of International Student Politics and the Cold War With Particular Reference to the NSA, CIA, etc.," *Ramparts,* 5 (March, 1967), pp. 29–38.

10. For example, before World War II, Soviet international sport participation was limited to the Red Sport International. Only after the war did the Soviet policy change and participation in sport activities with "bourgeois" sporting organizations begin. By 1952, the Soviet Union had joined practically every international sport federation. See Henry W. Morton, *Soviet Sport* (New York: Collier Books, Crowell-Collier Publishing Co., 1963), pp. 65–102.

Changes in Soviet and foreign policy after Stalin have probably led to an increased Soviet participation in NGO's. Soviet participation in the United Nations Specialized Agencies, especially UNESCO, is an indicator of these changes and probably was accompanied and followed by representation in various NGO's.

For an account of Soviet policy in regard to sociology and the initial participation of Soviet sociologists at meetings of the International Sociological Associaton, see "The Social Sciences in the U.S.S.R." *Soviet Survey,* No. 10 (November, 1956), pp. 1–19.

11.   An explanation of this attraction is suggested by Galtung. [See Johan Galtung, "East-West Interaction Petterns," *Journal of Peace Research,* 2 (1966), pp. 146–176.] He reasons that interaction between the top levels of two interacting social systems is more frequent than is interaction between the lower levels of the two groups or between the top level of one group and the lower levels of the other group. Smoker's analysis of international non-governmental organizations lends support to this hypothesis. [See Paul Smoker, "A Preliminary Study of an International Integrative Subsystem," *International Associations,* 17 (June, 1965), pp. 638–646.] The data in this paper have not been organized to test the above-stated hypothesis. Nevertheless, the reasoning and evidence of Galtung and Smoker help account for the finding reported here. The U.S. and U.S.S.R., as leaders of their respective blocs, have an interest in interacting with each other, *if* there is to be *any* interaction between the two blocs. As leaders, they have some like interests.

12.   From 1945 to 1948, many Communist and non-Communist trade unions belonged to the World Federation of Trade Unions. In 1949, the International Confederation of Free Trade Unions was founded without Communist trade unions. For an account of the international labor movement, see Lewis L. Lorwin, *The International Labor Movement* (New York: Harper and Bros., 1953).

13.   The distinction between NGO's formed by the confederation of pre-existing national units or by the establishment of national units by a parent organization is an important one. In many organizations, some combination of both sequences can be found. The consequences for the structure and authority system in these organizations is likely to differ. For analyses of the consequences of such differences within national voluntary associations, see, for example, Seymour M. Lipset, "The Political Process in Trade Unions: À Theoretical Statement," in Morroe Berger, Theodore Abel, and Charles H. Page (eds.), *Freedom and Control in Modern Society* (New York: D. Van Nostrand Co., 1954), pp. 82–124; and David L. Sills, *The Volunteers* (Glencoe, Ill.: The Free Press, 1957), esp. pp. 2–8.

Even when the national components pre-date the establishment of the NGO, another process may facilitate more consensus at the international level than an analysis of the characteristics of each national organization would lead one to expect. In the case of organizations established to meet the needs of the national members, the international activities may be peripheral to the concerns of the rank-and-file members and even of the organizations' leadership. In some such cases, at least, the staff persons or officials involved in international organization relations may have considerable freedom of action and be selected or self-selected because of their concern with international relations in general or because of their compatibility with the style and direction of the NGO.

Furthermore, leaders may share concerns and develop common understanding with leaders of other organizations which are not shared with their own rank and file members. See Louis Kriesberg, "Societal Coordination by Occupational Leaders," *PROD,* III (September, 1959), pp. 34–36.

14. *New York Times,* March 26, 1959.
15. Sills, *op. cit.,* Lipset, *op. cit.,* and Bernard Barber, "Participation and Mass Apathy in Associations," in Alvin W. Gouldner, *Studies in Leadership,* (New York: Harper and Brothers, 1950), esp. pp. 492–493.
16. In a bureaucratic organization, with authority flowing from the top down, a large number of levels may be considered to indicate decentralization rather than centralization. Many levels, holding the size of staff constant, would indicate dispersion of decision making. As Peter Blau has pointed out to me in a personal communication, this conceptualization underlies the treatment of a low ratio of managers to non-supervisory officials as an indication of centralization in the paper, Peter M. Blau, Wolf V. Heyderbrand, and Robert E. Stauffer, "The Structure of Small Bureaucracies," *American Sociological Review,* **31** (April, 1966), pp. 179–191.
17. Haas analyzes the role of committees in the formation of consensus in an international governmental organization with a legislative structure. He also points out some of the limitations of the resulting consensus. Ernst B. Haas, *Consensus Formation in the Council of Europe* (Berkeley: University of California Press, 1960). Also see Theodore Caplow, *Principles of Organization* (New York: Harcourt, Brace and World, 1964), pp. 248–249.

26. NATION STATE ESCALATION AND INTERNATIONAL INTEGRATION

Paul Smoker

1. INTRODUCTION

In this paper we shall be dealing with international integration and nation state escalation. Escalation is defined here in a rather broad sense to include the phenomena of the run-away arms race.[1] It refers to an interactive situation where increases of tension become manifest through increasing national defense expenditures.[2] International integration here means transnational bonds that bring individuals in one country into direct cultural and social relations with individuals in another country. While international integration as defined here can be exhibited through national behavior, as in the case of joint governmental cultural agreements, this need not be the case. Integration can also take place through non-governmental activity, such as international scientific conferences or football matches.

To clarify the theoretical argument that follows, we must define what will be meant by the "international" and the "nation state" systems, terms that are used here in a particular way for the sake of the theoretical argument. A nation state system is defined here as a system in which nations are the only actors, and, therefore, the nation is the only behavioral group[3] for the purpose of analysis. An international system, however, is defined to include a variety of actors, from individuals to nations to international organizations of both the governmental and non-governmental kinds.[4] Here there are many different behavioral groups, although one could, for example, take nations as the central actors and try to analyze behavior within the international context.

SOURCE. Paul Smoker, "Nation State Escalation and International Integration," in *Journal of Peace Research,* No. 1, 1967, pp. 60–74. (Footnotes abridged.) Reprinted by permission of the author and the International Peace Research Institute.

2. THE THREE WORLD ARMS RACES[5]

Richardson, in his analysis of arms races, worked within the nation state system framework. He assumed that in a two-nation arms race the rate at which the first nation arms depends upon the amount of armament the other nation has, the colossal costs of armaments, and the feelings toward the other nation (for instance, as expressed in treaties).[6] He expressed these assumptions in mathematical form and tested his mathematical model against the behavior of nations in the first and second world arms races.[7] Given the simplicity of his model and the many problems of measurement involved, the model was remarkably consistent with the facts. For the first world arms race, however, the agreement was better than for the second.

For a two-nation nuclear arms race within the nation state context, Richardson argued that a submissiveness or fear factor should be included to allow for the mutual fear induced by nuclear weapons.[8] This submissiveness model, when applied to the present arms race, for the United States and the Soviet Union suggested the possibility that this fear factor was completely absent before 1952 but came into being quite suddenly during that year.[9] In terms of the Richardson models, this meant that the present arms race behaved in the same way as the previous two up to 1952, in that the growth of defense expenditure was exponential; and then after 1952 behaved in a way consistent with the assumptions of the submissiveness model.[10]

This paper relates this change in behavior to the possible change from a nation state type of system to a kind of international system, and suggests a possible functional relationship between escalation and integration in this type of international system.

3. THE THEORY

To begin with we shall take an interpretation of Talcott Parsons' theory of social systems[11] and consider its relevance to the possible movement of a nation state type of system toward an international type of system. The four basic functional requirements of a social system suggested by Parsons—namely, pattern maintenance, adaptation, goal attainment, and integration—can at the national and international levels of analysis be very roughly equated with specific subsystems.

Thus, at the national level the nation can be viewed as individuals and groups who are mainly responsible for pattern maintenance through such activities as practicing cultural values and providing labor; an economy which is mainly responsible for adaptation; a governmental subsystem which is mainly responsible for goal attainment of the nation; and a cultural subsystem that is responsible for integration.

In a nation state system, it can be argued, the interaction is primarily an interaction of the goal attainment subsystems of each of the participating nations. A classical interpretation of such goal attainment interaction is pure power politics. There is, by definition, no integrative subsystem working between nations in a nation state system; the situation resembles a zero sum game in that "might is right."

In an international system we can assume that:

1. The pattern maintenance function may be characterized by individuals and families through that international system. The individuals might be referred to as "international man" and may represent, at present, a tiny fraction of the world's population.

2. The adaptation subsystem might be represented roughly by the international economic system, which includes international corporations. In the world of the future these corporations may play an increasingly important role, as giants like General Motors, whose sales in 1965 were more than the gross national product of the Netherlands and well over a hundred other countries, become more common.

3. The goal attainment subsystem might be represented by parts of the United Nations. Thus, some organs of the UN are concerned with world politics—for example, the General Assembly—while others are concerned with educational or cultural matters—such as UNESCO.[12] Thus, the General Assembly might be seen as characteristic of an international goal attainment subsystem.

4. The international integrative subsystem can be characterized by the various international cultural activities and may be indexed approximately by international non-governmental organizations[13] and international conferences.[14] The nonpolitical aspects of the United Nations and the family of international governmental organizations also might index the international integrative subsystem.

Figure 1 illustrates a three-nation nation state system within the context of three national systems. Interactions between subsystems (as represented by squares) are shown by arrows. This system defines nation state interaction as motivated purely by the goal attainment subsystems of the particular nations as illustrated by the shaded areas.

Figure 2 illustrates an international system as defined. Here goal attainment, pattern maintenance, integration, and adaptation are associated with international institutions and attitudes as defined above. Each of the four subsystems is represented by a circle, and the interactions between them by arrows.

Now, to put forward these two definitions is not to argue that such pure types exist or have existed in world affairs. However, it will be argued in the next section that there is evidence that world affairs are moving from a situation resembling that in Figure 1 toward a situation resembling that in Figure 2. It is not argued here that this gradual shift is as yet very great: on the contrary, the

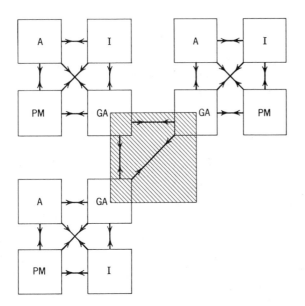

FIG. 1. A nation state system. A = adaptation subsystem; I = integration subsystem; PM = pattern maintenance subsystem; GA = goal attainment subsystem. The shaded area represents a nation state system.

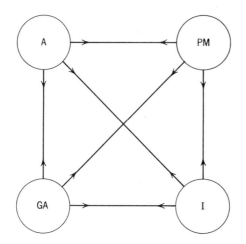

FIG. 2. An international system. A = adaptation subsystem; I = integration subsystem; PM = pattern maintenance subsystem; GM = goal attainment subsystem.

structure of the world society today is probably still like Figure 1 in many ways according to the theory presented here. It is not even argued that we will eventually reach the situation illustrated in Figure 2, the position of those who campaign for some kind of world government. Rather, it is suggested that the structure of the world community is likely to be an amalgam of both types as well as other major structural features, such as rank disequilibrium between nations and between international organizations as suggested by Galtung.[15]

For the purpose of this article it is sufficient to suggest that particularly since the Second World War, partly through the advent of modern communications, the international component of the world system has grown significantly. Here the world system is defined as the amalgam of the nation state and the international component parts and is illustrated in Figure 3. The relative importance of the nation state and the international components may change in time, it is suggested here, and such changes are likely to affect the relationships between variables in the world system.

The model of the world system, therefore, places considerable emphasis on the size of the two component parts. It is argued here, and subsequently investigated empirically, that as the international component grows in size, significant interactions between the international component and the nation state component become important in the analysis of the world system. Viewed in terms of levels

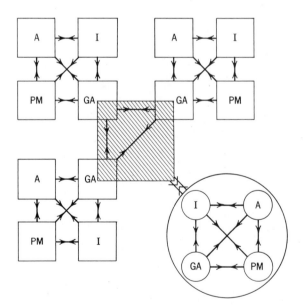

FIG. 3. The world system.

of analysis, this is to suggest that there are now interactive links between the nation state and the international level. For the purposes of this article, it is argued that the types of interactions depicted in the shaded box in Figure 4 are of particular importance to the arms race in general and nation state escalation in particular.

This is not to argue that the complete nexus of interrelationships presented in Figure 3 should not be considered; a complete analysis would have to include all the linkages. Rather, it is to suggest that in exploring the theoretical model put forward here, the particular interrelationships shown in Figure 4 are of interest. The reader, therefore, should bear in mind the partial nature of the empirical testing and theoretical argument that follows.

Figure 4 depicts a situation in which a three-nation state system is linked to an international system through the international system's integrative subsystem. While no integrative control operates within a nation state system, it is suggested here that the international integrative subsystem has increased in size and now exerts a controlling influence on both the international system *and* the nation state system. This is not to argue that the nation state system component (or

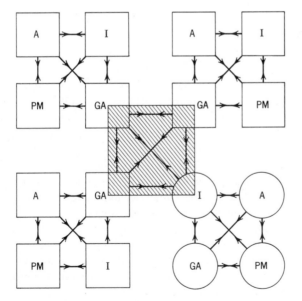

FIG. 4. The circular subsystems comprise an international system, the square subsystems national systems. The shaded area represents the escalation/integration space in which a nation state system interacts with an international integrative subsystem.

nationalism) is necessarily weakening, but to suggest that the international integrative subsystem has a greater controlling influence because it is now operating at a significant level.

However, in the same way that the old equation "hunger down equals war down" does not take into account structural properties of the situation, so the equally popular proposition "integration up, war down" fails to consider the nexus of interactions involved in structural relationships. When integration is operating at a low or zero level, as in the case of a nation state type of system, any increase in integration is likely to modify the power politics of simple goal attainment interaction. But when integration is operating at a relatively high level, as in the case of husband and wife, relatively high levels of tension become possible. The fact that husbands and wives murder each other with high frequency relative to other groups of people, even allowing for the increased opportunities, is consistent with the assumption that for high levels of integration the relationship between integration and hostility or violence is more complex.[16]

Consider now the situation in Figure 4: suppose that the nation state interaction of the goal attainment subsystems has entered an escalation feed-back process. That is, the Richardson equations:

$$\frac{dx}{dt} = ky - ax + g$$

and   (1)

$$\frac{dy}{dt} = lx - by + h$$

become relevant in that increases in defenses seem necessary to each nation to counter the rising tension and protect its interests. In these equations, x and y represent defenses; k and l defense coefficients that indicate the sensitivity of each nation to changes in defenses of the other; a and b fatigue and expense coefficients that indicate the economic and other restraints on building defenses; and g and h are grievances that indicate the feelings for each nation about the other. The Richardson equations show how these increases in defenses lead to new increases designed to protect each nation's interests, and the tension continues to rise.

Now, this is not necessarily a dangerous situation, for it could be that the increases in world tension due to an arms race are being matched by increases in the international integrative subsystem. This leads to a situation in which tension is rising, but where the system's ability to contain tension and avoid violence is increasing. The over-all strain on decision-makers may not, therefore, be increasing in proportion to the escalation process.

However, if a secondary feedback process is at work in which increases in tension adversely affect the growth of the integrative subsystem, then a drop in integration might occur, and, at the same time, the arms race escalation process may continue. From the point of view of actors within the system, the situation would have worsened; the strain would rise much faster than previously, and proportionately faster than previously, and proportionately faster than the tension. The effect of such an increase in strain on decision-makers, where strain is defined as the tension in the system relative to the strength of the system, will, it is argued, depend to some extent on the structure of the world system. Three distinct types of situation can be identified:

1. A world system which continues to contain a significant international integrative component.

2. A world system in which a significant international integrative component has become negligible as a result of the feedback effects of the arms race on the international system.

3. A world system in which the international integrative component was negligible even before the feedback process began.

This article argues that the three world arms races have, in some ways, produced each of these three types of situations. For the first world arms race, it is argued, the situation throughout resembled a nation state interaction process and the collapse of the significant international integrative subsystem was irrelevant to the outcome because the level of that subsystem was so low. For the second world arms race, it is argued, an international type of system collapsed into a nation state system; while for the present arms race during the period 1948–52 the drop in the integrative subsystem was not great enough to destroy the significant international component.

Of course, the argument presented here, and discussed in the light of empirical data below, ignores many important points and is based on a relatively simplistic theory. The question of alliances, for example, is not dealt with here in terms of our model. Nevertheless, the model put forward here is, in principle, susceptible to rigorous analysis and even in this simple form appears to be consistent with international and nation state behavior during the period 1900 to 1960 considered below.

4. COMPARING THEORY AND DATA

Integration and escalation

Two types of indicators are used to compare the theory with data. The first type of indicator concerns nation state escalation, the second international integration.

For nation state escalation the well documented data on the three world arms races have been used.[17] Thus, for the first world arms race, the defense expenditures of the Triple Alliance and the Triple Entente have been used; for the second world arms race, when the value of money was not so stable, defense expenditures for the ten nations, Germany, Russia, Japan, Italy, France, China, United Kingdom, United States, Poland, and Czechoslovakia, as calculated by Richardson in terms of defense hours worked in million person years per year, have been used; and for the present world arms race, defense expenditure for the United States and the Soviet Union in terms of Smoker's defense ratio have been used.[18]

In the case of defenses, the indicators used rest upon the justifications given by the authors and their relative success in describing the escalation in each of the three arms races. Because this part of the paper is concerned with a time series trend type analysis, the problem of intercomparability of units does not arise. The escalation process is indexed clearly in each case, while the relative magnitude of the process is conveyed very approximately by means of the respective scales used in Figure 5. In line with the Parsonian framework, the integration indicator used is the growth rate of international nongovernmental organizations (INGO's).[19] Some comparative data on the number of international congresses is used as background data, although for reasons discussed below the number of conferences is not suitable for our purposes here.

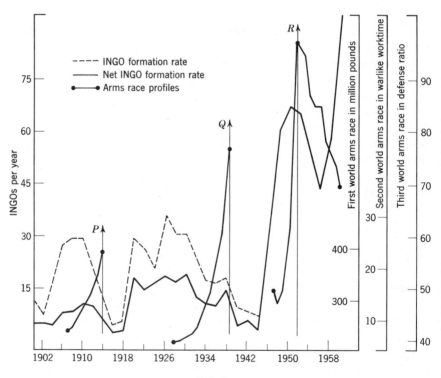

FIG. 5.

In the case of the integration measure, the need was for an indicator (1) relatively sensitive to short run fluctuations, and (2) relatively representative of over-all international trends. The number of international congresses per year does not seem to satisfy these criteria so well as the number of new INGO's formed per year. There are a number of studies which show that the number of international congresses show trends from decade to decade[20] not from year to year.[21] For example, in ten-year periods from 1840 to 1959 the number of international congresses held is 9, 22, 75, 149, 284, 469, 1,082, 974 (the period of the first world war), 2,913, 3,655, estimated 7,000, and estimated 9,600. However, year to year trends are often severely distorted by international exhibitions. From 1900 to 1960 there had been fifteen such international exhibitions. In every single case the number of congresses in the year of the exhibition was more than the number in either the preceding or the following year. Further, the percentage of conferences held in the town of the international exhibition was always more than ten per cent, and sometimes as high as eighty or ninety per cent. Typical examples, however, are the two Brussels exhibitions of 1935 and 1958, which attracted thirty-three per cent and twenty per cent, respectively, of the total conference universes for the year.

Because of this influence, the second criteria, that of reflecting over-all international trends, also is less well satisfied by international congresses than by INGO formation over the short run.

The relative inadequacies of the number of international conferences as an indicator should not obscure the approximations involved in using the rate of formation of INGO's as an indicator of growth in the international integrative subsystem. The indicator used here does not distinguish between large and small or rich and poor organizations; the considerable variance on these matters could very well affect the interpretation of trends.[22] However, for our immediate purposes the indicator chosen, rate of formation of INGO's, is assumed to be adequate, partly because of the relatively large numbers involved. In future studies better indicators might be developed.

Before proceeding to Figure 5, however, one further difficulty should be mentioned concerning the measurement of the rate of formation of INGO's: many of the organizations formed go out of existence after a number of years. Thus, up to 1951, 1,409 INGO's had been established; at that time, 905 remained in existence. Thus the net growth of the international integrative structure might be taken as an indicator, or the number of organizations formed could be taken. Although new organizations are being formed every year, in some years the over-all total drops because the disbanding rate is higher than the formation rate.[23] Thus, two INGO indicators have been used to 1944, namely the number of new INGO's formed per year and the net number formed from the point of view of an observer in the late 1950's.[24] Because the fall-out rate becomes significant only after a number of years, only the INGO formation rate as recorded in the tenth edition of the *Yearbook of International Associations* has been recorded after 1944.

Figure 5 shows both sets of integration indicators, the lower profile being the net formation rate, together with the three escalation profiles, one for each arms race. As explained above, the escalation indicators are not comparable in quantitative terms; they simply indicate that each arms race has been considerably larger than the previous one. The arrow P marks the outbreak of World War I, Q the outbreak of World War II, and R the point at which submission, or the fear factor, can be assumed to have come into being. We are able now to compare each of the three arms races with the theory suggested above.

For the first world arms race, the exponential escalation process began slowly in 1907, as shown by Richardson, and led to war in 1914. The rate of formation of INGO's, and the net rate of formation both showed a general increasing tendency from about 1902 to 1910.[25] After 1910, however, while escalation continued, the international integrative subsystem collapsed. Also the profile of the rate of formation after rising sharply up to 1906 seems to show signs of weakening from 1907–08 onwards. This is consistent with the feedback effect of the nation state system on a very weak international integrative subsystem. The World War I profiles are consistent with the assumption that a nation state system was dominant throughout; the collapse of the international integrative subsystem had no visible effect on the escalation process, due to the relatively insignificant level at which it was operating.

For the second world arms race, as mentioned above, Richardson did not get such a good agreement between his nation-state interaction theory and national behavior. In fact, he found it necessary to assume in his model that the second world arms race was in two parts, one up to 1932 and one from 1933 onwards.[26] After 1932 the acceleration was more marked and the escalation process typically run-away exponential.

The following assumption is consistent with the finding of Richardson described above, the theory presented in Section 3, and the integration and escalation profiles between 1926 and 1938 in Figure 5. That is, that the international integrative subsystem was operating at a significant level,[27] in that it was constraining the goal-seeking behavior to some extent; but then with the feedback process from the nation state escalation starting around 1930, the international control element became insignificant by the mid-1930's, and the national state interaction dominated. Certainly the collapse of the integrative subsystem is well marked in the Figure and to some extent reflected in such events as the decay of the League of Nations, which was in part a weak international goal-seeking subsystem.

As with World War I, the decay continued through World War II. Thus, even in 1947 there were fewer than 400 INGO's functioning as compared to about 600 in 1938. After the Second World War, however, the INGO profile shows a tremendous increase, such that by 1951 there were 905 INGO's, more than ever before.

However, the third world arms race had been under way since 1948; and the feedback, according to our theory, first became visible in the over-all INGO growth rate during the period 1951–52. The effect is even more visible in trans-cold war INGO's—that is, INGO's who have members living in any of the NATO, SEATO, and CENTO countries and in any of the Warsaw Pact or Socialist countries.[28] Our concern here, however, is with the general phenomena in the whole international system and not so much with effects on particular parts of the system. Obviously, such effects could be very important—for example, the tremendous integrative underdevelopment of South East Asia—but to consider them in this article would detract from the central point.

As stated above, a previous article argued that a fear factor came into being during 1952, having been absent previously, and caused the arms race to slow.[29] According to the profiles in Figure 5, it was during the period 1951–52 that the rate of formation of INGO's first dropped while the escalation continued. The fear factor finding, the theory presented in Section 3, and the profiles in Figure 5 are consistent with the following assumption: the international integrative subsystem was operating at a significant level in 1952, but due to feedback effects of the arms race escalation its growth rate had dropped. Despite this drop, the integrative subsystem still continued to operate at a significant level; and the nation state and international systems remained functionally linked to each other. The increase in strain relative to the increase in tension caused submission to operate on decision-makers of both sides.

To escalate in a situation with no interdependencies is, in other words, qualitatively different from escalation between interdependent parties. In the 1952 case, it is argued, a decrease in integration, coupled with a still significant level of operation by the integrative subsystem, contributed to a decrease in escalation because of the relative levels of tension and strain.

Trade and Defense

The argument outlined in the preceding sections concerns structural change. It suggests that because of the increasing international system, the nation state and international components are becoming progressively more linked over time. This increasing linkage is not, it is argued, a steady linear thing for during the three periods of nation state escalation considered feedback from the nation state escalation undermined the international integrative subsystem. However, it is suggested that the pre-World War I period, the pre-World War II period, and the post-World War II period will exhibit relatively increasing linkages between the nation state and the international systems.

In order to investigate in a preliminary fashion this possibility, it is of interest to compare the trade/defense relationships during each of these three periods. Trade can be conceived of as a part of the international adaptive subsystem to a first approximation, and has received increasing attention in the study of international relations.[30] One interpretation of international trade used Galtung's ideas on polarization[31] to construct a polarization index F_{mn} where:

$$F_{mn} = \frac{1}{2}\left(\frac{t_{mn}}{T_m} + \frac{t_{mn}}{T_n}\right) \tag{2}$$

Here t_{mn} is the intertrade between the mth and n^{th} nation, while T_m and T_n represent the total trade of the mth and n^{th} nations. This index tries to record the relative importance of intertrade between two nations. In the study where this index was suggested,[32] it appeared to give a reasonable indicator of polarization during the period 1948–62. This index is used here, however, simply to index intertrade between two nations.

Defense is measured here using the ratio Defense Expenditure/Government Expenditure. During the 1950's and early '60's this ratio appears to correlate with threats, accusations, and protests, while defense expenditure alone does not.[33]

The selection of nations for each period is as follows: For the first world arms race, Richardson's work suggested that the Triple Alliance and the Triple Entente were the dominant national actors. The six nations Germany, Austria-Hungary, Italy, France, Russia, and Britain have, therefore, been taken. For the pre-World War II period, five of these six nations (all but Austria-Hungary, which had ceased to exist) were taken, together with Japan and Italy. For the post-World War II period, the seven nations USA, USSR, UK, People's Republic of China, Federal Republic of Germany, People's Republic of Poland, and France were taken. The time periods taken are 1906–1913, 1929–1937, and 1952–1962, all inclusive.[34] Standard data sources are used.[35]

Table 1 shows the correlation by dyad of the trade ratio for the dyad against the sum of the defense ratios for the two nations in the dyad. The hypothesis concerning the increasing linkage between the nation state and the international systems is supported by this Table, for during the first period, 5 out of 15 dyads— or one third—exhibit a significant relationship;[36] during the second period, 10 out of 21—roughly one half; while during the third period, 16 out of 21—roughly three quarters—exhibit significant linkages.

A closer examination of Table 1 reveals that certain correlations, marked with an *, are positive. Before World War II, the USSR appears to have been improving its trading relations with the USA, UK, and France despite increasing nation state escalation. The same appears to be the case for Italy and Germany in their relations. For each of these dyads, trading relationships with eventual allies increased as the escalation increased. With the exception of the Japan/Italy dyad, all the other significant trade/defense relationships decreased as the nation state escalation increased and were associated with dyads comprising eventual adversaries. This is consistent with the assumption that those dyads that were operating under the constraints of the international system had trade/defense linkages consistent with the eventual alliance formation.

Since 1952, the USSR/Poland and the USSR/China dyads both show decreasing intertrade with de-escalation of the arms race, as does the USA/China dyad.

TABLE 1. Comparative Table of Trade/Defense Relationship for Three Periods in History

(The left-hand column shows the probability of such values of r arising by chance in an uncorrelated population of statistics. It merely serves as a method of comparing correlations from different sample sizes and should not be interpreted as a measure of significance.)

	1906–1913 Inclusive (N = 8)		1929–1937 Inclusive (N = 9)		1952–1962 Inclusive (N = 11)	
	Triple Alliance	*Triple Entente*	UK Japan		USA FGR	
	Germany	France	US Italy		USSR Poland	
	Austria-Hungary	Russia	Germany USSR		UK France	
	Italy	UK	France		China (Peoples Rep.)	
.001	Germany/Italy	−93	UK/Japan	−94	USSR/France	−95
					UK/China	−90
					UK/USA	−88
.01	Austria-Hungary/Italy	−85			Poland/FGR	−79
					USSR/Poland	+77*
					USA/FGR	−76
					Poland/UK	−76
.02			USSR/USA	+79*	France/China	−71
			USSA/Germany	−79	USSR/China	+68*
			UK/Italy	−76		
			UK/USSR	+75*		
			Germany/Italy	+75*		
.05	France/Italy	−73	USA/Japan	−71	USA/USSR	−67
			USSR/Italy	−69	USA/Poland	−67
					FGR/USSR	−65
					FGR/France	−60
.1	Germany/UK	−66	Japan/Italy	−64	USA/China	+59*
	France/UK	−62	France/USSR	+58*	FGR/China	−58
					USA/France	−56
Not significant in a random population of statistics.	Germany/Austria-Hungary	+55	France/Italy	−57	UK/FGR	−44
	France/Russia	+50	France/Germany	−53	UK/USSR	+08
	Italy/Russia	−46	Germany/UK	−52	UK/France	−17
	Germany/France	+39	France/UK	−52	Poland/France	+18
	Austria-Hungary/UK	−33	USA/Italy	−49	Poland/China	+05
	Germany/Russia	+27	Germany/Japan	−35		
	Italy/UK	−29	USA/France	+34		
	Russia/UK	+14	France/Japan	−29		
	Austria-Hungary/Russia	+08	USSR/Japan	+24		
	Austria-Hungary/France	+07	USA/UK	+06		
			USA/Germany	−05		

* indicates positive correlations.

To use Galtung's terms, this is consistent with the assumption that polarization within the Socialist nations has been decreasing as has polarization between the Socialist and Western nations, with the exception of USA/China, while polarization within the Western nations has been increasing with the following exceptions—

the UK/FGR and UK/France dyads have not followed this trend within the Western nations, UK/USSR and Poland/France between the two alliances, and Poland/China within the Socialist nations.

The over-all trends support the Galtung hypothesis that during this period, the international system was moving from its highly polarized state into a new pattern. The particular differences, however, argue that other factors may be relevant to the trade/defense relationship. That is to say, while it is obviously possible to interpret the deviants from the general trends in terms of political differences, it might also be possible to interpret them in terms of the over-all model presented in the early part of this paper.

For example, the international integrative subsystem is not, as observed above, uniformly distributed around the world. Such differential distribution is likely to influence linkages between trade and defense. Thus, in the case of the UK, the great increase in integration in Europe, other than the UK, is likely to influence such dyads as UK/FGR and UK/France. Future work using the model presented above will investigate such possibilities.

5. THEORETICAL IMPLICATIONS

The first implication of this paper suggests that the classic analysis of international affairs, simply in terms of the nation state, is likely to be less valid in the future, as an international type of system develops in the way suggested above. Multilevel analysis using many behavior groups and individuals is likely to be of more value in such matters.

Of course, it could be that the present analysis is inadequate or incorrect due to theoretical methodological mistakes. It thus goes without saying that all the conclusions in this and the next section need further consideration before they can be regarded as valid in any sense. However, the findings here suggest that any analysis of escalation or de-escalation that does not include the integration dimension of human relations as a functional component is likely to run into difficulties in interpreting international relations. Similarly, any analysis of international integration which does not relate to international power politics is likely to be in error. On the research side, it would seem from this rather limited article that detailed studies of intergration and its relationship to other variables are of some importance. For it can be argued that the simple formula "integration down, war up" is not sufficient if we wish to understand the complex structural relationships involved.

6. POLICY IMPLICATIONS

At the policy level this article, on a tentative basis, argues that the social context for escalation or de-escalation is important if control is to be retained. As mentioned, INGO indicators for certain areas of the world suggest a look of such international structures in these parts. Within such areas it might be argued that might equals right, but it is likely to be accompanied by force. Nor is it at this time clear how heterogeneous international integration, unevenly distributed around the world, will affect the functioning of the whole integrative subsystem.

At the world level, the possible success of the integrative system in 1952 might be interpreted as supporting evidence for a new brinkmanship. However, the eroding properties of feedback from the nation state system to the international system, as witnessed by the steady decline of INGO trans-cold-war bonding from 1952–59, should caution against such a view. It seems likely that increased integration, paradoxically enough, makes possible increased tension. Nuclear deterrence may only be able to function as a deterrent if the international integrative system is strong enough to contain and modify its power political use. But increased escalation decays the integrative subsystem and could in the not-too-long run lead to a dangerous situation. Any prolonged escalation, such as the Vietnam war, could do great damage in this respect.

On the positive side, the preventative approach to international conflict might be adopted on a large scale by governments through properly conceived technical assistance, cultural exchange, and exchange visitors. Besides this, those individuals whose professional or human concern lies in this area can contribute themselves to international integration by participation in activities of INGO's.[37]

A useful aid to those concerned with international integration might be the publishing of a monthly international integration index, together with a tension and strain index. Such information, even though crudely measured, might prove of value to those INGO's, peace groups, and politicians who are involved in action for peace.

NOTES

* This research was supported by JWGA/ARPA/NU project (Advanced Research Project Agency, SD 260) on Simulated International Processes conducted at Northwestern University, Evanston, Illinois, USA.

The author wishes to thank Professor Harold Guetzkow for his very helpful comments and suggestions during the execution of this study.
1. In many instances a distinguishing characteristic of an escalation process is its exponential character. All three world arms races have exhibited this phenomenon.
2. In the case of the present arms race, defense expenditures have to be corrected to allow for polarization using trade data if more than the two super-powers are included. Increase then refers to the corrected figures. For a description of this see Paul Smoker, "Trade, Defence, and the Richardson Theory of Arms Races: A Seven Nation Study," *Journal of Peace Research, 1965,* 2, pp. 161–176.

3. The term "behavioral group" corresponds to the usual term "behavior unit" and is used to avoid any misunderstanding of the word "unit" as it is used in measurement.
4. An international governmental organization is an international organization which is founded by treaty between at least two governments, and, as a rule, has as its members representatives of the governments involved. International nongovernmental organizations comprise all other international organizations.
5. The term "world arms race" is used here for those arms races leading to the first two world wars and the present arms race.
6. Lewis Richardson in *Arms and Insecurity* (Pittsburgh: The Boxwood Press, 1960), pp. 33-35, suggested that trade might be relevant also to the feelings between nations. This effect is now seen as related to the polarization phenomenon as explained in footnote 2.
7. See Richardson, *op. cit.,* chapters 2, 7, 9, 10, 19, and 20.
8. Richardson first suggested this possibility for a nuclear arms race in "Could an Arms Race End Without Fighting," *Nature*, September 29, 1951.
9. See Paul Smoker, "Fear in the Arms Race: A Mathematical Study," *Journal of Peace Research,* No. 1, 1964, pp. 55-64.
10. As pointed out in Paul Smoker, "The Arms Race: A Wave Model," *Peace Research Society (International), PAPERS, Vol. IV., 1966, Cracow Conference, 1965,* pp. 151-192, the decay of the arms race after 1952 is more consistent with an exponential decay process than with the Richardson submissiveness equations, which are not exponential decay in form. When seven nations are considered and allowance is made for polarization by the use of trade data, an exponential model gives a correlation of $-.95$ for the ten pairs of observations from 1952 to 1962, when the arms race accelerated once again, while the submissiveness model on the same data gives a correlation of $-.72$ and the unadapted submissiveness model a correlation of $.4$. Nevertheless, the argument here is not altered by a reinterpretation of the functional form of the submissiveness effect.
11. The interpretation used as a starting point is that of Karl Deutsch taken from *The Integration of Political Communities* edited by Philip Jacob and James Toscano (New York: Lippincott, 1964).
12. I am grateful to Robert Beattie of the Comparative International Processes project at Northwestern University for making this observation. In an earlier study, "A Preliminary Empirical Study of an International Integrative Subsystem in International Association," November 1965, a political/nonpolitical continuum was constructed on page 642 using empirical data on membership of international nongovernmental organizations.
13. The *Yearbook of International Associations* published by the Union of International Associations, Brussels, provides well-documented information on both governmental and nongovernmental international organizations.
14. The Union of International Associations published an annual Calendar also with details of international conferences and monthly supplements in their monthly publication, *International Associations.*
15. See Johan Gaultung, "A Structural Theory of Aggression," *Journal of Peace Research,* 1964, **2**, pp. 95-119.

16. Kenneth Boulding, for example, in "Towards a Theory of Peace," in Fisher, Roger D. (ed.), *International Conflict and Behavioral Science: Craigville Papers* (New York: Basic Books, 1964, pp. 70–87), distinguishes between the threat system, the exchange system, and the integrative system, and argues for functional relationships between all three.

17. For the first two world arms races, the data have been collected from the studies of Richardson, *op. cit.* For the present arms race, the data are given in Paul Smoker, "A Pilot Study of the Present Arms Race," *General Systems Yearbook,* Vol. VIII, 1963, pp. 61–76.

18. See footnote 9.

19. Collected from the *Yearbook* of the Union of International Associations.

20. For example, Genevieve Deville, "Les Reúnions Internationales en 1958," in *International Associations,* No. 6, 1959.

21. See footnote 19 and the two monographs "International Congresses, 1681 to 1899," and "International Congresses, 1900–1919" published by the Union of International Associations, Brussels, 1960.

22. For example, the forty largest INGO's in 1951 had a joint membership of 719,954,442 members, while the smallest INGO's may have only ten or twenty numbers. Similarly, while the estimated total budget of all the INGO's in 1960 was $306,150,380, two INGO's jointly handle more than $110,000,000 a year and others get along on less than $200.

23. For example, if all international organizations, governmental and nongovernmental, are considered in 1906 there were 160; 1912, 437; 1921, 321; 1926, 397; 1930, 524; 1938, 705; 1947, 416; 1948, 650; and 1951, 1020.

24. The tenth edition has been used supplemented by data from "The Development of the International Structure," in *International Associations,* June–July, 1952.

25. The year 1900 caused a certain disturbance in the rate of formation of INGO's because of its symbolic significance.

26. See Richardson, *op. cit.,* p. 225, footnote 7.

27. It must be remembered that the profiles show the rate of formation, not the number of INGO's in existence. By 1951 this was over 900.

28. See Paul Smoker, *op. cit.,* footnote 12.

29. See footnote 9.

30. For example, see Johan Galtung, "East-West Interactions Patterns," *Journal of Peace Research,* 1966, No. 2, pp. 146–177; Steven J. Brams, "Transaction Flows in the International System," *American Political Science Review,* LX, 4, (December, 1966), pp. 880–898; I. Richard Savage and Karl W. Deutsch, "A Statistical Model of the Gross Analysis of Transaction Flows," *Econometrica,* Vol. XXVIII (July, 1960), pp. 551–572.

31. Johan Galtung, "Summit Meetings and International Relations," *Journal of Peace Research,* 1 (1964), pp. 36–54.

32. See Smoker, *op. cit.,* footnote 9.

33. See Rudolph Rummel, "Some Dimensions of International Relations in the Mid 1950's," (New Haven, Connecticut: Yale University, Dimensionality of Nations Project, August 1964) (mimeo).

34.   For the present arms race, data problems for the period prior to 1952 prevented all the nations here being considered since 1948. However, for those nations for which data are available similar results were obtained over the whole period 1948–62.

35.   For the first world arms race the *Statesman's Year Book* was used. For the second world arms race the *League of Nations Armaments Year Book* and the *Statistical Year Book of the League of Nations* were used. The *Statesman's Year Book* compared favorably with these sources. For the present world arms race the *United Nations Statistical Year Book* and the *Series T Publication Direction of International Trade* were the main sources.

36.   "Significant" is used here in the sense that such a correlation would be significant in a random population of statistics. While this condition is not satisfied, it is still possible to take the correlation coefficient as a guideline in the sense that it enables comparisons across similar populations of statistics to be made.

37.   An earlier study, see footnote 12, suggests that the less political an INGO, the greater its integrative effect. Peace action INGO's are, therefore, less suited to this task.

CHAPTER NINE

Consequences of International Organizations

27. UNITED NATIONS PARTICIPATION AS A LEARNING EXPERIENCE

Chadwick F. Alger

Human organizations affect the societies in which they exist not only by making and implementing decisions that have social consequences; they also recruit members of society to play organizational roles that affect the present and future behavior of these persons—both in their organizational roles and in other roles. Writing after several years' experience in the permanent missions of their governments at the United Nations, two career diplomats suggest that the U.N. is not exempt from this generalization:

> In the U.N. . . . the word "diplomat" is rapidly losing its old connotation of elegance and wealth. As the U.N. security services have noted, "It is difficult

SOURCE. Chadwick F. Alger, "United Nations Participation as a Learning Experience," in *Public Opinion Quarterly,* XXVII (Fall, 1963), pp. 411–426. Reprinted by permission of the author and Princeton University Press. Copyright 1963 by Princeton University Press.

to tell the delegates from the visitors." Thus the U.N. has had an effect even on the appearance of U.N. Delegates, and by its methods of operation possibly on their characters. There is no doubt that the personal and parliamentary experience which delegates get at the U.N. may have long run consequences of value to the international community.[1]

This paper will present the findings from an investigation of the impact of participation in the United Nations upon national representatives.

THE RESEARCH DESIGN

As a result of numerous personal discussions with United Nations diplomats, five very general propositions emerged as the focus for the inquiry:

1. Participation in the United Nations changes notions about how the United Nations actually operates.

2. Participation in the United Nations changes notions about how the United Nations should operate.

3. Participation in the United Nations changes attitudes on particular issues.

4. Participation in the United Natons changes attitudes toward particular nations.

5. Participation in the United Nations influences the subsequent behavior of the participants.

A questionnaire was designed to be used in interviewing national officials participating in the United Nations General Assembly in 1959.[2] Each fall the permanent missions almost triple their number of personnel in order to meet the personnel requirements of participation in the General Assembly. In 1959 there were 1,380 members of General Assembly delegations, of which only 506 were permanently assigned to the U.N.[3] Of those delegates who came to the U.N. for the first time in September 1959, twenty-five were interviewed shortly after they arrived in New York and were reinterviewed two months later.

---

[1]John G. Hadwen and Johan Kaufmann, *How United Nations Decisions Are Made,* 2nd rev. ed., New York, Oceana, 1962, p. 54.

[2]The pre-test questionnaire had twenty questions, eleven of which were on the delegate's background, reasons for his appointment as a delegate, and his expected General Assembly committee assignment. The post-test questionnaire included sixteen questions. All questions except those on delegate backgrounds, etc., are quoted at the appropriate point in the discussion that follows.

[3]Compiled from *Delegations to the United Nations,* Fourteenth Session of the General Assembly, New York, United Nations, 1959, pp. 6–152.

Two interviewers conducted pre-tests during the two-week period that began a day before the opening of the General Assembly.[4] One delegate was chosen randomly from a list of new delegates for each nation. Since delegation lists did not become available until the period in which the interviews were conducted, the selection of those twenty-five nations included in the interviews was largely dependent on the order in which these lists became available. Other factors that determined whether particular nations were included in the sample were the time of arrival of selected delegates, some not having arrived when contact was attempted, and the ability of the interviewers to make contact with delegates. Early in the Assembly it is not easy to locate delegates, who may be at any one of a number of spots in U.N. headquarters, at their nation's permanent mission, finding living quarters, etc.

The sample of 25 had the following geographical composition: Far East-South Asia, 9 (Afghanistan, Australia, Burma, Ceylon, Indonesia, Japan, Malaya, Pakistan, Thailand); Europe, 6 (Denmark, Greece, Netherlands, Norway, Poland, United Kingdom); Middle East, 3 (Iraq, Israel, Lebanon); Africa, 3 (Ethiopia, Sudan, Union of South Africa); America, 4 (Canada, Haiti, Mexico, United States). Thirteen came from other foreign affairs posts (8 from their respective foreign offices and 5 from overseas posts). Of the remaining 12, 3 came from other government posts, 4 were parliamentarians, and 5 were private citizens.

The interviewed delegates served on all seven of the General Assembly committees. These bodies, with all U.N. members represented on each, provide the main scene of General Assembly activity. The distribution of interviewed delegates on the committees was as follows: Political (3), Special Political (1), Economic and Financial (4), Social and Humanitarian (7), Trusteeship and Non-Self-Governing Territories (5), Budgetary (3), Legal (2). One delegate did not have a committee assignment but handled public relations for his delegation.

Responses on each question do not total 25; in the pre-test the average number of respondents for each question was 17.5, and in the post-test it was 19.5. Occasionally questions were dropped because of limitations of time.[5] Usually, however, questions were dropped because responses to previous questions made them irrelevant. In addition, the maintenance of rapport with delegates from a variety of cultures required that the questionnaire be administered with flexibility.[6]

---

[4]I am exceedingly grateful to Professor James A. Robinson of Northwestern University, who collaborated with me in carrying on both the pre-test and post-test field work. In addition, Professor Robert Levine, University of Chicago, kindly performed two of the pre-test interviews.

[5]The length of interviews ranged from 10 minutes to an hour and 5 minutes, with an average length of 34 minutes.

[6]The writer knows of no previous attempt to use an interview schedule with "randomly" selected U.N. delegates. For a discussion of interviewing experience in 1960 with U.N. permanent mission personnel, see Gary Best, "Diplomacy in the United Nations," Evanston,

The difficulty of arranging interviews during the pre-test period, i.e., the early days of the General Assembly, prevented the acquisition of a larger number of interviews. The interviewers put in 18 man-days of work to get the pre-tests. In this effort they made at least 152 attempts to arrange interviews, not including the interviews themselves. They included at least 123 phone calls, 9 broken appointments, 16 face-to-face requests, and 4 contacts with intermediaries. The number of usable interviews was cut because only 25 of the 37 with whom pre-tests were conducted were given post-tests. This decrease in the sample by 12 occurred because 6 delegates returned home before post-tests were given, 2 were not approached again as a result of severe language difficulty, and 3 given pre-tests had servied in the General Assembly before.

Because of the low number of responses to each question and the fact that the sample of delegates is not completely random, statistically valid generalizations cannot be made about the learning experiences of General Assembly delegates. The questionnaire results will be reported in numerical totals, however, in order to give the reader an indication of the direction and dimension of change and an awareness of the size of the sample in each case. The major contribution of this research is a set of more specific questions about change that may be occurring in international systems through the impact on individuals of experiences in international organizations.

CHANGED NOTIONS ABOUT HOW THE UNITED NATIONS OPERATES

Five questions were used to find out whether delegates changed their notions about how the United Nations operates. One of these questions was asked only in the post-test: "In what ways was your experience here different from what you expected?" The other four questions were asked in both the pre-test and the post-test:

1. How will (did) your duties here differ most significantly, if at all, from your regular post?

2. Do you believe that your Assembly experience will (that you got anything out of your Assembly experience that will) make you more able to fulfill the obligations of your permanent post?

3. In what ways, if any, does the U.N. have an effect on issues of this type [i.e., an issue the delegate had chosen to discuss]?

4. What would you like to see accomplished (do you wish the outcome had been) on this issue during the Assembly?

6 *(Cont.)* Ill., Northwestern University, 1960, Chap. III, unpublished Ph.D. thesis. For an analysis of experiences with the use of an interview schedule in interviewing United States Congressmen, see James A. Robinson, "Survey Interviewing among Members of Congress," *Public Opinion Quarterly,* Vol. 24, 1960, pp. 127–138.

The four questions used in both the pre-test and post-test were designed to measure indirectly changed delegate notions about the operation of the U.N. The question used only in the post-test asked for this more directly.

Lack of knowledge about the General Assembly was most dramatically revealed by 4 delegates who indicated in the pre-test that they did not believe that their duties in the General Assembly would differ significantly from those of their regular posts. Two of these delegates had come from foreign offices, 1 from a parliament, and 1 from a consulate. All 17 delegates who were asked this question in the post-test stated that they saw a difference. A prominent difference between the pre-test and post-test responses to this question was the increase in explicit comparisons between regular posts and General Assembly posts. In the pre-test only 8 persons, of the 17 respondents, contributed such comparisons as: more specialized, you talk openly, part of a team, no negotiation, less routine, more academic, and world-wide perspective. In the post-test 15 of the 17 respondents mentioned such factors as: more individual initiative, less routine, faster decisions required, more personal contact, more need to persuade the opposition, etc. At this point it is not our purpose to emphasize the exact nature of the differences between General Assembly roles and the permanent roles of these delegates. The important thing is that after service in the Assembly almost twice as many delegates as before felt competent to make precise comparisons of their two roles.

Twenty delegates were asked in both pre-test and post-test whether they believed Assembly experience would make them more able to fulfill the obligations of their permanent post. All but one thought that the experience would be helpful in this regard. It is most interesting, however, that delegates volunteered information that revealed the importance to them of having the opportunity to get a better insight into the working of the U.N. Indicating in the pre-test the ways in which U.N. experience would make them more able to fulfill the obligations of their permanent posts, the largest number of delegates, 7, cited the opportunity to learn more in general about international relations. However, in the post-test the largest number of delegates, 8, cited the opportunity to get a better insight into the workings of the U.N. (3 more than in the pre-test). For example, in the post-test a delegate said that on his return to the foreign office he would now be able to suggest policy for his nation's General Assembly delegation "that can really be carried out." A delegate from another government department said in the post-test: "Before I came I knew that there were committees and I knew the general organization of the General Assembly but I didn't know precisely what they were doing and how things were done. Now I know procedure better and this will enable me to make better recommendations to the Foreign Office."

Asked in the post-test how experiences in the General Assembly had differed from their expectations, three delegates indicated that they had had no clear expectations at all; two of these were from foreign offices. Ten delegates responded that their experiences were no different from what they expected. One of these, from a foreign office, indicated that he had known exactly what his duties would be like. Amazingly enough, however, in the pre-test he had said that his duties would not differ much from his obligations in the foreign office, while in the post-test he said that his duties in the General Assembly were very different.

Of the twelve whose experiences differed from what they had expected, three delegates from smaller nations were surprised at the prominent roles small nations play in the General Assembly. They were surprised at "the willingness of larger nations of the West to listen to points of view of small countries," at the "big interest the United Nations has in small countries," and that "here the small nations have their say." A parliamentarian had thought that the General Assembly "would be a forum for speeches." But during his Assembly experience he found that "draft resolutions involve a good deal of lobbying and negotiation." He had "had no idea of this." A delegate from a foreign office found that "things that go on in the corridor seem more important" than he had anticipated.

The delegates were also asked, in both the pre-test and the post-test, how the U.N. affects an issue before the General Assembly that they had chosen to discuss, or issues before the General Assembly in general. One dramatic example of learning about U.N. processes was provided by the parliamentarian who responded in the pre-test that the U.N. has influence because "this is where decisions are arrived at on these [economic and social] questions." In the post-test, however, he replied that "the United Nations has an impact on these issues because those nations participating in General Assembly discussions have a moral duty to comply with resolutions and will over the long run."[7] Seven delegates voiced similar sentiments in their post-test. Resolutions were spoken of as useful in indicating "widespread support for particular positions," "meaning that world public opinion is behind them," "giving legitimacy to the aspirations of some of the smaller powers," and providing principles along whose lines "all nations will be obliged to legislate sooner or later." Only two delegates expressed similar sentiments in the pre-test.

CHANGED NOTIONS ABOUT HOW THE UNITED NATIONS SHOULD OPERATE

Along with remarkable lack of knowledge about the actual operation of the General Assembly in the pre-test, the delegates also offered very few suggestions

---

[7]The writer had an opportunity to talk with this particular delegate between the two interviews and found him rather negative toward the General Assembly because he thought the repetitious speeches were leading nowhere. His evolution from initial enthusiasm about the General Assembly, to a negative view, to a more positive feeling, is similar to the so-called "U-curve" of adjustment to foreign cultures, a recurrent finding in research on sojourners in foreign cultures. For a review of these findings see Eugene Jacobson, Hideya Kumata, and Jeanne E. Gallahorn, "Cross-Cultural Contributions to Attitude Research," *Public Opinion Quarterly,* Vol. 19, 1960, p. 193.

for change in the U.N. in response to the question: "How do you believe the U.N. should be changed, if at all, in order to make it more effective in this type of issue [an issue selected for discussion by the delegate]?" Of the 19 who were asked the question, 11 felt unable to make any suggestions in the pre-test, and 3 thought that change in the U.N. was not needed but rather change in the behavior of members. Of the 5 delegates offering suggestions, 2 wanted expansion of the size of the Economic and Social Council and the Security Council, 1 wished the Security Council veto removed, 1 wanted a convention on human rights, and 1 wanted aid to underdeveloped areas turned over to experts and taken out of "internal U.N. politics."

In the post-test 19 also were asked this question, and the number without suggestions dropped from 11 to 7. The number desiring the enlargement of the councils increased from 2 to 4. However, the most dramatic change was the fact that 7 suggested changes in General Assembly procedures. No suggestions of this kind were made in the pre-test. Three delegates thought that it would be useful to place limitations on debate. It may be significant that all three were delegates who had come from foreign office posts. One private citizen thought the session was too short to finish important business. A parliamentarian desired more "parliamentary-type debate"; only at the end of a daily session, when delegates exercise their "right to reply" to speeches, and just before an issue came to a vote did he find the kind of discussion that to him seemed to be essential in a parliamentary body.

The responses to this question also reveal considerable delegate learning about U.N. procedures, in particular the General Assembly. Although these delegates were already at U.N. headquarters as delegates to the General Assembly when the pre-test was made, they as yet had no suggestions for revising General Assembly practices. It was not until actual service that seven volunteered suggestions for change.

CHANGE IN ATTITUDES ON PARTICULAR ISSUES

In his study of the establishment of the International Finance Corporation, B. E. Matecki mentions "the profound changes that the personal contact of members of United States delegations to international institutions has wrought in their thinking and outlook."[8] He even cites examples in which United States delegates have been able, as a result of changed attitudes, to get United States policy changed.[9] In order to probe the possible impact of General Assembly experience

[8]B. E. Matecki, *Establishment of the International Finance Corporation,* New York, Praeger, 1957, p. 143.
[9]*Ibid.,* pp. 92, 142–143, 159–160.

on attitudes of delegates on particular issues, they were asked in the pre-test: "With which agenda item do you expect to be most involved?" Delegates were then asked 4 questions, 2 in the pre-test and 2 in the post-test, designed to measure indirectly attitude change on the specified issue:

1. What would you like to see accomplished on this issue during the Assembly? (pre-test)
2. What do you wish the outcome of this issue had been? (post-test)
3. What do you think will be accomplished? (pre-test)
4. What was accomplished? (post-test)

Quite unexpected was the fact that only 7, of the 23 asked to do so, cited a specific issue in the pre-test. Eleven were clearly unable to discuss a particular issue, with the remaining 5 not citing issues although their responses indicated that they possibly could have. Of the 7 who named an issue with which they were most concerned in the pre-test, only 1 person cited the same issue in the post-test. Thus, the data collected did not provide the specific kind of information sought. But it did, nonetheless, supply information on the level of knowledge of arriving delegates and the role of the U.N. in providing them with an awareness of and a common supply of information about particular problems.

In the post-test all delegates except the one who had not been assigned to a committee were able and willing to discuss a particular item on the agenda. A dramatic example of expanded awareness was the delegate from a Middle Eastern foreign office who indicated that he had never even heard of some of the African countries that his committee discussed. As an example, he cited the North and South Cameroons. He indicated that he now knew "how they emerged, what factors concerning them have political significance, and what the role of various blocs is in relation to such countries as these."

With so few supplying a specific issue in the pre-test, it was, of course, impossible to get many predictions on the likely outcome of debate on particular issues. Only four of the seven who cited specific issues offered predictions with much detail. The four predictions they made for their agenda items were: just discussion, nothing, expanded economic assistance, and satisfactory accommodation but not a complete solution. These predictions were in general accurate. Three of the four who felt able to make these predictions were foreign service officers.

CHANGE IN ATTITUDES TOWARD PARTICULAR NATIONS

In order to discern changed attitudes of delegates toward particular nations, they were asked, in terms of the issue selected by them for discussion, two questions in the pre-test and two in the post-test.

1. What nations will most emphatically oppose the accomplishment of your goal on this issue? (pre-test)

2. What nations do you believe most emphatically opposed the accomplishment of your goal on this issue? (post-test)

3. Why will the delegates of [nations specified by delegate] oppose you on this issue? (pre-test)

4. Why did the delegates of [nations specified by delegate] oppose you on this issue? (post-test)

Because of the inability of delegates to cite particular issues in the pre-test, these questions had the same limitations as other questions linked to specific issues. In addition, it seems not to have been a good strategy to ask delegates to cite their opponents. Perhaps they more willingly would have identified those expected to be in agreement with them. Nonetheless, thirteen delegates did indicate which nations they believed would oppose their goals in the General Assembly, either in terms of specific issues or just in general. Those cited were: East and West (3), East (3), great powers (1), United States and West (1), United States (1), United States and Israel (1), colonial powers (2), young nations (1).

Because pre-tests and post-tests were not often done in the context of the same issue, it is not feasible to follow individual change in attitudes; however, a few observations can be made about the total group of interviews. Seven more citations of opponents, or 20, were made in the post-test. New opponents added were: United States and United Kingdom, Arabs and Israelis, East and new nations, and the U.N. Secretariat. A remarkable shift was made by one delegate from the citation of the colonial powers in the pre-test to the new nations in the post-test. The addition of the Secretariat is of interest. In the Budgetary Committee the Secretariat occasionally becomes a common foe for all as delegates adopt the traditional attitude of parliamentarians toward executive expenditures. In addition, three delegates who chose to discuss the work of their committee in general indicated in the post-test that they saw no clear pattern of opposition. Scattered throughout the interviews are occasional comments by delegates indicating surprise at positions taken on issues by other nations.[10] At least in the context of these issues it is likely that this changed their attitude toward these nations. A Far Eastern delegate who had served in his foreign office for twelve years was surprised to find

---

[10]After their 1954 General Assembly experience, Congressman Bolton and Congressman Richards reported: ". . . surprise and to some extent a shock to realize that some delegates, who may be presumed to reflect substantial segments of opinion in their countries, harbor extremely inimical views about the United States." This surprise was registered despite the fact that Bolton and Richards had spent many years on the House Committee on Foreign Affairs. See Frances P. Bolton and James P. Richards, *Report on the Eighth Session of the General Assembly of the United Nations*, H.R. 1695, 83rd Cong., 2nd sess., 1954, p. 7.

that the white-dominated nations of the British Commonwealth did not vote as a bloc in his committee. An African delegate from one of the newer nations was extremely surprised to find that the United States voted with his nation on the South West Africa issue. An East European delegate was surprised to find that the Scandinavian nations sometimes "lined up with the colonial powers" in the trusteeship committee.

In addition, at least six delegates made general comments indicating how informative it was to hear delegates of other nations explain their policies and viewpoints. Several stated the value of learning about the problems of other nations and the effect of the policies of their own nation on these problems. Not all expressed it as dramatically as one African delegate, who said: "It has helped me to realize that they are, after all, human beings." For this delegate, some nations were formerly seen as negative stereotypes in which the policies of these nations were grossly simplified and exaggerated. Under these conditions, contact in the United Nations is much like other intercultural exchange in which "contact will provide richer and more accurate information about other people and will show them to be much like members of one's own group."[11]

For some delegates these contacts may develop into friendships that have some effect on politically relevant behavior. In an exceedingly informative first-hand account of U.N. political processes, two U.N. diplomats have written: "In many eyes the personal relationships established at the U.N. have as much, if not greater, importance than the formal decisions which are reached. Personal contacts at the U.N. can promote useful decisions both within the organization's framework and outside it."[12] Although the questionnaire did not have a question on this point, four delegates emphasized the importance of opportunities to establish personal contact with officials of other nations. At the end of his interview a Western European delegate volunteered this statement:

> On my committee men come year after year, and friendly relations continue despite disagreement over policy. It is very important that people in international conferences know each other well. It permits the reaching of compromises. One has choices of many kinds of words for stating the same thing. One can say the same thing in either very polite or very rash words. With friends, you are more likely to use friendly words. Therefore, it is useful to have friends negotiating in international conferences.

[11]Daniel Katz, "The Functional Approach to the Study of Attitudes," *Public Opinion Quarterly,* Vol. 24, 1960, p. 193.

[12]Hadwen and Kaufmann, *op. cit.,* p. 58.

CHANGE IN SUBSEQUENT BEHAVIOR

Commenting on the participation of Netherlands parliamentarians in international parliaments in Europe, Daalder writes:

Sometimes there tends to grow a psychological rift between the ordinary member of parliament and those who go to the foreign assemblies. Both groups may develop a different sense of priorities; the "foreign" members gets a little irritated with the "provincial outlook" of the domestic members insisting as it is said on discussing secondary matters as if they were of world-wide importance; the "domestic" member, on the other hand, deplores a tendency on the part of the foreign experts to deal in *grozen Worten*. At times they may even feel that the foreign members plead their own case. Although the expertise of the foreign members may be recognized and appreciated, it is sometimes felt to be of a slightly alien character.[13]

Since a follow-up study on subsequent behavior of interviewed delegates has not been attempted, consideration of impact of their United Nations experience on this behavior must be done in terms of delegate prediction and interviewer inference. Predictions by delegates were obtained by asking them, in the post-test: "Do you believe that your Assembly experience will make you more able to fulfill the obligations of your permanent post? In what way?" All but one answered in the affirmative; this one delegate considered his post as a judge to be too different to permit application of his General Assembly experiences. As was indicated earlier, the factor most cited as a help to delegates in performing their permanent roles was a better insight into the working of the U.N. Eight delegates mentioned items in this category. Six mentioned that they had acquired better knowledge of particular issues, and three that they had learned to know better the views and interests of other nations.

The fact that one-third of the delegates interviewed, including 5 of the 13 foreign service officers, considered that learning of U.N. processes would be important in the performance of their permanent jobs is one of the most significant findings of this study.[14] This was a volunteered response to a more general question—the

---

[13]H. Daalder, "The Netherlands," in Kenneth Lindsay, editor, *European Assemblies: The Experimental Period, 1949-1959,* New York, Praeger, 1960, p. 126. For a related discussion of literature on the effects of participation in "traditional diplomacy" on diplomats see Michael H. Cardozo, *Diplomats in International Cooperation: Stepchildren of the Foreign Service,* Ithaca, N.Y., Cornell University Press, 1962.

[14]Lord Ismay, former Secretary General of NATO, writes that the service of national officials in the NATO International Staff for two or three years "ensures that member governments have in their service an increasing number of officers with special knowledge of NATO affairs," See Lord Ismay, *The First Five Years of NATO,* Paris, North Atlantic Treaty Organization, 1954, p. 64.

question of U.N. processes was raised by the delegate and not by the interviewer. One delegate stated that when choosing from several alternative policies he will now be able to "choose the alternative that can be carried out in the United Nations." Another indicated both that his experience would enable him to "make better policy recommendations" and that it would "give greater weight" to his recommendations.[15] It can be inferred that in some instances better knowledge of the political processes of the U.N. may result in greater likelihood of officials using them. Greater knowledge would be expected to increase their ability to predict outcomes of these political processes.

The other two most cited items—better knowledge of particular issues and better knowledge of interests of other nations—can be discussed jointly with other factors cited as being of value upon return to permanent posts: better general international relations knowledge, wider perspective, and opportunity to speak to foreign delegates directly. In his permanent post, usually in his own national capital, the official is operating in an environment that structures his perceptions of the world in a particular way. This structuring, it appears, is much influenced by the well-known political alignments, which are largely shaped by geographical contiguity. The various regional organizations tend to intensify this selective perception of the world. Furthermore, many smaller nations have no diplomatic missions in many nations of the world. Even in national capitals where most nations are represented, it is reasonable to a ssume that interaction tends to follow the lines of geography, traditional friendship, and political alignments.

The interviews, however, tend to show that in the U.N. delegates get a quite different perspective of the world. The opportunity of the nations to reach each other becomes more uniform. In physical terms, within the U.N. Paraguay and Nepal are now as close as Nepal and India. Now Paraguay and Nepal may even become aware that, as landlocked, underdeveloped nations, they have certain interests in common. Existing alignments are not left behind when issues are handled in the U.N., but, more than is the case in other seats of diplomacy, nations have access to the entire world in explaining their policies and attempting to develop support. This does not necessarily mean that the delegate comes to view international relations in an idealistic "one world" sense. Perhaps more important is the tendency to see the world as a single political system.[16] A parliamentarian from

---

[15] For a more extensive analysis of some of the implications of multiple political roles, see Chadwick F. Alger, "The External Bureaucracy in United States Foreign Affairs," *Administrative Science Quarterly,* Vol. 7, 1962, pp. 50–78.

[16] This is similar to the finding of Pool, Keller, and Bauer in their study of the effects of foreign travel on United States businessmen, in which they report that "the cosmopolitanism of the much traveled lies not in the adoption of internationalist or liberal attitudes, but in their greater awareness of considerations lying outside their own immediate environment." Ithiel de Sola Pool, Suzanne Keller, and Raymond Bauer, "The Influence of Foreign Travel on Political Attitudes of American Businessmen," *Public Opinion Quarterly,* Vol. 20, 1956, p. 169.

a Scandinavian country stated: "I will go back with a clearer view of the fact that my nation belongs to the whole world. . . . Without the United Nations we would all live behind a curtain, more or less, and wouldn't have the opportunity to look inside other nations and see what they mean."[17]

Two United States congressmen, reporting on their experience as General Assembly delegates, have made a rather similar comment:

> We have been encouraged by the evidence that the United Nations, apart from its other accomplishments, has been serving as an effective training forum for the delegates from the newly independent countries—not only in terms of parliamentary procedures but even more in terms of the acceptance of responsibilities entailed in a constructive participation in the affairs of the community of free nations.[18]

This comment goes beyond that by the Scandinavian parliamentarian and asserts that General Assembly experience may not only give participants a feeling of belonging to a larger part of the world but a sense of personal responsibility to a larger part of this world.

Personal contacts developed at the U.N., discussed in the previous section, may also affect future behavior of delegates. These friendships sometimes link national roles that would not otherwise have intense first-hand contact. The participation of parliamentarians from a number of nations is particularly interesting because governmental foreign relations contacts are normally in the hands of the foreign office. After a Norwegian parliamentarian sits for three months next to a Pakistani diplomat in a General Assembly committee, what might their acquaintance mean when the Pakistani diplomat is sent to Norway? These lines of communication may be open when other official routes would not be used and may permit the transfer of information that other official lines could not handle.[19]

---

[17]For a provocative discussion of the potential consequences of a "systems-attitude," see Kenneth Boulding, "National Images and International Systems," *Journal of Conflict Resolution,* Vol. 3, 1959, p. 131, where he concludes: "The growth of a systems-attitude toward international relations will have profound consequences for the dynamics of the system itself, just as the growth of a systems-attitude in economics has profound consequences for the dynamics of the economic system."

[18]Clement J. Zablocki and James G. Fulton, *Report on the Fourteenth Session of the General Assembly of the United Nations,* H. Rept. 1385, 86th Cong., 2nd sess., 1960, p. 5.

[19]For relevant findings on the importance to integration of "mobility of persons" among nations, "at least in the politically relevant strata," see Karl Deutsch, *Political Community in the North Atlantic Area,* Princeton, N.J., Princeton University Press, 1957, pp. 53–54 and 68.

REACTIONS OF DELEGATES TO THEIR UNITED NATIONS EXPERIENCE

All but one of the delegates interviewed were asked: "Did you enjoy your Assembly experience?" All of them responded in the affirmative. Nineteen were asked: "Would you like to come back again?" and all but 4 said yes. Two of the 4 were undecided, and the other 2 said they would like to come back except for other commitments. The reasons most often cited by delegates who enjoyed the experience were: interest in the subject matter (4), the opportunity to experience the U.N. first-hand (4), the opportunity to have first-hand contact with other delegates (4), the educational value of the experience (3) and the opportunity to hear a variety of points of view (3). (Some delegates offered more than one reason.)

Despite the over-all positive reaction to the experience, there were negative comments. Three mentioned the inconvenience of being separated from families. One delegate did not enjoy life in New York. A delegate from South Asia devoted most of his response to this question to citing instances in which he had been irritated by "little stupid acts" of the United States delegation. Finally, four comments indicated considerable irritation with General Assembly procedures:

1. Sometimes the debates were insufferably dull.

2. The United Nations is a mob. . . . There are no negotiations carried on here at the U.N. Oh, there is some in the corridor, but mostly it is just a matter of speeches. You have an expression, "It's a hell of a way to run a railroad."

3. The work is interesting but with the exception of particular fields, it is somewhat disappointing. One would expect more rapid measures to be taken, but this is not the case. Some things come up year after year without improvement. Work doesn't move as swiftly as it should—it moves at a turtle's pace.

4. Speakers don't speak to the point and waste time. They raise matters in order to raise their personal prestige. There is no sense of responsibility. . . . At least one-third of the time spent in my committee was a waste of time.

These four negative comments were collected from the interviews without attention to the identity of the sources. Each came from a different continent of the world, but all were spoken by career foreign service officers—three from posts in foreign offices and one from an overseas diplomatic post.

This suggests that on first contact with General Assembly procedures those who have received their previous experience in foreign offices and embassies may feel less comfortable than do other delegates. Practitioners of more traditional diplomatic methods seem to prefer quiet negotiation with others who share their norms about how negotiation should be conducted. It is, of course, true that many career foreign service officers assigned to the U.N. for long periods acquire competence at utilizing the more varied political processes in the U.N., if they do not have these skills when they arrive. Parliamentarians, however, seem not to be so disturbed by the repetitive and time-consuming debate and the somewhat chaotic atmosphere of the General Assembly.[20] They realize that "dull and irrelevant" speeches and painfully slow deliberations may aid in the development of consensus and in the maintenance of the personal relations necessary for effective legislative action. The reaction of two United States Congressmen to their General Assembly experience serves to illustrate this point:

> Oftentimes, we are sure that many of us grew impatient with the length of some of the discussion to which we had to listen. We are equally sure that many of our foreign colleagues felt the same way about some of our own interventions. But if we are to encourage the continued development of voluntary cooperation among independent states, we must willingly and respectfully give our attention to the opinions of those who speak for these national units and who will be highly influential in determining the world's destiny.[21]

CONCLUSION

The data collected in this study make it possible to formulate a new set of propositions that will provide a more fruitful basis for further inquiry. Although the following propositions are not confirmed, they give a better approximation of the learning experience of General Assembly delegates than was possible before this study was made.

1. Participation in the United Nations provides the delegate with more precise knowledge about United Nations political processes than he had before.

2. Participation in the United Nations causes the delegate to perceive the United Nations more as an appendage of more proximate political processes and less as a distant island.

3. Participation in the United Nations causes the delegate to see it more as an instrument for gradual adjustment toward consensus and less as a device for producing immediate solutions.

[20]Ernst Haas writes of the reaction of European parliamentarians to their experiences in the Council of Europe: "Parliamentarians used to the powers and prerogatives of national legislative bodies and committed advocates of European unity share a feeling of frustration with respect to the labors of this interparliamentary assembly. . . ." See Ernst B. Haas, *Consensus Formation in the Council of Europe,* Berkeley, University of California Press, 1960, p. 1. The apparent difference in the responses of parliamentarians to these two international assemblies might be caused by different expectations of parliamentarians serving in the two institutions.

[21]Brooks Hays and Chester Merrow, *Report on the Tenth Session of the General Assembly of the United Nations,* H. Rept. 1980, 84th Cong., 2nd sess., 1956, p. 11.

4. Participation in the United Nations makes delegates more tolerant of the many speeches and prolonged negotiation of United Nations diplomacy and more competent in the practice of this diplomacy.

5. Participation in the United Nations expands the number of nations and the number of issues of which the delegate is aware.

6. Participation in the United Nations expands the number of nations and the number of issues with which the delegate feels involved and for which he feels some responsibility.

7. Participation in the United Nations changes the delegate's affective map of the world—i.e. alters his designation of which nations are the "good guys" and which are the "bad guys."

8. Participation in the United Nations provides the delegate with new personal contacts with officials from other nations that temper conflict with these officials, open new channels of communication with other nations, and keep channels of communication open with other nations when they might otherwise be closed.

These propositions can provide the basis for a more conclusive inquiry that discerns the nature of U.N. learning experiences after a longer period of service. This could be done by drawing samples of permanent mission personnel with short- and long-term service and comparing the two. It could also be done by making a similar comparison among persons who come to New York only for the General Assembly—the comparison being made between those attending for the first time and those who have attended several assemblies. Another useful investigation would be a comparison of national officials in a selected number of countries that have had U.N. experience with those in countries that have had no such experience.[22]

The findings of this inquiry suggest that the maximization of opportunities offered to a nation by U.N. participation requires more than the design of policies on issues on the agendas of the Councils and Assembly of the organization and strategies for getting these policies accepted. If it is a place where officials are educated and where new kinds of links between governments are initiated, these kinds of effects can be consciously shaped in desired directions.

Finally, it is likely that the findings of this research have relevance to other international organizations and to other political, and nonpolitical, situations where an effort is being made to bring separate social units into a more integrated social order. Whether it be a city council, the Democratic National Convention, the United States Congress, the International Chamber of Commerce, or the United Nations, the propositions generated by this investigation appear to be relevant. They predict that participants from individual units who participate in central

---

[22]For a report on interviews with United States defense officials on their views on the United Nations, see Richard W. Van Wagenen, "American Defense Officials' Views on the United Nations," *Western Political Quarterly,* Vol. 14, 1961, pp. 104–119.

institutions can be distinguished from those who have not participated by their concern about a larger number of units and issues, by their perception of the central institution more as an appendage of more proximate social processes and less as a distant island, by their tendency to see the other units more in varying shades of gray and less in blacks and whites, by their personal lines of communication to a wider variety of roles in other units, and by their greater facility in the social skills developed in the central institution for moving the units toward consensus. The creation of central organizations able to make decisions for fragmented social systems requires the development of an underlying social structure. Central organizations themselves, although limited in ability to make authoritative decisions, may play crucial roles in building such a social structure by the learning experiences they provide for those playing organizational roles, and by the new linkages they provide between formerly isolated roles in individual units.

28. SUPRANATIONALISM IN THE UNITED NATIONS

Hayward R. Alker, Jr. *

INTRODUCTION

In his *The Uniting of Europe,* Ernst Haas comments that "The 'good Europeans' [e.g., Jean Monnet] are not the main creators of the regional community that is growing up; the process of community formation is dominated by nationally constituted groups with specific interests and aims, willing and able to adjust their aspirations by turning to supranational means when this course appears profitable."[1] Applying the same perspective to the world arena, one may observe that "good universalists" such as Dag Hammarskjold and U Thant are not by themselves the main builders of a world community. Community formation is more the result of nations and groups of nations, willing and able to adjust their own aspirations, when such adjustments seem profitable, by turning to supranational means.

International community is a condition of international society in which existing attitudes and institutions assure peaceful adjustments of differences among nations.[2] It is a task of considerable importance to describe and explain the extent

SOURCE. Hayward R. Alker, Jr., "Supranationalism in the United Nations," in *Peace Research Society Papers,* III, Chicago Conference, 1965, pp. 197–212. Reprinted by permission of the author and publisher.

*This research has been supported, in part, by the Yale Political Data Program. The author gratefully acknowledges the research assistance of Raymond Hopkins and Douglas Condie.

[1]Ernst B. Haas, *The Uniting of Europe: Political, Social and Economic Forces, 1950–1957,* Stanford University Press, Stanford, 1958, p. XIV.

[2]I have purposely avoided distinguishing between amalgamated and pluralistic international communities because I do not want to rule out the possibility of peaceful adjustment of policy differences between sovereign nations under UN auspices. As a full-grown supranational organization, the United Nations may at some time foster and guide an amalgamated world polity. Before then, we can still talk about the peace-keeping contributions of partially supranational organization with nearly universal membership. Relevant literature on the definition of international or supranational political community includes E. B. Haas, *op. cit.,* K. W. Deutsch et al, *Political Community and the North Atlantic Area,* Princeton University Press, Princeton, 1957; K. W. Deutsch, P. E. Jacob, H. Teune, J. V. Toscano and

of supranational readjustments of national aims and practices and of resulting developments in international community.

The problem breaks down into several distinctive parts; each of which I shall briefly discuss. Specifically, if the United Nations is the major world-wide supranational mechanism involved in the satisfaction and readjustment of national aims, what indications do we have of a willingness to use supranational means for achieving readjusted national goals? Is supranationalism a factor in Assembly decisions? Secondly, if some evidence of supranational inclinations can be found, among which nations and for what reasons do such inclinations or predispositions occur? In other words, what considerations of profit lead to readjustments of national policies along supranational lines? Thirdly, since calculations of supranationalism are of necessity influenced by the environment in which they are made, what kinds of situations have led to supranational political responses? Finally, when supranational means have been used for achieving readjusted national goals, to what extent have these nations succeeded in laying the foundations of a world community?

Data and Methods.

Inevitably, data for answering such ambitious questions as these are not adequate. Nonetheless the records of the United Nations General Assembly are unusually valuable because they contain the official positions of a large number of nations on a large number of situations in which supranational activity is likely to occur. The institutional requirements in several ways aid the behaviorally oriented peace researcher: for example, all nations have to vote on exactly the same resolutions, copies of which are permanently available; whenever any one nation at any time calls for a permanent record of such positions, a roll-call vote is taken. Such roll calls force a nation to choose among four possible responses: Yes, Abstain, No, or nonparticipation in the roll call. Extensive verbatim and summary records indicate policy justifications of nations and their allies, *as well as* competing explanations offered by less charitable observers of these policies.

A body of records that are particularly suited to the search for the rudiments of supranationalism at the United Nations are those for the eight special and emergency special sessions of the General Assembly.[3] Such sessions have been called to

---

[2 (Cont)]W. L. C. Wheaton, *The Integration of Political Communities,* Lippincott, Philadelphia, 1964; and recent articles by Amitai Etzioni, especially "The Epigenesis of Political Communities at the International Level, *American Journal of Sociology,* Vol. 68, No. 4 (January 1963), pp. 407–421.

[3]The role of the Security Council on these matters has also been significant especially in Korea and in the first Congo crisis, when the Soviet Union did not veto the establishment of ONUC. But even before, and especially since the Korean War and the Uniting for Peace resolution, the Assembly has initiated or supported the major peace-keeping efforts of the United Nations.

deal with a variety of major threats to international peace; as such they may be considered an important test of the United Nation's peace-keeping capability, the core element, if not the main cause of international community.[4]

Emergency special sessions are called for by the Security Council (ironically, Yugoslovia first invoked the Uniting for Peace Resolution in the Suez crisis); "regular" special sessions are convened by a majority of Assembly members at the call of any one of them (as was done by the United Kingdom at the First Special Session on the future of Palestine). In chronological order these sessions are briefly described in Table 1. Fortunately, for all but one special session (the Third Emergency Special Session, which discussed Lebanon) one or more roll-call votes on final resolutions are readily available.[5]

Methodologically, I should like to illustrate a different research procedure for dealing with each of the four main substantive questions previously discussed. To see if predispositions to use UN peacekeeping mechanisms are a regularly distinguishable component of Assembly roll calls, I have applied the principal component method of factor analysis to a matrix of correlations among voting ranks on all non-unanimous special session roll calls. Even after the voting ranks of a very small number of absent states have been estimated, the main problem with such a correlation matrix is that the number of observations varies considerably from correlation to correlation. At the First Special Session 55 members were present; by the Fourth Special Session, Assembly membership had increased to 111. Nevertheless, the stability of UN voting alignments through the years allows for greater certainty as to the usefulness of this procedure.[6]

After the factor analysis, correlational analyses can be used to test various possible determinants of supranationalist predispositions, if at least to some extent, they appear to underlie Assembly voting alignments. Correlating national characteristics with supranationalism factor scores will help explain why UN instrumentalities are voted for.

Content analysis of Assembly resolutions may suggest answers to a missing link in the relationship between particular votes and general supranational

---

[4]Korea, Cuba and Berlin, prime Cold War crises, have not been the subject of special Assembly sessions; the omissions are significant ones in any over-all analysis of the United Nation's role. For a more detailed analysis of non-crisis Assembly sessions see H. R. Alker, Jr., "Dimensions of Conflict in the General Assembly," *American Political Science Review*, Vol. 58, No. 3 (September 1964), pp. 642–657, and H. R. Alker, Jr., and B. M. Russett, *World Politics in the General Assembly*, Yale University Press, New Haven, 1965.

[5]United Nations, *Official Records of The General Assembly*. Resolutions may generally be found in the Annexes of these documents.

[6]A more lengthy technical discussion of the factor analysis methods used below may be found in Henry Harmon, *Modern Factor Analysis*, Chicago University Press, Chicago, 1960 and Alker and Russett, *op. cit.,* Chapter 2. As a justification for using roll-calls from different sessions with different memberships, I am relying on the similarity of many of the voting factors identified below with those found in the previously cited analyses of votes in separate General Assembly sessions.

TABLE 1. A Chronology of Special and Emergency Special Sessions of the General Assembly

Session	Date	Topic	Result
First Special Session (SS 1)	Summer, 1947	Future of Palestine	Set up committee that recommended partition
Second Special Session (SS 2)	Spring, 1948	Future government of Palestine	Established UN Mediator
First Emergency Special Session (ES 1)	November, 1956	Suez Crisis	United Nations Emergency Force
Second Emergency Special Session (ES 2)	November, 1956	Hungarian Revolt	UN unable to enter Hungary; aided refugees.
Third Emergency Special Session (ES 3)	Summer, 1958	Lebanon and Jordan	Arabs pledged non-intervention; UN observation grouping set up by Security Council; troops withdrawn.
Fourth Emergency Special Session (ES 4)	September, 1960	Congo	Resolutions backed territorial integrity, asked for voluntary support of Congo operation.
Third Special Session (SS 3)	Summer, 1961	Tunisia	Urged negotiations for the withdrawal of French troops.
Fourth Special Session (SS 4)	Spring, 1963	Financial Crisis	Extended bonds; appropriated $33 million for ONUC through December, 1963

predispositions: why particular resolutions do or do not evoke supranationalist responses. Such a technique has rarely if ever been applied to General Assembly resolutions or debates. Nevertheless, I shall try to demonstrate how, in conjunction with factor analyses of final roll calls, it can shed light on diplomatic procedures for shaping perceptions of ambiguous crisis situations.

Finally, in a more historical and impressionistic vein, I would like briefly to comment on the characteristics of international crisis situations associated with greater national compliance with supranational initiatives.[7]

IS SUPRANATIONALISM A FACTOR IN ASSEMBLY DECISIONS?

Supranationalism means commitment to use and to be bound by political institutions transcending the nation state. In studying the European Coal and Steel Community, Ernst Haas suggested several structural characteristics of supranational institutions which, when joined to the supranationalism of national policies, lead to the sustained growth of supranational political communities. An international organization has become supranational, Haas believes, to the extent that it: (1) performs a wide range of governmental functions including peacekeeping and law enforcement, independent of those performed by nation states, (2) relies less on weighted majorities and national vetoes, (3) legislates on the recommendations of popular representatives independent of national governmental control, (4) produces a set of binding decisions that can effectively be carried out, (5) enlarges the scope of supranational power without requiring the consent of all member states, and (6) disallows unilateral termination of membership.

Assuming for the present that such a theory is relevant to a larger international context, we shall look for supranationalism, commitment to United Nations supranationality, in the decisions of the General Assembly sessions described above.

The Unrotated Factor Matrix

The conventional literature on factor analysis suggests two strategies for identifying principal voting components, exemplified in the unrotated and rotated factor matrices of Table 2 and Table 3. Entries in both factor matrices below may be thought of either as *correlations* between these hypothetical voting alignments and particular concrete roll-calls, or as *factor loadings* in the *factor model* that is assumed to explain particular voting alignments.[8]

---

[7] An important refinement of each of these procedures would be explicitly to allow for the interaction of individuals and subnational interest groups. See E. B. Haas, *op. cit.,* and C. F. Alger, "Personal Contact in Intergovernmental Organizations," to appear in H. Kelman (ed.), *International Behavior,* Holt, Rinehart and Winston, New York, forthcoming.

[8] If subscripts i refer to countries, j's refer to roll calls and k's indicate voting components (factors), the model assumes that the vote of a particular country i on roll-call $j (V_{ji})$ results from a linear additive combination of national positions on a small number of voting components (F_{ik}'s, called "factor scores"). Factor loadings (a_{jk}'s) may be thought of either as correlations between roll calls and factors or as coefficients of the factor model in Equation (1):

$$V_{ji} = \sum_k a_{jk} F_{ik} + U_{ji} \qquad (1)$$

The first strategy for identifying voting components emphasizes *frequent voting behavior*. The loadings in Table 2 are derived from uncorrelated hypothetical voting alignments, each explaining as much voting variance as possible. Factor loadings for the first five hypothetical factors (voting components) form the columns of Table 2. Note how the *most frequent voting factor contains nearly half (48%) of all special session non-unanimous roll-call votes*. The second, third, fourth and fifth most frequent distinctive voting components underlie 17, 7, 5 and 3.5 per cent of these roll calls. Three other factors, none of which had any loadings above 0.50 or explained more than 3% of the voting variance, have been omitted from the table.

Using the maximum voting variance approach, do we find common supranational voting predispositions across the different special sessions of the General Assembly? Unrotated Factor I certainly cuts across these different sessions, but seems to consist primarily of issues on which East and West disagree: Hungary, Soviet and Arab initiatives on Palestine, French attacks on Tunisia, and payment of Congo arrears. Thus half of special session votes reveal *"East-West"* alignments. If East-West issues could be solved in a United Nations context, international political community would be increased, but there is no striking evidence that such a trend has occurred or that commitment to a greater United Nations has played a dramatic role in such developments. Once East-West predispositions are taken into account, however, the second and third most frequent voting factors consist of issues showing a greater degree of commitment to use the UN and to obey its decisions.

Because of the content of the issues loading heavily on it, I would call the second most frequent voting predisposition, *"North-South"* inclinations. These predispositions have appeared in issues on which many "Northern powers" including the United States, the United Kingdom, France and the Soviet Union, have either positively agreed or negatively been forced into voting together: setting up adequate machinery for investigating the Palestine problem without crippling restrictions (especially votes 2, 12, 14 and 15), disagreeing (except for the United States)

8 *(Cont)* The U_{ji}'s represent the part of voting ranks that can not be explained by identifiable factors. In the present analysis only factors with variances equal to that of one roll call or more, and with loadings of 0.50 higher are considered identifiable. Even these relatively strict identification rules have produced communalities (h^2's, roll-call variance accounted for by factor loadings in the factor matrix) averaging around 80% of their maximum value (which is 1.0 or 100% in the case of no missing data).

Dynamically, Equation (1) suggests several ways of influencing national votes (V_{ji}'s) on a particular roll call *(j)*. Given relatively stable cold war and supranationalist predispositions (respectively, F_{i1}, F_{i2}), the neutralist diplomat, for example, tries to shape resolutions about a particular crisis so as to evoke favorable, supranationalist responses. His success would be indicated by a high supranationalism factor loading (a_{j2} bigger than a_{j1}) and by small particularistic voting components (negligible U_{ji}'s).

TABLE 2. Unrotated Factor Matrix for 52 Special Session Roll Calls

Roll-Call Description			I	II	III	IV	V	h²
SS1:	1	Omit Palestine future	70	35	04	17	09	65
	2	Omit religious concerns	−49	−07	−12	44	30	54
	3	Note religious concerns	42	14	29	−31	30	47
	4	Immediate independence	−83	−32	04	−02	10	81
	5.	Consider independent Palestine	−67	−21	24	−11	14	58
	6	Committee of SC members	−77	−05	12	22	48	88
	7	Committee of SC members	−76	−04	17	24	51	93
	8	Add 1 African member	−75	−05	15	19	48	85
	9	Committee of small powers	48	−35	06	02	−32	45
	10	End mandate	−72	−35	00	−14	−03	66
	11	Hear Jewish viewpoint	−46	39	23	−05	10	42
	12	Hear All viewpoints	46	69	32	−11	09	81
	13	Small power committee	91	14	13	−10	11	89
	14	Power to investigate	44	63	38	−09	12	75
	15	Palestine resolution	44	63	38	−09	12	75
SS2:	16	Jerusalem urgent	52	46	52	12	−04	76
	17	Charter OKs UN admin.	56	46	44	21	−01	75
	18	Use regular UN budget	53	57	26	35	−14	82
	19	OKs Unforeseen expenses	69	45	23	27	−24	81
	20	UN Commissioner	60	57	28	30	−16	89
	21	UN administer Jerusalem	58	58	29	29	−16	87
	22	UN Mediator in Palestine	66	−08	−01	35	03	57
ES1:	23	Urges Suez cease-fire	−29	−40	69	−38	03	81
	24	SG arrange cease-fire	−35	−38	48	−53	−21	81
	25	Asks SG for UNEF plan	44	−64	38	−17	−10	78
	26	Establishes UNEF	45	−58	48	−13	−15	81
	27	Organizes UNEF	66	−55	07	04	−08	74
	28	Withdraw forces	−29	−43	69	−38	10	90
ES2:	29	Notes Soviet repression	93	−04	−15	−17	17	94
	30	Hungary desires freedom	93	−04	−15	−14	18	93
	31	Intervention intolerable	93	−03	−17	−18	18	95
	32	Soviets violate Charter	92	−03	−14	−21	15	93
	33	Withdrawal necessary	93	−04	−15	−14	18	94
	34	USSR withdraw now	92	−05	−13	−15	16	92
	35	UN auspices for elections	79	−12	−15	−05	06	65
	36	Favors free elections	94	01	−11	−13	16	94
	37	Requests SG investigate	91	−07	−08	−11	12	86
	38	SG report compliance	92	−07	−10	−11	15	87
	39	Hungary resolution	91	−03	−20	−15	21	93
	40	Help refugees	92	−06	−10	−10	15	89
	41	Hungarian relief	55	−50	−23	03	−11	61
	42	Omit references to USSR	−83	−35	05	26	−13	89
	43	Withdrawal and relief	93	03	−09	−14	15	91
SS3:	44	Tunisia and France	−61	−36	24	16	39	73
ES4:	45	Noninterference: Congo	61	−72	−03	04	−06	89
SS4:	46	UNEF financing	65	−42	26	35	09	80
	47	Collective responsibility	54	−72	11	18	−01	85
	48	ONUC financing	68	−43	24	33	04	81
	49	Appeals for arrears	71	−37	26	32	06	81
	50	Bond sales extension	46	−72	08	35	00	86
	51	SG consider peace fund	49	−74	07	27	−01	86
	52	Continue working group	54	−73	12	20	−00	87
% Roll-Call Variance Explained			47.6	16.9	6.9	5.1	3.5	

(5 factors together explain 79.5%)

with Southern attempts to use the Secretary-General and the United Nations
Emergency Force to prevent Northern intervention in the Suez crisis (especially
vote 25), hesitating to support (except for the United States and to a lesser extent
the United Kingdom) United Nations Congo operations (votes 45, 47, 50, 51 and
52).

As the major alternative alignment to the East-West conflict in the General
Assembly, we should expect the North-South alignment to have differing substantive implications, including the possibility of greater use of and commitment
to United Nations decision-making machinery. The U.N.'s role in Palestine's partition and its aftermath, its intervention in the Suez and Congo crises do evidence
a considerable degree of supranational activity. Because several roll calls from
these crises do load on the North-South factors, supranationalism is clearly a
major part of this voting component; but because several apparently constructive
roll calls on these situations also appear to load more on the East-West factor, it
would be premature at this point to identify supranationalism with the North-
South conflict.

The third most frequent voting component reveals a different set of supranationalist aspirations. The three highest loadings on the third unrotated factor
(votes 16, 23 and 28) have in common a desire to prevent *"Arab-Israeli conflict."*
Vote 16 is a vote on Mexican text referring to the civil strife that broke out before Palestine's independence: "Whereas the maintenance of order and security
in Jerusalem is an urgent question which concerns the United Nations as a whole."
Votes 23 and 28 requested the cessation of hostilities and the withdrawal of
French, British and Israeli forces nine years later during the Suez crisis. Once
again, however, the substantive significance of this unrotated factor needs to be
sharpened, a task for which factor rotation is especially appropriate.[9]

The Rotated Factor Matrix

A second strategy for identifying voting components is to construct hypothetical voting alignments producing a substantively interpretable, *simply structured*
factor matrix. Such a matrix ideally consists of only very high factor loadings and
very low ones. It can be approximated by applying what is known as Kaiser's
"normal Varimax procedure" to the unrotated factor matrix. A factor can then
be simply identified from roll-calls with high loadings on no other voting component.

Hopefully, the rotated factor matrix will help distinguish more clearly among
the rather varied set of rollcalls loading on the unrotated voting components.
Comparing the rotated factor matrix (Table 3) with Table 2, clearer substantive

---

[9]The remaining unrotated factors do not seem to have appeared frequently enough to warrant
detailed discussion. Factor 4 seems to catch a lesser aspect of both the Palestine and Congo
situations, issues loading more heavily on the North-South and Arab-Israeli factors. Factor
5 distinguishes a special aspect of votes 6, 7 and 8. Unlike typical East-West alignments, Arab
states and some Asians abstained on these Soviet initiatives, to compose the committee considering the future of Palestine in a manner similar to the Security Council.

TABLE 3. Rotated Factor Matrix for 52 Special Session Roll Calls

Roll-Call Description	I	II	III	IV	V	VI	VII	VIII	h^2
				Factors					
1 Omit Palestine future	45	−15	−19	−41	−09	56	24	10	88
2 Omit religious concerns	−13	02	−24	39	56	08	−16	01	58
3 Note religious concerns	18	03	40	−43	−01	29	13	57	80
4 Immediate independence	−45	14	16	53	34	−49	−14	−07	91
5 Consider independence	−27	14	26	39	31	−69	06	−05	89
6 Committee of SC members	−20	22	06	46	78	−15	−04	−04	93
7 Committee of SC members	−15	21	08	46	81	−15	−04	−01	97
8 Add 1 African member	−18	23	10	44	76	−12	−05	−02	88
9 Committee of small powers	18	−44	08	−27	−38	−36	−28	09	67
10 End mandate	−41	16	23	42	17	−51	−31	00	81
11 Hear Jewish viewpoint	02	38	00	35	16	−28	47	−08	60
12 Hear all viewpoints	50	21	−02	−28	−15	20	69	03	91
13 Small power committee	39	−28	−02	−73	−22	05	32	02	91
14 Power to investigate	48	13	−00	−25	−13	08	76	07	92
15 Palestine resolution	48	13	−00	−25	−13	08	76	07	92
16 Jerusalem urgent	83	−00	16	−24	−01	11	22	−11	85
17 Charter OKs UN admin.	83	−05	06	−26	00	18	19	−06	83
18 Use regular UN budget	87	01	−22	−19	−12	−02	14	05	87
19 OKs Unforeseen expenses	84	−10	−14	−30	−25	14	06	−06	91
20 UN Commissioner	90	01	−16	−25	−16	01	10	08	95
21 UN administer Jerusalem	90	03	−13	−24	−17	03	08	16	95
22 UN Mediator in Palestine	43	−43	−22	−42	−05	−13	−21	28	74
23 Urges Suez cease-fire	−09	−11	90	24	13	−05	−03	08	92
24 SG arrange cease-fire	−27	−00	78	27	−18	−23	02	−00	84
25 Asks SG for UNEF plan	03	−62	53	−28	−09	−02	−12	−35	88
26 Establishes UNEF	10	−64	54	−20	−13	04	−00	−35	89
27 Organizes UNEF	05	−70	13	−43	−14	08	−11	−33	84
28 Withdraw forces	−12	−13	91	20	18	−08	00	06	94
29 Notes Soviet repression	19	−28	−08	−89	−18	07	03	−02	95
30 Hungary desires freedom	19	−30	−09	−88	−17	08	04	00	94
31 Intervention intolerable	19	−25	−08	−91	−18	06	02	−01	98
32 Soviets violate Charter	20	−24	−03	−90	−19	08	00	−03	95
33 Withdrawal necessary	19	−30	−09	−88	−17	08	04	00	94
34 USSR withdraw now	20	−30	−07	−87	−19	07	05	−01	93
35 UN auspices for elections	15	−34	−08	−67	−20	22	−06	03	69
36 Favors free elections	24	−29	−09	−86	−20	09	11	03	95
37 Requests SG investigate	21	−35	−06	−81	−20	08	08	−02	88
38 SG report compliance	20	−35	−07	−83	−19	08	08	00	90
39 Hungary resolution	18	−25	−10	−90	−15	08	−01	05	95
40 Help refugees	21	−35	−08	−82	−18	09	07	00	90
41 Hungarian relief	−14	−57	−11	−41	−22	−07	−17	−22	65
42 Omit references to USSR	−34	−04	04	79	26	−18	−20	−12	90
43 Withdrawal and relief	24	−28	−08	−84	−22	08	12	06	92
44 Tunisia and France	−29	−10	25	43	60	−14	−08	21	77
45 Noninterference: Congo	−15	−80	08	−40	−16	03	−14	−21	92
46 UNEF financing	20	−84	−03	−28	−01	−03	17	13	87
47 Collective responsibility	−07	−86	12	−27	−04	10	−13	−11	87
48 ONUC financing	20	−84	−02	−28	−08	−04	13	21	90
49 Appeals for arrears	23	−82	−03	−31	−09	−02	19	21	91
50 Bond sales extension	−07	−92	−00	−13	−02	05	−14	13	90
51 SG consider peace fund	−10	−90	04	−19	−04	04	−14	03	88
52 Continue working group	−07	−88	12	−25	−03	10	−12	−08	90
% Roll-Call Variance Explained (8 factors explain 87%)	14.2	18.5	7.0	28.3	7.5	4.0	5.3	2.2	

interpretations are indeed possible. Note, however, that the percentage of variance explained by these rotated factors does not correspond to the analogous figures for the unrotated matrix.

Rotated Factor 4, consisting almost completely of Hungarian roll-calls, seems quite similar to the East-West conflict, although Palestine and Congo questions no longer make sizeable contributions. I would use a *Cold War* label for it. Rotated Factor 3 appears to be a "cleaned up" version of unrotated Factor 3: it consists only of the Suez related Arab-Asian conflicts. Because previously noted votes 23 and 28, urging a cease-fire and troop withdrawal, now have extremely high loadings, perhaps an *anti-intervention* label is appropriate. Only colonial powers—France, Belgium, Britain, Portugal and South Africa among them—did not vote against Israeli-British-French intervention in the Middle East.

In a similar fashion, the second rotated factor seems to bring out more clearly the *United Nations supranationalism* predispositions contained in North-South alignments. *All* Congo and UNEF votes from two different sessions load heavily on this factor. Two other votes (no. 22 on a UN Palestine mediator and no. 41 on Hungarian relief) also have their highest loadings on this factor. In a modest way, like other supranationalist votes, they evidence national willingness to use and obey supranational instrumentalities.

The Palestine related votes loading on the unrotated factors can be distinguished into a number of substantively distinct components. Rotated Factor 5, like the fifth unrotated factor, pinpoints votes 6, 7 and 8, Soviet Bloc *r* solutions calling for a Palestine committee similar in composition to the Security Council. This attempt to keep Assembly decisions within a great power framework was resisted by Western states, while Arabs and Asians mostly abstained. The peculiar cross-pressures on Afro-Asian states in the Palestine context suggest, however, that Russian reluctance concerning what might be called *Security Council competence* might in other contexts appear on supranationalism issues.

A few of the remaining Palestine votes, appear on rotated Factors 6, 7 and 8. Only Factor 1 contains enough of these votes to require particular comment. Centered as it is on votes 16 through 21, the first rotated factor might be identified as *Palestine settlement* concerns. Voting alignments similar to these have regularly occurred in the General Assembly.[10] Because the main resolutions loading on this factor failed to achieve the required two-thirds majority, they failed to achieve even the status of internationally sanctioned recommendations.

---

[10] At the Sixteenth Assembly, for example, Palestine, Cold War, UN supranationalism and anti-intervention factors can be identified, as well as unrotated East-West and North-South alignments. The most significant omission to data from special session voting has been straight anti-colonial or self-determination resolutions such as occur on resolutions on the self-determination of natural resources or sanctions against South Africa and Portugese Angola. See Alker, *op. cit.*

The general effect of rotating the factor matrix (according to what is called the normal varimax criterion) was to sharpen the factor interpretations given to the first four unrotated factors.[11] Five such rotated factors were identifiable: Palestine settlement, UN supranationalism, the Cold War, "anti-interventionism" regarding Suez, and Security Council competence concerning Palestine's future.

Supranationalism in UN Voting

Given complementary pictures of "frequent behavioral" and "simply structured" components of General Assembly voting, we are now able to assess the extent of U.N. supranationalism. Implied by the definition of "supranationalism" as the "commitment to use and to obey supranational means" is the need to establish the degree to which the U.N. has acted as a supranational institution on these issues loading heavily on the supranationalism factor. The significance of such activities goes beyond the mere frequency of such votes to the resulting changes in the structure of the U.N.

In Haas' terms, both United Nations activities in recommending and overseeing the consequences of Palestine partition and its extended role in the Suez and Congo crises exemplify important increases in the range of functions performed and the scope of power exercised, often in spite of strong national opposition. Russia's decision not to veto the Congo operation, the extensive reliance of the Secretary-General on his advisory bodies for UNEF and ONUC, and the effective role of the General Assembly in both these situations once the veto had been exercised, are all radical departures from the 1-nation veto principle of the League of Nations in the direction of majoritarian rule.

If most U.N. representatives cannot legislate independently of their government's control, most supranationalism issues have nonetheless shown U.N. delegations and related interest groups in England, United States, and other countries to be significant influences on national policy-making. It is significant also, that none of the principle powers involved in these crises has publically announced its consideration of withdrawal from the U.N. because of the injustices it has suffered. Retaliatory action has always been less severe (often financial) and generally less successful.

A distinguishing characteristic of supranationalism resolutions has been the extent to which they have been binding decisions effectively carried out. After rotation, the Security Council competence factor "split" off from "supranationalism": it did not even receive a two-thirds Assembly majority—such a majority

---

[11]This conclusion is greatly strengthened by intercorrelation among the appropriate factor "scores" defined as noted in Table 4: East-West and Cold War factors, North-South and Supranationalism factors, Arab-Israeli and anti-intervention factor "scores" reveal paired correlations above 0.90. The rotated Palestine settlement factor correlates 0.62 with East-West alignments and about 0.60 with rotated Factors 5, 6, 7 and 8, all on different aspects of the Palestine situation.

did obtain, however, on the U.N. mediator vote. Anti-intervention votes also reflected supranational *aspirations,* but to become *effective,* resolutions establishing the requisite peace force were necessary; these roll-calls evoked a supranational alignment. Of the many votes on Hungary loading with exasperating futility on East-West and cold war factors, only the humanitarian issue evoked supranational responses and led to an effective charitable mission.

In sum, we find Haas' criteria of institutionalized supranationality remarkably appropriate for describing the intermittant strengths and the reoccuring weaknesses of supranationalism in the United Nations. Special Session majorities have not been able to legislate a new world order into being, but to varying degrees they have readjusted national policies on each of the main conflicts in the Assembly; cold war calamities have been humanized; Arab-Israeli conflicts have on certain occasions been radically transformed. nations have been successfully born in the struggle for self-determination.

WHAT DETERMINES SUPRANATIONALIST PREDISPOSITIONS?

The world is not ruled by votes in the General Assembly. Effective supranational decisions in the Assembly have resulted from readjusted calculations of national advantage.

Whatever progress may be possible toward the evolution of a larger role for such civilized devices in international life will be furthered by the development of a tradition of vigorous and meaningful contests for voting support by rival leaders, operating within the context of a General Assembly which is nobody's tool.[12]

Granting the realities of General Assembly politics, what kinds of states have evidenced supranationalist predispositions at its special sessions? Keeping with the above interpretation of the supranationalism alignment as the major evidence of such predispositions, one can test various possible voting determinants using correlational and related techniques. The discussion below will be only suggestive, not exhaustive.

National Characteristics Related to Supranationalism

Among the noblest ideals of Western civilization is the belief that nations with competitive political systems, democracies, are more peaceful than communist, autocratic or totalitarian regimes: "[Woodrow] Wilson, following the thesis laid

[12]I. L. Claude, Jr., *Swords into Plowshares,* Second Edition, Random House, New York, 1961, p. 459.

down more than a hundred years earlier by Immanuel Kant in his essay on *Perpetual Peace (Zum ewigen Frieden),* believed that world peace could be established only by a compact among democratically governed nations."[13]

A somewhat less classical argument embodied in the Covenant of the League and the Charter of the United Nations, is that Great Powers ought to be primarily responsible for the maintenance of international peace, presumably because they have both the required capabilities and intentions. Ever since two "International Peace Conferences" held at the Hague under the impetus of Russia's Czar Nicholas II in 1899 and 1907, smaller powers have taken a different view. Seeking voting positions equal to those of great powers, such states could argue that international organizations benefit appreciably from small power detachment and their real desire not to be destroyed by great powers.[14]

Three other national characteristics might also account for supranationalism predispositions. If we believe supranational issues to originate in Cold War debates then supranationalism voting may represent an extension of the Cold War into the General Assembly. Perhaps, too, ex-colonial states and underdeveloped states are using the Assembly for their collective security and economic development needs.[15]

The correlations and average supranationalism scores in Table 4 serve to test these various hypotheses. More than anything, supranationalism predispositions seem to be anti-communist ones. As Woodrow Wilson would have us believe, democracies are supranationally predisposed, but to a much lesser extent than communist states are anti-supranationalist. Western military allies, not all notable for their democratic systems, seem also to have moderatly positive supranational inclinations.

Great powers (as defined by a crude indicator, Gross National Product) appear to be resisting the supranationalism visible in the United Nations. Perhaps smaller powers are in fact more willing to use and to obey General Assembly resolutions.

[13] I. L. Claude, *op. cit.,* pp. 55-6.

[14] *Ibid.,* pp. 28-35. Small power attempts to enlarge General Assembly functions (the Uniting for Peace resolution) and to keep great powers ("members of the Security Council") off Assembly Committees indicate such feelings still exist.

[15] Ernst Haas, for example, has suggested the eventual possibility that revolutionary (usually anti-colonial) states will channel their collective security demands (as now done regarding South Africa) through the General Assembly. Beneficiaries of UN technical assistance programs have also submitted to supranational authority on numerous occasions in order to receive the desired assistance. The use of UN peace-keeping capabilities by the United States and its allies might also be considered in Haas' terming as "permissive enforcement." See E. B. Haas, "International Integration: The European and the Universal Process," *International Organization,* Vol. 15, No. 3 (Summer 1961), pp. 366-392, E. B. Haas, "Dynamic Environment and Static System: Revolutionary Regimes in the United Nations," in M. A. Kaplan, *The Revolution in World Politics,* Wiley and Sons, New York, 1962, pp. 267-309. Other references, as well as descriptions and justifications of the dichotomous coding procedures are given in Alker, "Dimensions of Conflict," *op. cit.*

TABLE 4. Relations Between National Characteristics and Supranationalism Voting
(Positive supranational scores represent high supranationalism predisposition)

National Characteristics	Average Supranationalism Score** of State Sharing the Characteristic	Correlation of National Character with Supranationalism Score**
Political democracy (N = 40)	0.34	0.29
National power (dichotomized at $10 billion GNP, N = 20)	*	−0.30 (estimate)
Economic underdevelopment (per capita GNP below $700 N = 95)	0.00	0.06
Western military ally (N =43)	0.29	0.23
Recent ex-European colony (since 1919) (N = 52)	0.31	0.29
Communist State	−2.38	−0.84
All Countries (N = 111)	0.02	*

*Not computed.
**Supranationalism scores are a weighted average of standardized scores for three different sets of Assembly resolutions: votes 1–22, votes 23–43 and votes 44–52. For each period standard scores have been computed from standardized voting ranks multiplied by factor loadings above 0.40 taken from the second column of the rotated factor matrix. Final scores are the result of weighting these period scores according to the amount of supranationalism roll-call variance for each period. These resulting scores are themselves nearly standardized (with a mean of 0.02 and a standard deviation of 0.93).

Finally, although economic development (as measured by per capita G.N.P.) does *not* seem related to supranationalism, ex-colonial background does. Not a little of the incisiveness of Suez and Congo resolutions comes from the anti-colonial as well as anti-communist feelings of newly independent countries.[16]

[16]I would like to illustrate only one of the many ways in which further multivariate explanatory relations among the variables in Table 4 could be developed. Consider the problem of adequately relating regional correlations to universal ones. Among Western allies (roughly, the "West" when OAS members are included), a correlation between communism and anti-supranationalism is meaningless because none of these states are communist. Among non-Western countries communism correlates −0.92 with supranationalism, ever higher than the universal 0.84 figure. For all 111 states ex-colonial status correlates only moderately (r = 0.29) with supranationalism, but belies a much higher relationship *among* non-Western countries (r = 0.61) than it does among Western countries (r = 0.16). In sum, *within* the West supranationalism is not an anti-communist reaction while among non-Western states

WHY DO PARTICULAR RESOLUTIONS EVOKE SUPRANATIONALIST ALIGNMENTS?

The factor model (given in Equation 1 above) implies that two sets of information are necessary to explain or predict voting positions on a particular roll call. First, one must know the various possible general voting predispositions, and why they are held. The previous sections of this paper have tentatively answered some of these questions. Before we can say that a particular resolution will evoke general supranationalist predispositions, however, another crucial piece of information is necessary. Looking at a factor matrix both the anti-behavioralist and the diplomat are likely to ask the same valid question: why did vote such and such (e.g., vote 48) load on the supranationalism factor? Factor analysis only allows us to say, *after the fact,* that such a loading did occur. We still need to know what characteristics of the resolution and of the situation it refers to to determine particular kinds of voting responses.

If we stress the determinative importance of reality *perceptions,* one fruitful area of investigation is to try and understand why and how certain situations are viewed in supranationalist terms. Interviews with diplomats and content analysis of their speeches and documents would be appropriate strategies. A preliminary study of the resolutions themselves may tentatively serve to indicate the usefulness of such an approach.

Distinguishing Characteristics of Supranationalism Resolutions

Table 5 contains data for testing several plausible hypotheses about the distinguishing characteristics of supranationalism resolutions. On the basis of the existing literature we might expect, for example, that resolutions must draw heavily on neutralists, democracies and ex-colonies as sponsors in order to achieve resounding supranationalist majorities.[17]

Several stylistic or wording characteristics of supranationalist resolutions have also been suggested: increased Charter references on successful task expansions tend to increase the legitimacy of the UN; the concept of supranationality implies more references to the role of the executive, the Secretary General, and/or to UN legislative bodies. One would also suppose that supranationalist resolutions avoid

16 *(Cont)* supranationalism is both an anti-communist and an anti-colonial disposition. For more detailed examples of relations among regional and universal correlations, see Alker, "Regionalism versus Universalism in Comparing Nations", in Russett, Alker, Deutsch and Lasswell, *World Handbook of Political and Social Indicators,* Yale University Press, New Haven, 1964.

17 Conor Cruise O'Brien, *To Katanga and Back,* Hutchison, London, 1962, refers to all of these characteristics of "good sponsorship" in Assembly politics. Ernst Haas, "Dynamic Environment," *op. cit.,* has stressed the need for support from revolutionary (anti-colonial) states on new tasks that increase the legitimacy and authority of the United Nations.

TABLE 5. A Content Analysis of the Sponsorship, Wording and Objectives of 52 Special Session Roll-Call Resolutions*

A. Sponsorship Characteristics:

Predominant Alignment:	Cold War Alignment			Democracy		Colonial Past		
	US Ally	Neutral	Soviet	Yes	No	Colonial Power	None	Ex-Colony
UN supranationalism	7†	8	0	8	7	6	8†	7†
Cold War	9	3	0	7	6	4	6	3
Palestine settlement	5	0	0	5	0	3	2	0
Anti-interventionism	3	2	0	2	1	1	2	2
Other (Palestine, etc)	7	4	7	9	10	5	10	3
Total	31	17	7	31	24	19	28	15

B. Wording Characteristics:

Predominant Alignment:	Legal Reference			UN References			Specificity		Critical	
	Charter	Other UN	No	SG	Other	None	Yes	No	Yes	No
UN supranationalism	4	7†	1	12	12	2	5	12	2	11
Cold War	3	3	11	6	9	6	12	4	9†	6
Palestine settlement	2	1	3	2	5	0	3	1†	0	6
Anti-interventionism	1	3	0	3	2	0	1	2	1†	2
Other (Palestine, etc)	1	0	13	2	10	3	9	6†	1	14
Total	11	14	28	25	38	11	30	25	13	39

C. Objectives Characteristics:

Predominant Alignment:	Action Required					Region			
	$	Troops	Info	Organize Discuss	Other	Eur.	N. East	Africa	Other
UN supranationalism	7	3	7	6	4†	1	6	6†	0
Cold War	0	0	4	1†	8	14	1†	0	0
Palestine settlement	3	0	0	3	0†	0	6	0	0
Anti-interventionism	0	1	2	0	3	0	3	0	0
Other (Palestine, etc)	1	0	6	9	2†	0	14	1	0
Total	11	4	19	19	17	15	30	7	0

*Data in tables above are frequencies of references to particular categories of sponsorship, wording and objectives. Because one resolution may have several kinds of sponsor, as well as require several kinds of action, it might be counted under more than one characteristic.

†Table entries marked by a dagger (†) were those more significantly increased on a subsequent recoding of the above information.

criticisms of specific states. Universalism of language and application is a definitional characteristic of the "rule of law."

Finally, concerning the objectives of supranationalist resolutions, we would expect increased task requirements in peacekeeping and other areas of international activity. Because of the UN's limited competence, such activities are not likely to occur in direct confrontations of the two super-powers.[18]

Despite the judgmental element of the content analysis categories used in Table 5 (two coders always agreed on more than 80% of the category assignments), these results tentatively corroborate most of the above mentioned hypotheses. Neutralist and excolonial sponsorships do seem to help produce supranationalist responses when such sponsors can be obtained. Democratic sponsorship is generally desirable in the Assembly on both supranationalism and Cold War alignments (note that democracies, although they form less than two-fifths of the membership, account for nearly three-fifths of the sponsorship).

Supranationalism resolutions, as expected, do have a larger number of Charter references than most other votes (Cold War votes do too), while references to Secretariat and legislative roles are also especially high. Supranationalism resolutions, although they *imply* criticisms of specific states, also usually do not use abusive language when referring to particular states.

Regarding the kinds of task expansion and the geographic areas appropriate for supranationalism responses, the sending of troops and the commitment of finances have obviously been important. Geographically, Hungarian aid, Middle Eastern and African peace-keeping forces have been possible in supranationalism terms.

SUPRANATIONALISM AND INTERNATIONAL COMMUNITY

Even though supranationalist predispositions have been formed and invoked with considerable success on several crucial occasions in the short period since the United Nations began, the above analysis does *not* prove that international community—peaceful relations among nations—has been brought closer to realization. The problems facing peaceful international cooperation and competition have also multiplied in the post-war period—perhaps even more rapidly the United Nation's limited supranationalist capabilities, which even now are being seriously challenged by great powers from both the East and the West.

[18]The above hypotheses have been drawn from previously cited literature or from conversations with UN diplomats. Most scholars seem to expect peace-keeping functions to grow more slowly than other informational economic and social ones. See in particular the fascinating varieties of this argument in terms of Parsonian functionalism in A. Etzioni, *op. cit.*; the present data is inadequate to test such theories about stages of supranational development.

Historically viewed, however, certain encouraging characteristics of the UN's modest supranational capability should be mentioned. First of all, it is sometimes said that the UN can only help settle disputes of small powers (such, in general, was the League's experience). The UN's record is a considerable improvement on such expectations: Britain was centrally involved in partitioning Palestine, Britain and France attacked at Suez, France fought with Tunisia at Bizerta, and Communist China battled the United Nations in Korea. The UN was unable significantly to affect outcomes only in major superpower confrontations, such as Cuba, Berlin and Hungary. Some small power problems, such as the current Arab-Israeli refugee problem, have remained intractable, but other crises in which great powers have been indirectly involved (such as the Congo) have been met satisfactorily. Significant UN successes have occurred on both small power and great power threats to peace.

Secondly, the analysis above does not take into account all community building capabilities of regional and universal supranational organizations: I have purposely limited myself primarily to General Assembly activities at special and emergency special sessions. The Secretary-General's individual intervention in the Cuban crisis must be remembered. Many of the less dramatic political, economic and social activities of the United Nations and of its affiliated organizations may also be helping to build foundations for world community.[19]

Finally, nonsupranational modes of moderating international conflict, however inadequate, must also be mentioned. American and Soviet calculations of advantage prevented the escalation of the Cuban, Berlin and Hungarian crises, even though justice was not always served. It is appropriate, therefore, to consider the United Nation's General Assembly as only one of several significant weapons in the arsenal of peace.

[19]Many observers have taken the view that economic development and technical assistance programs have, indirectly, been the United Nation's chief contributions to international community. When both Soviet and Western great powers have objected (as at the Sixteenth Regular Session of the General Assembly), these programs have also evoked North-South alignments. UN Supranationalism seems to be the more general phenomenon, embracing both peace-keeping and major developmental aspirations and achievements.

29. RESOLVING INTERNATIONAL CONFLICTS:
A TAXONOMY OF BEHAVIOR AND SOME
FIGURES ON PROCEDURES

K. J. Holsti

Incompatible objectives and policy actions between interacting states form the basis of most international conflicts. Governments pursue or promote a variety of objectives, some of which are readily identifiable—such as a demand for a piece of territory or the inclusion of rebel representatives in a coalition government—and others which are less tangible, such as the values inherent in the concepts of "peace," "security," or "a just international order." To achieve objectives, governments make different types of demands on their neighbors and on other actors in the system, some of which lead to conflict because their realization can be achieved only at the expense of the interests and values of other states. In other situations, of course, a demand or request by one state can increase the advantages of both. This is the basis for cooperative and collaborative interactions.

Relationships involving conflictful forms of state behavior can, however, be divided according to the sources from which they arise and the types of actions and counteractions they commonly result in. When observers refer to "international conflict" they seldom distinguish between the types of phenomena they label as conflictful. Is a border incident between Chile and Argentina involving the loss of several lives to be regarded as a "conflict" in the same sense that many aspects of Soviet-Chinese relations are conflictful? In this paper we will make distinctions between (1) *disputes* caused by accidents and minor provocations; (2) *conflicts* arising from incompatible collective objectives; and (3) more general *"tensions"* between two or more states. Disputes grow out of border incidents, diplomatic embarrassments, or unauthorized provocations made by military forces in a neighbor's territory. Presumably they are relatively easy to settle, because the causes are clearly identifiable and because they involve specific grievances—usually

SOURCE. K. J. Holsti, "Resolving International Conflicts," in *The Journal of Conflict Resolution,* 10 (September, 1966), pp. 272–296. (Appendices omitted.) Reprinted by permission of the author and the Center for Research on Conflict Resolution. Copyright 1966 by the University of Michigan.

to private citizens—rather than the incompatibility of collective, national objectives. To cite some examples: the accidental shooting of farm animals near the frontier by the border police of a neighboring state; the accidental destruction of fishing boats by another nation's naval vessels (the Dogger Banks incident); the violation of an international frontier by a group of armed bandits; frontier guards or patrols from neighboring states shooting at each other; or an armed aircraft accidentally destroying lives and property in a foreign state. When such incidents occur between states whose relations are already typified by hostile attitudes, they may lead to violent responses and even to war (the sinking of the *Maine* in Havana harbor provided the excuse for the United States to go to war against Spain), but generally they can be resolved through peaceful means such as indemnification of those who have suffered.

Most international *conflicts* also have sources which are relatively easy to identify. The most common cause historically has been the demand by one political group for territorial rights or resources controlled by another, or the effort by one society to impose military, political, or economic controls over alien populations. These demands cannot be satisfied except at the sacrifice of other states' "core" values and interests, and hence conflict arises and continues until the initiator withdraws its demands, or induces the other state to compromise, or forces it to submit through threats or military action. Another source of international conflict, and one which has appeared with increasing frequency, is the domestic rebellion which attracts outside intervention. Unlike the simple territorial conflict, there are usually four parties involved in the internal-international conflict: the domestic government and the rebellious faction, and two outside powers intervening to support either domestic group.

The type of relationship we have called "tensions" arises from a juxtaposition of historical, economic, religious, or ethnic conditions and is perpetuated by widespread and deep-seated public attitudes of hostility between two or more societies. Incompatible territorial and security objectives may, of course, be involved in "tensions" but by themselves they do not give rise to, or perpetuate, *all* of the forms of hostile behavior between the involved states. The Cold War and the Arab-Israeli tensions could not be resolved entirely by the settlement of just one of the component issues. The Korean armistice has had little effect, for instance, on hostile public attitudes in the main antagonists of the Cold War; and few believe that a future settlement over Berlin would end all the fears and lack of trust that typify the relations between the Soviet Union and the West. Sometimes, of course, a conflict over concrete objectives such as a piece of territory may become a symbol of a more complicated relationship and its resolution could begin a process leading to overall reconciliation. However, such territorial questions by themselves seldom cause the great religious, ideological, or national rivalries observed throughout history.

Since "tensions" have no single source, they are more difficult to resolve than those conflicts whose origins lie in expansive demands and in the incompatibility of recognizable objectives. Irrational fears, distorted perceptions, and traditional social hatreds between the French and the Germans, the Austrians and the Balkan Slavs; important trade and colonial rivalries; the Anglo-German naval armaments race; and more specific conflicts over territory such as Alsace-Lorraine—all these were important conditions underlying the crisis in the summer of 1914. The European system might have been capable of allaying the immediate crisis, if not all the hostile attitudes, had it been confined to the tangible rivalries. But by July 1914 there were few specific sources of hostility which could have become the subject of negotiation or mediation. Indeed, perhaps the frantic efforts of European diplomats to arrange negotiations while the military organizations were mobilizing as rapidly as possible failed because there were such pronounced hostile attitudes and so few definable areas of disagreement whose solution could have saved the peace.

The discussion that follows will exclude disputes and "tensions" and will focus primarily on conflicts which have identifiable causes, which involve the threat or use of force, and whose settlement usually signifies the restoration of friendly relations between states. Some of the specific Cold War crises will be considered also, though the Cold War itself—like the religious wars of the sixteenth and seventeenth centuries, or the hostility which resulted in the First World War—is not amenable to overall settlement by the resolution of specific issues. "Tensions" are resolved only within lengthy historical processes which lead either to eventual reconciliation or to cataclysmic wars.

BEHAVIOR LEADING TO THE RESOLUTION OF INTERNATIONAL CONFLICTS

A typical conflict arising from the incompatibility of readily identifiable objectives, interests, or actions may proceed as follows. One state presents demands or takes physical actions to change the *status quo*. Another party communicates to the first that these actions or demands are a violation of a treaty or some unwritten understanding, a threat to its security or "vital interests," or incompatible with its own aspirations. The first state responds by claiming that its actions or demands are fully justified according to various criteria, and that it has no intention of withdrawing them, although it is certainly willing to negotiate. The second party thereupon threatens to respond, perhaps by the use of force, to protect its interests or to block the fulfillment of the first state's demands. Moreover, the second party usually refuses to negotiate until the other party has first withdrawn its demands or physical presence from the field or area under dispute. The first government, however, is publicly committed to its demands or course of action and refuses to withdraw, though it still offers to negotiate. At this point the second party breaks diplomatic relations or institutes other countermeasures, including the use of force, if the other state is physically occupying an area not formerly its own.[1] What alternatives are there for resolving this kind of situation?

At least six theoretical modes of behavior and outcomes are available to two or more parties when they seek to achieve or defend incompatible goals, values, interests, or positions: (1) avoidance or voluntary withdrawal, (2) violent conquest, (3) forced submission or withdrawal, (4) compromise, (5) award, and (6) "passive settlement."[2] No matter which alternative is chosen by policy-makers, it is always the result of bargaining—the making of commitments, offering of rewards, or threatening of punishments or deprivation—between two or more governments (K. J. Holsti, 1964). This bargaining can be implied where, for example, two sides display their military forces, or it can be more explicit where they exchange written messages or negotiate directly through diplomatic representatives. In fact, bargaining in any conflict usually includes both kinds of communication. If one government mobilizes its troops, institutes measures of civil defense, or increases the size of its military budget after demands or actions against it have been made, it is signaling to its adversary that it is willing to use force to protect or extend its interests and values. A government bargains by making explicit threats or offers of rewards through written or verbal communications.

Avoidance

When the incompatibility of goals, values, or interests is perceived by both sides after bargaining has commenced, one alternative course of action is for one or both parties to terminate the conflict by withdrawing from a physical or a bargaining position, or by ceasing the acts which originally caused hostile responses. Although this may not seem a very common form of behavior, in fact it is probably the most common of all among governments that normally maintain friendly relations (Boulding, 1962, p. 308). This occurs when, for instance, one government initiates a proposal with its neighbors to make certain frontier adjustments. When the neighbors insist that the *status quo* must be maintained, the initiator may, not wishing to create bad relations, withdraw the demand and forget about it. In several instances since World War II, the major powers have voluntarily (e.g., not under threat of force) withdrawn from colonies or foreign military bases, thus avoiding friction with indigenous peoples. Or the issue may be more

---

[1] A similar situation and course of events can be observed in the following conflicts since 1945: Netherlands–Indonesia, 1947–1949; Iran–Great Britain, 1951–1953; Netherlands–Indonesia, 1954–1962; India–Portugal, 1961–1962; Berlin, 1961; Cuba–US, 1960–1961; Tunisia–France, 1961–1962; India–China, 1962; Algeria-Morocco, 1963–1964; Indonesia–Malaysia, 1963–1965.

[2] These are a modification and extension of Boulding's (1962) categories.

procedural: for instance, a proposal to hold a conference on some matter of mutual concern which, when disapproved by other states, is quietly withdrawn by the sponsoring government. Some recent examples would include the American government's implied abandonment of the multilateral force and the Soviet government's withdrawal of the demand for a "troika" arrangement for the Secretary-Generalship of the United Nations.

Conquest

A second method for resolving an issue is by physically overwhelming the opponent through the use of force. But even the termination of violent conflict involves some agreement and bargaining between the antagonists. One side, as Coser (1961, p. 349) points out, must be made to realize that peace, even under terms of unconditional surrender, is more desirable than the continuation of the violent conflict. This may be achieved in several ways: by making certain, for example, that the loser perceives that the possibilities of achieving even reduced objectives or successfully defending itself have disappeared. Such realization may come only after some symbolic military catastrophe—the defeat of the Spanish Armada, the Battle of Waterloo, the Nazi occupation of Paris, or the fall of Dien Bien Phu. The conflict may be terminated, also, if one side offers lenient peace terms, where the alternative to their acceptance would be more severe terms later on. Or the policy-makers of the losing side may be induced to believe that they can still salvage something—their military forces, an intact economy, or the avoidance of foreign occupation—by suing for peace. But no government arrives at such a decision easily.

Indeed, the most agonizing position for civilian and military leaders during a war comes when a decision has to be made whether or not to terminate armed resistance and capitulate to the enemy. No one can know for certain at what point the best terms of settlement can be achieved, and there are always those on the losing side who claim that further resistance can strengthen their bargaining position, just as some argue that immediate surrender will bring the most favorable terms of settlement. In 1940 the French surrendered quickly to the German forces, expecting that an early capitulation would lead to softer peace terms. This strategy, though considered by many as a blot on France's honor, succeeded in part because it enabled the French to keep their navy—an important bargaining instrument against Nazi Germany in the future—and to keep the southern portion of the country free of German occupation forces (Kecskemeti, 1958).

Submission—Withdrawal

A similar situation occurs when one party to a conflict decides to submit to the other's demands or actions even though no violence has taken place. The criterion used to distinguish submission from conquest is whether or not a threat to employ force is implemented. It could be argued that when one side submits merely to a threat, a peaceful settlement ensues. But in this discussion, submission resulting from military threats or *ultimata* will be considered as nonpacific modes of conflict resolution.

Conflict resolution through submission can also be analyzed as an example of effective deterrence: the second party, by raising a counterthreat, induces the first party to withdraw its "offensive" demands or actions. The deterrent, whether it is a diplomatic, military, or economic threat, attempts to persuade the antagonist that the probable risk and cost of pursuing its actions or objectives outweigh the cost of retreating or withdrawing. A threat of retaliation, according to Lieberman (1964, p. 111) is also designed, presumably, to prevent a future recurrence of the undesired behavior.

One problem with using the concept of deterrence is that most behavior in conflict situations involves calculations of risks and costs and threatening responses by other parties. Even in the case of avoidance behavior, elements of deterrence are always present—in the sense that the party making the initial demands or proposals concludes that their fulfillment is not worth the costs of alienating other governments. However, we shall use the concept of deterrence as a form of submission—withdrawal behavior only where the target of the initial demands or actions threatens to retaliate *with the use of force.* If, in the face of a large mobilization combined with a threat of retaliation, an initiator of demands or hostile actions withdraws them, we will assume that the withdrawal was primarily a response to the deterrent. For instance, though we have little documented proof, most observers believe that the Allied military buildup in Berlin and West Germany in 1961 induced the Soviet government to withdraw its actions aimed at signing a separate peace treaty with East Germany.

Compromise

The fourth form of settling international conflicts is through some sort of compromise in which *both* sides agree to a partial withdrawal of their initial objectives, positions, demands, or actions (Boulding, 1962, pp. 309–10). The withdrawal need not be of the same cost or magnitude (symmetrical) to both parties. Hence, some diplomatic compromises are often criticized by pressure groups, editorialists, and opposition political parties as being a "sell-out" to the enemy, a submission to its demands without receiving adequate compensation. Nevertheless, from a neutral observer's point of view, any agreement which entails some sacrifice of objectives, interests, or position by both sides can be considered a compromise even if one side seems to get the better bargain.

The major problem in resolving a conflict through compromise is to have both sides realize that the price of continued conflict is higher than the costs, whatever they may be, of reducing demands or withdrawing from a diplomatic or military position. Unfortunately, many international issues are not raised to be settled short of "victory."

Armchair observers of international politics frequently demand that the parties to a conflict should immediately begin negotiations. Negotiations are useful in a conflict situation if both sides maintain flexible commitments to their goals and if they are willing to accept some settlement short of their maximum objectives. But if a government places exclusive value on total "victory," negotiations are likely to lead either to inconclusive results or to capitulation by one party. European publics and statesmen were short-sighted in pleading for negotiations and compromise with Hitler over his demands upon Austria, Czechoslovakia, and Poland because he was absolutely committed to the destruction of those nations' independence, either through threats or through physical conquest. Hitler viewed the compromise at Munich as only a temporary settlement, while Daladier and Chamberlain believed that they had verbally persuaded Hitler to limit his objectives to the Sudetenland. The only way to have resolved the German-bred conflicts, short of submission by the victims, would have been the physical removal of Hitler or a combined display of military force which might have persuaded him that the personal and national costs of continued aggression would outweigh the advantages. In other words, compromise requires two agreements between the antagonists: both parties must initially agree that a partial withdrawal of demands or positions is preferable to continued conflict, and only after this decision has been reached can they begin discussing the substantive terms of a compromise agreement. There are, however, a number of characteristics of diplomatic behavior in a crisis situation, noted in both the theoretical and historical literature of international politics, which make these two types of agreement difficult to achieve.

One is the tendency for governments to attach symbolic value and importance to conflicts arising from rather simple sources. In our era, at least, conflicts tend to escalate not only militarily but also in terms of their diplomatic and public "ideology." As the issues in a conflict—often relatively simple at the beginning—become encrusted with ideological verbiage, they become harder to resolve through compromise because government officials and publics alike tend to regard any withdrawal as a sacrifice of some great principle. The conflict is seldom acknowledged as one involving primarily a piece of territory, for example, but is symbolized as the "defense of freedom," "defense against imperialist aggression," or the "vindication of national honor." The technique of escalating issues into matters of principle (Lieberman, 1964, p. 105) is useful in establishing a commitment to a bargaining position, but it is a double-edged sword which can also cut off escape routes and destroy bargaining flexibility.

The outbreak of violence has often been cited as another important impediment to compromise as a mode of conflict resolution. For example, Boulding (1962, pp. 323–24) has asserted that:

> . . . violence in itself prevents . . . conflicts from being resolved and indeed perpetuates them. Violence, for instance, creates an atmosphere in which

reconcilation is difficult and in which, indeed, each party is likely to move farther away from the position of the other. It likewise makes compromise difficult; one does not compromise with a man with a gaun, and getting a gun oneself does not assist the process of compromise either. One does not negotiate from strength; one may dictate from strength, but one does not negotiate. The only place where violence may have a part to play in conflict settlement is where there is a sufficient monopoly or preponderance of violence in the hands of one party so that settlement can come about through conquest or award. . . . Violence, in itself, because it cannot perform the reconciling and compromising function, leads to the suppression rather than resolution of conflict; it drives conflict underground but does little to eliminate it.

Many would agree that once antagonists attempt to induce submission or withdrawal by the use of widespread violence, it becomes even more difficult ultimately to resolve the conflict through processes aimed at compromise. But there are too many historical exceptions to allow us to accept this as a totally valid assertion. One can also argue that either the development of a military stalemate or the controlled display or use of force may actually help induce one side to conclude that a reduction of demands, a withdrawal from positions, or a partial settlement is preferable to continue violence (Coser, 1956, p. 137).[3] One example of this proposition occurred during the Korean war. No one was willing to discuss peace offers so long as either party was faced with submission or with the possibility of victory. When United Nations forces had occupied most of North Korea in the autumn of 1950, North Korea was no more prepared to discuss peace than it had been in the summer of 1950 when its own forces had occupied most of South Korea. But by late 1951 neither side had developed a capacity to overwhelm the other; a military stalemate ensued, and subsequently both parties were willing to discuss an armistice agreement which required each to withdraw from its original political-military objectives.[4]

Moreover, during the early stages of a conflict, one party may not be entirely clear how committed its opponent is to a stated position. It may then display or use controlled force to test the opponent's reactions and commitments. If the opponent responds by mobilizing forces, both sides may then decide that a compromise or withdrawal is preferable to war. A good illustration is the crisis over Trieste in 1953. This city had been a center of dispute between Italy and Yugoslavia for many years. A temporary solution was imposed by the Allies in 1948

[3]In industrial disputes the threat of a strike is an acknowledged stimulus for eaching a compromise agreement. For a contrary thesis, however, see Ann Douglas (1962).

[4]President Eisenhower's threat to use nuclear weapons in Korea may have been an important additional factor in inducing the Communists to agree to negotiate a cease-fire—that is, to withdraw from their stated objectives.

when they decided to make the port of Trieste a free city, with surrounding areas divided into two zones controlled respectively by Yugoslav and Anglo-American troops. Suddenly in 1953 Secretary of State Dulles and his British counterpart announced that the Allied troops would be withdrawn, to be replaced by an Italian occupation regime. This announcement implied clearly that Britain and the United States were prepared to give up their zone to Italian sovereignty without even consulting Yugoslavia, which itself claimed the area in dispute. The Yugoslav government let it be known that if the Allies withdrew from their zone and permitted it to be occupied by Italian officials, Yugoslavia would send in troops also, thereby making a war very likely between Italy and Yugoslavia. To back up the threat, the Yugoslavs mobilized their military forces. Once the American, British, and Italian governments were convinced that Yugoslavia would indeed fulfill its threat to prevent the Italian annexation, they became willing to negotiate a compromise. Ultimately the settlement approximated the one unilaterally declared by the Allies, but at least it was a settlement achieved through bargaining in which Yugoslavia was represented.

The decline of open communication among the disputants, another frequent characteristic of diplomatic crisis behavior (O. R. Holsti, 1965; Smoker, 1964), may be a third impediment against bargaining that leads to a compromise settlement. Though there is always implicit communication in the use or display of force, one of the first casualties of the outbreak of violence or the development of international conflict into the crisis stage is the breakdown or constriction of formal communications between the disputing parties. It is, for example, traditional diplomatic practice to sever formal relations even when serious disputes occur, and it is no less true during international conflicts. This act may be symbolic, designed to impress the other party with the seriousness of the quarrel, but it nevertheless decreases the possibility of exploring the actual degree of commitment the other party holds towards its position. Hence, the only way to judge that commitment in the absence of formal communication may be to take actions which should increase the likelihood of war. The importance of formal communication to compromise agreements can be seen in the frequent attempts of third parties to get hostile governments to discuss their conflict. Such efforts are usually based on the assumption that while the parties are conducting negotiations, they will avoid provocative actions.

A fourth characteristic of international crises which also impedes negotiations leading to compromise is the lack of trust between the antagonists. Though little systematic research on the element of trust in diplomatic bargaining has been completed, laboratory and game theoretical studies indicate that the lack of trust helps to prevent open communication and cooperative forms of behavior.

The theme of distrust toward the Soviet Union appears repeatedly, for instance, in the memoirs and statements of Western diplomats who have negotiated with the Russians, as well as in the statements of leading organs of public opinion

("You can't trust the Russians"). Having found, for example, that Stalin and Molotov used verbal agreements mainly as negotiating ploys rather than as genuine commitments, Western diplomats have often maintained that Soviet promises or oral agreements are worthless (Hepner, 1965). A similar indication of the lack of trust in Soviet-Western bargaining over political matters—and no doubt a further impediment to bargaining leading to compromises—is the view held by both sides, but emphasized more publicly in the West, that one can only negotiate successfully from a "position of strength," and that any military weakness would be exploited by the opposition (Bell, 1962). Among the persistent advice offered by Western statesmen such as Harry S. Truman, James Byrnes, Dean Acheson, John Foster Dulles, Adlai Stevenson, John F. Kennedy, and Winston Churchill is the one which states that the only way to achieve agreement with the Soviets is through displays of strength. Though it is undoubtedly true that Communist negotiators tend to exploit weakness, the assumption that settlements arranged through diplomatic bargaining are achieved more easily through threats of violence needs to be examined carefully before it is accepted. Certainly Communist governments have *submitted* and *withdrawn* in the face of superior strength and threats, but there is inadequate evidence to prove that they are more amenable to *compromise* as a form of conflict resolution when confronted with superior force.

If the absence of trust and communication inhibits diplomatic bargaining and compromise, then it would seem that where these are present—along with other variables such as the degree of responsiveness to others' needs and sensitivities (Pruitt, 1964)—willingness to compromise during a conflict will be rather pronounced. When contentious issues arise between allies there seems to be a strong presumption in favor of immediate diplomatic negotiations, a maximum of communication and explanation of positions, and a mutual willingness to reduce demands. A conflict or "misunderstanding" between Washington and London, for example, leads to the hurried dispatch of special emissaries to explain positions or to arrange meetings between the foreign ministers or the president and prime minister. Moreover, once negotiations have commenced, the informal and understood rules of procedure and etiquette are quite different from those in negotiations between hostile states. As Iklé (1964, p. 87) points out in an analysis of diplomatic bargaining, the element of trust in negotiations between friendly countries is maintained by scrupulous observance of certain unwritten rules, including the avoidance of lies, misrepresentation, and impugning of motives; the execution of all verbal or written agreements; the payment of debts of gratitude; and the maintenance of procedures which facilitiate rather than block easy communication. Such behavior, to be sure, arises from trust that already exists, but it also reinforces that trust and, hence, reduces hostility and presumably makes compromise easier to achieve. Behind this type of bargaining, according to Schelling (1960, p. 135), also lies the understanding that what the two governments might gain by breaking the rules would not be worth the damage to the tradition of trust that makes possible a series of agreements in the future as well.

Little needs to be said regarding the actual negotiation of compromise agreements. At some point in the proceedings, however, both sides revise their objectives, partly withdraw from their maximum demands, or remove themselves physically from a geographical position in return for some concessions from the other party. It is almost impossible to predict at what point a compromise is possible (even if there are theoretical points of agreement in laboratory games and simulations), since it depends upon variables that are difficult to measure—for example, the skill of the bargainers, the capabilities they can mobilize to offer rewards or make threats, the desire to reach agreement, and the diplomatic pressures of allies and neutrals.

Award

A further method for resolving international conflicts—where a third party has the authority to announce the terms of settlement—is through arbitration or adjudication. In such cases the decision or award is made to accord with certain prescribed rules found in specific treaties, in custom, or in general principles of international law. Most important conflicts are not, of course, resolved through this procedure because in arbitration or adjudication a state relinquishes the instruments of inducement to a third party which decides the issue on the basis of impartial law (De Visscher, 1957, p. 330). Moreover, conflict resolution through award requires at least three, and sometimes four, prior agreements among the disputants. First, they have to agree that some form of settlement—even one involving the loss of a position—is preferable to continued conflict; second, they have to agree to resolve the conflict on the basis of legal standards rather than according to military, political, economic, or social criteria; third, they have to agree to the jurisdiction of a specific court; and, if the case is presented to an *ad hoc* arbitral tribunal, the parties also have to agree on a neutral chairman for the court.

If parties to a conflict normally fail to maintain open communications with each other and lack trust in each other's motives and actions, it is little wonder that they do not accept judicial procedures for settlement, because such procedures imply considerable consensus among the disputants before the case is even heard. Moreover, if one of the parties in the conflict has a weak legal position, it is not likely to accept the jurisdiction of a third party and will continue to seek to achieve its objectives by direct bargaining. On the other hand, if a stalemate develops and if both sides trust the third party and expect a "fair" award, they might be induced to accept the impartial determination of the case by a court.

An award settlement need not, however, be made through judicial proceedings. As long as some external and impartial criterion for settlement is accepted by both sides, the settlement may be termed an award, even though it is administered by a nonjudicial institution. A plebiscite to determine the allocation of territory and population is an impartial device often used to settle both disputes and conflicts.

Again, however, both parties have to agree first that the criterion of majority will should serve as a basis for settlement.

"Passive Settlement"

Sometimes international conflicts are not formally settled through avoidance, submission, withdrawal, compromise, or award, but persist for a long period of time until the parties involved implicitly accept a new *status quo* as partially legitimate. When such a point has been reached, the involved states have quietly reduced the degree of their commitment to a specific objective. Some of the post-war territorial conflicts in which the Soviet Union and the United States have had a stake have been resolved through the slow acceptance of a new position rather than through formal agreement.

Consider, for example, the Korean problem. The division of that country at the 38th parallel after World War II was viewed at first as only a temporary arrangement, to be succeeded by negotiations leading to the unification of the country. By 1948, however, Communist and pro-Western regimes had become established in the two zones and neither would consent to the unification of the country on the other's terms. In 1950 the North Koreans attempted to unify the country by force, as did the UN forces before the intervention of Communist China. Since the armistice, both Korean governments have maintained at least a symbolic commitment to unification, but neither has taken realistic steps to achieve this objective. Hence, all parties to the conflict have more or less accepted the division of the country as a permanent fact, and Korea has been removed at least temporarily as one of the crisis areas of the Cold War. There have been no formal negotiations, no agreements, no explicit compromises, and no attempts at conquest since 1953, and yet all the parties have helped to resolve the issue by passivly accepting as permanent the decisions that were designed in 1945 to be only temporary. Other Cold War issues which have been settled in this manner include the Soviet acceptance of West Germany as an independent government and Western acquiescence to the Berlin Wall. Such settlements may never be very secure, of course, but since many conflicts have been temporarily resolved in this fashion, it suggests that a conflict often cannot be handled effectively when it has reached a crisis stage and that sometimes the least violent method of settlement—if it is a settlement at all—is the one in which both sides learn to live with their common problem until neither is tempted to impose a solution by force.

SOME FIGURES ON PROCEDURES AND OUTCOMES OF INTERNATIONAL CONFLICTS SINCE 1919

The tables and figures which follow are based on an analysis of most of the international conflicts which have occurred and ended since 1919 and which involved the threat or use of force. Each conflict is categorized according to (1) the bargaining and institutional procedures that the parties employed in the course of their quarrel, and (2) one or more of the six theoretical modes or outcomes of conflict resolution discussed in the previous section. Seventy-seven international conflicts (out of a total of eighty that were identified as conflicts rather than disputes) have been used as the basis of the figures. . . .

Three conflicts were omitted primarily because available information was inconclusive. The conflict between Kuwait and Iraq in 1961, for instance, was excluded because of contradictory interpretations of events. According to most British sources, England's intervention deterred an imminent invasion of Kuwait by Iraq; according to the Iraqi government, it had no intention whatever of using its military forces, though it claimed publicly that Kuwait legitimately belonged to Iraq; and while the Arab League acted by sending forces to Kuwait, its reports fail to spell out which actions, aside from Britain's intervention, were a threat to peace. The same sort of confusion was evident in a series of mobilizations and maneuvers between Turkey and Syria in 1957, and in a quarrel during 1960 between Haiti and the Dominican Republic involving squatters.

With the possible exception of the Corfu case between England and Albania, no *disputes* have been included as sources for the figures . . . . A conflict has been identified as a situation where one or more governments have made demands against another state, backed up with the threat of force, or where they have taken planned military or confiscatory actions which were a threat to the interests of other states. If hostile actions, often involving violence, were clearly unrelated to some governmental foreign policy objective, but were the result of some accident or the activities of groups over which the government had no effective control, the problem was placed in the category of a dispute. Using the criterion of government-sponsored and organized activity as against unauthorized hostilities, it was easy enough to place in the dispute category such problems as the sporadic clashes between troops of Poland and Czechoslovakia in the 1920's, Peru and Ecuador in 1954, China and Burma in 1956, Ethiopia and Somaliland during 1960–1961 (but not since 1964), and Argentina and Chile in 1965.

The conflicts . . . do not include colonial rebellions, except where they involved the active diplomatic or military intervention of third parties (as in Indonesia during 1948 and Indochina in 1954), or conflicts whose outcomes still remain in doubt, as in the Congo, Yemen, Cyprus, Vietnam, and Malaysia.

The figure on the conflicts . . . were derived from standard diplomatic histories, texts on international organizations, the *United Nations Yearbook,* the annual reviews of the Royal Institute of International Affairs, and summary reviews found in such journals as *International Conciliation* and *International Organization.*

Before examining the figures on procedures, behavior, and outcomes of international conflict, several problems in connection with the categories need to be noted. In the Nicaraguan problem of 1923–1927, and during the Lebanese crisis of 1958, for instance, the United States did not withdraw until an *internal* political compromise had been reached. The voluntary withdrawals were thus both a precursor to and a result of the domestic settlements. In both cases the settlements have been classified as voluntary withdrawals rather than a compromises because the antecedent arrangements constituted primarily a domestic, not an international, compromise. The Berlin problem was also difficult to categorize. The agreement ending the crisis in 1949 resulted in the lifting of the Soviet land travel blockade to the German city and a withdrawal of some Allied economic pressures, but otherwise both sides succeeded in achieving some of their objectives. As McClelland (1964, p. 212) points out, the Berlin crisis was peculiar in that various measures taken by both sides resulted in their physical separation, not confrontation. The pattern of behavior was also uniquely a "conflict of duplication," rather than a conflict of escalation over incompatible objectives. Since both sides learned to live with each other's hostile actions and political reforms—currency regulations, separate city governments in Berlin, and travel restriction—the settlement can be termed "passive," even though the immediate sources of crisis, blockade and counter-blockade, were withdrawn through a compromise arranged between Jacob Malik and Philip Jessup.

In some cases it was also difficult to judge whether a withdrawal was really a submission to force or threat, or whether it was a form of avoidance designed to alleviate tensions. The Quemoy crisis of 1958 is one example. We have therefore taken as a form of submission only those incidents in which one party withdrew in the face of an explicit ultimatum or violent retaliation or where most observers agree that a serious threat of retaliation in the form of a deterrent forced a withdrawal, as in the Berlin crisis of 1961. One might argue, however, that some of the cases listed as voluntary withdrawals were far from voluntary. This is a matter of judgment and the figures are open to correction.

Finally, in some cases it was difficult to distinguish between forced withdrawal and compromise. Some compromises could be classified as forced withdrawals or submissions because they did involve the evacuation of a previously held position under considerable duress (e.g., the Netherlands' evacuation of Indonesia and West Irian). However, they were classified as compromises whenever the second party conceded something in return for the withdrawal. In the Cuban missile crisis, for example, President Kennedy, according to Soviet statements, promised not to intervene against Cuba in return for the removal of the missiles.

The category of "frozen" dispute refers to those conflicts in which both sides have remained fully committed to their incompatible positions but where neither has yet dared to attempt resolution through accommodation, withdrawal, or military conquest. As distinct from "passive" settlement, these conflicts (such as Palestine, Kashmir, and German reunification) are *active* items on contemporary diplomatic agendas.

The category of "settlement attempts" in the tables that follow includes only *formal* efforts to use one or more of the established procedures for settlement or for terminating hostilities. These figures do not include all the informal attempts at settlement, such as offers of mediation which were immediately rejected, casual communication and bargaining in the form of press conference statements and speeches by government officials, or the unpublicized bilateral and multilateral discussions that occurred in the corridors and salons of international organizations. We also exclude informal bilateral discussions that may lead conflicting parties to submit a problem to multilateral institutions, though of course such talks may be a necessary antecedent to settlement.

TABLE 1. International Conflicts, 1919–1965

	1919–1939	1945–1965	Total
Number of conflicts	38	39	77
Military force employed	27	25	52
Formal settlement attempts*	57	73	130

*Includes peace negotiations after outcome of conflict had already been determined by war.

The figures in Table 1 indicate that the incidence of international conflict, excluding three that were difficult to classify, was about the same in the two twenty-year periods 1919–1939 and 1945–1965, and that organized violence occurred in a majority of these. More formal attempts at settlement were made in the postwar period, though the figure is not significantly higher. If we look at the modes of behavior or outcomes of conflict as categorized in Table 2, the picture appears more impressive for the period 1945–1965 than for the interwar era when the League of Nations operated. From 1919 to 1939, for example, 63 percent of all conflicts were resolved by military conquest, annexation, or forced submission-withdrawal, while the figure for the period in which the United Nations has operated is 33 percent. Military conquest as a mode of conflict resolution has declined from 42 percent to 15 percent in the post-World War II period. What is particularly significant in the latter period is the large number of "passive" settlements and voluntary withdrawals, conflicts which have never been resolved by formal agreement or in which one or both parties quietly withdrew from a geographic or diplomatic position, usually without making a formal agreement of settlement. Of the 39 identified conflicts in the post-World War II era, 26 percent involved the modes of behavior discussed under these two categories. The notable figure for the interwar period is the large number (21 percent) of conflicts resolved through awards of varous types.

TABLE 2. Outcomes of International Conflict, 1919–1965

	1919– 1939 (% of 38 conflicts)	1945– 1965 (% of 39 conflicts)	% of 77 conflicts
Conquest, annexation	42	15	29
Forced submission, withdrawal; deterrence	21	18	19
Compromise	13	26	20
Award	21	8	14
Passive settlement	–	8	4
Withdrawal–avoidance	3	18	11
"Frozen" conflicts	–	8	4
Total	100	101	101

The figures relating to the procedures employed for settling conflicts are also of interest. It is often asserted in texts on international relations that the diplomatic aspects of international conflicts are conducted primarily through formal bilateral negotiations, but the evidence in Table 3 indicates that, while attempts to use this procedure account for 36 percent of all settlement attempts, the figure for international organizations is comparable (see Table 6). Table 3 also reveals that once formal bilateral negotiations are undertaken they have succeeded (e.g., they have led to a final settlement) in 47 percent of the attempts. This is a rather high percentage considering the many impediments to explicit bargaining and communication that seem to exist in crisis situations. Finally, the number of successful bilateral negotiations (14 out of 26) is particularly impressive in the post-World War II period as compared to the interwar era, when eight out of 21 of the direct negotiations led to successful agreements and compromises.

Table 4 illustrates how infrequently mediation outside the structure of international organization is employed. For the period under analysis, only 7 percent of

TABLE 3. Settlement Through Formal Bilateral Negotiations, 1919–1965

	1919–1939	1945–1965	Total
Negotiating attempts	21	26	47
As % of all settlement attempts	36%	37%	36%
Successful negotiations	8	14	22
As % of all settlement attempts	12%	20%	17%
As % of negotiating attempts	38%	54%	47%

TABLE 4. Settlement Through Mediation, 1919–1965*

	1919–1939		1945–1965		Total	
Mediation attempts	5		4		9	
As % of all settlement attempts		9%		6%		7%
Successful mediations	—		2		2	
As % of all settlement attempts	—			3%		2%
As % of mediation attempts	—			50%		22%

*Does not include mediation by international organizations.

all formal settlement attempts took the form of mediation by a third power. There are not enough cases of mediation, therefore, to warrant any valid generalizations concerning the advantages or disadvantages of this procedure. The figures for this period suggest that it has succeeded in less than one out of every four times it has been attempted, but some of the successful mediations involved quarrelsome issues, such as the conflict over West Irian and the border fighting between Algeria and Morocco in 1963.

The formal multilateral conference, which can be considered a form of negotiation (though with problems quite different from those found in bilateral bargaining; for example, they often include an official or unofficial mediator), is still an effective procedure for resolving those conflicts which directly involve more than two governments. Though not many conferences were held between 1919 and 1965, 44 percent of those that were attempted led to successful agreement. As a percentage of attempts to successes, the figures for multilateral conferences compare favorably with bilateral negotiations (47 percent) and are higher than the ratio of attempts to successes for international organizations (35 percent). Nine percent (seven out of 77) of all the conflicts in the period were partially or entirely resolved in formal multilateral conferences.

As could be expected, the role of international organizations in resolving international conflicts has grown consistently, if not dramatically. For example, Table 6 indicates that while the L eague of Nations attempted only 18 settlements. the

TABLE 5. Settlement by Formal Multilateral Conference, 1919–1965

	1919–1939		1945–1965		Total	
Settlement attempts	8		8		16	
As % of all settlement attempts		14%		11%		12%
Successful conferences	4		3		7	
As % of all settlement attempts		7%		4%		6%
As % of all conference attempts		50%		38%		44%

TABLE 6. Settlement by International Organizations, 1919–1965

	1919–1939		1945–1965		Total	
Settlement attempts	18		30		48	
As % of all settlement attempts		31%		41%		37%
Successful attempts	7		11		18	
As % of all settlement attempts		12%		15%		14%
As % of all int'l org. attempts		39%		37%		37%

United Nations and various contemporary regional organizations have tried actively to resolve 30 crises in a similar period of time. It is difficult, however, to estimate the real influence of these organizations; in many instances a body such as the General Assembly passes resolutions "urging" the disputants to settle their quarrel without recourse to violence, or "deplores" noncompliance with such resolutions, without itself undertaking any steps toward mediation or conciliation. The impact of "opinion" resolutions on national governments cannot be assessed without full documentary evidence. In some instances these resolutions carry enough influence to compel governments to observe them while, unfortunately, there are as many instances when such resolutions had little effect on a government's policies. Thus the figures in Table 6 include only those occasions where international organizations *formally* took provisional measures, recommended terms of settlement, or established procedures for it. Any resolution or complaint which merely urged peaceful settlement or which only took note of a conflict was not considered a "settlement attempt." Nevertheless, even if we take this narrow view of the various international organizations, their effectiveness in resolving conflicts is about the same as formal bilateral negotiations between disputants. The interpolated figures in Tables 6 and 3 indicate that, during the period 1919–1965, 37 percent of the formal attempts to resolve conflicts were made through international organizations. This is one percent more than the percentage of attempts at settlement made through bilateral negotiations.

Moreover, the League of Nations and its universal and regional successors have been able partially or fully to resolve, through their own procedures, 23 percent of the conflicts that occurred in the period (18 of the 77), while 29 percent (22 out of 77) of the conflicts considered were resolved primarily through formal bilateral negotiations. Table 6 also points out that the League of Nations was slightly more successful than its successors in finding solutions to conflicts on its agenda. In the interwar period the League helped to fashion settlements in 39 percent of the conflicts referred to it, while the United Nations and various regional organizations have achieved agreements (exclusive of "passive" settlements in which the UN has played an important role) in 37 percent of the cases where they actually made an effort to propose terms or procedures of settlement. The

UN has been particularly unsuccessful at settlement of the many conflicts involving direct confrontations between the main protagonists of the Cold War. The only Cold War problems in which the UN played an important, though not decisive, role were the Soviet evacuation of Iran in 1946 and the Korean armistice negotiations.

But the conclusion that states have increasingly availed themselves of institutionalized mechanisms of conflict resolution is not substantiated by the figures in Table 7. These indicate that, during the past twenty years, parties involved in conflicts have used noninstitutionalized procedures—formal bilateral negotiations and *ad hoc* mediators or multilateral conferences—almost to the same extent that they did in the interwar period, relegating international courts and organizations to a secondary position. No doubt more conflicts could be referred to the UN and various regional organizations if there were not so many internal problems within such institutions. The veto, lack of funds for peacekeeping operations, and constitutional provisions which encourage states to settle their quarrels through *ad hoc* procedures have helped to prevent international organizations from intervening effectively in a majority of international conflicts involving the threat or use of force.

TABLE 7. Settlement Through Noninstitutionalized Procedures, 1919–1965

	1919–1939		1945–1965		Total	
Number of attempts	34		38		72	
As % of all attempts		59%		54%		56%
Successful attempts	12		19		31	
As % of all attempts		21%		27%		24%
As & of all noninstitutionalized attempts		35%		50%		43%

Moreover, these tables still do not indicate adequately the potential influence of international organizations in crisis situations, for there is no way to measure the informal pressures they place on disputants to resolve conflicts through, for example, direct negotiations. In addition, the UN has developed a set of means which, while not actually resolving conflicts in terms of formal settlements, have nevertheless helped "freeze" conflicts, isolate them, and impose controls on violence. By insisting on cease-fire agreements, by sending truce supervisory organizations to implement and police them, and by organizing international peacekeeping forces to separate combatants (and, in the case of the Congo, to help crush a secession movement), the UN has successfully imposed limitations on the scope of violence and on the number of parties becoming involved directly in international conflicts and domestic rebellions.

Indeed, Secretary-General Hammarskjöld admitted that "bloc" conflicts normally had to be resolved outside of the UN framework. The great contribution of the organization, he claimed, lay in its capacity to handle conflicts within and between nonbloc states and to isolate these from the intervention of the great powers. He argued (1960, pp. 4–5) that the UN "must aim at keeping newly arising conflicts outside of the sphere of bloc differences. Further, in the case of conflicts on the margin of, or inside, the sphere of bloc differences, the United Nations should seek to bring such conflicts out of this sphere through resolutions aiming, in the first instance, at their strict localization. Experience indicates that this preventive diplomacy . . . is of a special significance in cases where the original conflict may be said either to be the result of, or to imply risks for, the creation of a power vacuum between the main blocs."

In the Suez, Congo, and Cyprus problems, and during the crisis in the Middle East in 1958, the quick intervention of the UN forestalled initiatives by the great powers to introduce or maintain their own troops in the crisis area. By intervening in these conflicts, the UN had at least an indirect effect on bloc conflicts and tensions by preventing their extension into new areas. And while UN intervention has led more often to a stalemate between two countries or between two warring factions within a country, such an arrangement may eventually lead to "passive" settlements or to formal agreements, while unilateral intervention by outside powers usually has the purpose of gaining a clear victory for one side (Modelski, 1964, p. 144).

CONFLICT RESOLUTION THROUGH AWARD

In the history of international politics since 1919, at least 77 dangerous conflicts have arisen; of those that were settled by peaceful means or by negotiated peace treaties, a large majority employed the procedures of formal and informal negotiations and the services of international organizations or third party mediators. During the 1920s at least eight more conflicts were resolved by plebiscites or nonjudicial League awards. But what of judicial procedures? Certainly there has been no lack of opportunity to solve quarrels by delegating the power of decision to a court, for almost all conflicts involve important legal questions. Nor is there lack of institutions or conventions. Aside from various international tribunals, many states also have adhered to the Hague Convention for the Pacific Settlement of International Disputes, which calls upon its signatories to avail themselves of arbitral procedures where legal issues are involved.[5] And, according to Kenneth Thompson (1960, p. 208), from 1899 to 1933 a total of 97 additional international

_____

[5] As of 1965, however, only a few states had ratified the revised "General Act for the Pacific Settlement of International Disputes," drafted in the United Nations.

agreements for arbitration and conciliation were negotiated and ratified between governments. Today, over fifty treaties of alliance, amity, commerce, and navigation contain clauses stipulating that disputes over their interpretation or implementation should be referred automatically to the International Court of Justice. But what has been the record of settlement through judicial proceedings?

Table 8 reveals that these courts have successfully resolved or helped to resolve only five conflicts; that is, only nine percent of all formal attempts to settle international conflicts have been made through judicial institutions. Even if we consider the role of various international tribunals in disputes, as well as in conflicts, the figures are not particularly impressive. It is true that between 1920 and 1940 arbitral tribunals handed down 60 awards of some consequence (Jullin, 1954, p. 382), but the Permanent Court of International Justice resolved only 15 cases, while its successor has made only 14 decisions up to 1964, excluding advisory opinions and those decisions in which it ruled lack of jurisdiction. Of the many arbitral decisions awarded since the end of World War II, a majority have involved relatively minor issues, cases in which the interests of private citizens, rather than collective national goals, were at stake.

TABLE 8. Settlement Through Judicial Procedures, 1921–1965

	1921–1939	1939–1965	Total
Judicial attempts	6	5	11
As % of all settlement attempts	10%	7%	9%
Successful attempts	2	3	5
As % of all settlement attempts	3%	4%	4%
As % of judicial attempts	33%	60%	45%

Part of the explanation for this record lies, no doubt, in jurisdictional weaknesses of international tribunals. The gimmicks and ploys which governments have fabricated, such as the Connally Amendment, are well known and are sometimes used to justify a government's refusal to resolve either disputes or conflicts through the application of legal norms. But it is doubtful whether international tribunals would be employed more often even if their jurisdiction were more safely established.

More important reasons are involved here, reflecting ideological cleavages of our era, divisions of legal philosophy, and attitudes toward sacrificing the possibilities of achieving or defending positions through bilateral bargaining. International lawyers have for many years tried to draw distinctions between political and legal disputes, or between disputes and conflicts. Some have argued that only disputes as defined in this paper are amenable to the award mode of settlement.

Others point out that a dispute is one in which the two parties disagree over the meaning of *existing* laws or treaties, or where one party has violated its treaty obligations, while in a conflict a party seeks to *change* the other's rights, privileges, or obligations. Thus, a conflict—often termed by international lawyers as a political dispute—may have important legal aspects to it (witness the Berlin, Kashmir, Vietnam, and Malaysian problems), but obviously one or both antagonists do not wish to characterize the conflict in legal terms because their objectives and actions are incompatible with *existing* legal principles and treaties. No government, even if it can call up some farfetched or disreputable legal justification for its actions, is likely to accept legal criteria as a basis for settlement when it knows it has a weak case. Nor is it likely to permit the intervention of a third party if it is convinced that it will lose verything in an award. As one Canadian diplomat (Martin, 1964, p. 2) has recently stated:

> The fact is that international relations do not give rise to political problems which have a legal aspect, any more than they give rise to legal problems which have a political aspect. In my view, the basic distinction between disputes that are legal and disputes that are political is the readiness of the states concerned to regard them as legal, to consider them in terms of international law. But reluctance to think about and articulate problems in legal terms is not necessarily due to lack of interest in or respect for international law. It may arise because the realities of the issue are obscured, not clarified, by defining them in legal terms. Or the reluctance to litigate may be due to belief that the law, as it is, is unjust or inadequate and must be changed.

Indeed, this last point has been increasingly apparent as one of the problems of resolving both disputes and conflicts on the basis of legal criteria. Many of the new states are not enthusiastic supporters of certain doctrines of international law which originated in Europe and which are designed to protect the investments of European and American business enterprises or to provide a legal basis for colonial-type relationships (Röling, 1960, Syatauw, 1961; Sørenson, 1960). One can single out, in particular, the law relating to expropriation of private property and the question of using force to obtain independence or self-determination. The conditions and aspirations of these new states thus raise unprecedented problems for inducing behavior conforming to the award model; the history of cases before the major international tribunals reveals quite clearly that both states which have accepted an impartial third-party settlement have also accepted the legitimacy of *existing* principles of international law. Moreover, many of the disputes and conflicts submitted to international tribunals have involved states which normally maintain friendly relations—for example, Belgium and the Netherlands, the United States and Switzerland, Germany and Austria, Great Britain and France, France and Norway, and so forth. An examination of these disputes and conflicts also suggests that the importance of the issues to the litigants was quite small compared to their common interests.

CONCLUSION

The conclusion from this investigation is quite apparent. Most conflicts involve considerable bargaining between the antagonists and, in all the modes of resolution except award, that bargaining can continue until some point of accommodation or submission is reached. It is not unnatural that parties to a conflict expect to derive more benefits from their own actions than from decisions of third parties. Many, in fact, are quite willing to risk even conquest by the antagonist in order to attain or defend their interests, values, and objectives by employing a combination of verbal threats, offers of rewards, and retaliating actions. But in an award, bargaining ceases when both sides have agreed to resolve the issue on the basis of an impartial arbitrator or judge or by an objective criterion such as majority will. At best there is only a 50-50 chance of winning the award, and if the probabilities are different, it indicates that one side has a very weak legal case and will be, therefore, reluctant to agree to judicial procedures. But if there are no visible trends towards the increasing utilization of legal procedures for conflict resolution, other figures are more heartening. Compared to the interwar period, the record of pacific settlement (or in Claude's words [1959, p. 242], "pacific nonsettlement") has improved since 1945. No doubt where the vital interests of the major powers are directly incompatible, international organizations will continue to play a minor role. But if they can impose their presence in less awesome quarrels, isolate the areas of confrontation, and impose ceasefire and armistice agreements, they will have made an important contribution to the maintenance of international peace and security.

REFERENCES

Bell, Coral. *Negotiating from Strength.* London: Chatto and Windus, 1962.

Boulding, Kenneth E. *Conflict and Defense.* New York: Harper, 1962.

Claude, Inis L., Jr. *Swords Into Plowshares.* 2nd ed. New York: Random House, 1959.

Coser, Lewis A. *The Functions of Social Conflict.* Glencoe, Illinois: Free Press, 1956.

———. "The Termination of Conflict," *Journal of Conflict Resolution,* **5**, 4 (Dec. 1961), 347-53.

De Visscher, Charles. *Theory and Reality in Public International Law,* translated by Percy E. Corbett. Princeton: Princeton University Press, 1957.

Douglas, Ann. *Industrial Peacemaking.* New York: Columbia University Press, 1962.

Hammarskjöld, Dag. General Assembly, 15th Session, Official Records, *Annual Report of the Work of the Organization, 16 June 1959-15 June 1960,* Supplement No. 1 (A/4390 Add. 1), 1960.

Hepner, Edward. "Western Conceptions of Soviet Negotiating Behavior." Unpublished M.A. thesis, University of British Columbia, 1965.

Holsti, K. J. "The Concept of Power in the Study of International Relations," *Background,* 7 (1964), 179–94.

Holsti, Ole R. "The 1914 Case," *American Political Science Review,* 59 *(1965), 365–78.*

Iklé, Fred. *How Nations Negotiate. New York: Harper and Row, 1964.*

Jullin, L. "Arbitration and Judicial Settlement: Recent Trends," *American Journal of International Law,* 48 (1954), 380–407.

Kecskemeti, Paul. *Strategic Surrender.* Stanford: Stanford University Press, 1958.

Lieberman, E. James. "Threat and Assurance in the Conduct of Conflict." In: Roger Fisher (ed.), *International Conflict and Behavioral Science.* New York: Basic Books, 1964.

Martin, Paul. "International Law in a Changing World: Some Comments on the Value of the Old and the New." Speech delivered to the Toronto Branch of the International Law Association, October 14, 1964. In: Canada, Department of External Affairs, Information Division, "Statements and Speeches," No. 64/24, 1964.

McClelland, Charles A. "Action Structures and Communication in Two International Crises: Quemoy and Berlin," *Background,* 7 (1964), 201–15.

Modelski, George. "International Settlement of Internal War." In: James Rosenau (ed.), *International Aspects of Civil Strife.* Princeton: Princeton University Press, 1964.

Pruitt, Dean G. "National Power and International Responsiveness," *Background,* 7 (1964), 165–78.

Röling, B. V. A. *International Law in an Expanded World.* Amsterdam: Djambatan, 1960.

Schelling, Thomas C. *The Strategy of Conflict.* Cambridge, Mass.: Harvard University Press, 1960.

Smoker, Paul. "Sino-Indian Relations: A Study of Trade, Communication and Defense," *Journal of Peace Research,* 2 (1964), 65–76.

Syatauw, J. J. G. *Some Newly Established Asian States and the Development of International Law.* The Hague: Martinus Nijhoff, 1961.

Sorenson, Max. "The International Court of Justice: Its Role in Contemporary International Relations," *International Organization,* 14 (1960), 261–76.

Thompson, Kenneth W. *Political Realism and the Crisis of World Politics.* Princeton: Princeton University Press, 1960.

Author Index

Subject Index